PLAYA FIRE

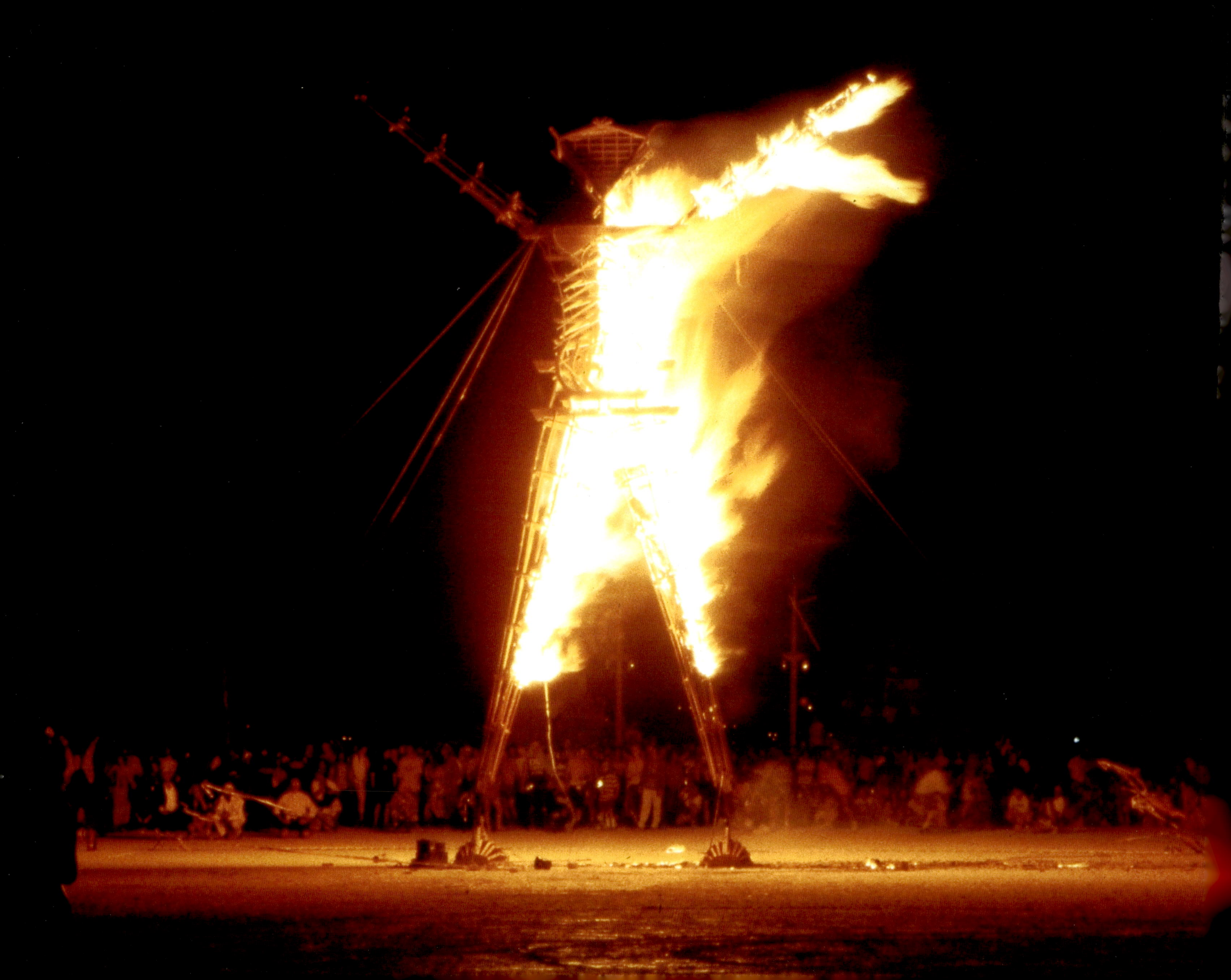

CONTENTS

FOREWORD

Spirit Flies Abroad

The experience of *spirit* is identified with breath. The word *inspiration* has a pedigree that extends back to the middle of the sixteenth century, deriving from the even more ancient Latin word *inspirare*, which means to breathe in, to draw air into the lungs. In this sense, we encounter spirit constantly in daily life in the form of sighs and sobs, snorts and gasps—any involuntary intake or expiration of breath. We speak of high spirits, low spirits, and spirited actions. We also know that spirit is highly contagious—it can spread with lightning speed through great assemblies—and it is identified with states of exaltation, as when we feel we rise above ourselves. Very often an excess of this feeling can produce an upthrusting of the arms.

One example of this aspect of spirit is revealed by an occurrence at the Temple Burn in 2016. For nearly a year prior to this annual ritual, a very lively debate smoldered like a creeping fire on Burning Man's discussion lists. The dispute involved community members who viewed this Burn as taking place on hallowed ground, as at a wedding or a funeral. Many were particularly impressed by the profound periods of silence that had come to punctuate the ceremony. Their adversaries countered this by advancing the principle of Radical Self-Expression, contending that everyone has an individual right to express him- or herself, which in extreme cases might include yelling profanities.

As with many such disputes, this ideological conflict belied a difference in sensibility; both arguments were tied to strong emotions, and after one long summer of intermittent sniping and shouting on the Internet, a breakthrough occurred. The spark that had originally ignited this controversy involved the loud playing of "Free Bird" and a fair amount of profanity, and one day a discussant directly addressed what had actually happened. The offending group was made up of members of the DPW, our Department of Public Works, he explained, and they were commemorating the death of a friend whose favorite song was "Free Bird." The raucous bellowing was of a piece with how this group sang birthday songs to one another. The contending parties did not exactly kiss and make up, but with this empathic insight they established an apparent truce.

This set the stage for the Temple Burn in 2016. This temple, choked with hundreds of remembrances of the dead, was being quietly readied for burning, when a series of unrehearsed actions occurred. The crowd, numbering in the thousands, had gathered around the Burn perimeter, when suddenly a sound arose, a sort of treble yipping, like the keening of coyotes; it traveled twice around the circle in a wave. Then a second wave of sound arose, this time pitched in a more dulcet tone, and rippled around the temple three full times before subsiding into silence.

The crowd then paused, as if in contemplation of itself, when suddenly a single person tossed out a profanity; it hung there in the air, as if it posed a question. Everyone appeared to wonder what might happen next, and then another shout was heard, but this was not a word, more like a stifled proto-word that stuck in someone's throat. Instantly it felt as if a spell was lifted, and moments later the temple erupted in flames. One could hear the fire soughing, as a great billowing wind rushed upward. It felt like a long and continuous sigh, a vast exhalation of breath. I was there to witness this, and it occurred to me: If this is not the action of spirit, alive and on the hoof, voiced and freely circulating, what else can it be?

Soul Remains at Home

Soul relates to experience embedded deep in our bodies. It is traditionally regarded as the source of human vitality and is associated with passionate prompts to action: it is muscular, emotional, and visceral. In our daily lives we speak of gut feelings, soulful looks, broken hearts, a catching of the throat, a shiver down the spine—and nearly everybody understands that the *Soul Train* is soulful. Perhaps most fundamentally, this process we call soul seeks always to attach itself to things, as when we love someone.

The founding ritual of Burning Man on Baker Beach expressed this sense of soulfulness in action. The group of carpenters who built the Man had hovered over every inch of it, and they had borne its weight on their shoulders. Carrying its dismembered parts down to the shore, they would assemble it, uniting legs and torso, arms and head. When it came time to raise the Man, they had so bonded with it that it felt like an extension of their bodies. These were people who had devoted their working lives to building balloon-frame houses—a wooden effigy built like a house required little explanation, and during these years on the beach no one ever thought to ask me what it meant.

We would raise the Man with a stout hawser, the sort of rope that's used for mooring ships, and we would attach it to the figure's solar plexus, since this was its center of gravity. This also meant we had to form a line along the rope that precisely aligned with Burning Man's spine. Dan Miller, who came to be known as the Man's man, would coach our effort. "Baby steps, take baby steps," he'd chant, as thirty pairs of legs edged backward. Viewing this from the sidelines, I saw tension sing along the tautened line, as if the Man transmitted energy.

When Burning Man approached the apex of its arc, it triggered very powerful emotions, made up in equal parts of awe and fear, since at that time the statue had no brakes. I watched their tense, vigilant faces fasten on to the Man, and as the massive figure teetered upward, it was clear that their entire nervous systems were entrained in one great effort; the straining of their limbs, the beating of their hearts, and their feelings roiling up from deep inside their solar plexuses had united them, as if they shared a common spinal cord—confronted by the Man they'd made, they had become him.

Is Burning Man a Religion?

> The practical needs and experiences of religion seem to me sufficiently met by the belief that beyond each man and in a fashion continuous with him there exists a larger power which is friendly to him and to his ideals. All that the facts require is that the power should be both other and larger than our conscious selves. Anything larger will do, if only it be large enough to trust for the next step.
>
> —William James, *The Varieties of Religious Experience*

There are two basic views of divinity. The first sees the divine as transcendent; the other views the divine as immanent. *Transcendence* is from the Latin word *transcendentem;* it means surmounting, rising above, as if to step up on a ladder. Immanence derives from the Latin *immanere* and evokes the feeling of an indwelling presence. It refers to all that is inherent in our being. For all practical purposes, the rituals I have described support these feelings and perceptions—they are very nearly textbook examples of religious experience.

The only thing this leaves out is supernatural agency, an external power that is said to hover over us and inform our deepest feeling of reality. William James has said, "All that the facts require is that the power should be both other and larger than our conscious selves." He adds, "Anything larger will do, if only it be large enough to trust for the next step." The Man we've made, of course, is not a god, nor is the burning of the temple evidence of supernaturalism. Energy did not flow from the Man into a group of followers. Rather it was their energy, their full-hearted participation that created the Man. When people joined in chorus around the temple, it was their voiced spirit, not divine afflatus, that united them.

Were we to remove all soul and all spirit from experience, we would be left with little more than what William James once called "a cold and a neutral state of intellectual perception." In such an arid landscape, there would be no urgent meanings, no riveting purposes, and the juice of reality would be squeezed out of the world.

Sometimes I am asked to speak in churches. Many people in religious communities seem to feel we might be on to something. I approach them with a proposition. "What if we gathered people of all faiths," I say, "and, placing them in a locked room, demanded they settle a question: Which Supreme Being, of all the millions of supremely potent beings humankind has worshipped, is really real?" I pause for a moment to let this sink in, and then continue, "Were we to leave and come back a day later, I am willing to wager that we'd find only hanks of hair and pieces of bone—so fierce would be the force of contradiction. Yet what if we here, now, were to reverse this word order and agree to simply say that being is supreme?" Then I see their eyes begin to faintly glint, their shoulders soften, and some people heave a little sigh of relief.

Larry Harvey

PLAYA FIRE

INTRODUCTION

THE ROAD TO BLACK ROCK CITY: 1990

The ten-hour journey from Portland, Oregon, to northern Nevada is more than a long transition from city to barren plain. It's a prolonged meditation on shedding the comforts and restrictions of urban life and embracing existence on an ancient terrain. Residential clusters give way to a vast pastiche of forest and farm; the patchwork of farmland gives way to scrub pine, broad random swaths of irrigated agriculture, and, in the far distance, the jagged plateau remnants of what was once Cascade lava.

Everything changes: Freeways transition to rural highways, then to country two-lanes, and occasionally to rutted and undulating ribbons of ill-repaired asphalt with the plinking din of recently applied oil and gravel. Urban clusters range from frontier cities like Klamath Falls and Bend to country towns with names that evoke bucolic slumber, like Sisters, Paisley, Lakeview, Chiloquin, and Cedarville. By the time the rhythmic arcs of field sprinklers bordering tiny Eagleville, California, disappear from the rearview mirror, we have departed the cultivated world of farm-to-table and entered a landscape as old as the jagged ridges of the Nevada foothills. Here, the roadway winds through mile after mile of rolling sage and deep ravines, havens for coyotes, herds of meandering cattle, and the occasional suicidal jackrabbit. Far beyond the arid sage shimmer the broad alkaline remains of prehistoric bodies of water, and that was where, in 1990, my son and I were headed.

As Bryan and I traveled to the first iteration of Burning Man on the Black Rock Desert, we had little idea of what to expect. While my son was an experienced back-roads driver, our old Texaco Western States map provided scant information to bolster my navigation skills. Once we departed the acres of water-dependent agriculture of northeastern California, the vast beige blob ahead of us in northern Nevada became a destination of mystery.

We had the camp coordinates my brother, Larry Harvey—who had cofounded the event five years earlier in San Francisco—had sent by mail, but little else. The fact was, he hadn't been there either and was following the lead of friends who had been there the year before. That same year, 1989, Bryan and I had attended what would be the last completed "Burn" on San Francisco's Baker Beach, but that had been a late-afternoon summer solstice art happening for urban hipsters. This was to be a four-day Labor Day weekend campout in the middle of a barren alkali wasteland—what would come to be known as "the playa"—and I was feeling apprehensive and ill-equipped.

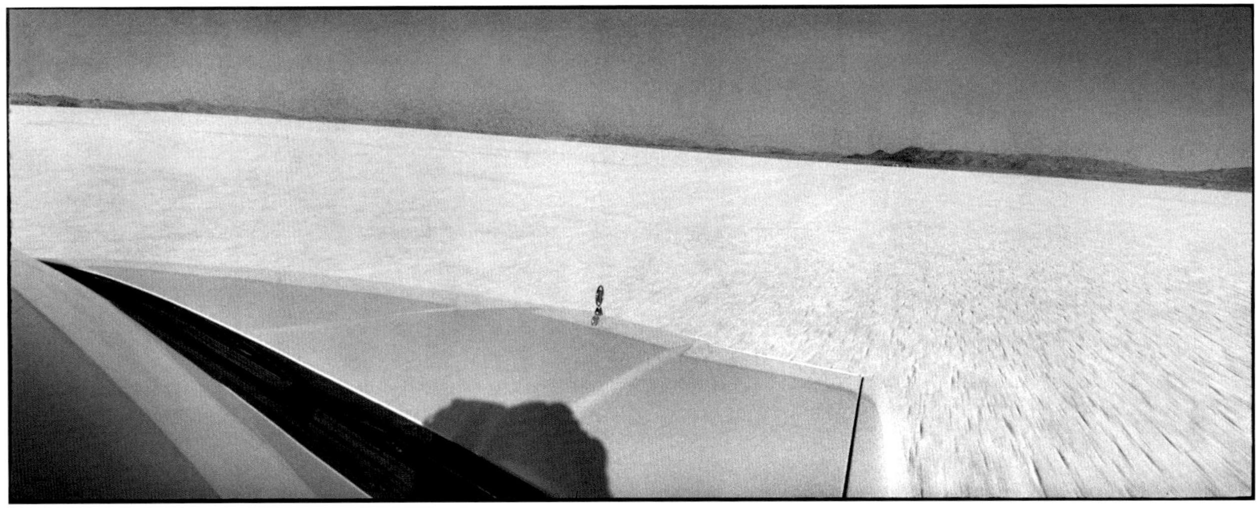

The Black Rock "playa" appeared to be little more than a lifeless expanse of parched crust.

I had chosen a route that would take us out Highway 26 past Mount Hood and down into the drier flats of central Oregon along Highway 97 to Klamath Falls, then across the corner of California near Alturas, and on into Nevada and its deserts. But we had taken far too long to pack up, and I soon realized we would never make the Oregon-California border before dark. The idea of heading into unfamiliar and rugged terrain at night was intimidating, so we began to look for a stopover site. Finally, as the afternoon light was beginning to fade, we pulled into the tiny wayside village of Chemult. The next morning, after a good breakfast, we were on our way once again toward the great unknown.

Frankly, we had little idea of what was ahead of us. Larry had given us his impression a couple of weeks earlier, but at that point he had yet to actually see the place. All he really knew was what he'd been told by Michael Mikel and John Law, two members of San Francisco's Cacophony Society, a cadre of notorious eccentrics who orchestrated renegade happenings at incongruous sites around the Bay Area. They had suggested that this was the ideal location for restaging their Baker Beach Burn, thwarted three months earlier. We had found Black Rock Desert on the map, but other than it being north of the small town of Gerlach, there was little save elevation to suggest its physiognomy. We had been winding up through a rocky pass for hours, and now we were following a ridgeline down into an area of sage and the occasional isolated, dismal-looking ranch. Finally, we crested a hill and I pulled into the first turnout. In the far distance the ridgeline came to an end, and beyond it lay a sliver of white and beige sand. It was our first glimpse of the playa.

We reached the bottom of the slope and the junction of Highway 447 and Route 34, the gateway to Black Rock. To the right we could see the trees and a handful of buildings that made up the town of Gerlach. We turned left toward our adventure. As we headed northward, we were scarcely prepared for what we were about to see. To the west was the backside of the ridgeline we had been following all afternoon; to the east stretched a vast lunar landscape. The Black Rock Desert is a massive alkali flat that encompasses nearly a thousand square miles. It's so flat that heat waves radiating from its surface create a mirage effect, and moving objects coming out

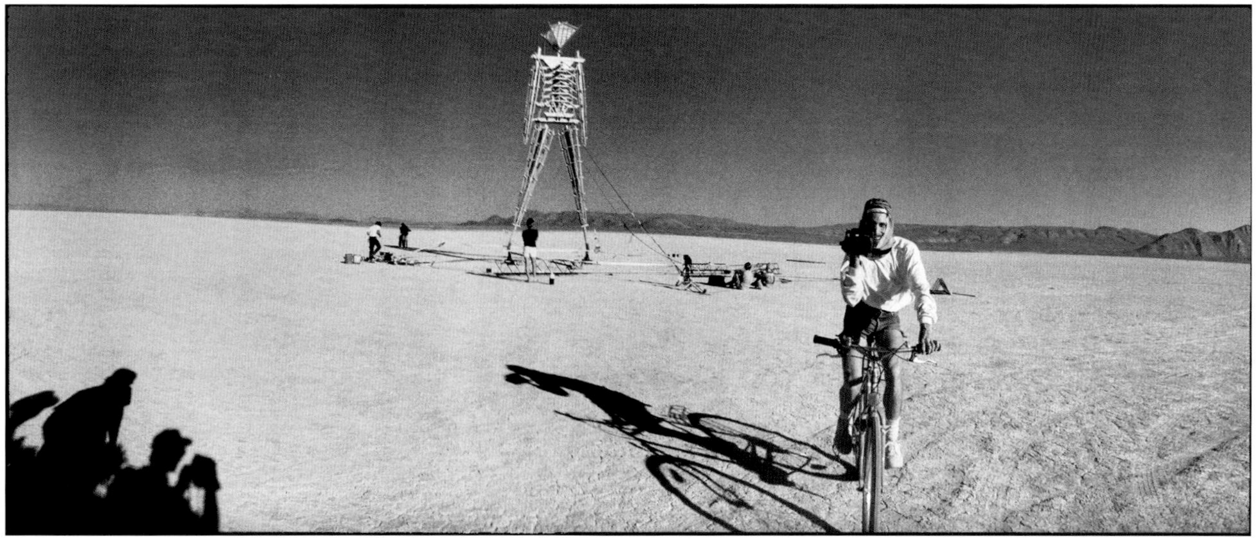

Outside the circle of camps stood a forty-foot-tall humanoid figure, and Dan Miller with his video camera.

of the mirage appear to be floating on a thin ribbon of sky—very disconcerting. To us, it seemed endless and otherworldly. We stopped at the roadside entry and gazed at tire tracks that splayed outward and then seemed to vanish in the glare of the afternoon sun. The playa appeared to be little more than a lifeless expanse of parched crust punctuated by cracks, wheel ruts, and windrows of powdered alkali. It looked like a place people go to vanish.

We began slowly crossing the barren surface armed solely with a compass and the coordinates Larry had sent by mail: "Head due east for six miles, and turn north for four miles." Bryan initially feared the crust might give way, but gradually he gathered speed. The hard alkaline surface invites speed—begs for it—so he stepped on the gas. Wakes of dust blasted high on either side of the car, adding to my giddy fantasy of careening across Mars. The sand rows deepened, and soon we were nearly upended when a particularly deep drift drove the car's nose down, spraying playa sand up over the windshield. It was time to get real.

After we'd completed six miles on the odometer, we turned north, or as northward as we could guess because the compass needle was wiggling back and forth. "Can you see anything?" Bryan asked as we neared four miles. I was busy alternating my gaze between the moving needle and trying to spot anything like our destination. The sun was diving toward late afternoon, and the desert's flat glare seemed as if it could swallow large objects whole. Unless we were within a mile of our destination, we might blow right by an encampment of hundreds. "Not a thing," I finally replied.

We were a few tenths past the four-mile indication when Bryan spotted a glint of sunlight off the side of a Ryder rental truck. In the distance sat a fully assembled and utterly out of place drum kit, seemingly poised for a spontaneous playa jam session. In the distance to one side of the drums towered a giant humanoid figure; to the other side a slender line of vehicles and tents blended almost seamlessly into the horizon. Above the cluster of tents a black pirate flag fluttered atop an orange-and-white parachute. With the benefit of hindsight, the scene loomed like a micro foreshadowing of the decades of unexpected Burning Man apparitions yet to come. Bryan altered our course by a few degrees, and we headed for it all.

It's difficult to overstate how the emptiness of the Black Rock Desert contributes to the mystique of Burning Man. Certainly the demand for a proportion that can compete with this seemingly endless expanse has influenced the construction of huge sculptures and mammoth theme camps, but scale is only part of the equation. The playa, with its ever-changing dome of sky, has provided a grand theater for ritualized expression for centuries. Many Burners are likewise inspired to perform the deeply felt. Of course we wouldn't start calling ourselves "Burners" for several years, a term that is now taken to mean adherents to the culture, but I also find it to be a useful descriptor because even in that first year, attending Burning Man on the playa required a much higher level of commitment than simply purchasing a ticket to become an "attendee." The prototypical urge for individual expression was there from the beginning as well. The wind-driven sand spreads outward to an infinite horizon, and we were swept up by an ageless desire to experience a reality beyond the surface of our planet. We may have been playa novices in 1990, but many of us were already well on the way to becoming "Burners" in our hearts.

When Cacophony Society mainstays John Law and Michael Mikel suggested bringing Burning Man to the Black Rock Desert, one of their compelling arguments had been that the horizon of the desert was much like the open expanse of the Pacific Ocean on Baker Beach, and they were right. Larry recalled years later, "The wide playa was like the ocean's broad undulating surface, but with one important addition—you could walk on it!" Indeed walking across the Black Rock Desert is endlessly stimulating. Contact with an ancient landscape activates primal instincts. The desert opened itself to us in 1990, and we succumbed to its sprawling embrace. We also felt the kinship of being with fellow travelers on a mythical voyage. It's one of the phenomena people talk about when describing their first experience venturing out onto the playa at Burning Man—the sense of walking alone on a boundless plain, and at the same time feeling bonded to the spirit of an ancient and invisible community.

Burning Man on the Black Rock Desert has grown exponentially and relentlessly from a relatively meager gathering of radical expressionists in 1990 into a bona fide international phenomenon. These days Burning Man is massively popular, drawing more than seventy thousand ardent attendees from around the world annually. These costumed and desert-clad

Burners jam themselves into a nine-mile perimeter of theme camps, gigantic works of art, and endless pageantry.

They arrive a week or so before Labor Day weekend in full creative mode bearing handcrafted gifts and hauling materials for art and living. They ride bizarro bicycles, drive fantastic "mutant vehicles," and pack in and out everything they need to thrive in an environment that is both harsh and miraculous. A relic of prehistoric Lake Lahontan, the Black Rock Desert becomes the catalyst for both transcendental personal experience and benevolent acts of communal spirit—often at the same instant. Much like the utopians of another age, Burners assimilate into a temporary culture that seamlessly encourages both individual expression and unconditional community support.

What we found on Friday of Labor Day weekend in 1990, however, was much more humble and modest. There were a hundred Burners alongside an appropriate number of tents, pickup campers, RVs, and a VW Vanagon or two with a Grateful Dead sticker plastered on a window or a dream catcher hanging from a rearview mirror. This tiny enclave sported very little of what would eventually become the enormous scale and neon glitter of Black Rock City with its elaborate performance-laden Center Camp, vast network of support structures, first aid stations, media center, post offices, radio stations, and endless lines waiting to get coffee or ice. What stood in its place was the droopy orange-and-white parachute, draped haphazardly over a crude shade structure and flying its forlorn pirate flag. Rather than a functioning town square or social center, this was little more than a visual curiosity.

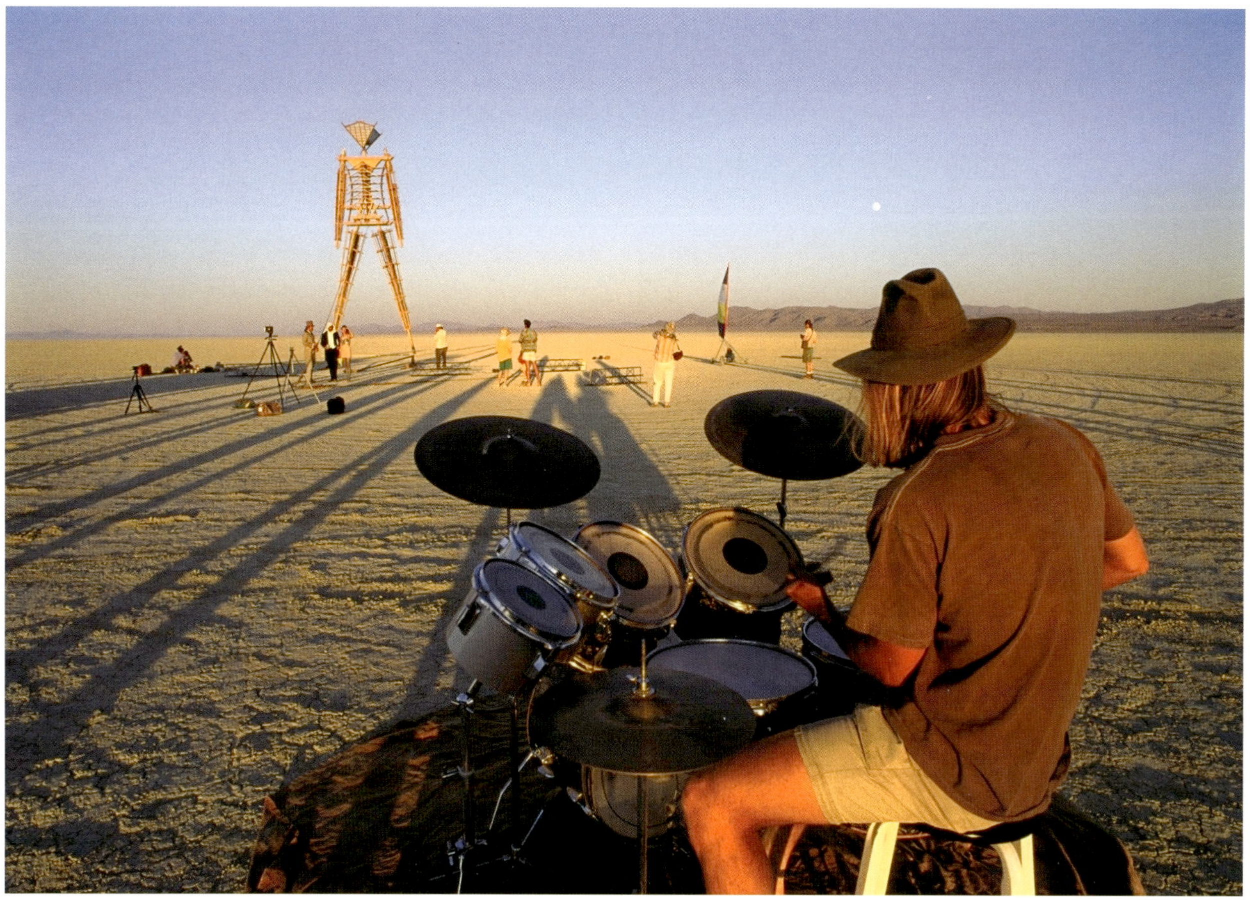

Dean Gustufson's drum called us to assemble in front of the Man.

Outside the tight circle of campers lurked an oddly comforting forty-foot-tall humanoid figure standing resolute against the desert skyline. Old friend Dan Miller bicycled toward us while filming our arrival with a VHS camcorder on his shoulder. The presence of the Burning Man on the flat expanse of the playa seemed completely natural and appropriate, yet it also evoked an uncanny resemblance to the kind of Hollywood hulks that dominated science fiction films of the 1950s. I know because I misspent much of my youth in the cool darkness of the Parkrose Theater on the rural outskirts of Portland, shrinking from alien monsters in *The Thing from Another World* or *It Came from Outer Space*. To my fantasy-addled mind, the Burning Man recalled the stoic and powerful robot Gort from the sci-fi classic *The Day the Earth Stood Still*. My motion picture analogy was further reinforced as Dan and I playfully photographed each other in our own fashion. It was my first panoramic image of the Burning Man on the playa; there would be many more to follow.

As the sun neared the horizon on Sunday evening of Labor Day weekend in 1990, Bryan and I, along with a hundred companions, gathered around the wooden guest of honor. The official signal had yet to be given, but we knew the burning time was near, and we were drawn by a sense of impatience. I had pre-positioned my tripod and camera equipment in a desirable spot, and we now enjoyed a few minutes together. This was the beginning of what would be an ongoing father and son odyssey to Burning Man, one that would bind us together in a special way for most of the following twenty-five years. For the Harvey clan, Burning Man has always been a family affair. One of the first sights we saw on the playa was Larry's son, Tristan—eight years old at the time—sitting with the ubiquitous Dan Miller on the Man's shoulder. These days our camp is a veritable circus of Harvey kin.

The staging for the first Black Rock Burn couldn't have been more ideal. A full moon rose to salute the Man. Amid the long shadows from the setting sun, Dean Gustufson's drum kit beat an insistent rhythmic call for us to gather together in common cause.

As was their custom, the pioneer Burners of the San Francisco Cacophony Society showed up sporting their finest party drag—costuming has been a tradition at Burning Man ever since. Nothing describes the evolution of Burning Man more succinctly than to say it is a series of individual and group inspirations that have morphed over time into community traditions. Radical Self-Expression, the most dynamic of the Ten Principles drafted by Larry in 2004 to articulate the most productive attitudes for people to embrace in order to engender a spirit of creative community, might well trace its roots back to Cacophony's penchant for dressing up.

Stuart Mangrum, who would go on to publish the first Burning Man newspaper, the *Black Rock Gazette,* insists that most of the Ten Principles were already a staple of Cacophony Society's mandate for organizing unconventional creative and mayhem-driven events. "Except for Civic Responsibility," he jokes. "Civic Responsibility was never a Cacophony value!" The involvement of countercultural groups in the early days of the Black Rock Burning Man made it clear that here a person's inner spirit was allowed out to play. San Francisco Cacophony and other groups like them generated an unmistakable synthesis between personal expression and group identity that has imbued the modern event with its most enduring ethos.

Often when people find out you've been to Burning Man, they will ask, "What does it mean?" The answer my brother gives is that everyone must develop their own interpretation of the event through vigorous participation. Although Burning Man channels many of the ceremonial aspects of religious ritual, it does so without an accompanying dogma. The closest one gets to an explanation of Burning Man philosophy may be found within the Ten Principles. These goals and objectives maximize one's experience at the event and keep people safe. They are also ideas already in practice at Burning Man more than they are a guru's pathway to heaven. Here's my thumbnail version:

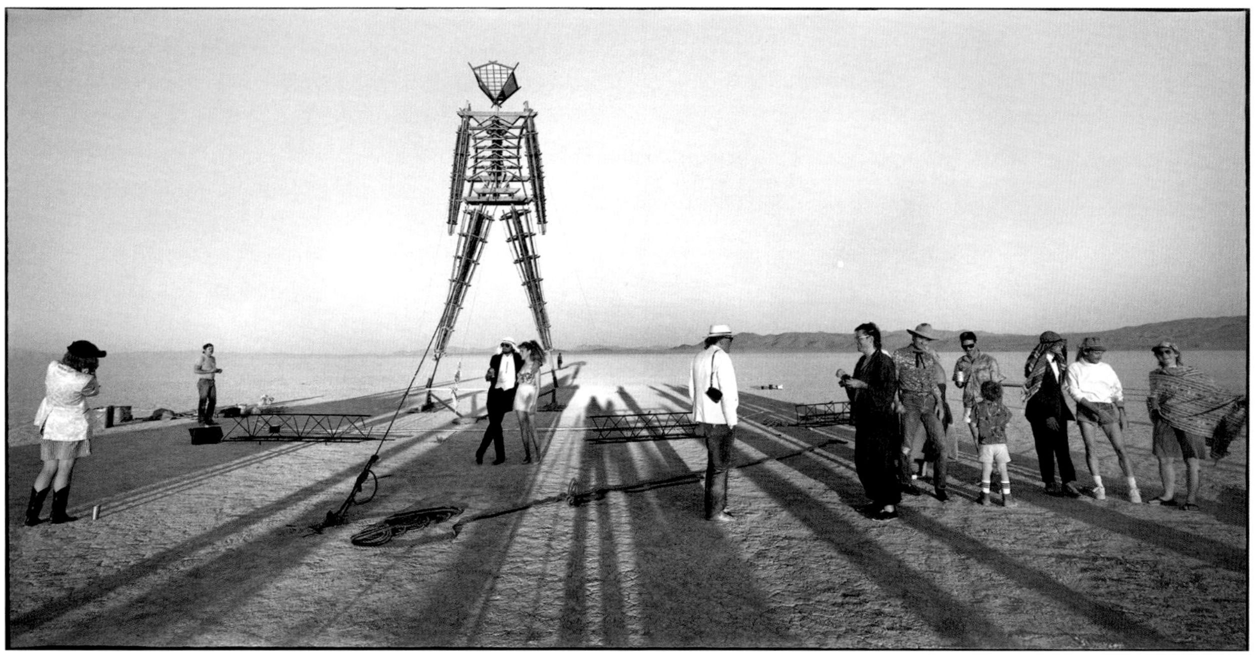

The pioneer Burners from San Francisco Cacophony showed up wearing their best party drag.

The Ten Principles

Radical Inclusion *(Everyone is welcome.)*

Gifting *(Every gesture should be a present to all.)*

Decommodification *(Purchasing is not an experience.)*

Radical Self-Reliance *(Trust your inner resources.)*

Radical Self-Expression *(Display your unique individual gifts.)*

Communal Effort *(Community is about collaboration and cooperation.)*

Civic Responsibility *(Assume responsibility for the welfare of all.)*

Leaving No Trace *(Respect and maintain the environment.)*

Participation *(We achieve our being through creative doing.)*

Immediacy *(Experience is the touchstone of our culture.)*

For the most part, the Ten Principles are a distillation of the social and survival skills ardent and creative Burners have been doing for years. The genius of my brother is his ability to understand both the practical and the philosophical aspects of large-group dynamics and to blend them successfully with the desires of creative people to express their individuality. He has a knack, as great men often do, of surrounding himself with diligent and dedicated associates. He and his able cofounders are constantly working to nurture individual inspiration and to make creativity a natural component of community culture. It's why Burning Man appeals to such a diverse audience and why the event is on its way to becoming an international institution.

As for the inaugural Black Rock Burn of 1990, it would be as it had been the previous four years on Baker Beach: a deceptively simple and incredibly moving ritual of destruction and renewal. The yearly reenactment is both timeless and utterly immediate, and it takes place in an environment that feels both otherworldly and familiar. Above all, it feels right to be there in that moment as the flames transport us to an experience that is personal as well as universal. The immutable landscape opens itself to us, engaging our primal desire for insight and revelation. Eventually, we succumb to that ancient longing.

The allure of fire has been with us from our first days on

Earth, when primitive people sat in caves and stared into a flaming pit hoping for deliverance or perhaps a supernatural sign. We are all subject to fire's attraction while we also live in fear of its deathly embrace. Hell would have little fury if not for scorching flame, yet the Burning Man fire beckons, calls us to gather around, to whoop and shout as a giant effigy is immolated before our eyes, or else to stare transfixed as if given a devastating glimpse into our own volcanic origins.

On a chilly evening in 1990, when a hundred eager souls gathered in front of a sacrificial giant and awaited the inevitable, we were just as affected, just as moved, as with any of the Burns that have happened since. I know, because I've seen most of them. The exponential growth and intensity of the modern ceremony doesn't seem to matter. In the present day,

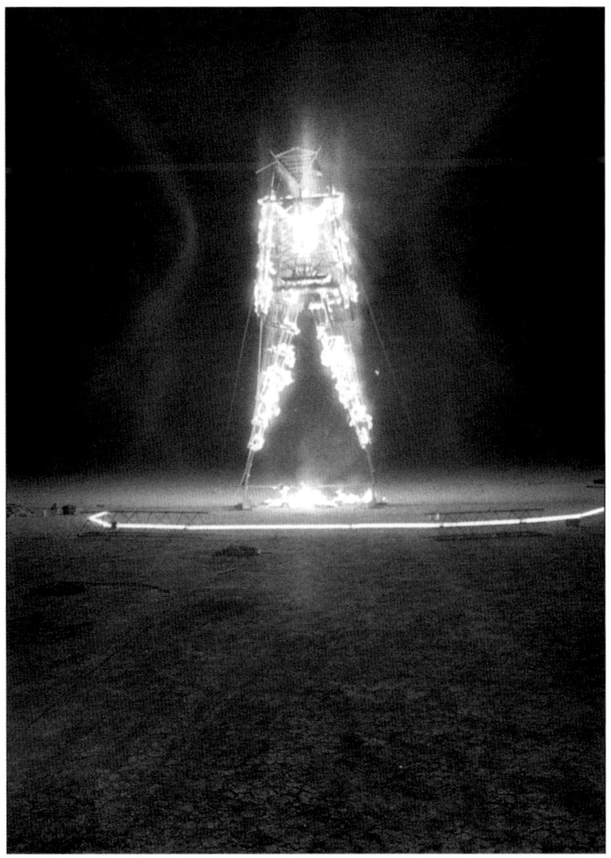

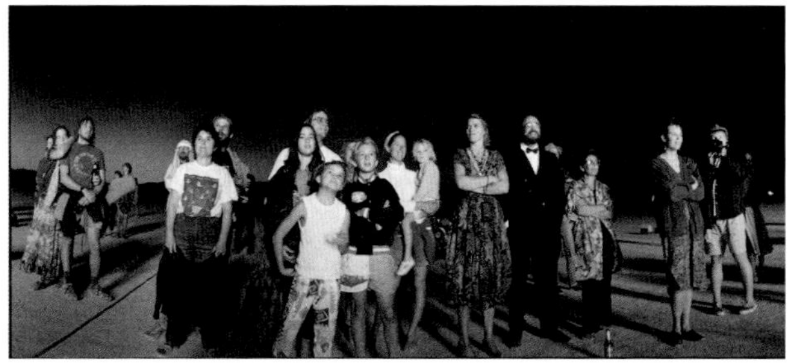

The allure of sacrificial fire is universal, and the response is as genuine today as it was in 1990.

there is an outsized amount of hoopla—enormous crowds, lots of noise, elaborate pageantry, huge fireworks—and yet at every burn there is a moment when the fire catches and begins to fully engulf the giant figure, a moment when there is only the sound of crackling flame consuming wood and the heat from that intense rapid oxidization on your face, and in that moment every Burn is equally personal and powerful. The intimacy between the fire-engulfed giant and the gathered multitudes creates a mysterious alliance, one that is reliable and constant. The look on the faces in a crowd of Burners is exactly the same today as it was that night so long ago.

Over the following twenty-five years I would witness the astounding growth and on several occasions the near demise of what has become a uniquely western festival. During this time the event has survived internal rebellion and conspiracies by local officials and national agencies determined to destroy or hold the event hostage. There have been civil lawsuits, and a legion of disaffected Burners who complain that the organizers have either "sold out" or hobbled the renegade spirit of the event through overregulation. Despite all of this, Burning Man has continued to grow annually and expand its influence globally. The factors that have made that growth possible are many and varied, but at their center is a fiery realization: the creative urge is present in the many, not simply in a gifted few, and when given the opportunity and enough space, we will often exceed our wildest expectations.

On the morning following that first playa Burn, after Bryan and I had packed up for the return to Portland, I walked out to the scorched remains of the previous night. By tilting my Widelux camera downward I was able to use its sweeping panoramic lens to create a simulation of Earth's curvature. It seemed a fitting finale, but not an ending—more like an incendiary beginning. Looking at that picture these many years later, I can't resist seeing it as a sign of the worldwide interest to come. Somehow my brother's intention—"to generate a society that connects each individual to his or her creative powers"—had found fertile ground. Ironically, that place turned out to be an empty and seemingly lifeless terrain. Time and time again people have looked into the flaming crucible of the Burning Man and renewed their creative spirit. I have come to appreciate just how constant and reliable that nurturing flame has become.

Bryan and I had been witnesses in 1990 to the ceremonial reenactment of an ancient ritual, and I knew then that we would return. The Man was rebuilt and burned the following year—and for decades thereafter. We returned again and again, but we were not alone. For a time the attendance at Burning Man doubled each year. Then it simply exploded. Each successive Burn offered something bigger, odder, or more fantastic. Yearly art themes were developed. The inspirations of individuals spread to their friends, and together they expanded them into parody camps, huge artful works, massive fireworks, big mutant vehicles, rolling dance clubs, audacious performances, and oversized innovations in technological whimsy. At the heart of this grand creative upheaval seems to be a need to reveal deeply felt expressions of self. This urge for unfettered expressiveness is nurtured by a rowdy, benevolent, and generously supportive community called Black Rock City. Thus begins the saga of Burning Man.

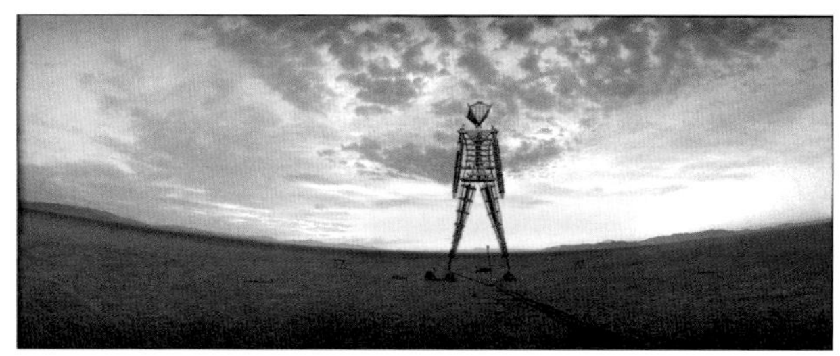

The Burning Man stood on the edge of a limitless horizon under an ever-changing dome of sky.

CHAPTER 1

RENDEZVOUS AT BAKER BEACH: 1986–1989

Burning Man was conceived and built in San Francisco, a city justly renowned for its bohemian culture and sexually liberal traditions going back to the gold rush days. By the time the Beats moved into North Beach in the 1950s and the hippies set up shop in the Haight-Ashbury neighborhood in the 1960s, San Francisco had become, hands-down, the worldwide epitome of Left Coast liberal nirvana. Of course there have been a few other bohemian magnet cities in the United States—New Orleans comes to mind, and New York—but San Francisco probably trumped them all in the 1960s by

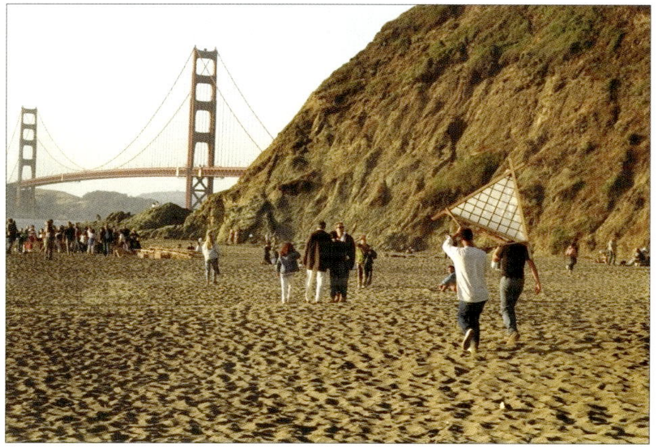

We carried the Man to Baker Beach in sections and assembled him in the sand.

offering all the right ingredients for a true bohemian mecca. In order for a city to emerge as a genuine attraction for artists and hipsters, it requires three relatively vital factors: an inclusive and tolerant social atmosphere; an established gentry to offer patronage, or at least an upwardly mobile economy; and cheap housing in its more colorful, slummier neighborhoods. The San Francisco of the late 1960s had it all in spades and was on the cusp of counterculture fame: it was hip, it embraced radical lifestyles, and Scott McKenzie had just recorded a song about it.

By the summer of 1967, my brother, Larry, could no longer bear the psychic restrictions of being raised by loving, though tightly corseted, midwestern parents in provincial Portland, Oregon, and he decided to follow the clarion call of the City by the Bay. I used to tell people that Larry went to San Francisco during the Summer of Love and never returned. In truth, he came back to Portland that fall and attended classes at Portland State University, where I was finishing up my degree. By then our lives had diverged. I had married Lynda Ann Seubert, a girl I'd met while I was stationed at a radar site in Cottonwood, Idaho, and Larry was in the midst of a search for self. San Francisco and its promise of a bohemian milieu had seized his imagination. It took a few hippie hobo years, and a loyal traveling companion of a girlfriend, but I was right: Larry and San Francisco were destined to be together, and his return to the Northwest was temporary.

Many questions remain unanswered when it comes to the genesis of Burning Man, and part of the reason is that my brother is either unable to articulate it or can't remember the whys and hows of it all. Creative inspiration is rarely delivered in a tidy package, I suspect, but in Larry's case the road is especially twisty, because he is a person who has spent most of his life trying to make sense of human existence, and he is voraciously well read on the topic. Human evolution is absolutely at the heart of Burning Man, as it applies to our role as both social creatures and solitary individuals who compulsively need to express ourselves. The truth is, the origin of Burning Man is a complex and convoluted story, and there are few cause-and-effect pathways to follow, but there are several significant signposts along the way.

One of the least known influences, I believe, is hidden within our semirural upbringing in Parkrose, now an eastern suburb of Portland, Oregon, as the adopted sons of Katherine and Author "Shorty" Harvey. They had migrated to the Northwest from Nebraska in the 1930s, and like many who had survived hand to mouth during the Great Depression, they arrived with a mistrust of banks, a relentless work ethic, and a strong sense of frugality. Much of what we ate, we grew in our field, and much of what we ate on, our father made in his shop. Dad was high-principled and self-reliant to a fault. To my knowledge, he never owned a credit card and paid cash whenever possible. If we couldn't afford something, we went without. Shorty Harvey based his life on a handful of cowboy principles: "A man's word is his bond" was one of them; "A

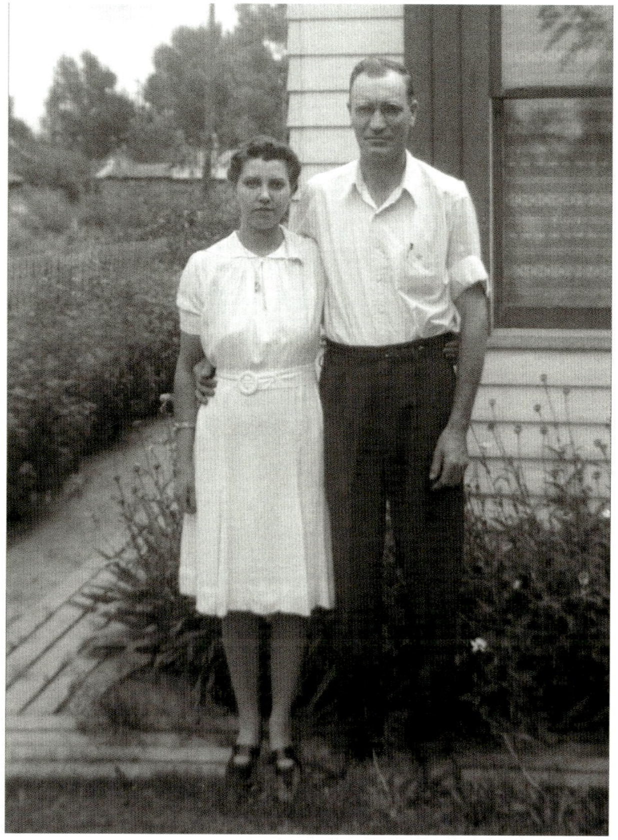

Shorty and Katherine Harvey (c. 1940)

man is only as good as his deeds" was another. Mom and Dad were upright in every sense of the word, and I rarely saw a photograph of our father or my Harvey uncles when they weren't standing straight-legged and proud—not rigid so much as self-assured and, to my eyes, stalwart.

Dad was six foot one and had gotten his ironic nickname by purchasing Shorty's Quick Lunch Café in Hemingford, Nebraska. By 1930, he was a successful businessman and a member of the Hemingford Chamber of Commerce. He proposed to Katherine in June of that year, and they honeymooned in the Black Hills of South Dakota. When the stock market crashed in October of 1929, he and other business leaders had refused to withdraw their bank funds, believing they needed to set an example of strength and confidence

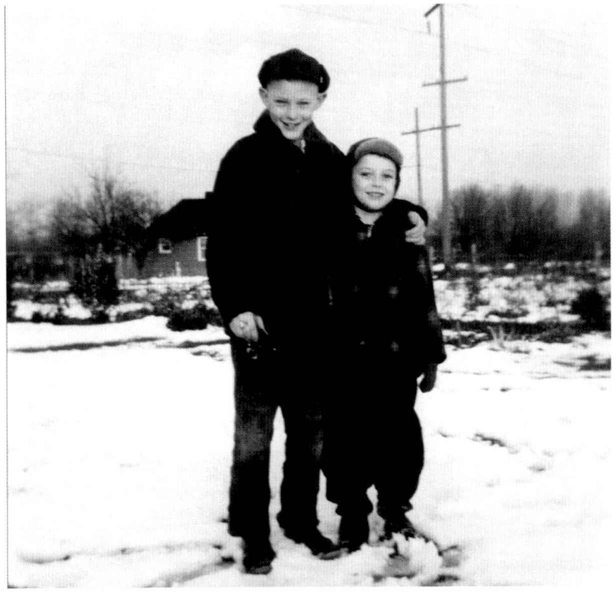

A splendid premonition in Christmas snow—
gift plastic camera and a smiling Larry and me.

to the community. When the bank closed its doors months later, they lost everything. Like Steinbeck characters, Katherine and Shorty loaded their belongings onto a Model A Ford and headed west. Dad learned carpentry on the road and joined a crew that was building grain silos across the country. The silo trail led them to Idaho, and when World War II broke out, they made their way to Portland to work in the Kaiser Shipyards. Dad had been too young for World War I, and at forty-one, he was too old for the World War II draft. By then the two had scraped together enough to buy a couple of acres of land, and Shorty began building a real home. I was adopted in 1945 at age two, and Larry was adopted as an infant in 1948.

In many ways it was an idyllic, though constrained, childhood. We had our own small patch of farmland, which produced mainly tomatoes, beans, and nectarberries, a large succulent hybrid berry our father had ordered from a midwestern agriculture catalog. The nectarberries looked like oversized loganberries and produced wonderful jams, jellies, and sweet runny pies. Why they never caught on I'll never know, but these days when you Google "nectarberry," you'll also find some tasty Oregon variety of legalized pot. Given Larry's early hippie enthusiasms and his eventual move to San Francisco in the 1970s, it's an irony I can't begin to resist.

Parkrose was an unincorporated area in those days, a mishmash of vegetable farms, small factories, and a handful of nice homes and shacks. As children, Larry and I spent hours entertaining each other, and being five years my brother's senior, I usually had the role of entertainer in chief. I would push him around the property in the garden cart as we took imaginary trips to magical places, and as we grew older and I started going to the Parkrose Theater, I would reenact movies for him scene by scene. He once told me that seeing these same films years later felt like déjà vu.

The gap between our ages began to show up when I entered high school. I thrived in the atmosphere of Parkrose, and I had several neighborhood friends my age. We dreamed of building hot rods and discovered girls. We used fake IDs to buy beer on the weekends, raised our fair share of teenage hell, and worked together in the fields in the summer. We swam in Mays Lake when we had a few hours off and played ball in the pastureland that bordered it. It was our own private version of backcountry bliss, only we could be "dragging Broadway" in downtown Portland in less than twenty minutes.

Larry was less enamored of this band of rustics, and in truth we were minor league hooligans. Heady and bookish,

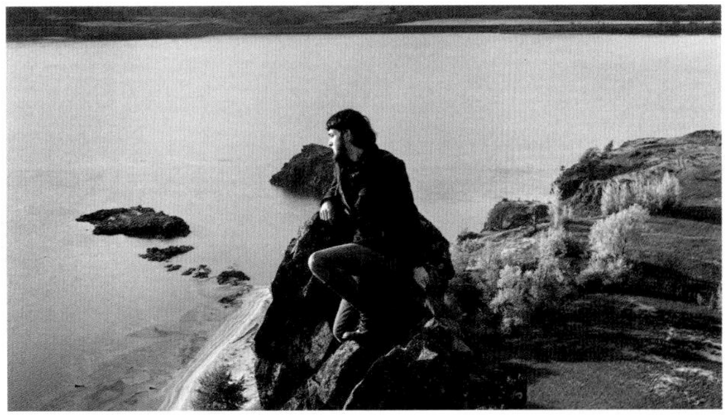

As a proto-hippie, Larry had an abiding belief
that nature reveals much of life's mystery.

Larry found himself marching to the beat of a drummer none of the rest of us had even heard. He yearned to break away from the dull ache of life on a pothole-ravaged street lined with produce fields and farm kids. While I was gravitating toward coming-of-age rituals and busy socializing with peers, Larry was experiencing the familiar isolation of a younger brother not yet welcomed to the party.

I joined the U.S. Air Force in 1962, abandoning Larry to his books and the wilderness of adolescence. His was the solitary quest for identity that virtually everyone goes through, but amped up by a precocious and persistent intensity, at the bottom of which was the shrouded mystery of having been adopted. Larry was focused on his origins—questions of identity colliding head-on with feelings of abandonment. How could he know who he truly was if he didn't know where he came from? He struggled with the image of motherhood and the mystery of paternity.

Larry was one of those teenagers who are determined to figure out who they are as individuals. He felt a desperate need for personal expression, though not from some inflated notion of being "creative." He longed to express the deeply felt, and that required a complete interior investigation. Headstrong and curious, he began to cultivate friendships with a cadre of psychedelic experimenters and would-be hippies. By this juncture, Larry was reading William James's *The Varieties of Religious Experience,* which extolled the possibilities of nitrous oxide for raising consciousness, as well as Timothy Leary's similar claims for LSD. He began pursuing his own quest for pharmaceutical revelations, and it put him on a collision course with our parents.

Mom and Dad were baffled by my brother. I had been a teenage knothead, but I was a typical teenage knothead. Larry was anything but typical. As a proto-hippie, he began to dress eccentrically and grew his hair to Beatle length before long hair became fashionable. He also evidenced a stubborn independence. He was well-read and an excellent student, and after disagreeing with one teacher's political message (in a Cold War–inspired class titled American Problems), he stopped going to the class altogether, choosing instead to spend the period in the library. Unfortunately, it was a required class, and as a result, he was not allowed to graduate with his classmates. It was devastating for our parents.

Dad was especially perplexed. He saw the world as populated by either honest, upright people or "shysters," and although dedicated to the concept of equality and fair play, he was quick to make judgments about character. As a result, he was self-destructively unable to compromise his values; he refused to work with contractors he felt weren't on the "up and up." Ironically, Larry's attitudes often mirrored Dad's. Even though they were totally opposite in their social orientations, and Larry was vastly better read and precocious, in terms of stubbornly held lofty principles, Larry and our father were the same man. But in everyday life those men had the devil's own time talking to each other, and it became a matter of regret for them both. For his part, Dad felt he had failed at parenthood, the one thing he most wanted to achieve, and though Larry knew in his heart that Dad loved him, his grief over the idea of the absent parent lingered unabated.

Shorty was an ardent Freemason. At the time, the Masonic Lodge in its various forms was still enjoying the widespread popularity it had developed in the United States in the era of George Washington and Andrew Jackson. Masons like to point to the number of U.S. presidents who were members of the Lodge, but what attracted Dad was the Masonic concept of God as the "master builder." It appealed to his personal credo that working with your hands is the highest form of creativity. True to that spirit, Dad made most everything in our house, including an amazingly agile desk at the far end of our kitchen. It had beautiful blond maple doors and drawers with hand-hewn pulls, but the true magic of his design was a pull-out table section concealed under the desktop. The table had two legs in front and sections in back that cascaded down like a roll top. When pulled out, it joined our dining table to extend its capacity by an additional four feet. (To this day, I still have that entire desk unit installed in our basement.)

The Masonic handbook also held a fascination. I remember him poring over the pages of this rather thin volume night after night, and I would peer over his shoulder at its mystical pronouncements, only to be disappointed that the book was written in code. While he would never divulge its

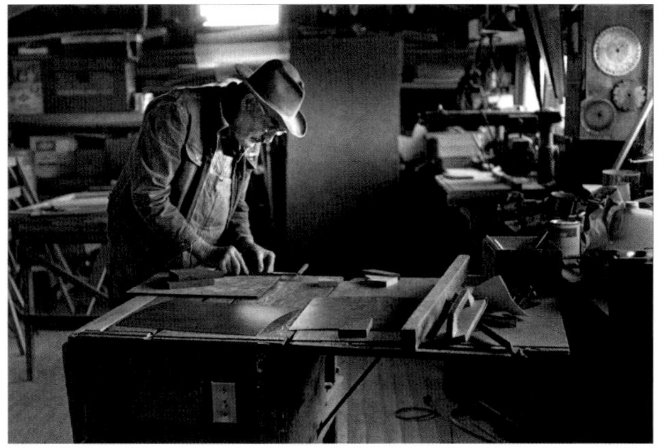

I told Larry, "Dad would have been proud that you conceived something so grand out of wood."

secrets, Dad assured me that the book contained everything a person would need to lead a decent and worthy life. What appealed to him, I believe, is that much of the sacred Masonic symbolism is rooted in the tools of ancient stonemasons—and by extension carpenters. These rudimentary tools represent the requirements of office and symbolize qualities of character—the most important symbol being the builder's square and compass, which are the central motif in the traditional Masonic emblem. In Masonic lore, the square stands for truth, and indeed one of Dad's best measures of a person's character was to decide if that person was "on the square."

Dad knew Larry was on the square because Larry was so open about his opinions and sincere in his quest for understanding, but Dad worried that he was heading down a dangerous road, and they wrangled constantly. While they never became estranged, it was inevitable that Larry would leave home as soon as he could, but he left with a reverence for nature that he assimilated from Dad. Decades later, it still bothers my brother that our father never lived to see him accomplish any of his dreams. We have often talked about what Dad would have thought of Burning Man, which still strikes conservative people as simply hedonistic and immoral. "Don't worry," I have assured him. "Dad would've admired Burning Man. He wouldn't have understood it, but Dad would have been proud that you conceived something so grand out of wood."

By the time I was discharged from the air force in 1966, the world I had left behind had irreversibly changed. Larry had developed a nature born of spending hours alone with his books, sharing the company of like-minded friends, and walking through a rapidly transitioning landscape. The old farms along our street were being sold to make way for Interstate 205 and the expansion of Portland International Airport. The sandy soil, enriched over centuries as a Columbia River flood plain before drawing Italian and Japanese farmers, was in the process of being paved over. Parkrose, which had seemed like a rural oasis in our youth, was on the way to becoming a seedy suburban backwater. (These days, our family home is somewhere beneath a Candlewood Suites, and Mays Lake forms a bramble-strewn apron for a nearby Home Depot.)

In the summer of 1968, Larry traveled back to San Francisco to get a second dose of hippie heaven, then he returned and moved in with the three of us in our tiny apartment in Northeast Portland. To Lynda's dismay, he showed up with what he claimed were 150 tabs of pink Berkeley acid, which he proceeded to store in our medicine cabinet. Bryan was barely four months old at the time, and Lynda had a fit over the "pills" being in our house. Larry went back to Portland State, and the Baggie full of pills soon disappeared. That was about the time Larry met and eventually moved in with a girl from Lebanon, Oregon, who would figure prominently in both his and Burning Man's gestation: Janet Lohr.

Jan had moved to Portland in 1968 and was intent on finishing her degree at Portland State when a mutual friend introduced her to Larry. By the end of spring term, in 1969, Larry had talked her into dropping out of school and heading out to discover America, or at least someplace where the living was free or easy. They were hippies to the core, and that summer they moved into a converted water tower on what turned out to be a marijuana farm in La Conner, Washington.

Unfortunately, they had to leave La Conner abruptly when the local authorities raided the pot farm and arrested their hosts. Larry and Jan had just returned from a visit to Portland and were inside their room when the police arrived. The agents had noticed their car parked by the water tower and briefly discussed checking it out, which gave Larry and Jan a

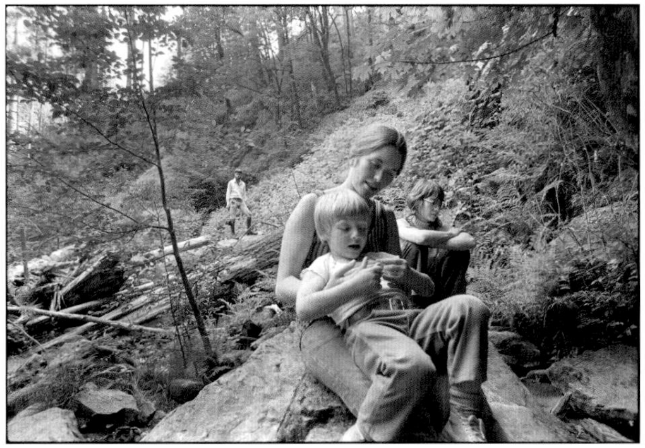

Jan teaches Bryan about the local flora in Coquille, Oregon. Lynda and Larry put up with being background.

fright, but the cops couldn't imagine anyone living in an old water tower, so the two of them were able to watch and listen to the whole thing unmolested from an upstairs window. After the raid was over, they hurriedly packed up and hightailed it back to Portland.

For the next couple of years, they lived in Corbett, located on the cliffs high above the Columbia River Gorge. Larry and I spent time hiking in the area, and I think it rekindled his long-held love of nature. Though they loved their hippie house in the Gorge, they were often at odds over where they were going. Jan wanted to return to college, and Larry was chronically unhappy about never being able to find his way to wherever it was he wanted to go.

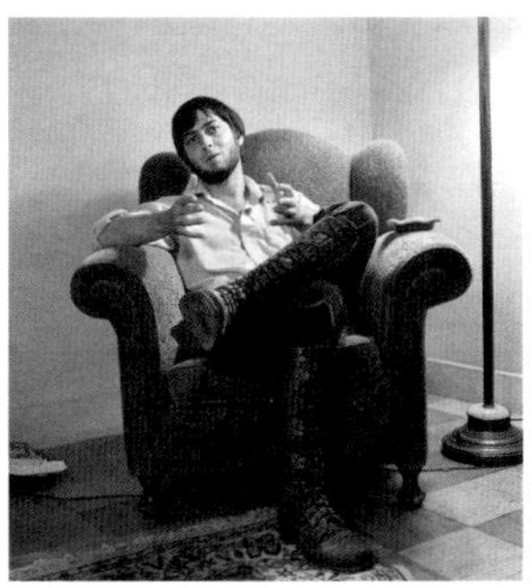

For the next few years, summer forays were the blueprint for their relationship. After a few roving summers, they stalled out in rural Montana, resulting in a brief separation. Jan then insisted they return to Oregon long enough for her to complete her degree, and she discovered a program in the remote town of Coquille, Oregon, where they could minister to both their needs. It was a perfect division of labor. Jan taught and studied for an education certificate; Larry set about learning the names of the coastal flora and fauna. It was the last and best of their country sojourns, and they relished showing us their favorite haunts on the Southern Oregon coast. It was our first look at the places we would grow to love: the sculpted rocks of Shore Acres, the delights of Golden and Silver Falls, and Eel Creek Dunes, and the button-cute seaside town of Bandon, where years later Lynda and I would buy a vacation home. Shortly after Jan finished her teaching program, they left Oregon for good and relocated to San Francisco—and their inevitable destinies.

When Larry and Jan moved to "the city" in the mid-1970s, their first home was an apartment on Ashbury Street just a few blocks from the Grateful Dead house. One of the charms of the city in those days was the ubiquity of artistic ambition. Everyone, regardless of their day job, seemed to be laboring away on some personal artistic project. In other words, Larry had found an enclave full of kindred spirits.

It was also a town full of cultural anarchists and political activism. I visited the two of them a few months after they moved to the city and was overwhelmed by the energized and vibrant life in "the Haight," most especially in the panhandle of Golden Gate Park. The panhandle was just a few blocks from Larry and Jan's apartment, and we would walk there most every day to watch the waning stages of the flower power era: people openly passed joints to one another; long-haired musicians strummed acoustic guitars while longer-haired slender maidens undulated to some interior and private rhythms nearby. On weekends, the San Francisco Mime Troupe often performed outdoor political theater, usually involving a polemic about corrupt city politicians and greedy landlords. The result of such liberal protests encouraged the city to adopt rent control. It's become an important contemporary issue, because rising rents have been driving the artists out of San Francisco for years, and that takes a toll on the city's ability to produce culturally edgy innovations like the Suicide Club, the Cacophony Society, and Burning Man, for that matter.

By 1981, Larry and Jan had broken up. They had moved to San Francisco with the intention of creating an adult life for themselves. After being there for nearly ten years, Larry didn't have all that much to show for it—except his son, Tristan. A few months after Larry and Jan had parted ways, Larry met and then briefly married a woman from Jamaica by the name of Patricia Johnson. Theirs was never fated to be a love match, and in fact they never functioned as husband and wife. But Larry deeply loved his son, and he was determined Tristan should not face the emotional isolation he had endured as a youth. In his mind, there could never be an acceptable scenario in which Tristan wouldn't be a part of his life. The ensuing years saw them struggle, as split families often do, but Larry always strived to be present.

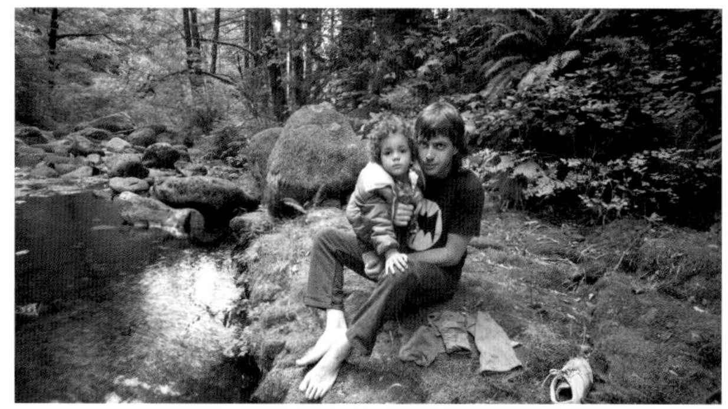

As a single father, Larry was determined to give Tristan nurturing love and principled guidance.

Propinquity has always played a vital role in the evolution of Burning Man, and San Francisco in the 1980s had many enclaves of radical art. After Jan and Larry had split, she was teaching ceramics classes at Fort Mason Center for Arts and Culture where she occasionally met sculpture students who were also studying under Stephen De Staebler at San Francisco State. De Staebler was an early enthusiast of found-object sculpture, and promoted the idea that temporary art was as valid as work created for the museum. He had a reputation for encouraging his students to make bold experiments in nontraditional forms. One of his students happened to be Jan's roommate for a time. She and her friends would go to the north end of Baker Beach and gather together driftwood and other sandy flotsam to create temporary sculptures. They would work during low tide, installing their creations at the water's edge. They would then take pictures against the panoramic shoreline and watch happily as the rising tide washed their assemblage away. San Francisco's blend of radical art and renegade culture was an ideal nurturing ground for Burning Man.

Another example of Bay Area temporal art took place on the tidal mud flats near Emeryville across the bay from San Francisco. There hundreds of odd wooden structures and creatures were erected by anonymous renegades in the 1970s and '80s. Some would disappear within days; others, like Tyler Hoare's WWI-style biplane, lasted for years. Baker Beach was also a favorite spot for annual solstice gatherings. A bonfire would be lit for warmth, and on occasion, people would bring objects to be burned. Jan Lohr remembers solstice bonfires all up and down the beach. It wasn't, as some have claimed, a prototype for Burning Man—after all, people have been setting objects on fire on beaches for centuries—but the precedent for creating temporary art or spontaneous happenings in the Bay Area was clearly thriving by the mid-1980s. And that fertile environment was ideal for Burning Man's emergence.

Roommates figure dramatically in another aspect of the Burning Man creation story. In the 1980s, Larry advertised for someone to share rent on his Alamo Square apartment using the old Roommate Referral Service, which employed handwritten binders in the days before the Internet. Dan Miller answered his request, and the two shared the apartment for nearly twenty years until Dan married and eventually moved to the small town of Willits in Northern California. Miller had been active in the San Francisco Cacophony. He was also dating Chrylu, a girl he had met at a bluegrass festival, and she had a roommate by the name of Paula Peretti, who would figure unwittingly in the annals of Burning Man lore.

Larry met Paula via Dan and Chrylu and became infatuated. At the height of their rather bumpy relationship, he took Paula and Tristan to one of the many Baker Beach solstice gatherings. They walked on the moonlit beach as a loving faux family, but the magic was short-lived. Their relationship soon ended ugly, and it rocked Larry's world in both a historical and a visceral sense. Lonely and brokenhearted, he plunged into a two-year psychic cul-de-sac. I remember stopping by to visit him during that period on the way back from a Friends of Photography workshop in Carmel. My brother was a mess. "I'm having a nervous breakdown," he blurted out when I asked what the hell was going on. Looking back on this period, I'm convinced there was more to his pain than an ill-fated love affair. A series of missteps had culminated in something of an existential crisis, and it would become yet another element in the mythos of Burning Man's creation.

By the time Larry began to recover, he was convinced he had to pull his life together. What he wanted was to establish a career and provide a nurturing environment for his son. He had been studying landscape design, and he had also made several friends in the bohemian community. One of them was a carpenter, Dan Richman, who, with Larry, formed a short-lived landscaping and pergola-design business with a decidedly literary name: Paradise Regained. The idea was simple. Larry would design and plant the garden, and Richman would build the decks and trellises. Richman was one of a genre of San Francisco tradespeople Larry began to refer to as the "latte carpenters." These were independent San Francisco workaday people who were typically college educated and literate, and who managed to supplement their artful aspirations with carpentry.

While Paradise Regained struggled and ultimately failed to establish a viable customer base, Richman, who Larry described as a "talented painter who also played flamenco," would hold bohemian-style salons at his home. It was at one of Dan's salons that Larry was introduced to another carpenter who also happened to be a single father with a son near Tristan's age: Jerry James.

Larry and Jerry became fast friends around their common bond of single fatherhood. They would often take Tristan and Jerry's son, Robin, to neighborhood parks or to the beach on their weekends with the boys. Larry and Jerry's friendship was complex. Larry was, as always, well read and charismatic. My brother can spin out elaborate ideas and philosophies

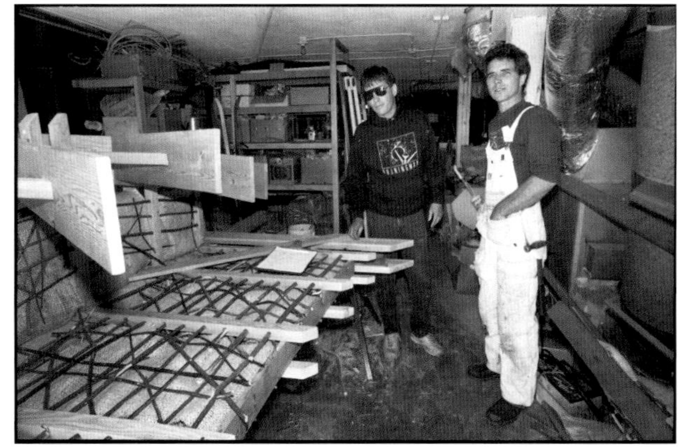

The relationship between Larry and Jerry James was always more complicated than it appeared.

at will, and Jerry saw him as an older sibling and mentor. It's a relationship model others have experienced. For his part, Larry was struggling to achieve a productive life. It was all well and good to have great ideas, but with a life adding up to a series of placeholder jobs and failed romances, the ideas were cold comfort. Also, it was June of 1986 and the solstice was approaching. The prospect of reliving the anniversary of his ultimately ill-fated beach reverie with Paula alone in his apartment was more than he could face. "I'd been moping around for two years, and I wanted to do something on solstice to expunge the pain of that memory," he said recently. "So I called Jerry and suggested building a wooden figure and burning it on Baker Beach." What he felt he needed was to reinvent the anniversary with a bold act of defiance and self-expression.

They agreed to meet at a friend's garage in Noe Valley, and they cobbled together a human effigy out of scrap in a single afternoon or so. It was a fairly crude figure: around eight feet tall with an upside-down pyramid for a head, burlap stuffed limbs, and pointed legs for jamming into the sand. Near six o'clock on the evening of the solstice, they loaded their "Man" into Jerry's pickup and drove to the north end of Baker Beach. They erected the Man at sunset, doused him in gasoline (a foolish move, Larry later admitted), and set him on fire. Two things happened: first, the wooden Man "incandesced won-

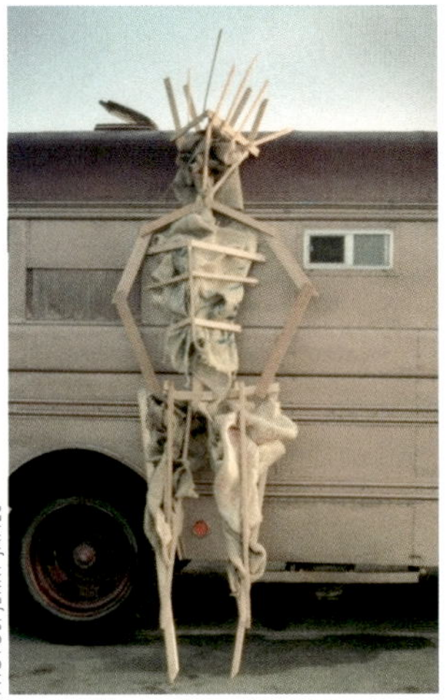

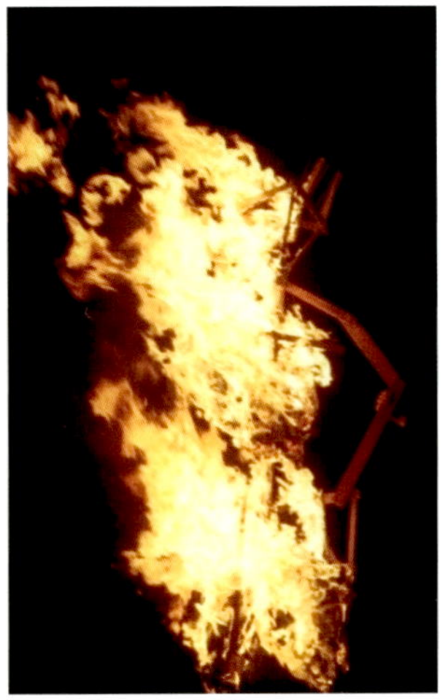

PHOTOS: JERRY JAMES

derfully against the evening sky," as Larry described it, and then the Man "instantly drew a crowd of curious onlookers." The wind blew the flames to one side. A young woman walked over and took hold of the nonburning arm, and posed for a picture. It was a pivotal response. Had people not been drawn to the flames, there might not have been the impulse to attempt an encore the following year.

Jerry recounts that Larry had been reading at the time Sir James George Frazer's classic work on magic and religion *The Golden Bough*, and he suggests that it may have engendered the impulse to build a human figure. Larry is certainly the best-read person in nineteenth-century literature I've ever known, and I'm certain he knows Frazer's book intimately, but while he'll entertain that references to Britain's "wicker man" might have had a subliminal effect, he was out to create a more personal gesture of fiery expression than to imitate a hoary legend from the distant past.

Larry gazed at this rudimentary spectacle as they set it alight and had conflicting reactions. First, he could see how dwarfed the near-normal-sized Man looked against the large dark horizon, and it would lead to his conviction that the Man needed to have a certain stature in order to compete with the ocean's panorama. But he saw also how brilliantly the flames were set off against the cobalt blackness of the night sky. There were elements of primitive magic in those flames, although it may not have been apparent to anyone at the time. It was over in a few brief minutes. Jerry says he thought it would be a one-off experience; Larry holds that he was already determined to repeat the ritual. The two met a month or so later and decided to try again the following year.

Their wooden Man grew to about twelve feet the second year, still manageable for a single truck. Jerry recounts that he was built out of scrap over two weekends. I've seen a picture or two of it, and his most distinguishing feature was that his arms were the jagged remains of stair supports. He was still modest and rough, but with decorative elements.

They had spread the word, and about thirty-five friends showed up. Despite a rather cold and foggy evening, and the same casual atmosphere as the year before, Jerry says he had the sense that there was a ritual element present and that this might be something they did again. What had begun as rather a lark was turning into a commitment. To announce this 1987 Burn, they produced a poster using Jerry's photo of the Man from the first year sandwiched with flames and a quote from one of Larry's favorite poets from his high school years, Dylan Thomas: "The force that through the green fuse drives the flower . . . is my destroyer."

The third edition of Burning Man, in 1988, proved a pivotal transition from a gathering of friends to something more serious and intentional. Jerry and his friend Mike Acker had formed a construction business, and Jerry enlisted the aid of Mike and other carpenter friends to assist in building segments of the Man because he was to be thirty feet tall—simply too large for the twenty-foot Lower Haight garage they were using as a construction site. By then they had employed the term "Burning Man" for their creation in an effort to counteract the wicker man movie reference being bandied about. Although Mike and Jerry crafted designs like the slanted support ribs and the famous upside-down pyramidal head, Larry had developed other very specific design ideas. He envisioned a tall, slender figure with raised arms, and though they had neither the means nor facilities to execute his vision, he was resistant to allowing issues of carpentry and budget to get in the way.

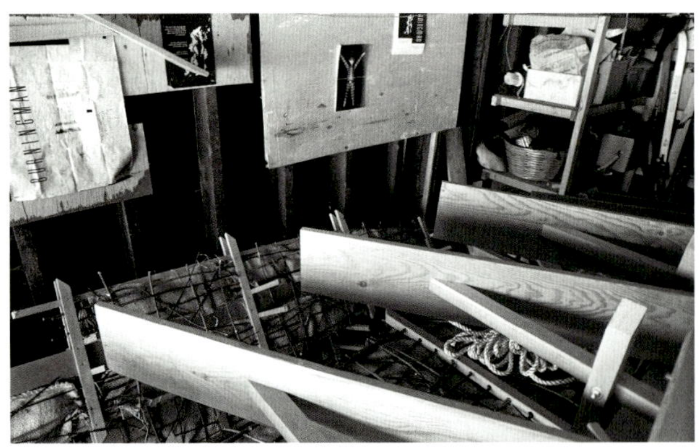

In 1988, Larry began drafting how their newly christened "Burning Man" should look.

The 1989 construction of the Man transpired in Jan Lohr's garage in Ingleside. Jan reported that there had been almost constant friction between Larry and Jerry during the several weekends it took to construct the Man. It seemed to be a continuation of the design disagreements in 1988 but elevated because this time they were working from Larry's new drawings. The particulars of such bickering are rarely worth analyzing, but what is clear is that there was a disconnect between Larry's design aspirations and the Man's construction at the hands of Jerry, Mike, and their crew of volunteers.

As I mentioned earlier, in terms of stubbornly held principles, Larry and our father were alike, but they also had many differences, and not simply because Larry was enormously well read. Their sensibilities were miles apart. Dad was a tireless worker and was forever making things for our home. Most of his designs had a sturdy practicality, but they were rarely graceful. He thought function trumped form. Larry believed form should follow function, but the goal was to render that function as artfully as possible, and he could be very emphatic about whether a particular form was successful. Unfortunately, he hadn't absorbed any of Dad's facility with carpentry, leaving his design notions tied to the dexterity of others. I think the underlying friction in 1989 had its roots in an internal conflict between Larry's desire for grace and his frustration at not being able to single-handedly master the practicalities of construction. The growing dysfunction in the Burning Man

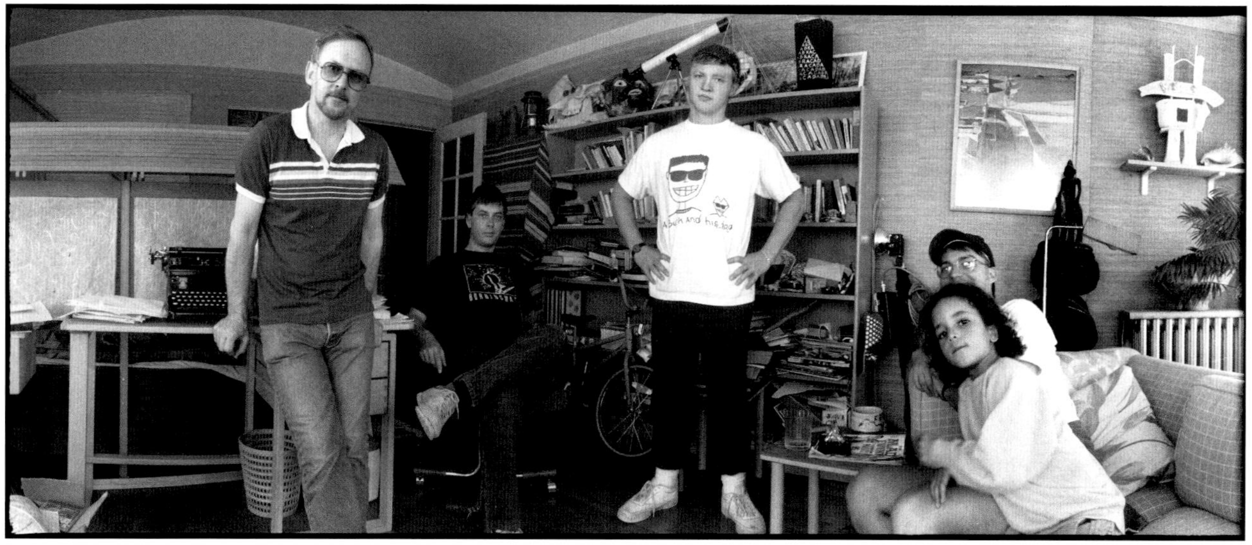

We'd heard enough about Larry's solstice bonfire that we paid him and Trey a visit.

collaboration was linked to a much older and much more private struggle with our father.

What had begun as a bit of artful tomfoolery between friends in 1986 had in a few short years transformed into a sterling example of pop-up art and theater. The first two Burns had been small gatherings of friends, but by 1989, the word had gotten out, and members of the Cacophony Society and others in the boho art community either had been to the 1988 Burn or had heard of it and were planning to make it to the 1989 festivities. Larry had been telling Bryan and I about his solstice bonfire for a couple of years, and so we finally decided to see what all the fuss was about. I volunteered to be the event photographer, and Bryan invited his longtime friend John Lance along for the adventure. After the usual packing hassles, the three of us set out on the ten-hour journey from Portland to San Francisco.

The weather was grand that week, and Larry spent a few days showing us around the city. We took in the Haight-Ashbury neighborhood and Golden Gate Park, and visited the Camera Obscura at Ocean Beach. This famous building-sized replica of a Leonardo da Vinci design was operated at the time by Dave Warren, aka Flamo LaGrande, who had agreed to ignite the Burning Man the following evening. Flamo was a bona fide San Francisco original. He would dress up in a vintage firefighter's hat and coat and reportedly could blow an arch of flame, the so-called Dragon's Tongue, fifteen feet long. He was also a founding member of the Suicide Club.

Larry also took us to Jan Lohr's garage to show us their creation. I remember taking a couple of shots of Larry and Jerry while I was documenting the setup before that evening's Burn. The mood was generally light, but when I look now at the picture of the two of them on page 13, I'm struck by the broad divergence in their dress. Jerry was a carpenter by trade, and when he showed up to take their Man to the beach, he was dressed in his worker-bee carpenter's drag: shop boots and bib overalls with tools on board. In contrast, Larry was outfitted for the show: black hooded Burning Man sweatshirt with a logo based on his Man design, pointy-toed oxfords, and aviator shades. He had clearly embraced his role as impresario and director of the event. It was an imbalance that would continue to fester until Jerry left the partnership the following year.

On the day of the Burn, when we returned to the garage to help with the load up, the forty-foot Man had been completed and was waiting for transport. The Man had been built in several sections, and those sections were loaded onto seven pickups. As a strictly guerrilla activity, the guys had concocted a stealth plan that involved each truck taking a separate route so as not to draw attention. The trucks would rendezvous in the parking area on the cliff above Baker Beach, and then a small army of volunteers would haul the heavy parts down to the beach for assembly.

We parked in the lot and began to slowly pick our way down to the sands of Baker Beach. It was slow going, but

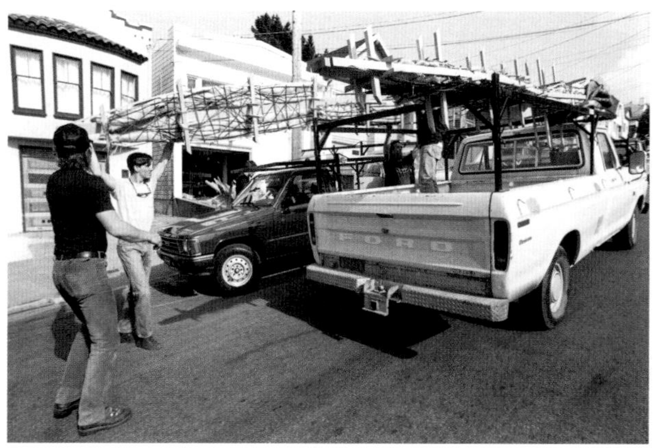

The Man was in seven parts and was loaded onto seven pickups for stealthy transport.

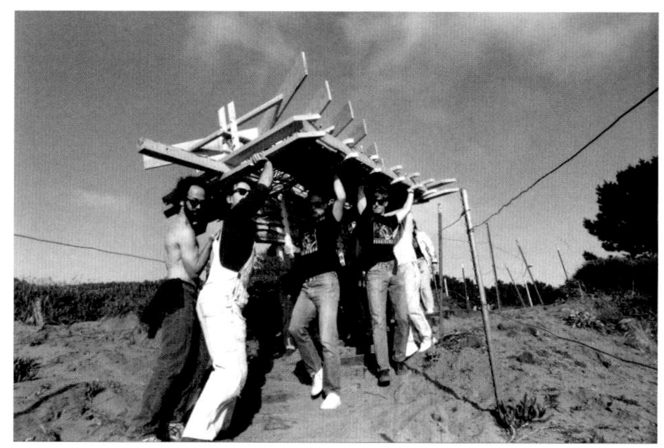

It took a dozen able and eager souls to haul the torso down the dunes to Baker Beach.

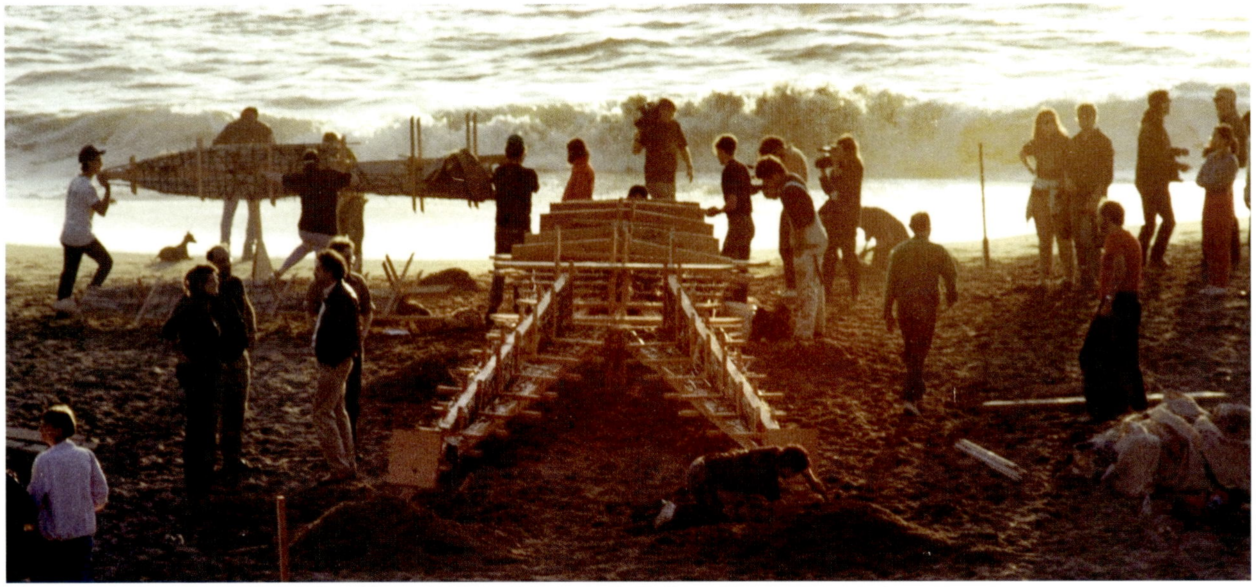

The Man was assembled in the sand on Baker Beach on the edge of a great ocean.

there was precision to the movements and a ceremonial grandeur to the setting. The headlands above the beach are a series of dune cliffs culminating in a single rocky ridge framed by the Golden Gate Bridge. The Golden Gate National Recreational Area authorities had built a set of steep stairs leading from the parking area down the sandy face of the cliff, and that was what the teams bearing the sections of the Man needed to navigate. Jerry James took the lead, guiding the torso down the steep sand-covered incline. It was a tricky enough descent for those two to four people hauling the lighter individual limbs, but the heavy torso required ten to twelve able bodies coordinating their movements and carefully wending their way down the grade without stumbling. That skewed ratio of a heavy midsection to lighter limbs would prove disastrous later that evening.

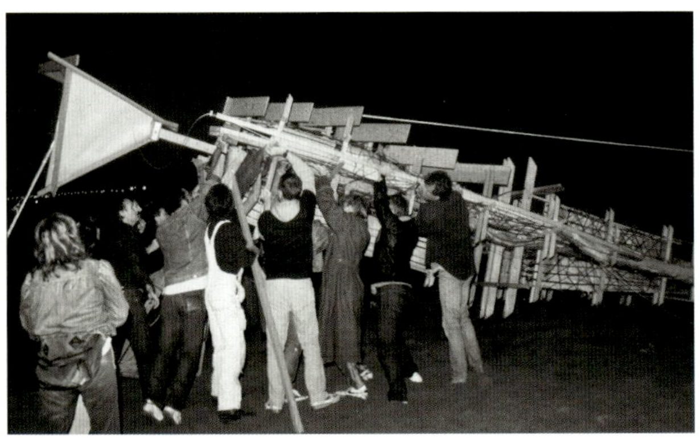

There was a structural flaw in the 1989 Man, and midway up something snapped.

The Baker Beach Burn was like most effective rituals: mysterious and utilitarian. I remember as a child going to my best friend's First Holy Communion. What intrigued me about the ceremony wasn't just the Latin, which I did think sounded mysterious and cool; it was all of the physical gestures—the raising of the chalice, the jingling of bells, and, after the wafers had been distributed to the eager seven-year-olds, the priest tidying up. I watched in fascination as he drained every drop from the chalice, carefully wiping the rim several times. *Wow,* I thought, *he's doing the dishes.* Thereafter I have believed that the most compelling spiritual mystery is the kind that's hidden within the practical, and every lasting culture is built in the same fashion: with communal effort. I don't know why, but there seemed to be a strong element of cultural magic built into the Baker Beach setting and ceremony.

Once all the parts of the figure were assembled, the central interaction—the one that unified the crowd in common cause—was to raise him from horizontal to vertical. The plan was to push the Man to a partial upright angle by hand and prop him there with poles. Then a hundred or so volunteers would pull him upright with a large rope by first dragging his feet into holes in the sand and, when the feet had caught, pulling him the rest of the way to vertical. Jerry described it as the way carpenters might put up a really long ladder, by having someone "foot" the base of the ladder while others push it upright. The reason the raising made for an effective ritual was because it required full community participation. As the rope is pulled, people automatically begin to applaud and cheer. By the time the Man is upright, virtually everyone present has committed to the ritual.

Unfortunately, in 1989 the weight of the heavy torso combined with a low rope angle forced additional stress to the joints, causing one of the legs to break. There was a loud crack and the Man came crashing back to Earth, nearly impaling some of the volunteers on its spiky details. The head shattered at an odd angle, and the entire torso twisted.

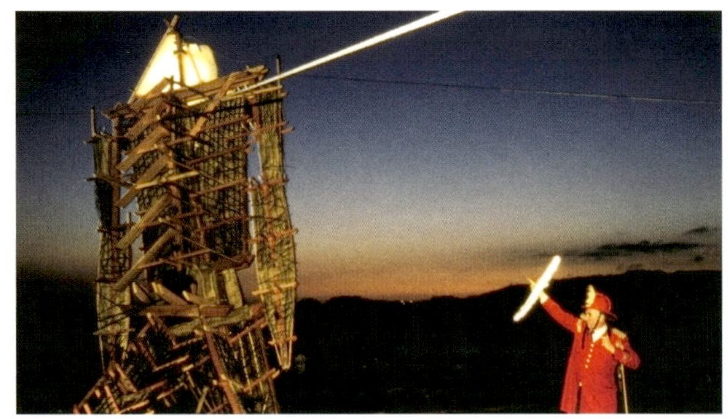

Flamo LaGrande's fiery coup de grâce was a fitting end to the Man's raising ordeal.

Jerry says now that he made the mistake of building the legs in two parts in order to keep the size of the limbs within the limits of the garage. For a moment it looked like the entire evening would be a failure, but then someone realized that we could simply break the other leg, prop the Man into a semi-seated position, and burn him anyway. Undaunted by the Man's maimed form, the team went about erecting the Man with cables. Flamo LaGrande set the damaged Man afire, and the crowd went nuts.

It was the sense of communal involvement that again captured my attention. From the very onset, with the crew of carpenters loading segments of the Man onto the wood racks of the pickups, to the people bearing those limbs down the steps of the cliffs, to the gang of volunteers assembling those parts on the sand, the event relied on the efforts of a cadre of volunteers. This is what the bohemian tradition in San Francisco had come to stand for: artists and others working together to create something artful in the world. These days the extraordinary amount of volunteer activity impresses virtually everyone who goes to Burning Man, and it was already present at Baker Beach. Larry would see it as a key element in building a community of Burners. Eventually, it would be called Participation—one of the Ten Principles—and while that might be anything from wearing a costume to building a camp or car, the highest contribution is performing services vital to the needs of the community.

The fire, when it fully engulfed the broken figure, completely masked its infirmities, and for several minutes the Man blazed gloriously. As Bryan, John, and I watched the flames from the hillside, we felt more than we'd expected. Despite all the problems, the Burn itself was breathtaking. There is something enormously powerful about the image of a human figure on fire. What I'd envisioned as a bunch of San Francisco hipsters gathering for a solstice bash and a bit of new age mumbo jumbo had turned out to be much more dynamic and moving than I could have imagined. I'd never envisioned the collective will and cooperative spirit needed to make such an event happen, and we all had been completely unprepared for the mesmerized reaction of this crowd of passionate onlookers.

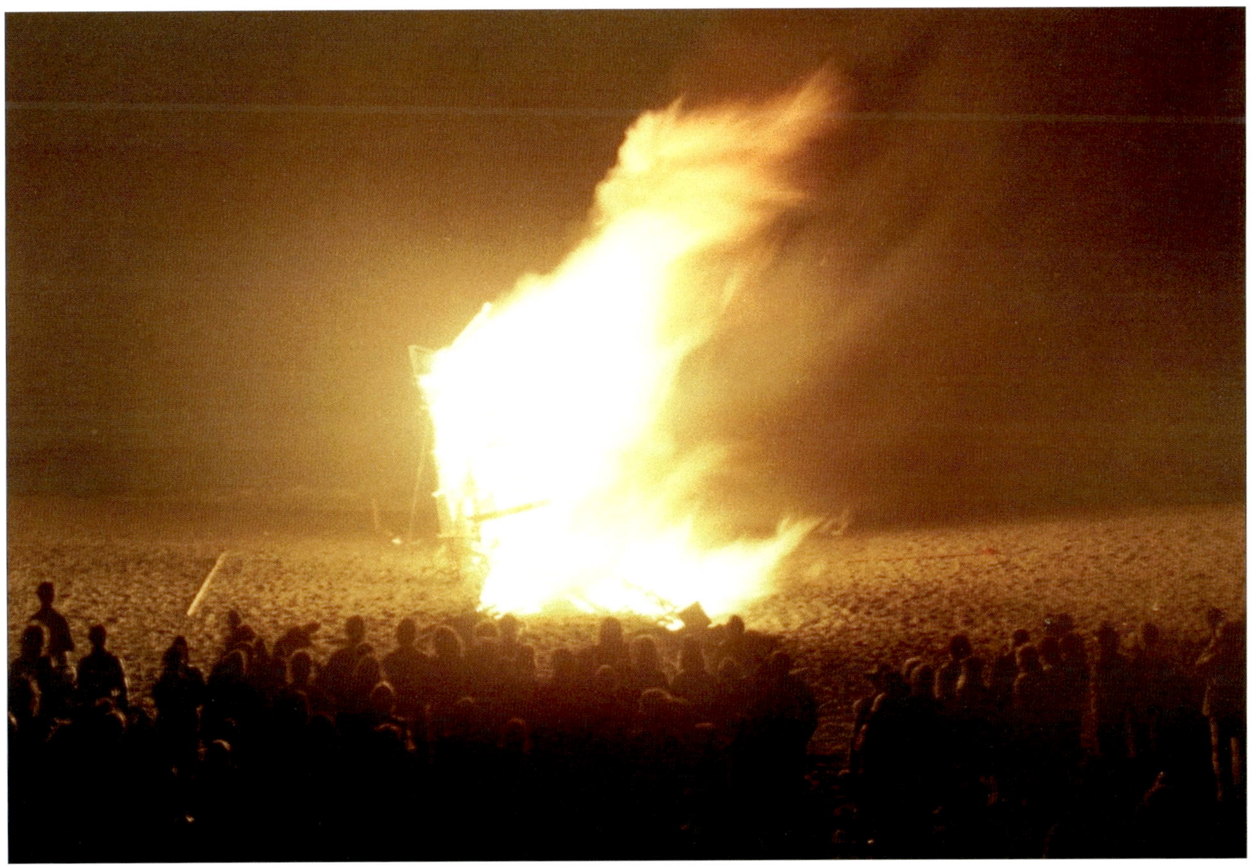

The experience of participating in that Baker Beach Burn was more than we had anticipated. The intensity was genuine, the emotions were raw, and the sense of being a part of something larger than life was very real. It was the kind of experience that transcends buying a ticket and sitting earnestly in an audience. It was the kind of experience that you can only have by grabbing on to the end of the rope and hauling on it with all you've got.

Bryan, John, and I returned to Portland feeling we'd witnessed something special, something beyond our abilities to describe. Flawed and failed as it was in its execution, the Baker Beach Burn was utterly moving and uplifting. There was a sense of it being both neo-hipster and as old as the grains of sand on the shore. We had witnessed a nascent phenomenon, bringing people together to collectively explore the origins of culture. Somehow my brother had figured out the alchemy of creating new raiment from ancient cloth: to reenact and collectively explore passionately that oldest of dreams—that what we create today in this hour is for us and all others to share. We will do this for ourselves and for one another, and out of this experience will come a personal revelation. The group will explore this art together, and out of that will come what each person seeks alone. It's an ancient formula.

> Immediate experience is, in many ways, the most important touchstone of value in our culture. We seek to overcome barriers that stand between us and a recognition of our inner selves, the reality of those around us, participation in society, and contact with a natural world exceeding human powers. No idea can substitute for this experience.
>
> —Larry Harvey

GOD'S ANVIL

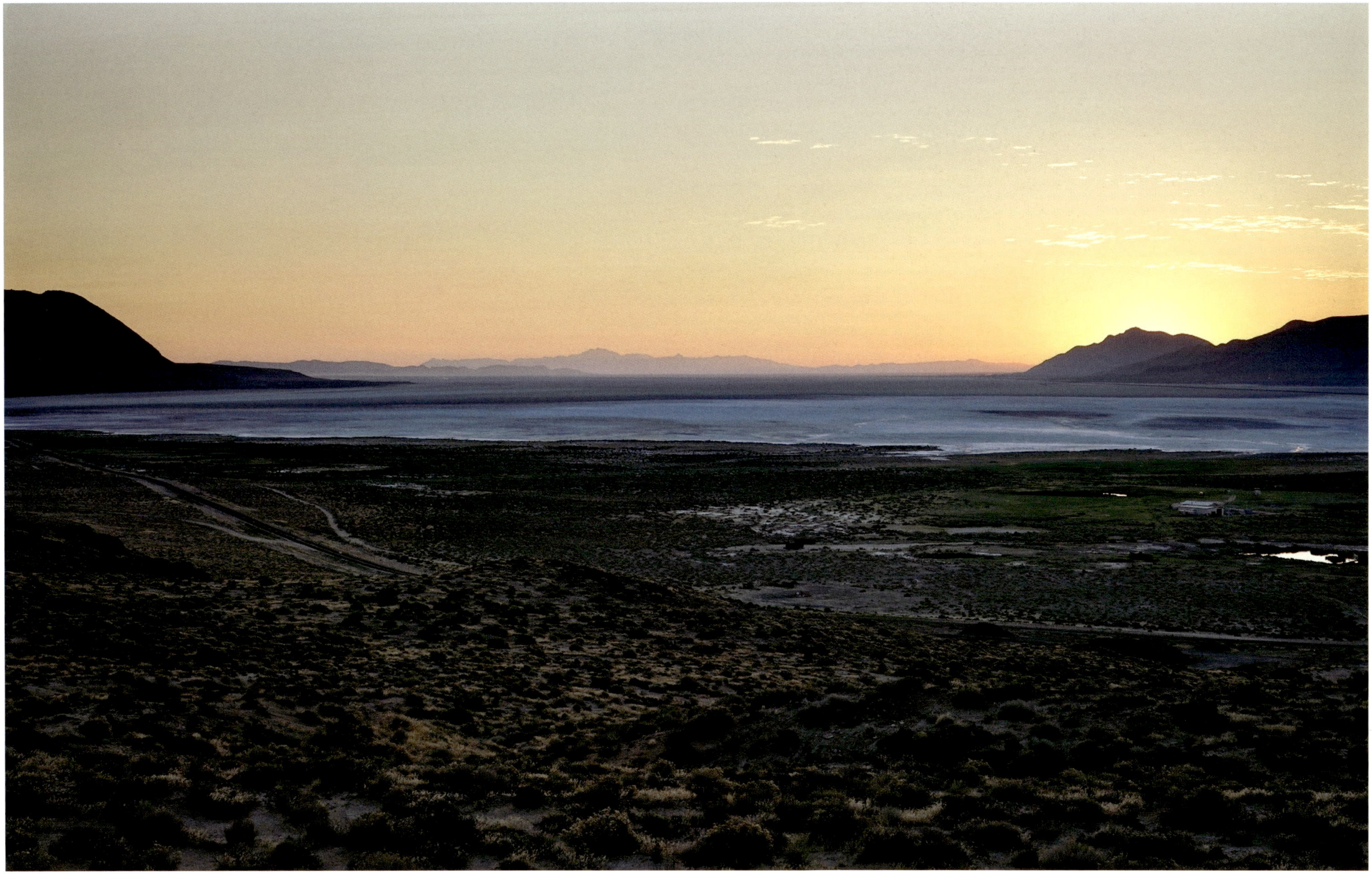

Black Rock Gateway, 2016

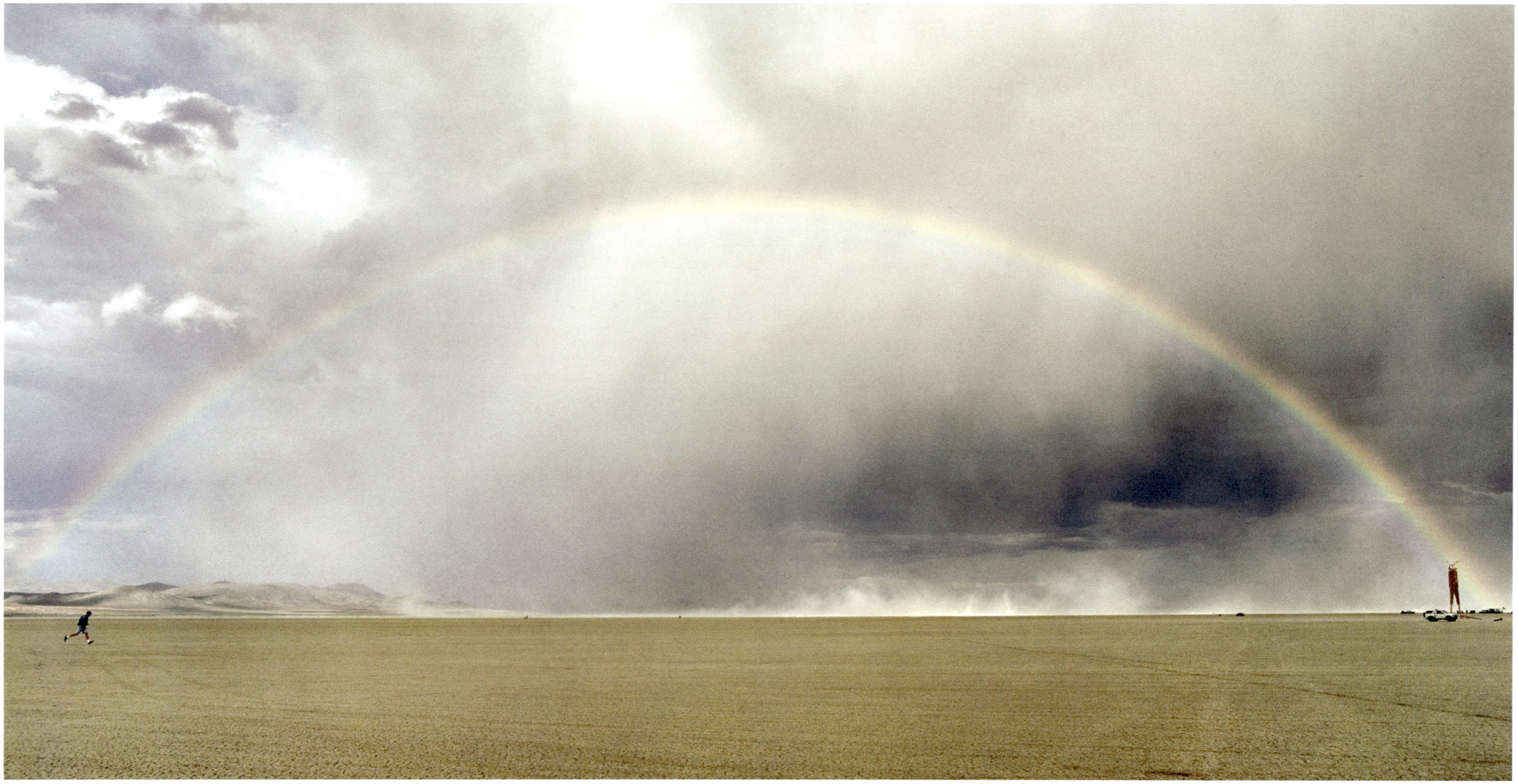

Rainbow Runner, 1995

The Black Rock Desert snared our attention from the first moment we set foot on its hard expanse. The event hadn't yet grown so large that it could possibly distract us from the dynamics of a vast flat surface and volatile weather. Veteran Burners like to reminisce about the wild ol' days of the event, when there were no roads or a perimeter fence to corral us, and the playa was our endless playground. In those days we drove our cars fast across the alkali flat, lolled away our afternoons at Fly Hot Springs, and at night followed lasers through the dark to rave camps. Everywhere we looked, there was unlimited opportunity. Even today individuals bike or jog out by the orange boundary and imagine a world without restrictions. On the playa people traverse the edge of a world without apparent limitations, and many cannot wait to embrace that creative possibility. Here is a place for personal expression of an unparalleled magnitude, and we are sometimes amazed to find a bit of deep playa art apparently made for no one except the most adventurous. We venture across the surface of God's great anvil, praying for a spark of genius.

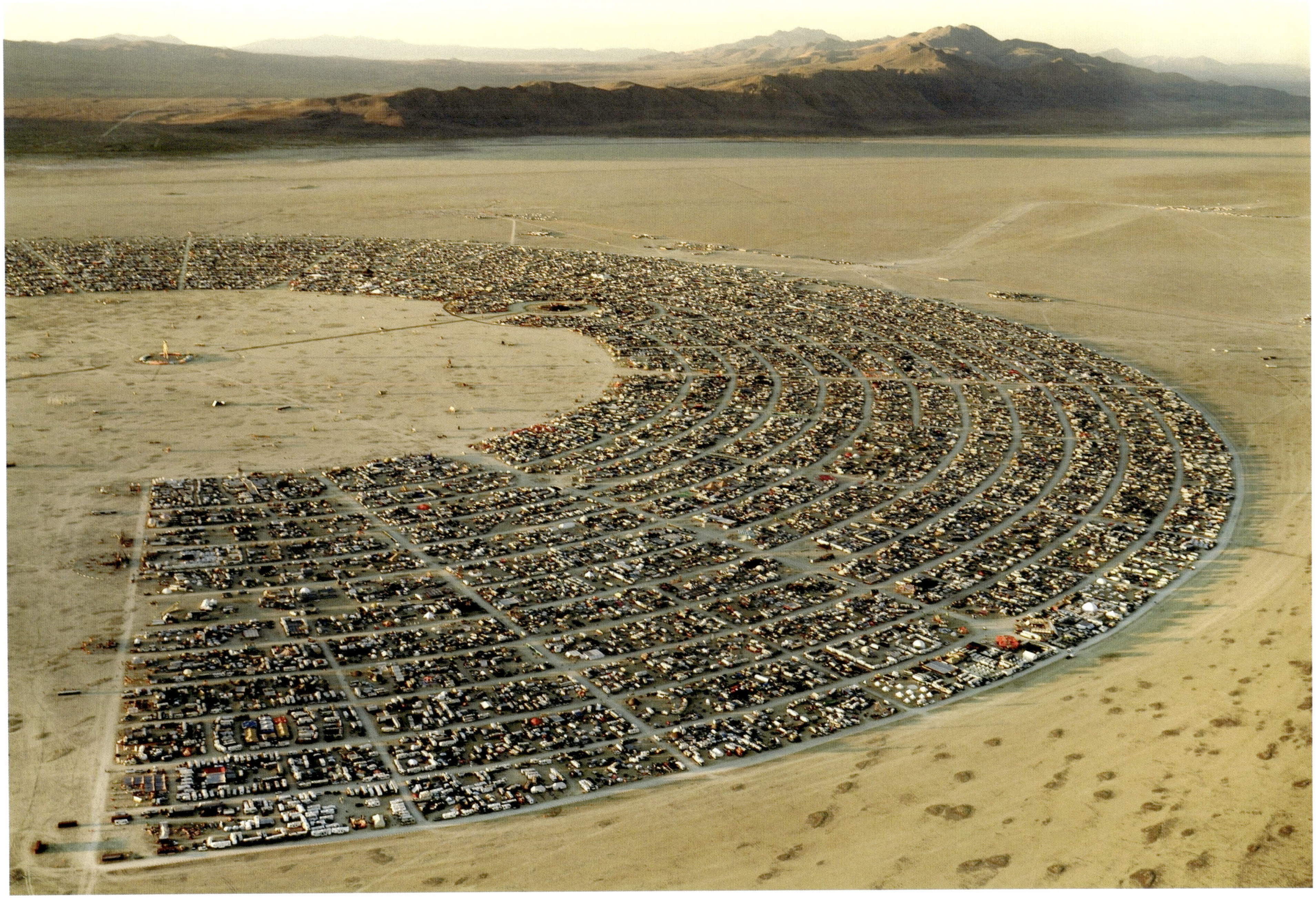

Black Rock City, 2014

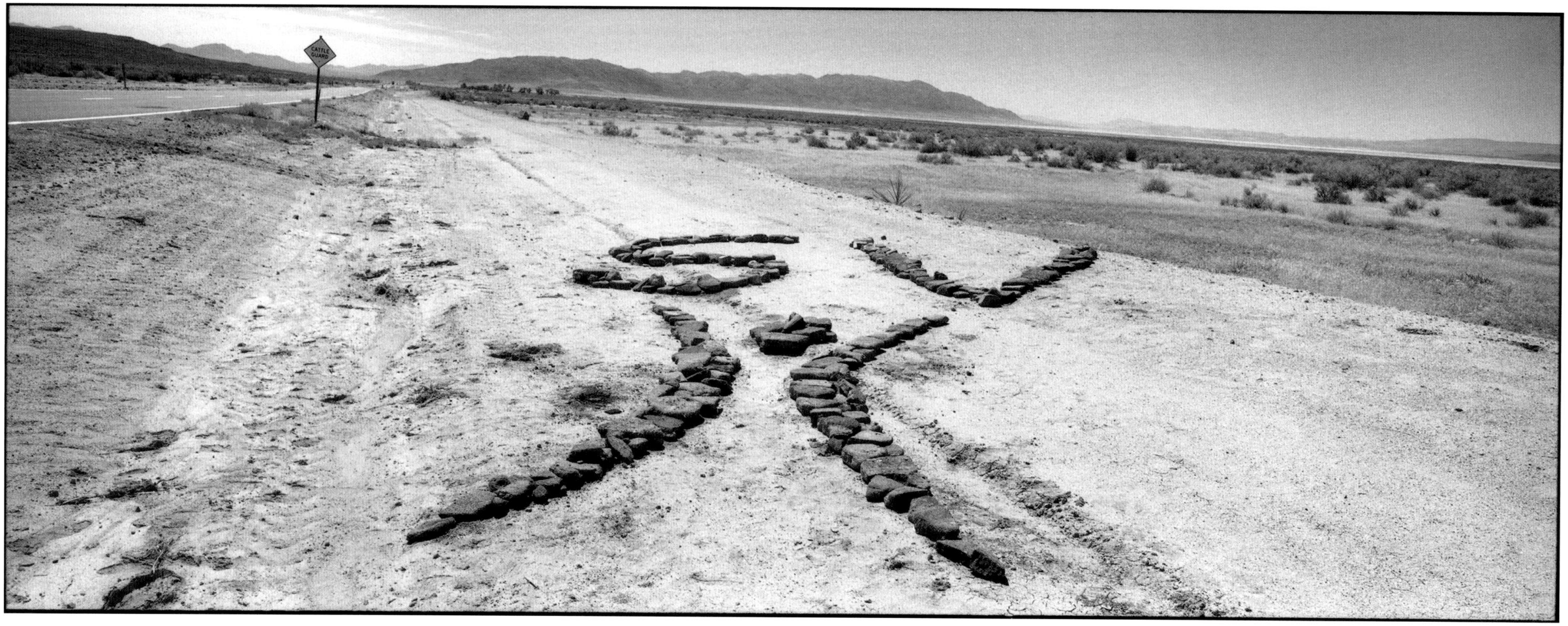

Road to Black Rock, 2003

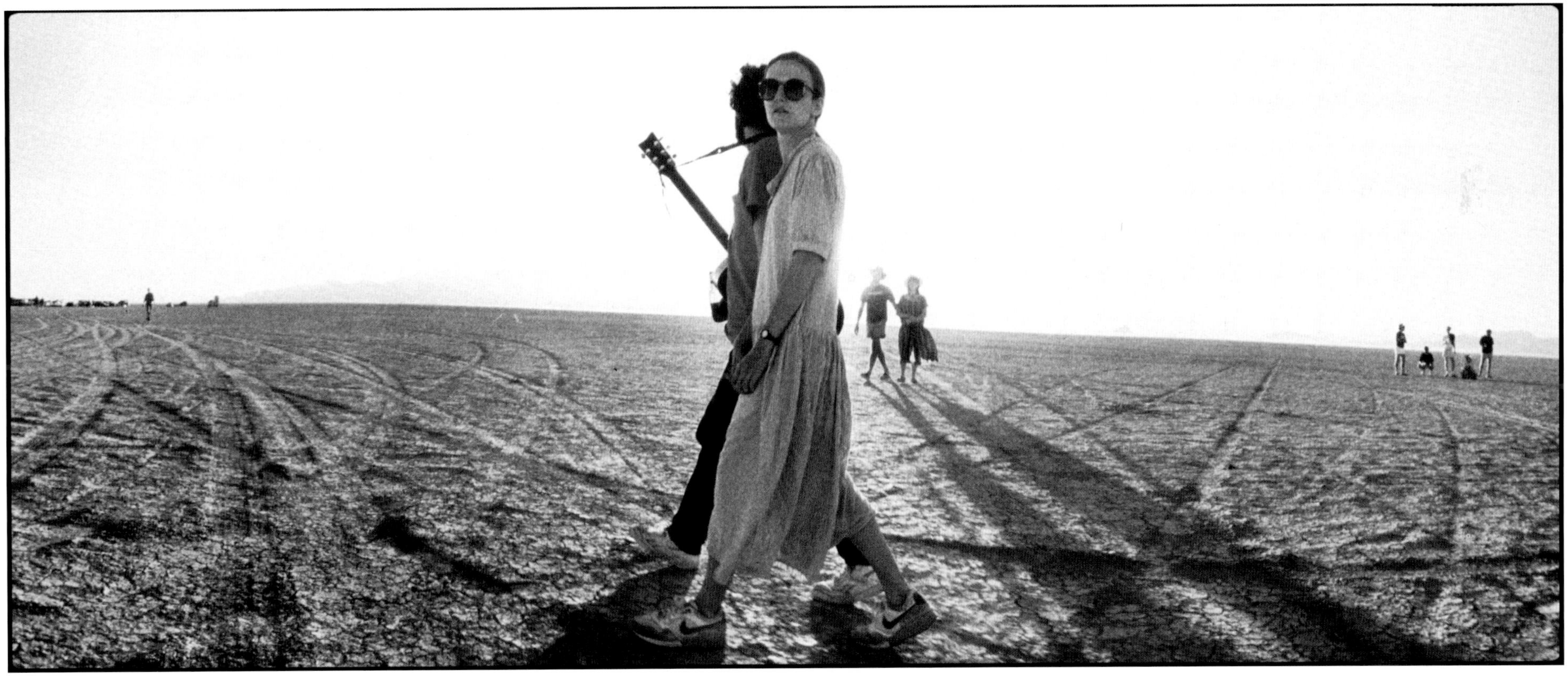

Playa Walkers, 1990

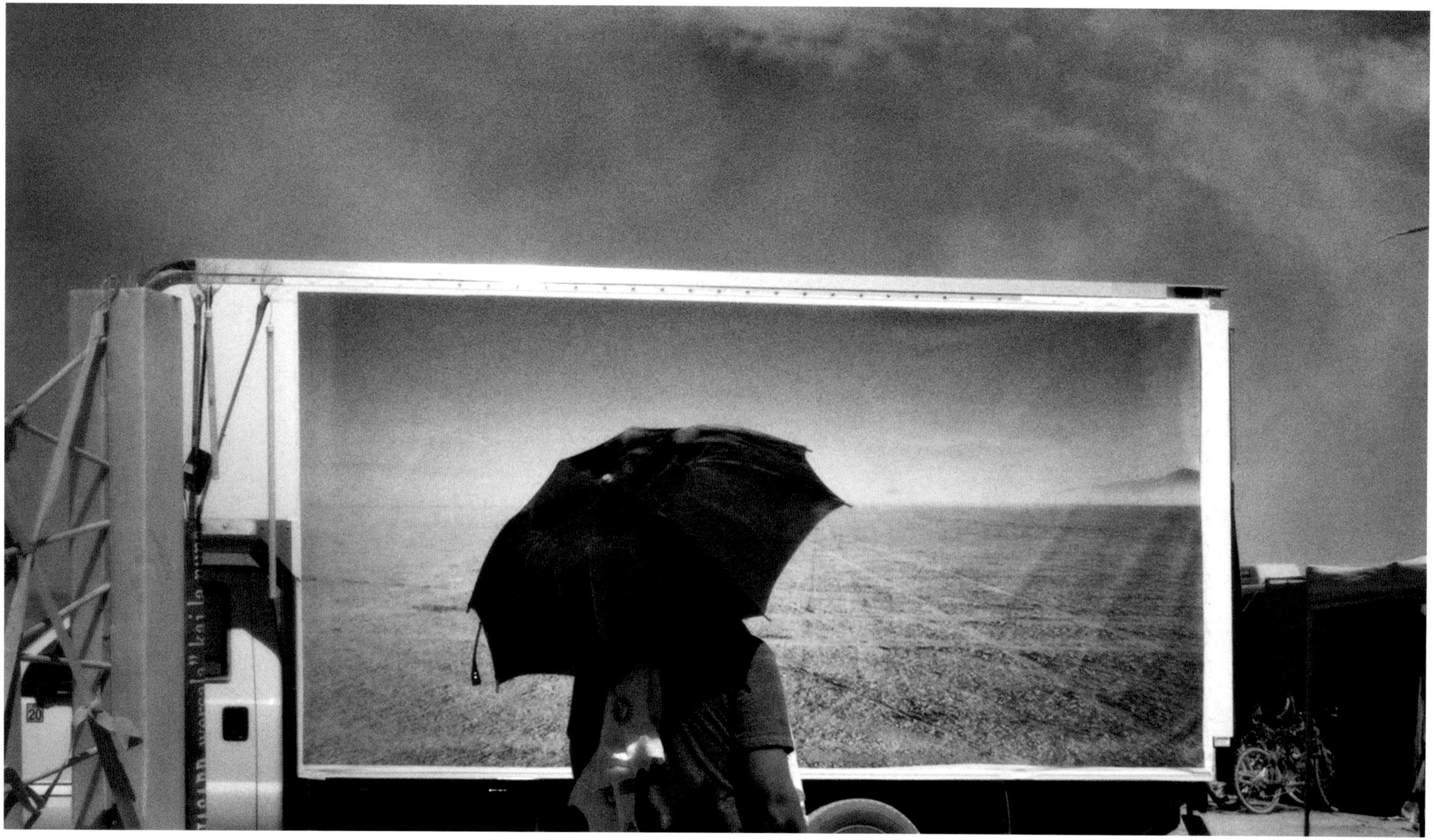

Truck Mural, 2012

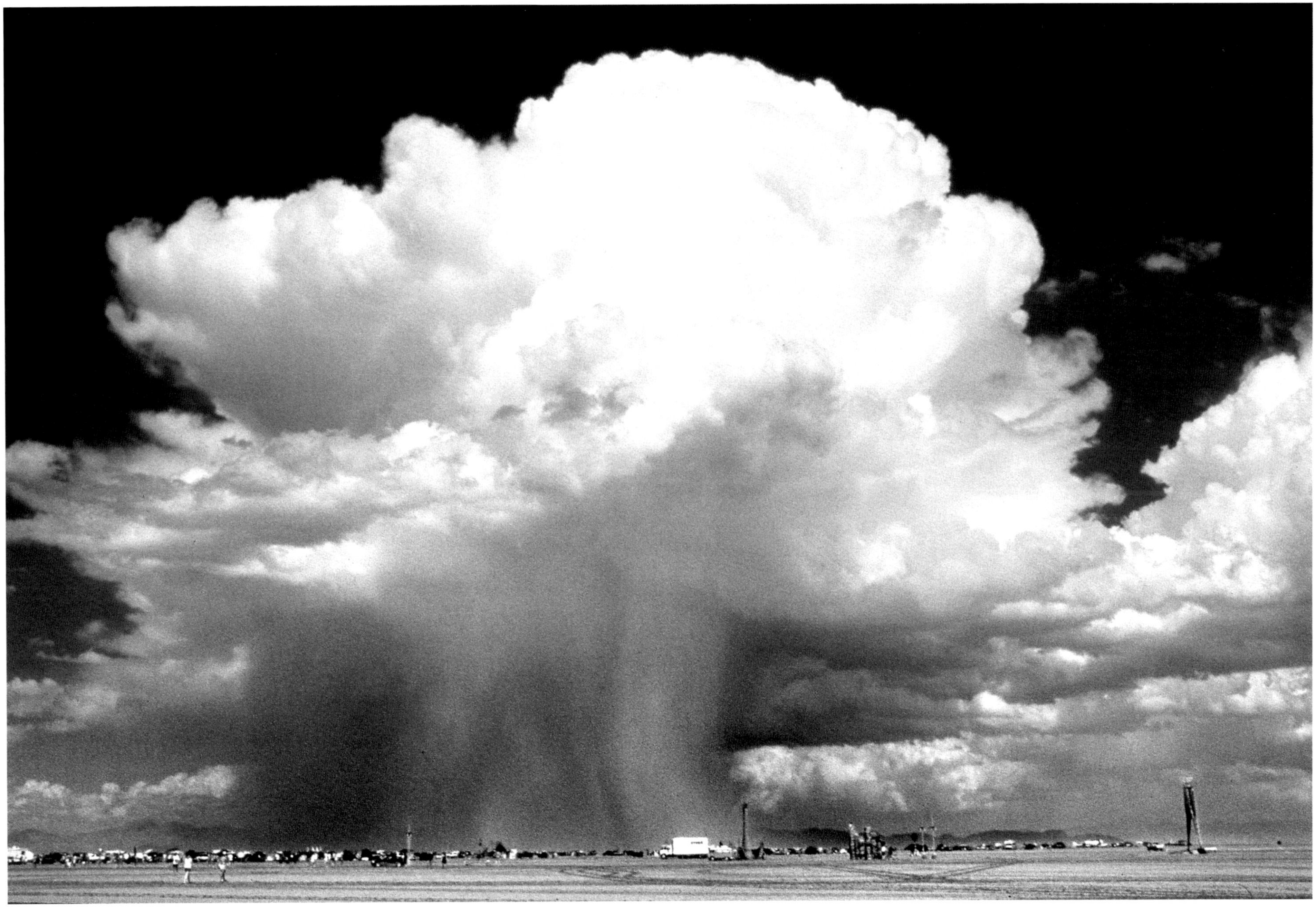

Storm Cloud, 1995

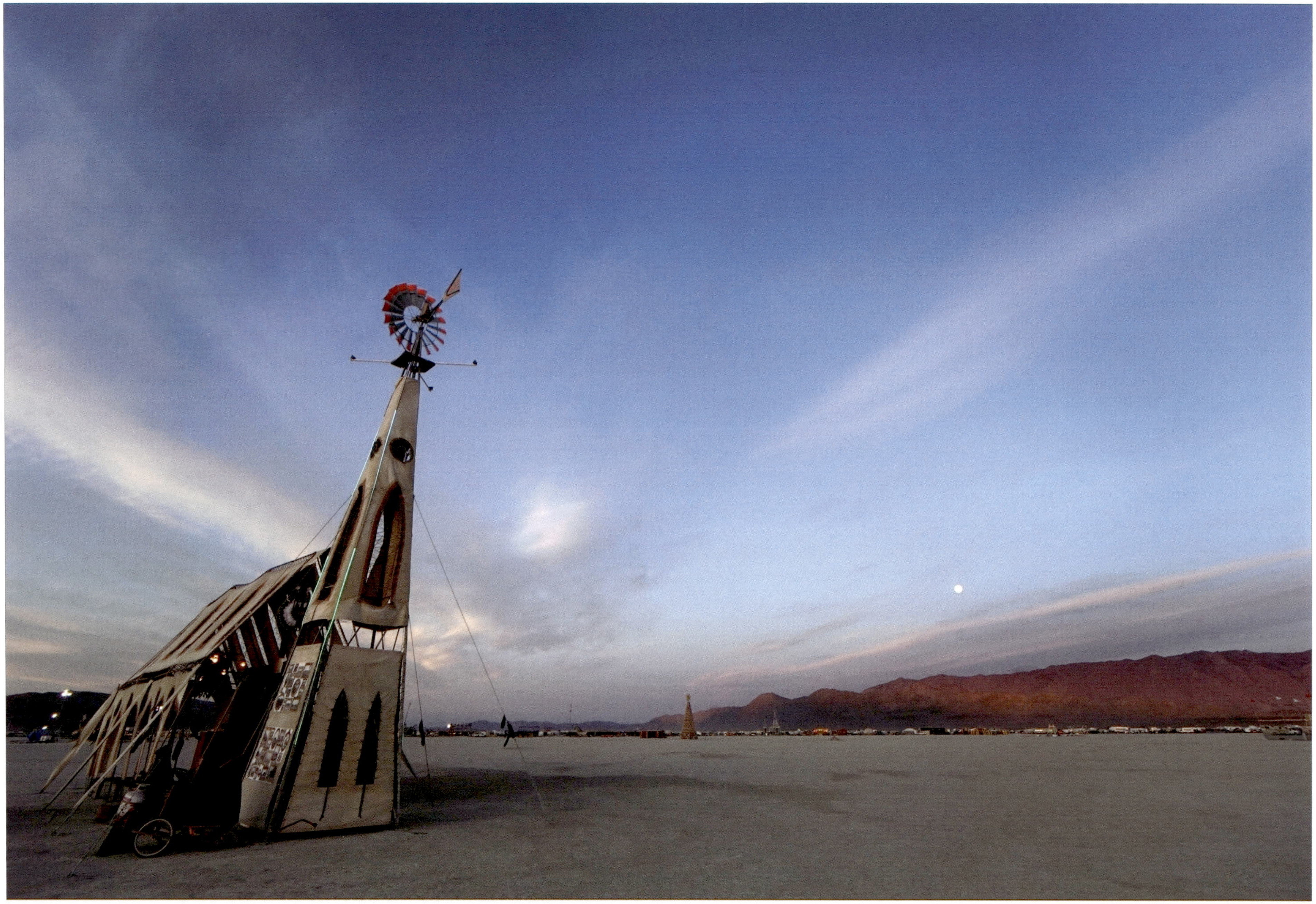

Prairie Wind Chapel, *2015*

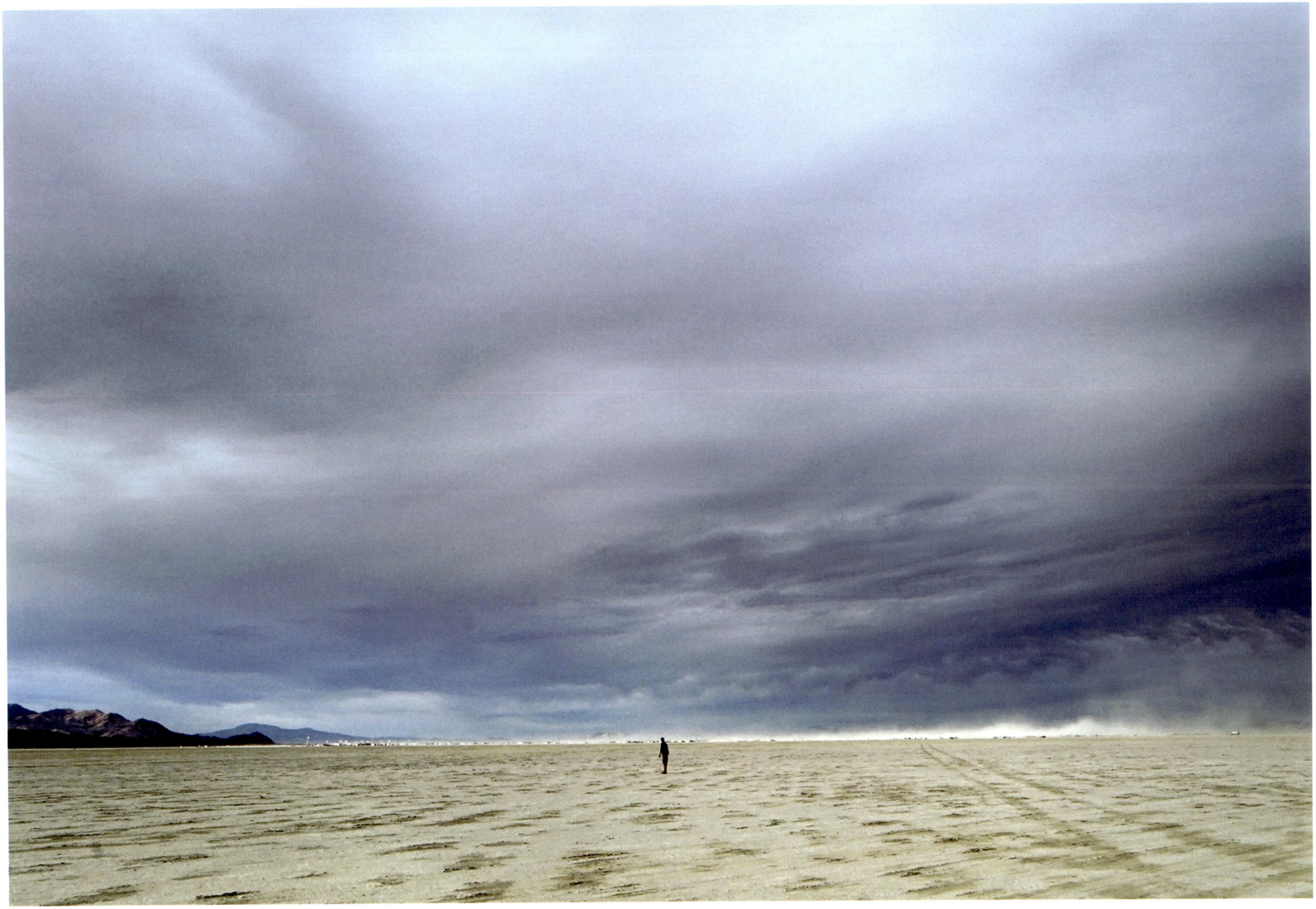

Evening Playa Sky, 2015

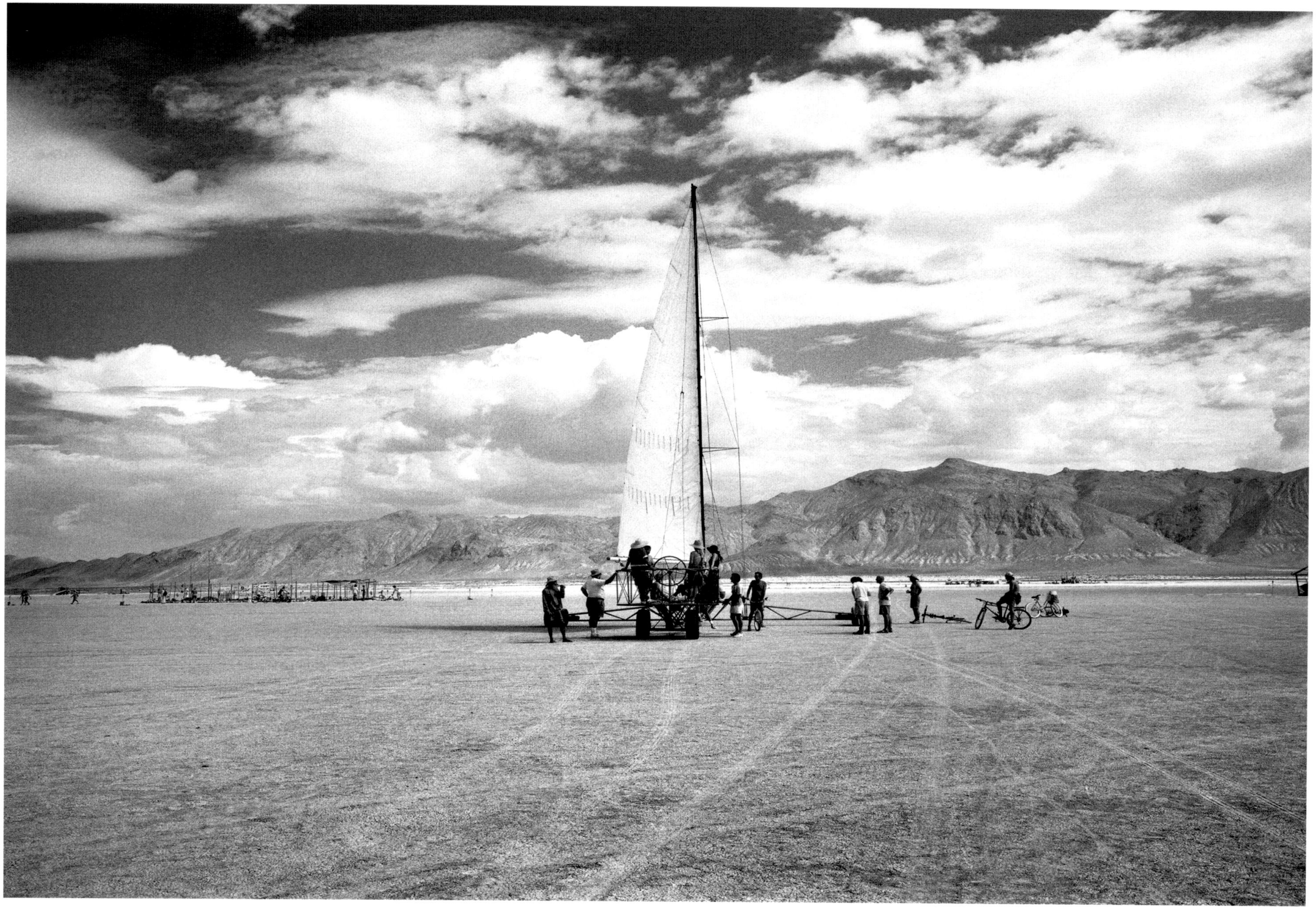

Wind Sailors, 1998

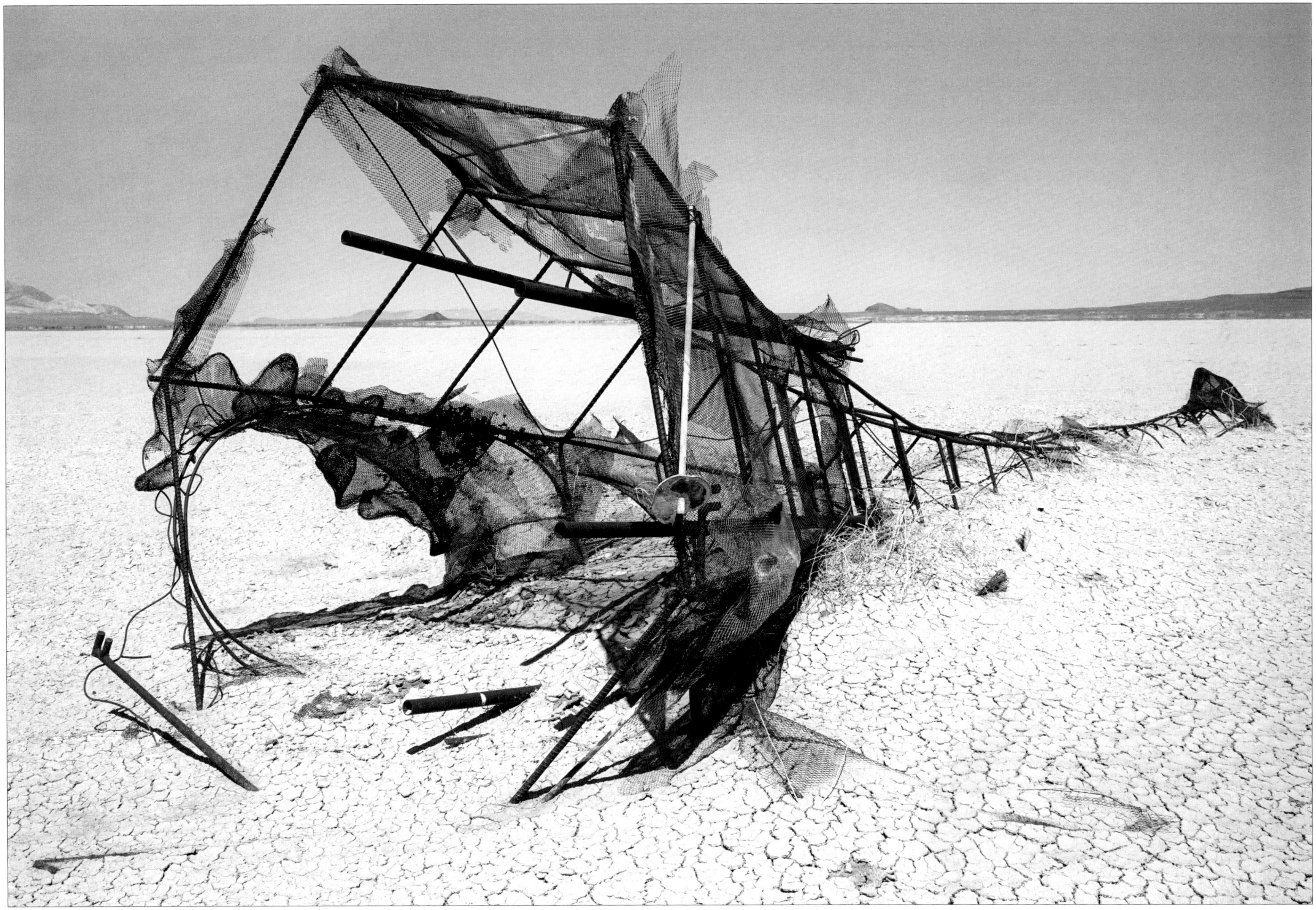

Pepe Ozan's Hualapai Relic, *2016*

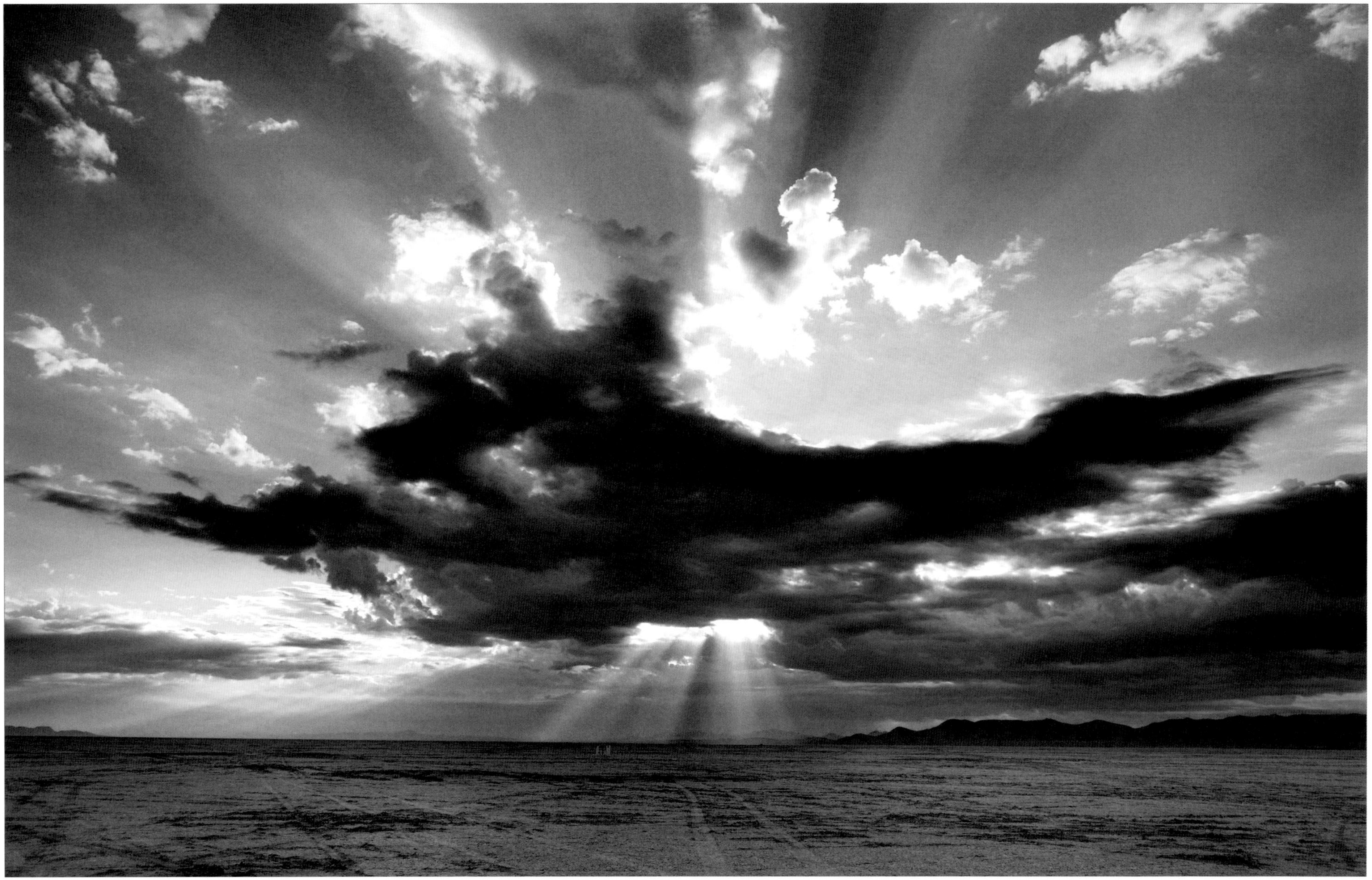

Morning Clouds, 2014

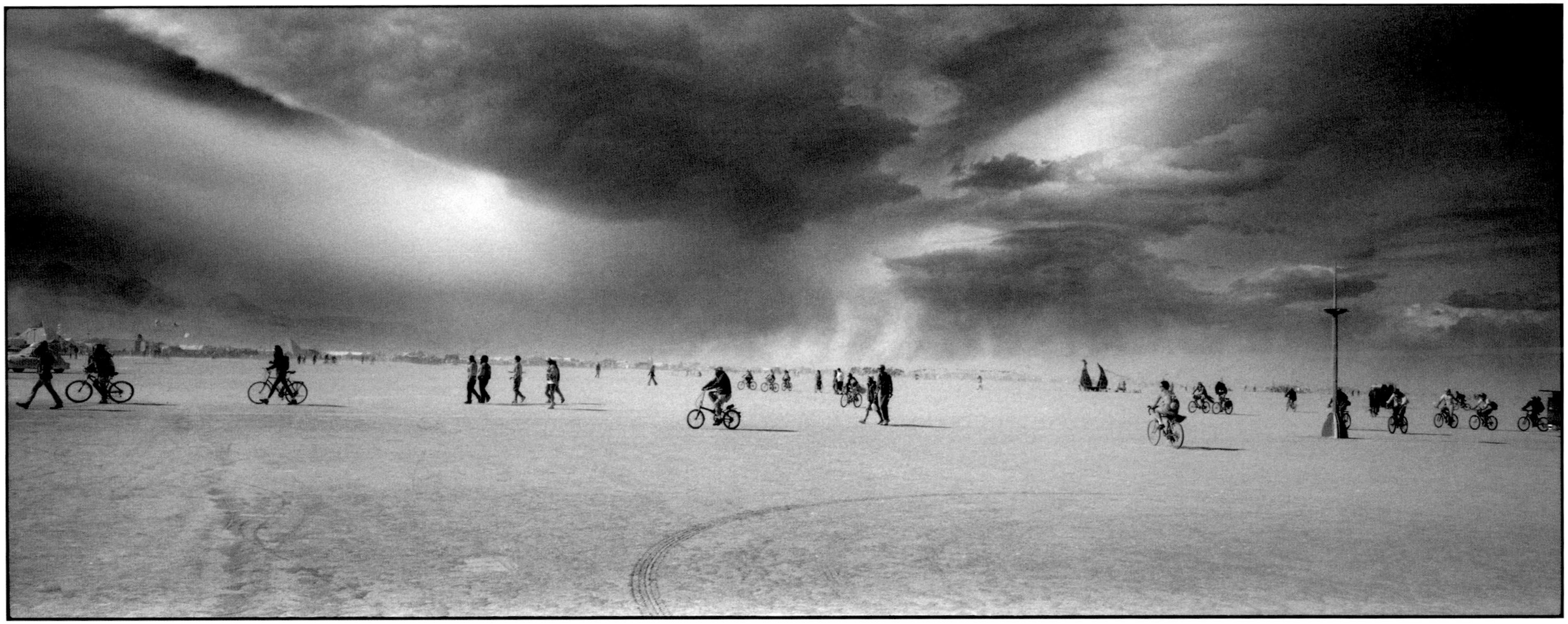

Approaching Storm, 1999

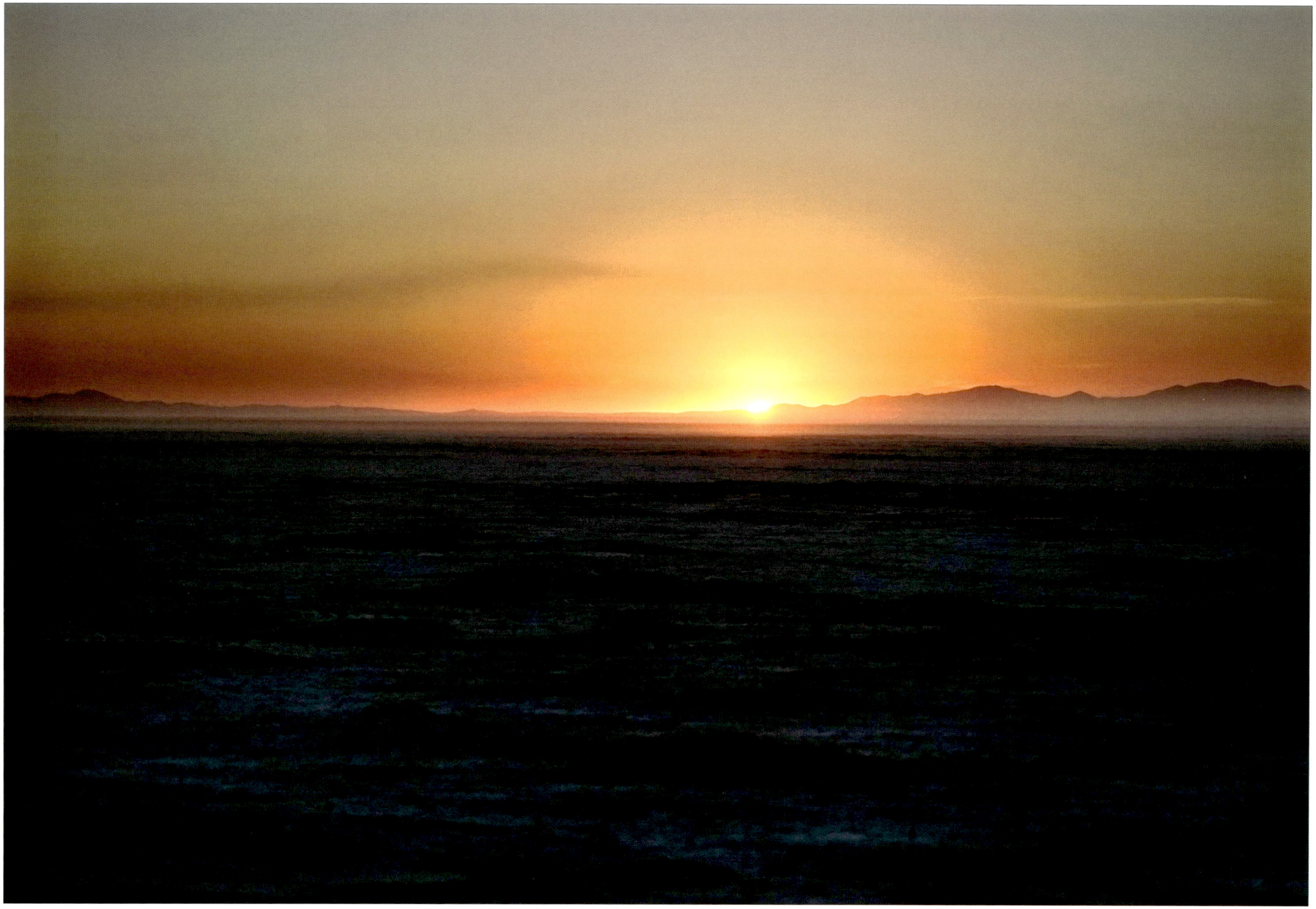

Playa Ocean, 2016

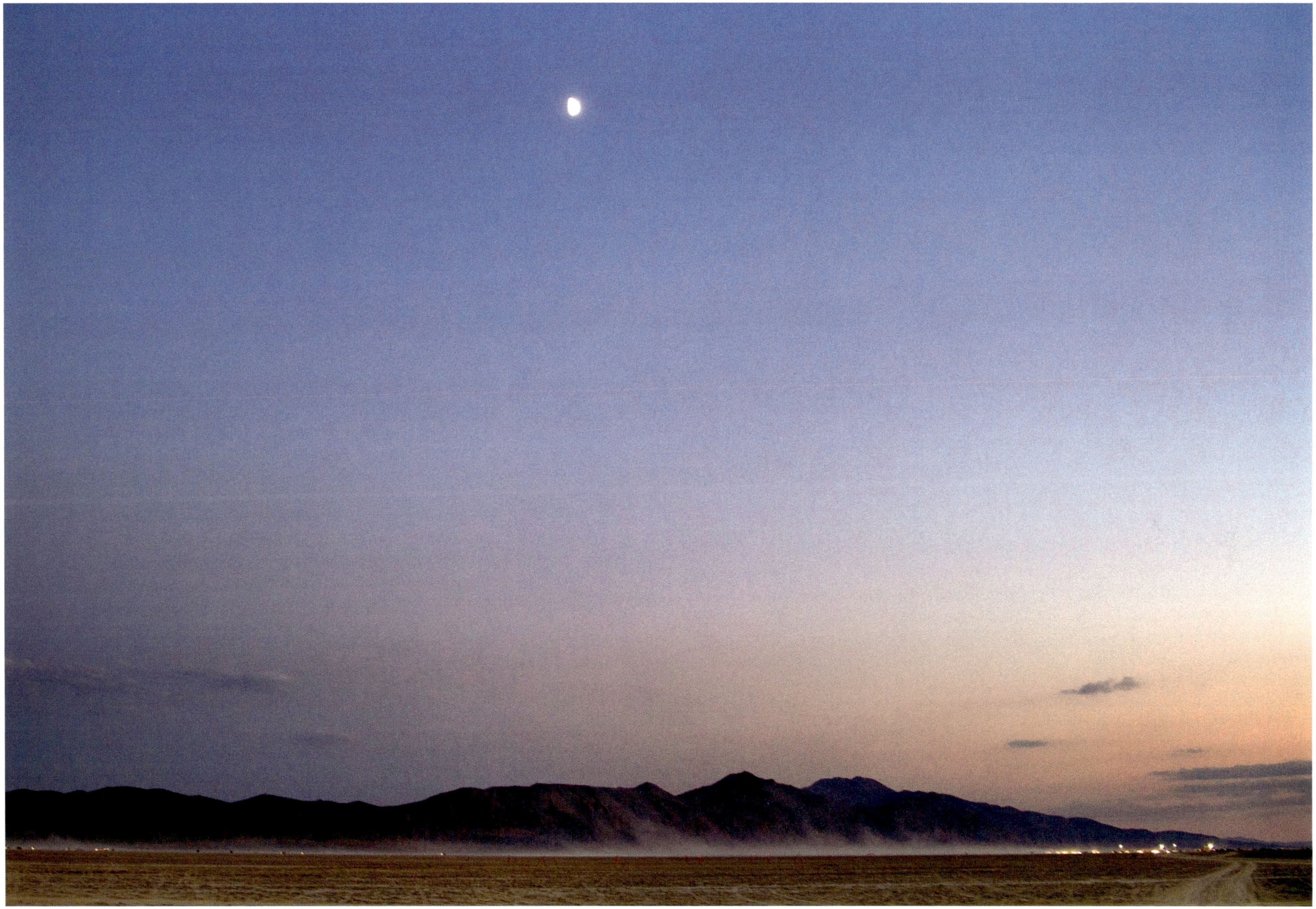

Early Arrivals, 2012

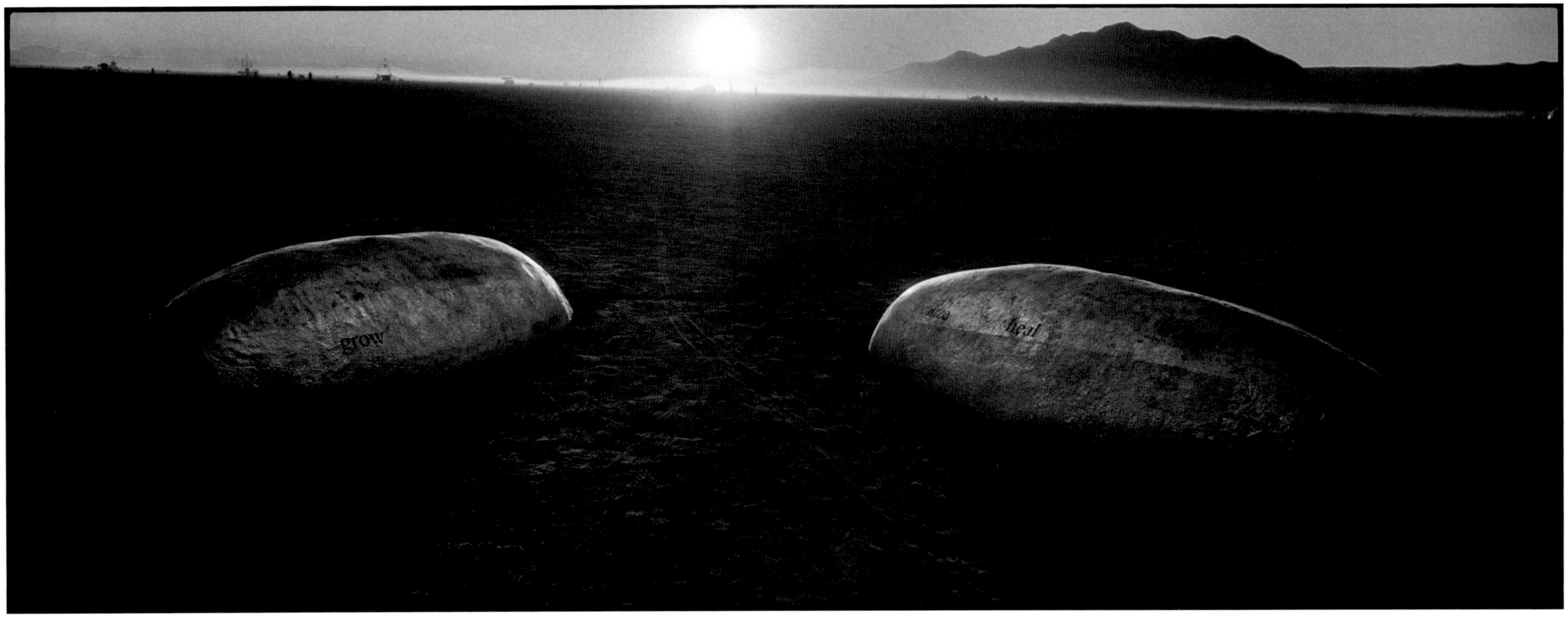

Linguistic Islands, *2009*

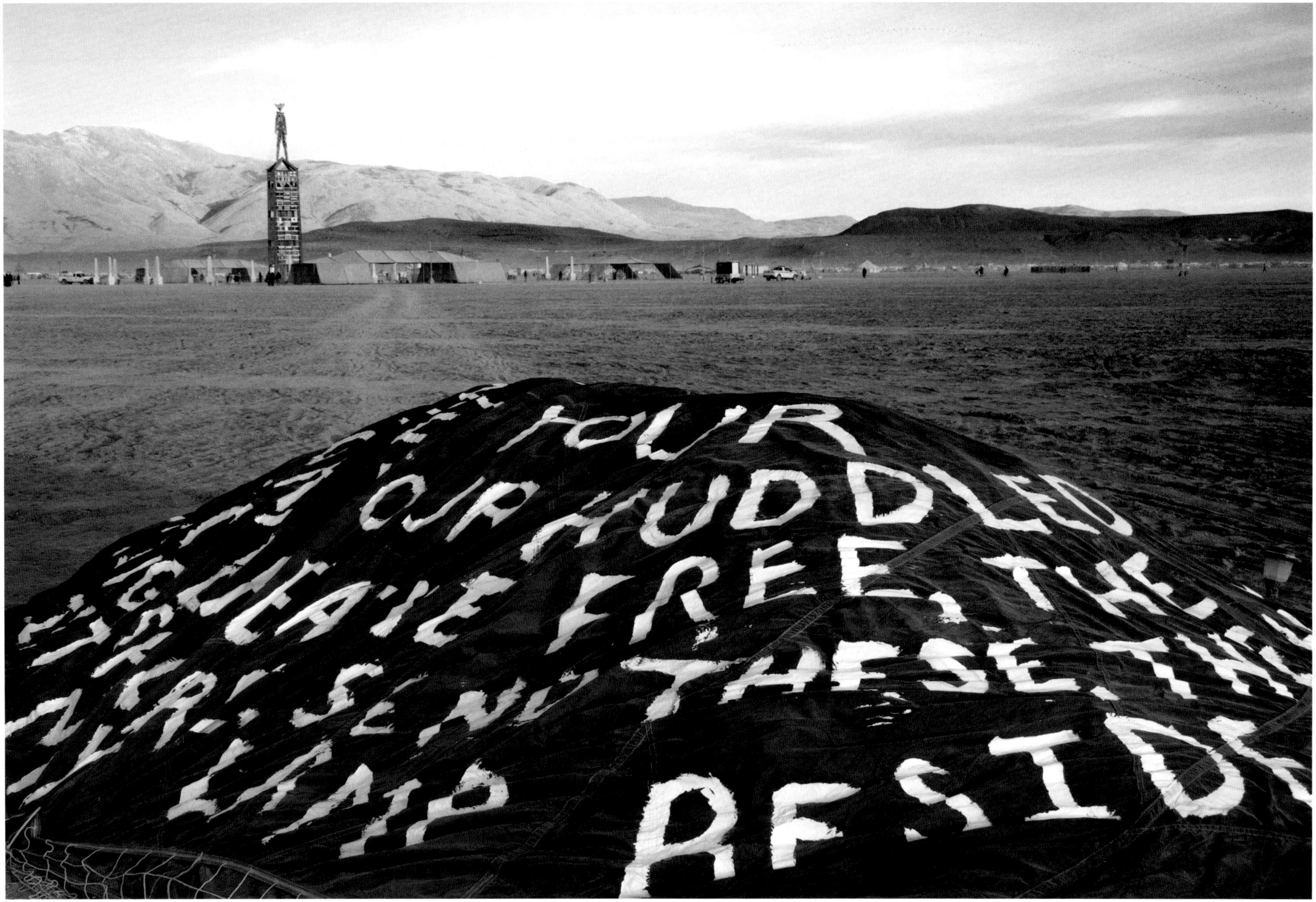

Our Huddled Free, 2008

Dust Storm Duo, 2014

The playa has many faces and infinite moods. Dust storms can visit their rough magic without warning, and those who have ventured far from camp endure or head for shelter. Newbie Burners wear or carry dust masks and goggles at all times. The dust-averse or ultra-sensitive might wear the bulky cylinder masks favored by painters, but veteran Burners are a foolhardy bunch, and many opt for the simplicity of sunglasses and a bandana. Photographers often wrap their cameras and lenses in duct tape and plastic sheeting, but diehards always go out in the worst conditions because dust storms generate an array of visual effects.

In a playa dust storm the placid becomes mysteriously animated, figures transpose into graphic elements, the atmosphere shifts dramatically—provoking a surreal curiosity. Sometimes, of course, the dust is being pushed by approaching rain. Playa weather can be fickle, and it changes rapidly. Like sailors on a placid sea, Burners scan the sky for signs of an approaching gale. The vacant playa, like the negative space between stars, provides a backdrop for our most outrageous apprehensions and an enduring context for our most creative mythologies.

Dust Storm Cuddle, 2016

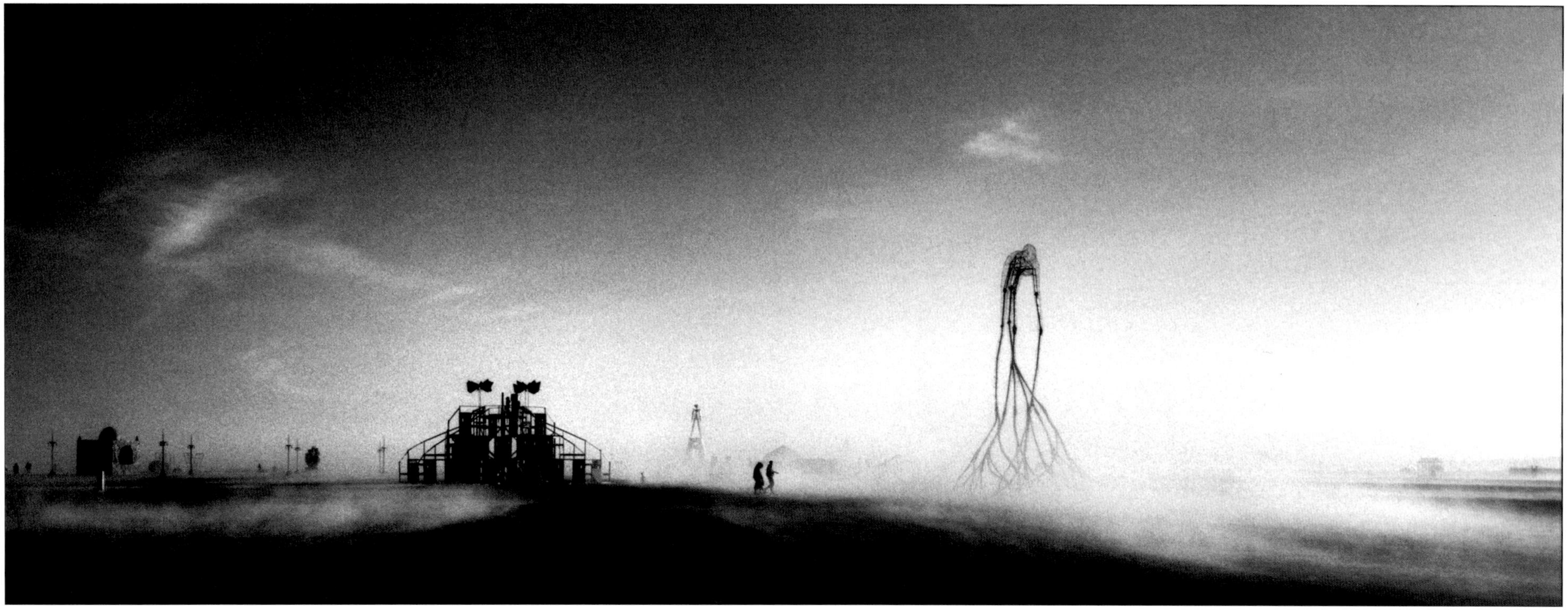

Flock *Horizon, 2001*

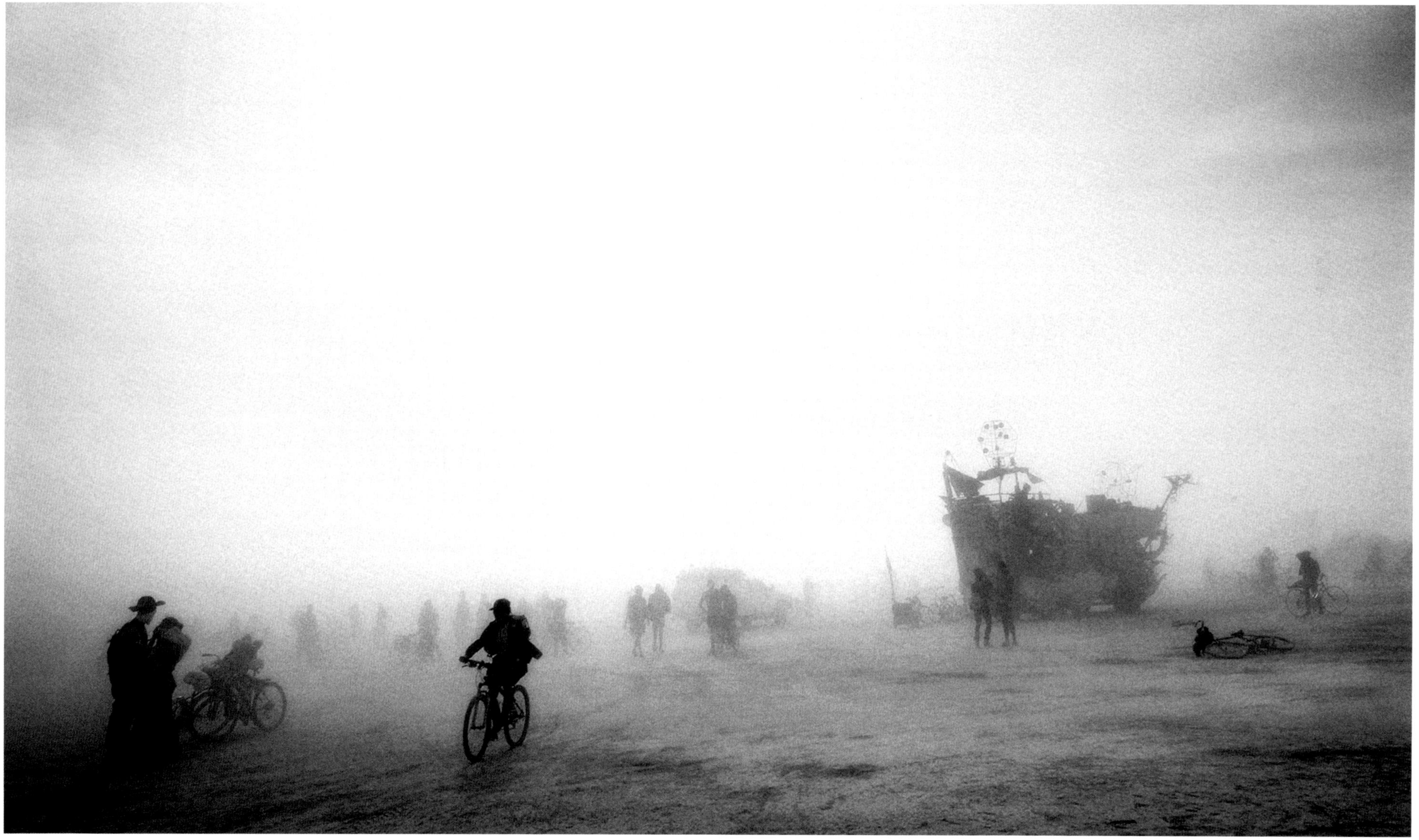

Dusty Sun, 2014

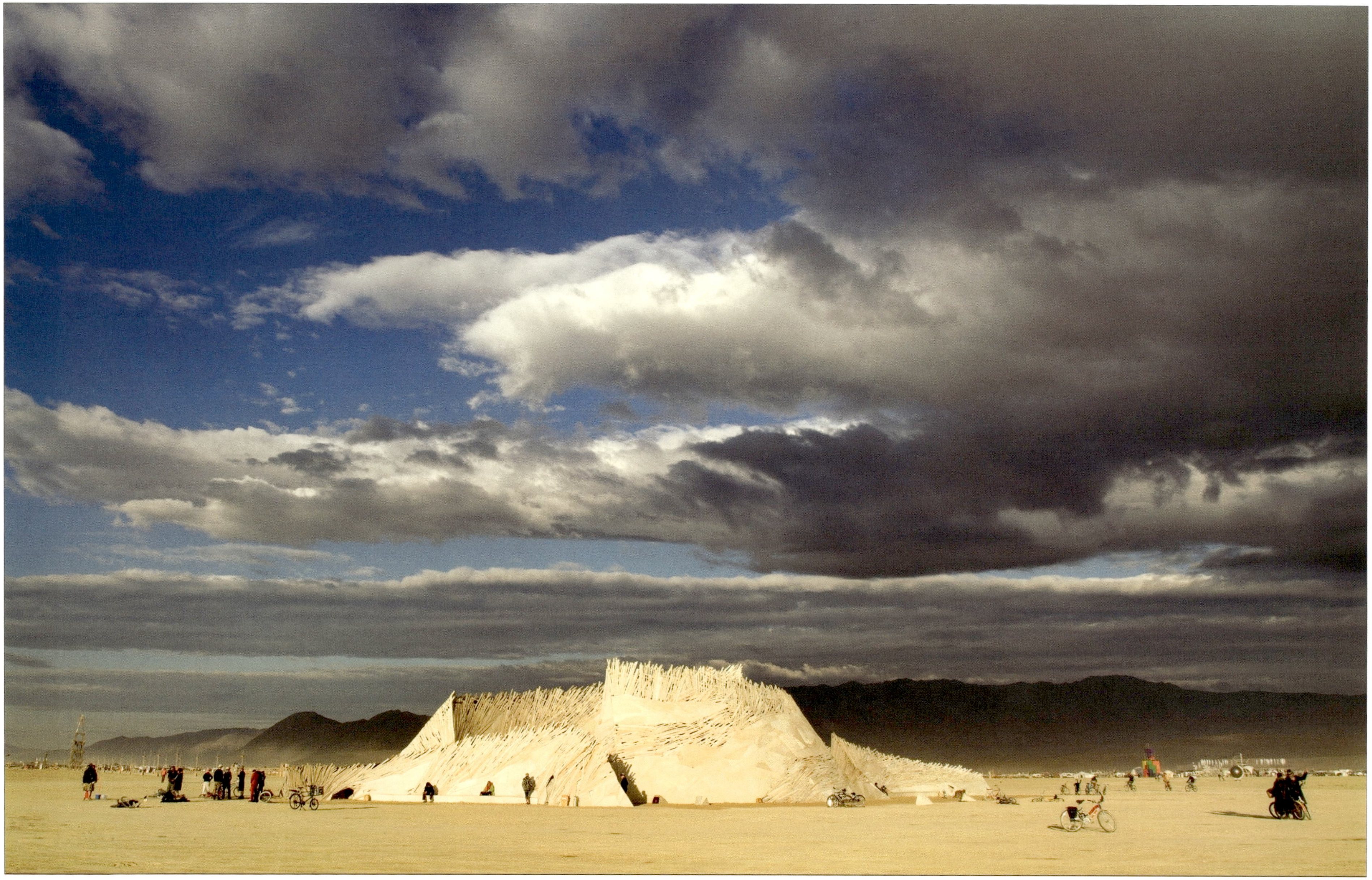

Temple of Flux, *2010*

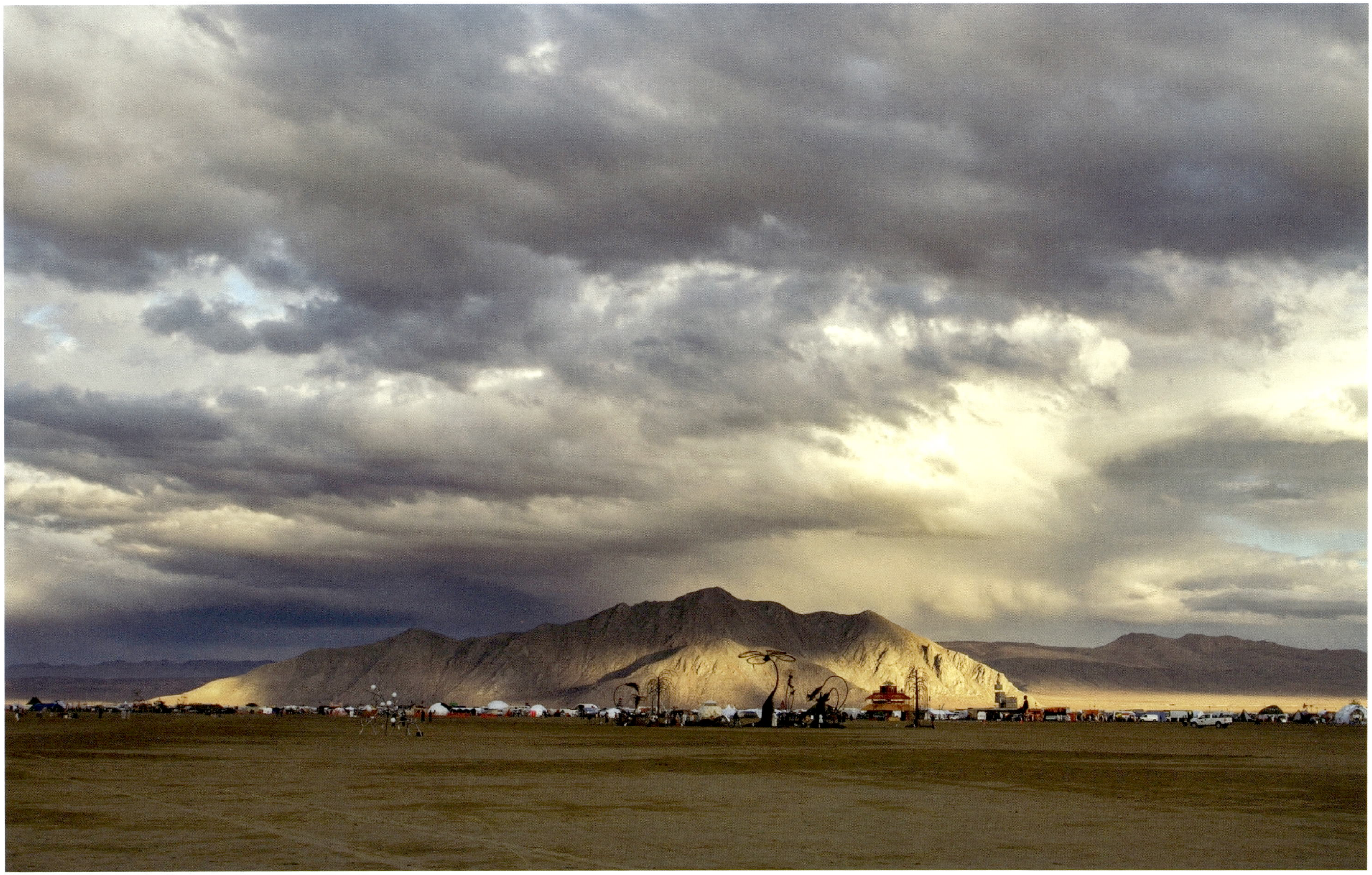

Twilight Camps, 2010

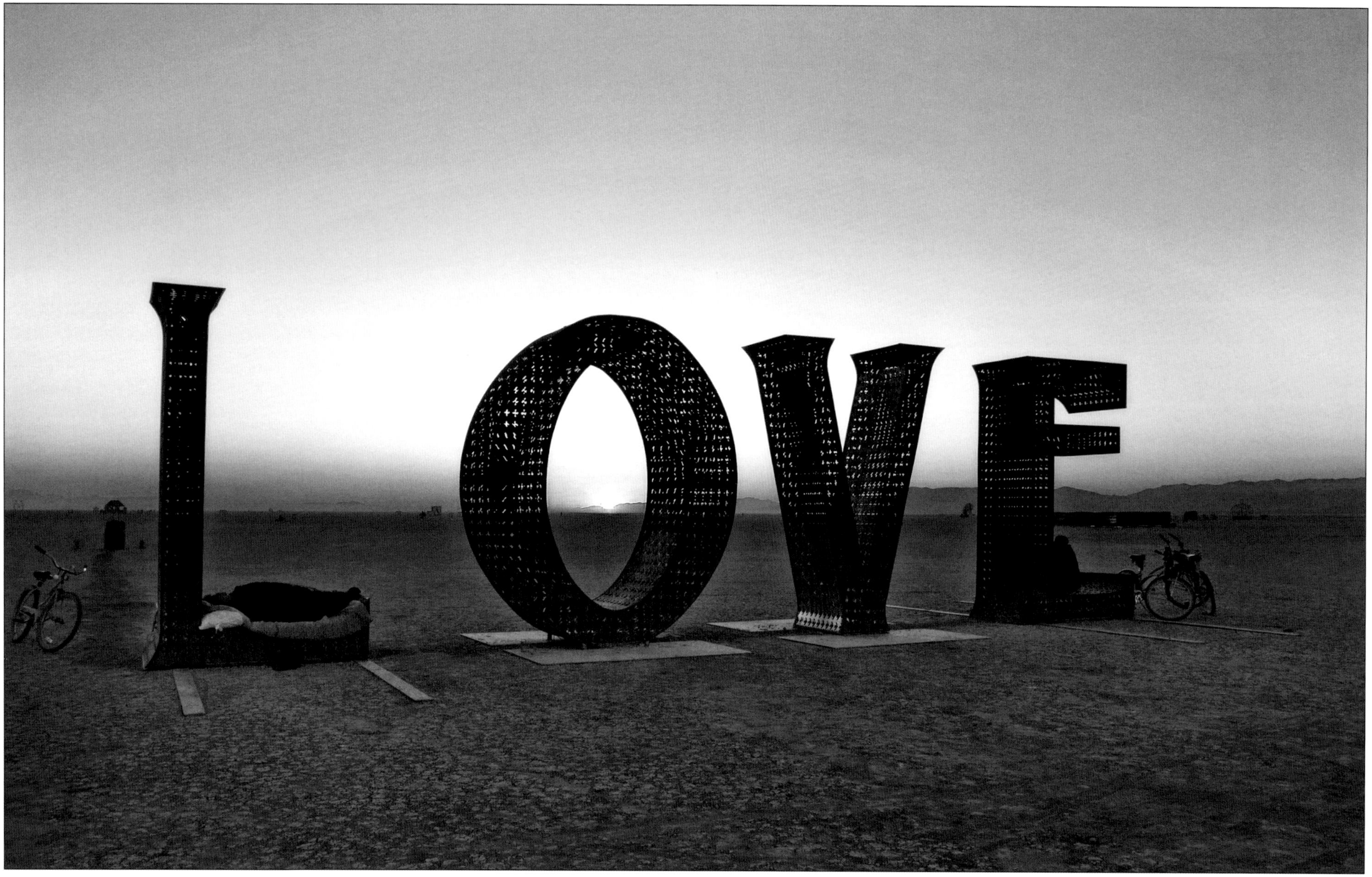

LOVE *Sleeping, 2012*

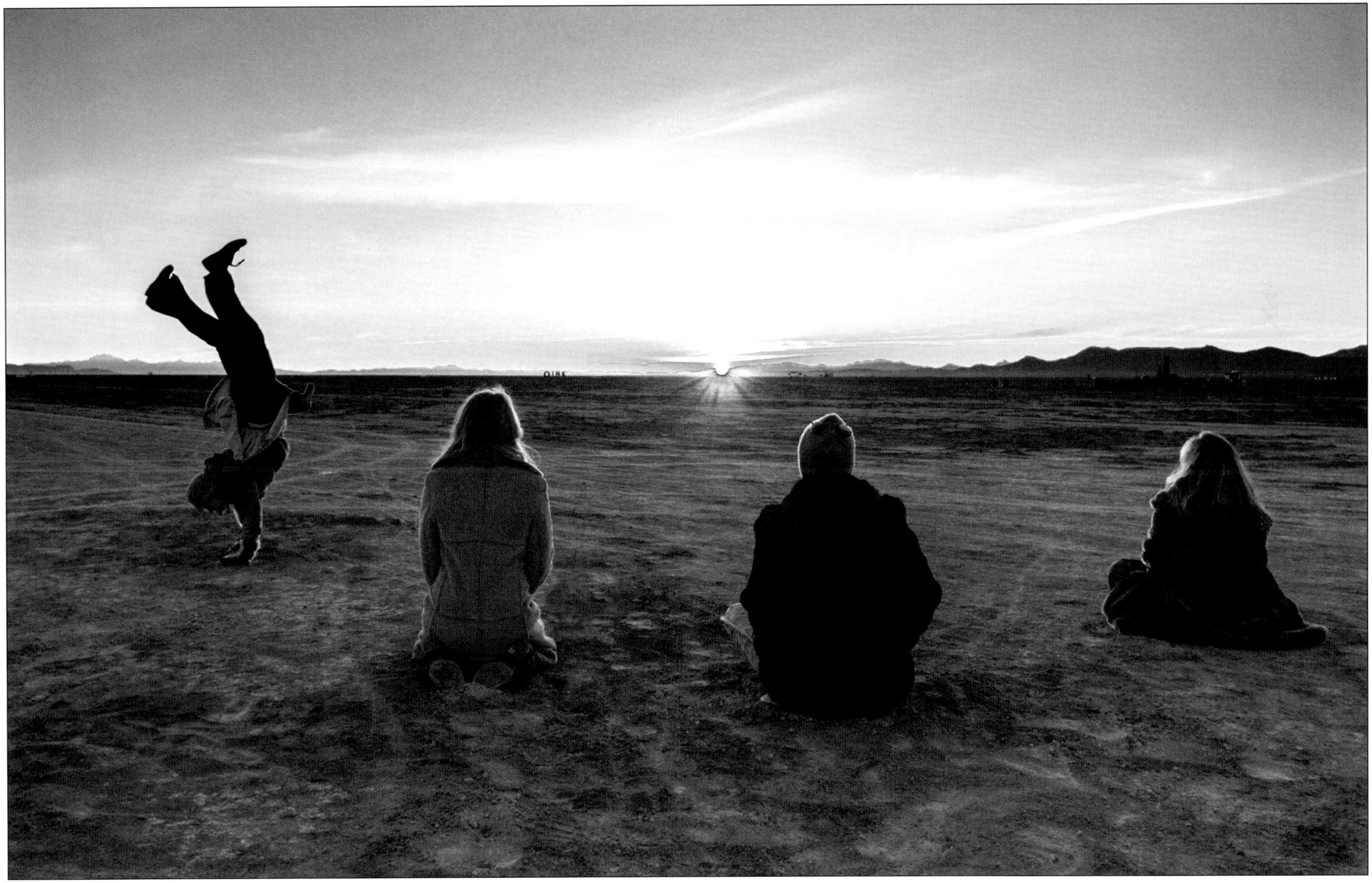

Sunrise Handstand, 2010

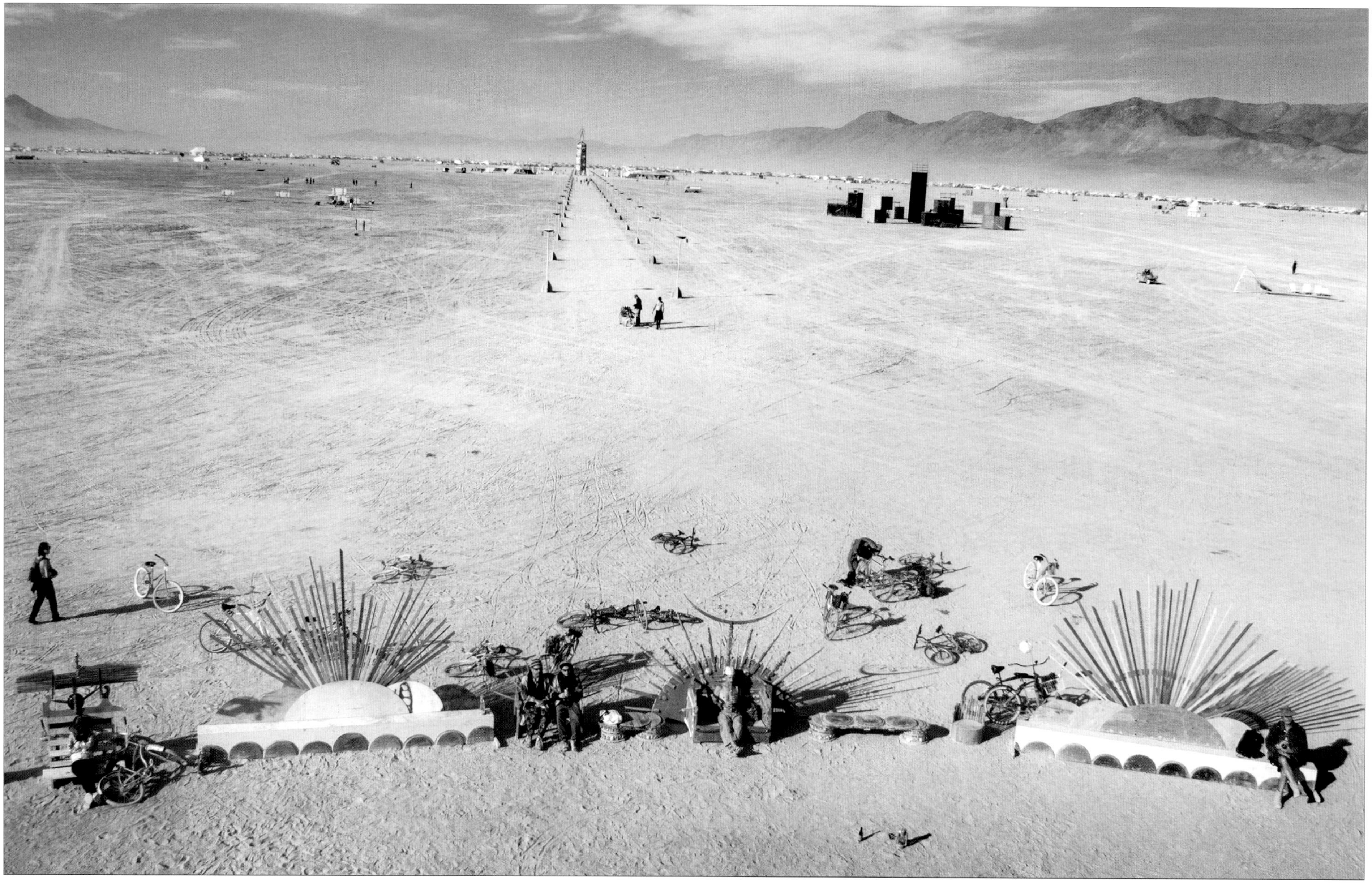

Early Risers, 2008

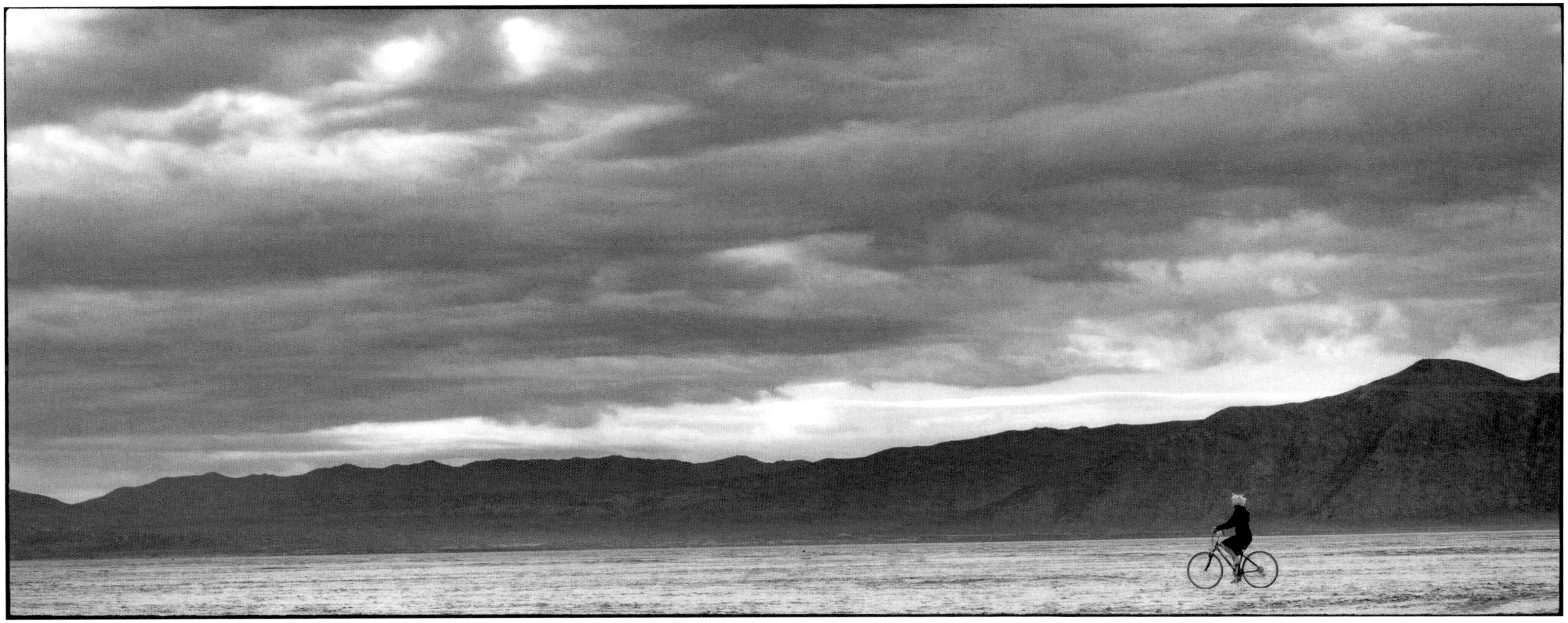

Playa Biker, 2014

Solitude and an unfettered sense of tranquility are the great promises of the early morning playa. They prompt city folk to get up bleary-eyed, pull on a sweatshirt and leggings over and under last night's dancing costume, and head out for a solo bike ride in the chilly nip of dawn. True solitude is a fruitless illusion, for you are never far from company. There are always fellow pedalers out there hoping for the thrill of navigating a brave other world, and of course there are the all-nighters still dancing their weary butts off to the flagging beat of dark reverie; but if you ride far enough away from the din of the city, the playa will open its wide expanse, and you can lose yourself in the unseen mysteries of vast empty space. It is then when the true isolation of a desert landscape can be felt. The stillness is tactile, and every sound becomes amplified by contrast. In that emptiness, only your breathing and the crunch of breaking playa crust disturb the quiet. There is much beauty in such a solitary sojourn, and many of these early-bird bikers come back to camp with tall tales of meeting oddball world travelers or having an extraordinary or even transitory experience. It can be a heady addiction.

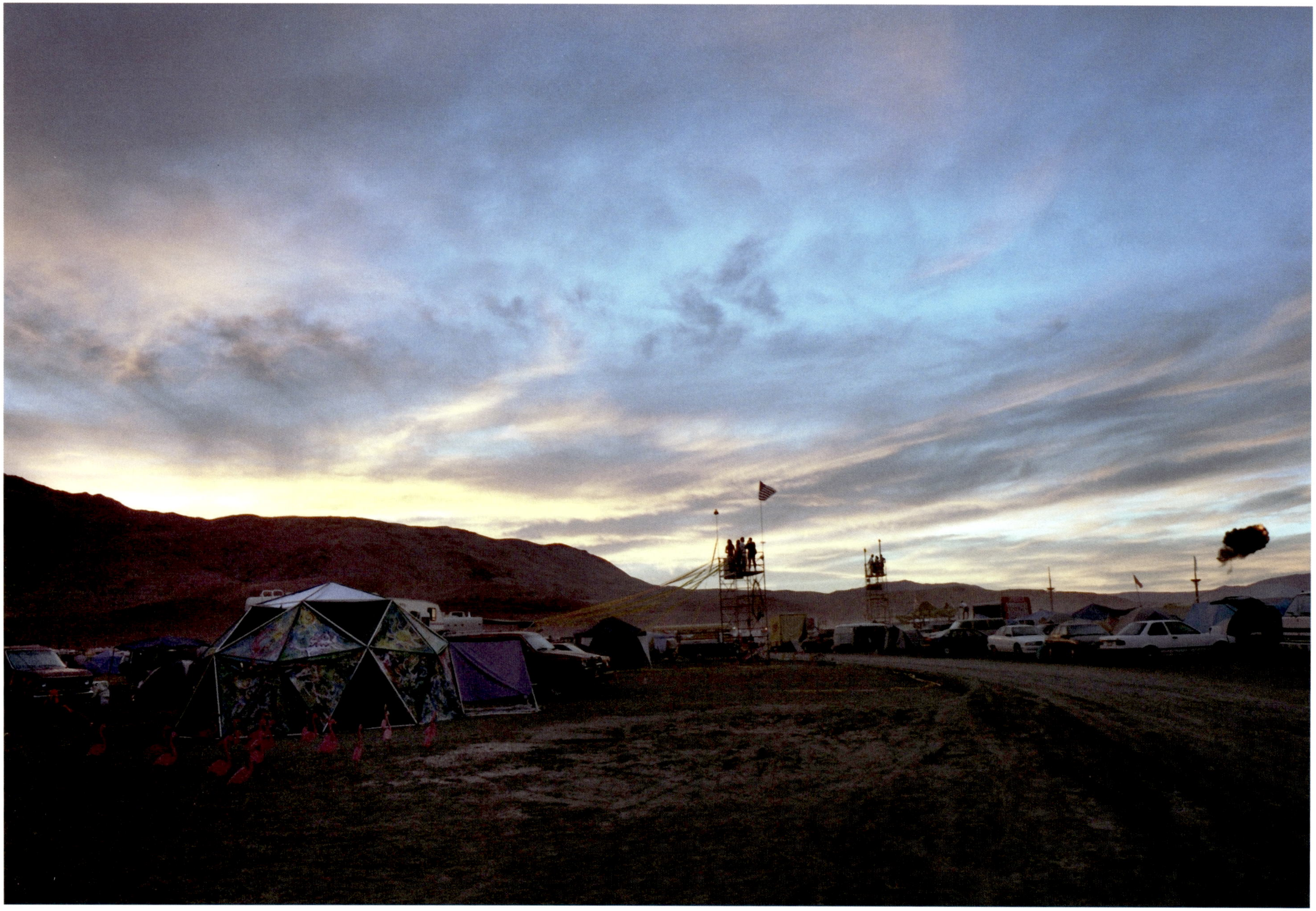

Twilight Camp, 1998

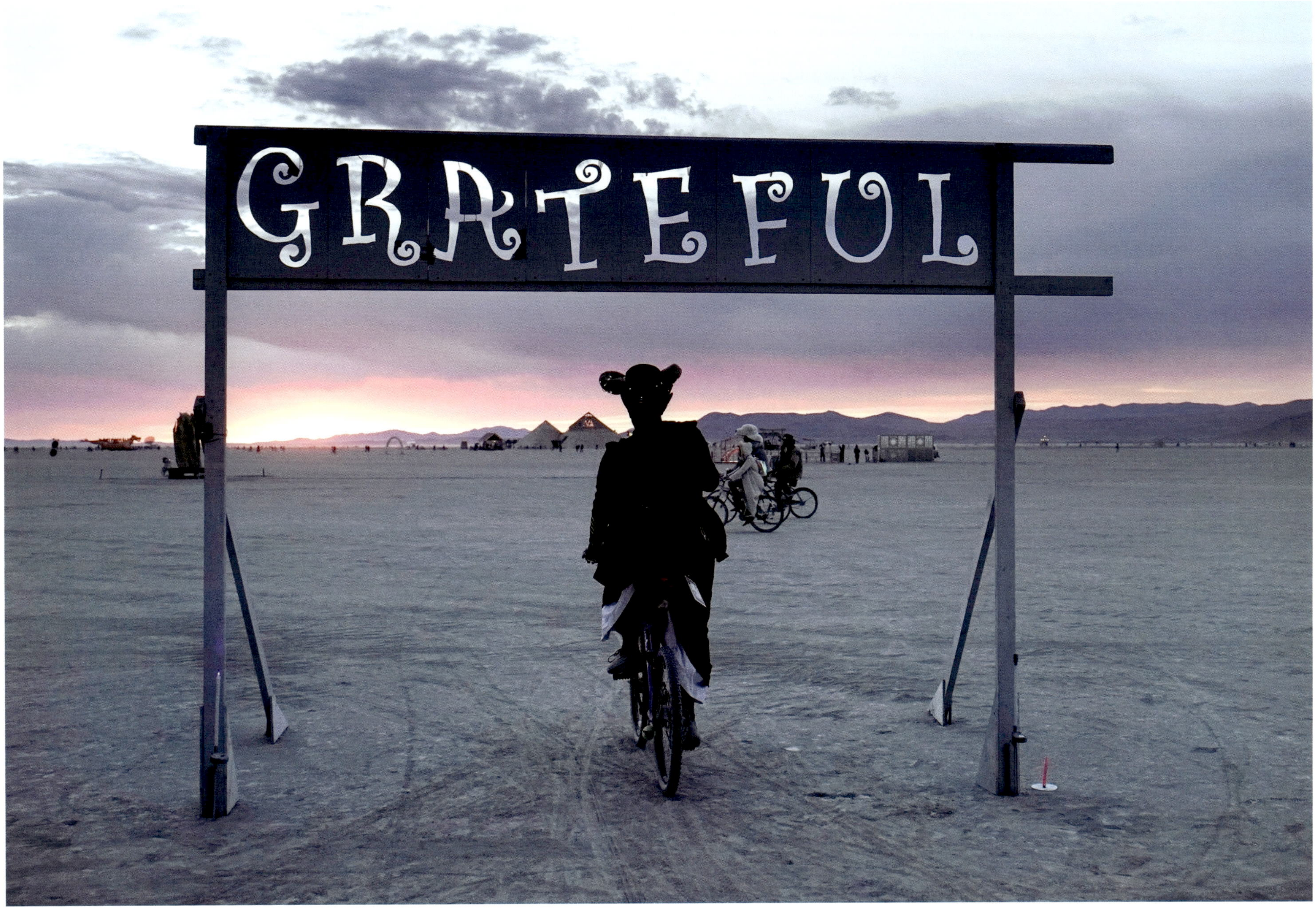

Grateful, *2016*

CHAPTER 3

NO SPECTATORS: 1990–1995

Moving the Burning Man to the Black Rock Desert in 1990 began with a series of dramatic events in San Francisco. The first was a further deterioration in the relationship between my brother and Jerry James. They had clashed openly and often over what they were actually trying to accomplish, personality issues, and a deadly mistrust about intentions. As the "visionary" of the event—a term he would grow to loathe over the years—Larry was increasingly in the spotlight. When a news team arrived to film the Burn in 1989, it was Larry who provided an articulate on-camera interview, while Jerry stood to the side looking, as he himself described, "like a deer in the headlights."

Larry learned a great deal from his initial contact with the media. "It was a great lesson," he said. "I was embarrassed that we'd had so much trouble with the Man, but the reporter carried on as if it had been a great evening. That's when I realized, from where the camera stood with the Man engulfed in flames behind us, you couldn't tell he was broken, and for the media, all that counted was what was on the camera at the moment."

My brother has always given a great interview and still spends many of his waking hours during Burn Week talking to one journalist after another, but other issues were driving a wedge between the Burning Man partners. Jerry and Mike Acker were trying to manage their fledgling construction business, and Jerry began to feel he was being asked to make economic and time sacrifices in order to further Larry's growing fame. They also had different agendas. Jerry had seen Burning Man as a bohemian lark; Larry was following a siren song. As the time drew near for the 1990 Baker Beach Burn, the two were barely speaking.

The one thing that had become obvious after the Man broke down in 1989 was he needed more competent engineering. The first four versions had more or less been cobbled together on the fly, often out of available scrap lumber. Fortunately, another group of latte carpenters stepped forward to help with structural advice. Dan Veale, Steve Donovan, Mike Acker, and their friends understood more about structural engineering than Larry and Jerry. With their structural advice firmly in mind, Larry, who had studied drafting in school, produced a complete set of architectural drawings

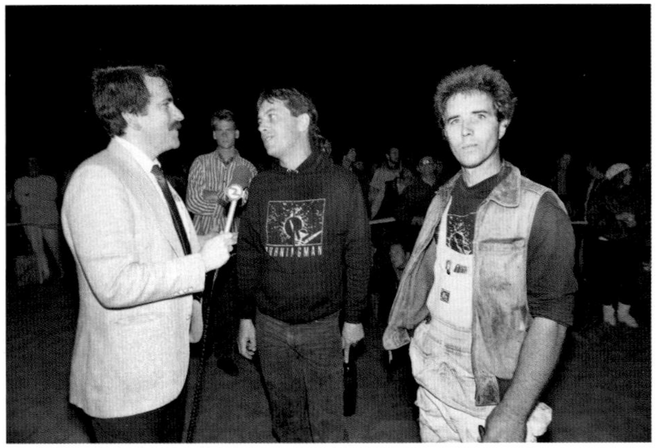

Larry seemed to be a media natural, but Jerry felt more like a deer in the headlights.

that articulated in precise detail the features and elements of a phenomenal new Man. The result was a strikingly balanced and rather svelte-looking giant that would remain unchanged for the next twenty-four years.

Dan Miller recalled that the second great innovation to grow out of the construction meetings with the latte carpenters was they invented a method for raising the Man that would properly distribute the forces on the various limbs, and it would do so without endangering the volunteers. Dan remembers it was Steve Donovan who first suggested a large A-frame boom attached to the front of the Man's feet. It would rise as the Man was lowered and act as a brace to improve the angle of the rope. It would also act as a cantilever to stabilize and assist in pulling the Man back upright. Dan jumped on the idea immediately and built a scale model out of Lego blocks to demonstrate how it would function. It would prove to work perfectly when they eventually took the Man to the desert three months later.

Like the year before, the planned 1990 Baker Beach Burn would be dogged by a series of catastrophes. The first was a failure to launch. The reputation of the renegade celebration had spread, due in part to the previous year's media coverage of the already notorious event. By solstice eve, there were a thousand or so volunteers and spectators lining the dunes or clustered on the beach. There were also the authorities. Reports vary. Some say there were police and firefighters. Others suggest representatives from the army, since Baker Beach was officially still part of the Presidio at that time, a military fort. The unit Larry negotiated with included representatives of the Golden Gate National Recreational Area. They eventually allowed the team to erect the Man, but Larry had to agree not to set it afire. In fact their negotiations had centered not on whether the authorities would grant permission to burn but on how to manage the restless audience of hundreds watching. When the crowd realized there would be no burning, they booed, and then a "Burn the fucker" chant began to build from the rowdy crowd. Dan Miller suggests that part of the problem was they had no direct means of public address—no center stage—no bullhorns. After Larry and the authorities had come to their agreement and the representatives had left the scene, John Law and several members of Cacophony insisted they could burn the Man anyway, but Larry held resolutely to his promise. "I thought that if we burned it, we would never be allowed back on Baker Beach again," he said. "Of course, we never did go back, but that wasn't the point. I had given my word."

Finally, the crowd thinned and the gathering grew more congenial. P. Segal, a roommate of one of the Cacophony members, remembers tugging on Larry's arm that evening. "Let's take him to the Black Rock Desert," she yelled. She also reports that Cacophony's John Law chimed in, "Yes, let's take him to the desert." Larry stared at them blankly. "What?" he finally said, but the moment passed. Later, referring to John Law, whom he had yet to meet, Larry asked Dan, "Who was that pushy guy with the handlebar moustache?" It was his intro to someone who would figure largely in the immediate future of Burning Man. Michael Mikel remembers the involvement of Cacophony differently. He says he first attended the Baker Burn in 1988 and felt all along it was something that fit the Cacophony philosophy. He and other members of Cacophony had helped publicize the 1989 Burn, and they were running around with radios, performing security duties, on the night of the 1990 Non-Burn. Dan Miller remembers seeing them there as well and thought they looked kind of spooky—like spies or undercover cops.

San Francisco Cacophony existed to produce radical and *outré* events for one another, and they were always looking for new ideas. In 1989, Cacophony Society members Kevin Evans, along with his roommates Miss P. Segal and Dawn Stott, had attended *Ya Gotta Regatta—The Breakwind Dance,* a wind sculpture event on the Black Rock Desert that had been organized by Bay Area sculptor Mel Lyons (aka Mel Function) and cosponsored by John Bogard of Planet X Pottery. Planet X sits ten or so miles outside of Gerlach, Nevada, and it has been a welcome landmark on our trek from Portland to the playa from the beginning. It's that milepost you most look forward to seeing near the end of a long journey—the official signal that you've finally made it through a hundred miles of sage, and your destination is near.

Mel Lyons had distributed postcards advertising his wind sculpture event around San Francisco, and Kevin thought it sounded like a good Cacophony-style adventure. The roommates set about fashioning a canopy bed out of PVC pipes and bedding. They even tucked a mannequin under the covers. P. Segal says it had wheels and was responsive to the wind, thus qualifying it as a wind-driven sculpture. Then they strapped the bed to the top of Kevin's car and headed to Nevada. Kevin was very impressed with the playa, as were the others. "It's so empty, it's full" was Dawn Stott's now well-reported comment. Though no one could have envisioned the impact the playa would have on the future of Burning Man, Kevin returned to San Francisco convinced that it would make the perfect location for a Cacophony "Zone Trip."

Kevin Evans had been reading Hakim Bey (Peter Lamborn Wilson) and had become intrigued with his notion of the Temporary Autonomous Zone. Carrie Galbraith, who along with Kevin and John Law edited the book *Tales of the San Francisco Cacophony Society,* reportedly created the notion of the "Zone Trip." She related in an interview on KBOO radio that she got the idea from Andrei Tarkovski's *Stalker,* a film in which the "Zone" contains a room where one's utmost desires are fulfilled. The Cacophony version was a simpler but compelling concept: choose a mysterious or unusual place, a place where anything can happen; make a collective journey to that zone; and experience what happens. Evans's immediate reaction to

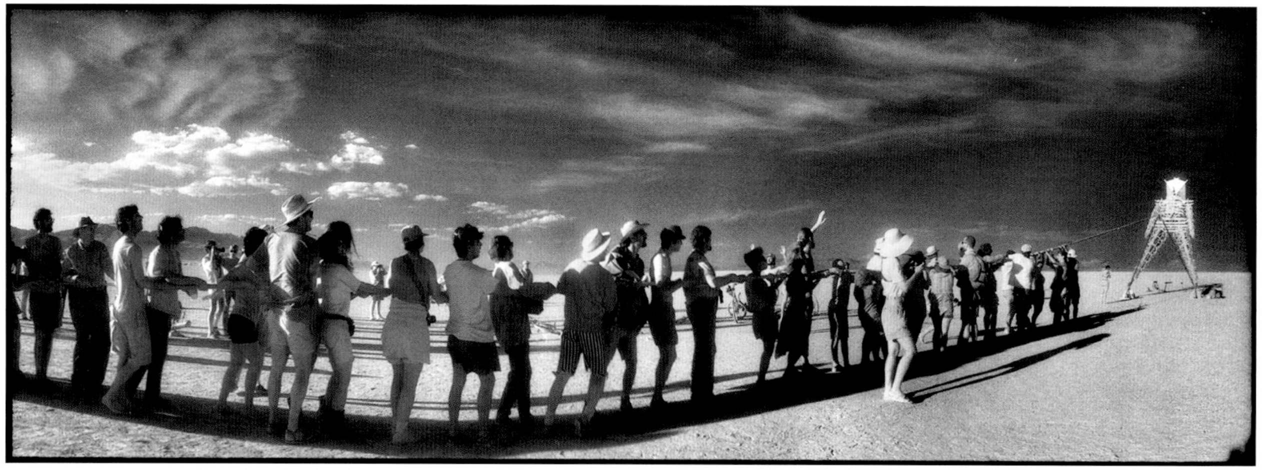

Two hundred volunteers would lower the Man for fueling up and then raise him for the Burn.

the Black Rock Desert was that here was such a place.

Cacophony Society members made up a solid percentage of early Burners in the first playa years, and they organized themselves around the idea of creating participatory events as a means of mutual entertainment, but the origin narrative around Burning Man and the San Francisco Cacophony Society is murky at best. I would not agree with claims that Cacophony in any way "founded" Burning Man. Jerry James and Larry Harvey founded the event on Baker Beach in 1986. What is true is that Burning Man had enjoyed early support from them because the surreptitious nature of the event was akin to a typical Cacophony night of renegade antiestablishment fun. After Burning Man lost its Baker Beach home in 1990, the renewed version of the Burn on the Black Rock Desert was an obvious and natural collaboration.

Coincidentally, Jerry James had also attended the *Ya Gotta Regatta* event in Nevada, and it had been his introduction to members of the San Francisco Cacophony Society. In 1990, he arranged for a meeting between Larry, himself, John Law, and Michael Mikel. Shortly after the meeting, in which they all agreed to take the Man to Nevada on Labor Day weekend, Jerry discovered that half of it had been cut to pieces in the shop parking lot where it had been stored. The head and arms had been stored in Jerry James's garage, but the legs were twenty-four feet long and the torso was fourteen feet long and bulky. They ended up in a parking lot behind the shop where the Man had been built that year. Unfortunately, the parking lot manager mistook the pieces for a bunch of scrap wood and sawed them up to make parking curbs. It was the last straw. Jerry simply did not want to invest the time and money into a rapid rebuilding, and at that point he withdrew from the partnership. Clearly, if John Law and Michael Mikel hadn't proposed the notion of bringing the Man to the Black Rock playa, the evolution of Burning Man would have taken a much different path. They also were in a position to step into the vacuum left by the demise of the partnership between Larry and Jerry, forming what Larry would somewhat derisively refer to as the "Temple of the Three Guys."

Once Larry was able to borrow money and enlist the aid of Dan Miller in rebuilding the Man, a series of planning meetings were held at P. Segal's apartment at 1907 Golden Gate Avenue to organize Zone Trip #4: Bad Day at Black Rock. Miss P. pointed out that this was much more than the typical Cacophony outing, which often entailed just a few hours or, at most, a weekend at a Motel 6. "We met at the ball diamond at Golden Gate Park," she remembered. "We had an ill-sorted bunch of vehicles and a Ryder truck with John Law at the wheel." Kevin Evans added, "We met under the *toaster.*

Cacophony inspired many ongoing renegade art projects," he explained. "One of them was to find small appliances and fasten them to power poles. Most would be removed by the city, but there was a toaster that had been nailed high up on a pole next to the ball diamond in Golden Gate Park that stayed there for years. We'd often meet under the toaster for Cacophony outings." After hours of delays, a caravan of vehicles struck out on Zone Trip #4. In the lead was the yellow Ryder truck, and in the back of the truck were the disassembled parts of the rebuilt Man and all the major camp equipment.

The Cacophony party drove out to the desert in a group. "We did a head count of eighty-nine when we left San Francisco," P. Segal said. "John wanted to make sure we had eighty-nine on the return as well." Once they reached a pile of tires by the side of the road north of Gerlach, they turned toward the playa and the unexpected. After they began crossing the playa, Michael Mikel sped up into a position next to the truck, yelling that everyone should stop. Michael drew the now legendary line in the sand, long enough to accommodate them all standing side by side. It was to symbolize the point of entry into their next adventure. "On the other side of this line," he intoned, "everything will be different. Reality itself will change." Then the line of Cacophony pioneers joined hands and crossed into the Zone together. "And it did change," Michael added years later.

In 1990, Bryan and I had discovered the Black Rock playa as an important and vital setting to the Burning Man pageantry, and we had returned to Portland feeling as if we'd experienced something primal and revelatory. The second year of Burning Man on the playa in 1991 was in many ways a repetition of its predecessor, but there were significant changes as well, one of which was an organized effort by individuals and small groups to creatively engage with one another in a mutually beneficial community of artists and imagineers. The event would always be a place to play, but that play would have a purpose and a promise.

The Black Rock Desert would in time give birth to Black Rock City, and like the Man himself, BRC would need to be built, to disappear, and to be rebuilt year after year—without losing its cultural integrity. Of course in 1991 the "city" was still merely a cluster of campsites, barely a village, truth be told, but what changed that year and contributed significantly to the event that followed was an attitude people had packed in along with their tents. That attitude is now summed up in the single most dynamic of the Ten Principles: Radical Self-Expression.

I can remember talking to Larry a few weeks prior to Labor Day in 1991; I wanted to verify that we were actually going back to the Black Rock Desert for the event. He assured me we were, and then he shared with me some of his many ideas for what Burning Man might become. Frankly, I've forgotten most of what he said those many years ago, but one notion stuck. He foresaw an event that would be driven as much by the creative urges of its participants as by the ingenuity of its organizers. It's a concept that has baffled and intrigued observers to this day, and it is a dominant factor in the longevity of the event. What it requires above all else is a constituency of participants rather than an audience. The problem with an audience is that it arrives with a built-in expectation of being entertained, and that was the antithesis of what Larry had in mind. He was looking to build a community based on the idea that everyone should become an equal partner in realizing the full potential of their experience at the event. It would take a few years for such an optimistic notion to fully take hold, but there were definite signs of it by that second year at Black Rock.

In truth, the 1991 playa gathering was a bit of a new age affair. People erected and displayed indigenous peoples' iconography, organized drumming circles, and shook the playa with "primitive" dancing. Although this new age sensibility was a short-lived phenomenon—and soon gave way to rave music, interactive art, and mutant vehicles—there is little doubt that in 1991 neo-pagans came to interact with one another and play. In fairness, there continues to be hippie-influenced elements to much of Burning Man, but the neo-paganism of the early 1990s annoyed the satire-driven auteurs from Cacophony. John Law reportedly suggested the idea of a bumper sticker that would read NO DRUM CIRCLES. Another Cacophony wag proposed creating a "New Age–Free Zone," but of course that would have gone against their inclusive Cacophony catchphrase: "You may already be a member."

In 1991, the population of the Black Rock village doubled, and that trend would continue for the next few years. It was still primarily an event organized by Larry and the San Francisco Cacophony Society, but it was also beginning to attract attendees from other parts of the Left Coast. Michael Mikel, with his background in the fledgling tech community, was actively promoting the event through *Rough Draft*, Cacophony's newsletter. Cacophony was growing, and there were chapters in LA, Seattle, and Portland. John Law, who was naturally charismatic, had become a driving force in the group, and as Burning Man became more of a focus for them, he began to exert considerable influence. Larry had initially reached out to Cacophony in a desperate attempt to find a home for his Burning Man ritual, but for better or worse, the Cacophony Society was beginning to think of Burning Man as *their* major event of the year. The difference in the perception of who produced Burning Man in the early 1990s would lead to confusion and dissonance in the historical narrative of the event, which will likely never get sorted, but there is no disputing the contribution Cacophony made to the perception of Burning Man, much of which is still widely held by the general public.

Many hallmarks of Burning Man can be traced to its Cacophony connection in the early 1990s. For Cacophony, "dressing up" was de rigueur, and they always wore some version of thrift-store chic to social functions. The list of Cacophony events is long and for the most part consists of a series of hilarious acts of establishment nose tweaking and culture jamming. Burning Man has benefitted from many such traditions with its emphasis on cultural parody, but Cacophony has a self-limiting stance in that it was organized around a series of individual events, which were relatively small in scale. In the end, Cacophony is and was a relatively small group of pranksters, who for a time played a significant role in Burning Man's development.

Interestingly, it was the new-age Burners who pioneered creative participation as the mainstay of Burning Man. Eventually someone hung a NO SPECTATORS sign in Center Camp—a public testament to the new credo that at Burning Man, "there is no audience; everyone is the show." It was a groundbreaking idea that has been Burning Man's distinguishing philosophy ever since, and it was the Burners of 1991 who got that party started. In 1990, Bryan and I had both thought Cacophony oozed a clubby vibe—non-hostile but equally non-inviting. That had all changed by 1991—a positive result of the new-age drumming and group dancing. There was a clear movement toward inclusive involvement. Everyone was invited—nay, cajoled—into joining the circle. There was a general, though unspoken, notion that if you weren't part of the performance, you really didn't understand the ethos of the event. That sense of being part of an expressive community was apparent with our first steps onto the playa. A clear invitation to both collective and individual *participation* heralded the enduring zeitgeist of the event.

For me, the 1991 Burner desire for self-expression reached its zenith on a windy Saturday afternoon. I was busy tightening our tent supports when a lithe woman wearing multiple layers of white linen strode by. I grabbed a camera and followed her as she walked out to the Man and climbed up onto one of his legs. With the wind whipping her winged costume into a gossamer frenzy, she began a slow, acrobatic ballet. For the next half hour, the graceful Crimson Rose (who would go on to become a co-founding board member of today's organization) and the Burning Man engaged in a pas de deux. In the ebb and flow of playa wind, people gathered around like acolytes. Some stood or sat cross-legged on the ground, transfixed at the sight of this utterly unexpected act of grace. While Crimson's spontaneous exhibition wasn't a formal art piece per se, there is little doubt in my mind that her ballet was the first example of performance art at Burning Man. It also set a precedent for self-expression to be an act of generosity to the assembled throng.

Another foreshadowing of the contemporary event was when camp identity evolved as a natural outgrowth of the desire for group expression. It's actually self-expression in the plural, and I witnessed this phenomenon from the earliest days. Individual costuming is clearly an example of self-expression, but thematic costuming is a step in the direction of creating a theme camp. Bringing along a croquet set for recreation is simply a desire for entertainment. Adding appropriate Victorian garb turns the game into a desert parody of the English lawn party, and that's the kind of gentle satire upon which most theme camps were founded. Theme camps would become well established by the latter half of the 1990s, encouraged by newly recruited Black Rock City manager Harley K. Bierman (later, Harley K. Dubois). By the contemporary era there would be more than one thousand registered and placed camps. Many would center on an exaggerated cultural or social idea, others would perform services to the community at large, but at their heart, theme camps evolved from simple acts of group role-playing and communal identity.

Although it wouldn't be made official for a couple of years, the leadership of Burning Man would evolve in the early 1990s into a triumvirate consisting of Larry, John Law, and Michael Mikel. Larry continued in his role as the innovator and chief architect of the event, John took over the organizational and logistical operations, and Michael primarily dealt with publicity and financial management. Their roles were imperfectly balanced, and they each brought in their own network of lieutenants. Both Larry and John were strong personalities who were used to running whatever show in which they might be involved, and they clashed often. The softer-spoken Michael often found himself in the role of mediator. A power struggle was inevitable.

Burning Man has typically attracted people with shared social values, and many Burners were ardent feminists. Janet Lohr, Larry's former companion and our family friend, keenly felt the overt expression of male dominance at the center of the event. It was, after all, called Burning *Man,* and that was symbolically a challenge to her and her compatriots' sensibilities. These days it will be argued that the effigy is without gender, and that is certainly the intent, but in 1991 there was a desire to introduce something that felt female and nurturing to this overtly man-centered gathering.

They also wanted to do something that was equally ancient and ceremonial. What they chose to do was build a kiva-style oven and bake loaves of rotund female-shaped bread with the same wood-fueled fire that would soon consume the Man. The idea was to break the bread into Communion-sized pieces and distribute them to the masses. Baking bread was a thematic masterstroke, and it conjured up ancient ritual, but

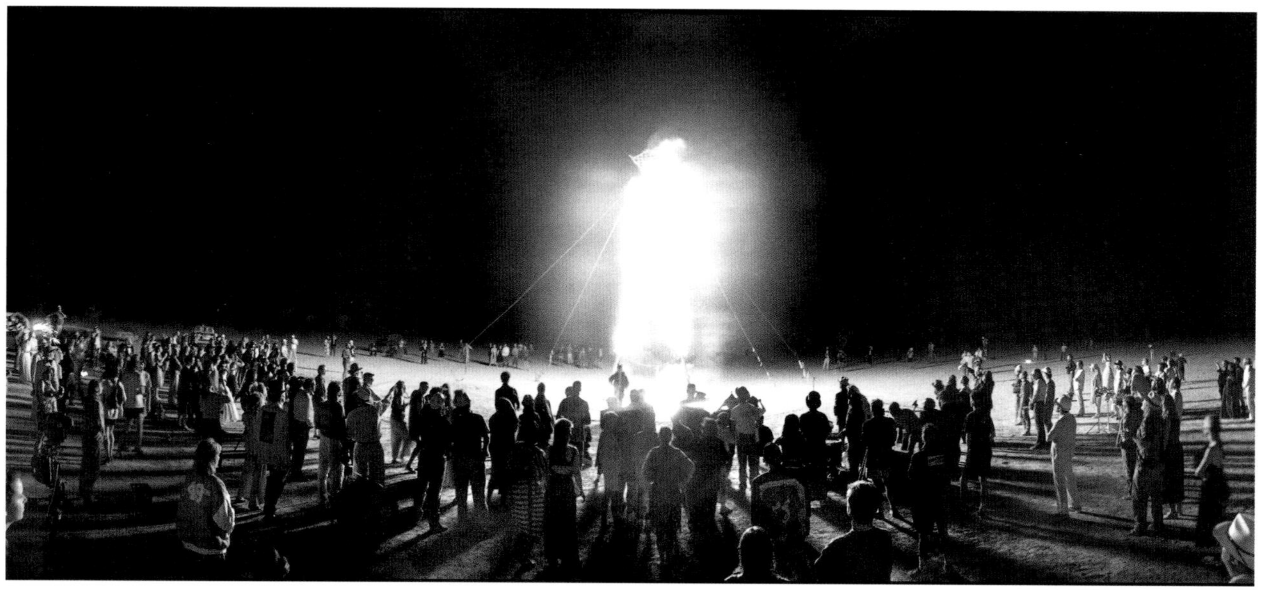

Our close proximity to the 1991 Burn provided an intimate experience with ritual fire.

passing the bread chunks to even a couple hundred people was a logistical nightmare. Though the bread-baking ceremony never reappeared, impractical in the face of a burgeoning population, many camps today exist solely to gift food or drink to the multitudes. I certainly think their gesture brought a necessary awareness to the event and gave rise to the idea that ceremony is at the core of the fire. I also like to imagine that those long-ago loaves of bread helped to shape the principle of Gifting at Burning Man.

In 1991, modest pyrotechnics were added to the Burn, and these blossomed into the extravagant fireworks displays people have come to expect at the modern spectacle. In advance of Flamo LaGrande doing the actual lighting in 1991, Crimson Rose performed a nude fire ritual in front of the Man, carrying a bowl of fire. It turned out to be a prototype for her Fire Conclave performances of fire spinners and fire dancers that have been a staple of the Burn for over twenty years.

An important characteristic of those early Burns was that the Man was standing on the ground just a few dozen feet away from the circle of witnesses. There was usually some kind of perimeter of caution tape, but for the most part the only thing between the flames and the crowd was a modicum of common sense. At one point during the 1991 Burn a woman rushed from the crowd and headed toward the flaming figure. It caught everyone by surprise, and no one was quick enough to stop her. She ran straight to the Man and threw something into the flames. I was told later that it was a manila envelope that contained her x-rays. She had recently been diagnosed with cancer, and this was her defiant response.

These gestures were another in a series of extraordinarily powerful acts that for me defined the importance of individual expression. Veteran Burners sometimes complain that today's Burning Man has too many rules, and they reminisce about a dimly remembered time when the event was a Wild West monument to the credo of "Anything goes." I'm not sure the event was ever so unbridled, but I will say the immediate access we had to the Burn made it a deeply intimate experience. I could easily walk as close to the flaming figure as common

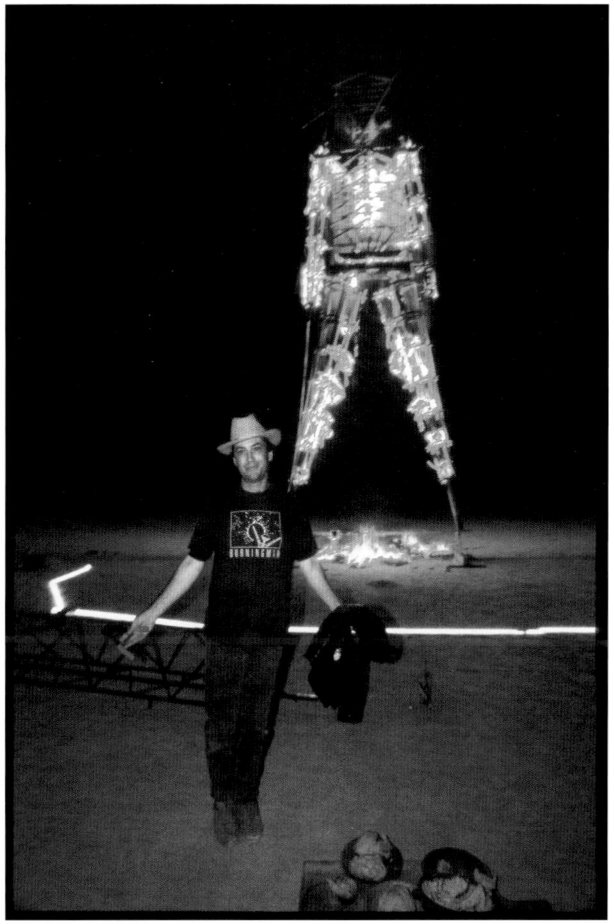

It was clear my brother had found his rather improbable niche.

sense and the heat on my face would allow. Of course modern safety concerns exist because with the large contemporary population, not everyone at the event will exercise common sense, or be able to feel their faces, for that matter.

I remember taking a parting photo of my brother at the end of the 1991 Burn. He was getting ready to sever the support wire, which would allow the Man to fall. Larry is notoriously self-conscious in front of the camera, but in that moment he spread his arms and opened himself. It's a simple portrait caught at a rare moment when he was pleased and willing to show it. I love the elements of the picture: his T-shirt from a Baker Beach Burn, leftover ceremonial bread from the kiva oven, and the first of his soon-to-be-famous hats. This hat was his original Stetson, called "Open Road." It had belonged to our father and turned out to be the same model worn by President Lyndon Johnson. Sadly, it was lost in a playa dust storm a couple of years later, but there would be many more Stetsons to take its place. Bryan and I returned to Portland that year with the understanding that his "hippie uncle" had somehow found his rather improbable niche.

I think of 1993 as the year that individuals made a lasting impression. Walking eastward from our cluster of tents and campers that year, I headed directly toward the stolid wooden giant standing at the apex of the rising sun. Getting up to photograph the sunrise at Burning Man is a habit I acquired my first year on the playa, and it's one I maintain to the present day. Bryan and I had missed the 1992 Burn, and so I was anxious to reconnect with that exquisite playa experience once again. Initially excited to be seemingly the only photographer up that early, I thought it might be my best opportunity to get a pristine view of the Sunrise Man. I was disappointed to realize a distant intruder was in that glowing ribbon between earth and sky. Even though he was moving right along, I knew there was scant possibility he would escape the sweeping lens of the Widelux before the sun finished rising, so I shot. These days encountering throngs of sunrise trekkers is commonplace at Burning Man, and the idea of seeing only a single individual would be a rarity. Today, while I still enjoy the quest for an image of the pristine Man uncluttered by throngs of people and their bicycles, it's that resolute hiker on the horizon that resonates in my memory. I feel a kinship with him and his need to explore deep playa.

The following morning Jan Lohr and I were out near the Man because we'd heard a rumor about a strange creature making a sunrise appearance to dispense coffee to hardy souls brave enough to get up at first light. At first, we stood alone, but gradually a few sleepyheads made their way out, a couple of other photographers, and some individuals packing personal mugs. We stood shivering and feeling a bit foolish in the half-light. Finally we spotted a horse-shaped vehicle bearing what appeared to be a black-clad bovine superhero, followed by a faithful sidekick pushing the rig slowly toward us. This was my first sighting of Java Cow, who would become the first of many celebrated characters at Burning Man.

Java Cow was an invention of Kimric Smythe, who would create several firsts for the event. He became the first to load pyrotechnics into the Man, and he would perform as the Exploding Man during the pre-Burn ceremony of many early Burns. Although his bovine visage was striking against the playa horizon, Java Cow's morning ritual was simple and homespun. After his trusted assistant passed out paper cups and handed him a large thermos, Java Cow intoned, "Does anyone want cream or sugar?" Our scripted reply was "No, sir, we want it black!" With that, the coffee would be poured, and the ceremony was over. Of course it's easy to see Java Cow as the first of a multitude of such playa personae, but there was much more to this beloved critter than meets the camera's eye. Java Cow's sunrise ritual reinforced the burgeoning notion that at Burning Man each individual's creative gesture should be a gift to all.

It was also Kimric Smythe and his father who cofounded the Drive-By Shooting Range in the early 1990s, and though it was located miles away from the main camp, and you had to know where to go to participate, it still sounds badass to modern Burners. Shooting at stuffed animals from a bike or pickup certainly added to the Wild West mystique of those early Burns, but it was a short-lived and relatively benign phenomenon. Ever the restless creator, Kimric went on to help introduce steampunk to the playa, and he is part of the team that produced *Neverwas Haul,* a steam-powered rolling Victorian house that is certainly one of the great mobile works of art at the event.

It's true guns were a small but significant part of the early Black Rock scene. At least some of the early Black Rock Rangers—a group that was formed by Michael Mikel in 1992 to keep Burners from getting lost or injured—carried firearms. Northern Nevada wasn't a benign tourist destination. It still isn't. The then-seven-mile perimeter fence surrounding the encampment wouldn't be built until the late 1990s, when Rod Garrett designed the modern city complex. Before that, people could travel in and out of the camp at will or strike out

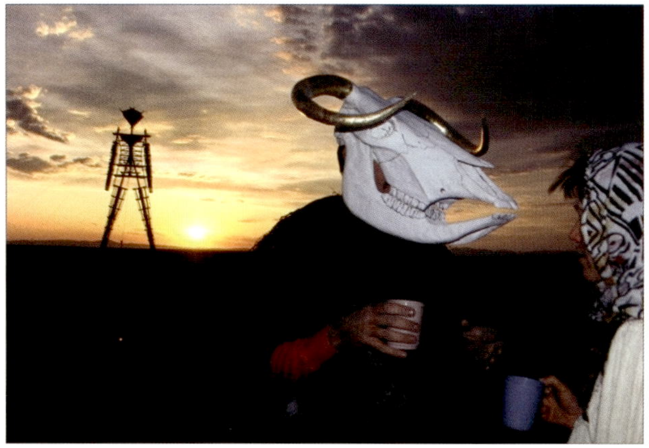

The Java Cow offered coffee at sunrise.

onto the fifty-mile-wide playa surface, looking for adventure.

In those days Rangers roamed the outer reaches of the encampment keeping an eye out for stranded rigs. Dan Miller recounted driving out on perimeter sweeps and being plagued by the limited range of their two-way radios. "We only had a mile or so of radio range," he remembered, "and when voice contact would fail, we developed a system of clicks with the on/off button as a way of extending our communication." People would also wander out on bikes, looking for Fly Hot Springs, and blow a tire because of the hot playa sand. I had a Portland friend who did exactly that and had to push his bike six miles back to camp over scorching playa. He could barely move the next day because of the severity of his blisters. The principle of Radical Self-Reliance would derive from two factors that were obvious in our first playa years: arrive prepared to survive for several days in challenging conditions, and don't be stupid. Most of the injuries I've witnessed over the years resulted from ignoring one of these factors.

Fly Hot Springs was our personal oasis in the early days of the event. The multicolored fountains are the result of errant geothermal drilling in the 1960s. A company was drilling a test well and hit a reservoir of 200°F water—hot, but not hot enough for their needs. The result was the beginning of a geyser. A slender monolith called the "Wizard" also stands like a monkish sentinel over the springs, a remnant of similar drilling done in the 1950s. Thereafter the tricolor cones have been growing each year. The three knobbed spouts are the source for a series of radiating pools of boiling to spa-like water. The farther the pools are away from the geyser the more comfortable, but the pool nearest to the spouting water will blister your feet. Since the water temperature shifts drastically, testing the water is mandatory. Occasionally a drunk or foolish person would step or, worse, jump into a scorching pool, which ended up generating an emergency flight to Reno. Of course that was the darker possibility, and there are many other ways for the unaware to sustain an injury at Burning Man, but the vast majority of the time we enjoyed a sanguine and refreshing dip into nature's most pleasurable bath.

Not only did Michael Mikel (aka Danger Ranger) create the Black Rock Rangers, he also brought the first official "art car" to the playa in 1991. True, it wasn't a plastic-fantastic, kitsch-covered, Texas-style rolling collector's dream like Harrod Blank's *O My Gawd!* or a critter-inspired satire like Michael Gump's Beetle-topped van *The Host,* both of which appeared a couple of years later. Michael Mikel's *5:04 PM* was a "circumstantial" phenomenon. It was the exact moment an earthquake hit the Bay Area during the warm-up for game three of the 1989 World Series. During the quake a brick wall toppled onto a 1978 Oldsmobile Cutlass Supreme, caving in the back of the roof and the trunk lid. Michael offered to buy it, and then drove it to the playa.

Art comes in many forms at Burning Man, and playa art was even then attracting international attention. The same year Michael Mikel drove the first art car to Burning Man, international artist Serena de la Hey installed three wicker figures on the playa. However, it was Argentine artist Pepe Ozan's 1993 innovative lingam series of mud sculptures and elaborate opera sets that would dominate art on the playa for years.

Today's theme art at Burning Man is mandated to be inclusive and interactive, but by 1993, several people were already in the process of establishing that tradition, organizing fashion shows, parades, and performances. The clearest indicator was the large NO SPECTATORS sign in Center Camp, of course. Larry was always dismissive of the term. "If there weren't spectators, why would anyone do anything?" he wondered. I take his point, and the truth is, photographers are the largest body of spectators in the world, but I also understood that the sign was an admonishment for everyone to participate.

When Bryan and I arrived at the playa entry road in 1993, we found a scrappy-looking trailer serving as a ticket booth and gate shack. It was dubbed the Trauma Unit and still resides at the Burning Man Work Ranch. (This is where they store some of Burning Man's most hallowed relics of the wild ol' days.) At the Trauma Unit we paid for entry and were given the official coordinates for finding the encampment, but the trailer also offered some vexing information. Next to the door was a disclaimer to the effect that filming would be going on at the event, and our entry implied our consent to be filmed for commercial purposes. The outside world had gotten wind of the event, and an independent film crew was on the playa intent on documenting this renegade happening. Suddenly we were going to be not only *the show* for one another but also performers in an early form of reality television! As veteran Burners, we were nonplussed.

Their presence turned out to be a mixture of annoying intrusion and low comedy. The film crew scampered around between groups of Burners, dragging cameras, cables, and boom mics. Whenever two or more interesting-looking Burners flocked together, there would come the crew. Naturally whatever spontaneous activity was afoot immediately dissolved into stilted self-consciousness. Now, I know nothing about how this episode of *Playa Gone Wild* was supposed to turn out, but I'm pretty sure the filmmakers had hoped for more. What they got was a performance piece featuring

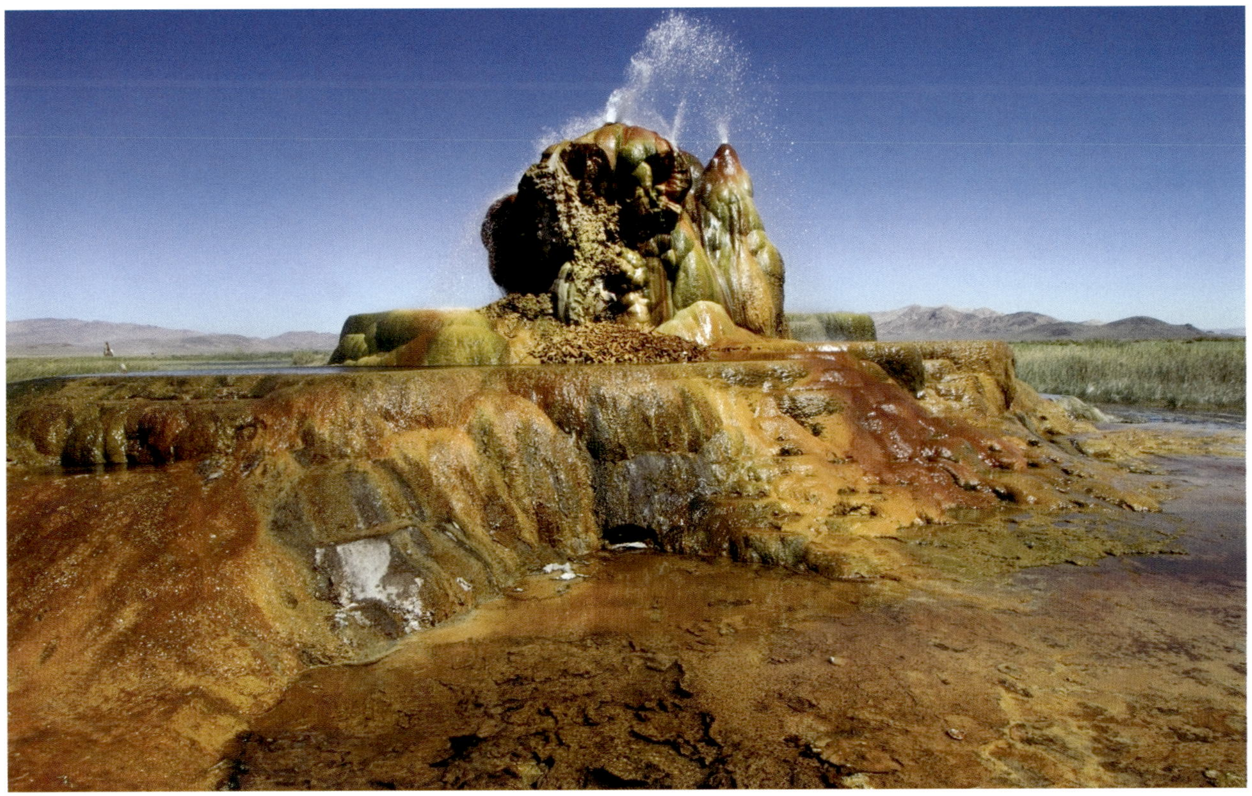

Remarkable Fly Hot Springs provided pleasures and dangers in the early days of Burning Man.

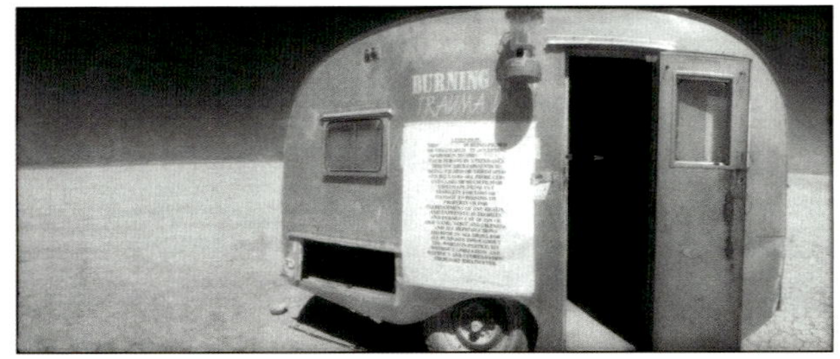

The Trauma Unit is almost as hallowed a Burning Man artifact as the Bone Tree.

several dozen people gathering in Center Camp to witness a staged act. Someone had scripted a mythological pageant complete with costumes, music, and a large dose of hokum. I can't swear it was a deliberate *punking* of the Hollywood rubes, it being the 1990s and all, but I'd never seen anything quite like it at Burning Man before or since.

Although no doubt many people resented the film crew pushing their way into every activity, in the end there was a general willingness to tolerate these outsiders with the same spirit of inclusiveness that has evolved into a valued Burning Man tradition. Though common today in the era of YouTube, commercial video seemed to us at the time to undermine the free-spirited spontaneity we all craved. As a photographer, I was suddenly acutely self-aware when I realized I was being filmed while taking photographs. I had never experienced being one of the participants and also a documentarian—this was something different. This was participatory media, and it gave me a taste of my own medicine.

As we prepared to watch the 1993 Burn, I realized that the event had transitioned from a loose gathering of Cacophony Society friends into a unique entity. By then many of the signature aspects of the event were in place or were prototype activities evolving into traditional elements: self-reliance, participation, individual initiative and invention, performance, costuming, universal inclusion, gifting, interactive art, and radical self-expression. All of these were natural outgrowths of attracting a random gaggle of creative people to this ancient desert incubator. I think of those early years of Burning Man on the Black Rock playa as the gestation period of a profound legacy—an event allowing individuals the freedom to express their inspired selves.

The weather that evening seemed relatively clear to the east, but something odd and uncomfortable lurked along the western horizon. Bryan and I had noticed a weird kind of air stagnation in the late afternoon. A thin veil of dust seemed to hang several feet above the ground throughout most of the evening as everyone got dressed for the Burn. The holy terrors of Burning Man—the natural conditions most reviled by modern Burners—are wind, rain, and *dust.* These elements had been relatively absent for the most part in the first couple of years. We had afternoon winds in those days, but they were pretty benign by modern standards. That all changed in 1993.

Whether they were inspired by the presence of the film crew or their numbers had grown to critical mass, the crowd at the 1993 Burn was much more raucous and out of control than in previous years. After the Man had fallen that evening, people rushed forward and began dancing around and jumping over the figure. This was an old tradition that had begun at Baker Beach and would continue even as attendance grew to today's number, but this year seemed more frantic and dangerous. As we moved in closer to the Man, I became aware of lightning moving closer, and the wind had picked up dramatically. I looked nervously down at the metal tripod I was toting and decided it was time to head back to camp.

In those days when the Man went down we lost our primary directional landmark. I had been stumbling forward, head lowered into the wind, toward where I imagined our camp to be, when suddenly I was blinded by dust! I hadn't realized in the dark that the gale was pushing a wall of dust directly at us. This was to be my first desert whiteout, and I had absolutely no idea where I was going. Finally, I caught a glimpse of headlights and a man kneeling next to his Datsun pickup frantically trying to stake down his tent. We secured his tent, and he invited me into the pickup to ride out the dust storm. I looked down at my clothes in the dim light from the dashboard and was startled to see that I was chalky white from head to foot.

As the whiteout subsided, I looked out the dusty windows

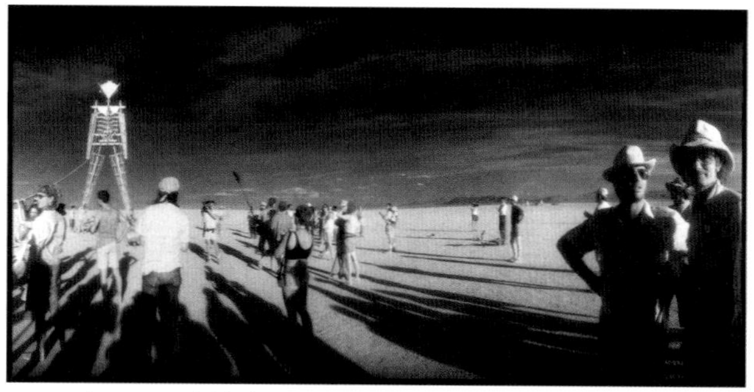

Larry and Michael project a confidence that belies the shaky underpinnings of the organization.

of the pickup, trying to figure out where in the murky darkness lay the remnants of our camp. "I think I know where I'm going," I announced as I opened the door. "Good luck," he called as I walked out into the darkness. I had made it only fifty feet or so when I felt the first drops. Within moments I was engulfed by torrential rain. When it rains hard on the playa, everything turns to sticky clay. The only thing to do is hunker down in the closest shelter and wait for it to dry out. In the din and shimmer of the driving rain, I saw the faint outline of a van. It was filled with equally wet refugees, and I got to wait out the rain in a camper full of Burners. Fortunately, they had plenty of beer.

The Hollywood intruders, however—panicky at the thought of getting their expensive gear soaked—tossed everything into their rental truck and made a run for it. We saw them the following morning. In their blind frenzy to escape the wind and rain, they had driven straight into the path of the storm. Ironically they had ended up stranded, their abandoned truck mired to its axles in playa muck. It was there for us to pity as we all headed for home. As for Bryan and the band of Burners who had been dancing around the fallen Man, when the dust and rain hit, they had just taken off their shoes, covered their heads, and kept right on dancing. It's the way veterans deal with the weather at Burning Man.

The organization that produced Burning Man on the playa in those early years primarily consisted of my brother, John Law, and Michael Mikel. By 1995, they had formalized a partnership and trademarked both the image and name of Burning Man. But Larry and John Law had opposing views on the future of Burning Man, and nearly everything else, for that matter. The three men had no sooner signed a partnership than it all went to hell.

A major problem seems to be that John Law and Larry had widely divergent views on the scope of the event. John apparently saw Burning Man as a continuation of the kind of outside art happenings he'd been party to: the Suicide Club and the Cacophony Society. The Suicide Club had always been a secret cadre of daredevils who kept their climbing of bridges and buildings on the down-low. They also had a rather secretive membership. Michael Mikel said, "The Suicide Club was so far underground I couldn't find it!" The Cacophony Society, in contrast, was ready to embrace anyone interested in planning an edgy and original frolic. Their slogan—"You may already be a member"—allowed for unlimited growth, but they generally confined their urban-centered events to evenings and weekends. Burning Man on the playa held much greater potential, but John and Larry had radically conflicting aspirations for the event. John Law saw Burning Man as another renegade San Francisco enterprise destined for legendary obscurity. Larry Harvey had a much grander, world-scale vision.

Looking back on those first years on the playa, I'm left with a compelling question: How does a gathering of like-minded renegades transform itself into a national phenomenon? Parsing the relationship between the Burning Man and the Black Rock playa seems one way to understand the growth and evolution of the event: The desert is a vast, harsh environment, a place where survival is a genuine issue. It conjures for us a sense of primal wonder and a deep respect for natural forces. It also feels boundless. Everything on the playa needs to be large in order to achieve significance. The event itself compels us to participate in a large, instant community and to be self-expressive. "Here is your big canvas," the event suggests. "Now do something big with it." It took years to fulfill that potential, but the experiment succeeded because an enormous primitive space encourages limitless

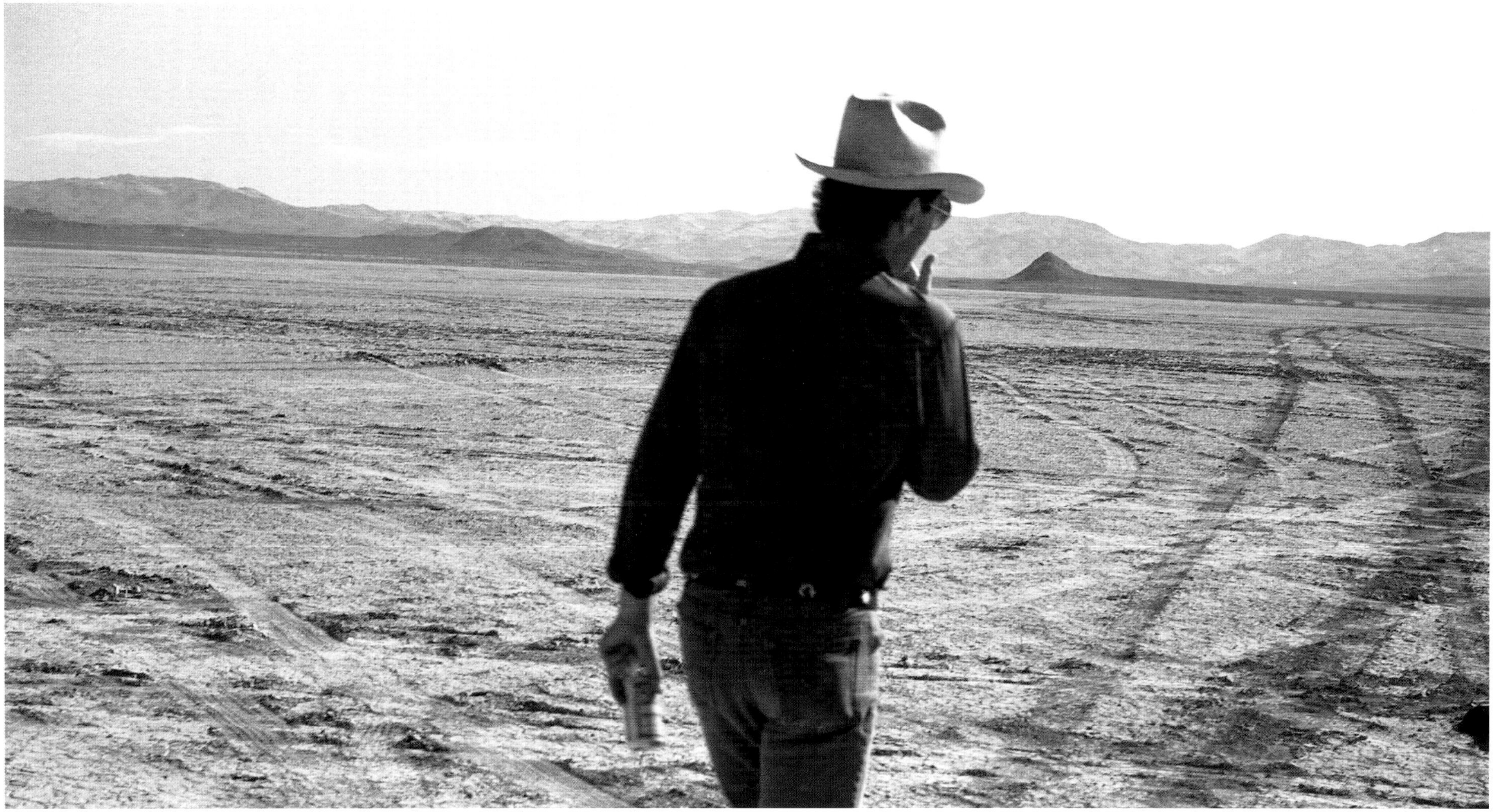

The first time my brother laid eyes on the playa it fired his imagination.

creativity and unrestricted scale. "Build it bigger, build it bolder, build it better," the desert seems to suggest. It's the playa that encourages us to dream large and to stretch our imaginations, and this feeds the world's perception of the event.

Being able to leave the playa at will was the quintessential symbol of the Old West era of Burning Man. Once in a while in those halcyon days of the event, Larry and I would travel the twelve miles to Gerlach for necessary supplies or to catch a quick beer at Bruno's Country Club. It was an overdue respite from the heat and sand, and I looked forward to being with my brother. By then Burning Man had purchased a house in town that was used as a makeshift office. I'm not sure, but I think Larry's old friend Flash Hopkins lived there at least part of the time. Larry was usually overloaded with responsibilities during the event, so such a trip allowed us an opportunity to talk. I remember asking him one afternoon before the Burn how long he planned to continue with Burning Man. The question had all of the subtle implications of a father asking his son how long he planned to be the lead singer in his garage band. Larry gave me a look that suggested this particular band might very well be the E-Street Band. "We're just getting started," he said, smiling. "I've got plans!"

CHAPTER 4

EXPRESSION

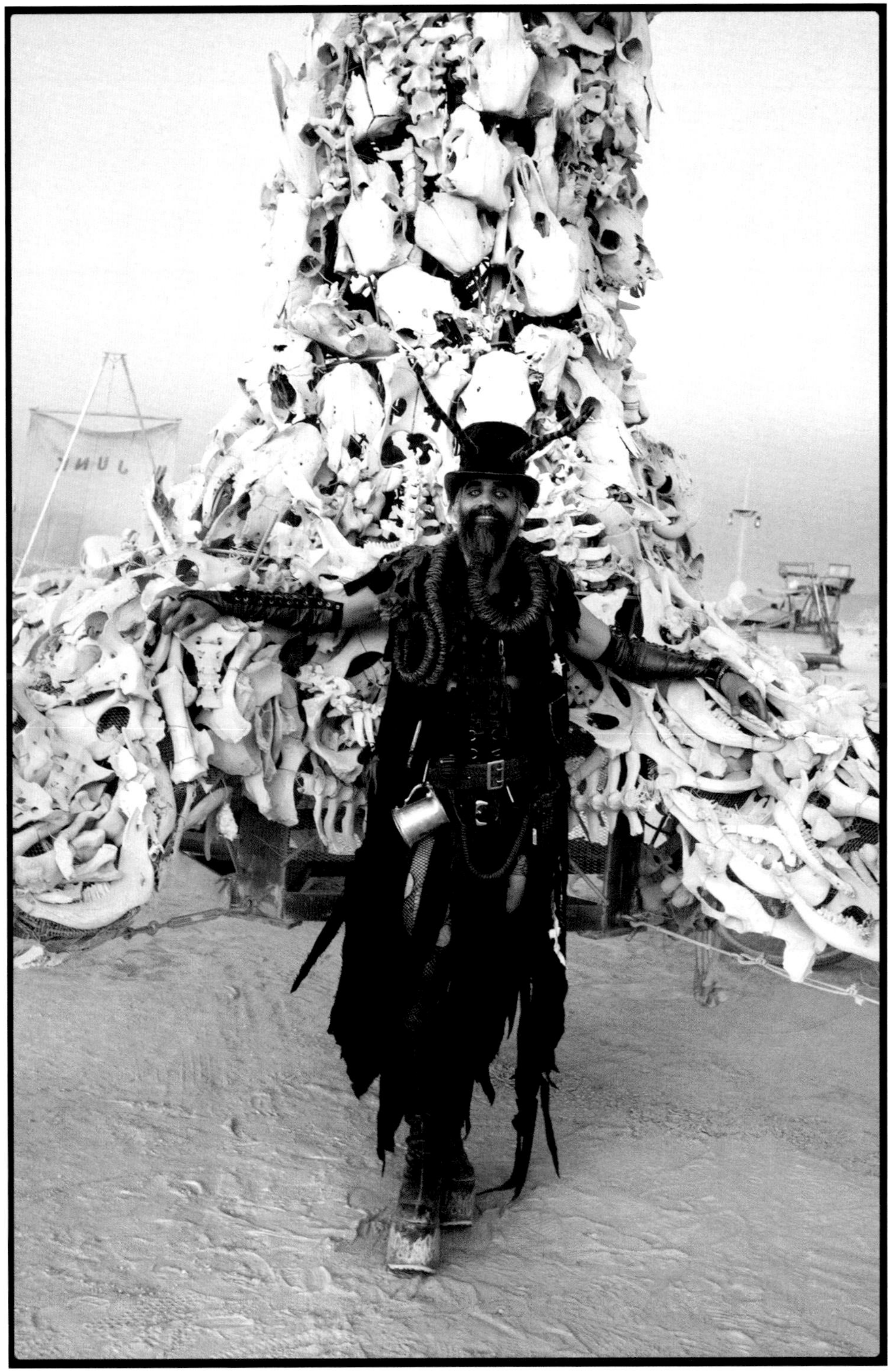

Steven Ra$pa, 2011

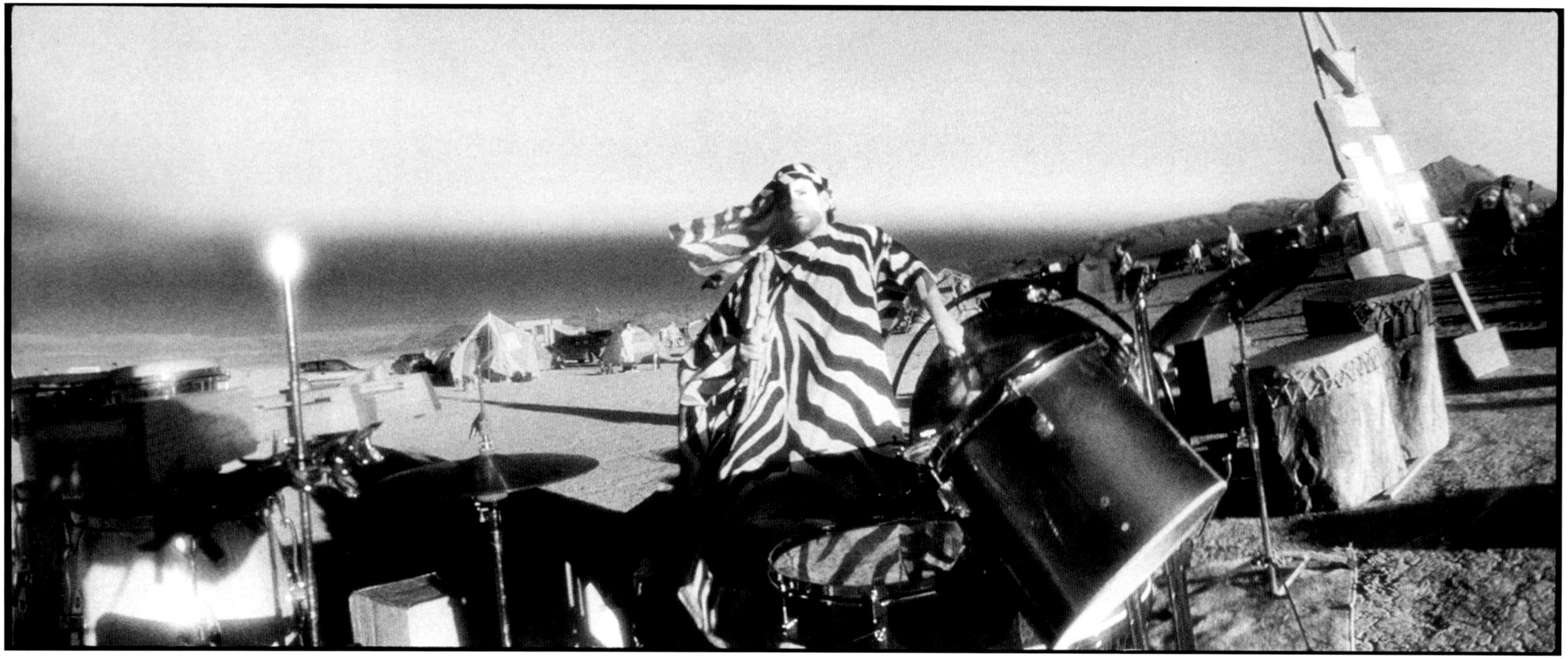

Playa Drummer, 1991

Participation is a principle that is often dated to when someone hung a NO SPECTATORS sign in the central area of camp in 1993, but there were examples of individual and group expression from the first year. Certainly Crimson Rose's ballet on the Man in 1991 is evidence, but she was not alone. Cacophony people were costuming the night of the first Burn, and there were new-age drummers and feather-bedecked dancers aplenty by the second year. Expression is a two-headed creature. There is what we express as individuals and what we manifest as a community. At the heart of participation at Burning Man is a willingness to allow the deeper sense of ourselves out to work and play.

Many artists will say that much of what is personal and artful comes from a sense of play, or at least from allowing oneself to play around with an idea long enough for something personal to happen. Sculptor David Best has said that much of what drives artful expression is a sense of generosity—the willingness to share the intensely personal with the community. My high school drama teacher taught us that performance was an outward expression of an interior reality. It's the willingness to expose the deeply felt, whether that be an act of play or a protest. "No spectators" isn't a statement of audience contempt; it's a challenge not to be content with watching when participation is so much more rewarding. If you can't let that inner person out at Burning Man, you'll miss one of the best opportunities for Radical Self-Expression you'll ever find.

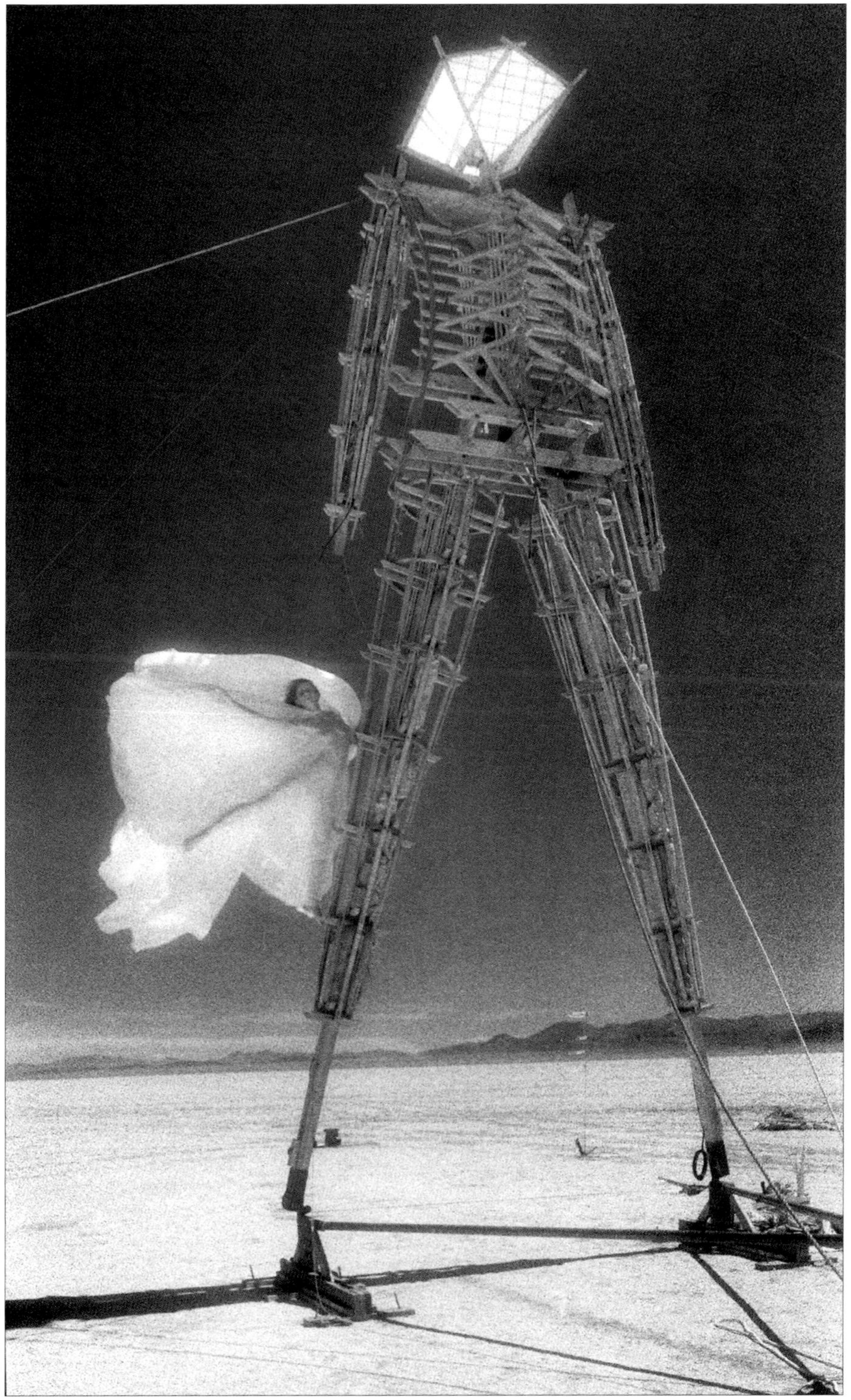

Crimson Rose Ballet, 1991

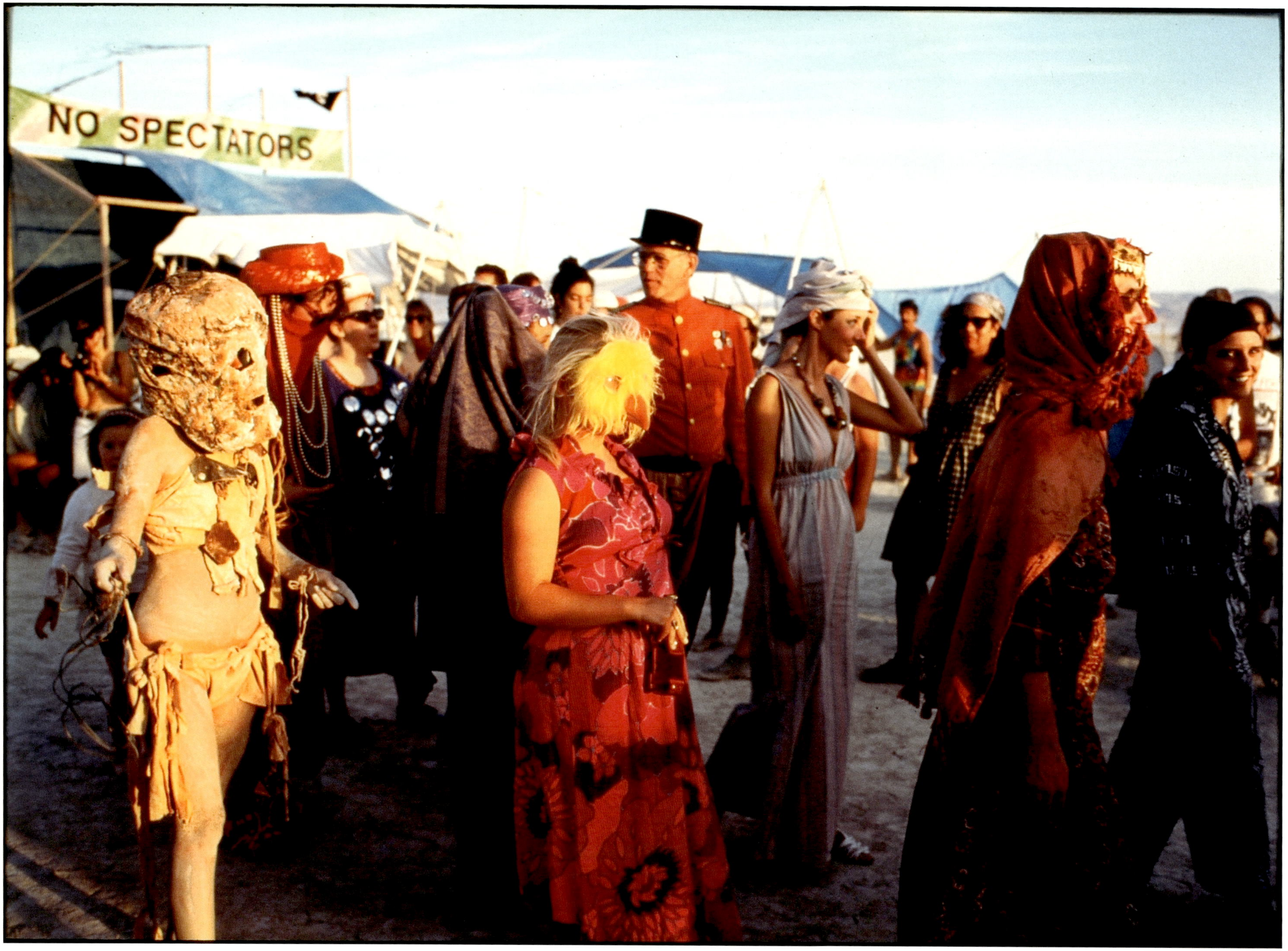

NO SPECTATORS, 1993

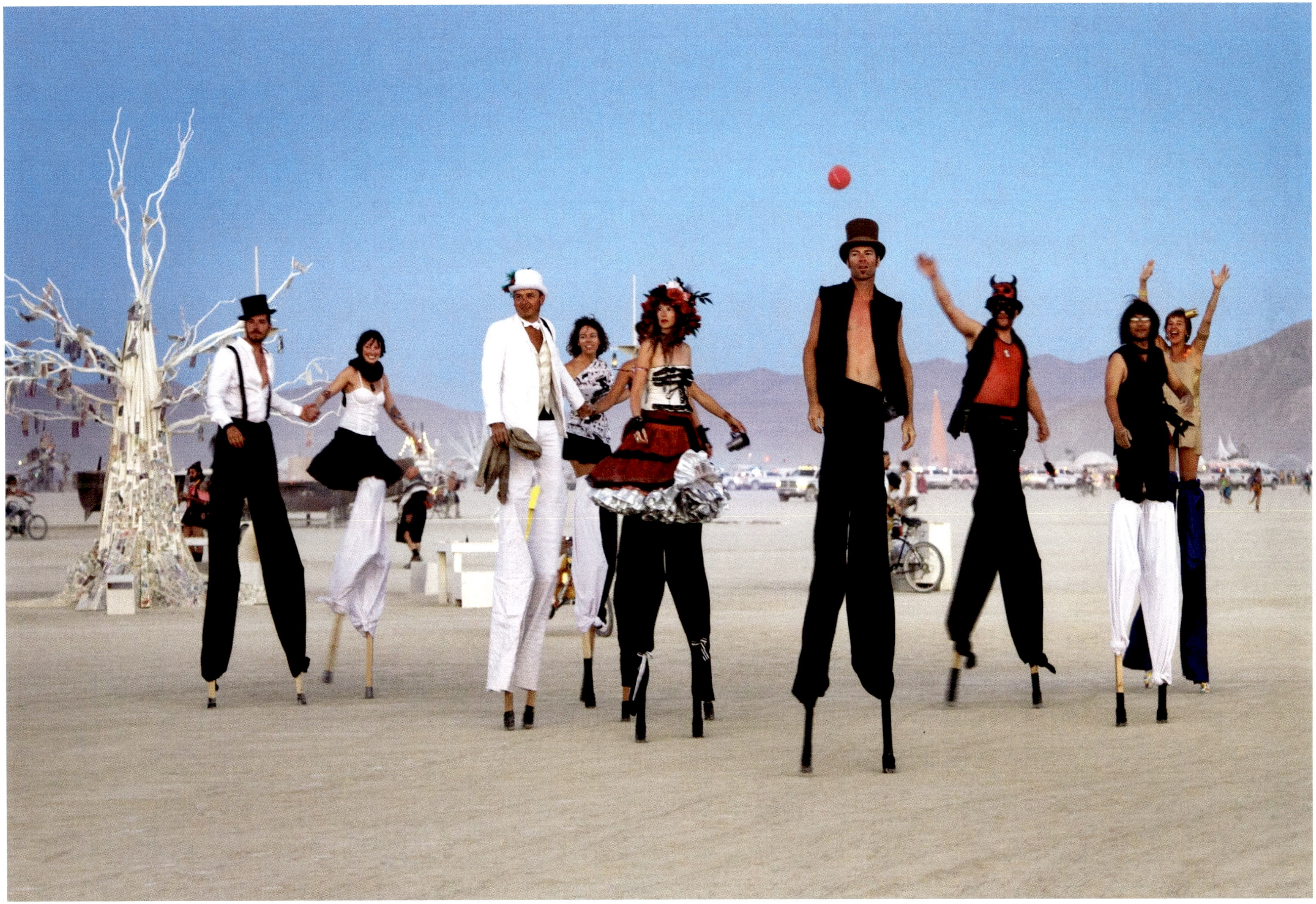

Stilt Walkers, 2012

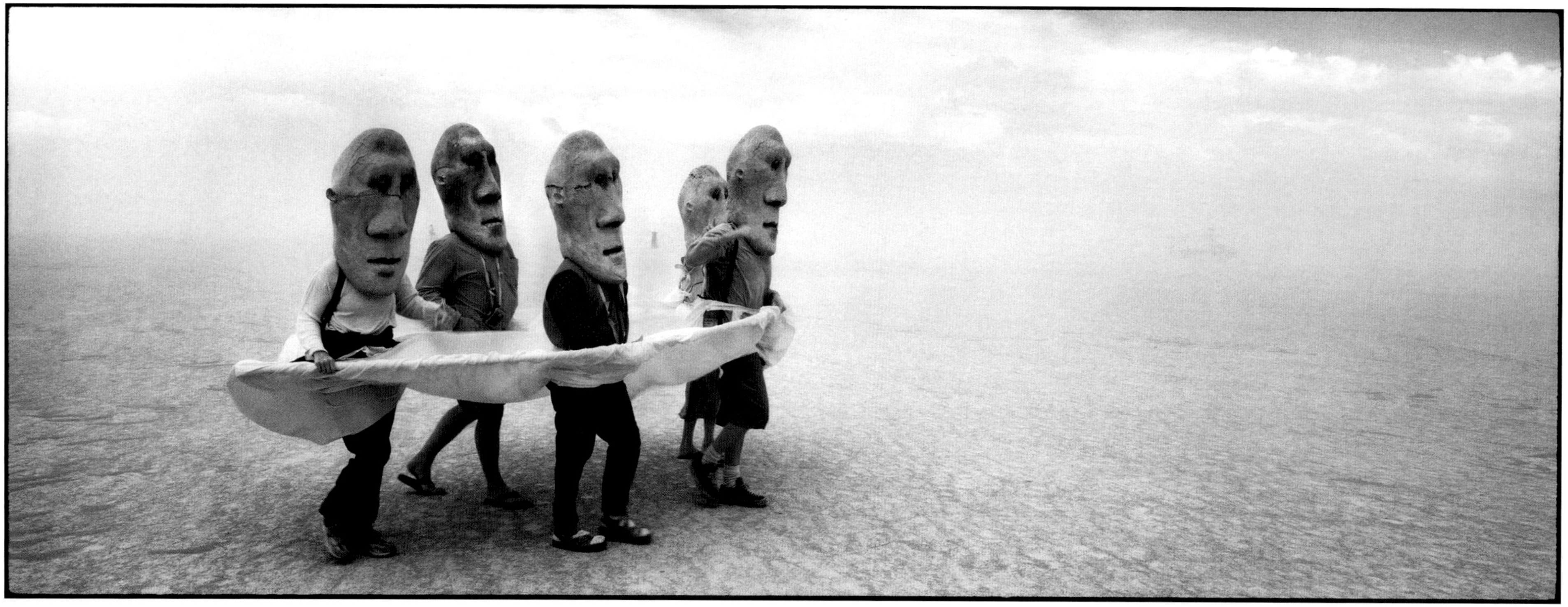

Whimsical Travelers, 1999

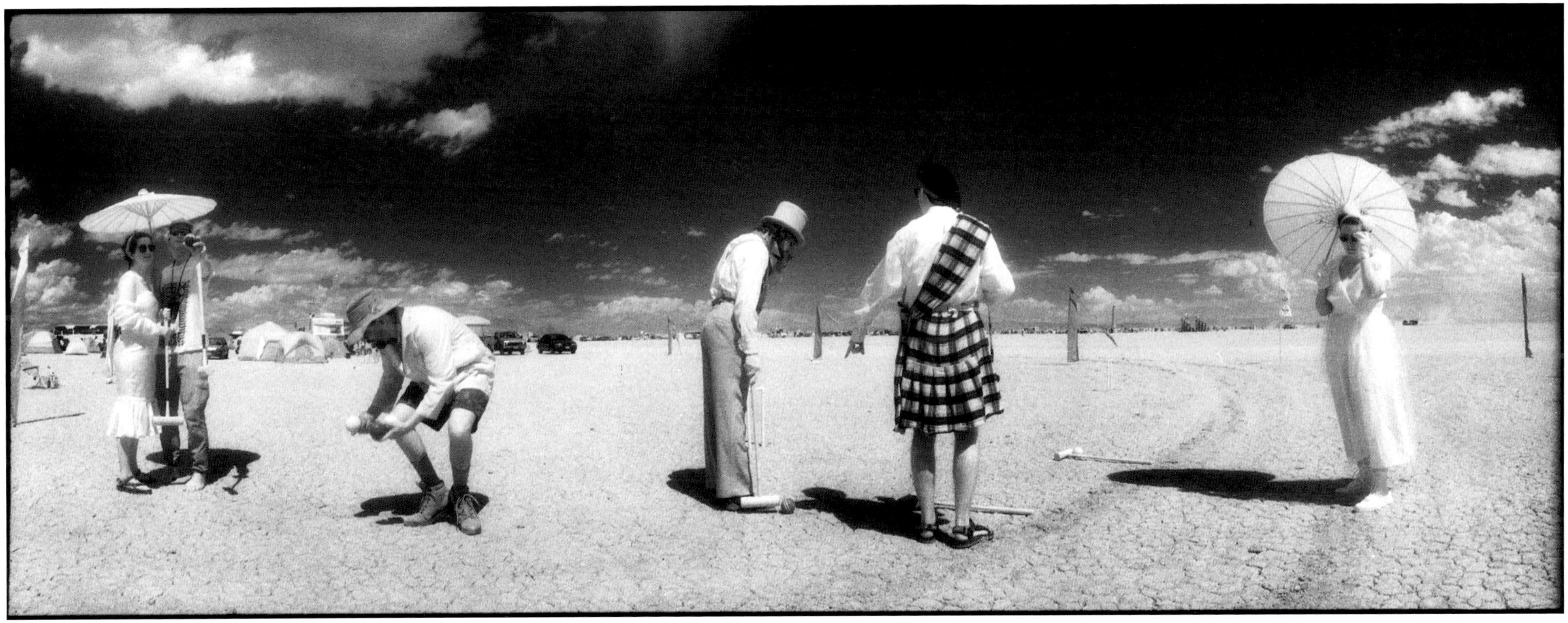

Croquet Players, 1995

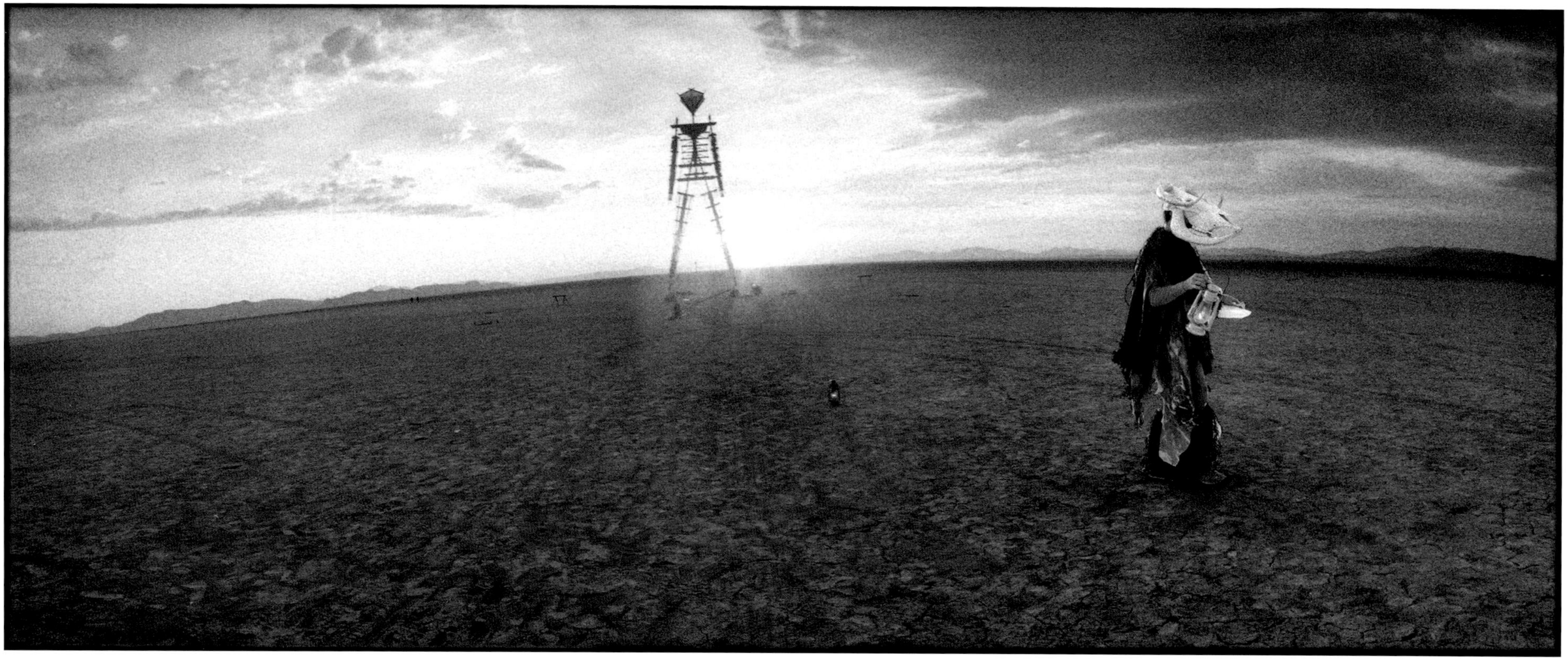

Java Cow Ritual, 1993

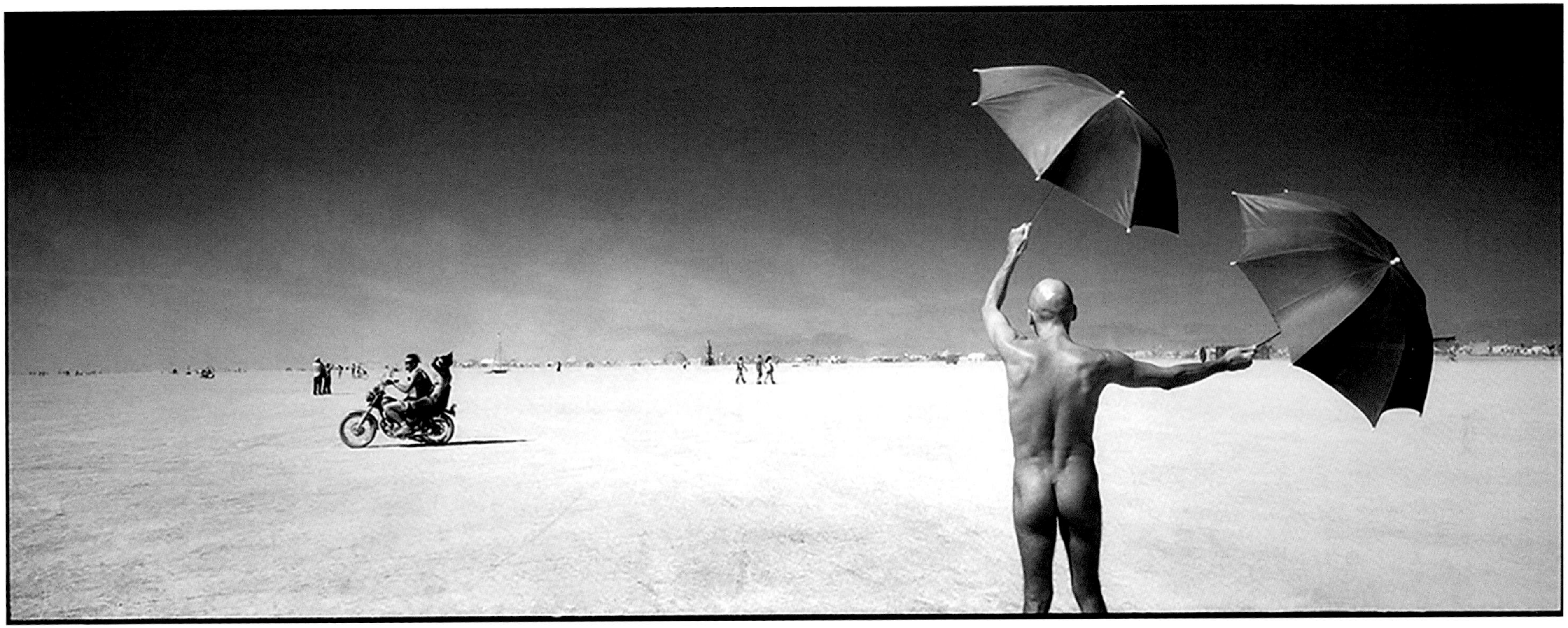

Umbrella Man, 2005

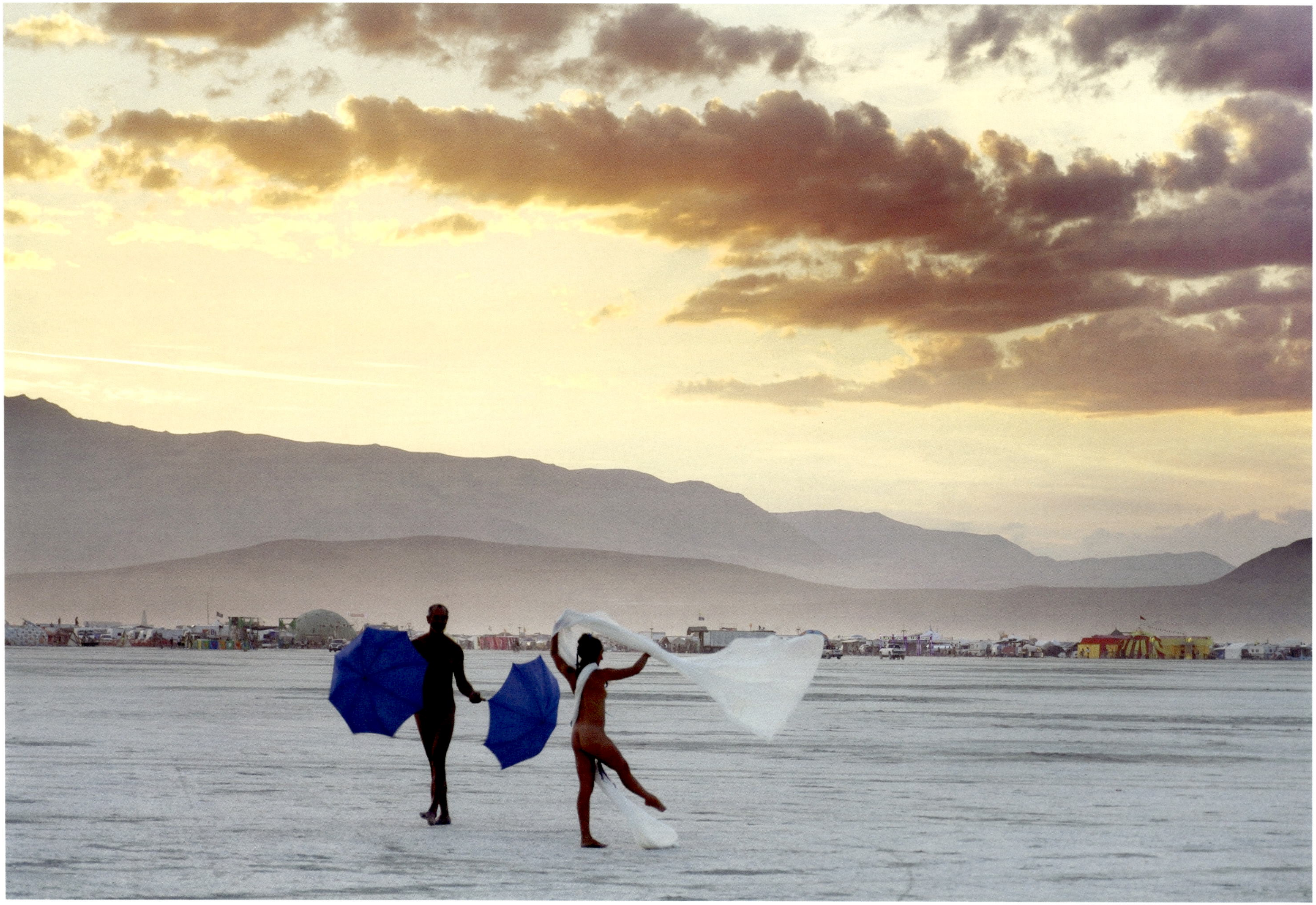

Playa Pas de Deux, 2014

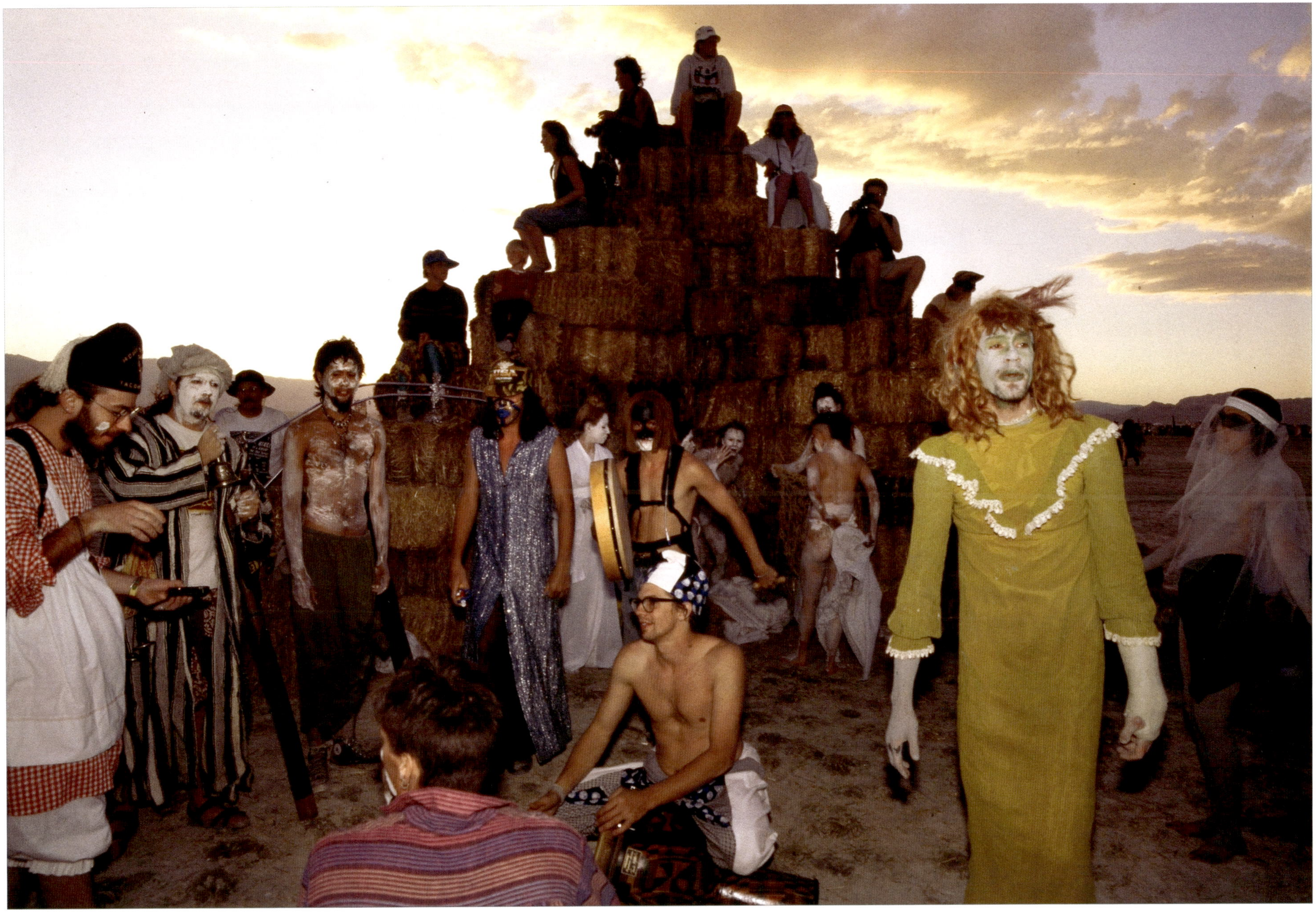

Pageant Rehearsal, 1995

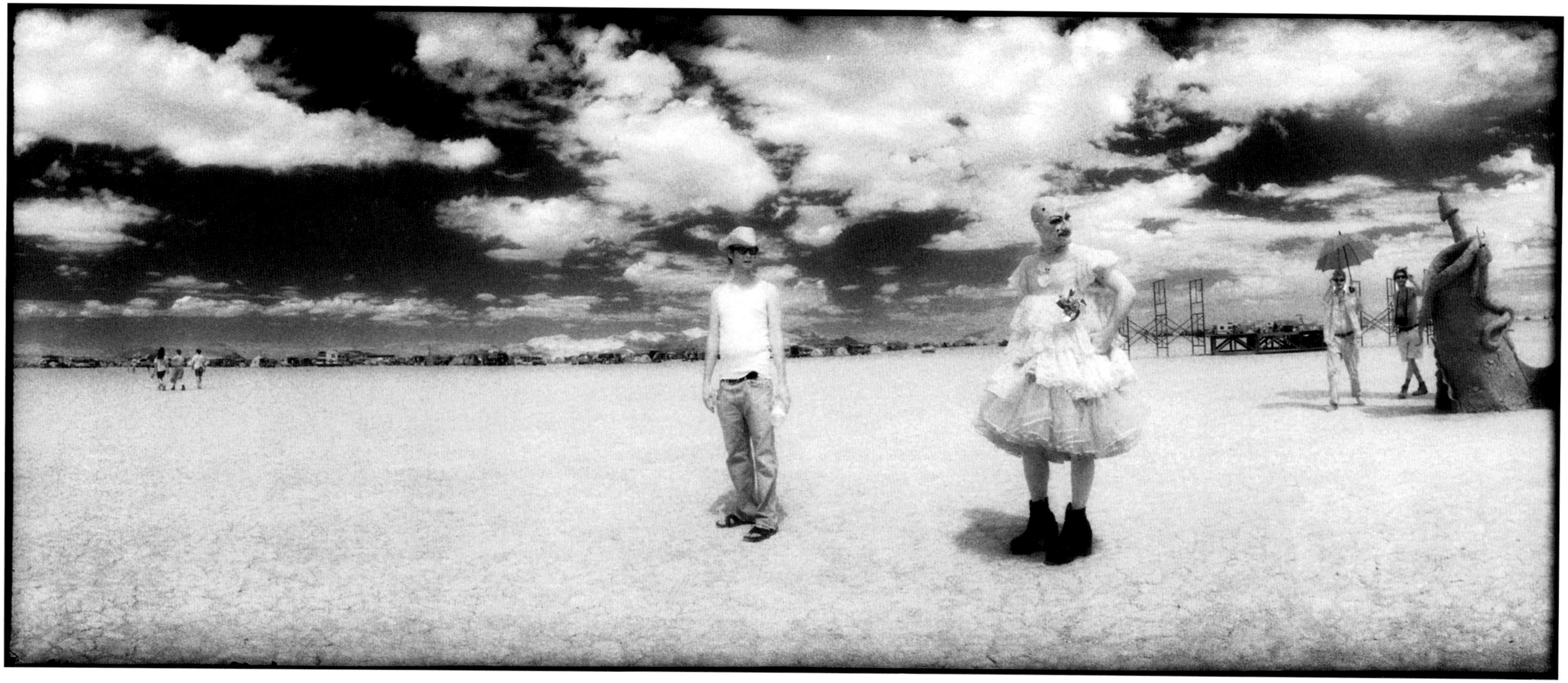

Playa Encounter, 1995

The remarkable thing about Radical Self-Expression is how naturally it occurred. Exhibitionist drag is a contemporary cliché at Burning Man, but we were a bit more buttoned-down in the nineties. Yet the desert conspired with those who felt the urge to express themselves by providing an alien setting, and the event's countercultural heritage added another layer of permission. If you had a whim and it didn't hurt anyone, you indulged it. When you and a bunch of strangers got mired in the playa mud, you turned it into a mosh pit. If people couldn't behave with abandon on the playa, where else could they? The not-so-deep secret of Radical Self-Expression on the playa was opportunity.

I was a middle-aged man from Portland, Oregon, and Portland wasn't as yet all that weird, but I could feel the rush of unbridled freedom the moment we got out of the car. In fact, speeding across the sand drifts was an ample prelude to a sense of having entered an autonomous zone where most conventional restrictions had been left back on the interstate. It wasn't so much wild and untamed as it was open and accepting. The event offered an open invitation to be whoever we imagined ourselves to be, and that was not only okay, it was an expectation. We were curious travelers who'd stumbled upon the land of unabashed humans, and they often turned out to be reflections of our interior selves.

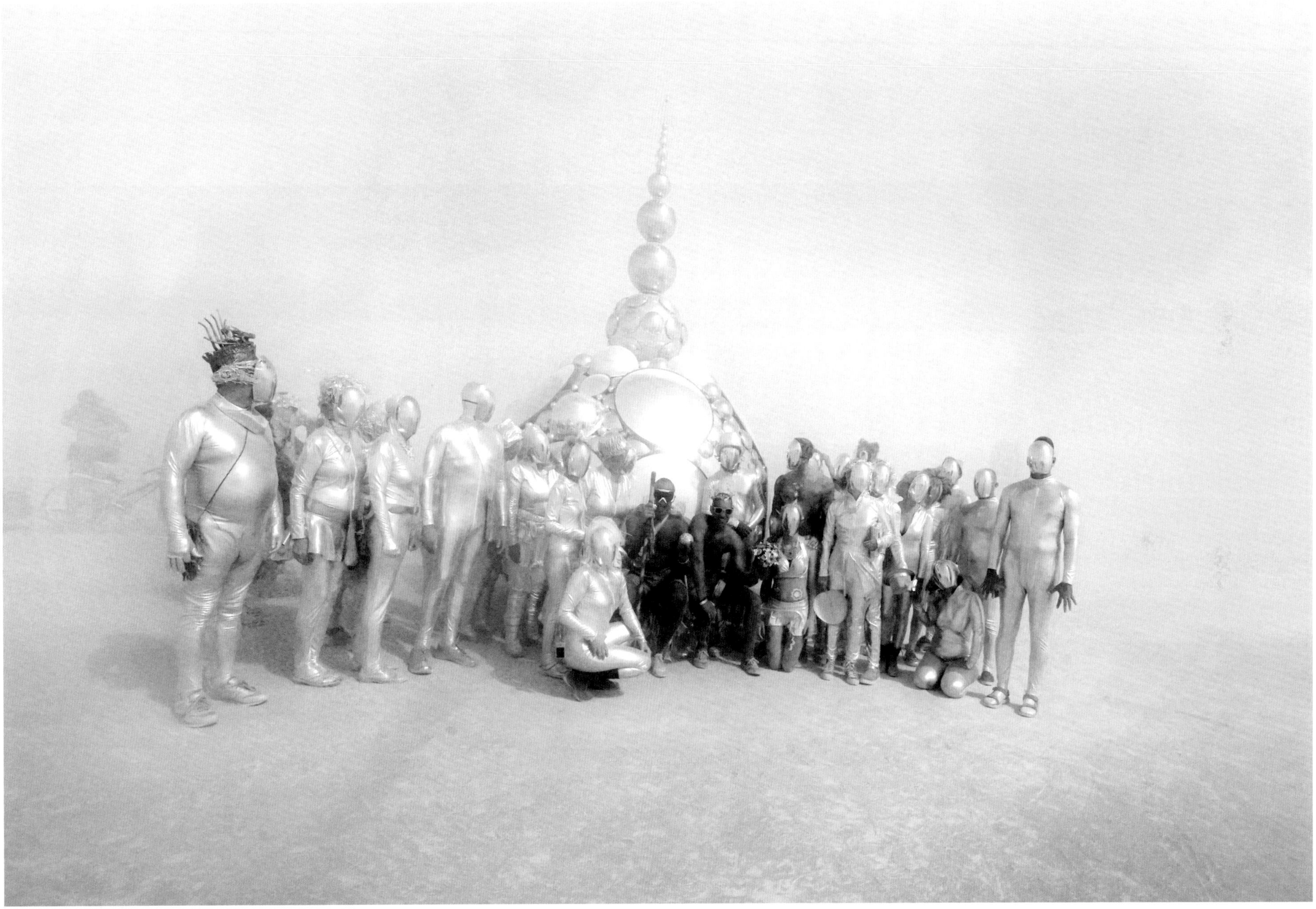

Looking Glassholes, *2015*

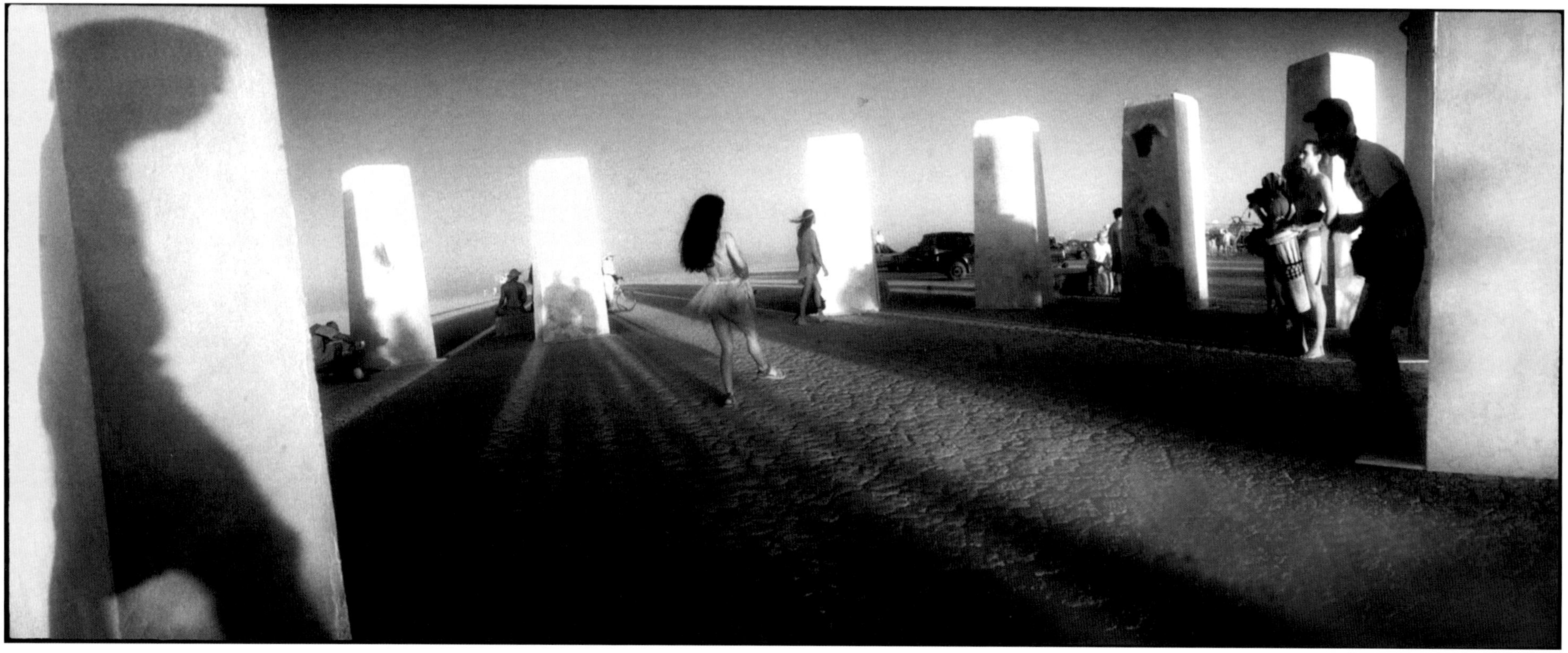

MudHenge, *1996*

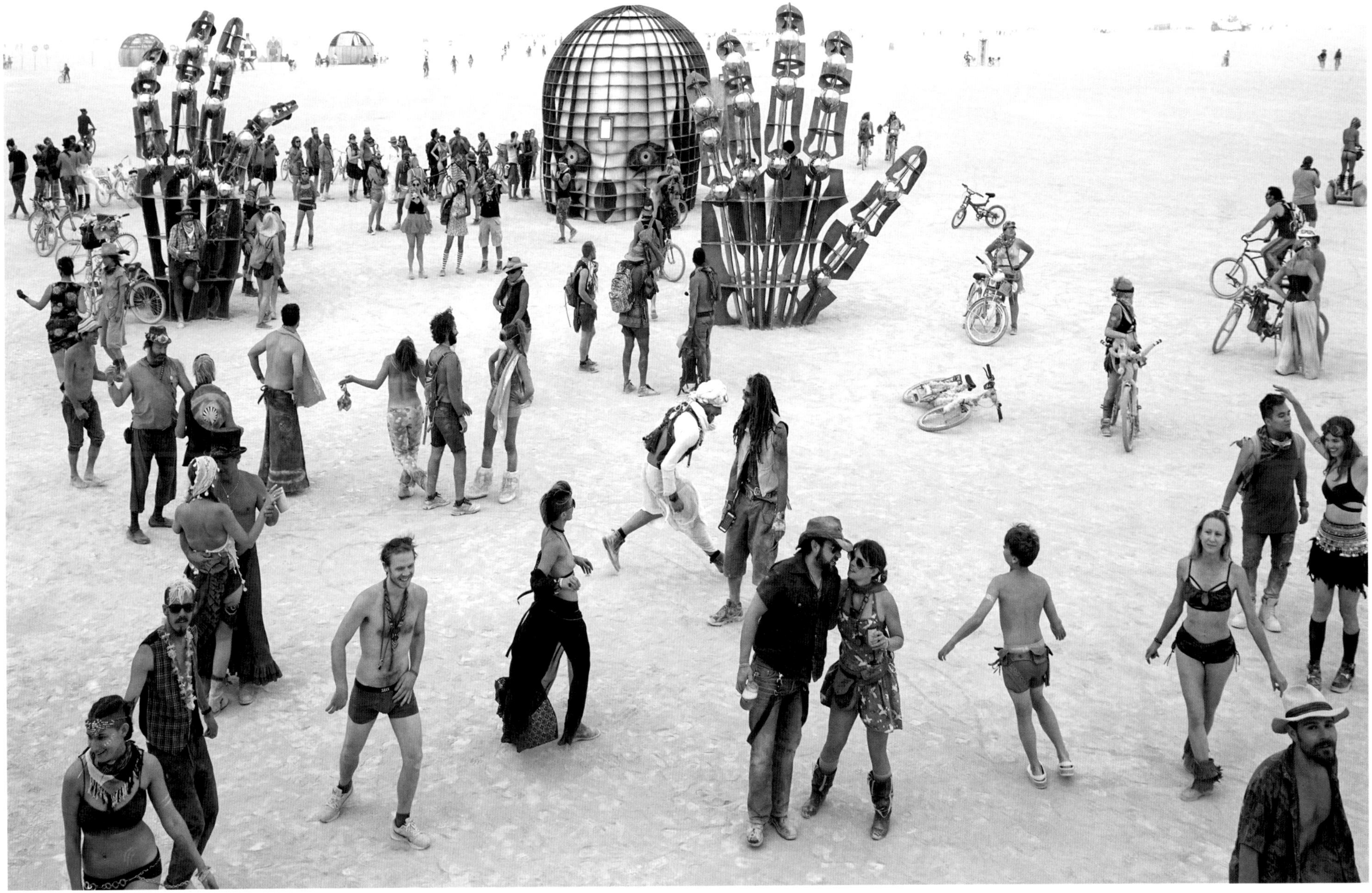

Playa Pas de Dozens, 2016

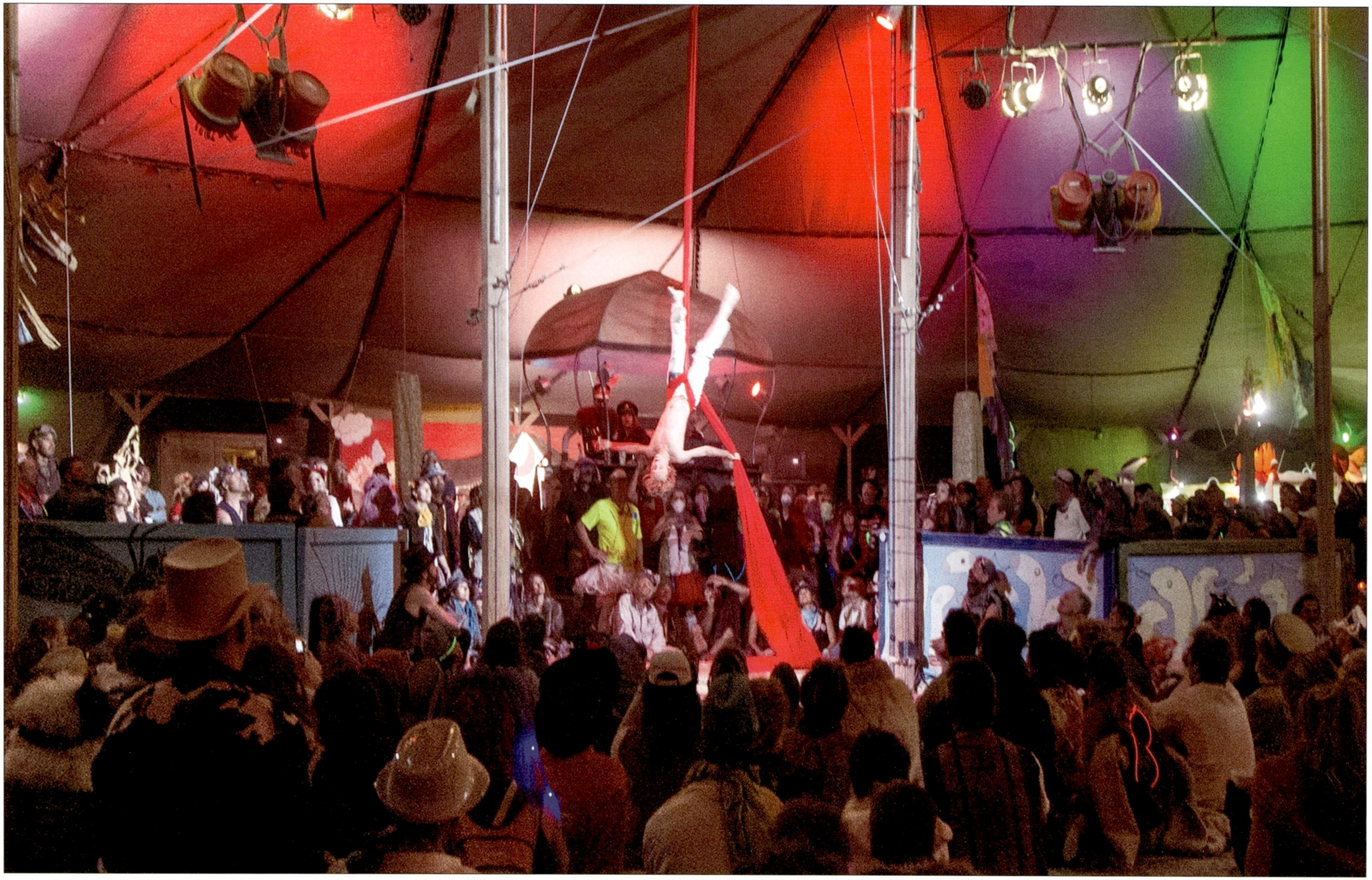

Aerial Silk, 2012

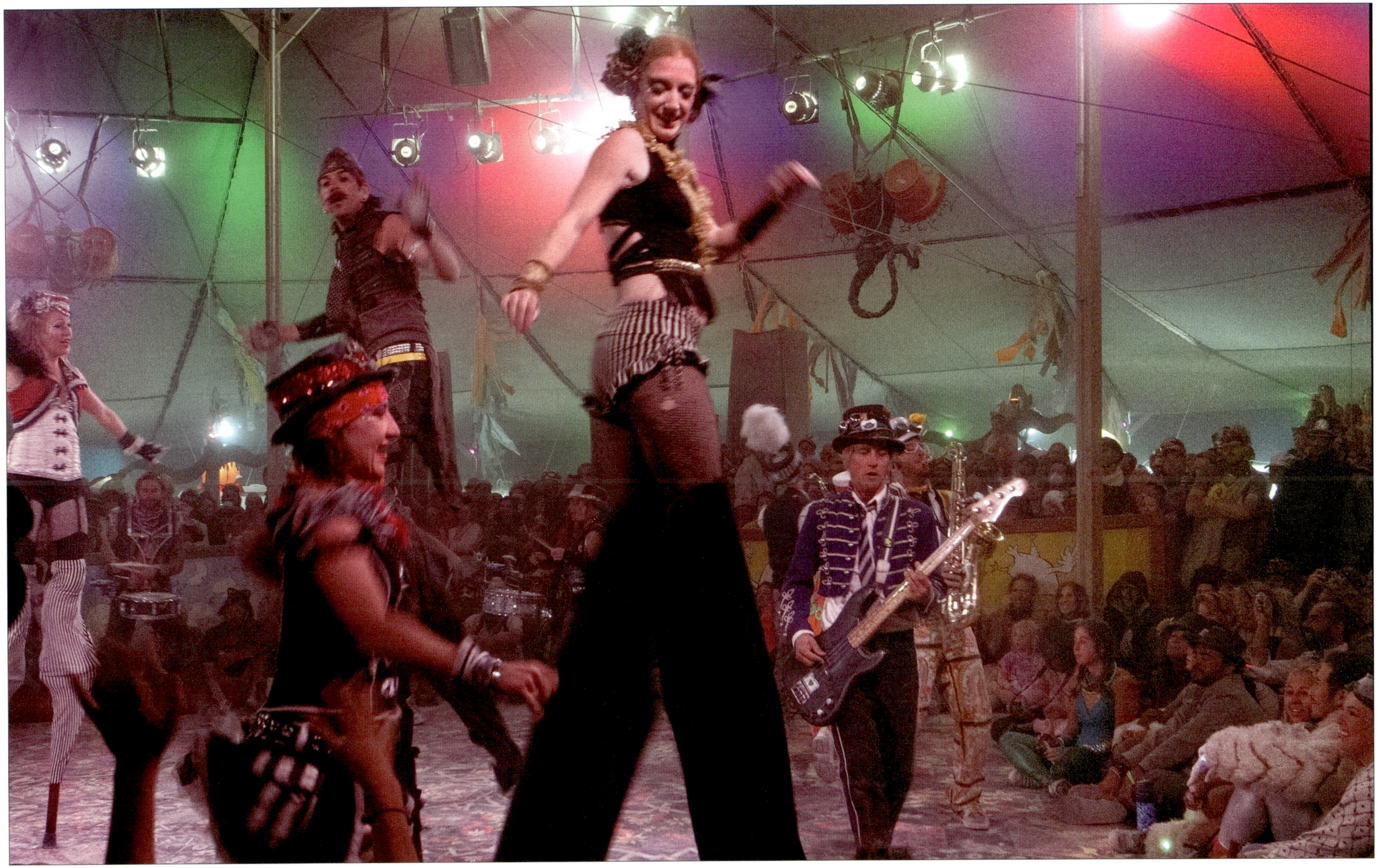

MarchFourth Dancers, 2012

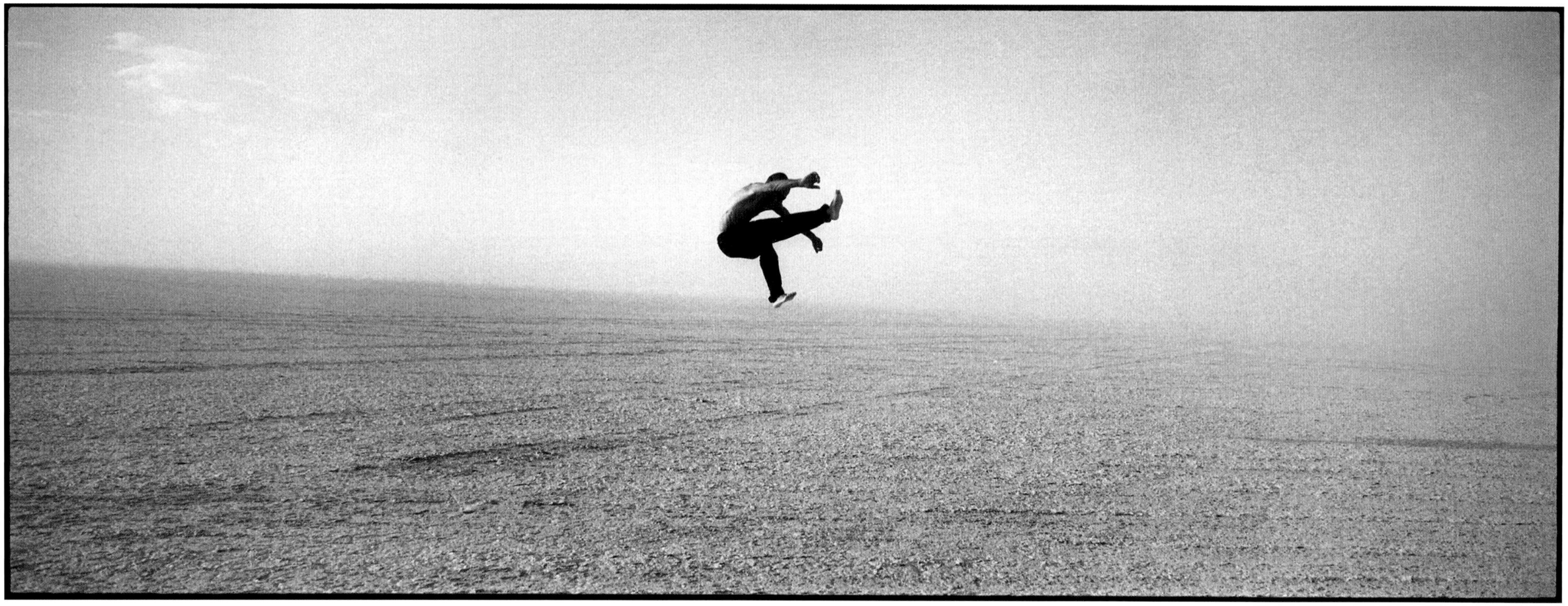

Zen Kick, 2008

Without a doubt the most reliable reaction to setting foot on the Black Rock Desert is that one is almost immediately overcome with the impulse to play. It's virtually instantaneous, and I liken it to stepping onto the widest and longest beach in the solar system, but on Jupiter or some other far-flung planet. My buddy Jim Bocci showed up with golf balls and a driver the first time he drove down with me to Burning Man in 1995. Of course the quintessential example is when Apollo 14's Alan Shepard hit a golf ball on the moon. It's not that he hit a golf ball. What ten-year-old wouldn't want to hit a golf ball on the moon? No, it's that the experience of standing on the lunar surface inspired him to do such a frivolous and playful thing.

Play is at the heart of Burning Man. Theme camps are mostly childish exaggerations of our inventive inclinations; even the more serious-minded art and parody are typically rendered in a style that is cartoonish. But play can go beyond artful aspiration; it can speak internationally. There is a universal language of play we relate to because we all wiggled our toes the same way at our first encounter with a wave-washed beach. Play is a truly universal experience, and even at its most intense, setting a humanoid effigy aflame in the middle of a dry lake bed with seventy thousand of your closest friends is still, at its core, a gonzo beach bonfire.

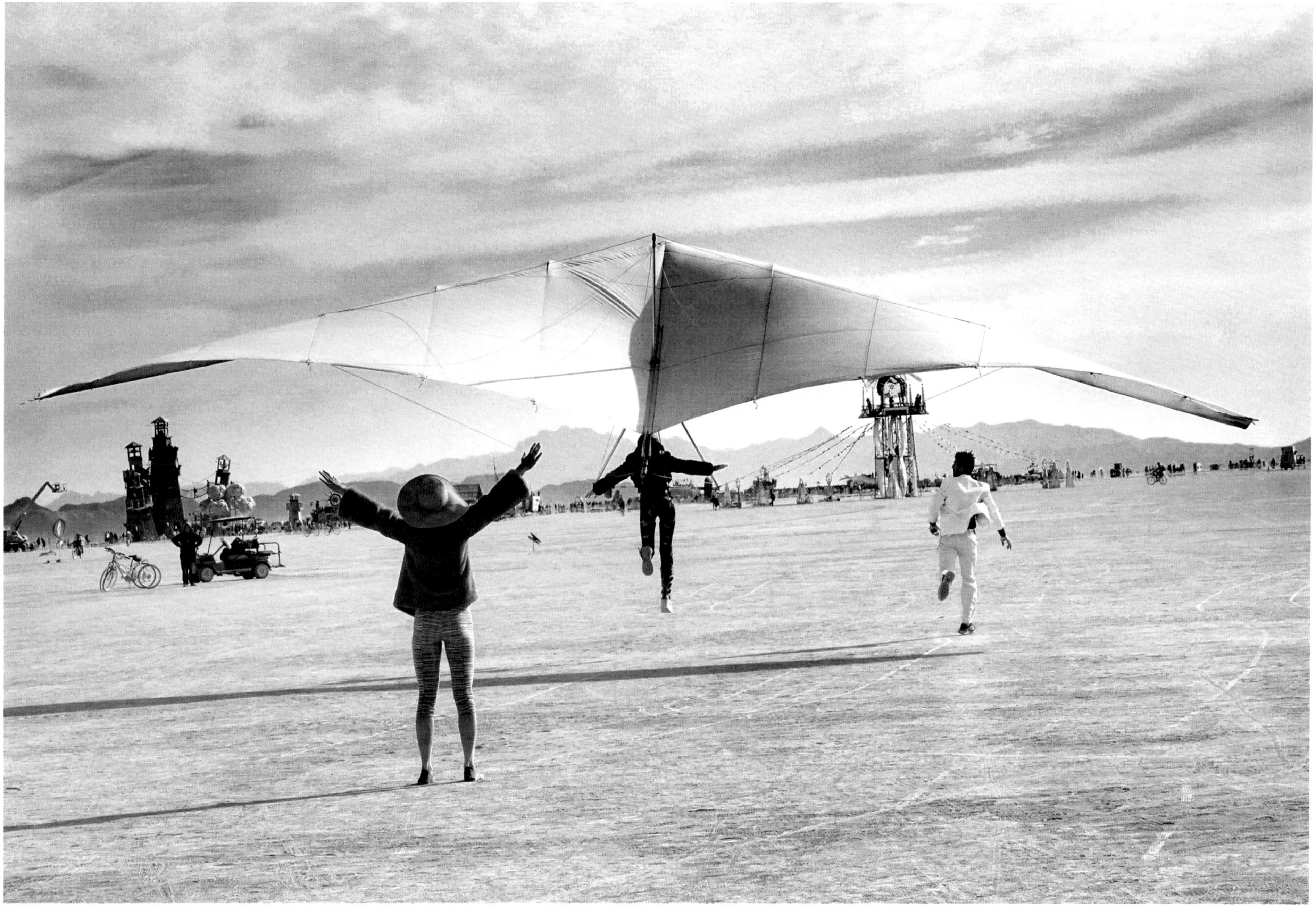

Playa Flight, 2016

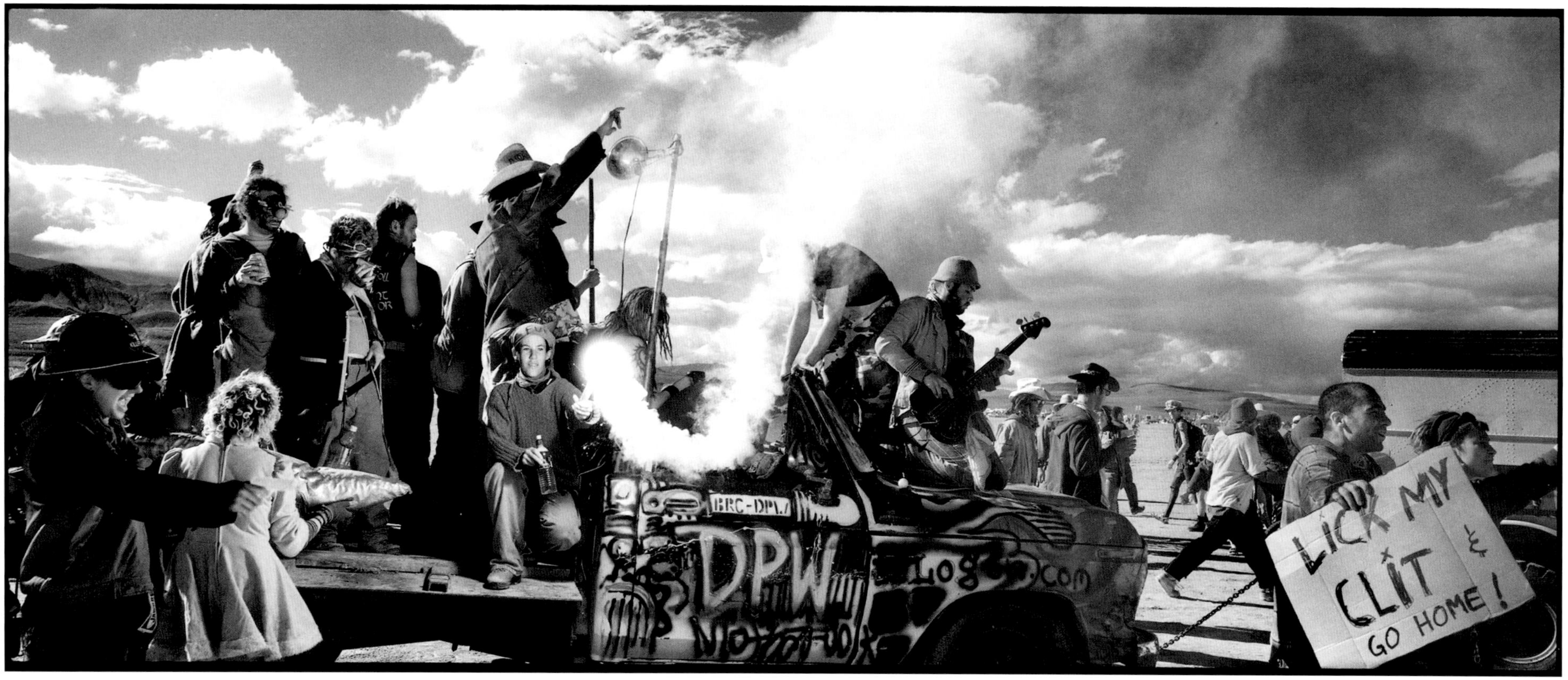

DPW Parade, 2000

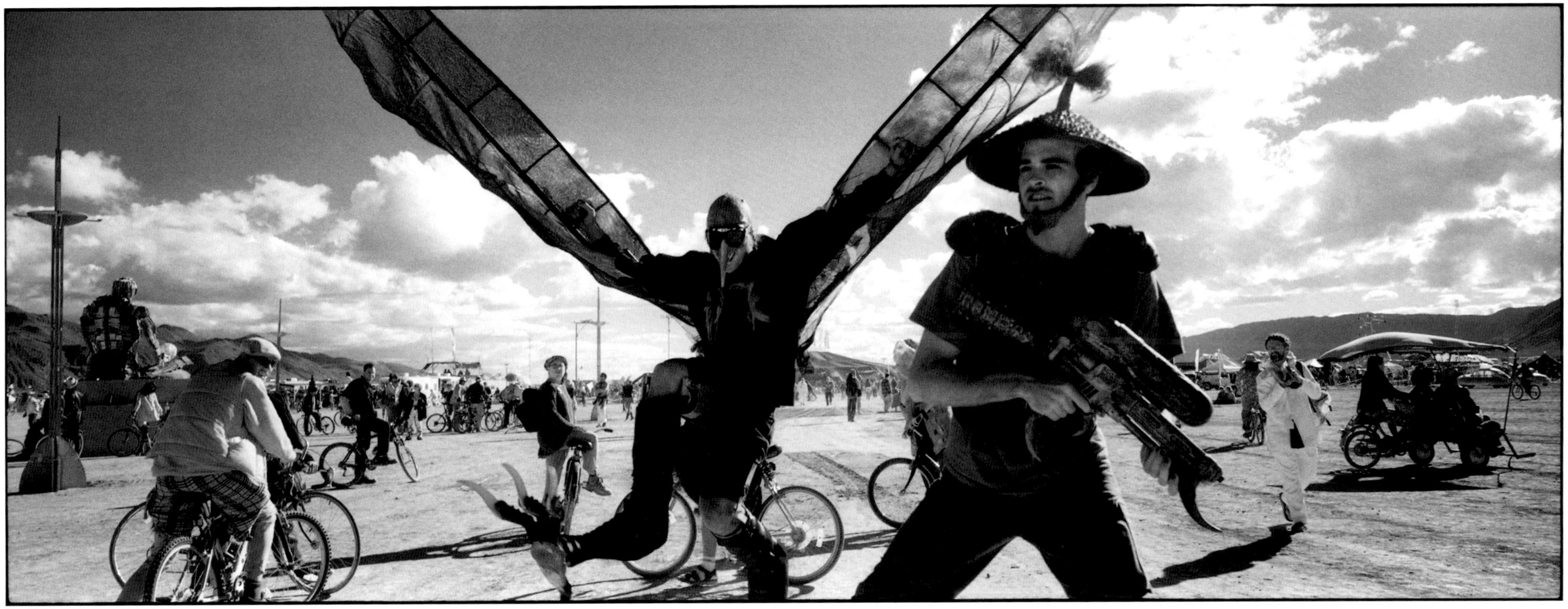

Birdman and Sidekick, 2000

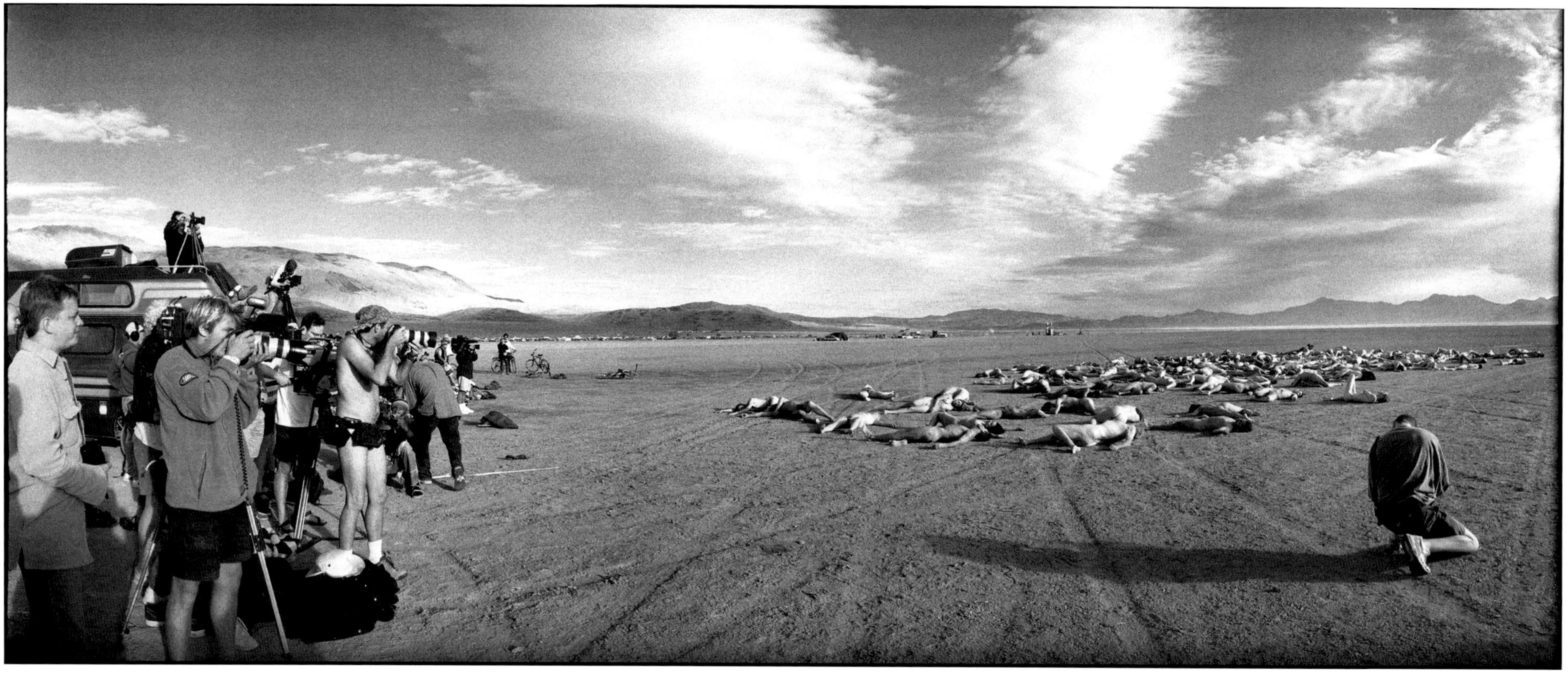

Nevada, 1997

The broad expanse of the desert awakens within many the desire to leave their mark. Indeed the urge for both art and expression seems to spring quite naturally to many who venture onto its inviting flatness. We are dwarfed by its resolute scale, and as a result we attempt to enlarge our footprint. It's as if the very barrenness of the plain challenges our being, and we feel compelled to make an existential statement. The most obvious examples are the many giant sculptures or art cars, but sometimes it simply takes the form of an individual's declaration of passion and identity.

Artist Spencer Tunick visited Burning Man on Hualapai Flat in 1997 and staged a couple of different nude groupings for his *Naked States* book. He liked the playa so much that he returned to the Black Rock Desert to stage photo shoots in 1999 and 2000. In 2013 he returned once more to stage one of his most spectacular arrangements. The playa was the perfect setting for his sculptural groups, and I'm sure the enthusiasm of hundreds of naked volunteers added to the attraction. Tunick is but one of many professional artists to respond to the playa's clarion call, but I persist in celebrating the persistent amateurs who come to this place and fall in love with what seems to be nature's great blank canvas. Here they rush to build something, or dance, and they leave their marks as crudely or as elegantly as they are able.

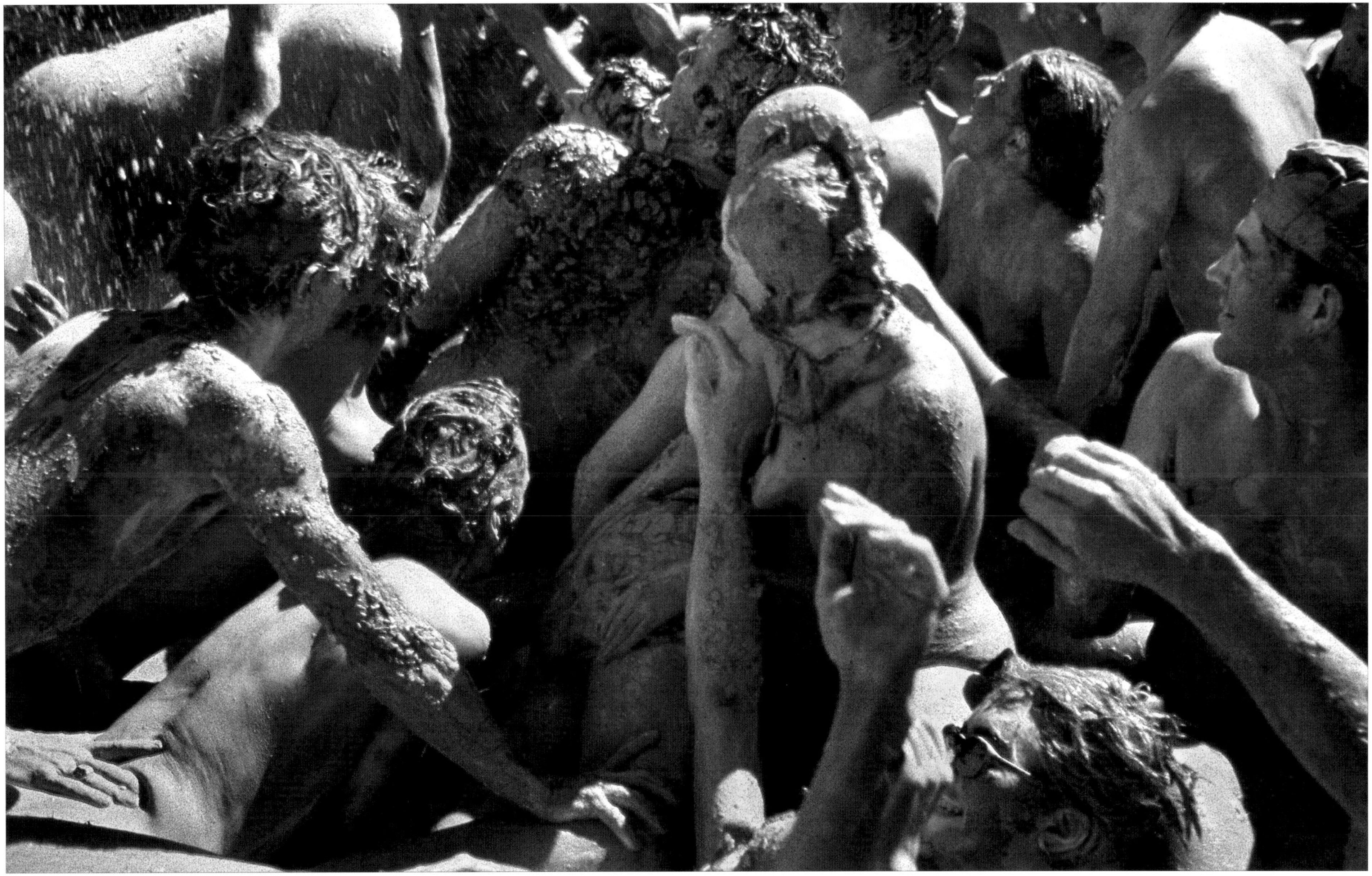

Mud Wallow, 1995

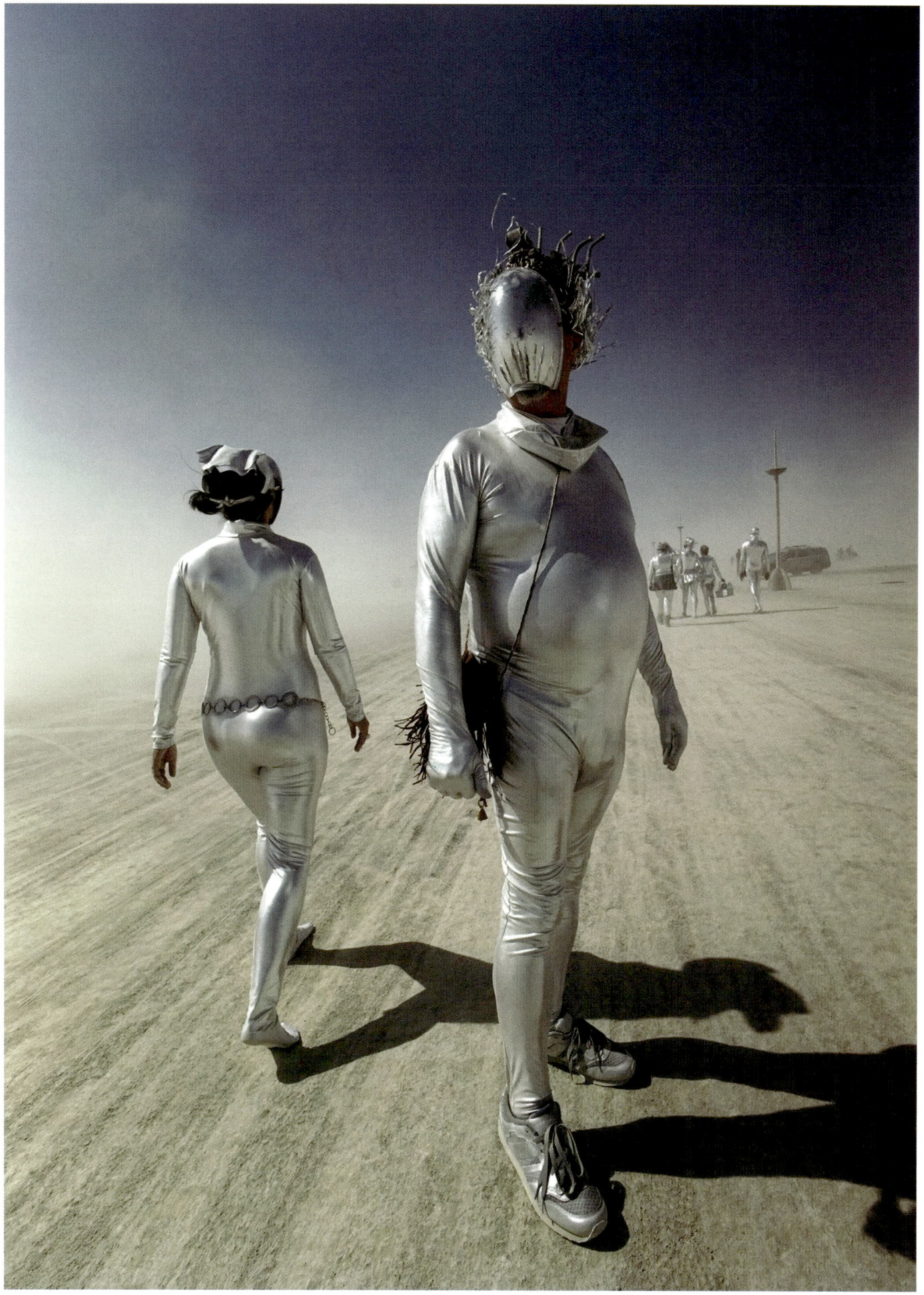

Silver Couple, 2015

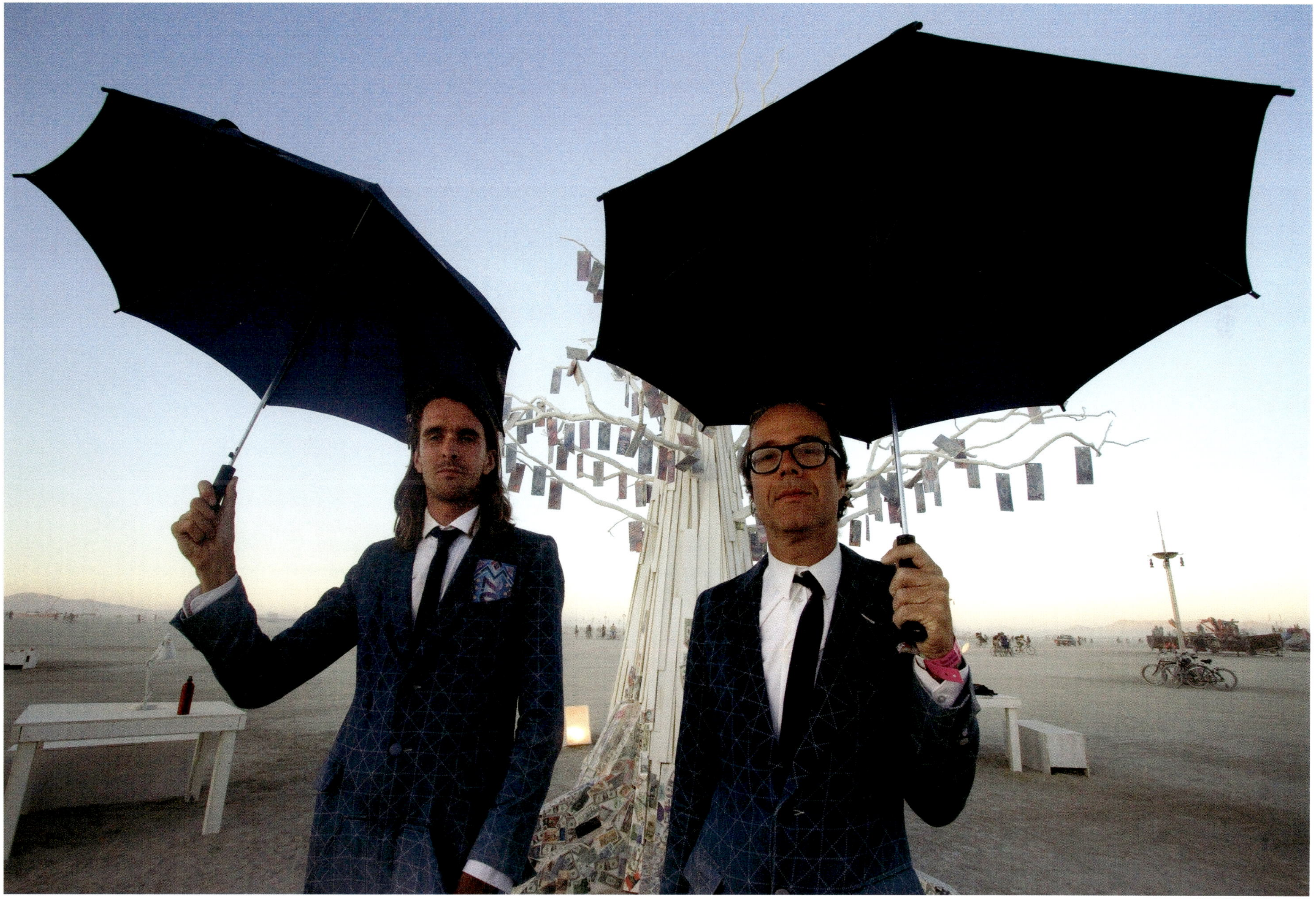

Transformoney Tree *Bankers, 2012*

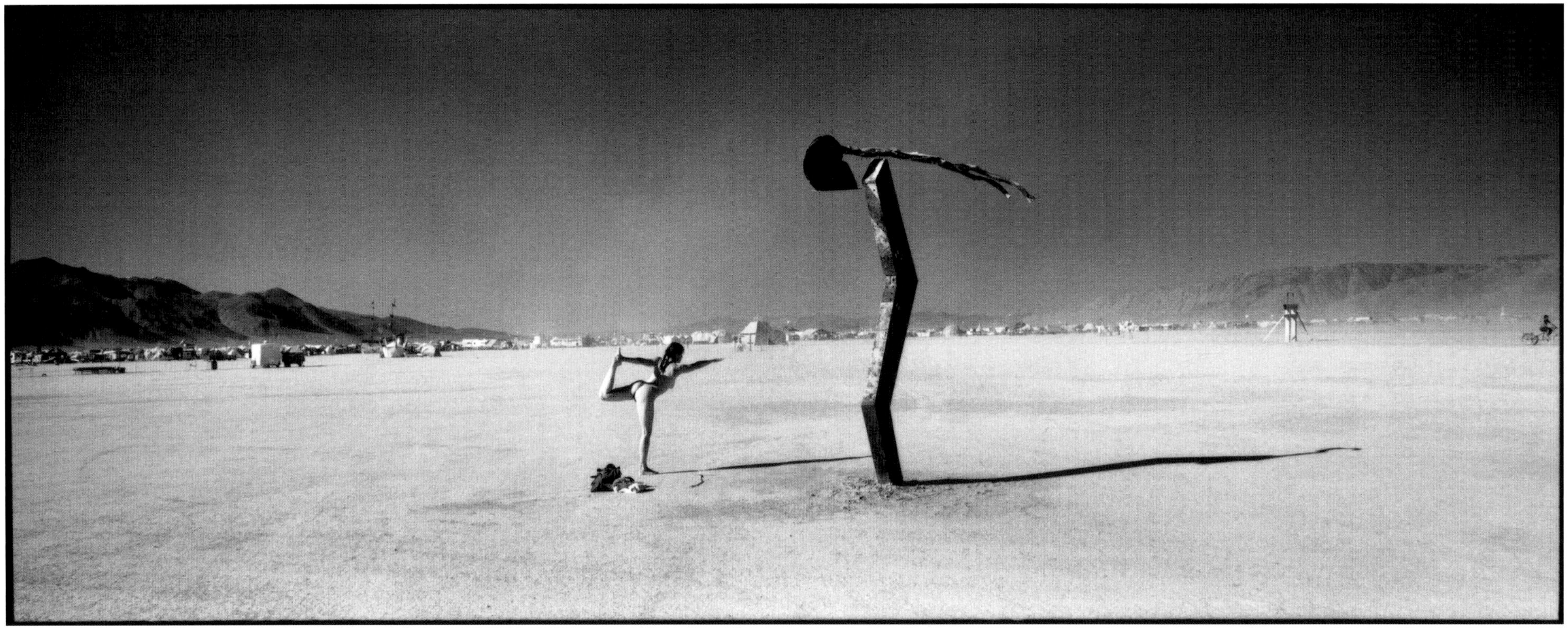

Yoga Pose, 2003

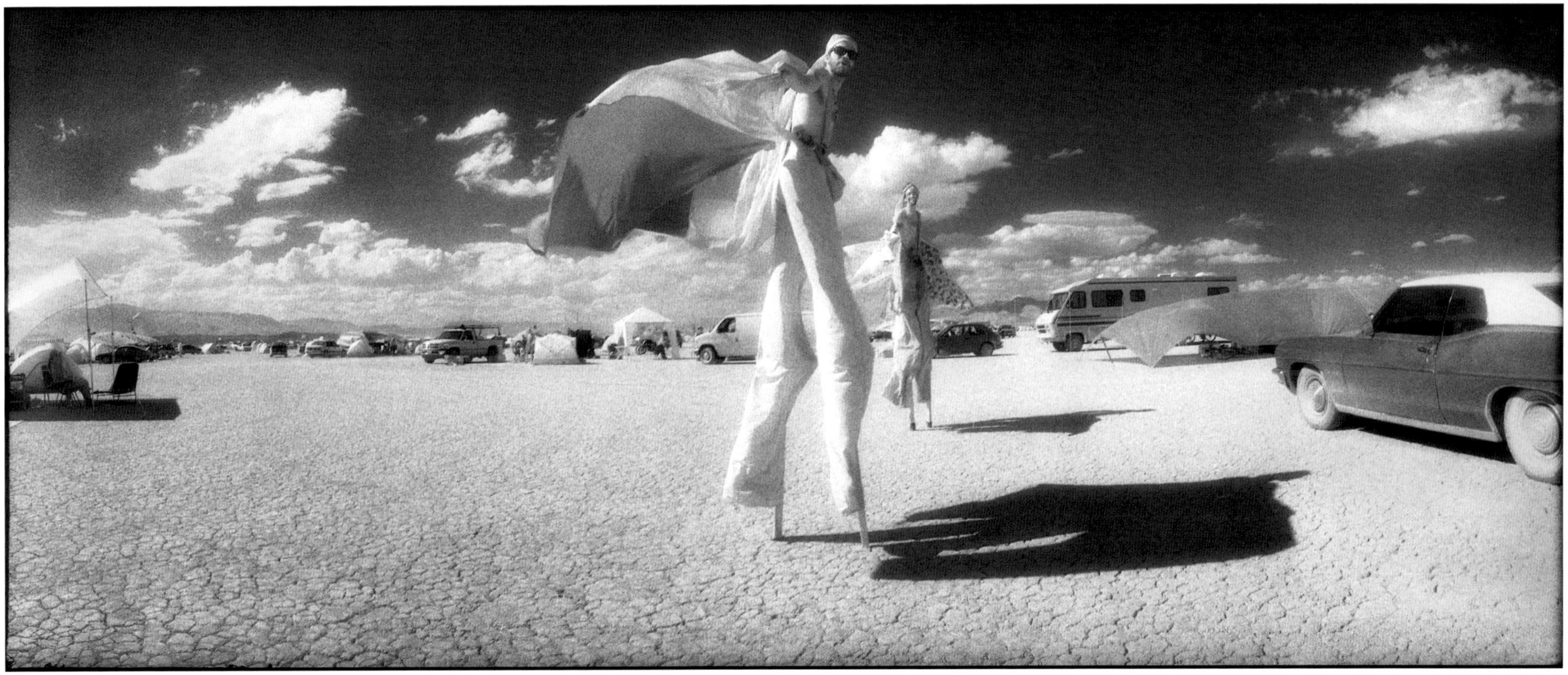

Stilt Walkers, 1995

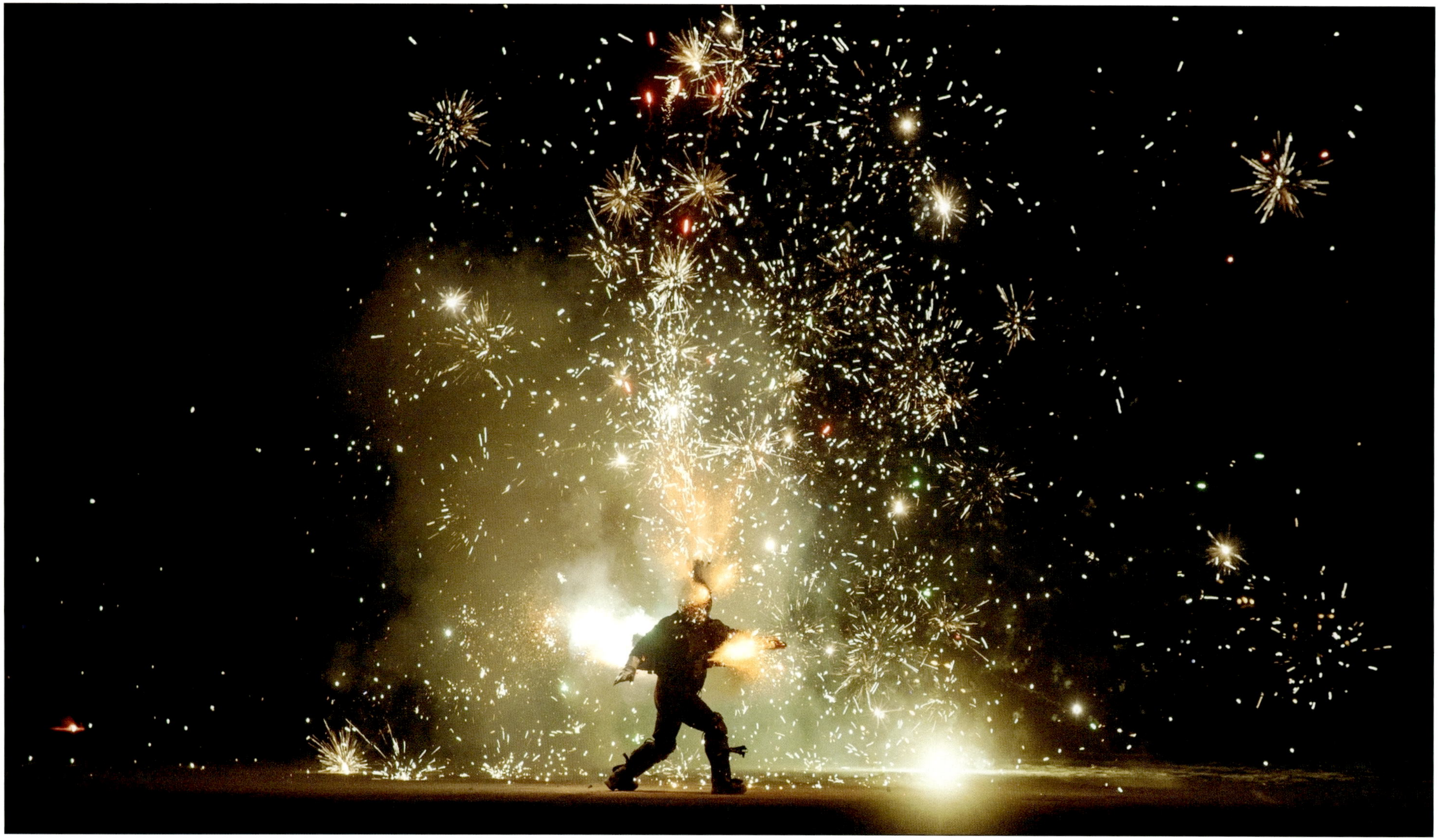

Pyro Man, 2012

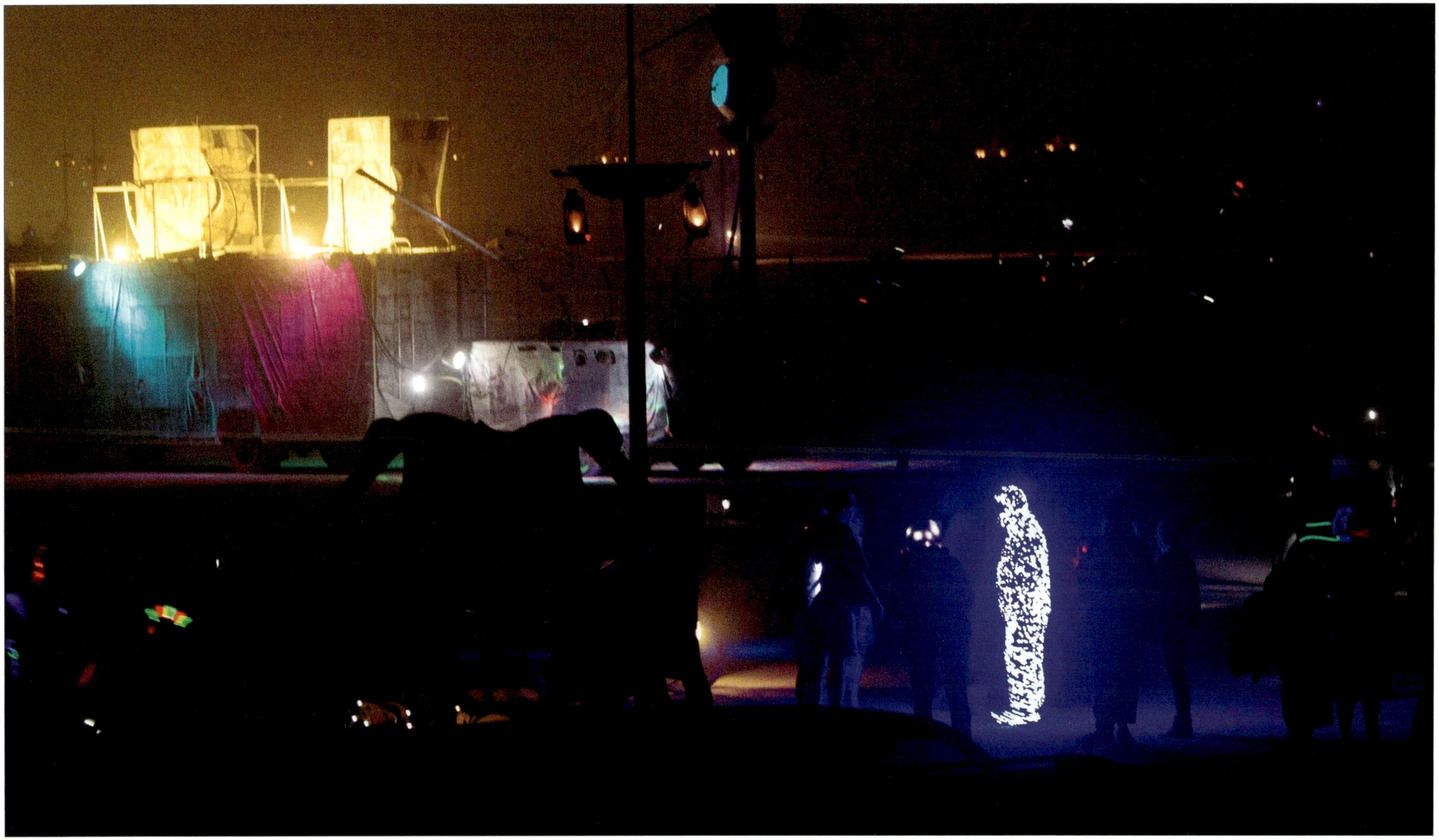

Blue Man, 2012

CHAPTER 5

BRIGHTEST DAYS, DARKEST NIGHTS: 1995–1997

Communal society was blossoming at Burning Man by 1995. The population had doubled to four thousand, and would double again the following year. The random collection of tents and RVs began to form into clusters that resembled villages of the like-minded or represented regional collections of friends. Camp identities were forming, and as the Man was still the central locus by which all activities radiated, the camp cluster began to take on a somewhat circular shape. By then there was also a thriving Center Camp Café, founded and managed by Miss P. Segal. Community was becoming a viable concept at Burning Man.

Miss P. and her apartment mates have always loomed large in Burning Man's Cacophony era, and one of them, Harley K. Dubois, was at the head of the list. Her first job was manning the Burning Man Hotline: 415-TO-FLAME. "We had two lines: one for ride share and one for volunteers to help build the city," she said. "Finally, they put me in charge of a bunch of those volunteers, and I became the city manager." Harley would go on to found many of the critical institutions at the event: Theme Camp Placement, the Greeters, Playa Info, and Burning Man Information Radio (BMIR). These days she is known as one of the six founders of the contemporary organization, and she is also the only member of that group besides my brother and Michael Mikel who has roots going back to those first meetings at 1907 Golden Gate Avenue.

Burning Man was also beginning to experience growing pains. Every year from 1990 the population had doubled, and this resulted in an embarrassment of riches. Cash at the gate was the norm since this was the era before Internet sales. Besides founding the Black Rock Rangers, Michael Mikel had also functioned as the bookkeeper and financial manager for the leadership triumvirate from its beginning, but securing large amounts of cash in a volatile environment was always a worrisome task. Hauling a safe out to the playa was a reasonable option, but in the early days of limited resources, people tended to make do. Michael's idea was to create a vault by burying a stovepipe in the playa sand. It was a simple and relatively easy solution, but it had a built-in flaw. During wet years, the rainwater settled into playa aquifers, some of which lurked just below the surface. Whether the water came from a hidden spring or a high water table, the pipe filled up. "All the funds were muddy and soaked," Harley joked later. "We actually had to launder the money!"

Larry reports that in those days there was still wide disagreement amongst the faithful about whether to allow just anyone to attend. San Francisco hipsters can be as clannish as anyone, and the event, which would build itself around the notion of Radical Inclusion, struggled in the beginning to keep from becoming exclusive to the Bay Area "in crowd." Most of the antecedents to Burning Man were loosely formed hipster groups like Cacophony or party-driven conclaves like Anon Salon. Fund-raising had always been an issue, and so Burning Man partnered with Bay Area groups to stage fund-raising parties. Anon Salon parties, which aspired to "blur lines between performers and audience," were virtually a monthly affair in the 1990s—gatherings such as Flambé Lounge, the afterburn Decompressions, and Heat the Street Faire. As a result, people at Burning Man congregated together in clusters based on friendships or common interests. The core discussion between Burning Man organizers and longtime supporters was what kind of event it was going to be: secretly exclusive or broadly inclusive. Larry favored the latter.

From my point of view as a Portland outsider, inclusion wasn't a problem—I wanted inclusion—but there was an obvious disconnect between people who "got" the spirit of the event and those who did not. It's no secret that many people in Gerlach and rural Pershing County initially looked at Burning Man with a jaundiced eye. Pershing County was an impoverished and very conservative hunk of territory. Many of its citizens saw the event as a threat to law and order, and their religious way of life. The conservative county sheriff's office became an anti–Burning Man voice in the area for years

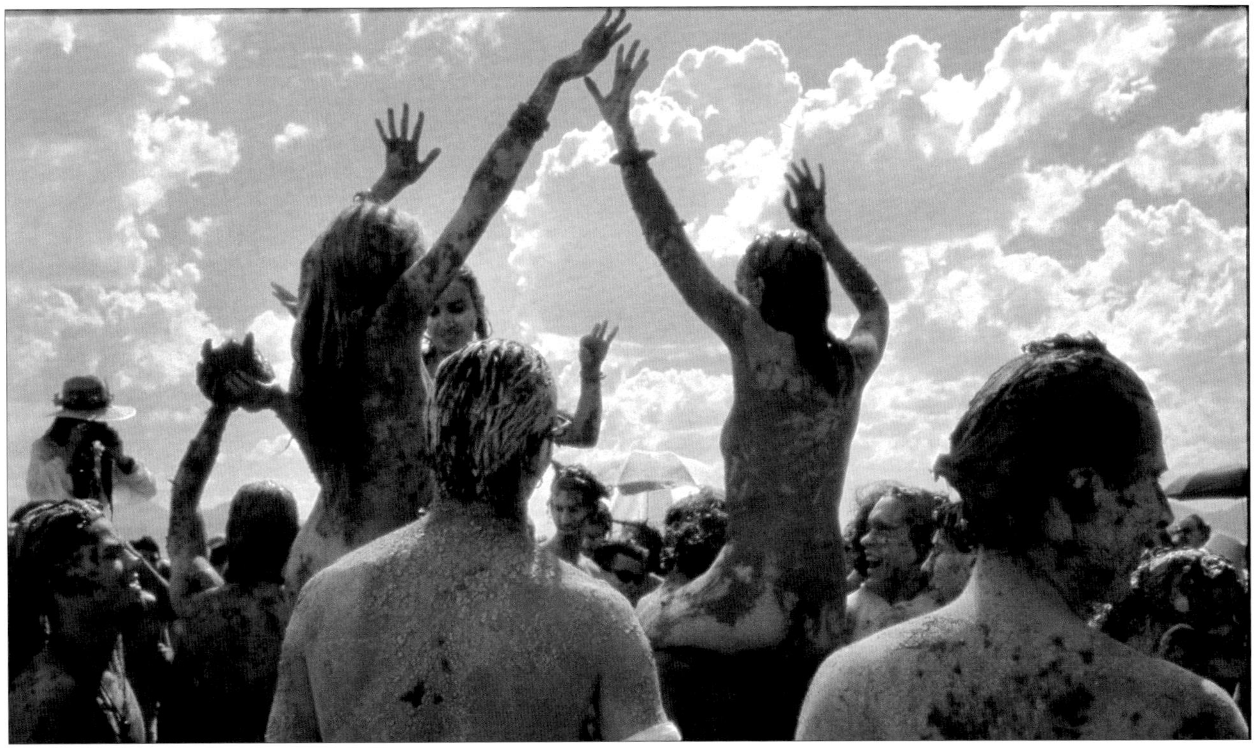

For an hour or so we danced the dance of pagan exuberance over nature's bounty.

and tried, unsuccessfully, to thwart the event at every turn. As a gesture of neighborly goodwill, Burning Man would open its gates in the early years for locals to attend free of charge on the Sunday night of the Burn, but many of the young locals had a warped notion that this "satanic ritual" was an open opportunity to enjoy a bit of forbidden fun. There has always been an unwritten mandate that no campsite should be permanently located east of the main enclave, which would thus ruin the sunrise view of the Man, and cars were never allowed into the central area surrounding the Man, but I remember several pickups loaded with hot-blooded local boys driving around the central camp shouting, "Show us your tits!"

Nature itself drove some of the evolution of Burning Man culture. The frequent rainstorms of 1995, for example, would eventually lead to the advent of one of the Burning Man clichés most repeated by the non-Burner public: public nudity. That summer volatile thunderstorms swept out of the northeastern skies and slammed into us at regular intervals. Most of us were woefully unprepared. I had designed a shade structure for our camp using plastic tarps and stanchions. When the first gusts of wind and rain hit, my blue shade cover filled with air and blew into the sky like a kite. After the wind subsided, we rebuilt the structure, driving the stakes deeper into the playa and lashing everything down with more rope. We also tied it to the open hatch of our station wagon. That lasted until the next storm. Bryan and I spent the next hour frantically clinging to the tarp in an updraft or pushing it up in the middle to keep it from filling up like a bowl in the driving rain.

Wind on the Black Rock Desert is easily the most destructive to camps and artwork, and dust is certainly the most irritating, but rain can bring daily existence to a standstill. When it rains hard on the playa, its surface becomes a mucky clay that sticks to everything. Bike tires instantly cake with mud, swell by six inches in diameter, and then grind to a stop. Everyone clumps about in Frankenstein shoes, and clothing quickly becomes plastered and useless. Fortunately, the sun dries the playa surface as hard as pavement in a reasonably short time. Veteran Burners sometimes characterize each year at the event as a good biking year or a terrible biking year. When it has been a wet winter but the playa surface has been able to bake into hardpan before the trucks and equipment arrive to build the city, it can be a great biking year. If it rains after the city building begins, it usually leads to terrible biking conditions. If people and vehicles continue to move about the wet playa surface, it becomes chunked up with muddy clods that are as unforgiving as quarry stone, which renders bike riding next to impossible. On the plus side, wet playa mud is also incredibly slick and inviting. Veterans caution newbies to simply stay put in a brief shower, seek shelter in a lightning storm, and if a downpour is here to stay, just strip off and enjoy some slip 'n' slide fun in the mud!

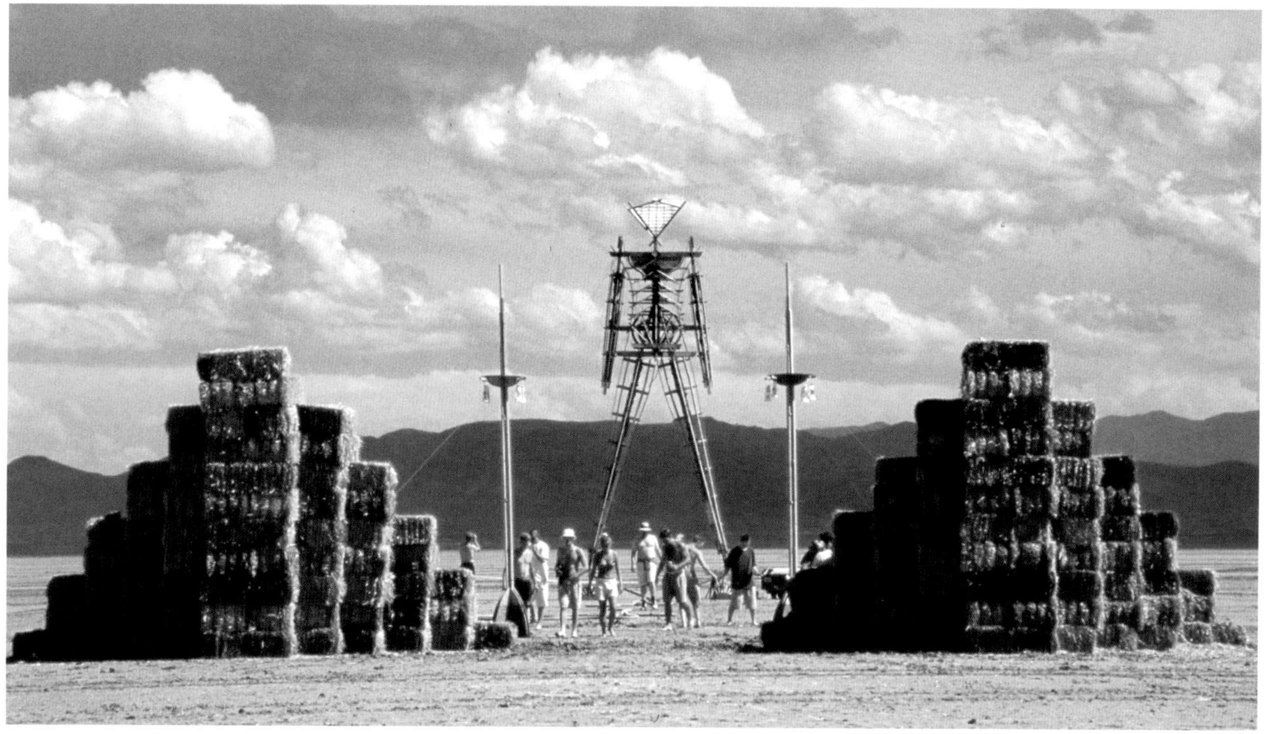

Stacked bales of hay created bleachers for viewing the Man in 1995.

And so, after the series of heavy rainstorms in 1995, burners did the playful and logical thing: they stripped off their clothing, began sliding around in the slippery muck, and gave one another therapeutic mud rubs. It was so much fun that the following year a group of smarty-pants brought a tanker truck full of water and created a public mud pit. Nudity hadn't really happened all that much prior to 1995, but it became commonplace in the following years. Once that freak-flag-waving genie escaped the clothing-optional bottle, nudity at Burning Man became an enduring activity. I say, blame it on the rain.

Bryan and I had missed the 1994 Burn, and it would be the last miss for me. We returned in 1995 to find that once again the population had doubled, and there were key baby steps being taken to centralize the camp in relation to the Man. That year would be the last year the Man stood flat on the playa surface, instead of being elevated on a raised platform. The notion of elevating the man came to Dan Miller in 1995 after someone else had the idea of twin stacks of hay bales as symmetrical bleachers facing the Man. Dan liked the hay bales so much that the following year he would create the first elevated platform for the Man, using a combination of hay bales and plywood. Those platforms would grow in height each year, usually by adding another row of bales, until 2000. Dan recalled the combination of bales topped with plywood would create a "secret room" inside the bales for blunt Burners in the know. "It was the coolest and safest place to smoke weed." My guess is that it stopped being cool on Burn night.

The hay bale bleachers became a natural place for people to congregate and take in the sights, and created the kind of interactive space beneath or adjacent to the Man that is a hallmark of the contemporary event. It was rare to pass them in 1995 without seeing a group of Burners. The thunderstorms of 1995 brought a new and unexpected dimension to the hay bales. It turned out there was a simple, but problematic, support system for these stair-stepped seats: rebar. Each bale was connected to the bale above and below it with long rebar stakes that went from top to bottom and were driven into the ground. They kept the bales from tipping over and formed the structural skeleton of the design. The problem was that the rebar also attracted static electricity. I took a picture of Bryan atop the stack of bales one sultry afternoon as storm clouds were gathering. He raised his arms in a climber's victory salute. A few minutes later, as we were talking, I looked at a woman sitting across on the opposite pile. Her long hair was rising straight up! Then we realized it was happening to everyone with longer hair. "I think you all had better get off these bales," I shouted. "That's a thunderstorm headed our way, and the rebar in these bales is acting like a lightning rod!"

The year 1995 also marked the transformation of the rave scene on the playa from fringe activity to a playa stalwart. The first rave campers were typically a handful of guys and gals with huge speakers in the back of a pickup truck. In the first couple of years rave and techno camps were most often relegated to the outskirts of the main camping area and considered by mainstream Burners to be a fringe activity happening "out there somewhere," but by the mid-1990s their camps—complete with outsized sound systems and DJs with names like Turbo Ted and DJ Niles—were getting larger and much more sophisticated. They presented something of a love/hate conundrum at Burning Man from its earliest days on the playa. Organizers would usually ask them to set up a mile away from the main camp so as to modify the sonic intrusion, but that worked only so long as the rave camp consisted of five guys and gals with a pickup sound system parked in deep playa. A couple of the more state-of-the-art music camps came equipped with lasers and strobe lights to complement their humongous speaker array. The faithful would follow the pulsating green rays to their bass thumping, Ecstasy-fueled lairs in the dead of night.

Rave music was always a mixed blessing at Burning Man. The San Francisco techno scene was very instrumental in bringing people to the event. They would advertise extensively in the Bay Area underground papers, and despite some initial rejection by the hippie elements on the playa, the rave scene by 1995 was bursting at the seams.

Live bands were also present early on. In 1993, a nerd-rock group called Three Day Stubble put on several teeth-grinding shows. Frankly, music as outsider art is often pretty hard on the ears, at least on my ears, and I found thumping techno blasting all night was as welcome as a toothache. Today music camps have grown into highly visible sonic behemoths and are located at the farthest ends of the horseshoe with their speakers pointing outward, but they were a big draw by the mid-1990s.

By 1995, Harrod Blank and friends had established Art Car Camp, and this added to the idea that Burning Man was becoming a collection of creative communities. Some of the early art cars also came loaded with substantial audio systems, and those eventually blossomed into mobile sound camps. The first iteration of art cars were typically American sedans with all manner of vintage flotsam glued to their surfaces. We initially thought of them as visual curiosities, but as they became larger, they also became more purposeful. Later versions would become sound-laden people movers fabricated from bus and truck chassis. As they grew in popularity and size, their mobility allowed them to roam wherever the spirit and whim might dictate, as cruising nightclubs or mobile dance clubs. Eventually they became Burning Man's monsters of midway: mutant vehicles. Because they could roam at will and park by someone's campsite, they at times became more of a nuisance to the sleep deprived than the big techno camps. Some literally would drive around all night long. Soon these mobile dance clubs were restricted as to where they could

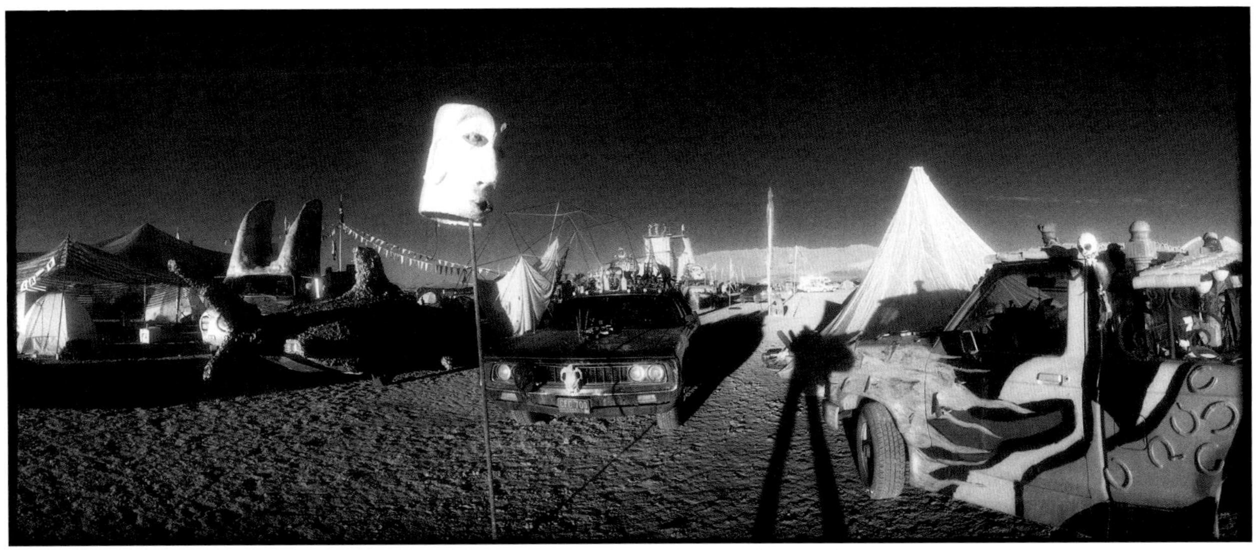

Art Car Camp modeled the coming synthesis of personal art and creative community.

roam and for how long, and these days they set up near the deep playa art, fueling late-night-into-sunrise dance parties for the sleepless.

The music scene always beckoned when the sun went down. I remember one evening in particular. It was late, and in our current inebriated state a bike ride onto the dark playa rave scene seemed like a timely notion. There were four of us fools, I think, and after a few hundred feet of plowing through chunky crust, the midnight bike ride was getting tiresome. About that time a pickup full of Burners passed us on the right, and we all yelled in unison, "Give us a ride!" Some guy yelled back "Grab on!" as the pickup slowed to a stop. We each grabbed a corner of the pickup bed and held on tight. I cannot begin to describe how unnerving it was to hold on to a speeding vehicle with one hand and attempt to steer a bike through cloddy sand with the other. It was akin to out-of-control skiing, when you know if you try to stop, you'll crash for sure, but you also know if you hit the wrong bump or a tree, you'll crash harder. Somehow we made it all the way to the rave camp and back unscathed. "I've never ridden in a rodeo," I remember telling someone later, "but I think I know the feeling."

Several things in 1995 were clear indicators of where Burning Man was headed. Artwork was going to be an essential element, as the open playa simply demands to be filled with creative expression. Pepe Ozan's lingam series became more elegant and suggested the sensual mythic motifs that would transition into elaborate sets for his eventual Burning Man operas. In the coming four or five years, these wire and playa mud constructions would become featured set pieces for the event. A persistent component to all Ozan's playa constructions was that they were designed to burn. His first lingam was shaped like a lumber mill's wigwam burner, which any person from timber country would recognize. Even as his forms became more fluid in shape, they were all still fundamentally a tall chimney with a hollow potbellied base intended to be filled with wood. The overriding aesthetic trends at Burning Man in those days seemingly evolved directly from the explorations of temporal art that had occurred on Baker Beach. The unspoken rule of art at Black Rock Burning Man was that all playa creations should be consumed by fire—a concept that would be challenged in the coming year.

"Art" at Burning Man in the early 1990s was considered temporal and disposable. Usually after the Man went down people would run around looking for more stuff to burn. It could be a rather hellish spectacle. Ray Cerino had allowed his *Water Woman* shower to be burned in 1995, but his enlarged version for 1996 was much more elaborately structured. He wanted to deconstruct it and bring it back as a yearly piece, but its positioning just behind Lisa Galli's *MudHenge* made it vulnerable to the mob. *MudHenge* had been designed to be burned, so when the crowd was finished running through the *MudHenge* fire, they reflexively turned their attention to *Water Woman*. Some of the frenzied mob began picking up flaming sticks, intending to set her ablaze. A group of Ray's friends stood in front of her, forming a barrier, saying in effect, "This is his art, and it should only be burned with his permission." Thereafter, only those designated pieces of art were torched.

By any estimate, 1996 should have heralded Burning Man's coronation as a fully formed, thematically inspired, satirical arts extravaganza, and in many ways it was. While the population at the event had doubled from the previous year, the pieces of featured artwork had quadrupled. The camp was laid out on a discernable axis, signaling its transition from random camp clusters into a designed layout, and most importantly, there was the first of what would become the organizing aesthetic of each year's event: a theme. Larry had been arguing for some time that the organizational structure of their operation needed strengthening. As the founder of the event, he still held the nominal position of director. "First among equals" was John Law's retort. John persisted in seeing the management of the event as some kind of exercise in rebel democracy. Regardless, Larry moved forward with the formation of a committee to plan and oversee the operation. He had Michael list him as chairman on the roster, and he remembers John attending and scowling his way through only one planning meeting, evidently seeing it as the dawn of dreaded bureaucracy at Burning Man.

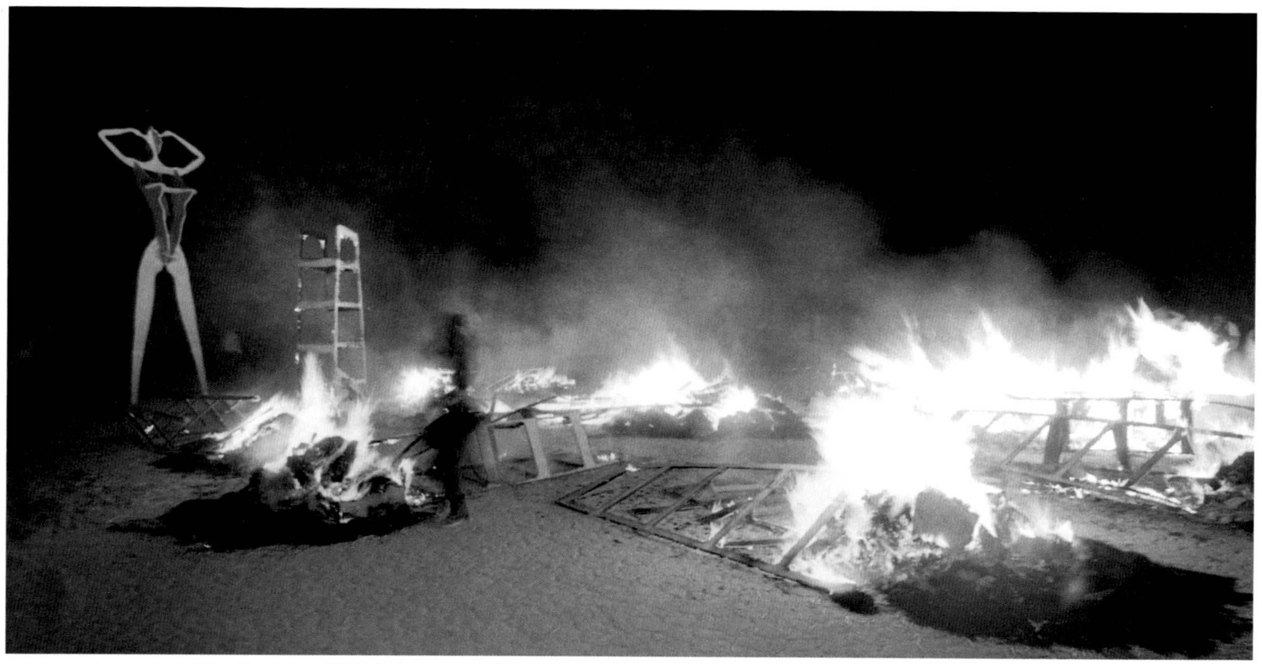

The Burners of MudHenge *tried to include* Water Woman, *but Ray's friends protected her.*

In reviewing the bulk of conflicting statements surrounding this critical juncture, I'm left with this: Burning Man in 1996 was poised on the cusp of its future success as a radical arts and culture movement; it was also in the midst of organizational chaos. At the heart of the conflict was the nature of the triumvirate. Larry, Michael, and John had never shared a unified vision for what Burning Man should be. John, and to a lesser extent Michael, saw the event as a continuation of the radical culture jamming they had engineered in San Francisco. The whole point was to stage a countercultural parody of the default world and use it as a means of protest. John's perspective seems to me to be that rebellion and culture jamming can only be carried out by a core group of creative outsiders. The minute a movement gets too large, it generates the most negative aspects of the establishment: oppressive politics and bloated bureaucracy.

Larry always saw the event in a much larger context. He didn't want to rebel against society so much as he wanted to influence the cultural norm and reshape it, and he understood from the beginning that to effect change globally he would need to develop a world-scale platform. Broken down this way, it's not hard to see that the individual perspectives of John Law and Larry Harvey were completely incompatible. The problem for my brother was that he had gotten into the partnership to rescue Burning Man from a premature demise at Baker Beach, and now it was being threatened from within by the dysfunctional power struggle between him and John Law. Both marshaled their factions. Larry formed his planning committee from people who were already doing solid administrative work at the event, and John relied on a cadre of Cacophony cronies and the playa roustabouts who had helped him set up the city. He also installed Vanessa Kuemmerle as head of the Rangers (displacing Michael Mikel). It was a case of John working from the nuts and bolts outside and Larry controlling the political inside. To this day people continue to debate the aftermath of that struggle.

Officially the inaugural theme for Burning Man in 1996 was "The Inferno." Larry had concocted a mock news exposé about a planned takeover of Burning Man by Helco, a multinational corporate entity whose intent was to engineer a coup and then infect the event with a deadly dose of consumerism. The "Helco" theme—as everyone insists on remembering it—brought together a legion of Burning Man contributors. Flynn Mauthe designed and built *Helco Tower,* which was the mythical headquarters for corporate greed. There were contributions and performances by Kimric Smythe, John Law (a streak of flame riding a zip line from the tower to the gate below), and a host of others. The LA Cacophony Society created *Tinseltown,* featuring a sacrificial burning of freestanding cutouts of Marilyn Monroe, Mickey Mouse, and other nostalgic stars. There was a strip mall with corporate parodies, such as Starfucks, Joe Camel, Submit, and Caca Bell. Several pieces of playa art also followed the theme, such as Kal Spelletich's *Cerberus,* a three-headed hound from hell.

"The Inferno" was a stunning success as a theme. In the contemporary era, the theme informs virtually every aspect of the event for that year, and "The Inferno" established that pattern. Pepe Ozan took his lingam motif and enlarged it into a gargoyle-bedecked stage set, and then he wrote and recorded the music for his first Burning Man "opera," *City of Dis: The Arrival of Empress Zoe*. For the remainder of the decade, his operas became featured performances at the event. They followed a formula: A host of naked and semi-naked fire performers would dance around the perimeter of his sculptural stage set. A droning soundtrack would evoke the somber portent of grand opera, though sadly without the orchestral brilliance of a master composer. Lastly, there would be a crescendo of destruction, and everything would dissolve into hellish flames. In *City of Dis* a woman (Empress Zoe?) gets carried into hell. At least I think so, as I could never make sense of his librettos. Pepe was a lovely, lovely man, who put his heart and soul into each creation. His zeal modeled the best tradition of Burning Man artists, who labor valiantly and give generously of their talents each year. The mythic exaggerations in Pepe's constructions were such that they often looked as interesting after they were burned as before. I used to love going out the morning after one of his performances to rummage around the charred remains of his opera set, looking for evocative details. They always seemed to possess a sense of melancholy and poignancy.

A good many of the featured works that year were a satire on the Hades of consumer culture. My brother's long-time friend Flash Hopkins had come up with a brilliant way to honor the theme, feed the multitudes, and maybe stick a buck or two in his pocket. Flash became the proprietor of McSatan's and sold burgers as fast as he could make them. Soon after, all vending would be prohibited from Burning Man except for coffee and chai in the Center Camp lounge and ice at Arctica, which were considered social necessities on the playa, but in the hands of a brilliant farceur, vending is a metaphor unto itself. While much of the art was intended to be a riff on bankrupt consumer values, there was also an element of dystopian pain.

When I look at my photos from that year, I'm struck by how many exhibit an ominous feel. Even an early morning study of a rehearsal at *MudHenge* takes on an eerie ambivalence. There was something off about the entire experience that year, something Bryan and I had felt as we traveled through the smoldering trees near Warm Springs, something in the harshness of the oppressive heat and dust of that year, and something in nearly getting lost in the darkness as we reconnoitered our way to the camp one night—a premonition felt, but not yet known.

I awoke to the *thwap, thwap, thwap* vibration of a medivac helicopter, flying directly over my tent early the next morning. It felt ominous and chilly and utterly wrong. I punched my head out of the tent flap just in time to see the whirring shape disappear to the north, where the rave camps were located. We'd already heard rumors of a motorcycle death prior to the opening of the event, and on this sad morning we would soon learn that an inebriated driver had run over a tent in the early morning darkness and seriously injured the people inside. He had then veered head-on into a car, scalding the woman inside with steaming radiator fluid. The specter of tragedy was becoming an indelible part of the 1996 event.

The death of Michael Furey on a motorcycle had been an utterly preventable tragedy. Though it had happened several days before we arrived, I talked to a number of people who had been there, and while the story varied, all agreed that large amounts of alcohol had been consumed at Bruno's in

Gerlach; several patrons and friends had tried to persuade Michael not to ride his motorcycle back to the playa; and he had died playing "chicken" with some of his friends, who were driving a van. Most of the stories I heard maintained that Michael had made several passes at the van, each time veering off at the last second, and he misjudged the distance between them on the fatal last pass. A recurrent, and unsubstantiated, rumor that I heard at the time was that the van had turned its lights off. Beyond the fact that this was a tragic loss of one of the Burning Man crew, the reverberations from that incident destroyed friendships, altered relationships, and damaged reputations.

What made the incident even more problematic is that my brother was quoted as saying, "There is no blood on our hands." I know he said it, because he said it to me as well, and it caused a firestorm between opposing factions within the Burning Man organization. Larry says he intended to defuse concerns that they were somehow responsible because Michael had been there to help set up the event—that it was a tragic but personal accident. John Law felt Larry was more concerned about liability than the loss of one of their own. In later writings he said it was one of the reasons he and Larry parted company. There is no way to know anyone's intent when they make an ill-received comment, but I know my brother, and while he is a pragmatist, he is also a person of deep convictions with an exaggerated sense of responsibility. I feel he may have been trying to allay concerns over liability, but he is not a person who will evade responsibility. Michael Furey's death was a sad and unnecessary tragedy, and the relationship between John Law, Larry Harvey, and Michael Mikel was never the same again—and neither was Burning Man.

In many ways the ugly incident of a drunk running over an occupied tent early on that fateful morning shook the organization even more profoundly. This was a tragedy that was very much a result of decisions made and not made within the Burning Man hierarchy. The ongoing battle between rave camps and Burners hoping for playa peace and quiet had culminated into what has been described as the "techno ghetto." This was a cluster of tents adjacent to the rave stages, located about a mile away from the central camp.

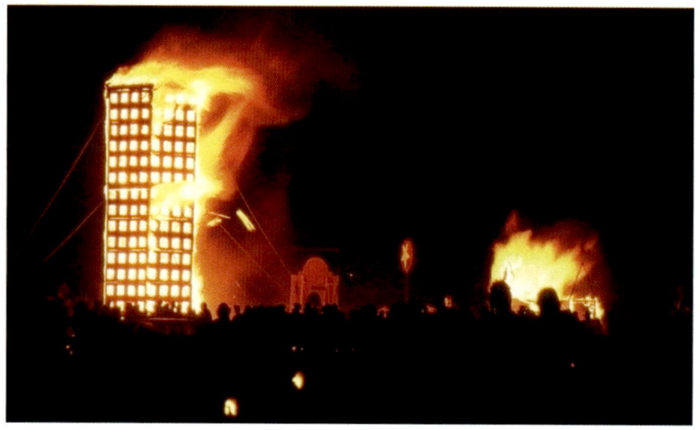

"The Inferno" was Burning Man's first successful theme, but it foreshadowed tragedy.

The ghetto comprised the living quarters of the music crews and the genre's most ardent fans. While the mile-from-camp decree had been the default solution to the noise issues from the beginning, it had also created a busy traffic corridor between the main camp and the rave scene. Vehicular freedom, the heart and soul of the wild ol' days, was on a collision course—literally—with the expanding population of the event, and the need to restrict traffic was becoming an obvious necessity.

The tickets at Burning Man always come with a disclaimer on the back: "The ticket purchaser or holder (you) voluntarily assume all risk of property loss or damage, personal or bodily injury, serious injury or death, which may occur by attending Burning Man. . . ." It's a fairly standard obfuscation of responsibility that lawyers like to write into such disclaimers, but it does underline a single salient fact: the playa and the event can be a dangerous place, and you can die there—some people have.

Remarkably few, given the rough conditions and the wild and wooly nature of the event in its earlier years. No death is ever acceptable at an event designed to provide a good time, but any venue that hosts seventy thousand or more attendees each year can expect fatalities or serious injury on occasion. Given the level of radical behavior at Burning Man, its safety record is actually quite good, and part of the reason is that the tragedies of 1996 forced event organizers to grow up and provide competent support services in matters of safety and security.

The aftermath of the tragic incidents in 1996, and the resulting lawsuit, forced Burning Man to examine its guerrilla heritage. The event entered into a critical and transformational period. John Law quit and took almost all of his most ardent supporters—what my brother refers to as the anarchists' wing—with him. Using what was left of the executive committee, Larry frantically tried to reorganize and restructure the event to make it safer, but transitioning from a renegade to an established contemporary operation would take more than reorganization; it would take a complete political makeover. One of the brighter aspects to this upheaval was that Larry was able to recruit several of his most loyal and creative supporters to join him in fashioning a new Burning Man organization—among them were Harley K. Dubois, Michael Mikel, Crimson Rose, Will Roger Peterson, and a recent arrival to the scene, Larry's girlfriend, Marian Goodell. This group would become the nucleus of a groundbreaking organization that not only redefined the conception of mass public gatherings but also turned Burning Man into a model of subcultural inspiration in the twenty-first century.

A nervous Bureau of Land Management (BLM), spooked by the pending litigation as a result of the recent accidents, seemed hesitant to allow Burning Man a permit to hold their event on the Black Rock playa in 1997. Previously, John Casey, the owner of Fly Ranch, had approached Larry about relocating Burning Man to the ranch, which was just twelve miles north of the Black Rock Desert and adjacent to a much smaller playa in Washoe County called Hualapai Flat. On the surface at least, the offer seemed like an ideal opportunity to avoid future government red tape.

Moving the event to Fly Ranch seemed initially to have many advantages over dealing with the regulation-heavy and increasingly greedy BLM. Not only did it border the small though adequate-sized playa, but also a ribbon of the ranch extended into the playa far enough to allow the Man to be placed on a private swath. Meanwhile Burners as private citizens could mill about or camp on the Hualapai playa surface because it was public land. It seemed like they would enjoy the best of both worlds.

Difficulties arose when Burning Man attempted to secure an event permit from Washoe County. Washoe County is home to Reno, and it is vastly more sophisticated when it comes to drafting regulations governing private facilities that host public functions. It also proved much more adept at figuring ways to "generate revenue" than impoverished Pershing County had ever been. The key piece to the revenue puzzle was that the country around Fly Ranch was awash in grassland and sagebrush, and Burning Man was a fire-based gathering. It opened the need for many additional permit requirements.

What had originally looked like a respite from all the federal regulations imposed by the BLM became a quagmire of urban-centered event stipulations. Events staged in cities come with built-in infrastructure: sidewalks, curbs, street lighting, fire hydrants, and medical facilities. Many of Washoe's requirements had been drafted with those assumptions in place. Fly Ranch and Hualapai Flat had few or none of these amenities, and so Burning Man was faced with a lengthy negotiation with the county over which regulations would be enforced and a frantic push to satisfy the regulations that remained. One requirement on which the county refused to budge was the submission of a city plan. That turned out to be the proverbial blessing in disguise because it forced the drafting of a blue print for how Black Rock City would be designed.

The Washoe County Commission didn't like Burning Man, or at least saw it as an event that was unpopular with their conservative Nevada constituents and therefore an easy mark. After they applied regulations that had been drafted for urban events, such as Reno's Hot August Nights, requiring Burning Man to provide similar services, they took steps to ensure they would be compensated for the enforcement and infrastructure costs associated with what they were demanding. Some of the regulations, such as street lighting and sidewalks with curbs, were deemed ridiculous for a desert event. Others—having streets with addresses so emergency vehicles could find an injured or ill party—made sense in light of the previous year's accidents, but how would that work in a city full of tents?

Because Fly Ranch had grass and sage land adjacent to the playa that was being used for camping, it was red-flagged as a fire hazard, and so the commission instructed the fire chief to demand that a contingent of thirty firefighters be on hand 24/7. The county bean counters crunched the numbers, and the amount they requested for all the additional county services was $350,000. That was way more than Burning Man was projected to take in. The person in charge of keeping order and making sure these amounts were paid to the county was Sheriff Dick Kirkland. The initial agreement with the county was that a portion of the receipts would immediately be dedicated to paying for its services, but someone in authority began to fear the entry totals weren't adding up fast enough and ordered the sheriff to occupy the ticket office in order to ensure the county got its money—and that's what he did. Deputies moved into the ticket office and confiscated every nickel. It created an immediate cash-flow crisis.

Over the next three days deputies confiscated 100 percent of the ticket money that came through the gate. The negotiations with the county had left a public impression that Burning Man might not get their permits. With all the confusing

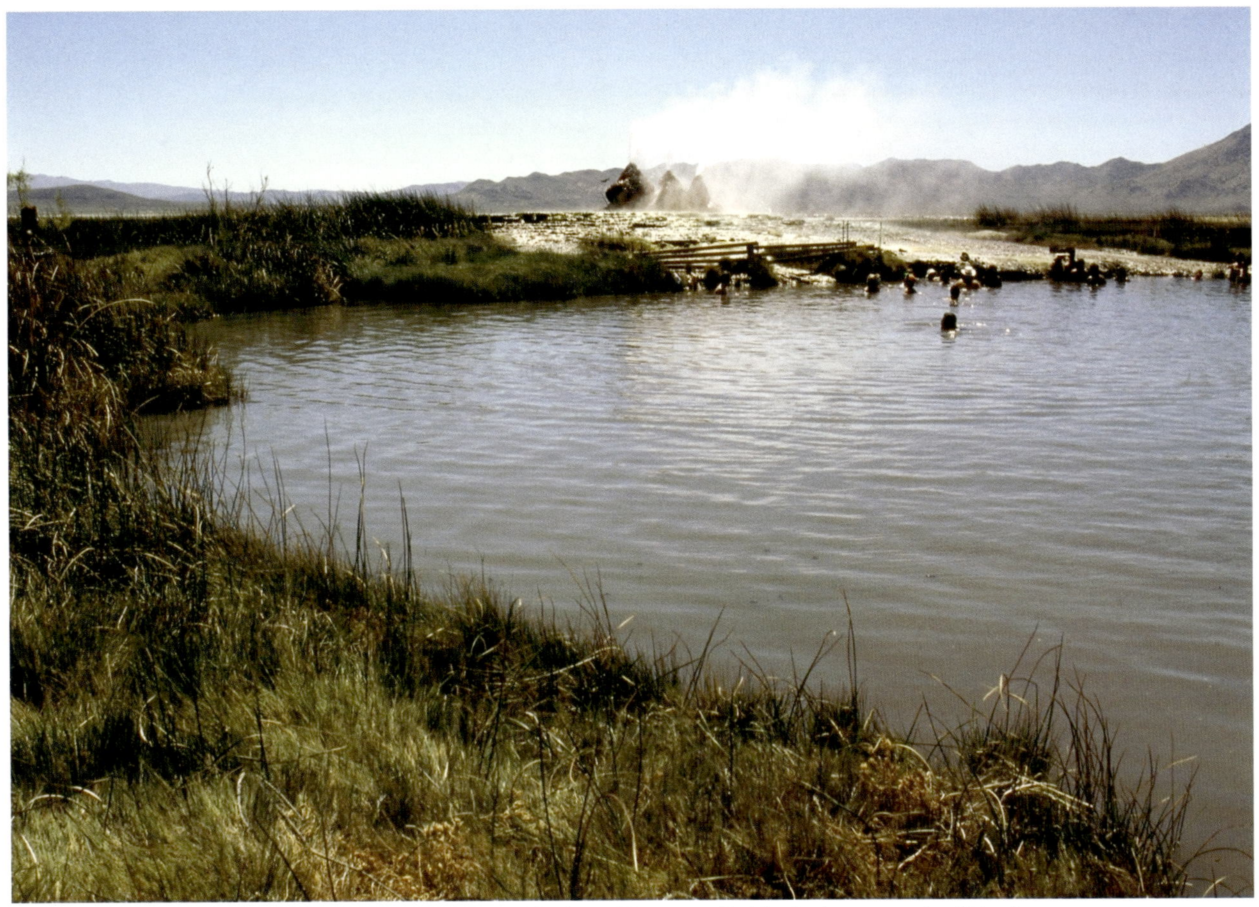

In 1997, Burning Man moved to Hualapai Flats near Fly Hot Springs—a mixed blessing.

publicity and the change of venue, attendance in 1997 leveled off at ten thousand, which was a modest uptick from the year before but nowhere near enough to meet the organization's financial obligation to the county. Moreover, without the gate, Burning Man had no working capital. It had artists who'd arrived—some from out of the country—expecting to receive a stipend. It had expenses for rental equipment and food for its workers and staff. They couldn't even pay to have their porta potties serviced! In desperation, Larry made a speech to a couple hundred Burners for financial assistance, and that's when we discovered the broad economic scale of the people who come to Burning Man.

I remember two things about Larry's speech that year. First, he made the speech under Michael Christian's *Bone Arch,* which was Michael's first piece of Burning Man art. Michael would go on to contribute many more, but that wasn't the memorable part. The bones of Fly Ranch cattle littered the area. I'm not sure if those bones were used by Michael to decorate his arch, but the following year Dana Albany, with the help of Flash, used them to create her *Bone Tree,* which has been a symbol at First Camp, the site's headquarters, ever since. The second thing I remember about Larry's speech altered my perception of Burning Man. A young man walked up to Harley after the speech. In his hand he held a check for $25,000. He introduced himself as "Dan" and said he preferred to remain anonymous, but he wanted to give the check to Larry personally. Dan wanted to be sure it went to the right place. It was a wonderful gesture and would go down in the annals of Burning Man, but in the end the event would still owe vendors a debt of $220,000.

It turned out the experiment on private land would nearly bankrupt the organization, but for all its subsequent tribulations, Larry looks back on 1997 as the year when Burning Man came of age. Many of the things the event was required to do helped map out an effectively designed Black Rock City. "The blueprint for our future was fashioned out of that trial, and our determination to survive it," he said. "I told the county that if they wanted me to eat an alligator, I'd get three guys to hold him down and one guy to hold his jaws, and we'd eat him!" The county had required a city plan. So first Harley drafted a city plan, and then, as she said, designer Rod Garrett "changed it all!" The best break of all came because it was necessary to carve a roadway from the ranch to the Hualapai surface, and that meant Burning Man for the first time would firmly control access to the event. Controlling entry would be the key to making future events profitable.

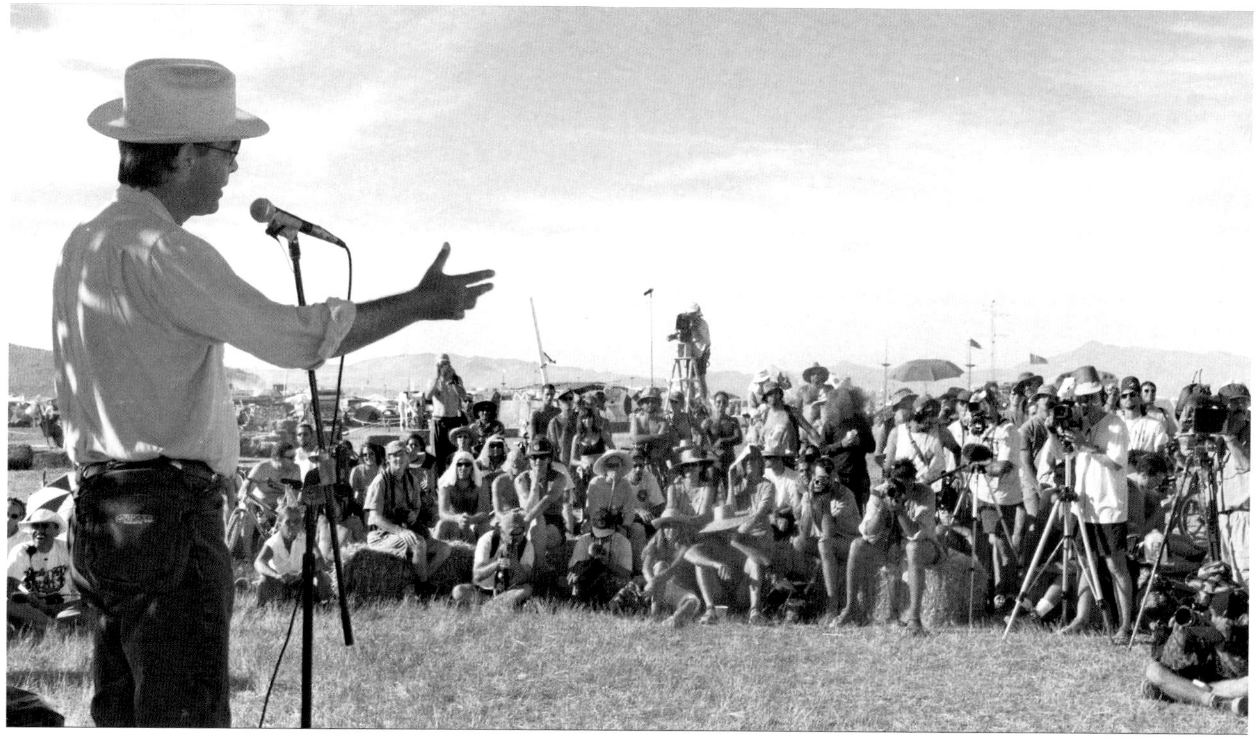

With Burning Man nearly bankrupt, Larry made an appeal for funds that raised $80,000.

The gift from "Dan" was only the tip of Burning Man's reach even then. Larry's speech had kept the wolf from the door. By the time they were gearing up for 1998, they had paid their debt to all of their vendors and artists in full. They had raised a significant amount from individual donations, but another type of benefactor became an even more profound partner in the event's growth—not so much as a monetary resource but as fertile ground for the spread of Burning Man culture: the regionals. Just as Cacophony Society had founded chapters in cities like LA, Portland, and Seattle, Burning Man followers throughout the country were beginning to form regional gatherings. Today there are over a hundred affiliated regional Burn groups in every state and throughout the world. The early versions of these groups did fund-raising and made personal donations to bring the event back to the playa. In his speech Larry had offered a "lifetime ticket" to anyone giving $500. Those thirty-four lucky people are smiling *big* these days.

Several factors went into Burning Man's rescue that year. The spectacle and allure of fire was as powerful as ever, and most Burners simply embraced the event as always. Also, the national media were beginning to take notice of this strange bit of cultural upheaval in the desert. In 1996, *Wired* magazine published the first cover story on the event, called "Welcome to Burning Man," and I was lucky enough to be part of that cover. Their publishing wing followed up with the first photography book on the event. National artists like Spencer Tunick also made an appearance. In 1997, his first massive nude landscape on the playa generated art media interest. Plus, several news organizations ran stories that year about the conflict in the desert, but none was more important than *Nightline*.

At the height of the crisis with Washoe County, *Nightline*'s television crew showed up to film an entire thirty-minute segment on the event. Forrest Sawyer narrated the first network coverage of Burn weekend, and it couldn't have come at a better time. They not only gave national exposure to Burning Man but also helped shine a light on the exploitative treatment of the event by Washoe County. Though the County Commission may have been calling the shots, the authoritative face of law enforcement that year was Sheriff Kirkland. At first Kirkland took an aggressive stance. Like members of the County Commission, he had a jaundiced view of Burning Man. He and his deputies not only detained Burners for minor infractions but also constantly prowled the playa with a helicopter and patrol wagons. Burners complained they were flying low over Fly Hot Springs to ogle the naked swimmers. Their presence created the dampening effect of an occupying force.

As often happens with law enforcement at Burning Man, a metamorphosis took place. Politically conservative elements typically arrive with a skewed view of what the event represents, but then they are amazed to discover creative and enthusiastic participants, walking about with smiles or engaged in projects, instead of an unruly mob of riotous and disruptive hooligans. I've seen this shift year after year. The look on the faces of the authorities softens, and so do their attitudes. Burning Man could be a big neighborhood barbecue in the town park or a concert on the waterfront. Since nothing sinister is going on, they begin to feel a little foolish. Occasionally they get to bust someone for walking around with a joint, but they actually have to work harder than they expected to find lawbreakers. There's nudity and noise and cavorting and shenanigans galore, but it hardly rises to the level of a venial sin much less disorderly conduct. I remember a tall naked guy walking by a couple of BLM officers in full riot gear. It was midafternoon, and the weather was dusty and sweltering. "You dudes look hot," the naked man said with a wave. "We are," they replied in unison, and I thought I detected a trace of envy.

By the time the *Nightline* piece aired, the narrative was already beginning to change. When the authority figures were interviewed at the beginning of the piece, everyone was stressing their mission, which was public safety—law and order. Later in the program, when the firefighters were asked what they had needed to deal with at the event, they admitted, "Not much." When a medical staffer was interviewed about medical treatments, he said, "Mostly heat-related or dehydration issues. A few burns—mostly minor." When *Nightline* host Forrest Sawyer recounted the fees that Washoe County had leveled against the event for public safety, it was beginning to sound suspiciously like Burning Man was being grossly overcharged. Tellingly, when Sheriff Kirkland was asked what he thought of the event, he looked straight at the camera and said, "All I just see is a bunch of people out having a good time!"

As a result of the increased publicity in 1997, people in the default world were beginning to get the idea Burning Man was doing something original. They weren't at all sure what it was, but they understood it was unique. The event was also beginning to attract people from around the globe, and the world's sympathetic response to the conflict with Washoe County was energizing. Publicity—primarily in the form of the Internet—became a conduit between the event and the outside world. The organization reached out to this pool of potential Burners and invited them to join an experiment based on experience and an expressive community culture. People started coming in droves, and the need for security and reasonable regulations became more acute.

Despite its crippling financial challenges, Burning Man emerged from its ordeal with Washoe County stronger and politically wiser. More importantly, Larry assembled a new generation of executive founders. Michael Mikel, Crimson Rose, Will Roger Peterson, Harley K. Dubois, and Marian Goodell would not only take the necessary measures to adequately protect the health and well-being of the attendees of Burning Man but also produce a revolutionary new model for the way art- and community-based events would be administered. Rod Garrett's Hualapai camp design would morph into a dynamic city plan that was both symmetrical and expandable. Larry and Will would search for an alternative event site, but in the end, the team would elect to return to the BLM and the Black Rock Desert.

In 1998, the seeds for the modern event were sown, and Burning Man would emerge from the dark times and begin the long steady climb to becoming the kind of innovative and high-principled event my brother and his partners had always dreamed it could be. What they eventually would create was a fantasy-laden mega event that provides a kickass good time, and along the way they would make room for individual expression and engender a mammoth community of the spiritually rich and the artfully gifted. Of course that meant establishing both responsible guidelines and commonsense rules that would cause the wild ol' boys to roll their eyes and cluck their tongues in disgust.

But times change. John Casey died, and Fly Ranch was sold in 1998. The new owners required special permission to visit Fly Hot Springs and limited the numbers. There was something about diving into those primal waters that had energized our sense of autonomy and freedom in those early years. The ensuing many-year hiatus from Fly Hot Springs was, for me, the symbolic end to the wild ol' days of Burning Man. The increased security and the interminable slog in and out of the contemporary event have lent strength to the notion that modern Burners have lost some precious liberties in the transition to a bigger event—but that's true only to an extent. We were always bound by common sense and the desire to be safe. In place of imagined lost freedoms exists a much more exhilarating personal experience. It's a bit like leaving Mayberry and moving to Hollywood. You lose something precious, but you gain considerable opportunity. A group of us were lucky enough to visit Fly Geyser in 2014 and again in 2016 after Burning Man announced it was going to be able to purchase the property. We walked on planks around the geyser and splashed around in the largest pond. It felt like taking a nostalgic vacation in our old hometown. While many of our childhood friends had moved away, the kinetic memories of our Burning Man adolescence persisted and were as warm as the spring itself.

CHAPTER 6

LIFE ON THE PLAYA

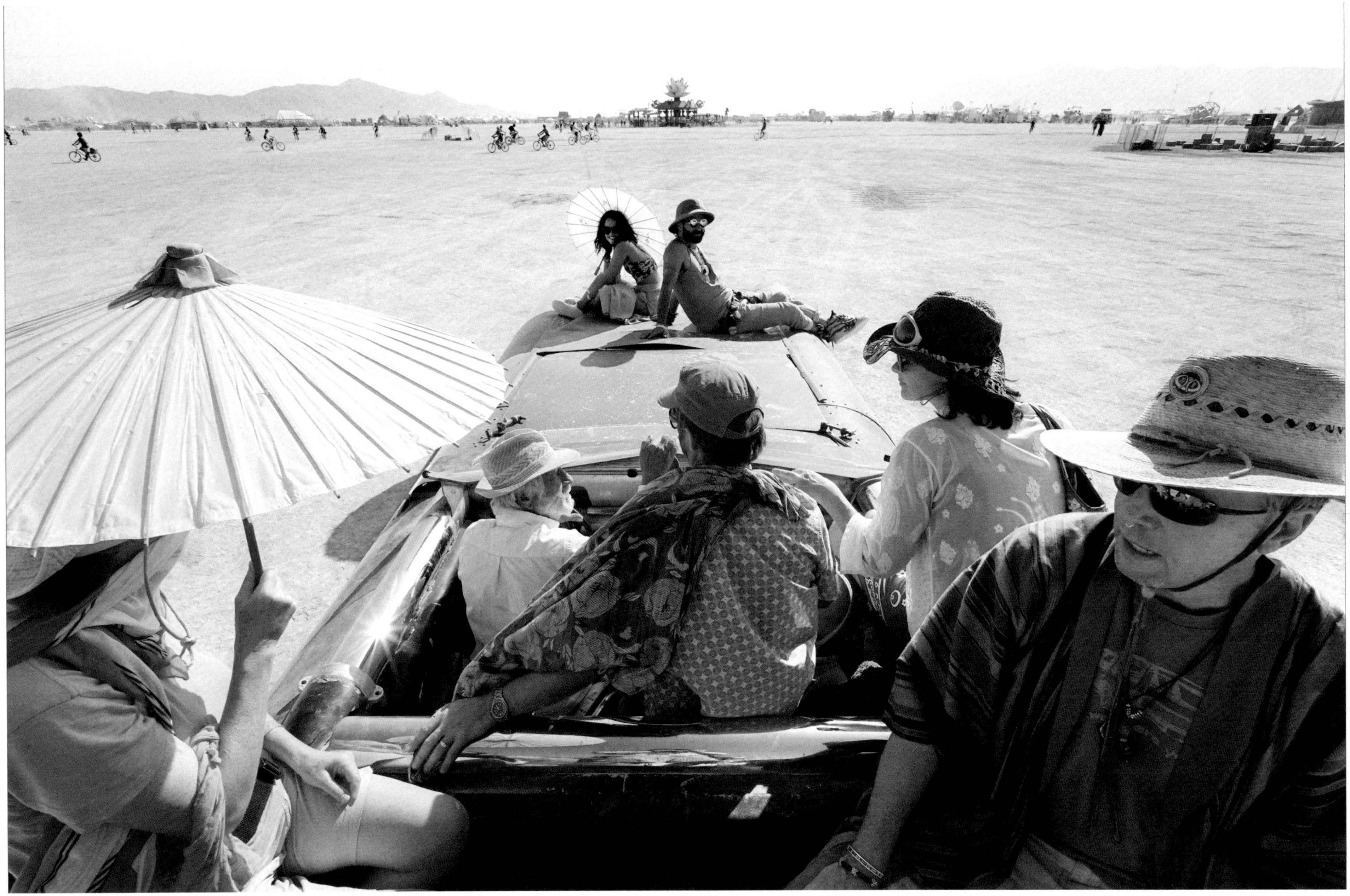

Rocket Car *Tour, 2015*

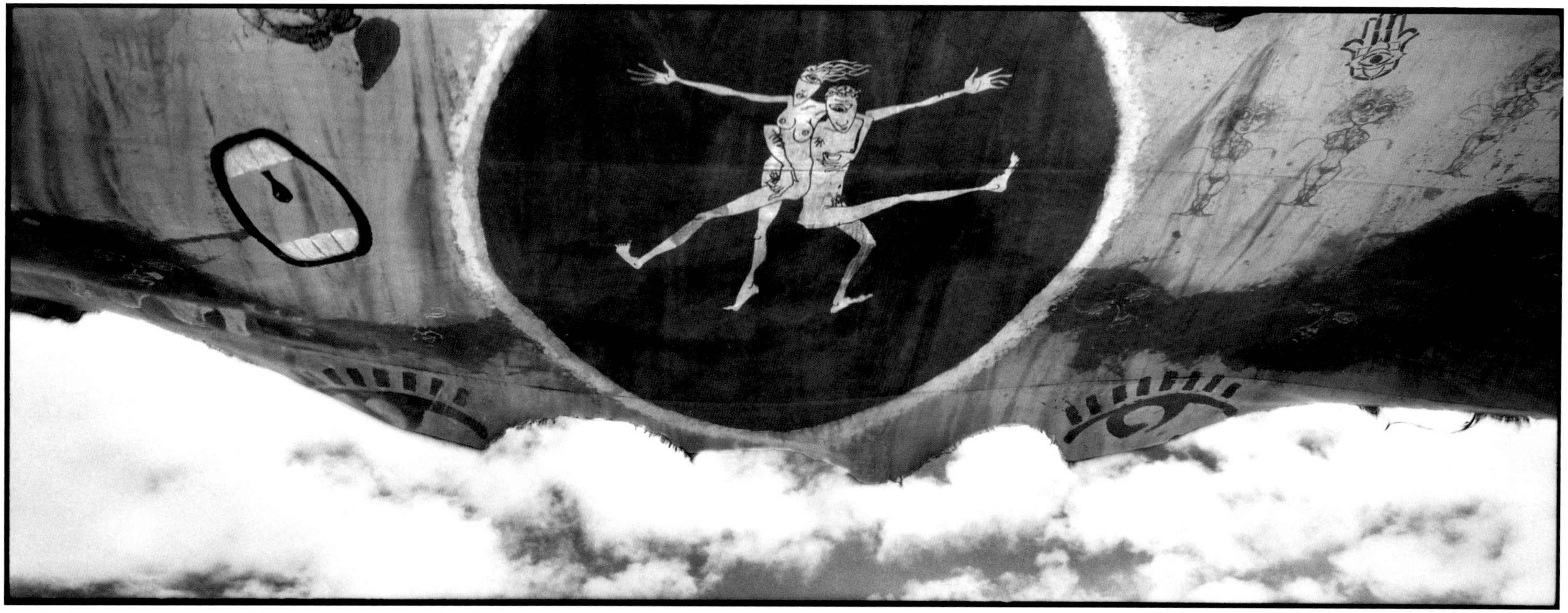

Bodies in the Wind, *2000*

A day at Burning Man is a series of dramatic events, and it begins at dawn. Sunrise is a transcendent moment. Many burners stay up all night just to howl like wolves and then toddle off to bed. The first blush of dawn against the desert sky inspires a timeless reaction, and there is hardly a person who doesn't experience a tingle at the first glimpse of this familiar friend. But there's more. There's something about a Black Rock sunrise that feels eternal as the dust. It may involve the same giant red orb that rises elsewhere in the world, but it feels special, and that rewards this journey to the edge of civilization. It's the most exquisite beginning to a day on the playa.

Late morning into midday is all about rest and recuperation. Many burners have been up all night, and as the temperature goes up, they go to sleep or for coffee in Center Camp. Afternoons are an adventure. New arrivals are eager to bike out to see the art, but if the wind picks up, as it often does in the afternoon, there can be blinding whiteouts. As the week progresses and hundreds of vehicles grind more playa crust into a fine white powder, the dust becomes oppressive. Afternoons are often about sightseeing, but they can also be an exercise in survival.

Nighttime is lights time. People dress in outlandish costumes and get their glow on. Then they stroll or bike out into a swirl of activities. It's a gaudy, glittery, noisy, and boom-boom bass world of fire spitting, Thunderdome battles, techno dancing, and party busing. If you're older, you can always sit on a dusty couch in Center Camp and watch the Battle of the Marching Bands or listen to mellow music in the Jazz Café. You can't make a wrong move. There are wonders and delights everywhere you go.

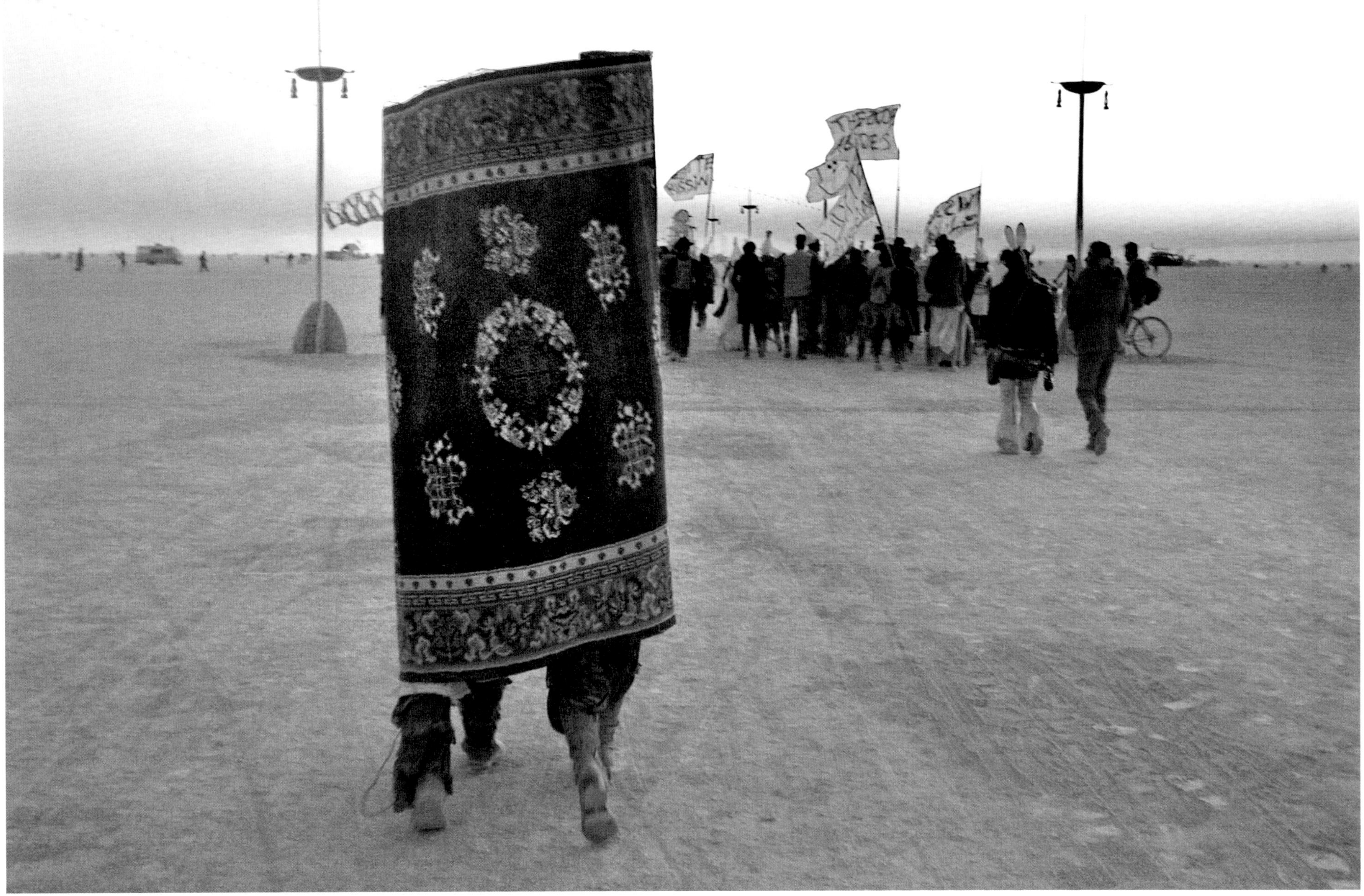

White Russian Parade, 2011

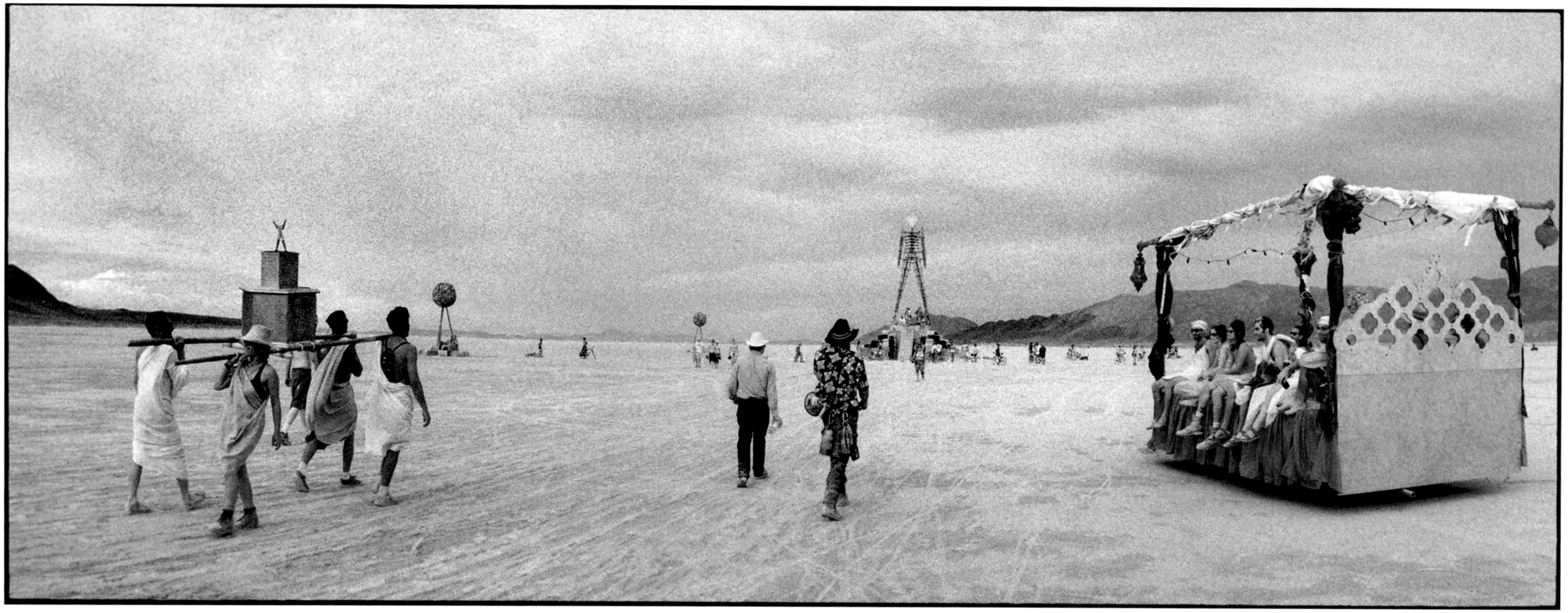

The Little Man, 2000

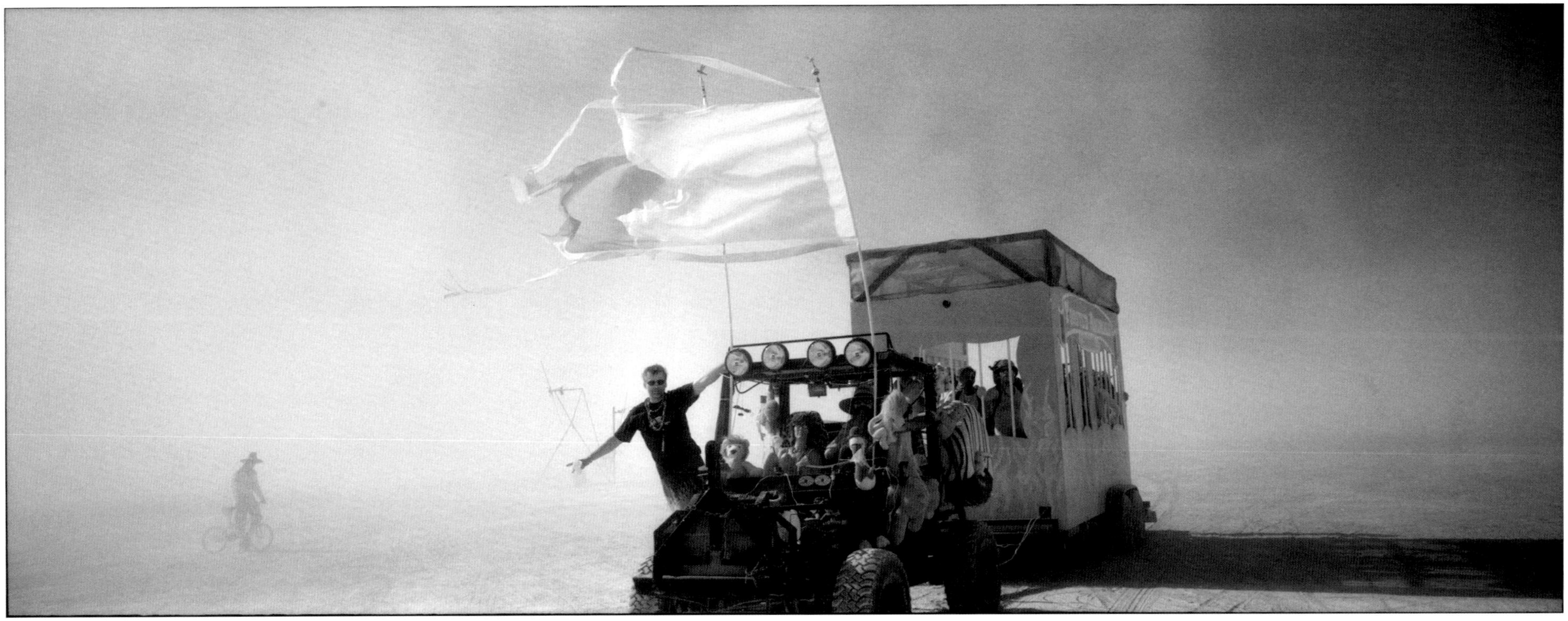

Toasted Animals, 2002

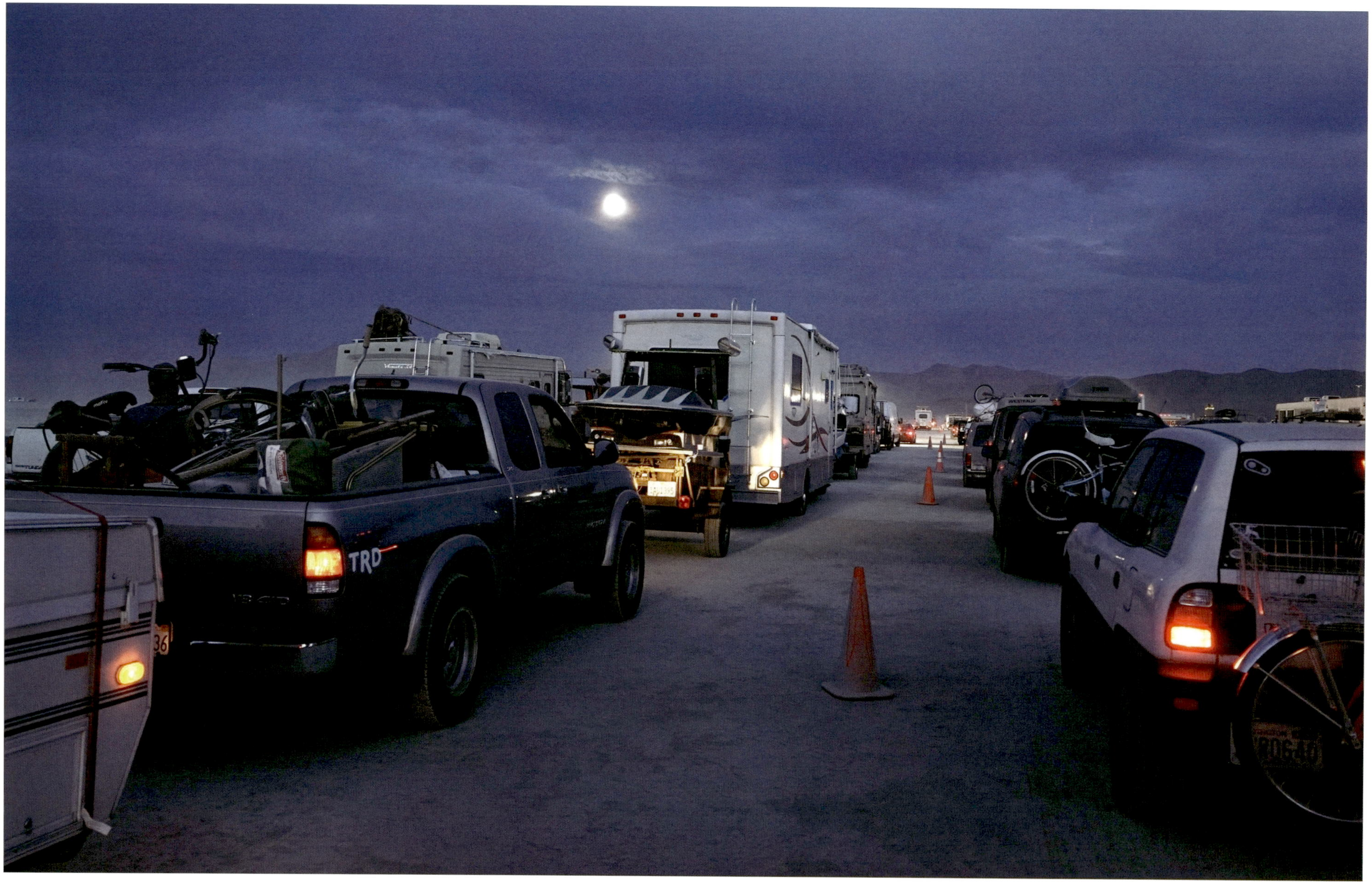

The Line In, 2015

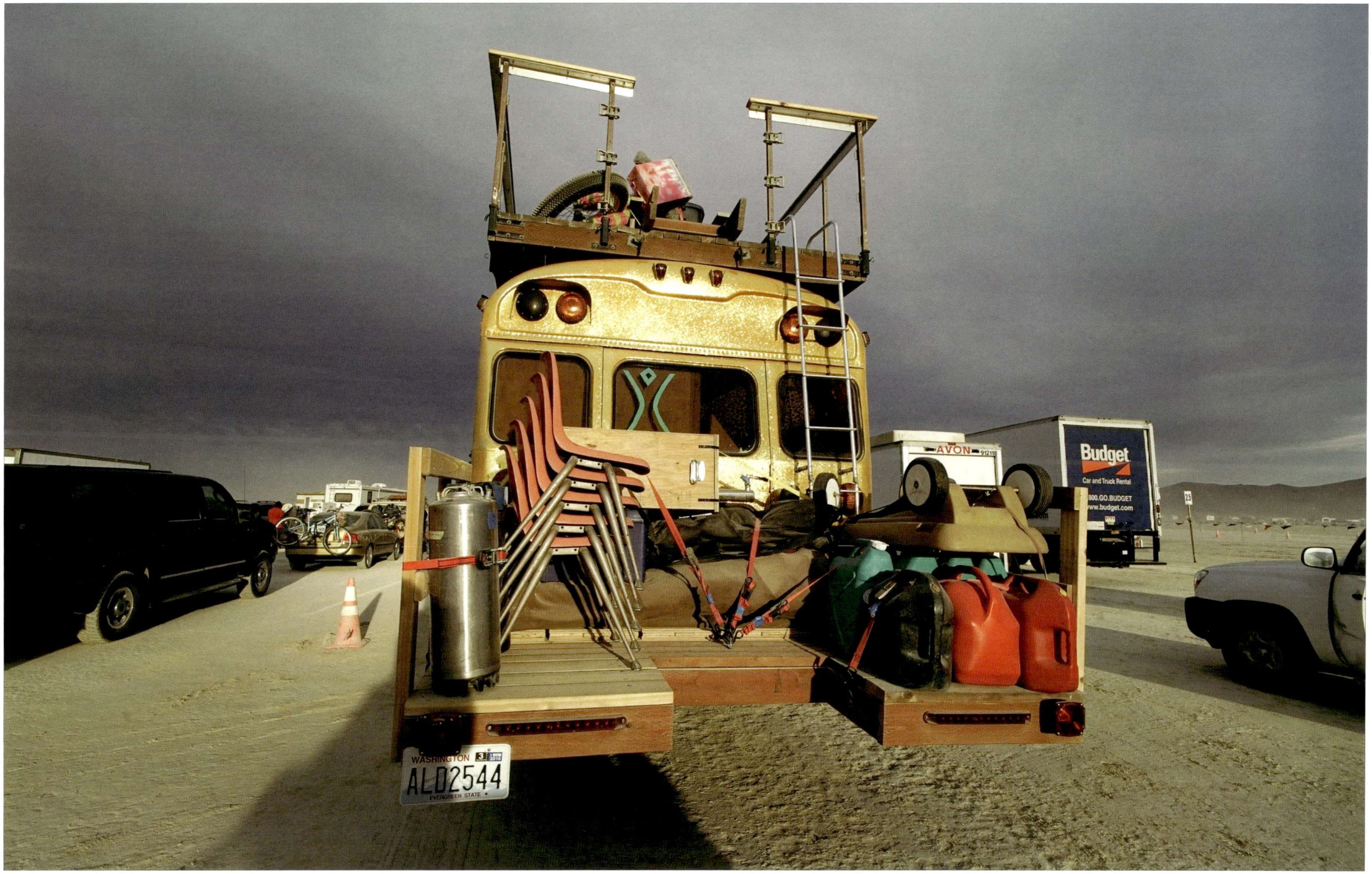

Sparkle the Bus, 2014

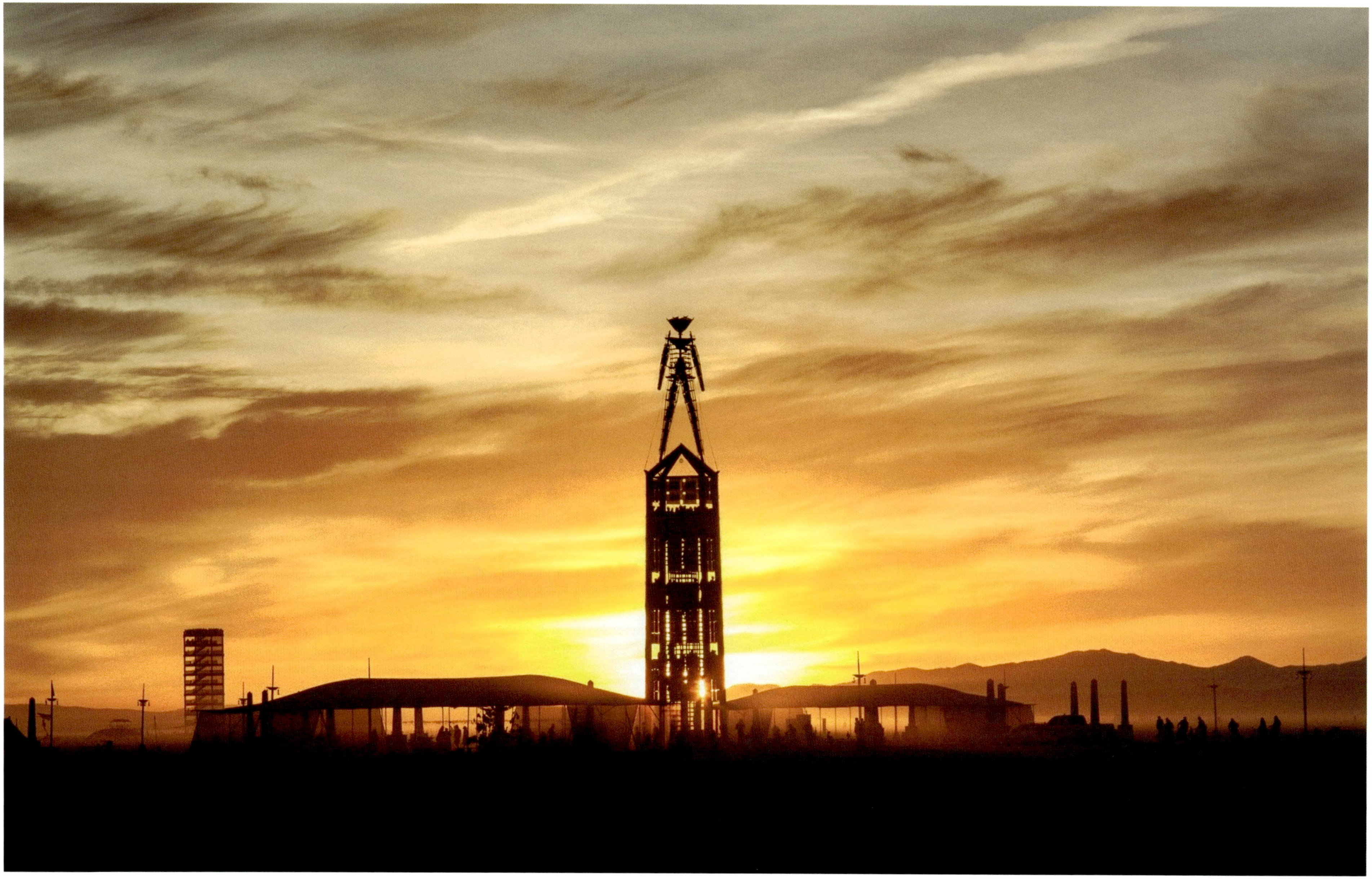

American Dream Sunrise, 2008

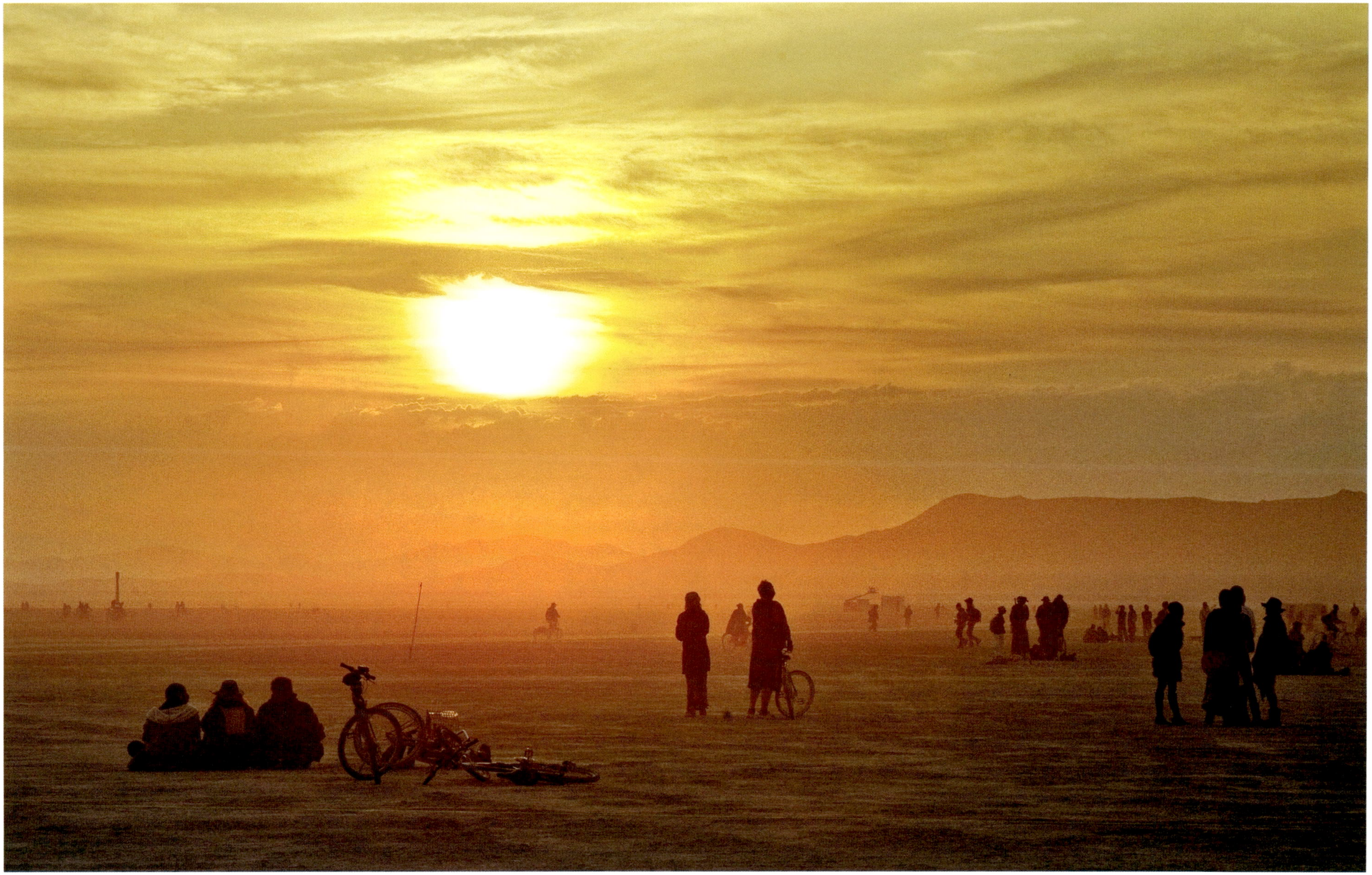

Burning Dawn, 2009

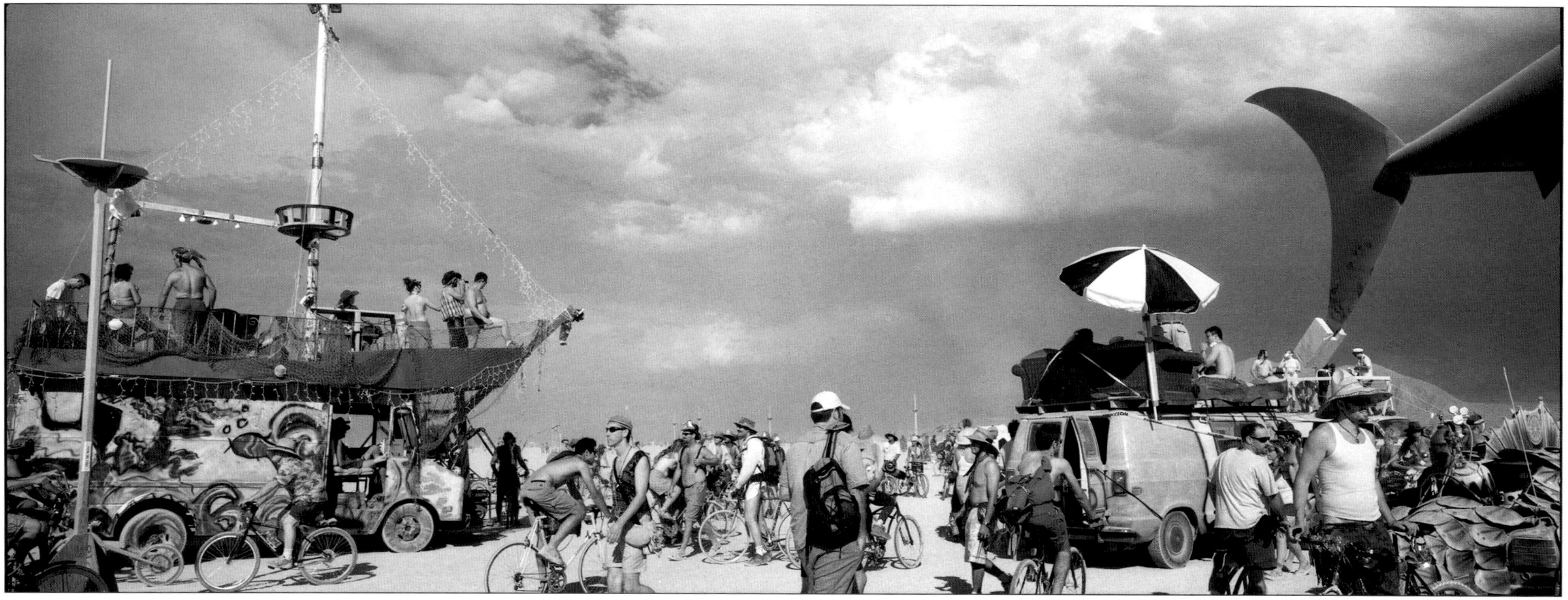

The Floating World, 2002

Community life at Burning Man is often crowded and chaotic. It is, after all, an instant city with upwards of seventy thousand souls, and daily life often consists of navigating through the melee. Within that challenging mishmash, however, hides an abundance of community-initiated activity. Parades are popular. Some—like the Bunny Parade, the Critical Tits bike ride, and the infamously abusive DPW Parade—are annual events. But it is the never-ending parade of average Burners who create the ultimate show. They stroll, bike, or ride in outlandish style around the Esplanade—the circular inner boulevard that separates the central city from the perimeter of camps—for hours.

Little is sacrosanct at Burning Man. Playa art typically pokes fun at life in the default world. On the other hand, playa motifs often reference the movies. Attend often enough and you're likely to see a version of every spoofable character or idea that has ever flickered across a screen in the dark. Occasionally life imitates art, and for a brief millisecond the chaos resolves itself into a semblance of order. The aimless vehicles and random wanderers maintain their orientation just long enough for the camera to portray an incidental moment as visually profound. In that moment we sometimes feel as if we've been granted a glimpse behind the cosmic mask. It's when playa photography approaches art.

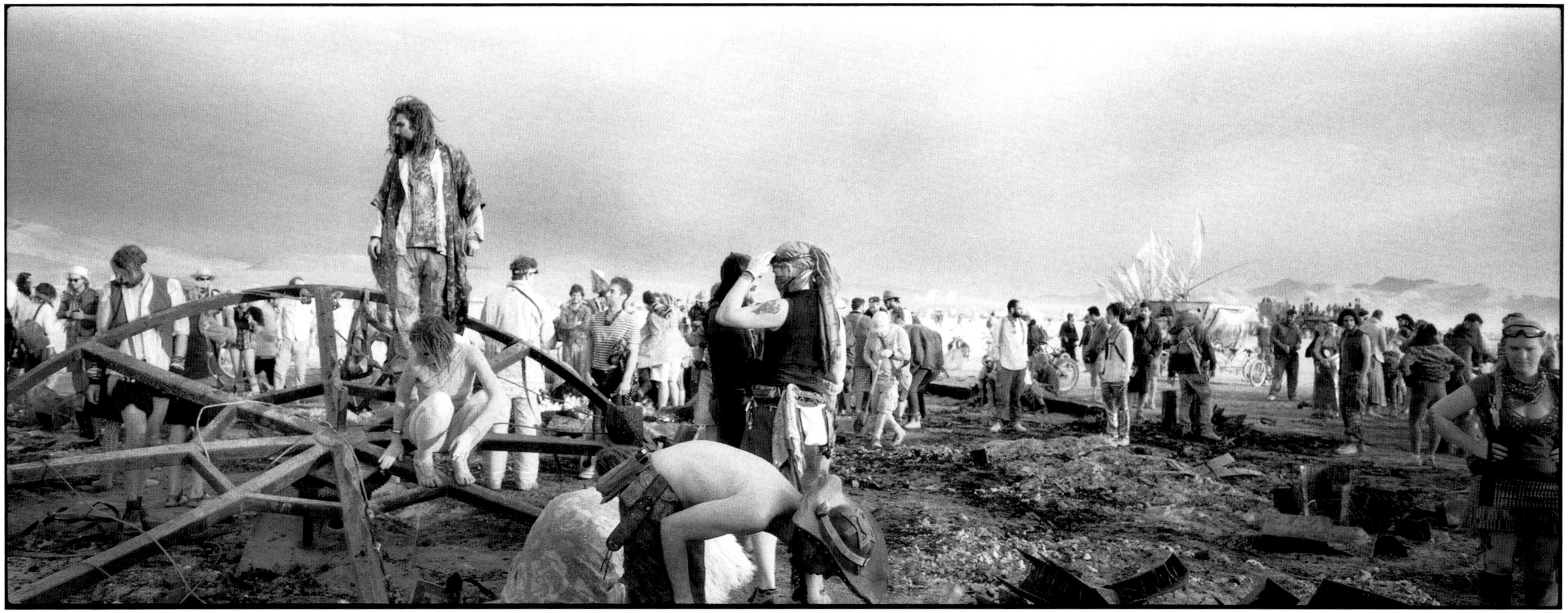

Burn Aftermath, 2014

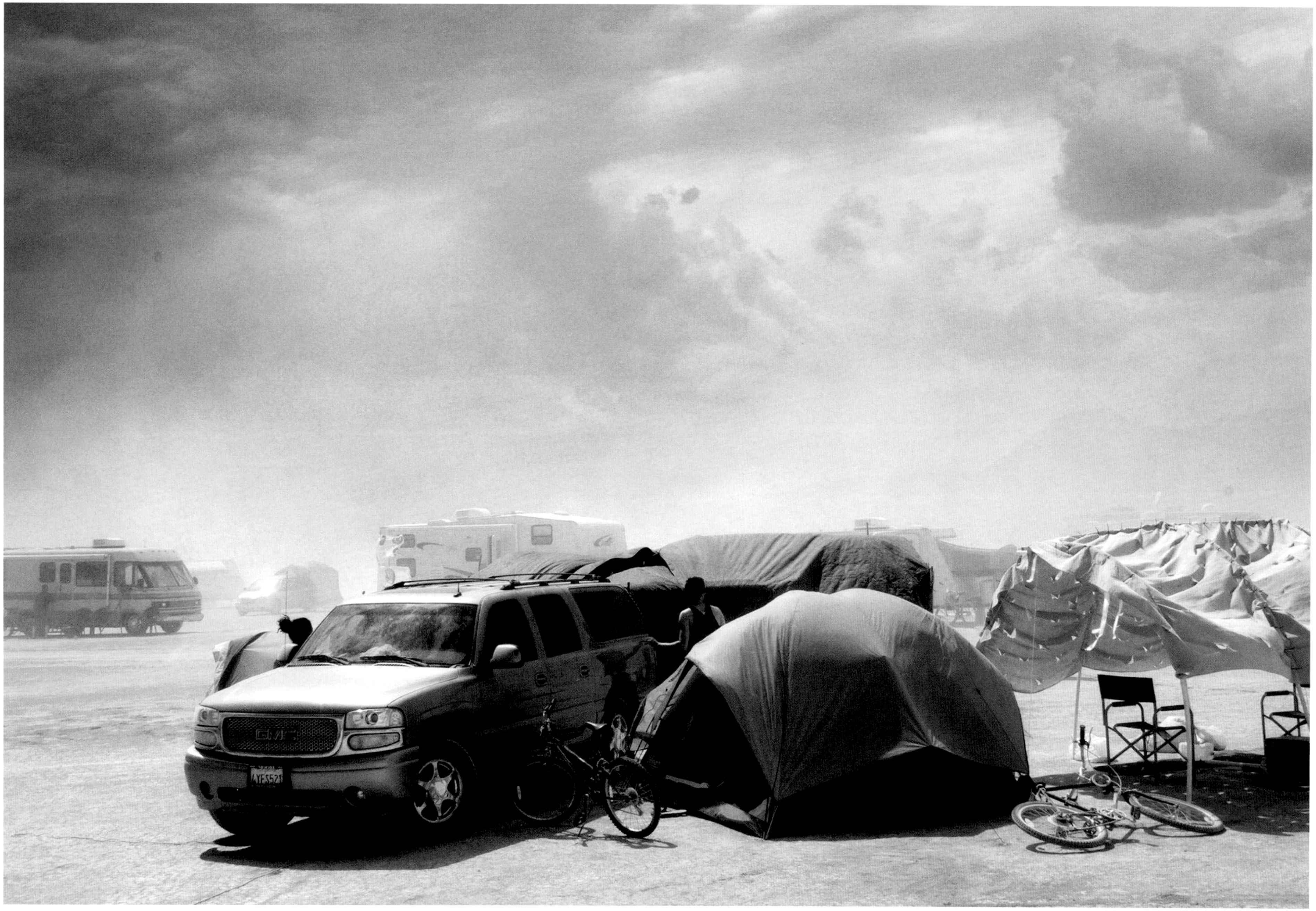

Approaching Storm, 2007

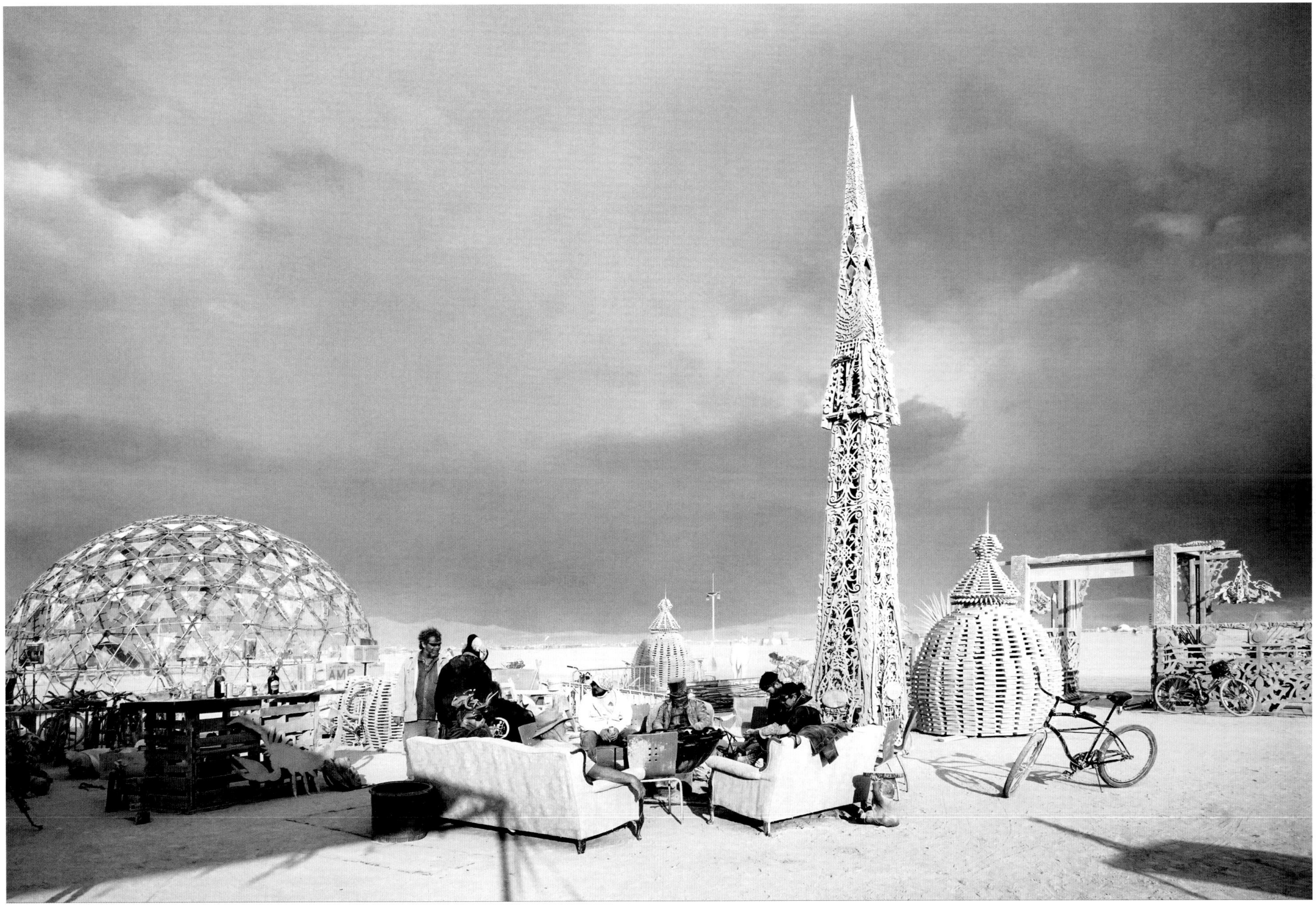

Temple Camp Storm, 2016

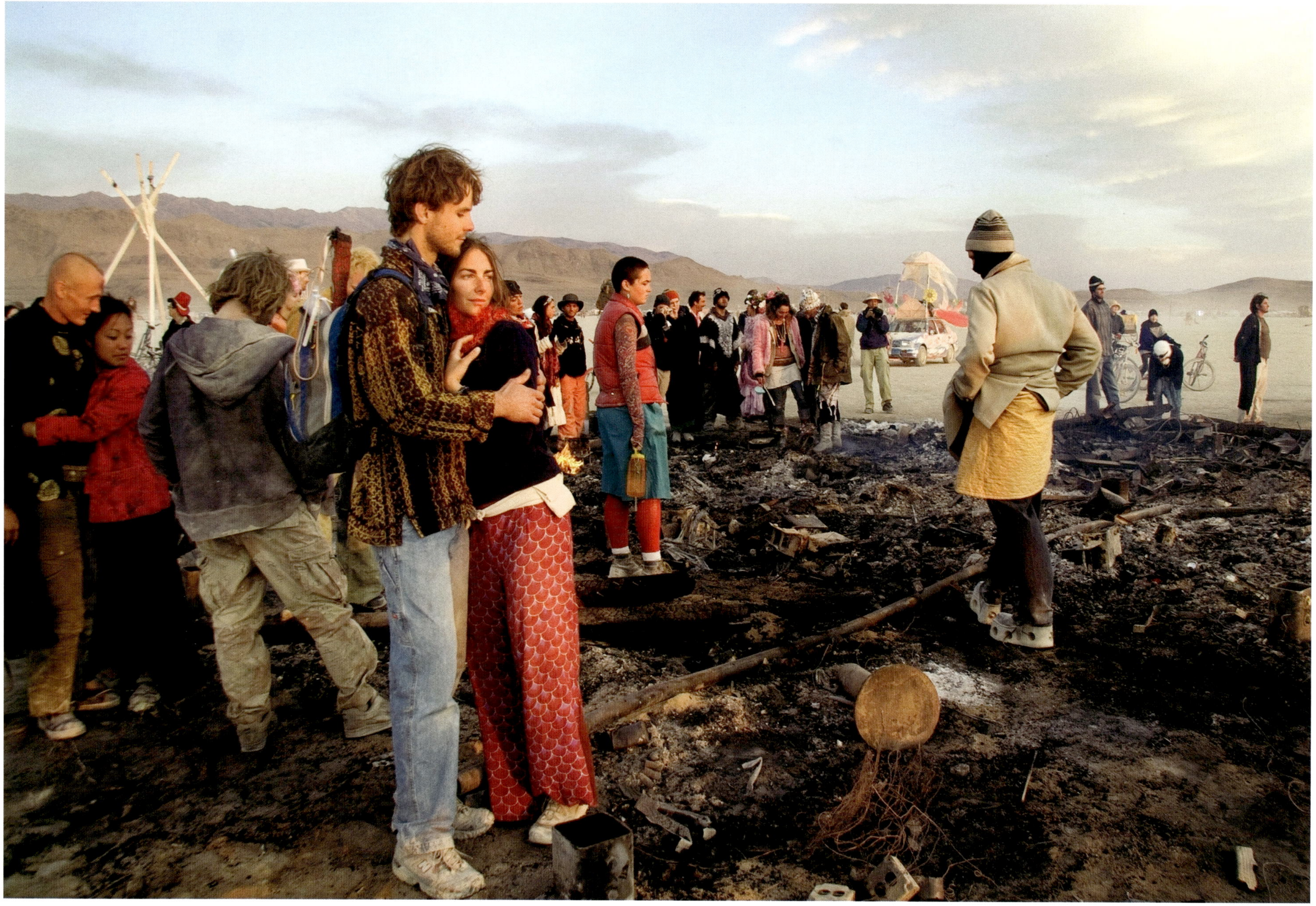

Afterburn Couple, 2005

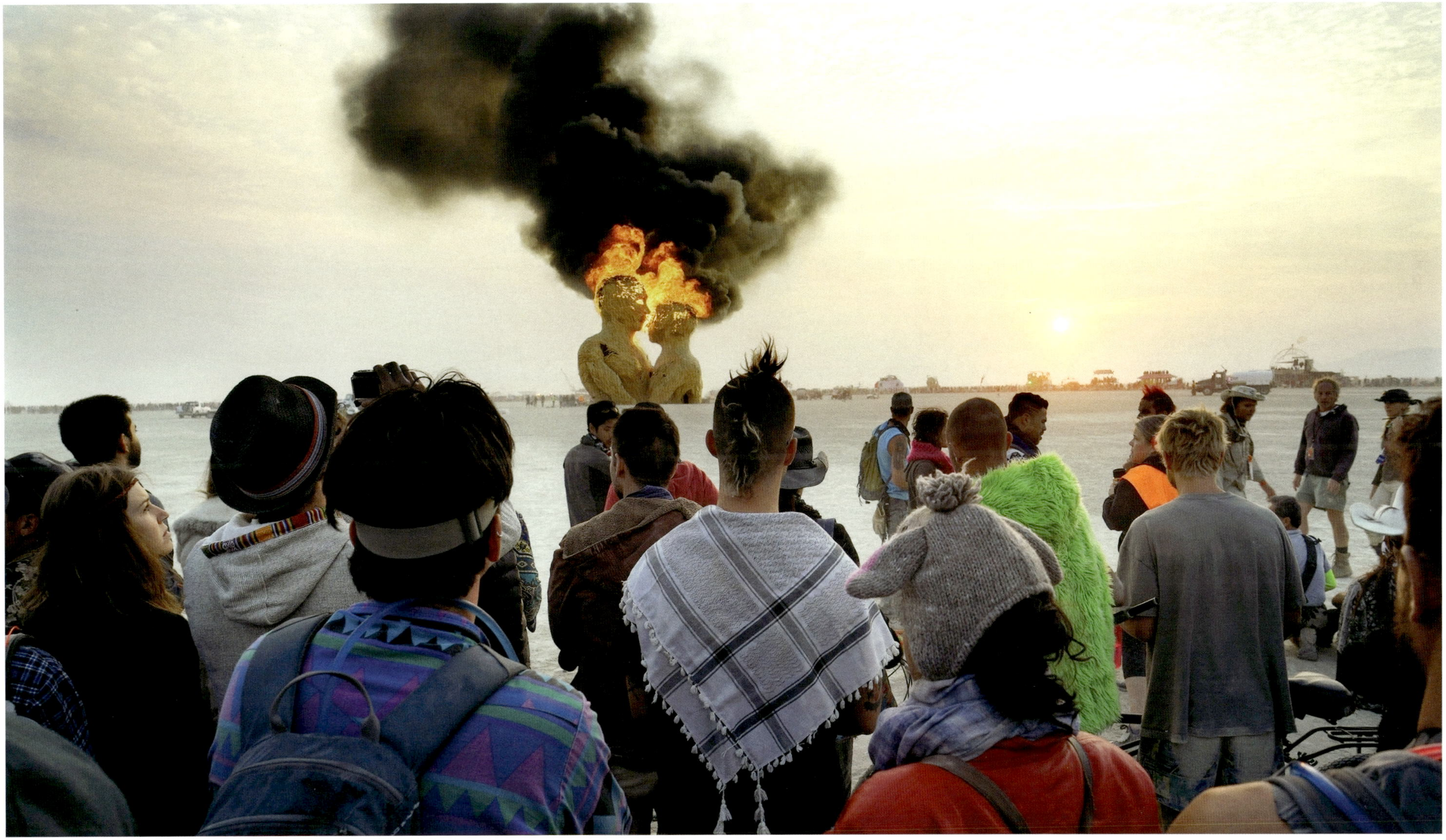

Embrace *Morning, 2014*

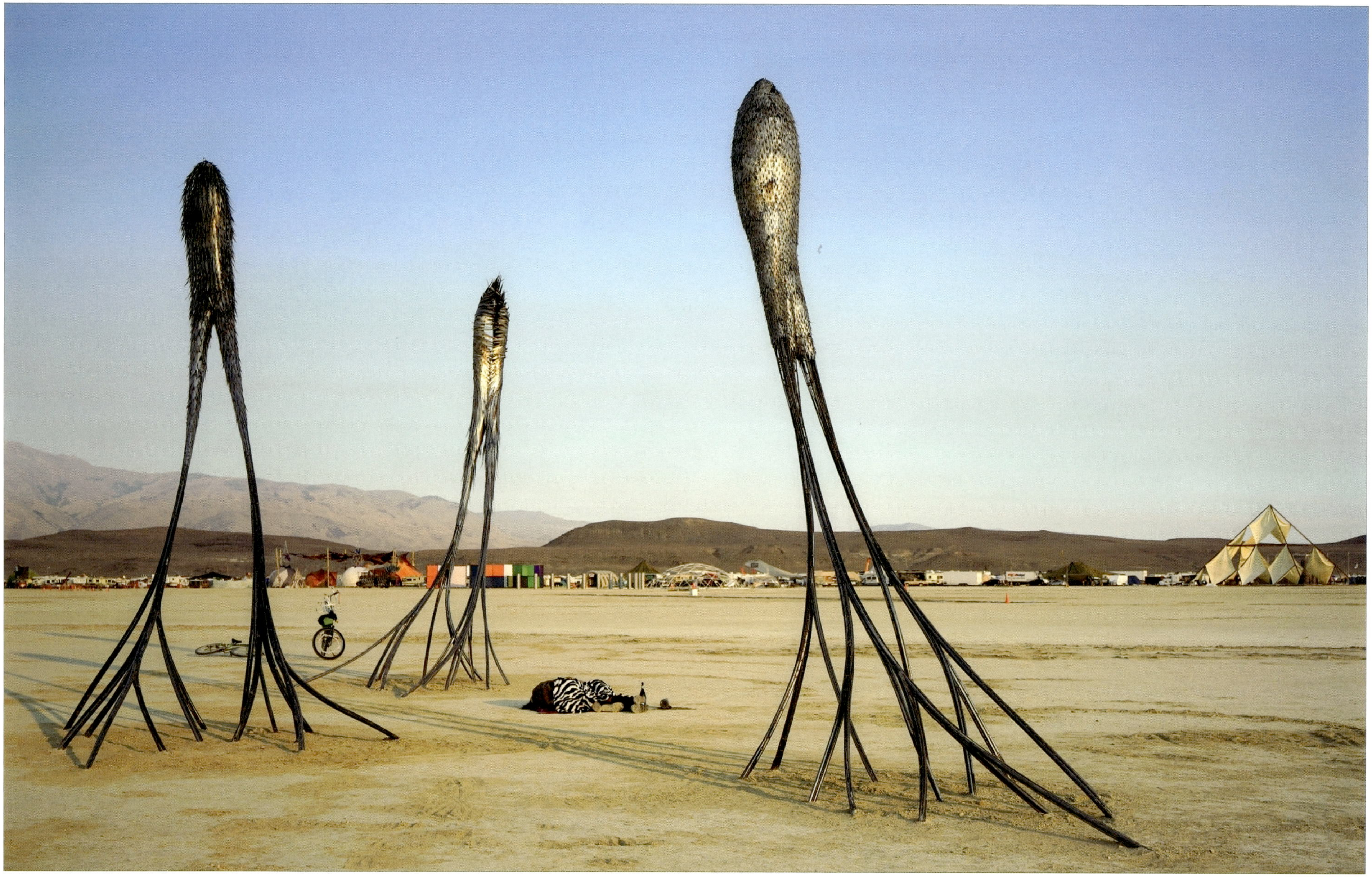

Curious Drifts, *2013*

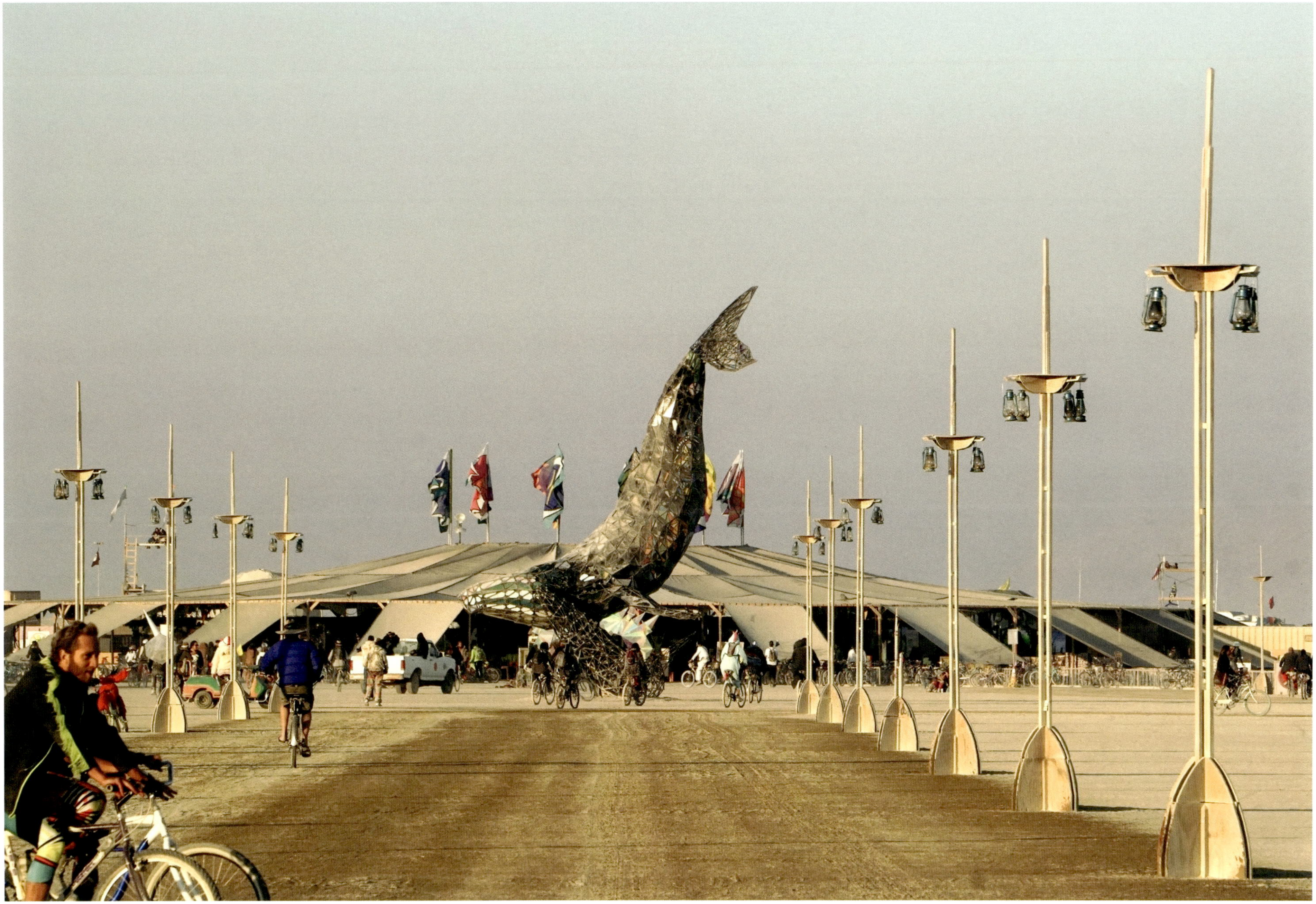

Center Camp Spires, 2016

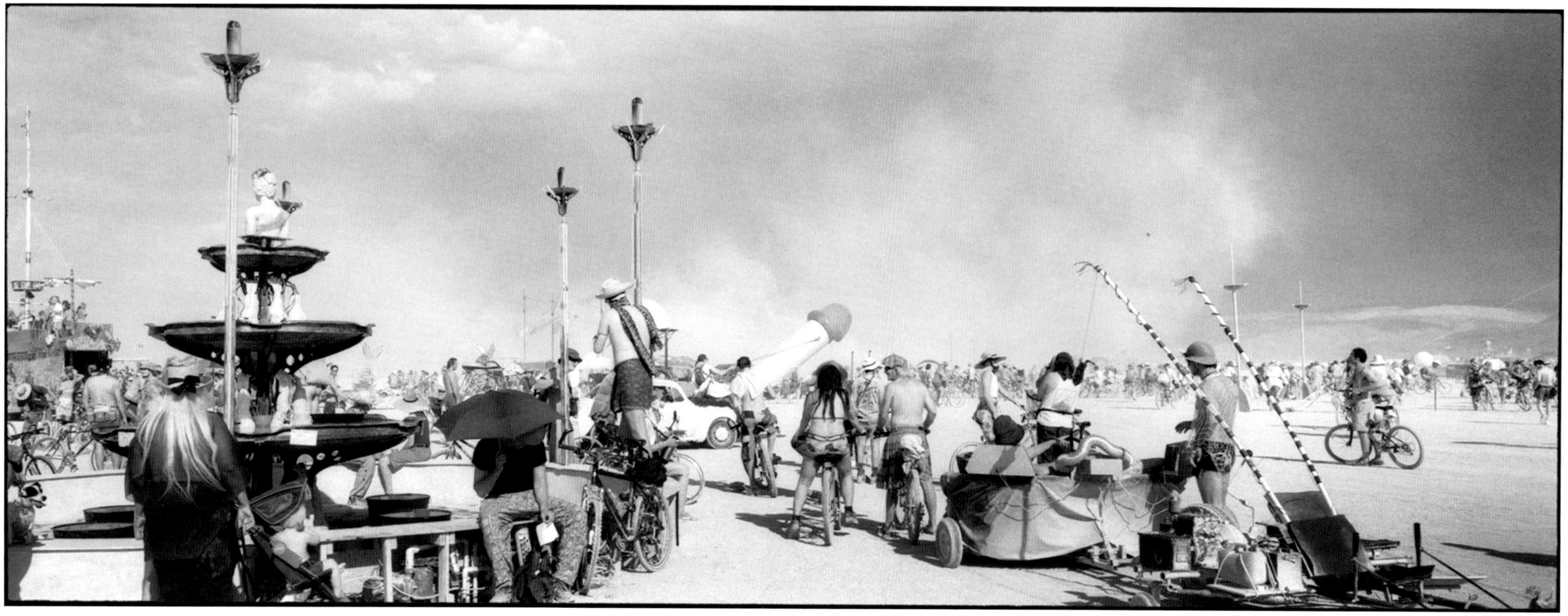

DPW Parade, 2002

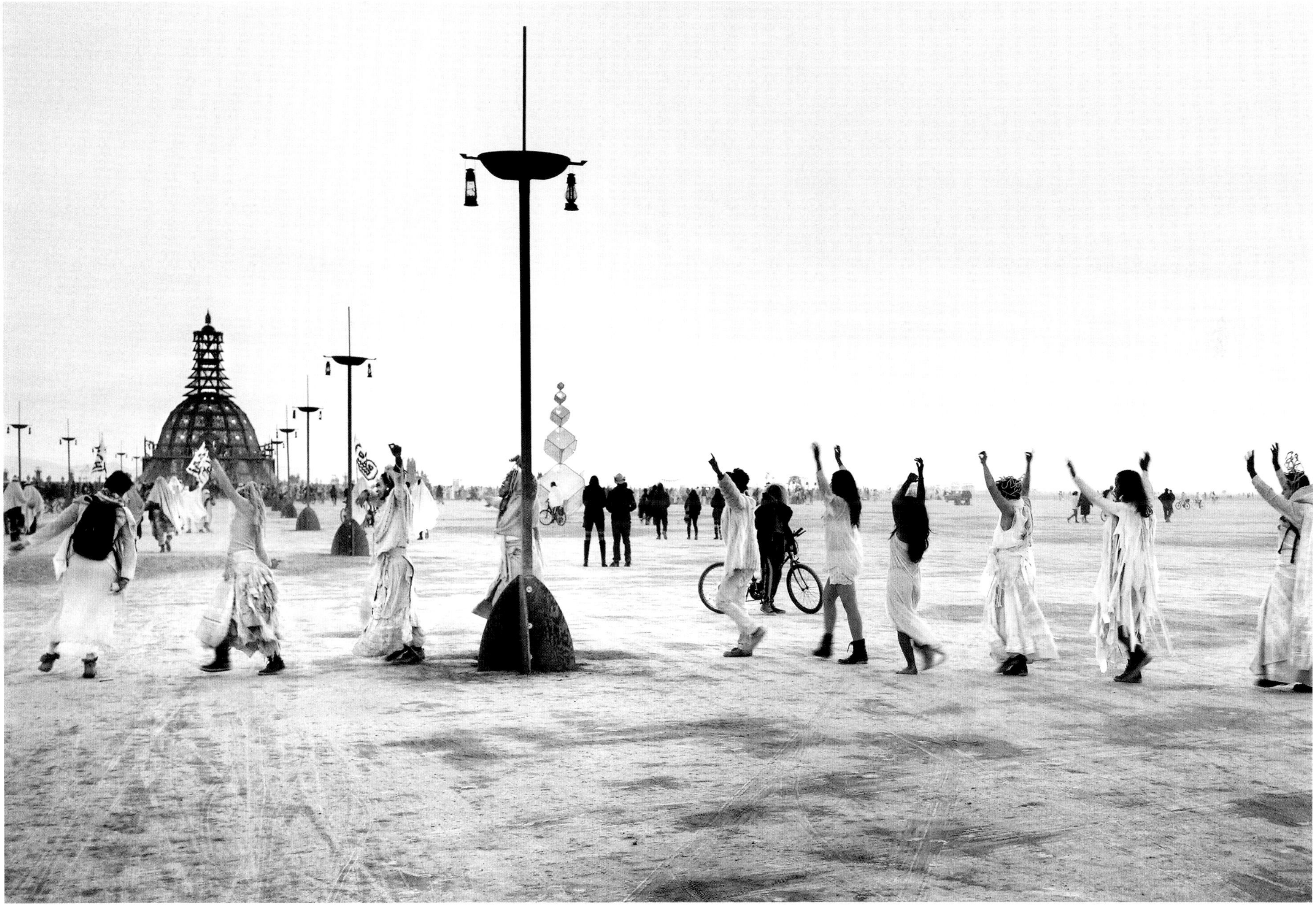

Sunday Morning, 2014

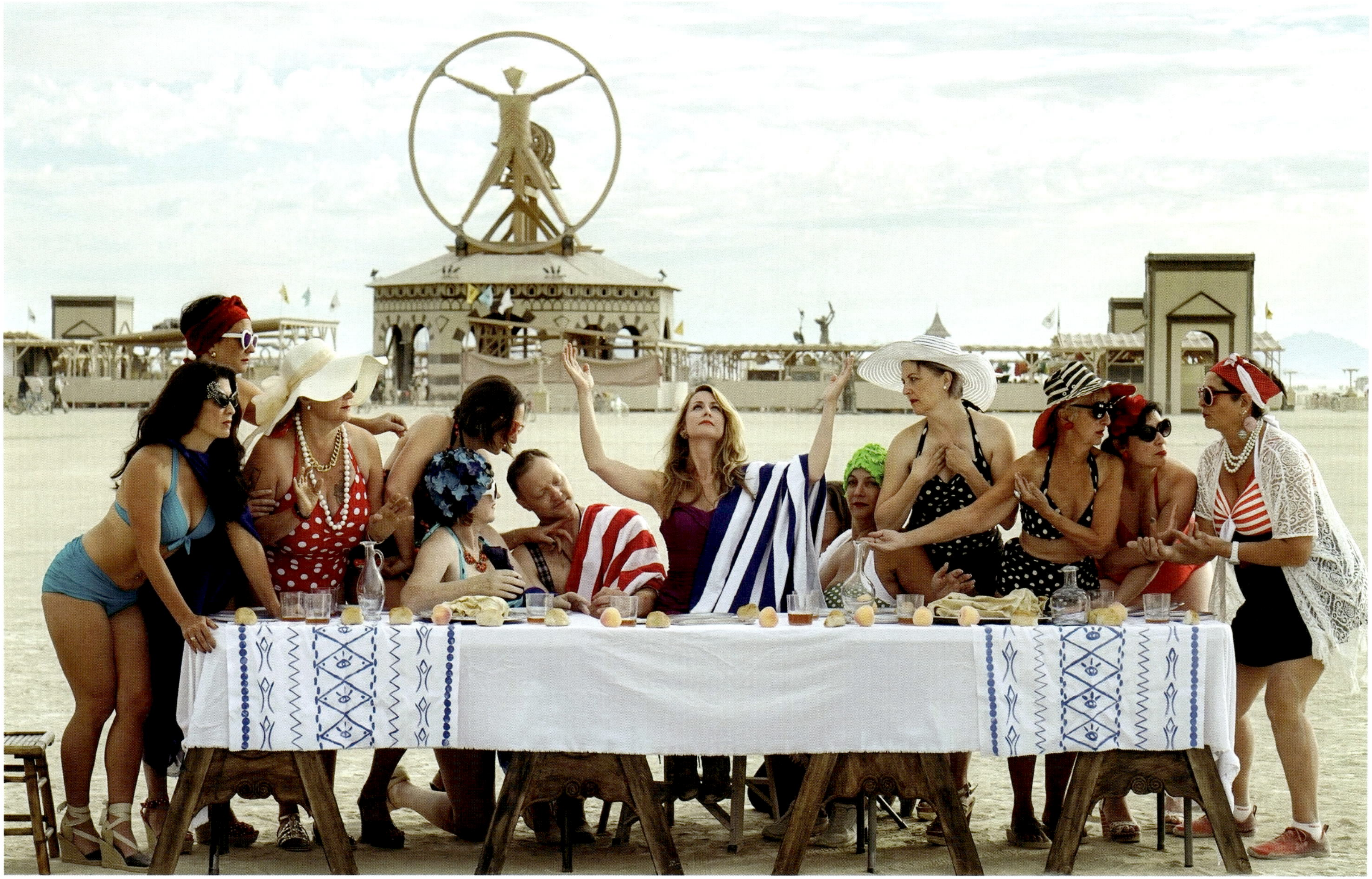

The Last Summer, *2016*

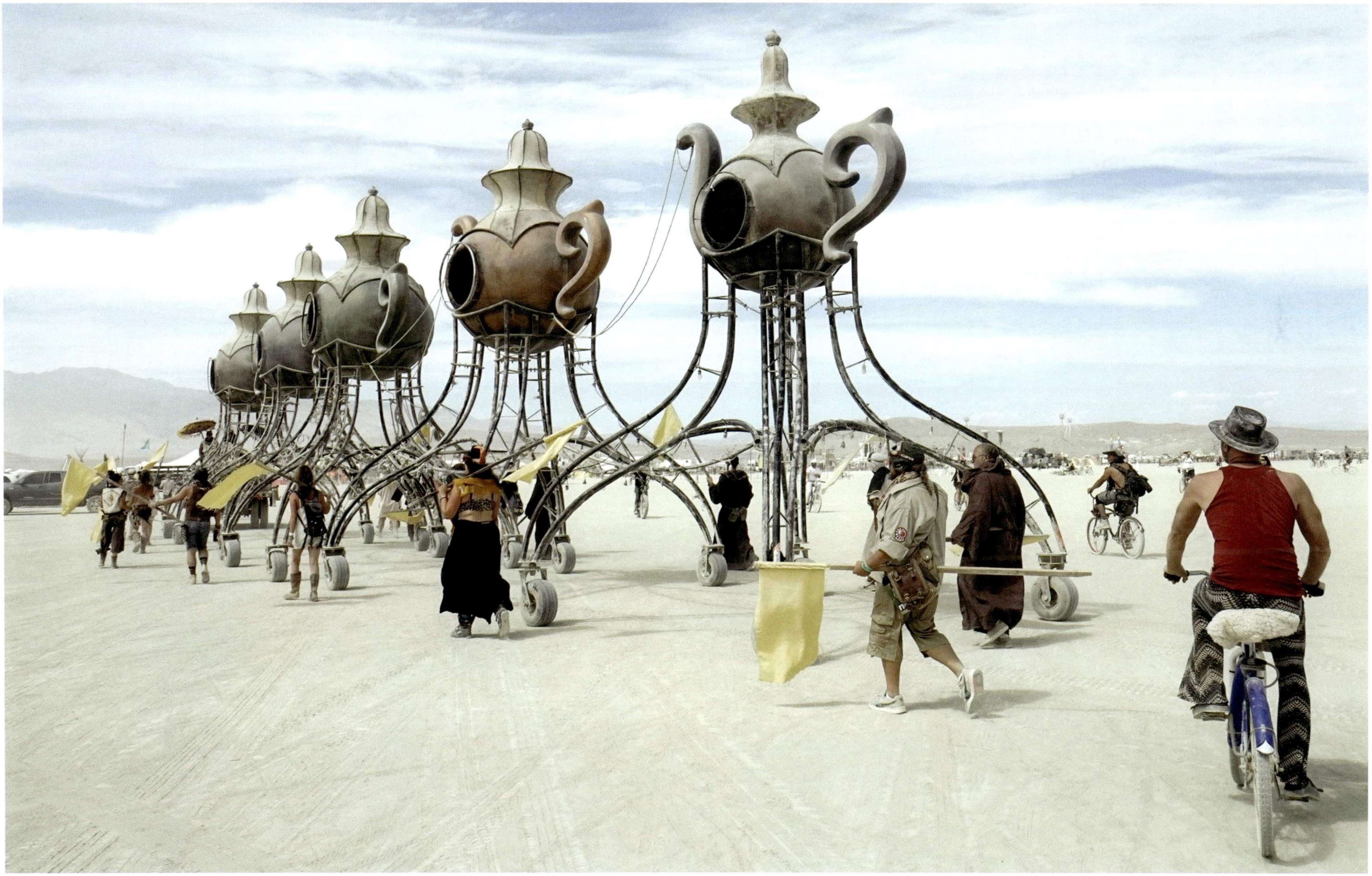

The Lost Tea Party, *2016*

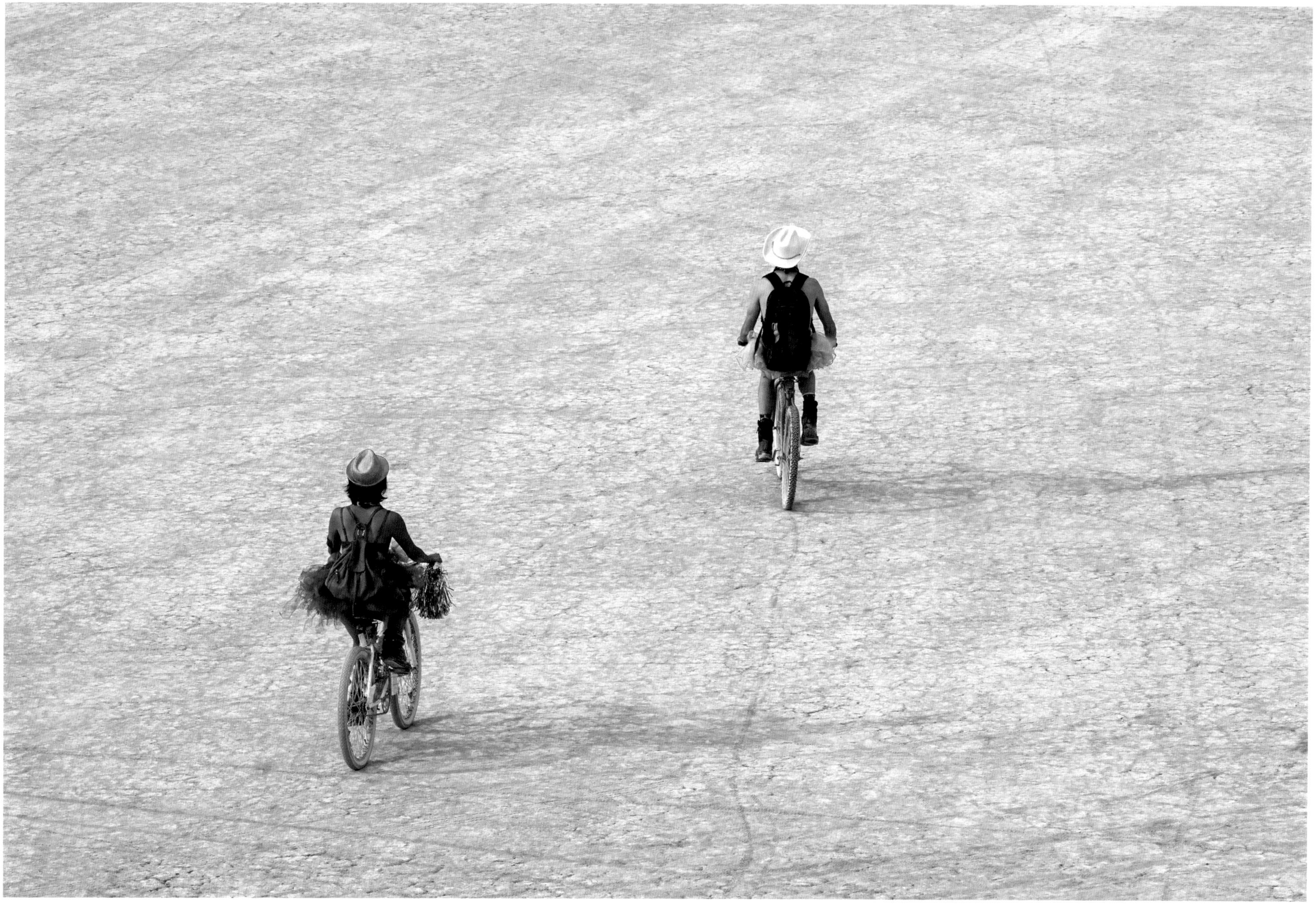

Playa Bikers, 2015

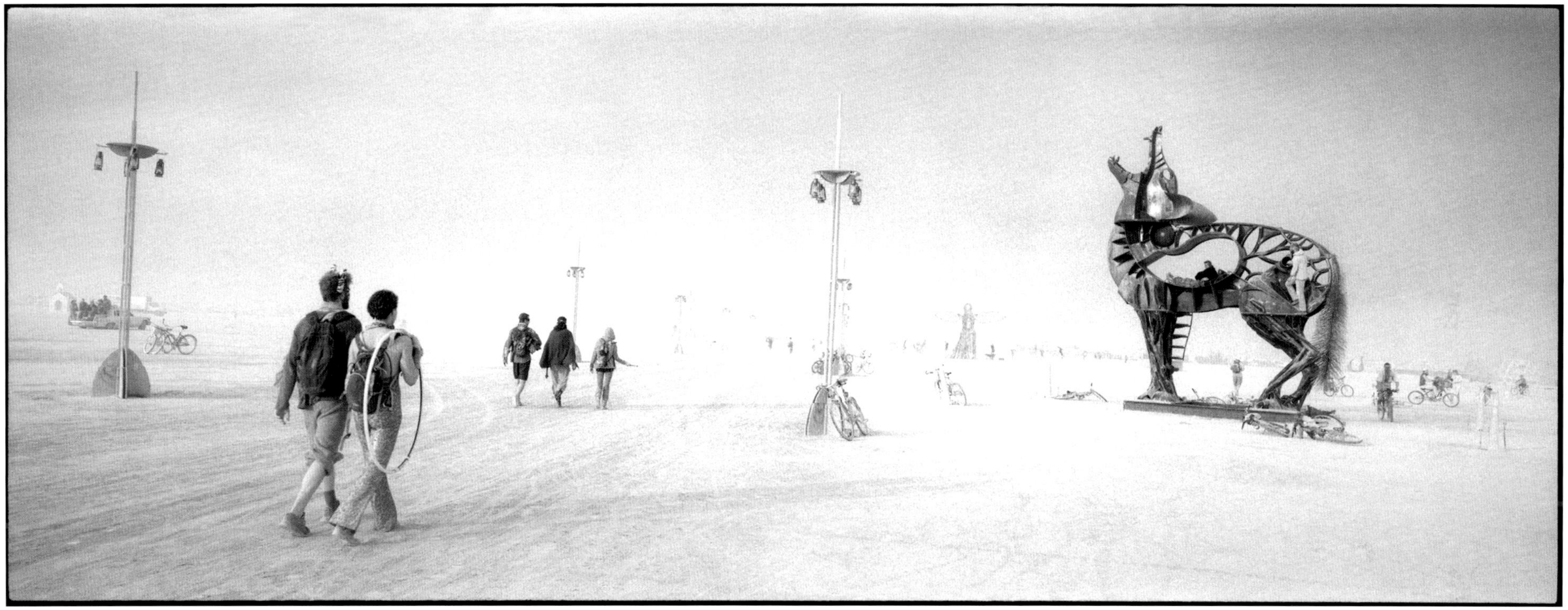

Coyote *Walk, 2013*

The perimeter fence around Black Rock City is now nine miles long. The diameter of the area between the outermost roads is over two miles. Often the wind blows across the hot playa surface, pulling the California coastal air east like a magnet. Hidden in the corona of heat and dust are the jewels of creation that are deep playa art. Burners spend a lot of time walking and biking around, and it's sometimes a trial. The dedicated strike out early; the tardy wait until it's stifling. The attraction is undeniable. Hundreds of hidden treasures are way out there or tucked away in the myriad streets that begin with A and often sprawl outward to J or K. For midafternoon dancing, nothing beats the scene at Pink Mammoth, and you can usually find a delicious libation at Martini Village, but you'll first have to venture into the "burbs." It'll be worth the effort.

A tour of the deeper playa usually results in a surprise. It's why experience is the central ethos of the event. Everyone must be the author of their own adventure in Black Rock City, as there is little in the way of scripted activity, and you're probably already late for whatever is on the schedule anyway. Camps list their offerings in the yearly guide, but it's an intention at best. Burning Man isn't an outdoor art gallery so much as a "happening" in the avant-garde 1960s sense of the word. You might stumble upon a parade of giant teapots, or Joanna Priestly and the Children of Chaos staging a parody of Leonardo's *Last Supper* with gender-swapped apostles in swimwear. The unexpected is de rigueur at Burning Man. Looking at others' pictures once I get home, I'm always amazed by what I've missed.

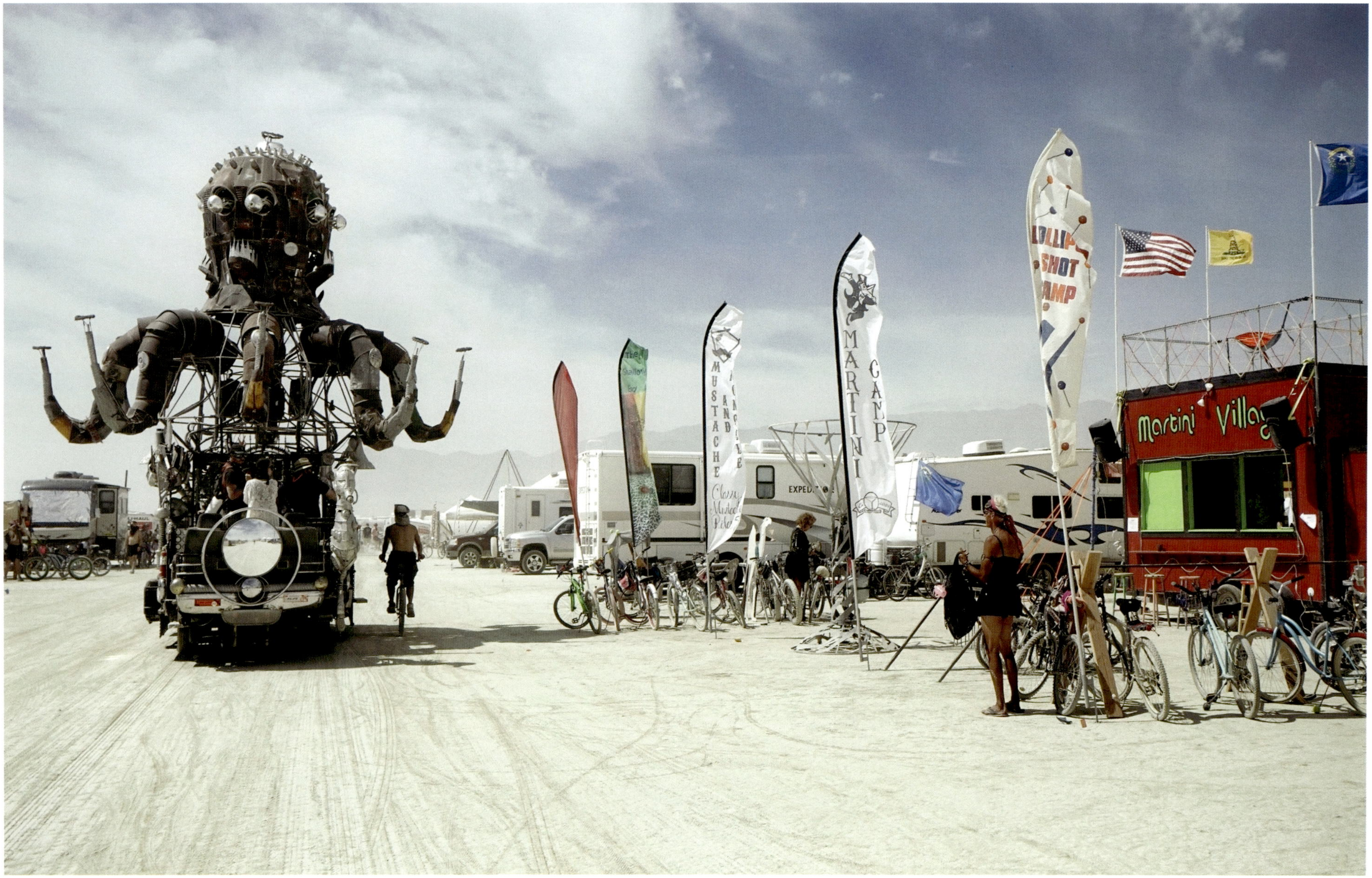

The Burbs, 2016

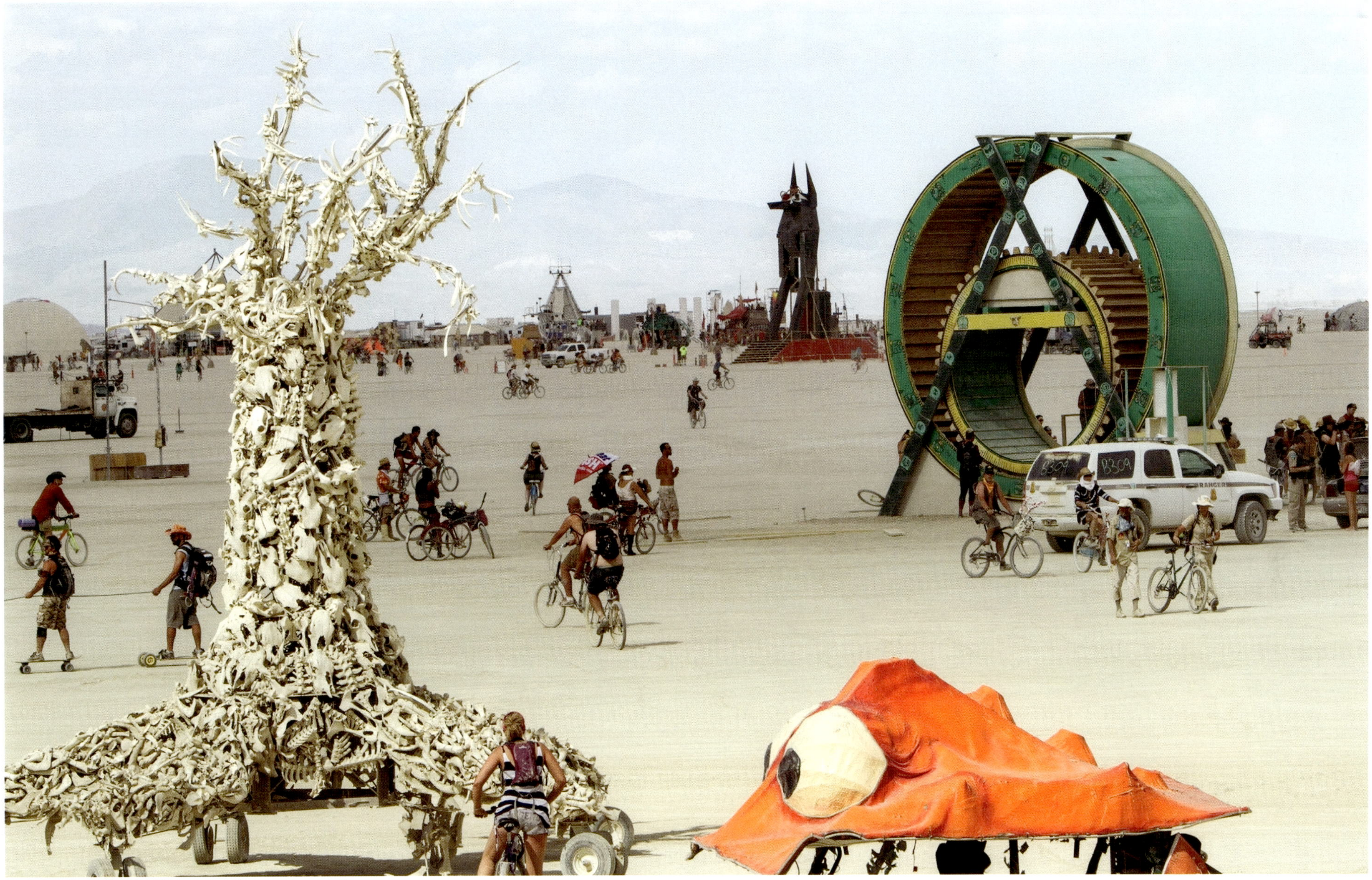

Bone Tree *Scene, 2012*

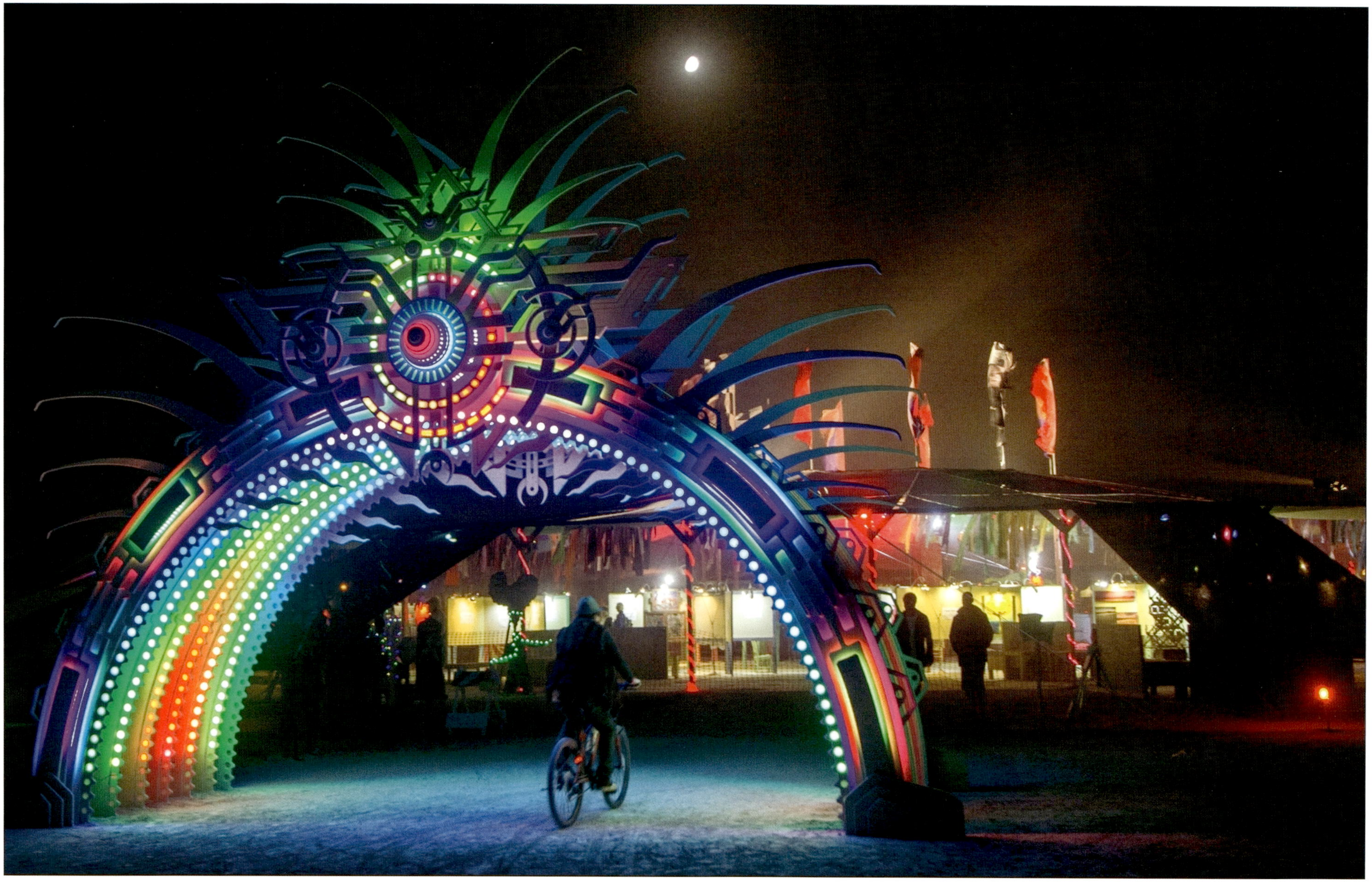

Star Portal, 2012

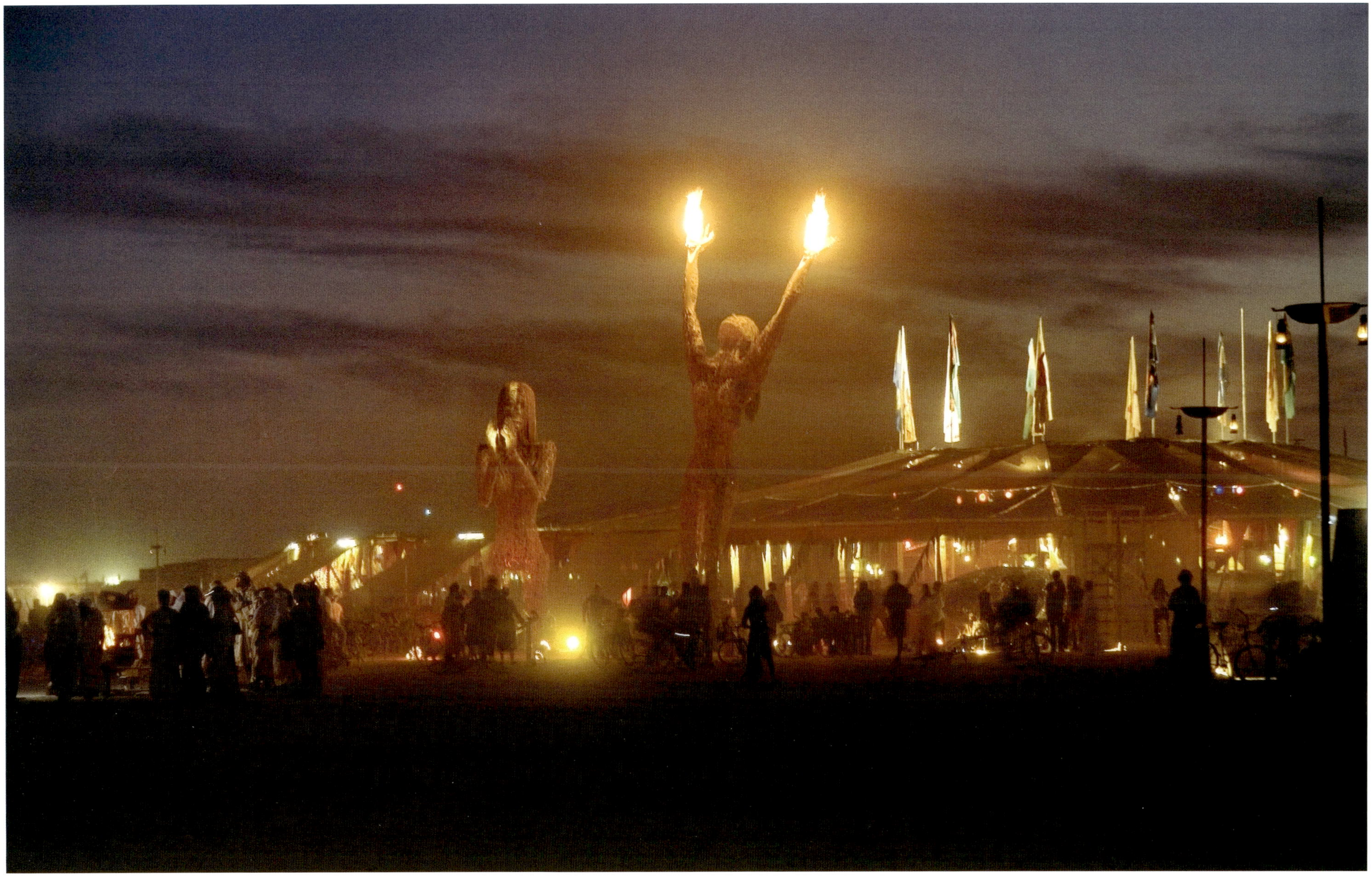

Leaping Giants, 2006

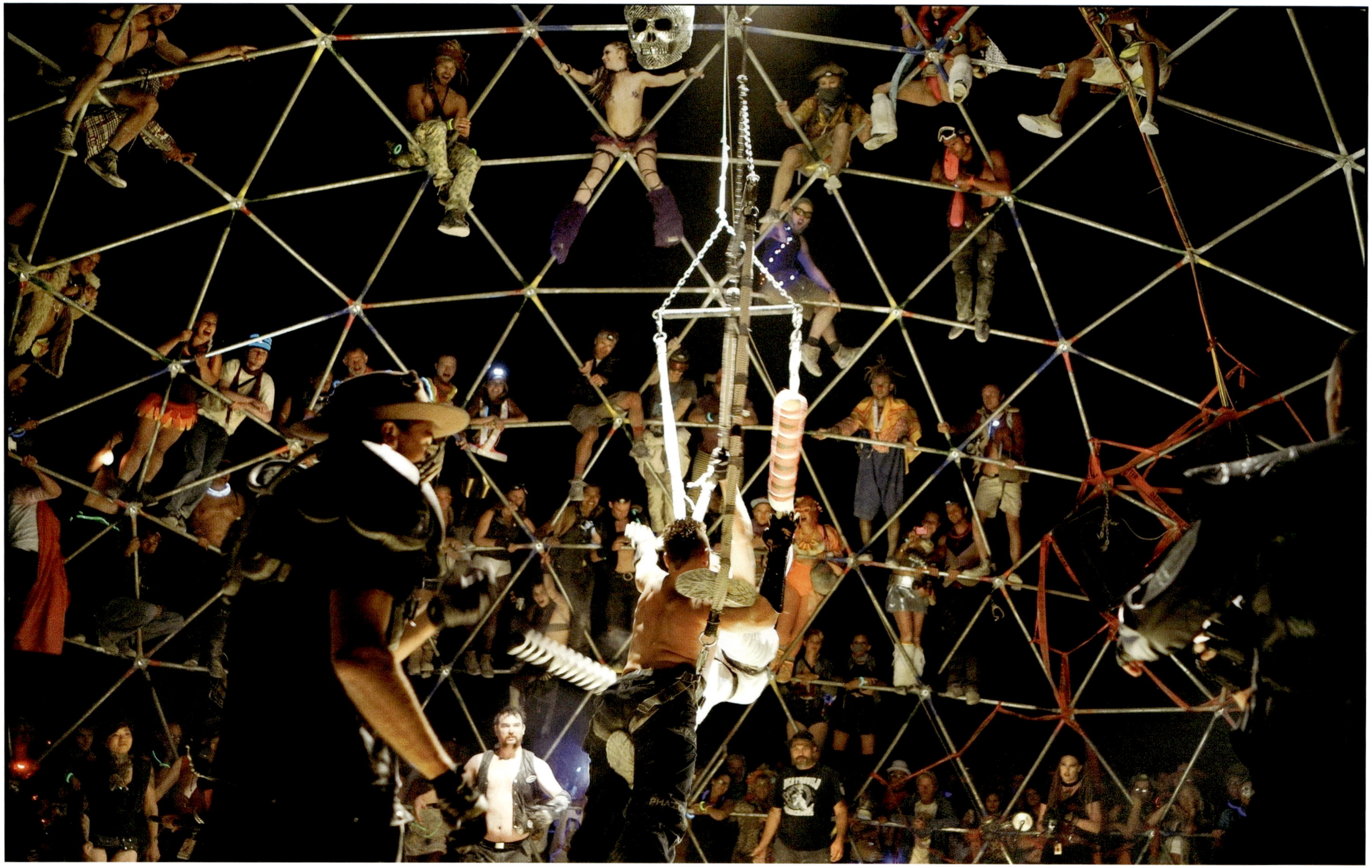

Thunderdome, *2013*

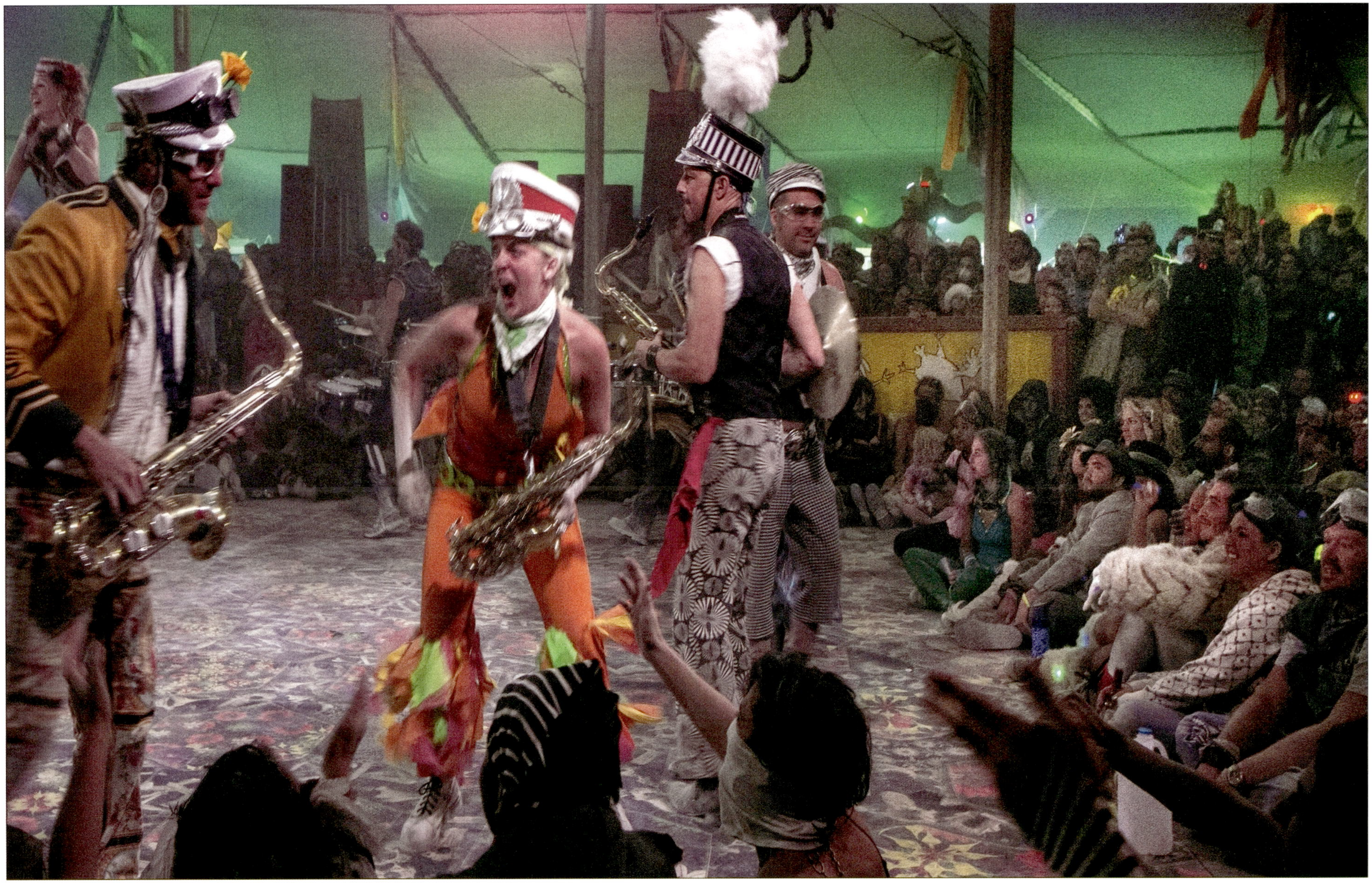

MarchFourth, 2012

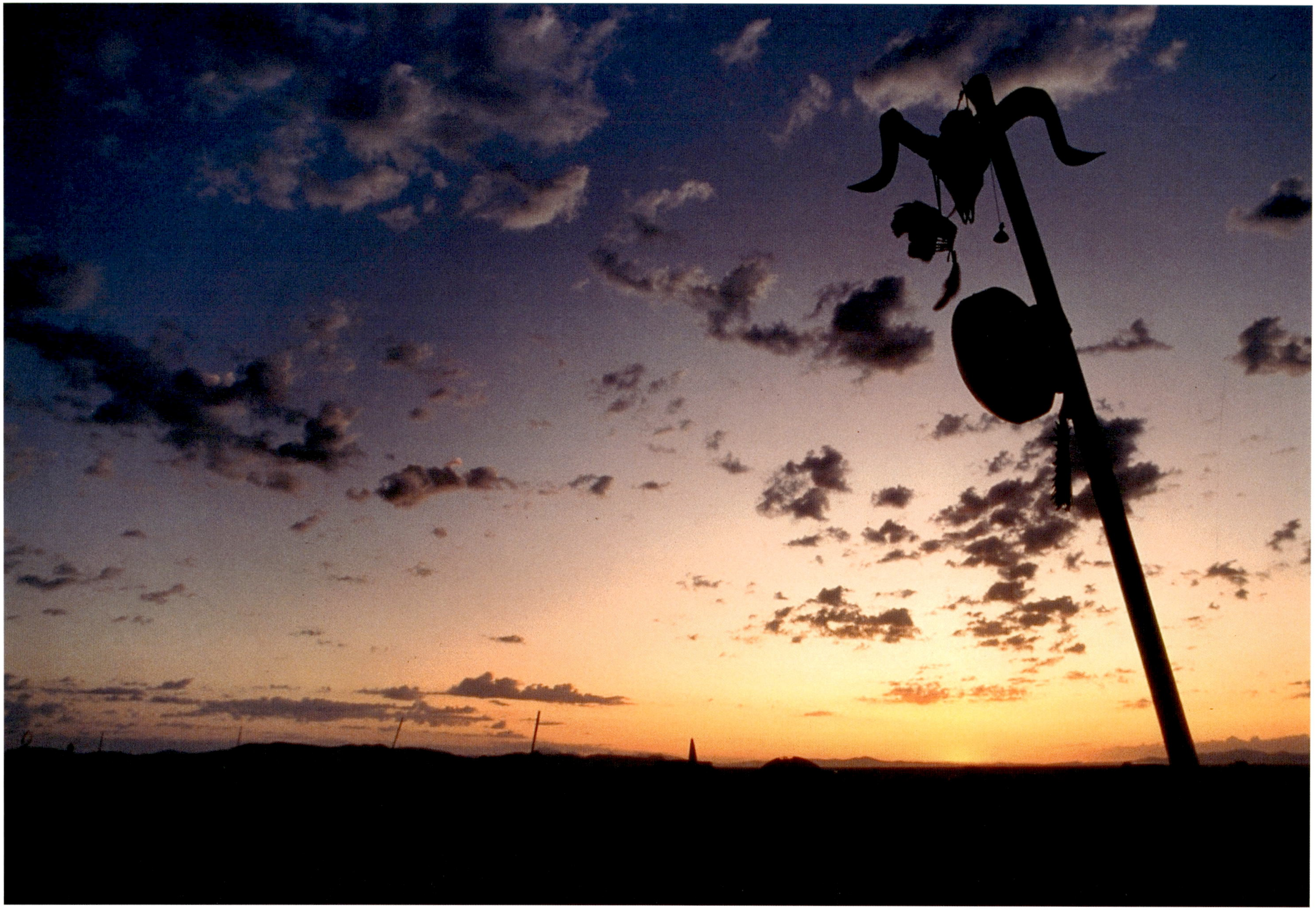

Sunrise Totem, 1993

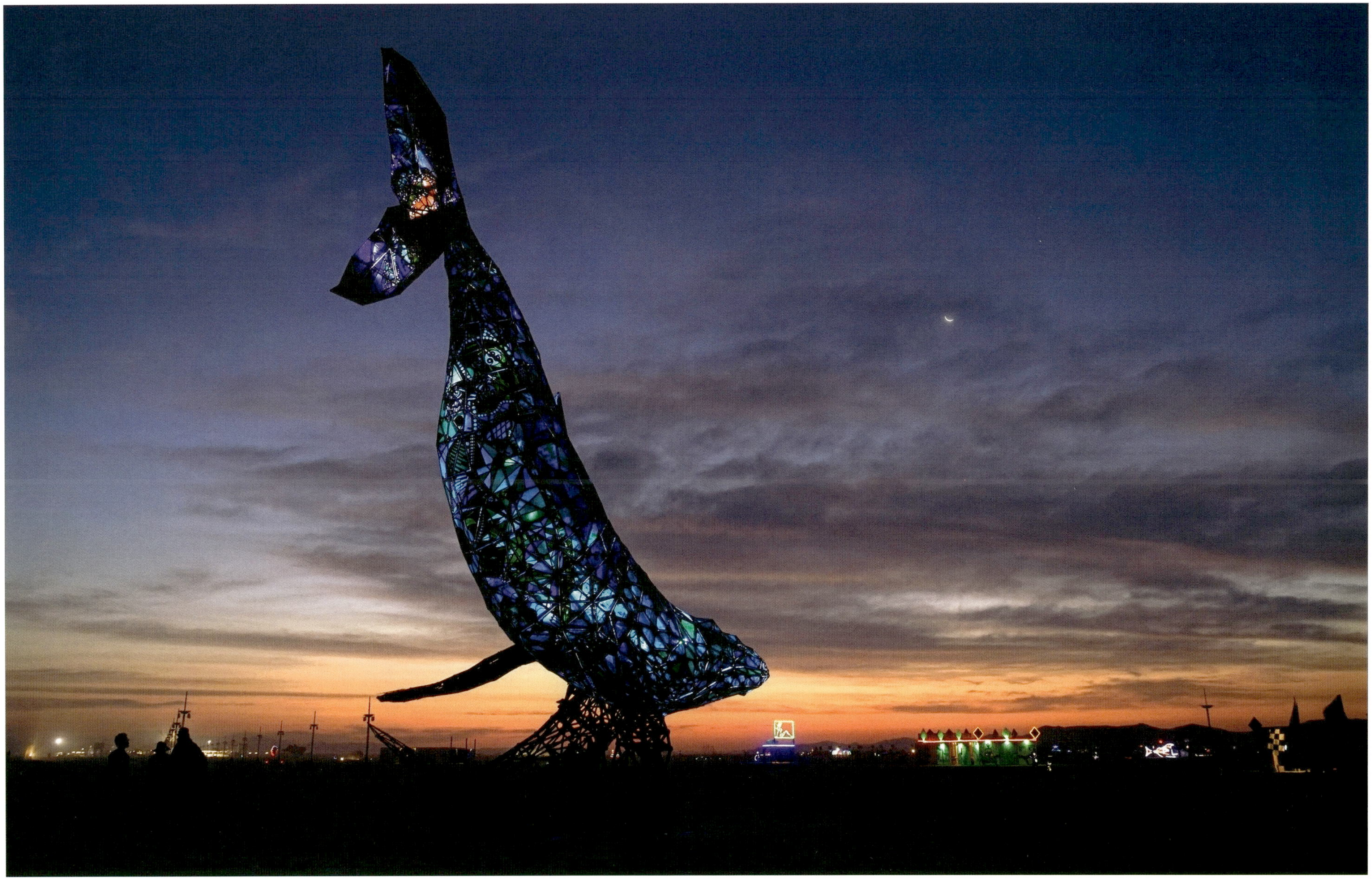

Space Whale, *2016*

CHAPTER 7

AMEN CORNER: 1998–2000

In 1998, Burning Man emerged from the debacle of the previous year wounded but undaunted. The move back to the Black Rock Desert would initiate an internal restructuring and a top to bottom reassessment of what the future of Burning Man was to be. Over the next four years virtually everything that has come to symbolize the character and consequence of the organization would be in place, or at least well on the way. The new century would introduce an era of expansion and rediscovery, and Burning Man would emerge in 2001 with a fully realized model for its future. While authentic experience is still the ultimate goal of attending the event, the means of attaining that experience would gradually shift away from free renegade expression to a more community-based culture of creativity and ritual performance. The idea wasn't to stifle individual expression but rather to influence that creative outburst toward the enrichment of the entire community.

What was abundantly clear after the tumultuous years of 1996 and 1997 was that Burning Man had to not only achieve more effective administration and fiscal control over the event but also do so without killing individual initiative. Larry had lobbied hard after the collapse of the triumvirate in 1996 to recruit a support team from the most involved personalities on his committee. Several members of this new board of directors emerged to form a powerful management unit, and their performance in the wake of Washoe County's heavy-handed treatment had solidified their knowledge and resolve. The experiment on Hualapai Flat had been a financial disaster, and Larry understood more than anyone that if Burning Man were to survive and grow it must return to the Black Rock playa. Initially, the BLM was resistant. At first, they claimed they were too busy to review Burning Man's requests for a permit, but the organization that had responded effectively to the bureaucratic maneuvers of Washoe County was acquiring a strong political acumen. They effectively lobbied the BLM, and soon thereafter Burning Man was back on the playa.

The serendipitous component to this new administrative ensemble was that each of the six would evolve niches that reflected their strengths. Aside from Larry and Michael, who continued in their traditional capacities, the others developed specific areas of expertise that were sorely needed to jump-start the twenty-first century edition of Burning Man. Crimson Rose, who had initiated the first artistically driven performances at Burning Man, focused on the other aspects of art at the event. Her most renowned contribution was of course as a fire performer. In 1991, when she debuted a fire ritual as part of the lighting ceremony, she enlisted the support of others to perform with her, and this she dates as the beginnings of the Fire Conclave, which now involves sixteen hundred performers from thirty-two chapters around the world. Aside from recruiting art for the event, Crimson Rose brought with her a highly evolved sense of ritual. Fire and ritual are as inseparable as baptism and water, and it's thanks in no small measure to Crimson Rose that reverence for ritual has become an engrained component of Burning Man's ethos.

Michael Mikel described the early managerial styles of John Law, Larry Harvey, and himself as "loose." Then he added, "We each did what we did." That may have worked in the wild ol' days, but it would have been woefully inadequate for an organization that was trying to learn to play hardball with politicians on the county, state, and federal levels. The new Burning Man organization knew that every facet of the event had to be competently overseen, and each person in authority had to become the absolute master of their bailiwick. Safety and security at the event depended on it, but more importantly, if Burning Man was to be more than a hedonistic jam session, the organizational spirit required radical reshaping.

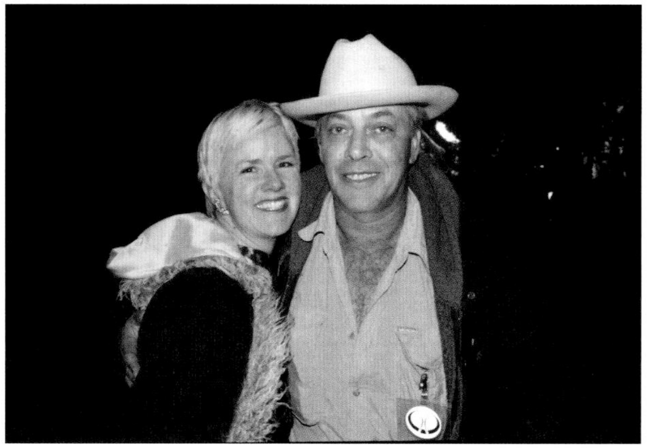

Burning Man apparently thrived on nepotism and administrative hanky-panky in 1998.

Initially, Michael put Harley K. Dubois in charge of the volunteer hotline. Burners had mostly camped together based on who they knew, but when people would call to volunteer to do things or help build the city, Harley would ask them what kind of a camp they were planning. This was a transformative approach because it often planted a seed that their camp could be more than a tent and shade structure. It could be as expressive as them. She might also help people think about giving their camp an identity centered on some form of community interaction. If they were willing to create expressive digs and offer services, Harley would offer to place them near the front of the city. Out of that gentle encouragement came an array of bigger and more innovative theme camps.

By 1998, the Esplanade had become the Broadway of Black Rock City, and Harley began reserving space along it for the most expressive theme camps. Two of the firsts were Birthday Camp and Santa Camp. They were simple manifestations: at Birthday Camp every day was your birthday, and at Santa Camp every day was . . . well, you guessed it. Another aspect that Harley brought to the idea of camp placement was determining which camps would work best next to each other. Theme-based camps had been around as ad hoc affairs early on, but what Harley brought to placement was a kind of curatorial community zoning. As early as 1995 she was stringing certain camps together to form something like districts and neighborhoods, and of course neighborhood is the quintessential ingredient for a collaborative community.

One of the more fortuitous requirements from Washoe County had been submission of a city plan. Harley had worked up a design, and Will Roger recruited his friend and designer extraordinaire Rod Garrett to refine it from an engineering standpoint. Crimson Rose had introduced Will to Burning Man, and he had taken over the building of the city after John Law departed the scene. Will began to assemble a gang of volunteers, many of whom were not refined characters. They would become the famously antisocial DPW (Department of Public Works). Of course Fly Ranch had turned out to be a unique space. The central city had to conform to the topography of the grassland. Will and Flash Hopkins used a piece of earth-moving equipment to create a roadway from the ranch to the playa, which was a controversial approach because it tore through a swath of sagebrush, but it also created a controllable gateway. After the event, Marian and Harley organized a group of volunteers to repair the damage. It was only partially successful, but that group of environmental repair specialists became the Earth Guardians, who pioneered the principle of Leaving No Trace.

The final piece to the administrative remodel that year came in the form of Larry's romantic partner, Marian Goodell. That's right. My brother brought his girlfriend on board! This should have been a disaster of the highest order except that Marian possessed badly needed communication skills and a finely tuned sense of political savvy. She also exhibited the acumen of a detail-oriented, kick-butt executive. The first thing she did was create an overdue web presence: Burning Man.com. Then she authored the famous *Jackrabbit Speaks* newsletter. She also proved to be a shrewd negotiator and a charming schmoozer at collaborator functions. She was, as they say, the complete executive package. Today, she is the CEO of the entire Burning Man organization. Another of her unique managerial gifts is that she can see both the big picture and the small details equally well, which enables her to be adept at both strategy and tactics. Though she and Larry stopped being a couple after a few years, Marian turned out to be an example of romantic nepotism gone right.

The return to the Black Rock Desert pushed the event's growth faster, with the vastness of the playa attracting people the way the prairies of the nineteenth century drew pioneers, its scale exciting imaginations to bigger and bolder deeds. A handful of large art pieces had already made their appearance in previous years, but the move back to the playa signaled an uptick in scale and artist enthusiasm. The year 1998 saw a surge in both artist and regional contributions. Pepe Ozan created his largest opera set to date: *The Temple of Rudra*. Its stage was framed by four smokestack-like supports with a swarm of wire insect-headed creatures guarding the entire piece. One of the earliest regional collaborators was the Mystic Krewe of Satyrs from New Orleans, who brought *Le Boeuf Gras d'Or*, a ribald Mardi Gras–style

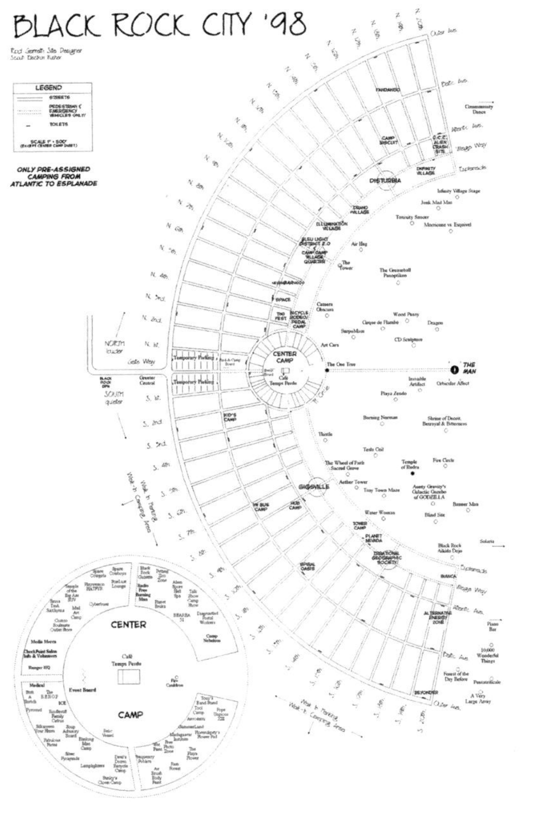

The genius of Rod Garrett's city plan was that you could always find your way home.

float in the form of a golden bull with oversized gonads and a large human penis. It was their second float. Bay Area sculptor Finley Fryer and his crew built a two-story *Chapel of the Burning Book* out of interior illuminated recycled plastics, which featured poetry readings and music performances on the second floor.

The year 1998 also saw Rod Garrett's first design for a city on the Black Rock playa. The famous 10:00 to 2:00 increments laid out in a horseshoe shape wouldn't make its appearance for another year, but most of the classic features of Rod's design were already present. The Man was located at the center of an imaginary circle. Behind him the eastern horizon presented a broad apron for the rising sun. At the 6:00 position was a keyhole leading to a second circle. This was Center Camp, with P. Segal's Café Temps Perdu in the middle, surrounded by all the essential services as well as an array of smaller theme camps.

The mastery of Garrett's city plan was that the circular roads follow an arc that radiates from the Man. The innermost road—the Esplanade—would function in two dramatic ways. First, it would form the front yard of the city and allow Harley's theme camp placement to take on a visual continuity. Second, it would be a great boulevard for a constant stream of Burners intent on seeing the magic of their neighbors' creations. Rod's design would also mean that Will and his DPW crew would have a crucial survey point with which to locate and lay out the city. The intersecting streets in the early version were numbered 1 through 20 in each direction from Center Camp, which would prove too restrictive, as many camps soon outgrew their lots. Thereafter the intersecting streets were laid out at half-hour intervals, but when you look at the overall design of 1998, the essential genius is evident: No matter how large the city grew, you would still be able to find your way around.

The 1998 theme was "The Nebulous Entity," and frankly it was a nebulous theme based on a complex sculpture by Michael Christian. It looked like a combination tree and sea creature, and was intended to support interactive performance. I'm not sure it really achieved liftoff. It was a fine sculpture, but as a theme it didn't inspire much. Nudity, which had been a by-product of rainstorms, was still being encouraged by sculptural showers. *Water Woman* was a recurrent fixture for years, but 1998 saw an even larger water feature by Dan Das Mann called *One Tree*.

While nudity and sexual parody are commonplace at Burning Man, the majority of the people I encounter could be at any music festival or carnival. Burning Man has a reputation for over-the-top sex, but it's largely overstated. There are camps that may encourage open sex inside their compound, but for the most part the playa is pretty tame. At Burning Man you expect to see the radical and the unconventional. It's one of

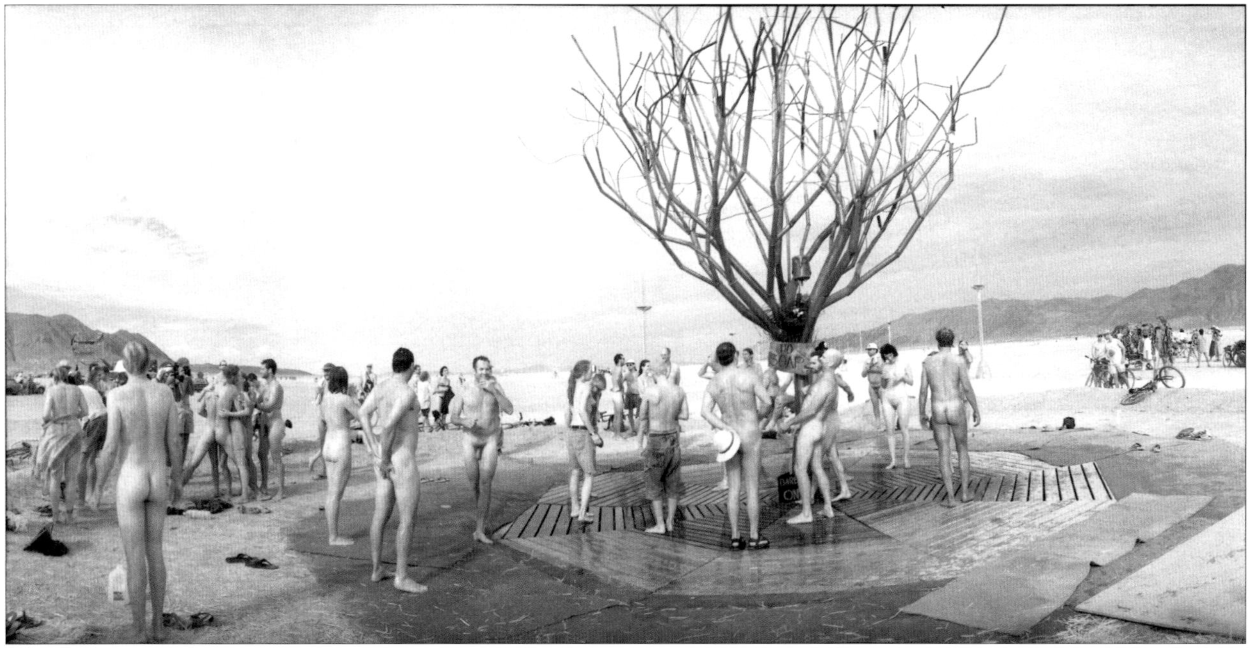

One Tree *was a shower sculpture that achieved a balance between art and utility.*

the attractions, and it's important not to impose conventional mores at an event that challenges people to be expressive, but there are standards for behavior. Ticket purchasers are expected to follow Nevada law, which prohibits lewd and lascivious behavior in public. In fact, these days it's pretty easy to tune the provocative out, or at least not to pay conspicuous attention, but in the late 1990s it was still a bit of a surprise to be standing in the porta potty line next to a naked guy with hunks of metal piercings on every private square inch. Ever the unhip rube, I might blurt out, "Dude, do those things get hot in the sun?"

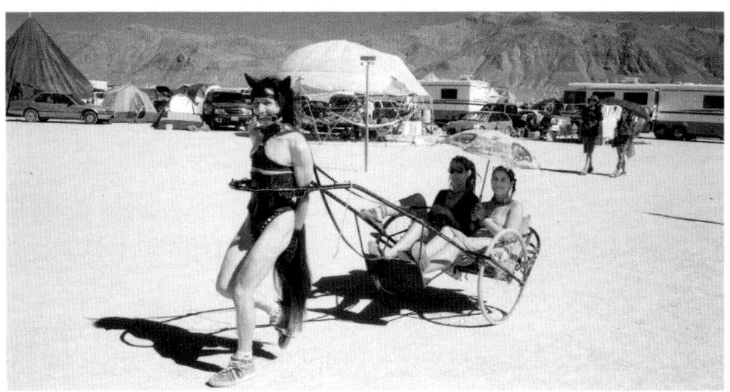

Being radically inclusive means you never know who's going to gallop by next.

However, nudity is more than mud-induced high jinks or a playa perversion; it can also be a vivid gesture of personal expression and community bonding. One instance from 1998 lingers: I remember walking out on my usual morning photo ramble and seeing an older naked man pushing himself along with a walker. His head was thrust forward in determination as he made for a tall wooden sculpture supporting long red banners. The sculpture was called *Sharon,* the work of Michael Taluc. If I were to speculate based on his knobby form, his saggy haunches, and his disheveled white hair, the old man's age was near ninety. It had been a cold, wet year, and the playa surface varied from choppy hash to crunchy powder, thus pushing his walker along was a struggle. The little wheels simply couldn't rotate on the playa crust, so he would lift the walker, plant it a few inches ahead, and then take a step or two forward. It took him a very long time to get to *Sharon.* I stood watching in stunned admiration from a distance as he moved relentlessly toward his goal, and I stood with him in spiritual solidarity as he gazed upward in rapt fascination at those marvelous blowing folds.

In the late 1990s, if someone had said the wild ol' days were behind us, we'd have laughed him out of camp. Casual driving in civilian cars had been banned, but the Burn was as crazy as ever. Art cars just got bigger and badder and became mutant vehicles. One major loophole then was the definition of an art car. Today, a mutant vehicle has to go through an inspection at the DMV and receive a permit. In the late 1990s, you only had to create a gestural "art vehicle." If a guy with a dirt bike hung a set of antlers on the front end, that might qualify as "art" enough. Some didn't even bother to do that.

The 1998 Burn ended on a high note. Indications were everywhere that the event was back on level ground. Larry and I decided to go into the fire circle. It's not something I do every year because it's a limited view. Once you get inside the circle, you're stuck. On the other hand, it's the best seat in the house. As per normal, there was incessant drumming and the rising excitement that builds toward the pending fireworks and burning. Having the Man on a platform had reduced the intimacy of the event, but it had increased the spectacle. Attendance had risen to fifteen thousand, and that number had pushed the circle out farther and the rows of people deeper. A photojournalist began taking pictures of Crimson Rose just before the annual Fire Conclave was to begin. My flash failed when I took a picture of Larry, but it turned out I had taken the shot simul-

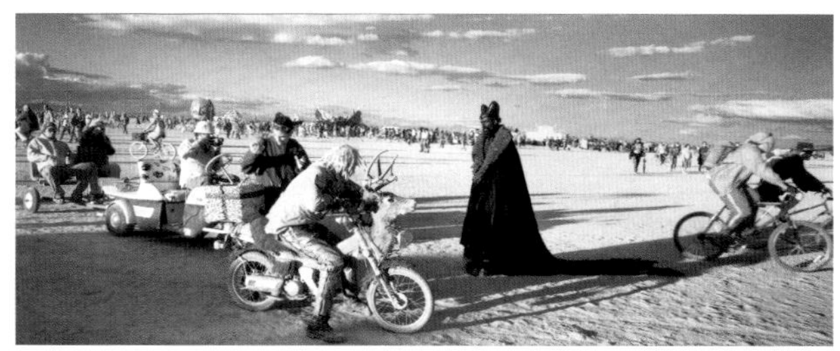

In the 1990s every dude with a dirt bike and a deer head could claim to be an art car.

taneously with the photojournalist. I was pissed at the time, thinking I had blown a good expression, which for Larry is few, but even though the negative is technically flawed and grainy, it was a wonderful moment.

In his 2010 essay "Designing Black Rock City," Rod Garrett provides a description of the 1999 plan that is as straightforward and unassuming as the design itself: "In 1999, we oriented the blocks annularly in order to better provide for future expansion. The theme that year was the 'Wheel of Time.' As the radial streets had been laid out in 15-degree increments, we were prompted to name them for the numbers of the clock face. When combined with the concentric street names, this turned out to be a conceptually graphic and easy-to-use system of location. Although the theme changes each year, we continued with the time analogy in naming these streets."

Rod's city plan for 1999 would be the enduring model for Black Rock City for the foreseeable future. His inspiration to use a clock face as the model for the radial streets was an elegantly simple model for navigating the city. "We're at 4:30 and B" is an amazingly simple and completely foolproof way to help your friends find your camp. The great advantage of Rod's scheme is that it has allowed for expansion of the city

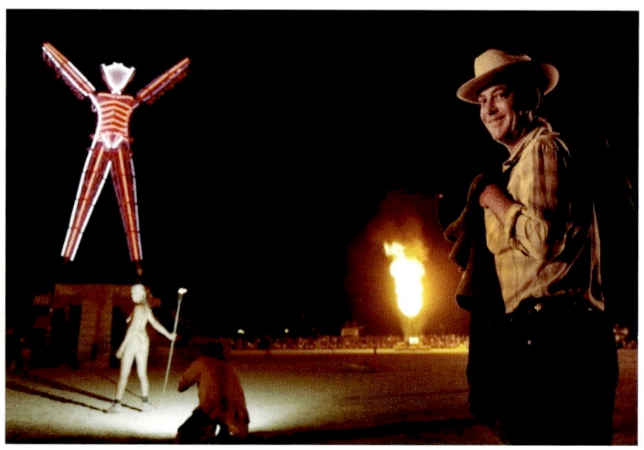

By 1998, Burning Man was back on track, and better days were just around the corner.

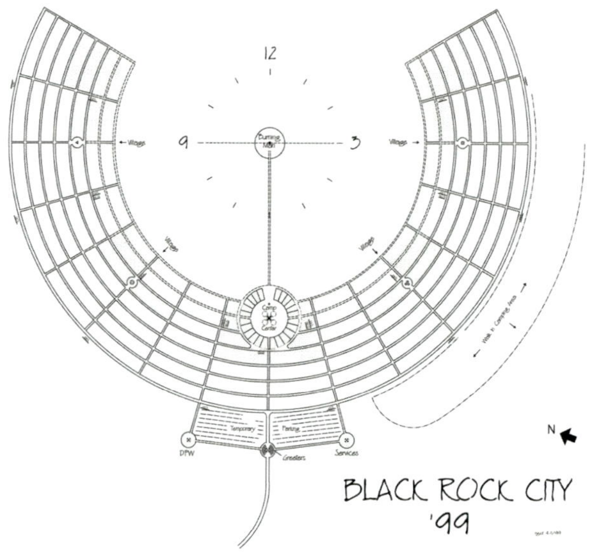

without losing that navigation tool. Over the years plazas were added at 3:00 and 9:00, and recently at 4:30 and 7:30, yet it's still easy to find your way home.

"The Wheel of Time" produced some good moments, but it was an abstract theme that contemplated space and time with an emphasis on the coming millennium. There was pageantry, but it didn't seem to inspire much of a response from Burners. Instead it put all the creative effort on the organization and the installation artists. It might have worked better in later years, when Burners better understood how to use the theme as a guide for personal projects. "The Inferno" in 1996 had worked because people instantly got the idea and could join in the satire. Over the next two decades, Larry would generate the themes and write an accompanying essay outlining them. They have become crucial to the perceived success of a given year. If a theme resonates with Burners, they will arrive packing innovations in camps and clothing, driving their new rolling monument to hubris. My feeling is that the best themes were the ones that produced the most enthusiastic responses, the ones that encouraged activity in the suburban areas of the city as well as the central playa. The themes for 2000 and 2001 would set a high mark for all of this and help springboard the event into its modern era.

"The Body" was a marvelous theme in 2000. It was playful and organic in the most creative sense of the word. In a pattern similar to 1999, the theme art was arranged in four sections along a spinal axis of the Man. The idea was to take a journey through the body beginning with the anus (an entry into all things organic) and then proceed to Pepe's large male lingam and a corresponding female yoni. An additional area would represent the heart, and then finally an artful encounter with the brain. Installation art located within each of these areas was expected to address that sector of anatomy. The reason this was such a fruitful theme is that it worked on so many levels, and it appealed to both esoteric and carnal sentiments. Such a classic motif frees artful urges naturally, and it stimulated the Burners in unforeseen directions for self-expression.

As a theme, "The Body" could have been fairly prosaic, and indeed many people responded with variations on the obvious, but what made it successful was that Larry's essay encouraged people to contemplate a broad range of response, and seemingly everyone jumped on the bandwagon. Because of that, "The Body" became another of the great teaching moments at the event. Following the confusion and melodrama of the mid-1990s, participation had been more of an idea than a general practice. "The Body" opened a floodgate

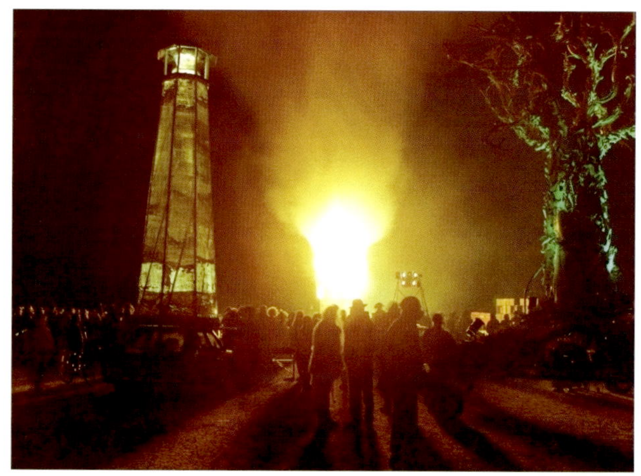

"The Wheel of Time" illuminated a mobile lighthouse and Bone Tree *along the playa.*

of participation. There was lots of nudity, of course, but the theme also provided a readily understandable panoply of imaginative possibilities.

On Thursday night of Burn week, *The Greater Spine* showcased performances and installations, and the Friday night pageant was *A Tour of the Spine*. Larry's essay spelled out opportunities for fully expressing the theme:

> The entire spine of this body can be regarded as a grand harmonic scale. The vertebrae, on which the centers of our nervous consciousness are strung, are like the keys of a piano. Ranging from the darkest roots of our awareness to the sublime projections of the mind, each key in its succession strikes a different tone. We will arrange art installations of all kinds along this scale. . . . Artists wishing to participate in the Greater Spine should consider a simple exercise. Touch that place along the axis of your body that you wish to occupy, as if sounding a single note, and see what feelings and ideas arise. . . . Would you like to be a virus or an antibody plying the great oceanic space of this corpus of work? Have you an affinity for the breasts or the hands or the feet? Do you wish to create a work not literally related to a position, function, or part of the body that exemplifies some other aspect of corporeal being? All such ideas are welcome.

Theme camps were also very active and fun. There is nothing like the body to bring out the least esoteric forms of parody. While Reincarnation Location might have been a tad obvious, the idea of making reference to a "womb with a view" was pretty amusing. It was a great theme because it allowed everyone to have some fun with a topic that is always ripe for a laugh, and if you don't believe me, just check out any of the most recent feature-length animated movies for children. Fart jokes, anyone?

One of my favorite experiences with "The Body" was in a theme installation I cannot name. I'm not even positive it was in 2000, but it would make sense in light of the theme. I entered a room and followed a long serpentine line that circled around a platform. Atop the platform was a four-foot-high viewing apparatus that looked like it might have come from the conning tower of a submarine. From the platform, steps led up to the apparatus, where I could bend over to

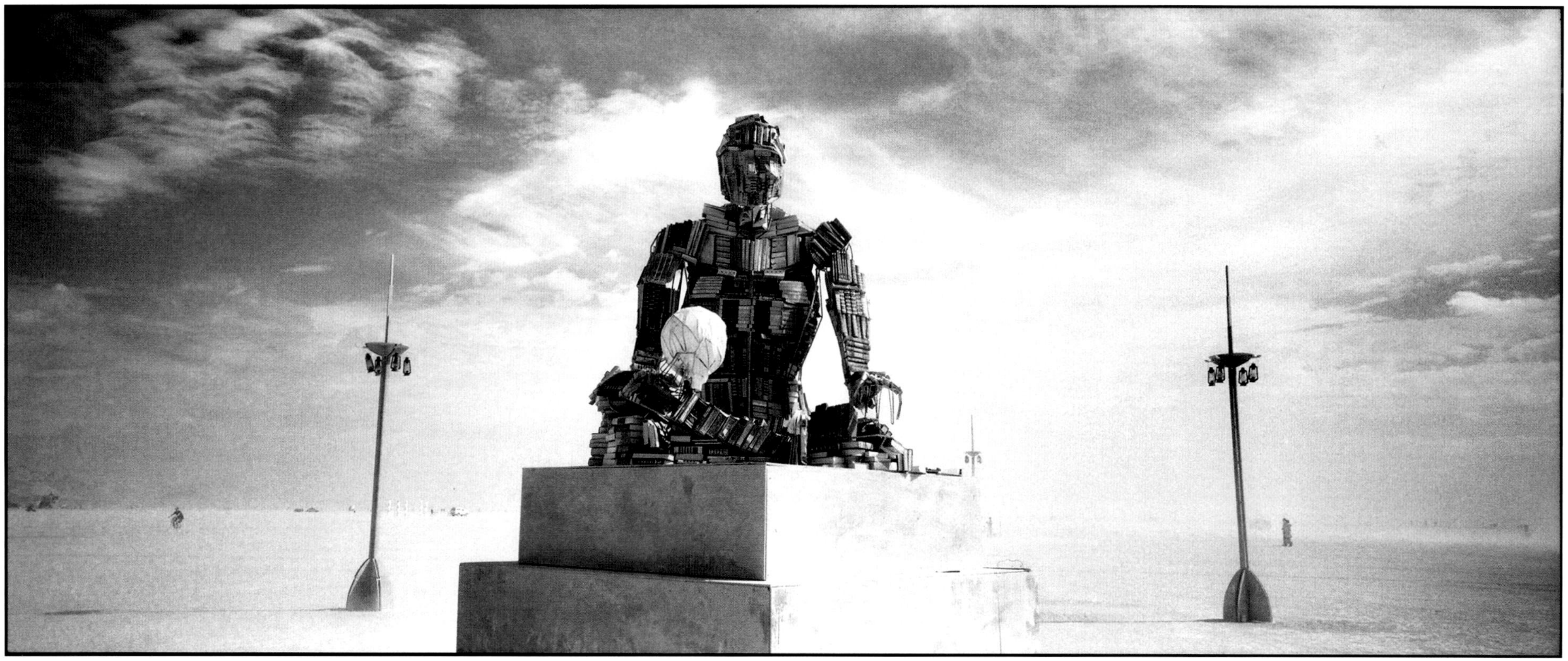

Body of Knowledge *sat like a weary sentinel amid the excesses of bodily humor in 2000.*

look down into it. What appeared on the screen inside was a closed-circuit view of my ass, taken with a camera mounted somewhere behind me. When looking at a view of their own ass, most people will instinctively start wiggling and shaking their butts. It seems to be a universal reaction. "Hey, that's my ass. I wonder what it looks like when I shake it?" Afterward I looked up and smiled, and then moved off the platform and followed the line into the next room. In that room was a group of previous ass shakers laughing up at a large screen showing the current ass shaker on the platform!

As entertaining as "The Body" turned out to be, on a personal level it became an agonizing experience. This was a year when all my friends had bailed out. Bryan and I shared a rental RV with two of his school buddies. Being the old man in a camp of thirty-somethings piqued my vanity enough that I indulged in some foolishness. As we headed to the playa Thursday afternoon we encountered a stranger bearing an array of cups. The idea was liquor tasting of some sort, and the drinking that day had started early. Later the four of us went out on the town. One of the highlights of *The Greater Spine* was that it provided a series of body-related art installations one after another. The effect was similar to a carnival midway, and you entered the whole thing by going through *Anus*. This was a huge fabric orifice atop a platform with giant legs splayed on either side. When you reached through the "sphincter" of the orifice you could feel a horizontal bar. The task was to grab the bar, swing yourself through the "anus," and then down a chute into a box below filled with hay. It was a not-so-subtle entrance into the body. The problem was that each of the young guys tried to create more sliding speed down the chute by swinging harder and faster. Naturally, I didn't want to be the old duffer, so I gave myself an extra-hard swing and then held on to the bar just a bit too long. The result was I launched myself too high into the air. For a brief second I saw my feet against a blur of stars, and then I slammed down hard midway on the slide. The next thing I felt was landing smack on my tailbone at the back of the hay box—where most of the hay had been kicked out. For a few seconds I was seeing stars again. It felt as though I would never stand again, and I was positive I'd broken my tailbone! It turned out to be just a bad bruise, but it rendered the rest of my weekend a painful expedition.

The year 2000 saw both the ending of the hands-on Burning Man and the dawn of a new mechanized era. We participated in the final raising of the Man by hand, and it seemed a fitting farewell to the old method of doing things. The following year the team of hardy volunteers once needed to raise the Man would be replaced by a crane.

Despite some cool weather, the theme had been a great success, and we all felt that Burning Man was on the rise. This was a brand-new millennium, and the event would enter into an unprecedented period of growth. The following year would introduce substantial changes. The Man would gain an additional twenty feet in height, thanks to a bold A-shaped plinth. Over the next decade Larry's themes would become a driving force both in developing formal installation art and in shaping a community based on expression and participation.

But before we bid a formal farewell to the wild ol' days, there was one last gasp of renegade tomfoolery. We gathered for the Burn in 2000 expecting to bid a raucous welcome to the millennium, and indeed the professional pyrotechnics were spectacular. The organization had passed the point where Kimric's amateur pyro and John Law's bits of neon would satisfy the expectations of larger crowds. There were safety concerns as well by then, so from that point on the organization hired "pros from Dover" to wow the attendees. With the crowd roaring and fireworks spouting like a fountain from ports all up

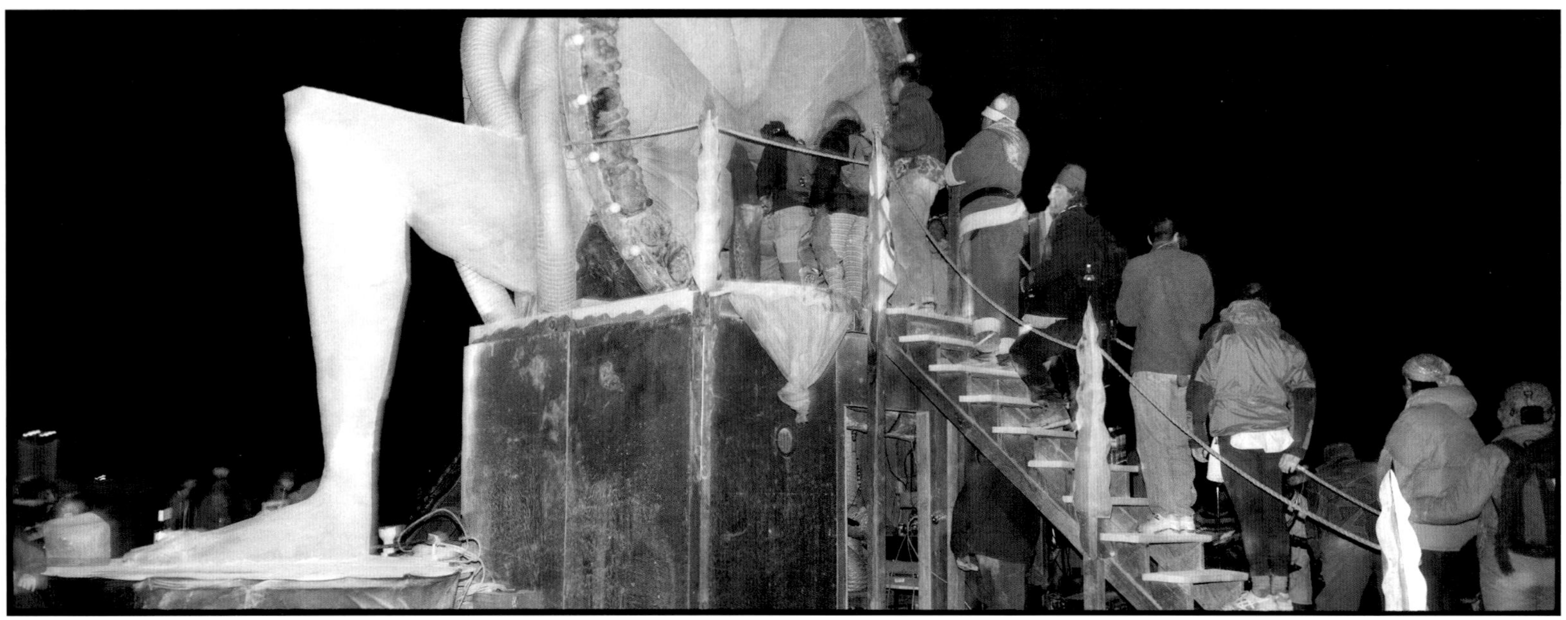

A journey through Anus *could turn out to be a long slide to a bruising finale.*

In the distance shimmered an elegant edifice, and it offered a respite and succor to all.

and down the figure, a naked streaker ran up the back steps, raised his arms in triumph, and then ran down the front steps, where he was tackled by firefighters. I imagined this as a naked "Body" running amok in a blazing homage to the frontier days of Burning Man.

There has always been a metaphysical aspect to Burning Man. It's in the way people respond to their first steps on the playa and the way they sit transfixed by the rising sun as if they've never really seen it before. Of course it's been there from the beginning in their emotional as well as visceral responses to fire. There was never a Burn that didn't touch the crowd and strike a spiritual chord. At least it did with the ones sober enough to appreciate it. This is ancient stuff, and virtually every Burner feels a twinge of emotional rapport with the Man when he is fully engulfed in flames. However, there was never a spiritual or meditative means to express those deeper sympathies when the majority of the crowd was screaming their brains out.

Part of the city plan for Hualapai Flat had required street lighting, and there had always been a need for visual guides at night. Larry had designed the first lantern spires in 1993. At first the twenty-four kerosene lanterns simply designated the four quadrants of the circle. With ever-expanding roadways in the city, the need for lighting kept growing. Steve Mobia gathered together a cadre of flame-robed volunteers to perform the nightly task of hanging the lanterns, and as Black Rock City expanded over the coming years, the number of lanterns and spires continued to grow. These days over a thousand lamps must be distributed at dusk and then retrieved again at dawn. The volunteers who do this work are called Lamplighters, and lamplighting has become one of the great cultural models in Burning Man's development. Being a Lamplighter is strictly a voluntary opportunity for vital participation at the event. Every year hundreds of Burners sign up to do a shift, or even several days. They often labor in the oppressive conditions of heat, blinding dust, and occasionally a slog through mud, but it is the most noble of Burning Man traditions, and those who participate say it is the most spiritually rewarding.

When David Best and Jack Haye built a modest *Temple of the Mind* as a tribute to their fallen friend Michael Hefflin in 2000, no one could have imagined how profoundly it would affect Burners who saw it. When the artists returned in 2001 with a larger, more pagan-inspired *Temple of Tears*, it inextricably altered the experience of attending Burning Man thereafter. This was art with a universal purpose, and because of their insight and efforts, sacred ritual on the playa had found its home.

CHAPTER 8

JOURNEY OF THE MACHINE

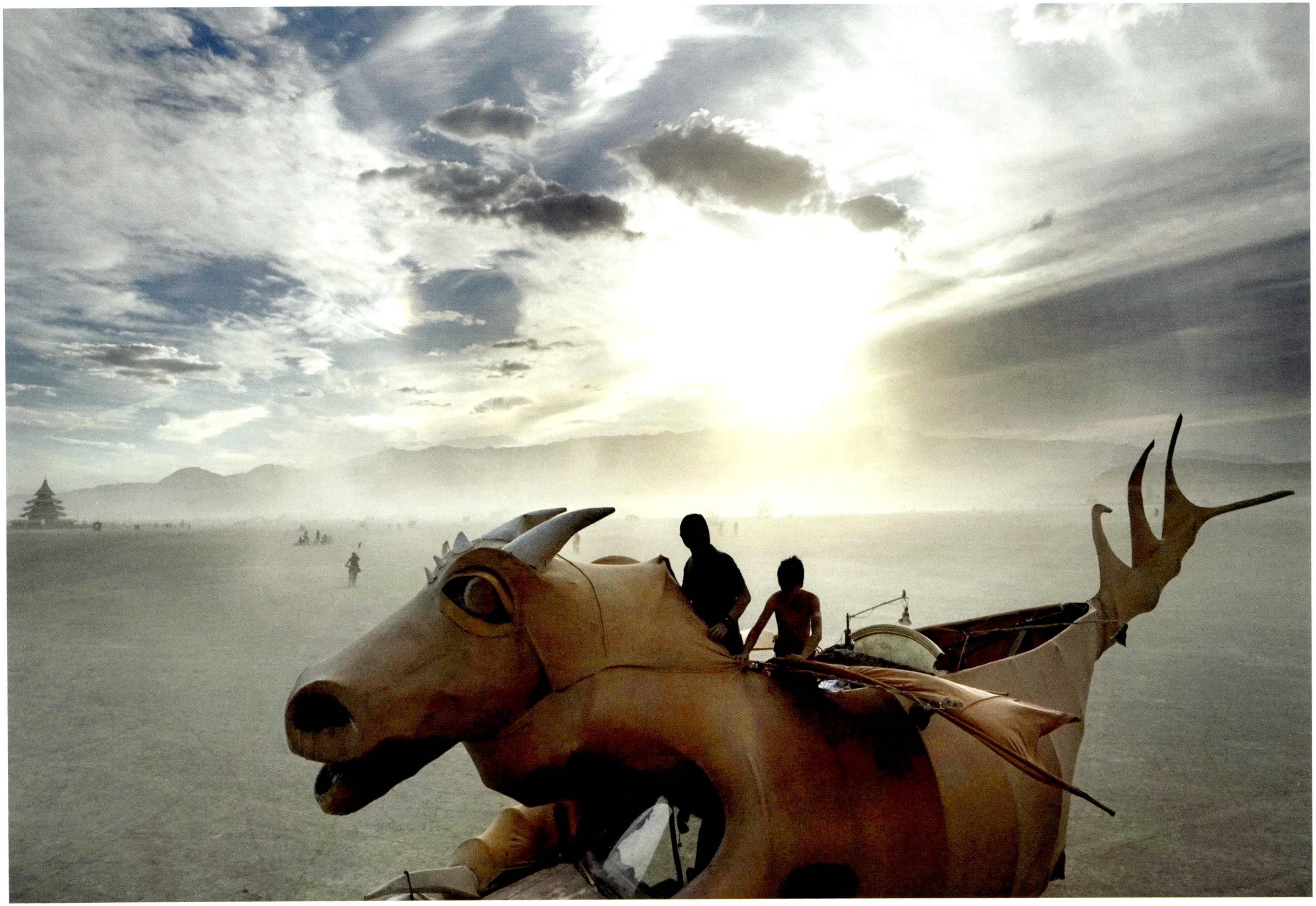

Baby Abraxas, *2016*

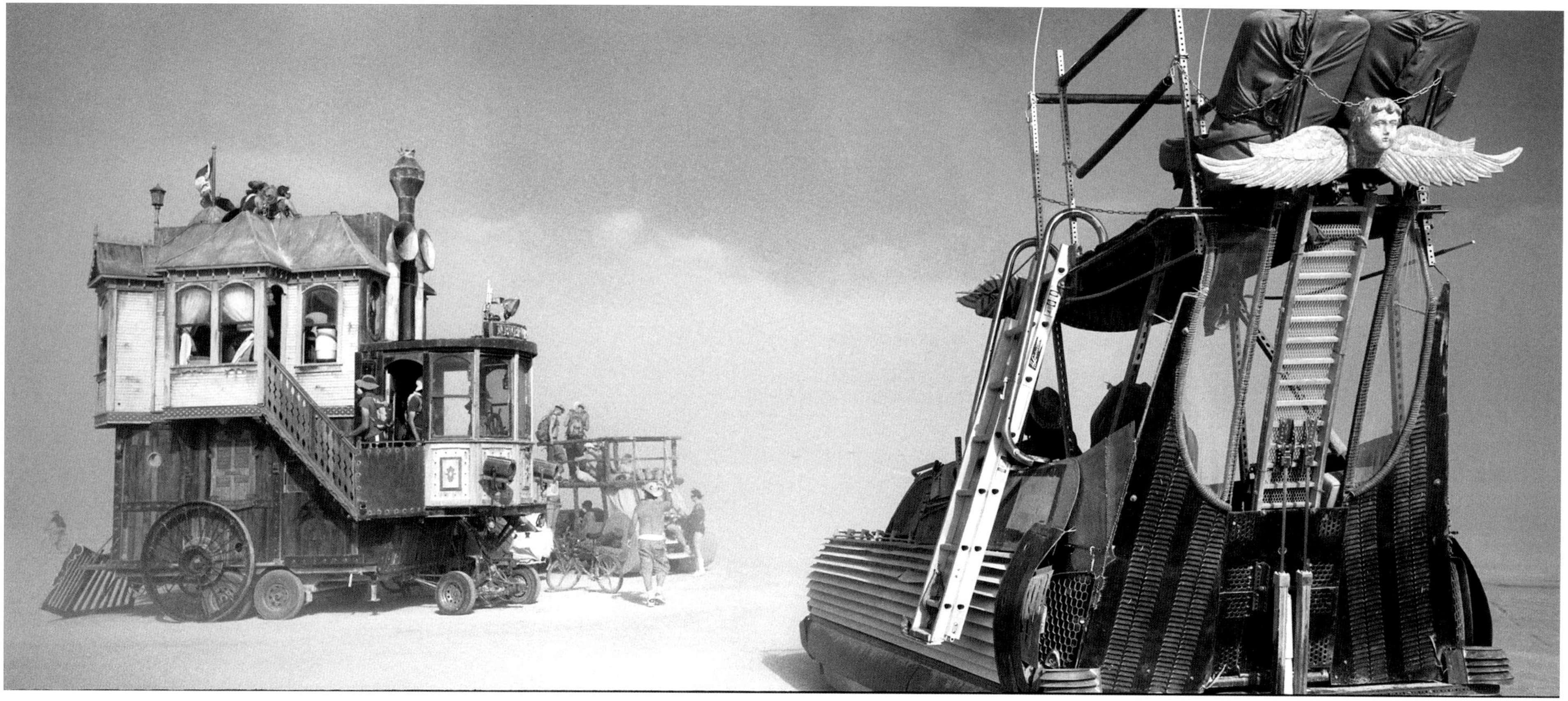

Mutant Vehicles, 2009

Art or Ego? Mutant vehicles are star attractions of the modern event—a synthesis between individual expression and community interaction. In 1991 Michael Mikel drove the first official "art car" onto the playa, his *5:04 PM,* which was the crumpled result of San Francisco's 1989 earthquake. Although most early art cars were vintage American sedans covered with layers of plastic statuary, *5:04* was created by a chunk of building falling onto its trunk lid. Like the infamous mullet, the front end was an ordinary 1970s Lincoln junker, while the back was where lucky Burners could snuggle in the cavernous cavity and party across the playa. While the appearance of a mutant is the artful expression of its creators, the essence even in the early days was as a means of communal interaction.

These days the playa is crisscrossed with mobile contraptions depicting every visual parody known to humankind. Two of the most venerable are *Neverwas Haul* and David Best's *Rocket Car.* The *Rocket* was built on an old Cadillac chassis and still turns heads. *Neverwas Haul* is a rolling steampunk Victorian mansion and has been a major playa attraction for several years. Mutant vehicles have also morphed into mobile techno blasters, which attract thousands of all-night dancers. *Abraxas the Golden Dragon* has been rockin' the playa since 2006. It joins sonic-enhanced mobile dance wagons like *Robot Heart, Dancetronauts,* and *Mayan Warrior* in shaking the playa till sunrise. They will blast EDM (electronic dance music) all night long, and their bleary-eyed, exhausted fans will straggle home looking like they've paid a hefty price for the honor.

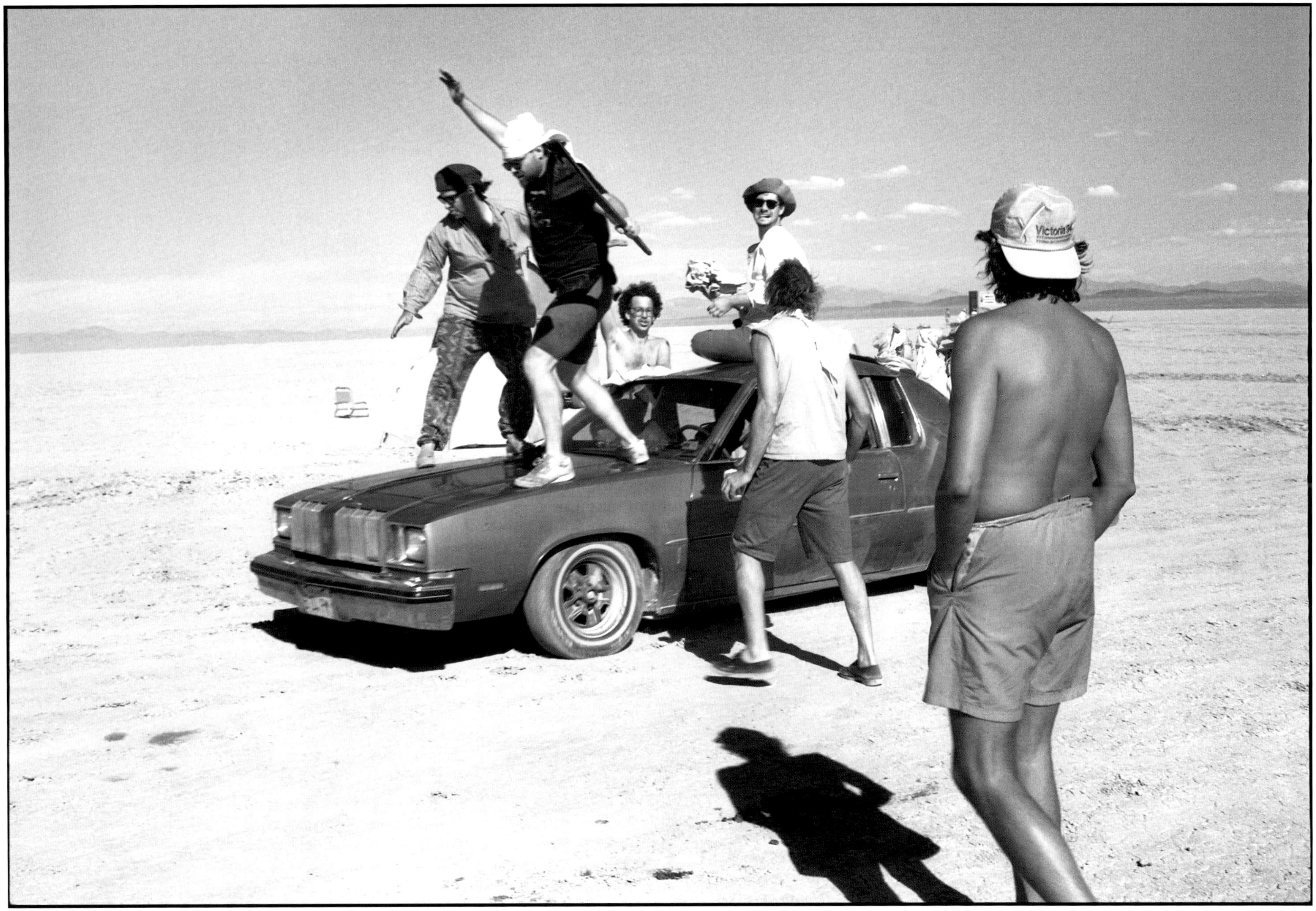

5:04 PM *Ride, 1991*

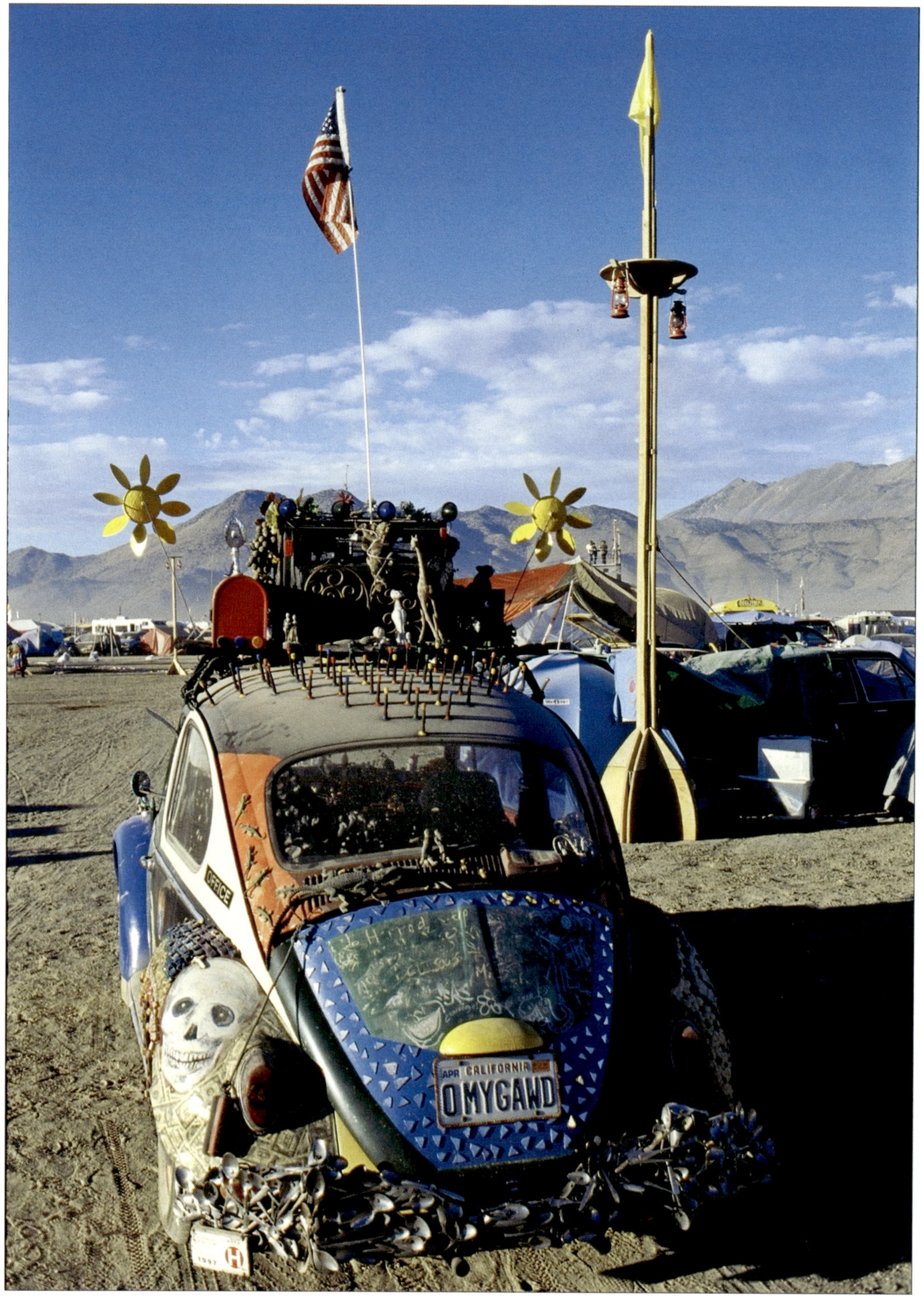

O My Gawd!, *1995*

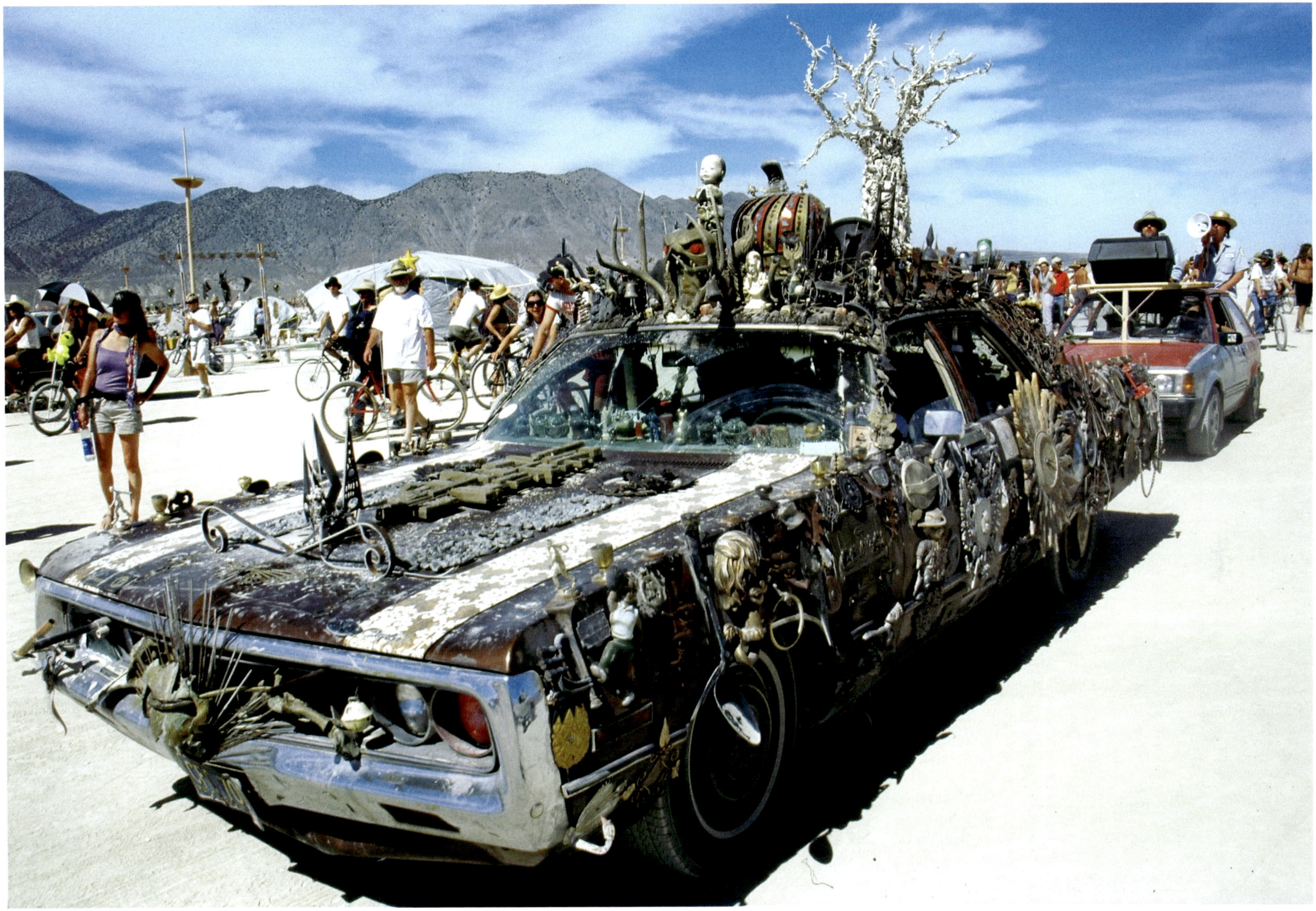

Jesus Chrysler Art Car, *1998*

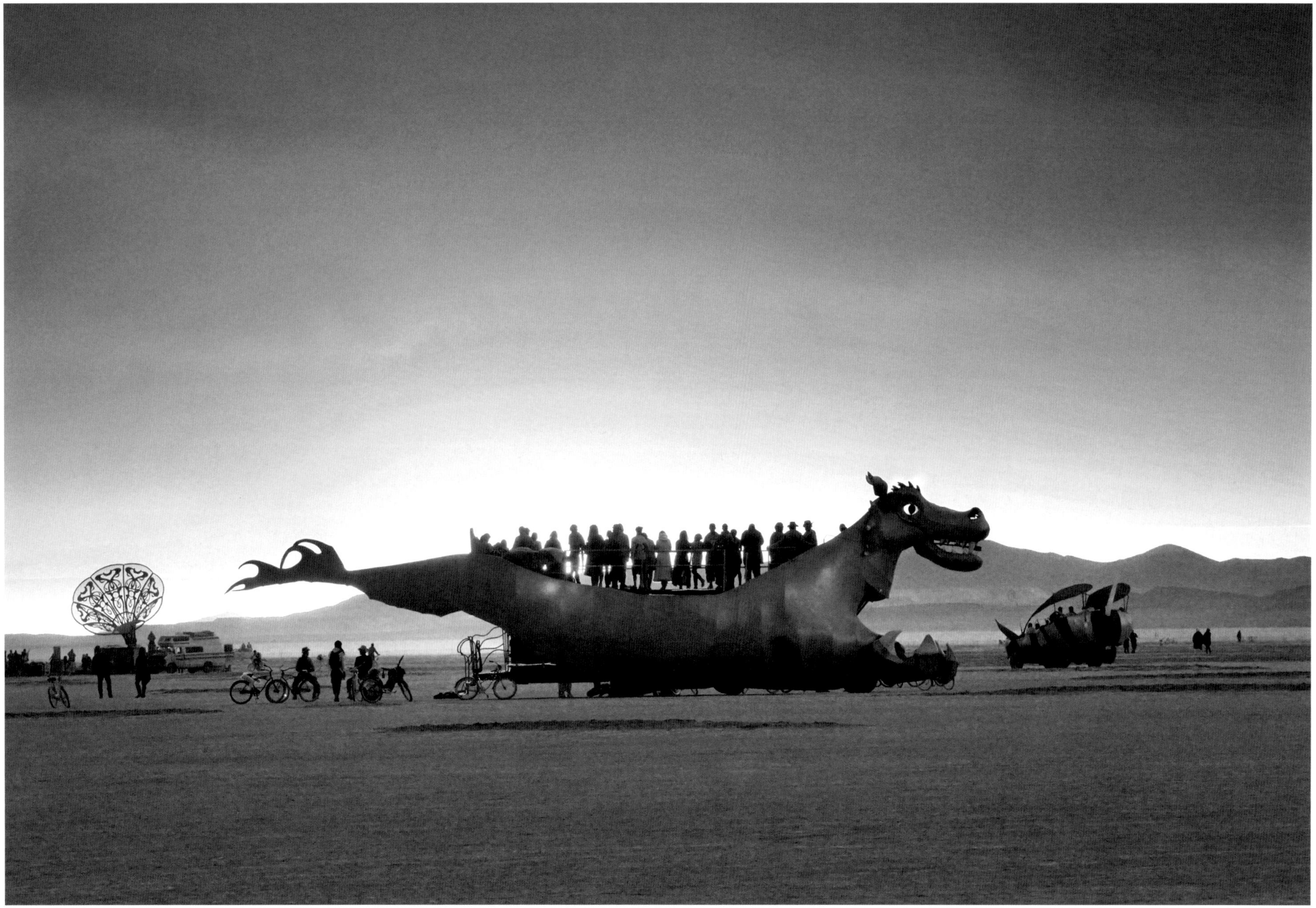

Abraxas *Sunrise, 2016*

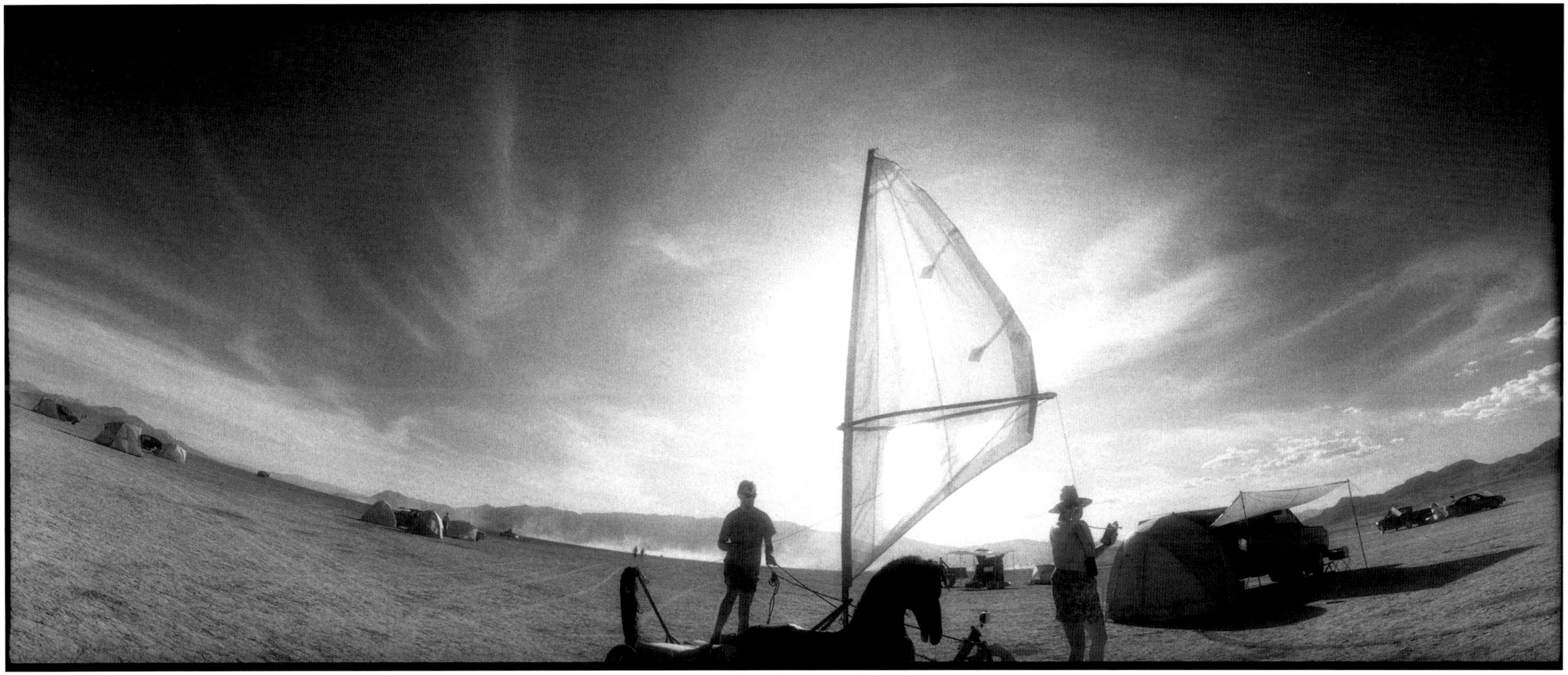

Myra the Horse, 1993

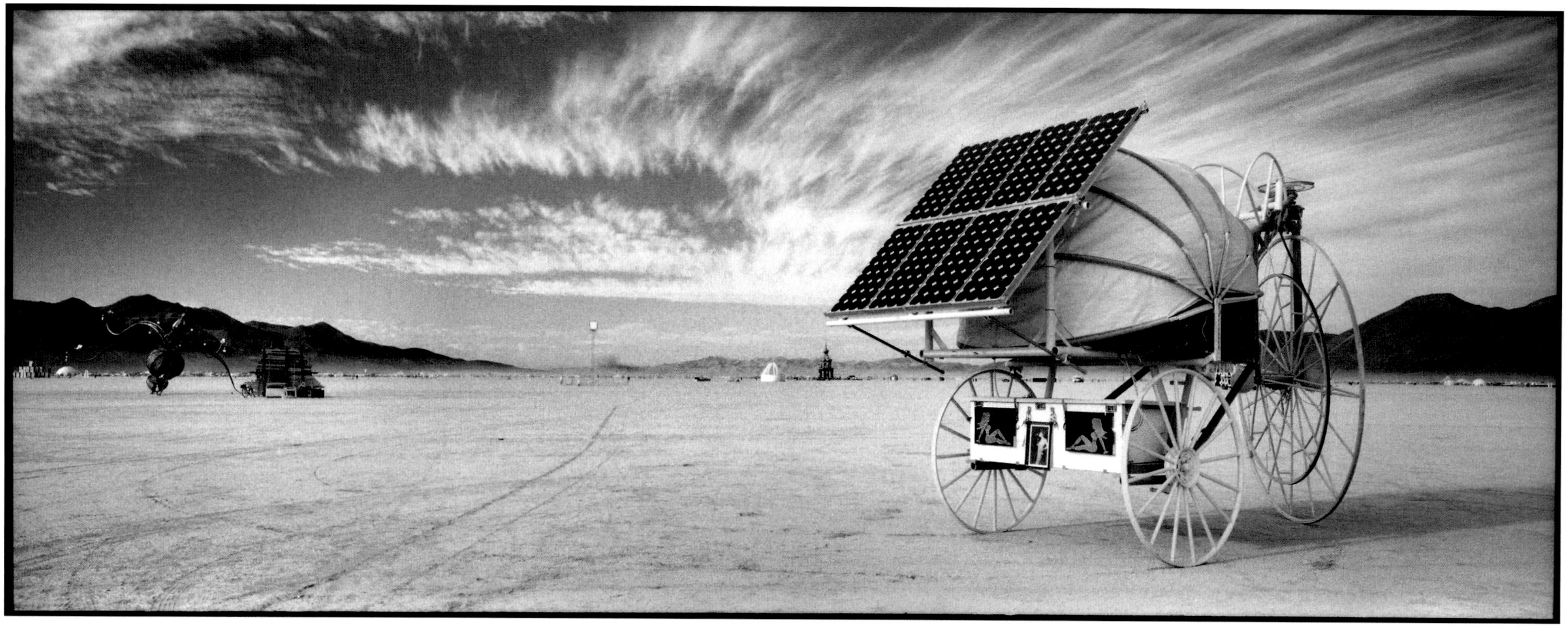

Daisy Solar Wagon, *2003*

Art cars were in existence before Burning Man moved to the playa. The famous Houston Art Car Parade originated in 1986, ironically the same year as the first Baker Beach Burn. I'm not sure of the year for the playa's first decorated car, but I believe there was an Art Car Camp in 1995, and I remember taking a picture of Harrod Blank's *O My Gawd!* that year. There was also Tom Kennedy's *Ripper the Friendly Shark*. Mutant vehicles morphed from art cars, and my simple definition is that Harrod's globe-festooned VW was an art car, and *Ripper* was a mutant vehicle. One is an elaborately artified car; the other resembles something other than a car.

My favorite mutant vehicles are expressions of the owner-artist's personality. I remember one three-wheeled wagon that was a totally individualized combination of steampunk buggy and solar-powered trike. I loved its balance of vintage design and contemporary engineering, and with its girlie mud flaps below an array of solar panels, it managed to look both sexist and progressive! One of the contemporary playa's perennial favorites is our friend Jeannie Schulz's *Pig Pen*, a tribute to her beloved husband, cartoonist Charles Schulz. Regardless of the level of execution, the mutant vehicle represents one of the purest forms of Gifting on the playa. The largest are basically musical people movers. Most welcome strangers aboard, and many drivers spend hours roaming the playa with Burners hopping on and off at regular intervals. During the Burn many hundreds hang on to every available inch of the taller mutants in hopes of getting a view above the multitudes.

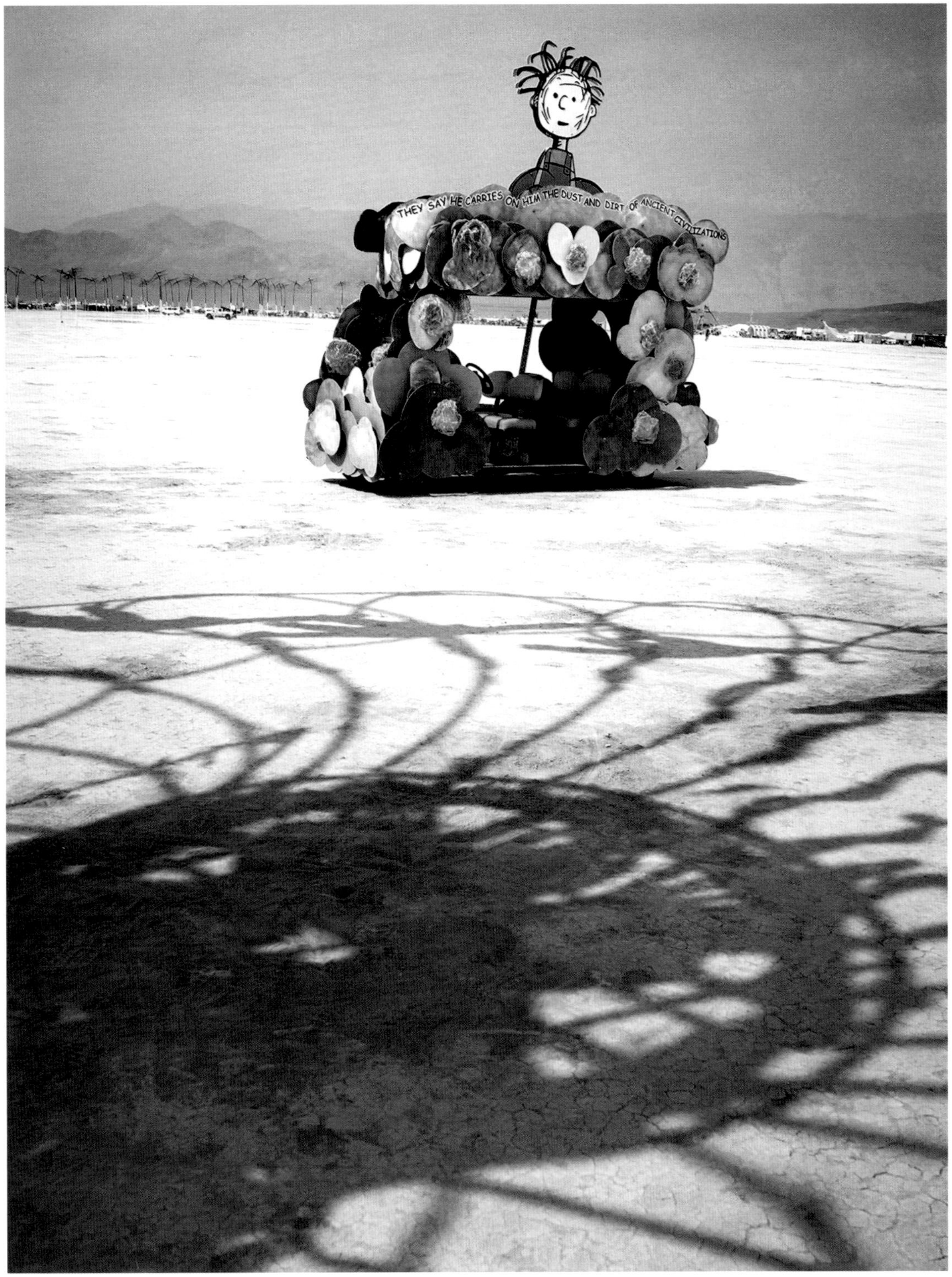
THEY SAY HE CARRIES ON HIM THE DUST AND DIRT OF ANCIENT CIVILIZATIONS

Pig Pen, *2012*

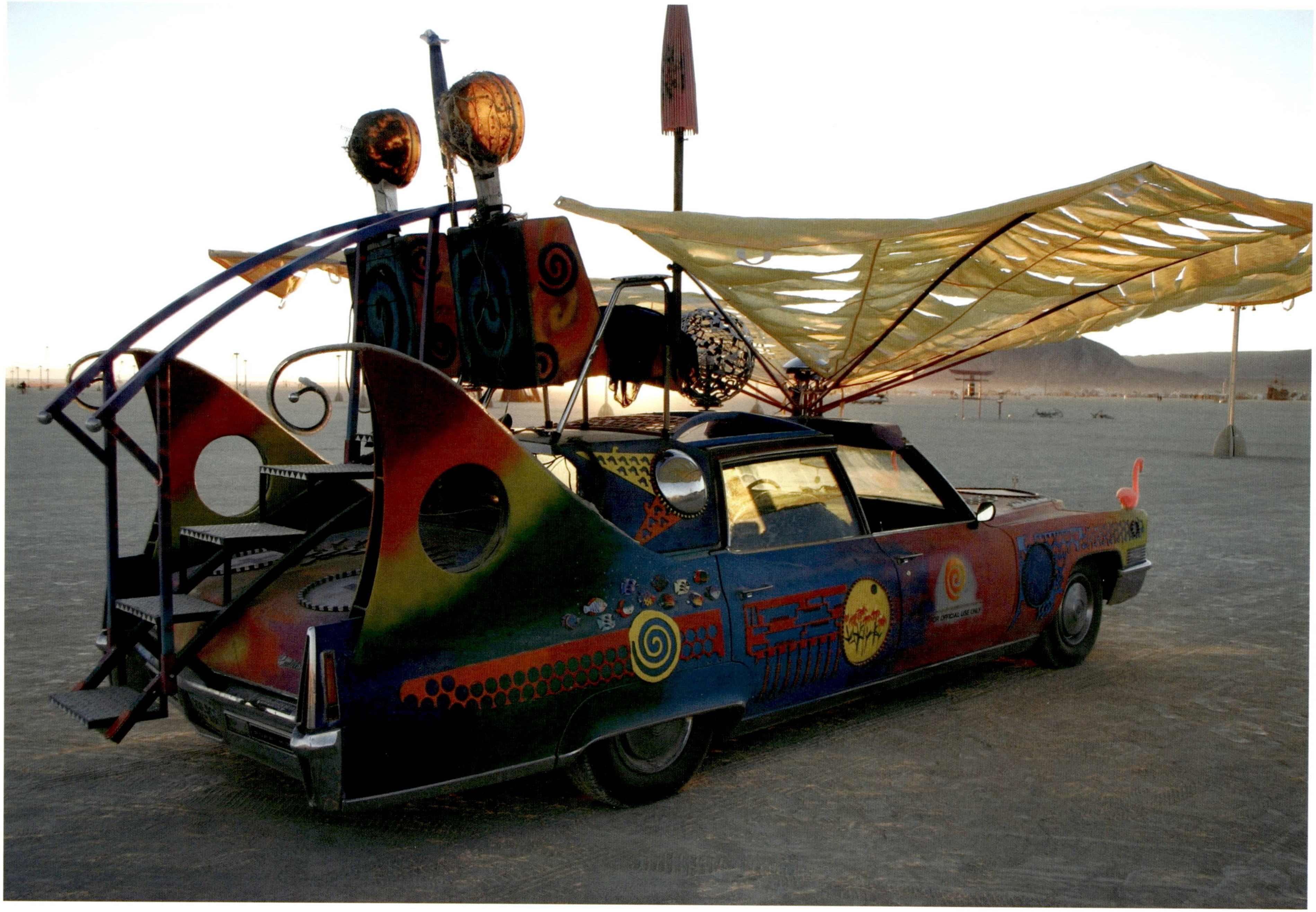

Sunrise Caddy, *2005*

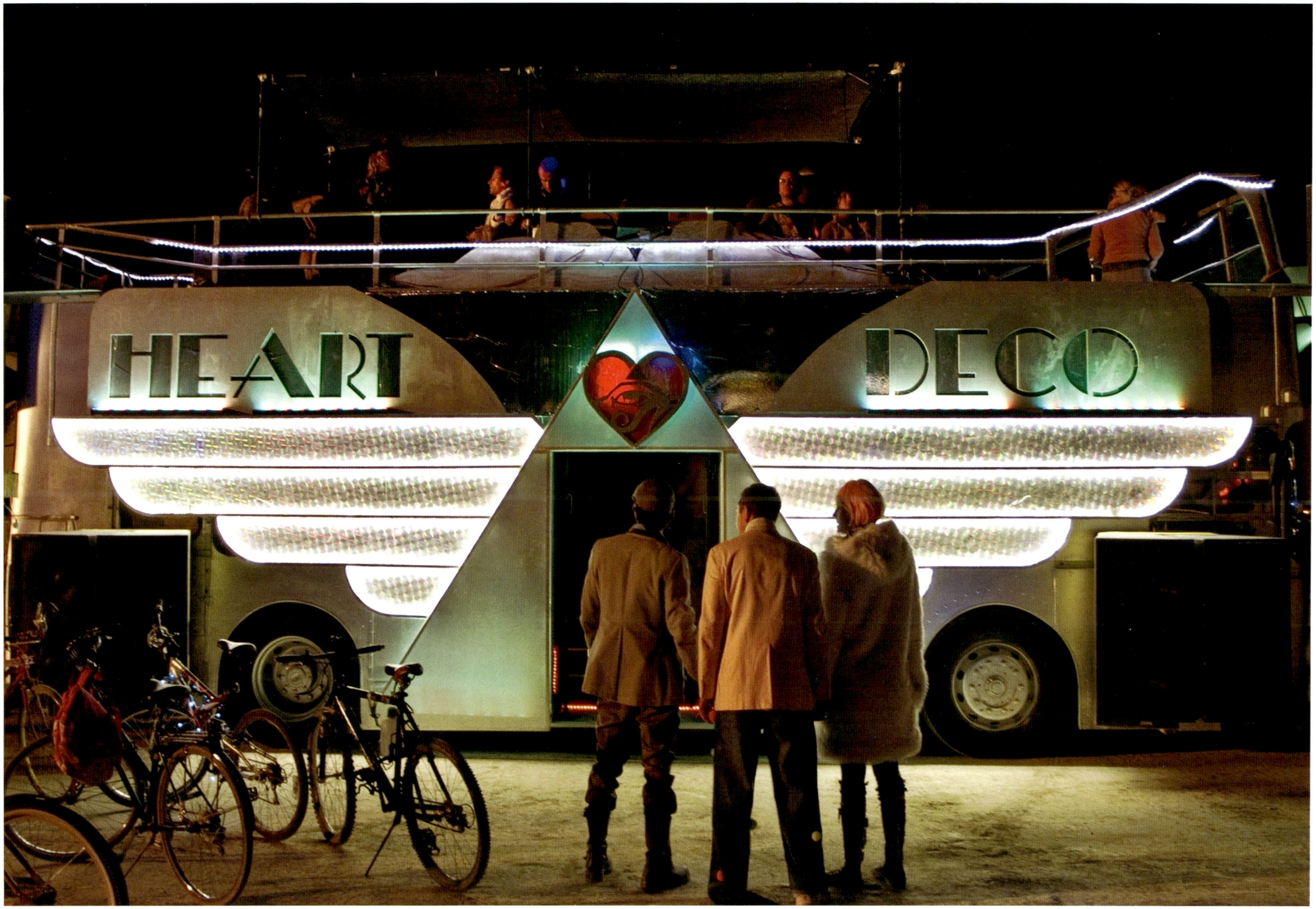

Heart Deco, *2011*

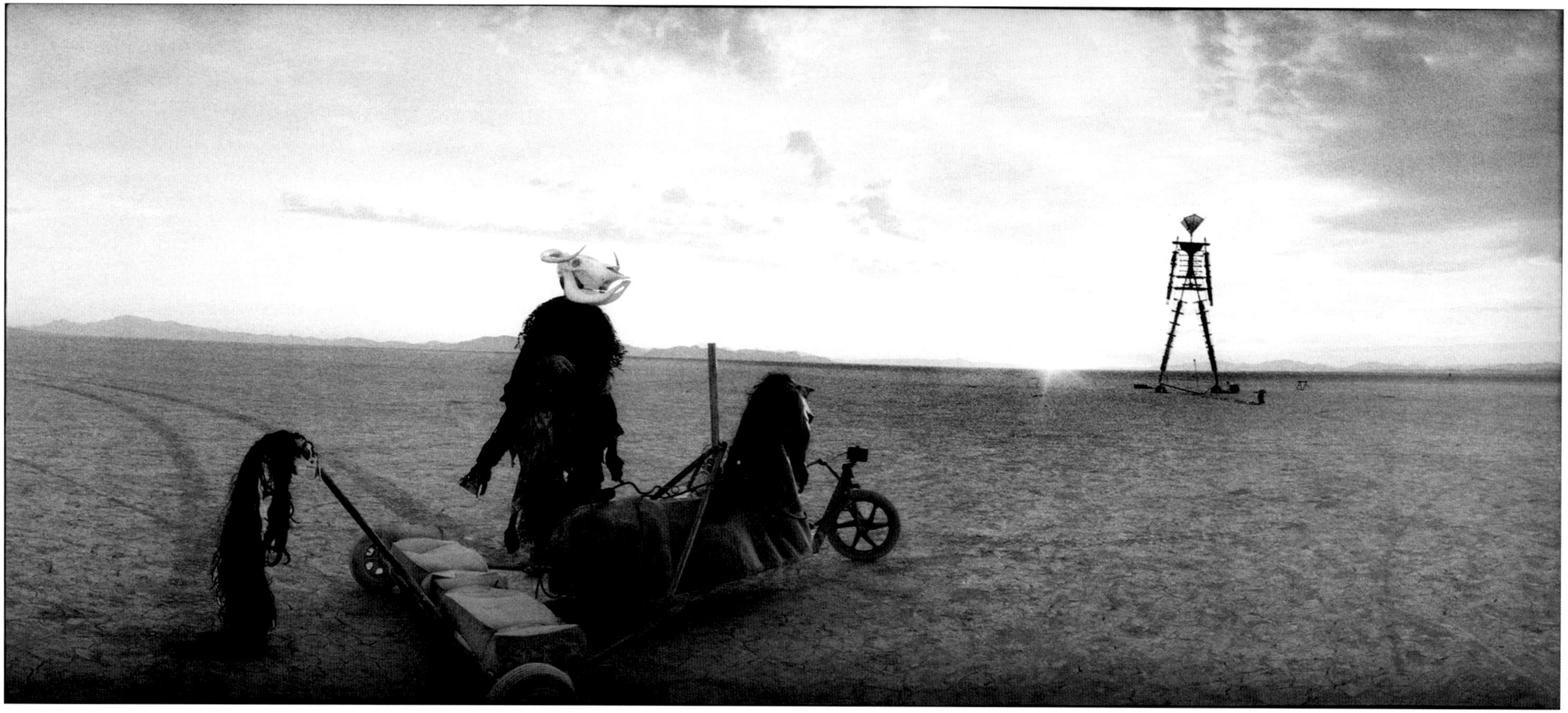

Java Cow Sunrise, 1993

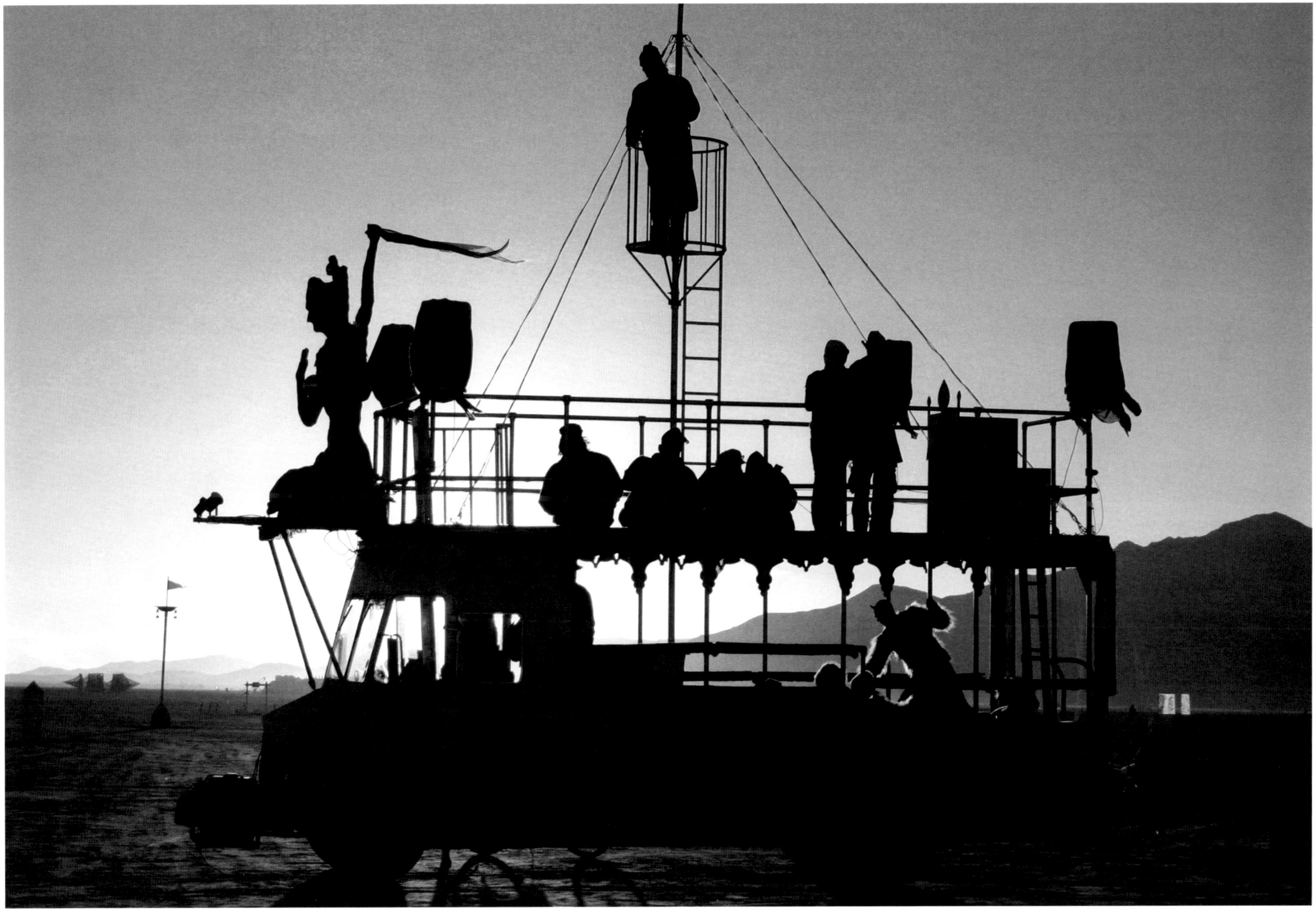

Karma Kar, *2004*

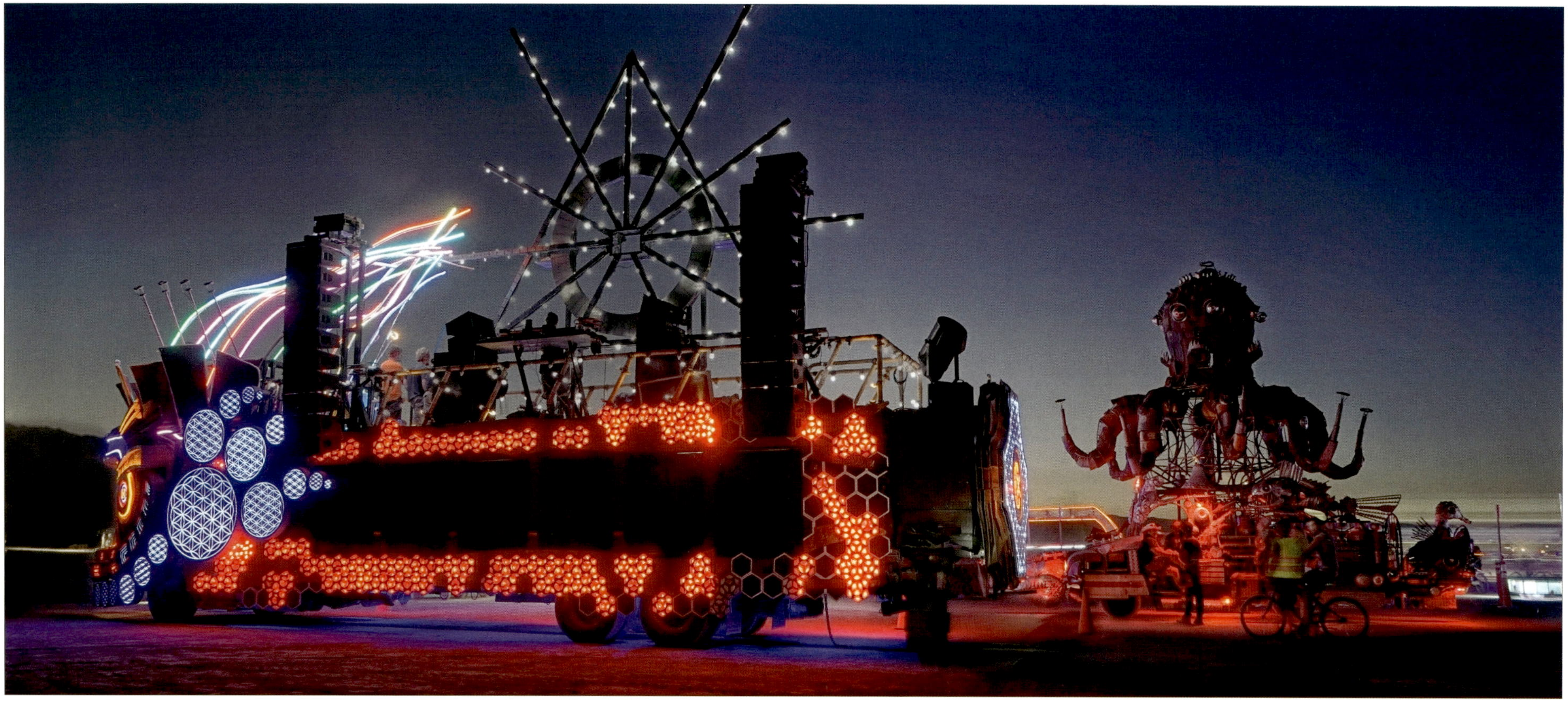

Mutant Encounter, 2016

Clever is the key to a successful mutant vehicle, and the best ones reflect the builder's personality. Modern soundscape behemoths are often the result of spending lots of money, but putting the array of high-tech audio gear aside, the very best show the hallmarks of individual inspiration. This year I was wandering the line of mutant vehicles waiting for their night-light inspection when I happened upon the sleek new *Mayan Warrior* near *El Pulpo Mecanico*. The *Warrior* is an impeccably designed concept vehicle and sports a best-in-class audio system. It will no doubt take its place as techno royalty, but there needs to be more than dazzling style and audio excellence to become a playa classic. It requires, in my opinion, the hallmark of hands-on craftwork.

El Pulpo Mecanico in all its salvage-yard glory is in a class by itself. The brainchild of Arcata artist Duane Flatmo and flame engineer Jerry Kunkel, El Pulpo is a unique blend of salvaged materials, sculpted castings, stellar propane technology, and articulated movement. With a four-sided face, eight bulging eyes, gaping mouths, and articulated flame-spouting tentacles, *El Pulpo Mecanico* roams the playa with aplomb. Everywhere it goes it draws a crowd. It's an artist-made creation, and that's the key to being a playa legend—the likes of Loadie Camp's *Shark*, David Best's wooden cut-out festooned *Temple Bus*, Harrod Blank's *O My Gawd!*, Pepe Ozan's *Narwhal*, or any of the robotic fire belchers by DPW. The key to mutant vehicle immortality is the artist-mechanic's quirky ingenuity.

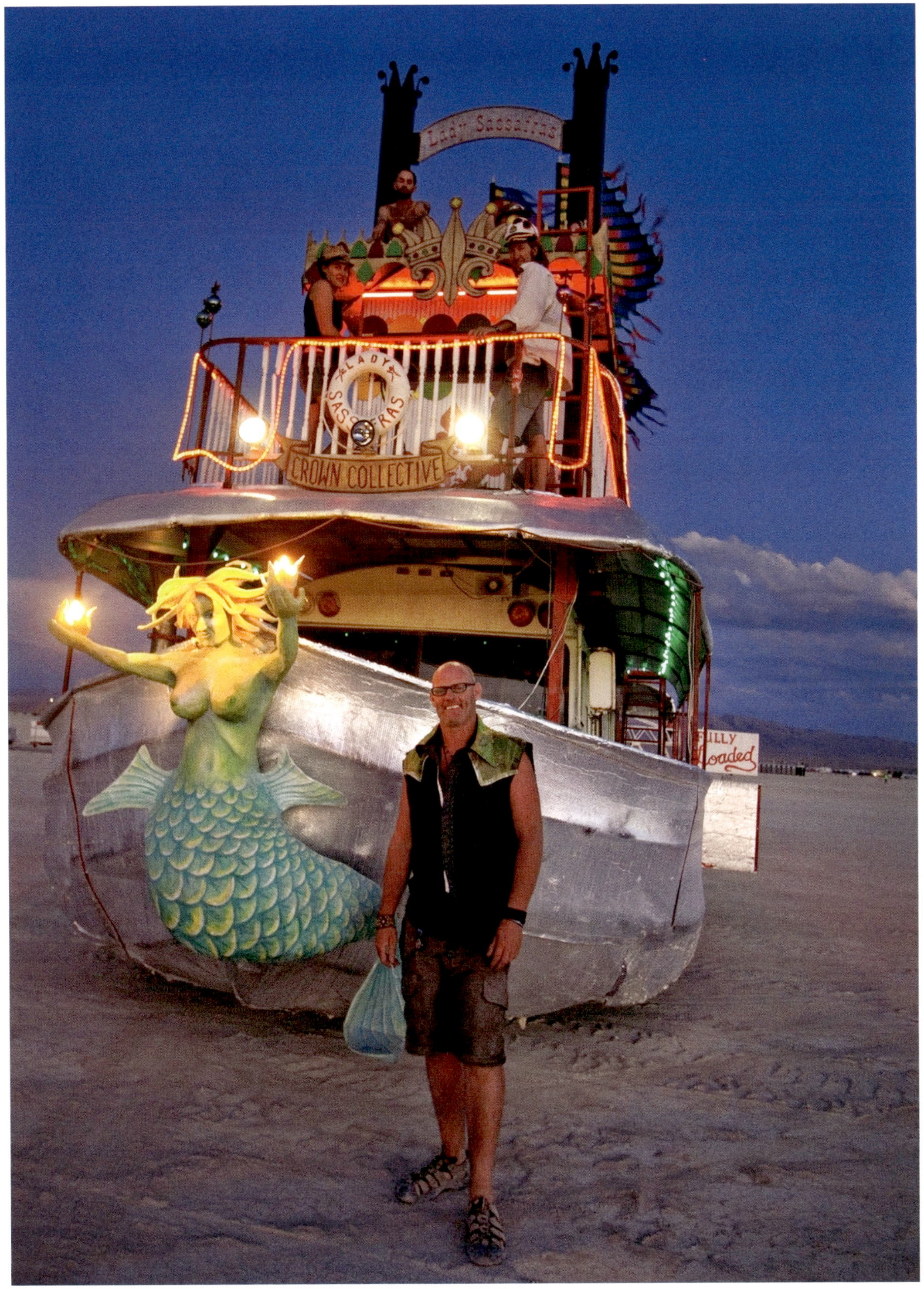

Lady Sassafras, *2011*

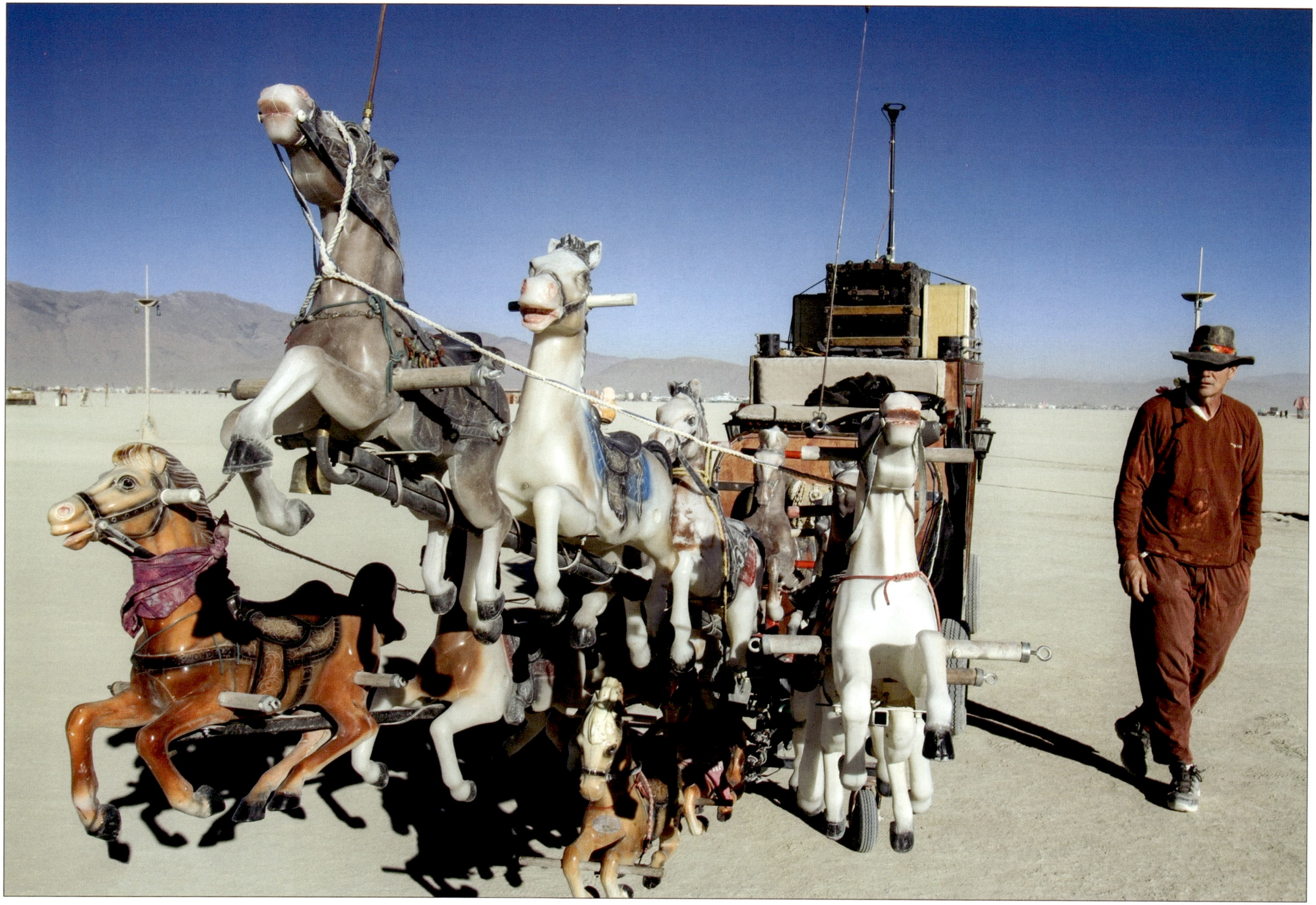

Wonder Wagon, *2012*

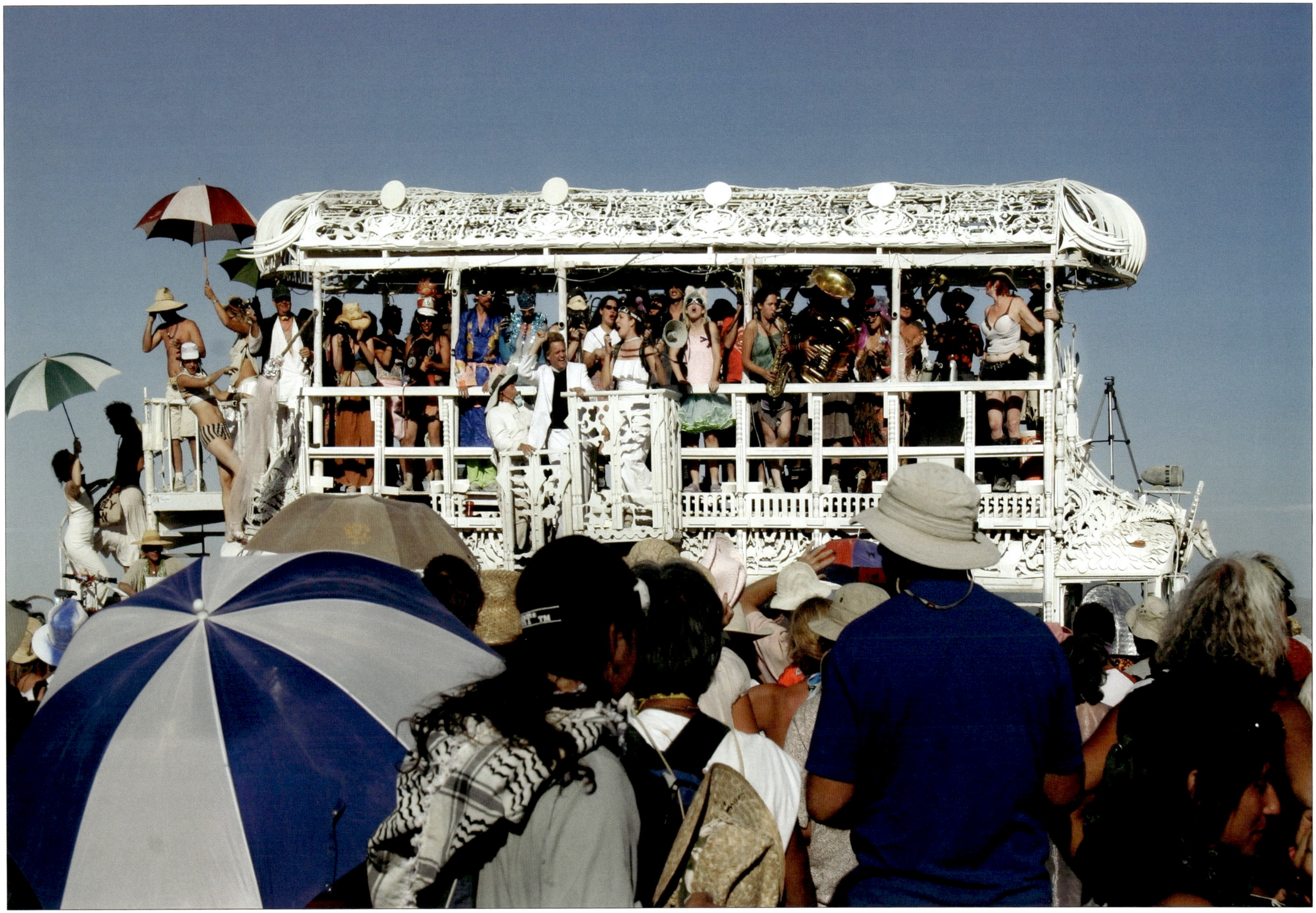

Temple Bus, *2005*

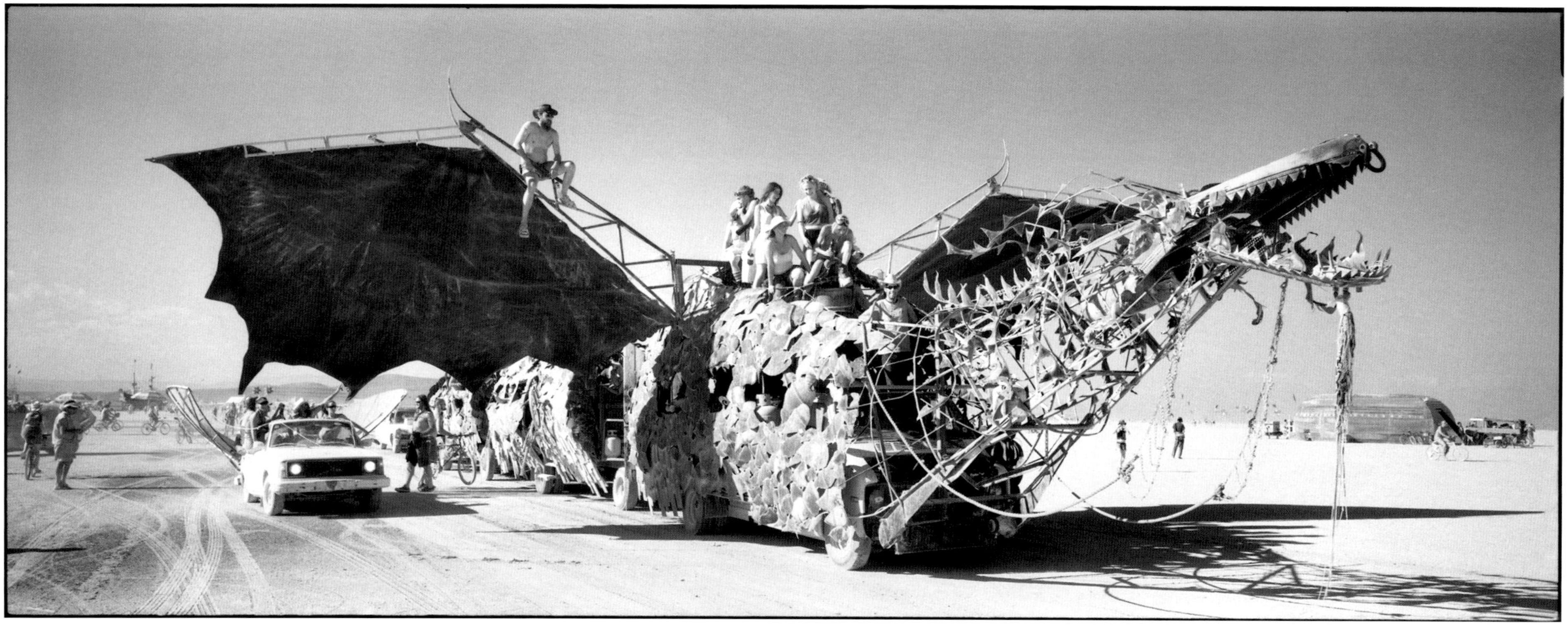

Flaming Metal Dragon, 2002

The mishmash of individual inspiration at Burning Man could generate a graduate paper on creative diversity. That's especially true when it comes to the plethora of vehicular contraptions. At midday it can be difficult to cross the Esplanade, for it is choked with a never-ending gauntlet of pedestrians, bikes, and random rolling inventions. However, mutant vehicles are more than a creative indulgence; they are the ever-present unexpected encounter and the spice that flavors the event. In a dust storm, they emerge like mythological beasts out of the swirl, and we are transported to the land of childhood fantasy. At night they are an explosion of neon and a fire-spouting beastly brigade.

Times change. The Texas-style plastic-laden sedans have given way to over-the-top behemoth sound machines, designed in Bay Area custom shops, and to artist-rendered concept vehicles, such as Andy Tibbets's *C. S. Tere* and Tom Bates and Gretchen Roosevelt's *Wonder Wagon*. These are typically the products of dedicated individual builders or a camp culture. At the other end are machine-shop monsters, which often center around fire effects, many of which are the efforts of DPW motorheads. Then there are the "jankymobiles," which are barely disguised golf carts or scooters that display minimal effort but often present parody humor and are able playa transportation. I'd personally prefer to see a majority of mom-and-pop projects to balance out the $300,000 custom-designed techno blasters. Expression must remain individual, and "artist-built" has been an enduring aesthetic from the earliest days of Art Car Camp.

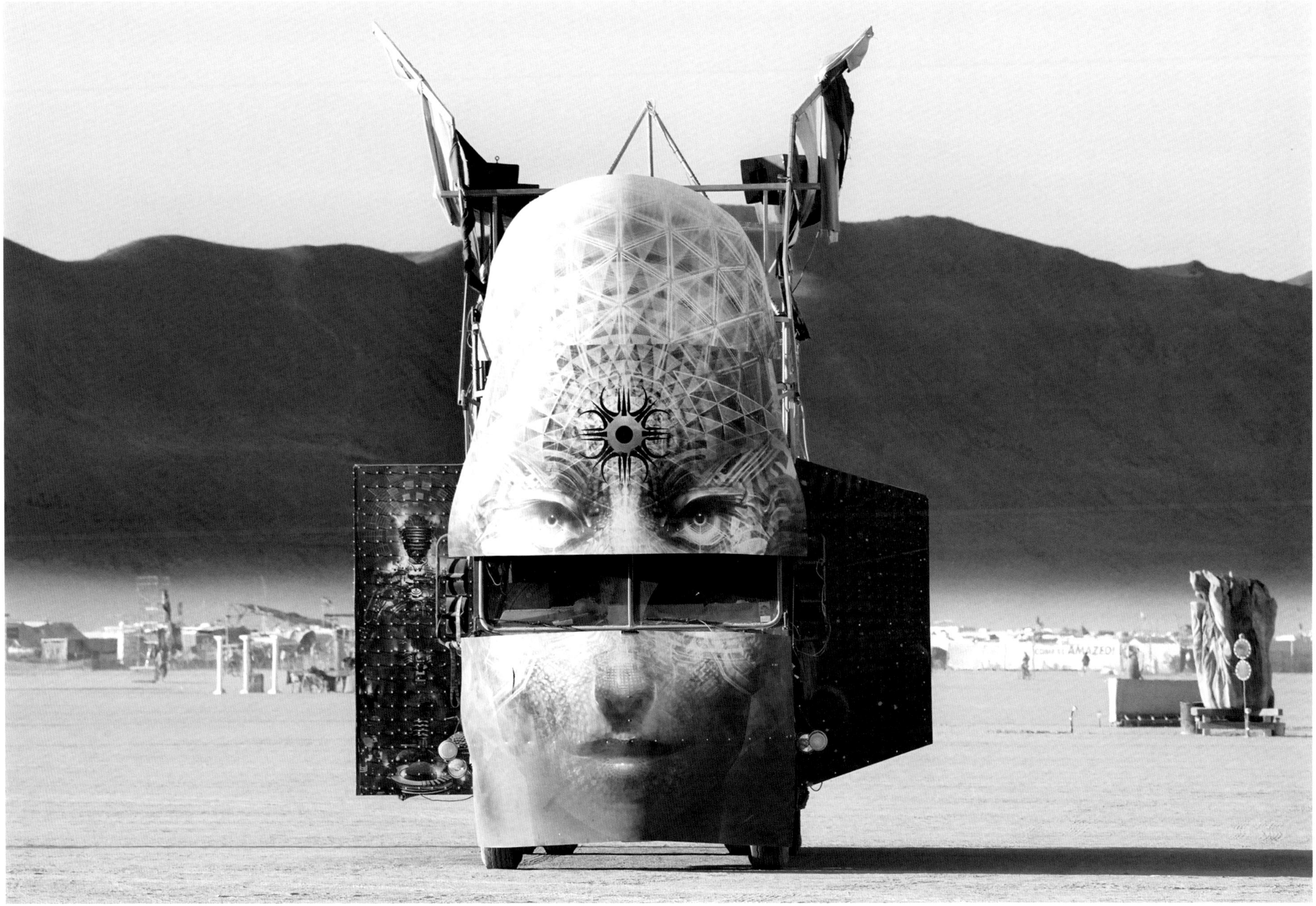

Mystic Flyer, *2016*

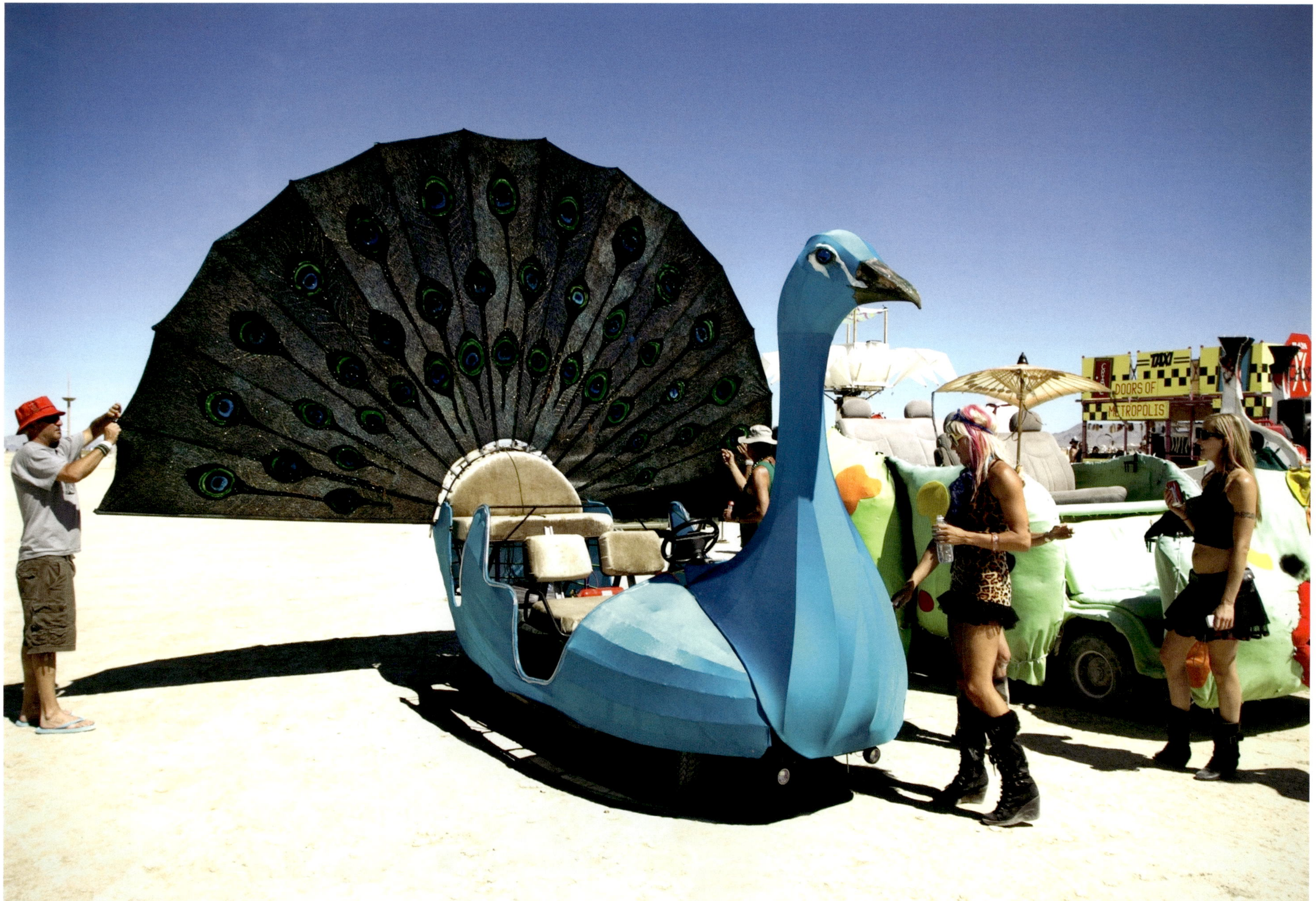

Blue Peacock, *2010*

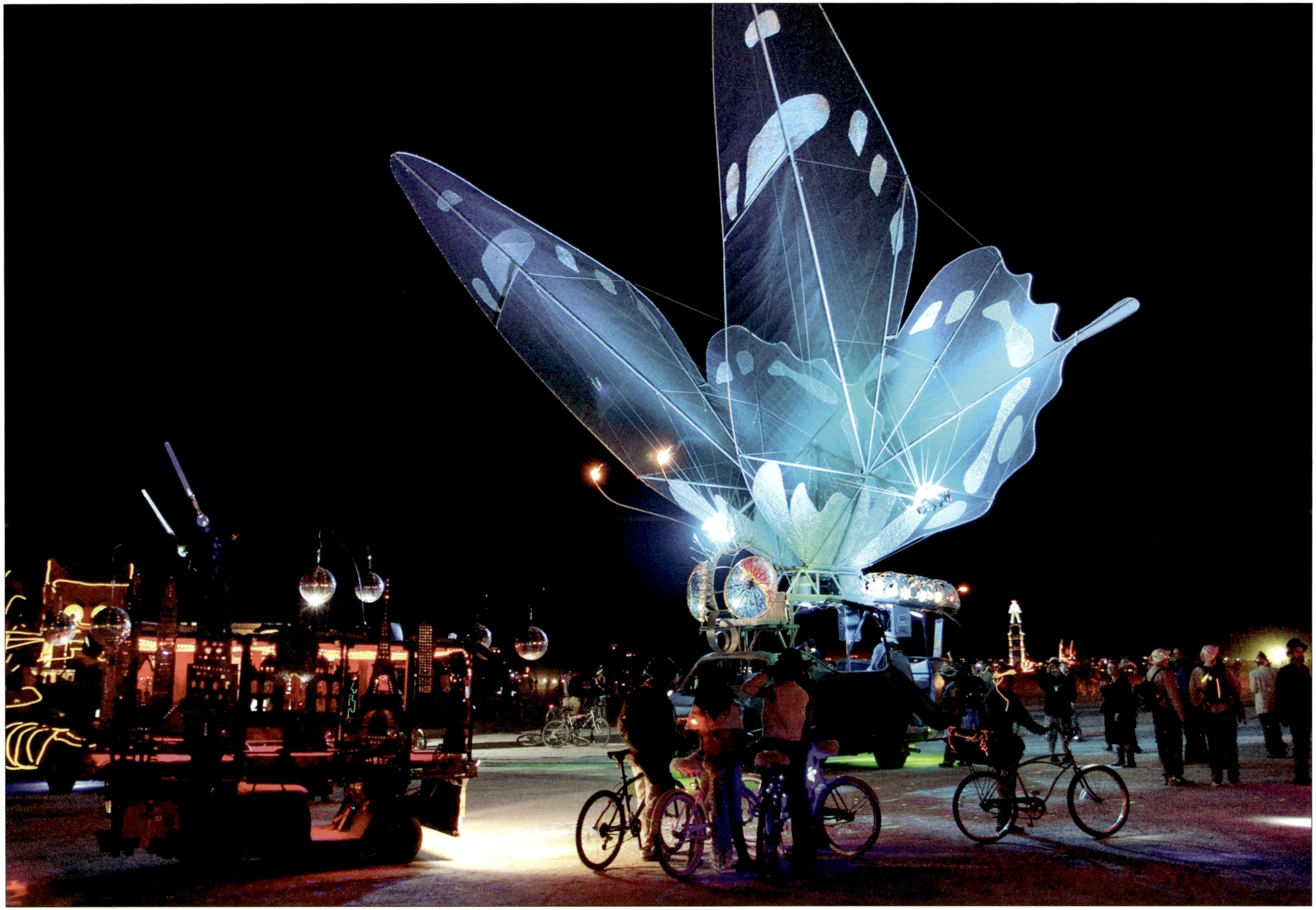

Lepidodgera, *2011*

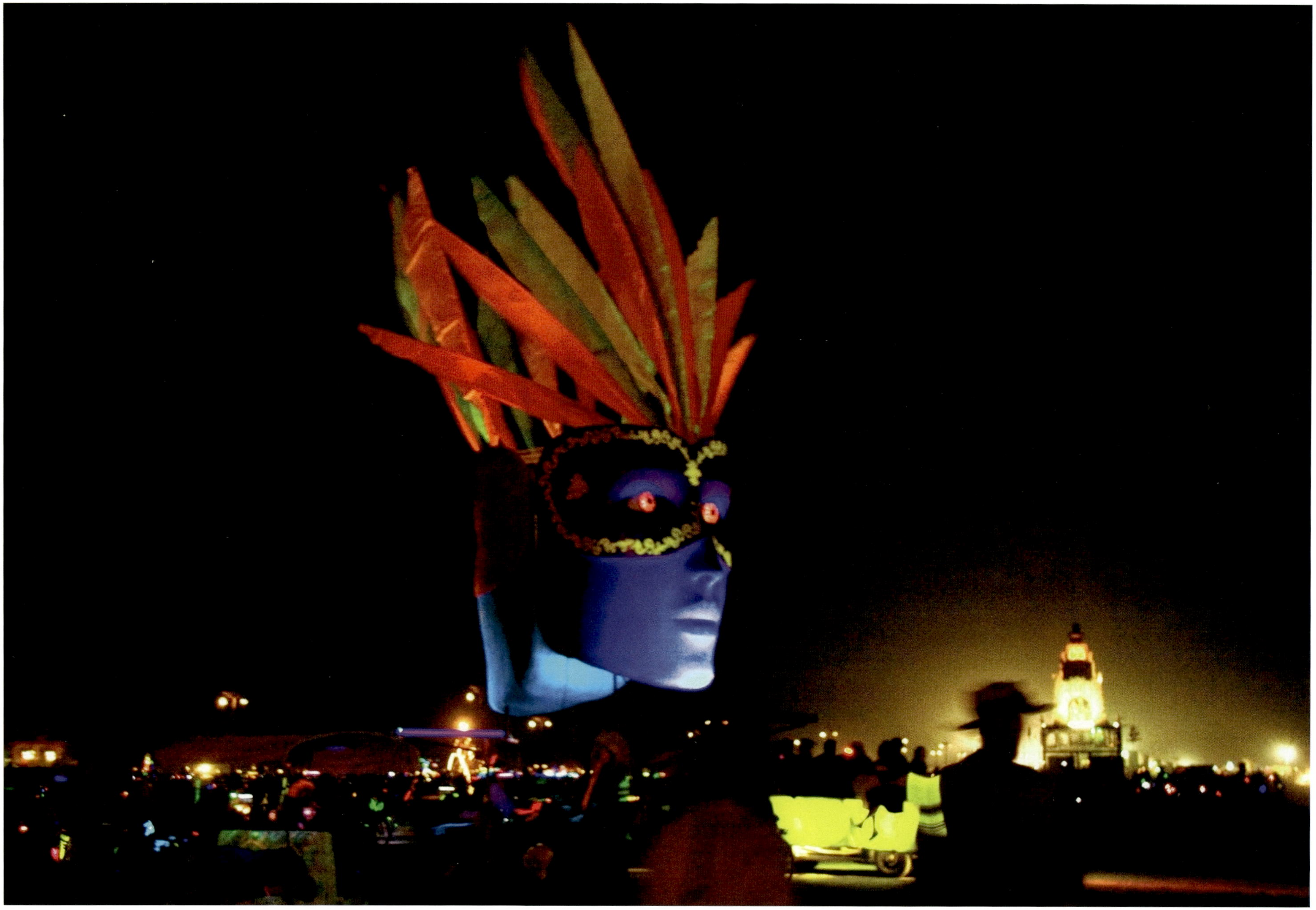

Medusa Train, *2007*

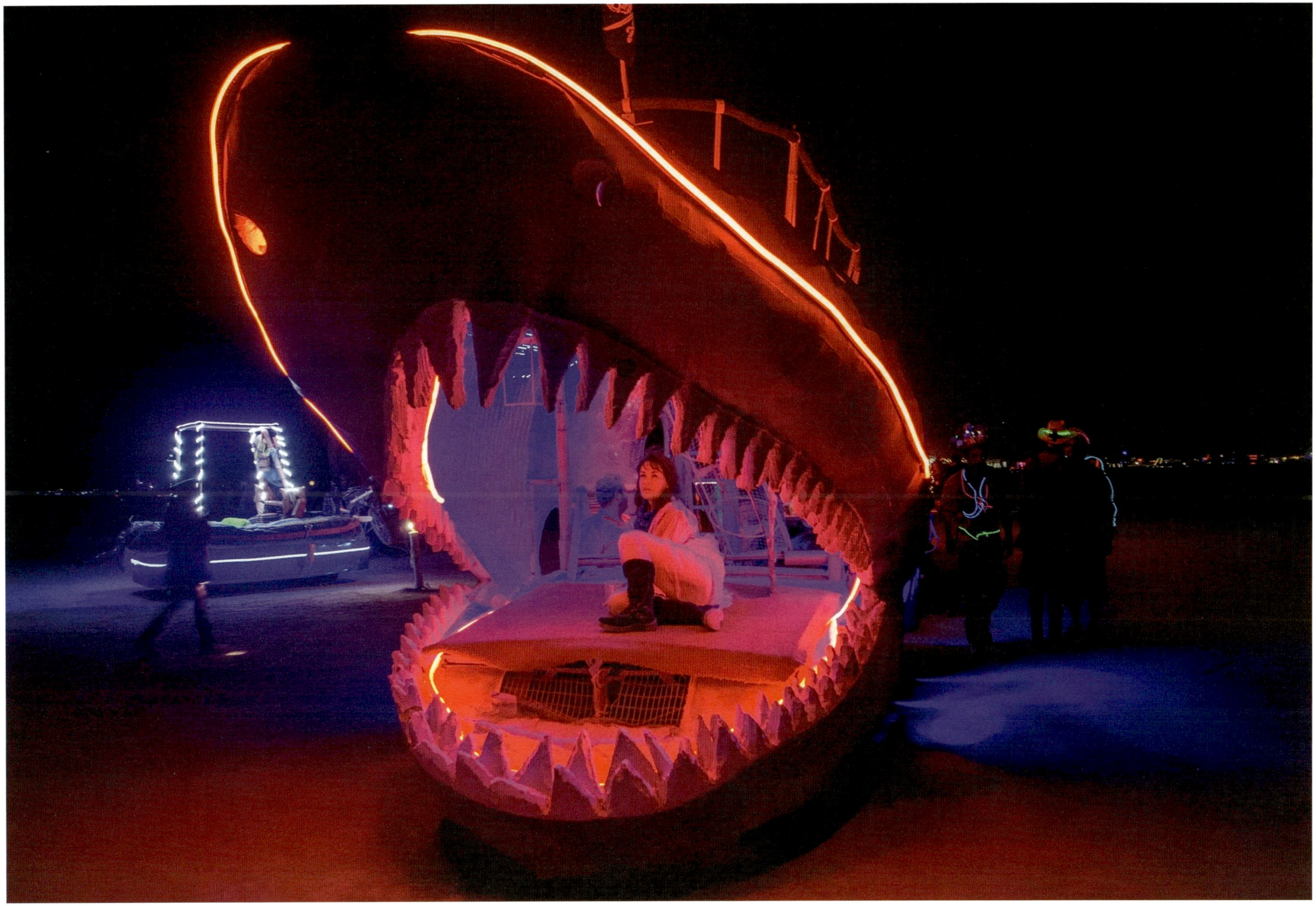

Shark Car *Maiden, 2012*

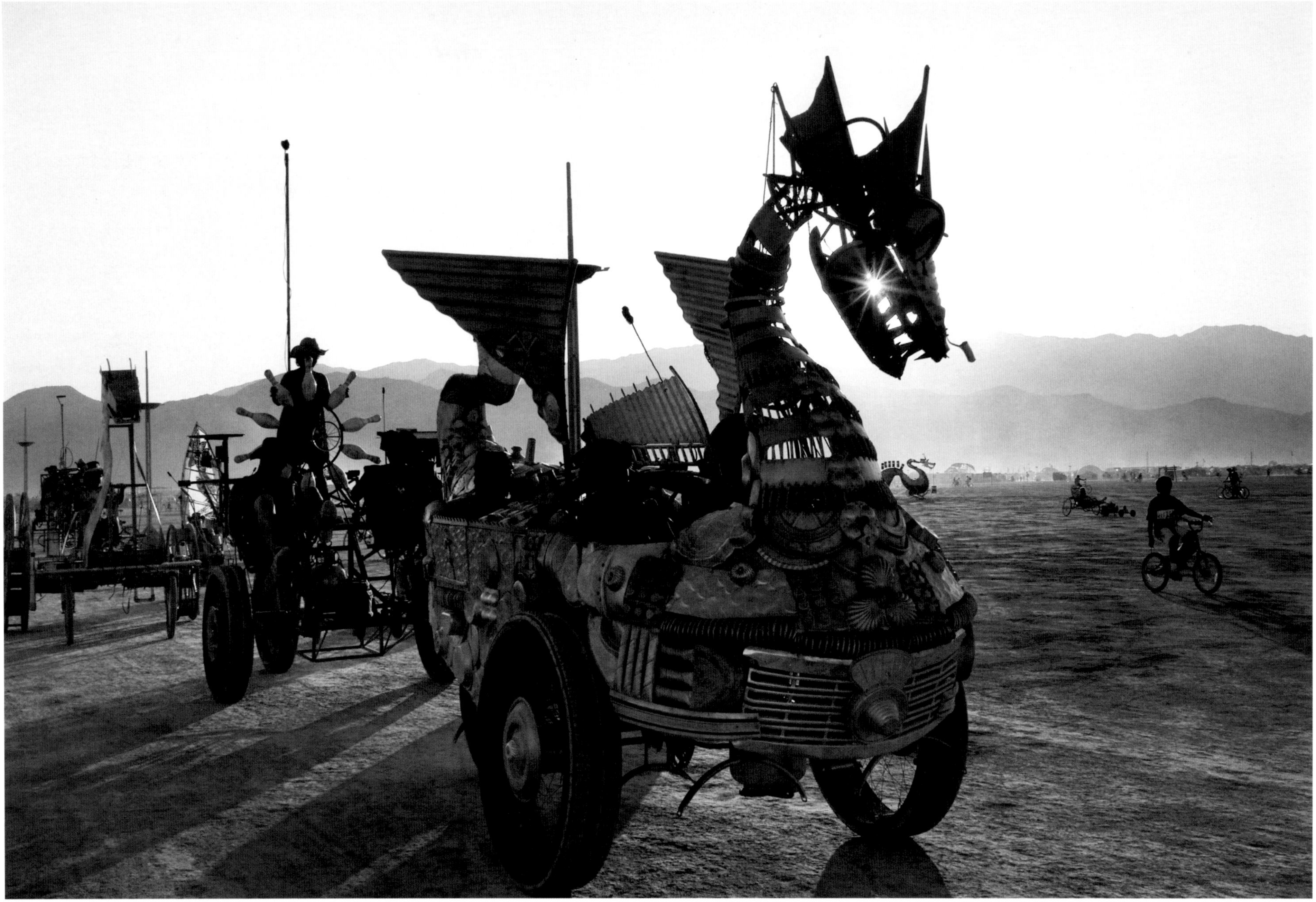

Tin Pan Dragon, *2009*

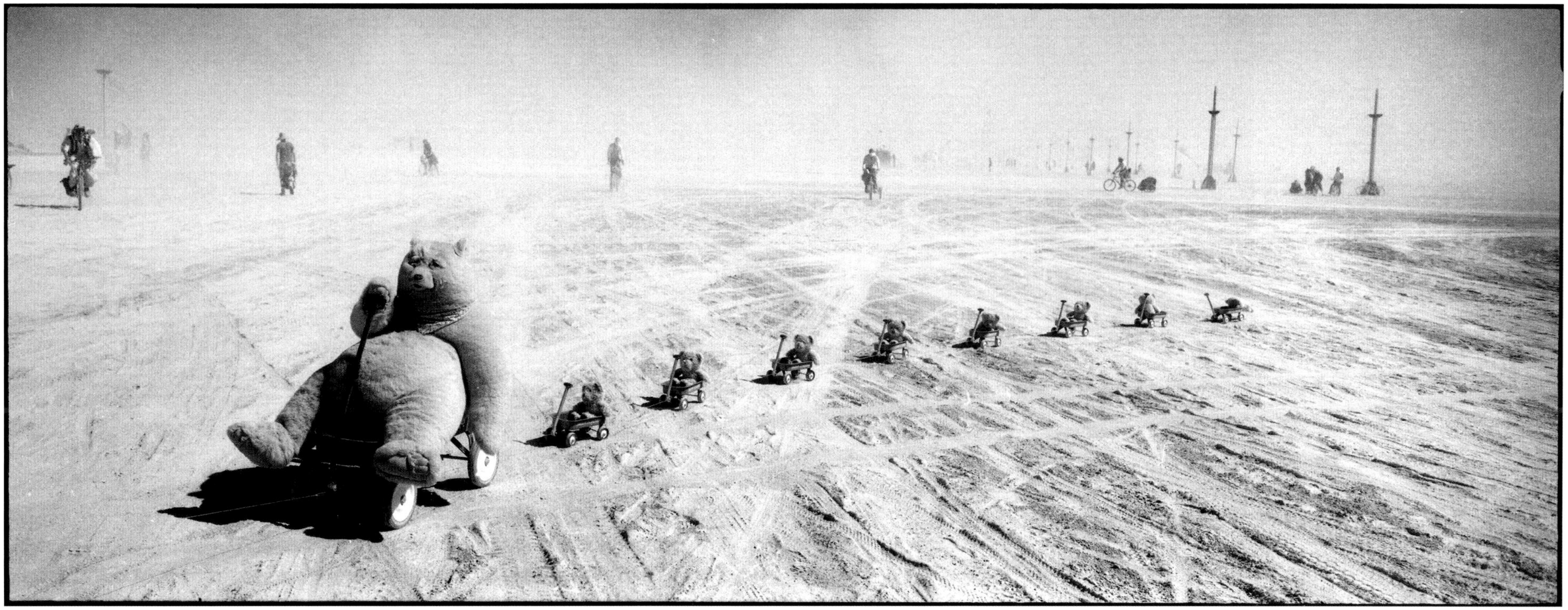

Teddy Bear Train, *2008*

Mutants are technically motorized car- or truck-based vehicles that need to pass a DMV inspection and be licensed for either day or nighttime playa driving, but I've always been attracted to oddball mobile works of art. Animals and replica ships seem to be the most ubiquitous forms of art on wheels at Burning Man. Once car artists got past the "plastic fantastic" phase of sticking hundreds of figurines and trophies all over an American '70s beater, vehicle crafters began to allow their imaginations to run wild. Soon sharks, whales, narwhals, pirate schooners, and rocket ships were turning the playa into a semblance of the back lot at Warner Bros.

Of course the Bay Area is a breeding ground for all things technological, and many of the most imaginative wheeled creations involve radio control. One of my early favorites was a motorized couch that the owners could ride around the playa using a remote control to steer. That wasn't all: behind the couch was a lit floor lamp on a wheeled base that was tethered to the couch electronically. Whichever way the couch moved the lamp would follow. I saw a similar assembly a few years later that featured a bear in a red wagon being trailed by several little cubs in wagons. The marriage between technology and motor vehicles is alive and well on the playa. Many of the earliest playa cruisers were pedal- or hand-powered. It's all a manifestation of creative participation as the next best step in experiencing Burning Man.

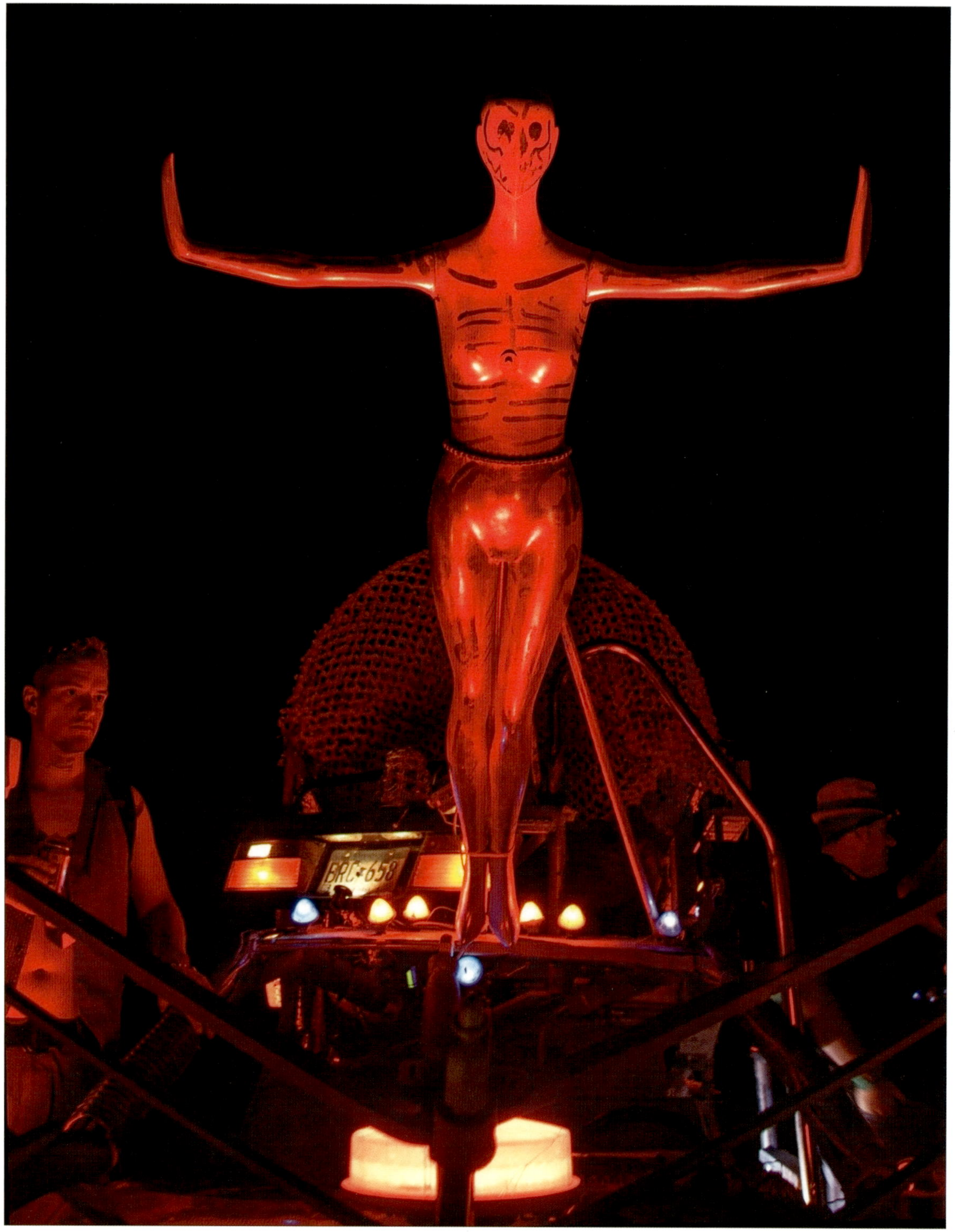

Hood Ornament, 2008

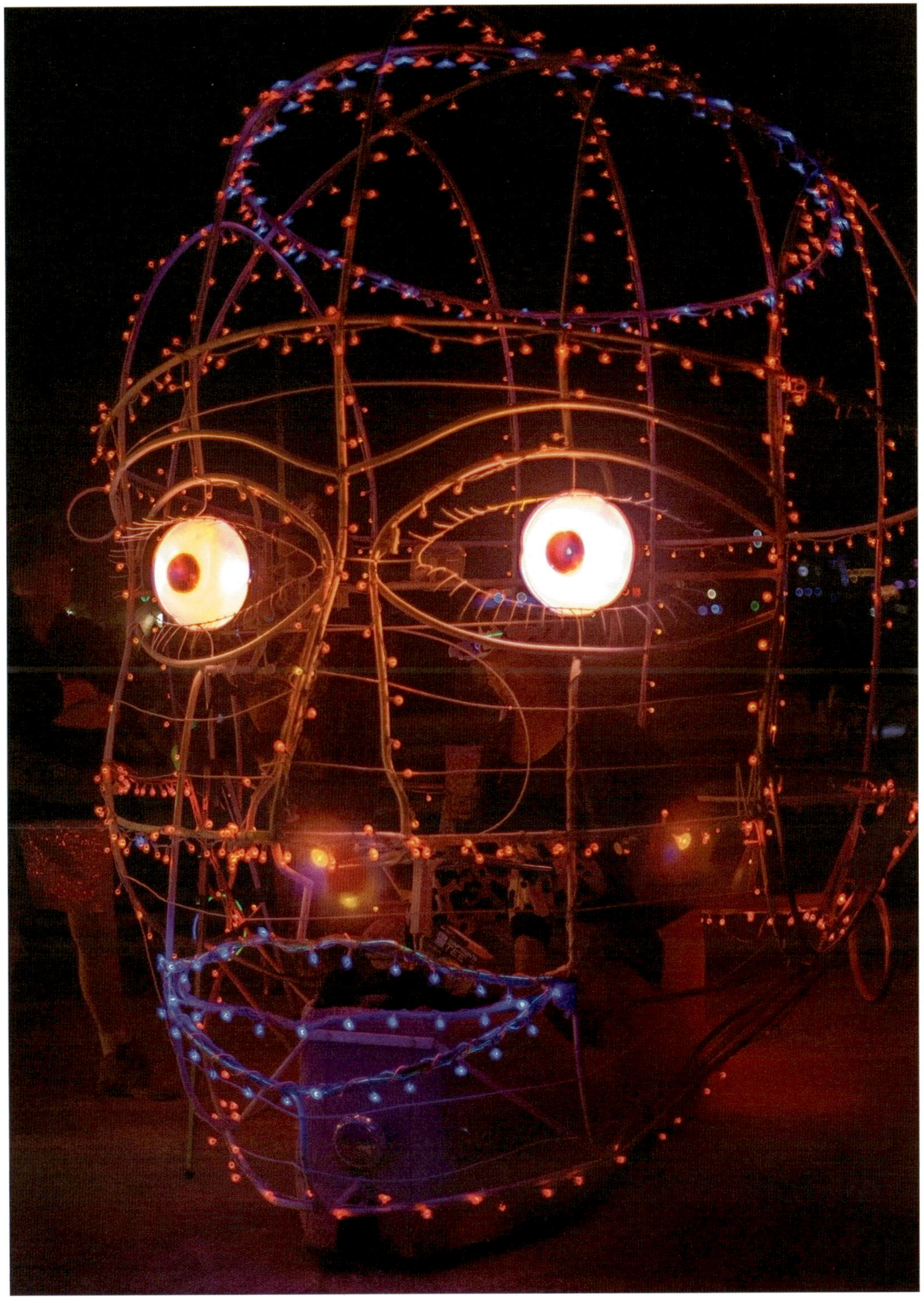

Big Giant Head, *2009*

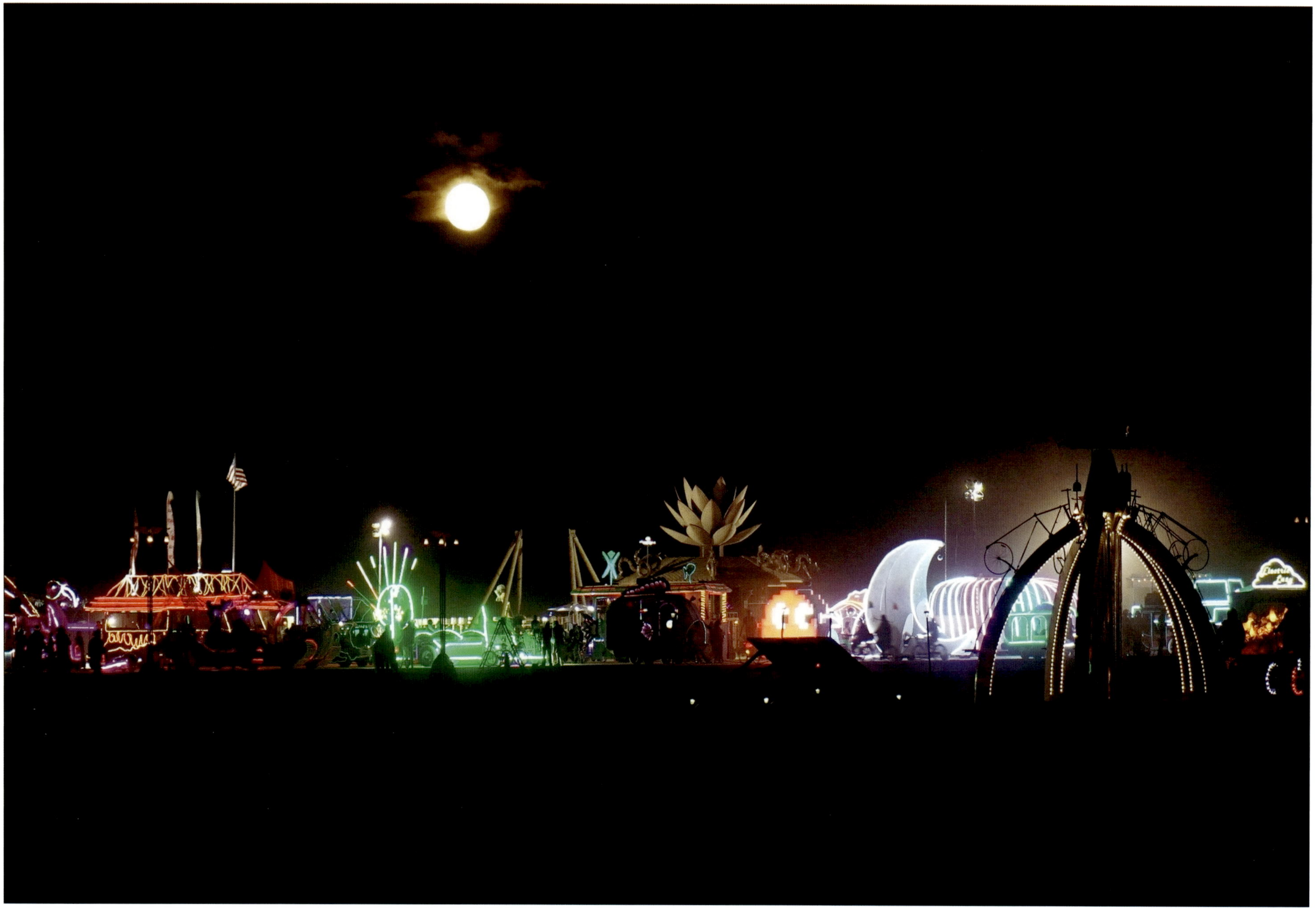

DMV Lineup, 2015

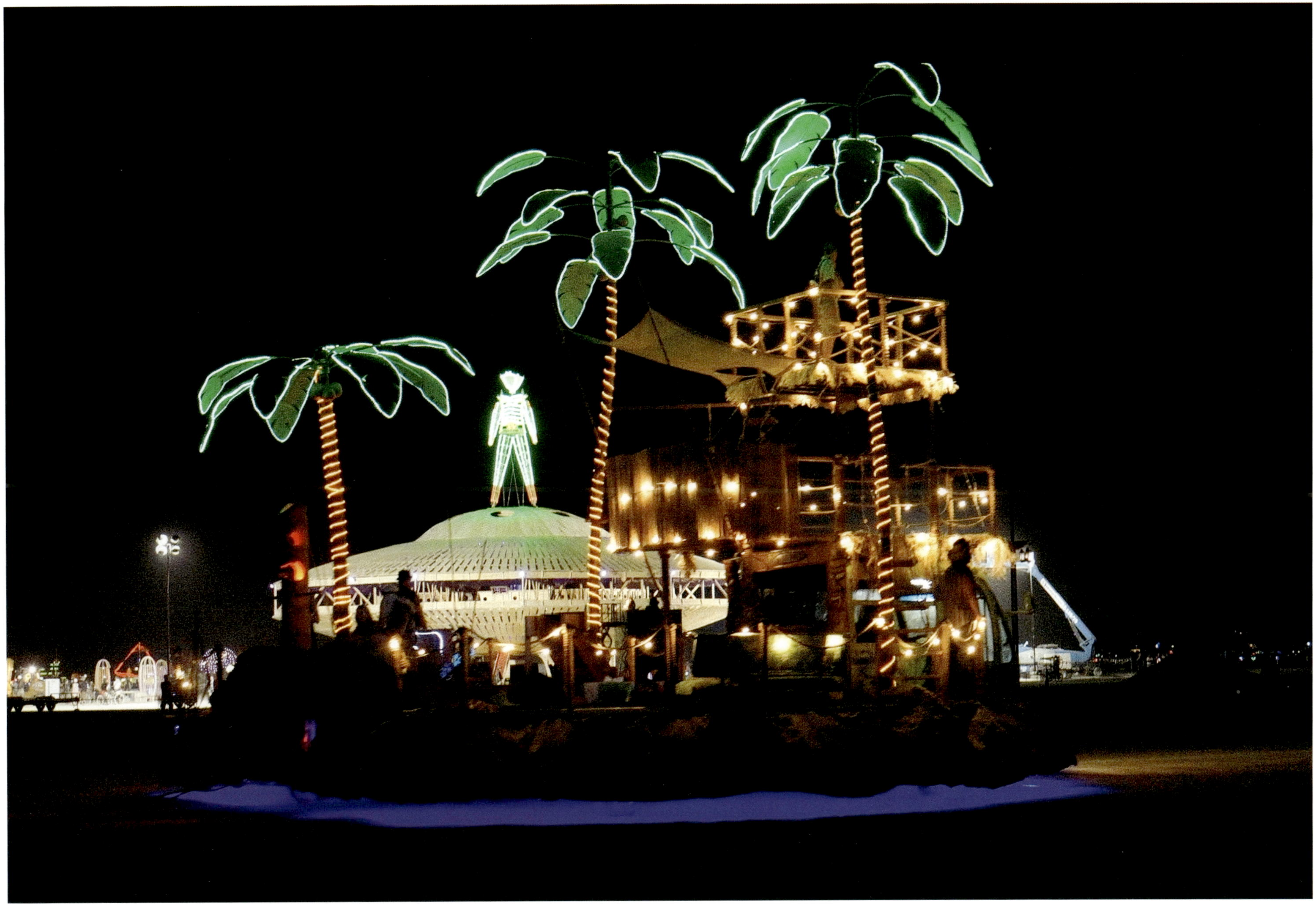

Tiki Island, *2013*

CHAPTER 9

THE RISE OF RITUAL: 2001–2004

Ritual behavior comes naturally on the playa. People instinctively understand this is one of nature's special places. Sunrises are often magical, and walking out onto the early morning playa is something that is truly a touchstone activity for all. Ironically, blowing dust, which is an irritant to everyone, also creates an aura of mystery and transforms the playa into a transcendent dreamscape. Harsh but compelling, it's the near-perfect environment for metaphysical investigations or personal meditation.

A visual artist from Kyoto, Ken Hamazaki, has been performing the traditional Japanese tea ceremony in front of the Man every year since 2000. For Ken, the ageless expanse of the playa offers the perfect setting for reenacting this ancient piece of performance art, and he does it at the same time each day during the week. He is but one of a multitude of individuals who feel compelled to engage in ritual activity at Burning Man. For some it's a spontaneous gesture inspired by their first experience on the playa or an impulse to design a spiritually grounded theme camp. For others it may manifest as a desire to volunteer as a Lamplighter or Greeter.

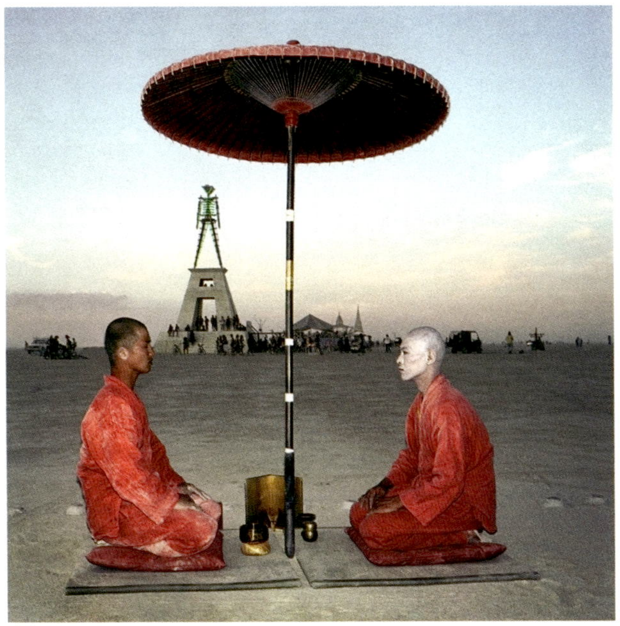

Ken Hamazaki and assistant perform the tea ceremony, 2001.

Burning Man is at a remove from everyday life and thus the perfect opportunity to access an area of the psyche that is often under attended. Watching Ken on the playa is in itself a lesson on the nature of ritual. What I find intriguing is that this time-honored and reverential ceremony is performed in front of a horde of dusty Burners. It is a solemn rite that is utterly conspicuous and out of place at that moment in that place, yet Ken manages to create an appearance of complete privacy. People bike past in droves, and many stare or take snapshots, yet Ken maintains his composure and attends to the details of the tea ceremony as if the vast playa is his own personal sanctuary.

Ken began his annual tea ceremony the same year David Best and Jack Haye were inspired to build their first temple, *Temple of the Mind*, and I assume that was to connect it with the 2000 theme, "The Body." There is something about temples in the context of the human psyche. Something about their architecture, their spires and domes, or the inordinate amount of filigree or ornamentation: you automatically know it's a place of enrichment—you feel it deep in your being.

I'm not using the term "temple" in a religious context, because there are many very compelling temples that aren't conventionally religious at all. The Capitol in Washington, DC, for example, the Louvre, and certainly the Lincoln Memorial are all temples as far as our senses are concerned. I've heard it said about certain ballparks, and some people feel that way about the Indianapolis Motor Speedway and Churchill Downs. It's a visceral sensation. Your body feels different when you enter the space, and you know this is a place that has something spiritual to say to you—if you'll listen attentively. The playa's a temple. When a temple is built on the playa—well, that's a temple atop a temple that's on sacred ground!

Burners understood the *Temple of the Mind* was such a memorial, and they responded respectfully. The following year, Burning Man approached David and Jack about building a larger temple for their 2001 theme, "The Seven Ages," referencing Shakespeare's "seven ages of man." The concept was to set seven birth-to-death theme areas along a corridor from 6:00 through the Man to 12:00. For example, "The Mausoleum" would be at the 12:00 position as the representative seventh age and death. Best and Haye's resulting Asian-inspired structure—*Temple of Tears*—was as peaceful as a Buddhist monastery, though embellished with enough pagan elements to charm Attila the Hun. As with any memorial, it inspired people to inscribe personal tributes to loved ones on every surface. Burners also brought pictures and personal artifacts as memorials.

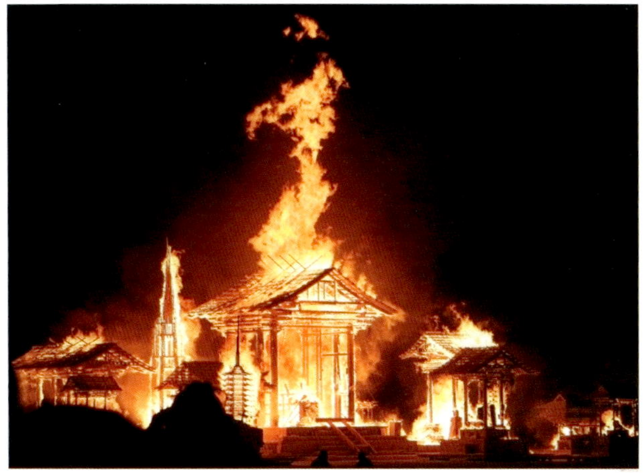

The temple fire becomes a life-affirming denouement to the Burning Man experience.

Originally conceived as theme art, the temple at Burning Man became an inextricable part of the ritual and pageantry that would come to define the event. Virtually overnight the temple became an instant tradition, and the Temple Burn resonated so intensely the organizers moved the burning of the Man to Saturday, allowing the Temple Burn its own night. After ten years of building toward becoming a culturally significant event, Burning Man achieved its goal by taking on its metaphysical counterpart: the body made spirit.

Though the Burning Man temples have varied greatly in style and shape, they always evoke the same reaction: people treat them as sacred spaces. The common denominator we share as human beings is we each suffer personal loss and pain. What the temples provide is an opportunity to expiate that pain with a positive and creative gesture. All during the week Burners create memorial altars, bring pictures, or inscribe messages of hope and mourning on the temple walls. People pray and shed tears openly; they laugh and tell stories about loved ones to strangers; they linger in the throes of precious memory. Casual visitors are usually quiet and respectful, sensing this is a place unlike any other they will encounter on the playa. While much of Burning Man is a gaudy display of expression and celebration, the temple is about reflection and reverence. When the Man burns, it's a raucous melee of immolation, but the temple crowd is silent. This Burn transforms that energy into a life-affirming denouement. By then, nearly every person has contributed a memorial token to the pyre, or at the least scrawled the name of a loved one on a section of wall. It's the quintessential finale to Burn week.

Over the years, David Best, with the help of a dedicated temple crew, has built nine Burning Man temples. He has also constructed a number of temple installations in significant places around the world, including Derry in Northern Ireland and Kathmandu in Nepal. The temples of Burning Man are quite simply the apex of what ritual is all about. Not simply repetitive pageantry, which can become rote and lose meaning, but individualized and personal. Each person makes an emotional contribution in their own way and gets from the temple what they will.

Black Rock City is a ritual unto itself. From the moment of its inception with Rod Garrett's plan for Hualapai Flat there has been a revered methodology to the building of the city. Will Roger Peterson originally headed the construction team, which would become the enduring and notorious DPW, and today Tony "Coyote" Perez is the chief shepherd of these noble hooligans. On an appointed day in late July a core cadre of the "early Man crew" assemble on the barren playa to survey and stake out that year's city. Using an impressive combination of traditional and digital tools, Tony establishes the symbolic center of the city, which is where the Man will be sited. There they drive in the "Gold Spike" with an accompanying ceremony. It is both serious and as much of a parody of ritual as you can imagine. From this central spike all aspects of the city will be surveyed. The perimeter fence is built, roads and streets are established, and all essential features of Black Rock City are staked out.

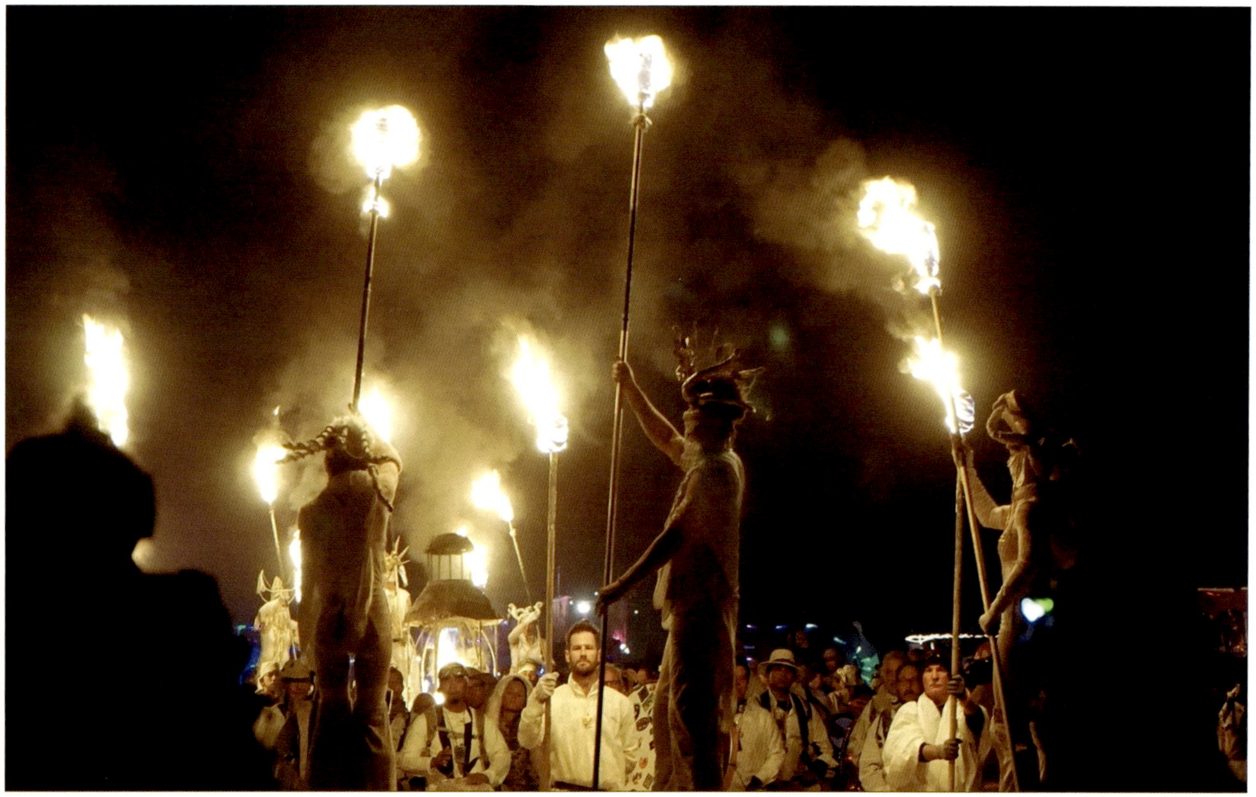

Crimson's Fire Conclave adds a ritual mystique to Burning Man's titular ceremony.

Ritual evokes the visceral response we all felt that first year on the playa, and it has continued unabated every year since. For multiple reasons 2001 coalesced those ritual elements and transitioned the event into its contemporary iteration. The raising of the Man onto a plinth added immeasurably to the theatricality of the Burn. It also provided a means to unify the figure with the yearly theme. The temple established sacred territory on the playa and focused the emotional rapport Burners instinctively felt about this ancient landscape. Burning Man was on the cusp of a mature realization of what Larry sought when he first laid eyes on this exotic topography. This was the year when spiritual and creative inclinations were fully joined, and Burning Man's celebration of art and community culture could begin in earnest.

The truth is, if you give people an opportunity at Burning Man, they will create a yearly tradition on the spot. This is especially true when it comes to theme camps, which stage annual parades and giveaways. These aren't rituals in the classic sense, but they display many of the elements of ritual. An annual parade often forges the members of the camp into a communal unit that will share their performance with the outside world.

There are even rituals connected with entering Burning Man for the first time, and these are in the hands of the exuberant gang of volunteers people meet just prior to entering Black Rock City: the Greeters. Greeters, like their counterparts the Lamplighters and the Temple Guardians, are volunteers who play an important role in setting an example for community culture. This friendly bunch is the welcome wagon committee for the playa, and in true Burning Man fashion combine hugs for veterans with ritual hazing for newbies. They have been functioning since 1997, when they transitioned from the Rangers, who were the first official gatekeepers. The Greeter station makes up the final checkpoint before entering BRC. (As the Burning Man population grew, it became obvious that gate duties needed to be subdivided among specialists. Harley K. Dubois created most of these specialty groups as part of her role as city manager. First there were ticket takers and a second group in the Will Call area. Vehicles would then need to be searched for stowaways and contraband.) Greeters set the tone for people's expectations, and they hand out an important information booklet on navigating the city, safety concerns, and a daily schedule of events happening all around the city. There is also a map with the location of all theme camps and art works, and some swag in the form of stickers.

To satisfy the strong desire for a ritual of passage into Black Rock City, the Greeters commissioned a Reno artist to create a Burning Man bell. He produced long steel Buddhist-style bells that could be struck with a hammer or even a piece of rebar. The first question a Greeter will ask is "Have you been to Burning Man before?" If your answer is yes, they will reply with the long-standing salutation reserved for all veteran Burners: "Welcome home!" You are then welcome to ring the bell, or if you're a grizzled veteran like me you're happy with just a hug. If you are a "virgin" Burner, you're in for a bit of an initiation ritual. The Greeter assumes a more commanding tone, and you are usually ordered to get down on the playa and make a dust angel. Once you've produced a well-defined angel, you are allowed to ring the bell and are officially welcomed into the city. The dust angel is just an initiation haze, but ringing the bell is the ritual signal that you've finally arrived at your destination.

For me, the most compelling examples of ritual behavior at Burning Man are when individuals create their own meditative solitude in the midst of the chaos. I've seen it too many times to ignore the obvious conclusion that the playa is one of the best places on Earth for meditation and personal contemplation.

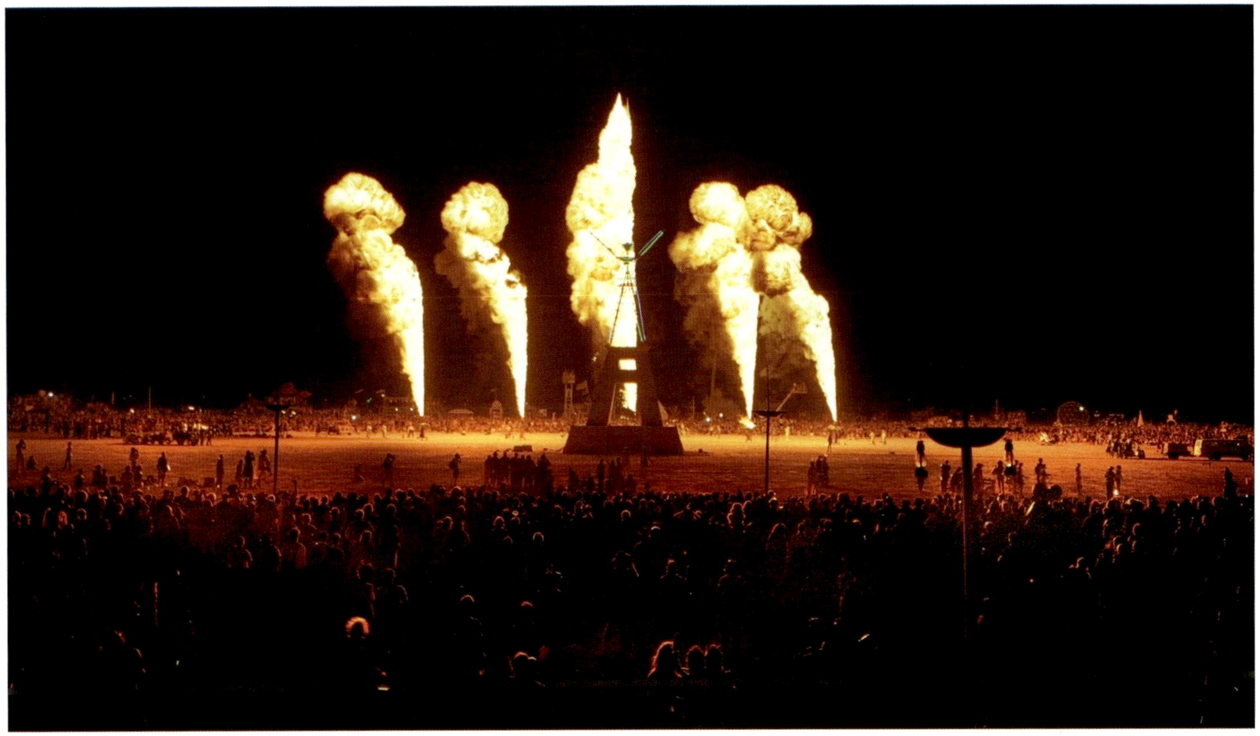

By 2001, Impotence Compensation Project's Fire Cannons *were illuminating a growing multitude.*

I encountered one such fellow in 2001. He was sitting on a mat a hundred feet from the Man in the early morning light. I remember his name because I wrote it down—Henry Mah—but I don't remember another thing about him. We exchanged pleasantries for a few minutes, and then I left him there to meditate and be alone in a way that can only be achieved in a place such as the playa. These days I see people every morning sitting on mats in a tranquil state. A crucial attitude that Burners ought to bring as a prerequisite to fully enjoying their experience at Burning Man is captured in one of the Ten Principles: Immediacy. This imperative to tune in to each moment with complete attention describes a state of awareness that's almost always available during a Black Rock sunrise. I've watched many times as the morning sunlight washes over Burners like a warm bath, and their faces open to every nuance and possibility in life.

Personal ritual is virtually automatic at Burning Man. In fact, Sallie Edmunds, one of the two people I've been camping with at the event for the past few years, goes to a yoga session almost every morning. This kind of group meditation is commonplace all across BRC. But what intrigues me aren't the formal yoga sessions, of which there are probably a half dozen or so going on at any one time; it's those solitary individuals like Henry Mah who walk out onto the playa, sit on the ground, and contemplate their being. That kind of ritual occurs every day as well. Not only is it the essence of Immediacy, it's also certainly a most individual form of Participation. The ethos of the event blends seamlessly with the solitude of the place, and those who allow themselves to absorb that reality will have gotten all the reward they need for having made the long journey so far from their homes.

The year 2001 was very mixed for the Harveys. It was the first year I would attend the Burn without Bryan, who was battling leukemia. He had gotten sick that spring, just two

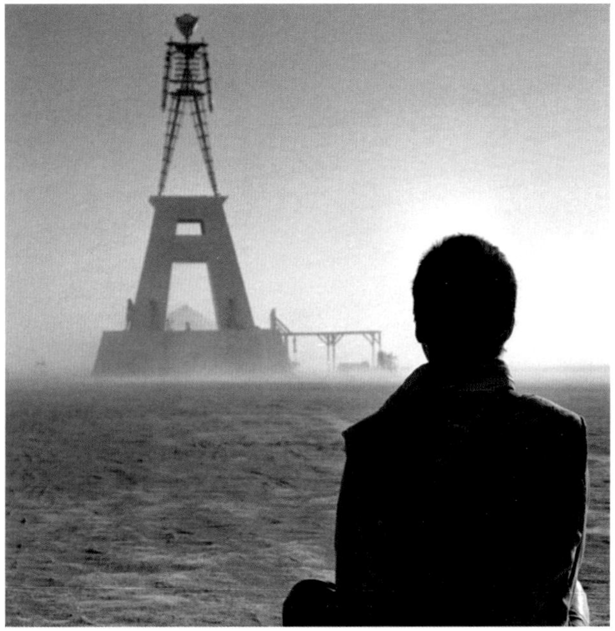

In 2001, I chanced upon a fellow sitting quietly on a mat in front of the Man.

months shy of graduating with an engineering degree from Oregon State University. It was an unbelievable, arduous, and gut-wrenching time for us all, and Burning Man was the furthest thing from my mind, but Bryan had responded well to chemo, and so he and Lynda insisted that I make the trip and put our names in the temple for good luck. A day after I arrived, I hated it. All I could think was that I was there without Bry, and it simply didn't feel right. Then Larry as well as Marian counseled that I should give it a day or two. They felt I should use the time to recharge, take stock. It was good advice.

I spent quite a lot of time on the playa alone myself that year. For the first time the Man had been placed on an A-shaped pedestal, and it added immeasurably to his dynamic against the horizon. Like Henry Mah, I sat on the playa for more than one sunrise, and I got to know the play of early morning light on the desert surface most intimately. It's probably the reason I feel so strongly about the playa being a place of spiritual healing. I especially found myself hanging out at the *Temple of Tears*. It fit my somber mood, but it also lifted my spirits. By the time I returned to Portland, the doctors at OHSU had declared Bryan cancer-free. The 2017 Burn will be my twenty-seventh, and happily, it will be Bryan's twenty-first.

The theme for 2002 was "The Floating World." I'm not positive, but I seem to remember that originally, Larry intended to play on the Japanese ukiyo-e style of art from the lavish Edo period. By the time the theme essay was written, however, it had become a treasure hunt on the high seas, and so the playa that year was filled with ships and pirates. One of the great adventures was a treasure hunt for gold doubloons, which depicted a treasure chest on one side and the symbol of the Man on the other. If you found a doubloon, you could keep it, use it to gain admission to the lighthouse base of the Man, or gift it to someone else. I still have one somewhere with our other Burning Man memorabilia.

"The Floating World" was notable in that it produced some of the most spectacular seagoing vehicles to ever sail the playa. The most notable was a battle-scarred vessel of considerable scale: *La Contessa*. It was massive, and of course it had a sound system. The creators of it—Simon Cheffins and Gregory Jones, along with dozens of others—were very generous with their time, and by the week's end, nearly everyone on the playa had had a ride. It came back for many years and was easily one of the best "playa schooners" to sail vast old Lake Lahontan in decades. There was also a giant white whale that Flash Hopkins drove around, and Pepe Ozan's opera set piece *Narwhal*, which resembled a friendly sea mammal and has also returned to the playa many times.

What Burning Man offers is a world apart from the one we live in from day to day. It is a world of fantasy and imagination, and in it we are transported to a head space long dormant in urban adult life. I think the reason spiritual elements appear so effortlessly on the playa is that it is so removed from the relentless commerce of contemporary America, where our senses are bombarded with the thousand inane trivialities of daily living, and the only way out seems to involve buying, booking, or subscribing to something. I think it's why people spend so much time staring at an image of a cute kitten on their cell phones or laughing at a YouTube video of their friends cavorting on vacation. "Please let me be there," they seem to be saying. "Let me be any place but here!" Burning Man offers a destination that is far beyond our wildest expectations—a genuine out-of-the-mall experience.

"The Floating World" was one of those themes that simply stirred everyone's imagination. I suppose it was an easy one to

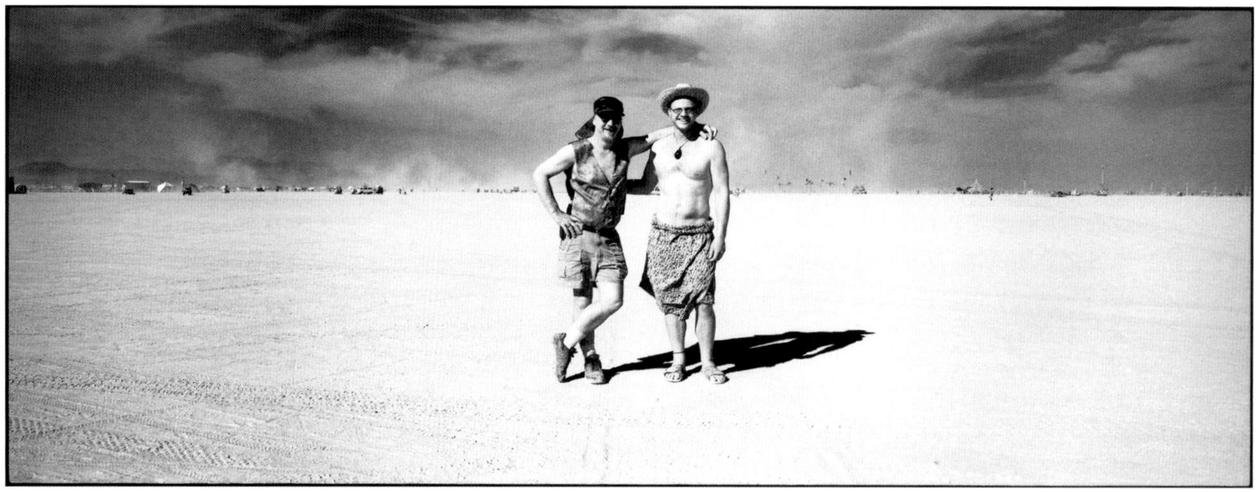

A healthy Bryan and being together on the playa in 2002 floated our world.

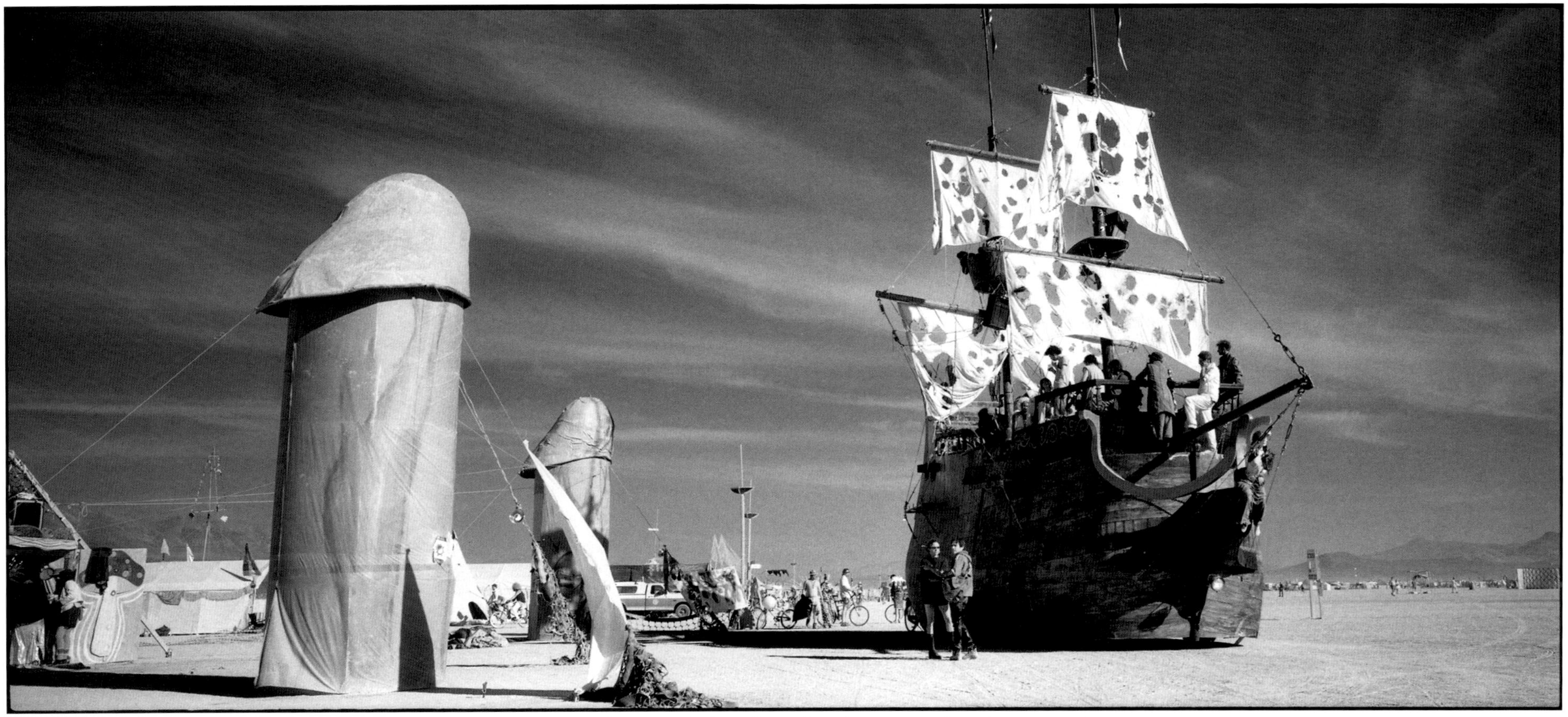

The good ship La Contessa *docks in front of two large penis-shaped camp sentries.*

translate into colorful objects, but 2002 sticks in my memory as a happy combination of art and whimsy. There was *Anas Vulcanus* (more commonly referred to as "Ducky") by Aaron Muszalski, a yellow duck-shaped casino parked out in deep playa, which became the hot ticket for clubbers. Its size strictly limited the number of patrons, and there were always fifty people outside trying to get in. It's customary to bring a bottle to playa bars, and there would always be some guy trying to jump the line, yelling, "I've got Gold Label!"

One of the advantages of an infectious theme is that it lends itself so well to parody, and parody is the highest form of expression at Burning Man. Steven Carthy's *Floating Larry* certainly fit the bill. An uncanny steel and wax replica of my brother was mounted atop an SUV that traveled around the city broadcasting long-winded speeches. It was a perfect rendering, and the figure received his just deserts by going up in flames. It was a fitting prelude to the following year's theme: "Beyond Belief."

Spiritual philosophy was very much at the heart of the 2003 event. The Black Rock Desert has been inspiring spiritual reactions since its crossing by the earliest indigenous people of this country, and we latter-day pilgrims on the playa often lie on our backs, staring up at a universe of stars that feel close enough to touch. They hang there like bits of tiny fire, and we are alternately warmed and chilled in the sure and sudden sense of being small in their presence. It is an alien world out there, and it beckons seductively in the cool of the night air. Larry's theme essay for 2003 echoed a thesis I'd been intuitively feeling for years about the sacred nature of the playa:

> Sacred things appear to come from some profoundly other place that is beyond the bounds of space and time. It is as if a window is opened on another world that is too real to be real. This place is absolutely unique. Like all sacred places, it releases powerful emotions: joy, wonder, dread, and—most transcendently—pure exaltation. The sacred speaks to us of vastness and of union with a power

larger than our conscious selves. The sacred provides access to a greater sense of being. Yet whether sacred things are literally real is always open to examination. "Beyond Belief" asks two related questions: How does the sacred exist, and where might it be found?

Burning Man has always held steadfastly to its egalitarian and inclusive mantra—all philosophies are welcomed and appreciated. This is the place to experience the greater unknown, and we present the sacred openly, to be taken or left as you choose. Experience is at the heart of why we come to Burning Man. We hope to experience what has been hidden or stifled in a world dominated by commercial interests. By eliminating the power of commerce, Burners are free to explore alternative avenues of happiness. What "Beyond Belief" did was open the playa to every manner of spiritual exploration and comment. Larry makes it clear in his essay: "Our theme will occupy that ambiguous territory that lies between reverence and ridicule, faith and belief, the absurd and the stunningly sublime."

"Beyond Belief" also saw the first creation of a supporting base for the Man that was fully interactive. The base was much more than a supporting plinth. Though the base from the year before had doubled as a "lighthouse" you could enter and climb, it had ostensibly been a reward for finding a doubloon. The 2003 base was designed in the form of an Aztec pyramid open to all. Around the perimeter of the sacred pyramid were alcoves with manned volunteers giving presentations about various forms of spiritual practice. The pyramid also featured wide steps—again in the manner of the Aztecs—that allowed people to climb up to a viewing platform. In the forecourt of the base stood Todd Dworman's *Labyrinth,* an eighty-foot maze of electroluminescent wire, which could also be illuminated at night. *Labyrinth* and the alcoves returned a level of interactivity to visiting the Man, which had been eroding in favor of the temple.

In 2003 Burners were encouraged to treat the Man as they would another piece of interactive playa art. The Man had originally been the only piece of playa art, and small design cues each year had addressed the theme, but the problem with raising the Man above the modest height of the hay bales of the late 1990s was that it took away the intimacy of just hanging out with the big guy. There had been benefits to raising him seventy feet above the playa to be sure, but reinvigorating the sense of interactivity was crucial to keeping the Man in the forefront of his own party. From 2001 forward, the Man and his base were considered the principal articulation of that year's theme.

Art installations from 2003 were likewise inspired by the world of belief: Peter Hudson's zoetrope playa swimmer was called *Sisyphish,* alluding to Greek mythology. Will Atkinson positioned a working drinking fountain in deep playa to refresh the thirsty pilgrim. Want to stop off on your journey to enlightenment and talk directly to the man upstairs? *Phone Booth to God,* by a group calling themselves the Ojai Bureau of Pleasure, became a regular feature on the playa. There was never a guarantee that God would be on the line, but often someone was there! One of the most spectacular feats of artistry and engineering was *The Temple of Gravity* by Zachary Coffin. Five granite slabs reportedly weighing eighteen thousand pounds each were suspended from a five-spoke steel arch in a seamless blend of art and science designed to inspire belief in the laws of physics that might exceed our imagination. The claim was that you could fill each slab with as many people as it could possibly hold, and you wouldn't increase its weight by more than 10 percent.

What "Beyond Belief" accomplished to a lasting effect at Burning Man was that it made clear that matters of the spirit were a natural part of the playa experience. The theme also generated profound respect for many ritual activities that were beginning to develop serious traction as annual rites of passage. People were beginning to see participating in such activities as vital in their quest to fully experience the event. It could mean actively working in a fully evolved theme camp, such as the Black Post Office, or volunteering in some capacity on one of Harley's many civic crews, whether that meant cleanup and playa restoration with the Earth Guardians or service as a Greeter. Without a doubt the highest of such callings is to become a Lamplighter. For lamp lighting is an authentic daily ritual and has a legendary heritage.

Because ritual has always been an intrinsic part of Burning Man, traditions like raising the Man by hand and the nightly procession of Steve Mobia's flame-robed Lamplighters held a ceremonial place of honor from their outset. Lamplighters are the Shaolin monks of the playa, and over the years their presence has grown into a symbol of the spiritual nature of the event itself. Just when Burners are gearing up for a night on the town or lining up for their evening meal, you can hear their distant clarion call: "Make way for your Lamplighters. Make way for your Lamplighters." There is no ritual at Burning Man that garners more universal respect. I've seen Lamplighters making their rounds when the dust is absolutely blinding and the wind is whipping their flame-embellished robes into a blur. They walk slowly, often to the beat of a single gong or drum, each with a shoulder yoke with a dozen lanterns. Every night they parade their way in monkish silence bearing light in the growing dusk. Burners understand and honor their service to the greater good, often with applause. It is tiring work, and it requires a strong commitment to volunteerism and community service that transcends the self-indulgent entertainment side of the event. Moreover, Lamplighters are a daily reminder that Burning Man embraces ritual traditions that evoke time-honored social and cultural values.

Rituals take many forms, and there are ritual activities that happen every year on the playa that have nothing to do with sacred space. At least not in the traditional sense of the word. The ritual tour, for example. This usually takes place on a bike or maybe an art rig, but it's a daily occurrence. People walk around the Esplanade in droves, looking at camps and art, but also just being out and about in their best playa drag. Sitting around camp may be acceptable at midday, but even then you feel you might be missing out on an important experience.

Burning Man playa art can sometimes present images critical of traditional religions. While others poke gentle fun at the expense of popular mythologies, playa artists often perform satirical impressions aimed straight at conventional religious stereotypes. Reverend Billy (from the Church of Stop Shopping) is a recurrent playa character that's a hilarious wedding officiate, who also does a great Burning Man–

influenced revival preacher: "Playalujah!" Crosses have often been used in art installations, usually as an antiauthoritarian parody or to otherwise criticize a commercial society that denigrates women or demands conformity. I remember one cross that was plastered in popular glamour magazine covers and wrapped in chains.

One "Beyond Belief" theme artist utilized a fourteen-foot cross covered in pieces of broken mirror. David McParland's *Cross Dress* was designed to stimulate an interactive self-discussion by the viewer regarding their faith or lack thereof. When the viewer stood on the nearby podium/pulpit with their arms outstretched, they saw their distorted reflection on the cross. The podium possessed a dual nature as well. When you faced the cross, it became self-evaluative, but when you faced the opposite direction, it became a pulpit for delivering a sermon to the nonexistent multitudes. I especially liked how the cross reflections blended into the playa and sky. I thought it worked just as well viscerally as it did metaphorically.

The year 2003 happened to mark my wife Lynda's second trip to Burning Man (in 2002, Lynda had been so thrilled with Bryan's recovery, she vowed that if he was going, she was going). By then, we'd been married for thirty-three years, since 1967. Marriage encompasses a lifetime of personal rituals, of course. We met when I was stationed on a tiny radar site in her hometown of Cottonwood, Idaho, and began dating when she was a senior in high school. I even took her to her senior prom. There was a segment in her little Catholic farming community who really hated the idea of local girls dating airmen from the base, and at the Saturday night dances there were often parking lot battles between the "scope dopes" and the town boys. Dating a GI was a significant social risk, but Lynda has never lacked for the courage of her convictions, and her family embraced me. We got married when she turned twenty, and Bryan arrived within a year. Working full-time and raising a child while your husband is struggling through college makes for a tough beginning. After graduation, I taught part-time and began photographing weddings. As our principal support, Lynda continued to work full-time. We survived and eventually prospered, but after thirty-five years of toil and Bryan's harrowing recovery from leukemia, our marriage had stumbled through its fair share of dysfunction and despair. I began to sense we were overdue for a little recovery of our own.

I decided I wanted to reaffirm my love and commitment to this plucky woman who had worked tirelessly all her adult life to make a future for us, and at the same time assisted me in trying to make something of myself—no mean feat. We had

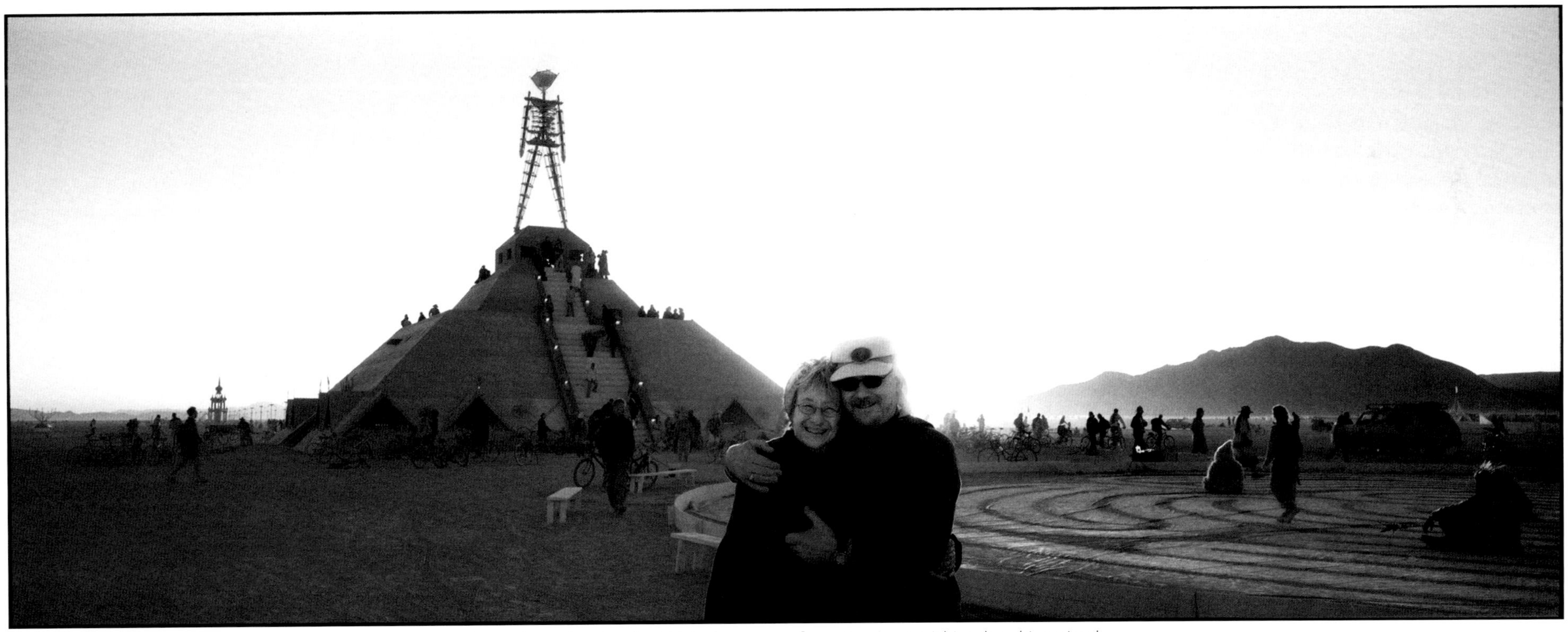

Proposing to Lynda after thirty-five years of marriage was trickier than I imagined.

never had a formal engagement, and consequently Lynda had never been given an engagement ring. By that time we had a jeweler who was a tenant in a retail space that was part of our studio building. I asked him to fashion a ring out of some small diamonds, and I brought it with me to the playa in 2003 with the intention of asking Lynda if she would marry me all over again. My somewhat ill-considered impulse was that the perfect time and place would be at sunrise in front of the Man.

The one hitch was that Lynda is not exactly a "morning person." I began the night before, spinning yarns about the glories of the playa sunrise and how she should get up early "just once" to see it for herself. She agreed reluctantly, but faced with a bone-chilling six A.M., she had a complete change of heart. "Come on," I pleaded. "Just stand out here beside the van." She finally agreed to get dressed and stand by the rig. Once out there, I started urging her toward the Man to get a better view. "Let's get closer to the Man," I urged. "We can stand by the van!" she snapped. "Just a little closer," I cajoled, dragging her along as I spoke.

Finally, as the first glint of sunlight peeked over the hills, I stopped at the nearest artwork and pulled out the ring box. "Will you marry me all over again?" I blurted. She didn't say anything, and she didn't look particularly happy. I tried again, only this time I went into a longer spiel about how much I appreciated everything she'd done for us. "Huh?" she replied with a vaguely disoriented look in her eyes, and that's when I realized that she was still half asleep! Finally, a look of recognition began to play across her face, and she smiled. After she allowed me to put the ring on her finger, we walked the rest of the way out to the "Beyond Belief" pavilion. We asked a friendly fellow to snap a couple of pictures of us. He was shooting into the sun, but the moment was exquisite.

"Vault of Heaven" in 2004 completed a cycle of themes that encouraged explorations of the great unknown, artfully synthesizing mythic cosmology and the science of astronomy. The Man was placed atop an Observatory, a dome made of open geodesic triangles that crowned a museum of cosmic wonders.

When Larry and I were kids, we shared a bedroom that was part of an addition Shorty built to the house in the 1950s. We got to pick out the wallpaper, and as space travel was all the rage then, we spent years living with Buck Rogers–style spacecraft and planets. I wouldn't rule out that it had a subliminal effect on Larry's adopting this science-fiction-influenced theme.

"Vault of Heaven" should have worked better than it did. The Observatory was a magnet for Burners, and it also provided one of the better pre-Burn fireworks displays, but there were other aspects of the theme that simply didn't jell, and while it should have carried forward the metaphysical discussion of the previous couple of years, it veered more toward science and politics. Astronomy was a natural focus, given the big skies of the playa, but there were also myriad political parodies as a result of the recent escalation of the Iraq War. People brought telescopes or paraded as caricatures of the Bush-Cheney administration. One of my great pleasures that year was to climb a ladder next to an eight-foot Dobsonian telescope trained on Saturn. This wasn't my first view of that celestial beauty, but I never tire of its symmetrical perfection. I always think the same thought: "It looks just like our wallpaper!"

Geographically themed camps were also on the rise, and it was clear that Burning Man was developing an international following. I remember walking by a camp on the edge of the Esplanade early one morning. It was an hour before sunrise, and the blue-black sky was deep and subdued. The entrance to the camp was formed by a serene torii gate that glowed deep red from within. Behind the gate sat a square pavilion with rice-paper shades. Even the tents were spare and in neat rows. On the outside of the gate was a Shinto bell hanging from a frame that was inscribed with kanji letters. The entire presentation spoke of a firm purpose and

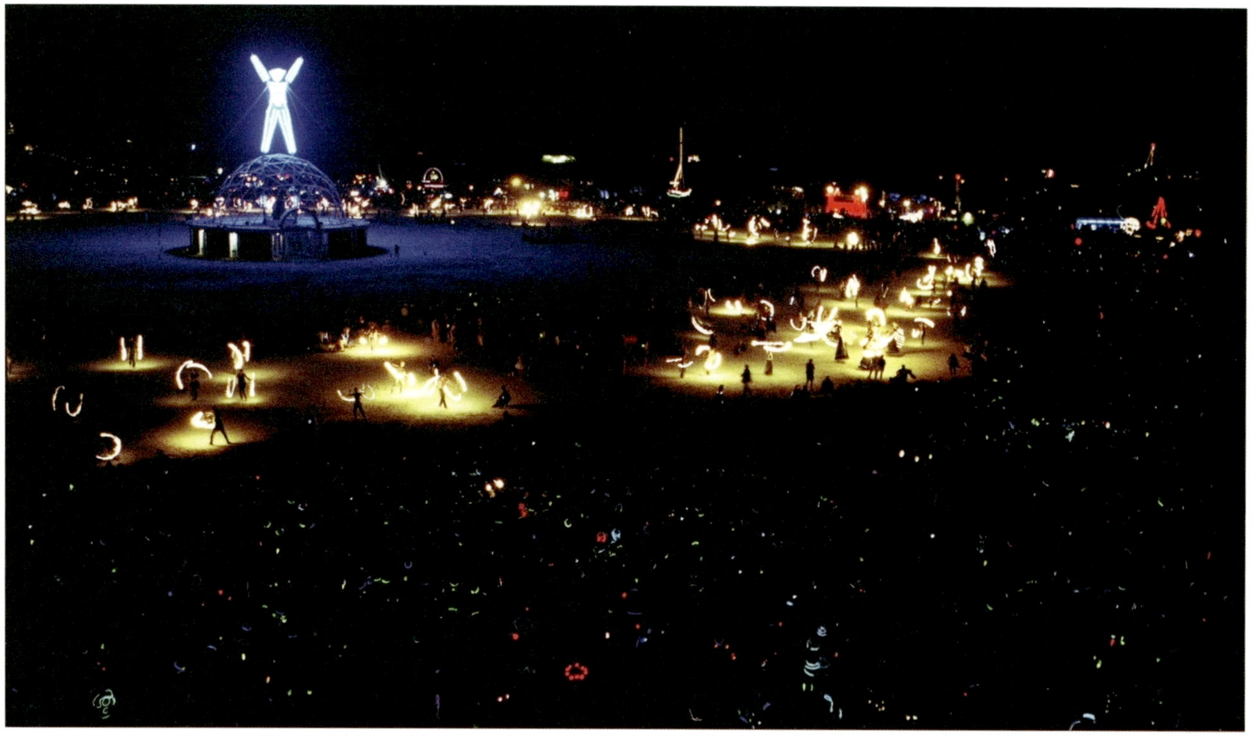

"Vault of Heaven" themed Burning Man's quest for cosmological enlightenment.

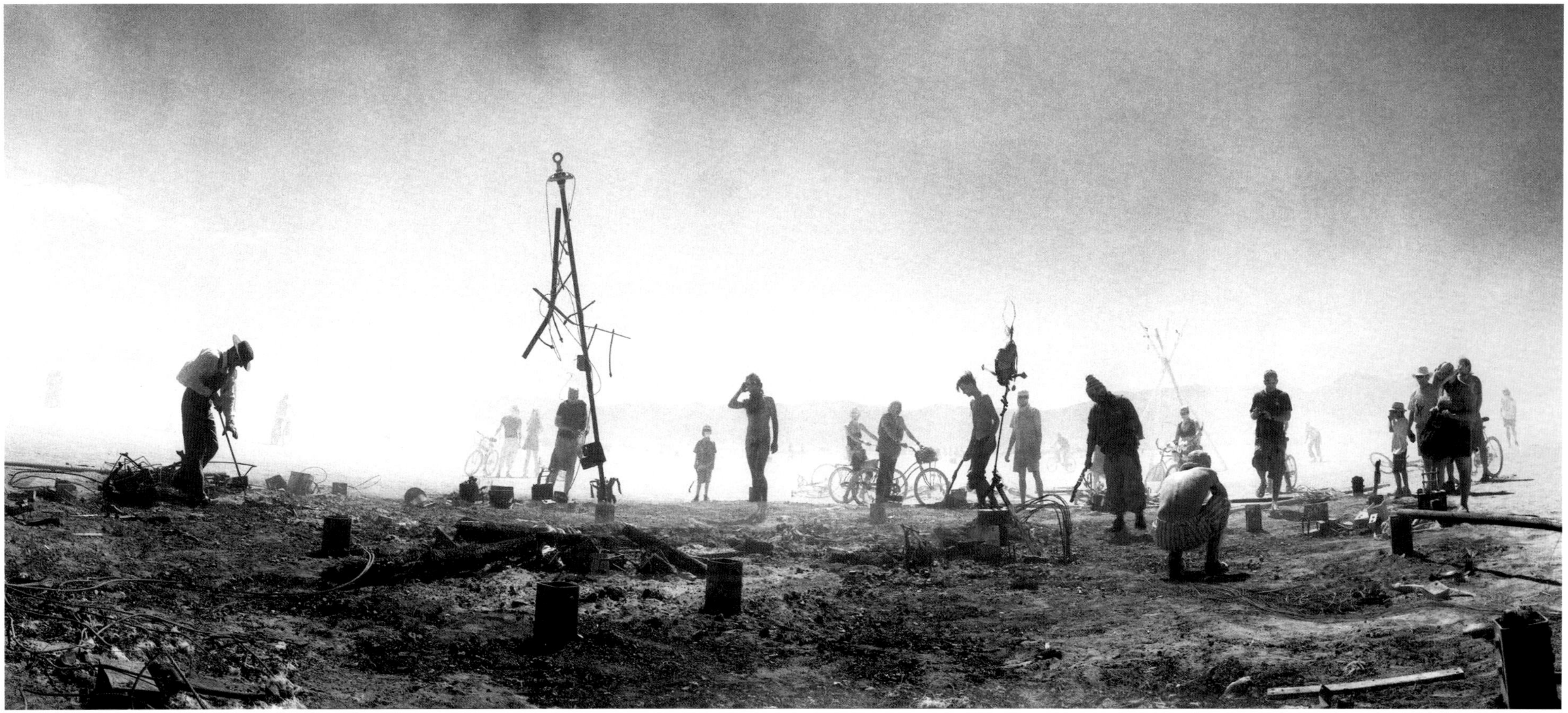

a deep respect for cultural and spiritual heritage. At least that's what I imagined as I stood silently while the souls within the tiny village slept.

There is one last ritual that needs to be reprised, and it's one that goes back to the first playa Zone Trip. The morning after the Burn, people go out to the remnants of the pyre and pick through the ashes. It's a scavenger hunt for a bit of the Man. It's a quest for a talisman from the previous night's version of sacred ceremony. It's a memorial to the spirit of the wooden giant they have witnessed in ritual sacrifice. It's also part of our collective conscience. Someone or another is always dying for our sins. Taking a piece of that sacrifice home is a sign of respect. This ritual collection has always been as spontaneous and as reliable as rising for sunup. The unexpected part is how much like a wake it feels. We grieve the loss of that central figure, which for the better part of two weeks has been our host, our guide, and our larger-than-life compadre.

By the end of 2004, fantasy and wonder had become the expected experience at Burning Man, but an even deeper component had been added as well. Burners began going to the event to plunge deep into their craving for an enlightened existence. The inclusive culture of the event will always introduce a wider and ever-increasing variety of experience. In that way Burning Man will never be exactly the same as it was the year previous. Each year my brother searches for a theme that will excite attendees to new perspectives and discoveries. This is the secret of the growing success of the event in a widening sphere of global appeal. In 2004 Larry would articulate for the first time the ten governing principles for the event. These were precepts and codes of behavior that had been Burner traditions going back to the Cacophony era, but by translating them into the formal Ten Principles of Burning Man, he created the basis for both growing an arts culture and establishing a global community of shared values.

> Uniquely expressive acts get transformed and elaborated into social rites, and through participation they accrue a breadth and depth of meaning that can only be produced in a communal setting. It is the primal process by which culture is created.
>
> —Larry Harvey

CHAPTER 10

SACRED SPACES

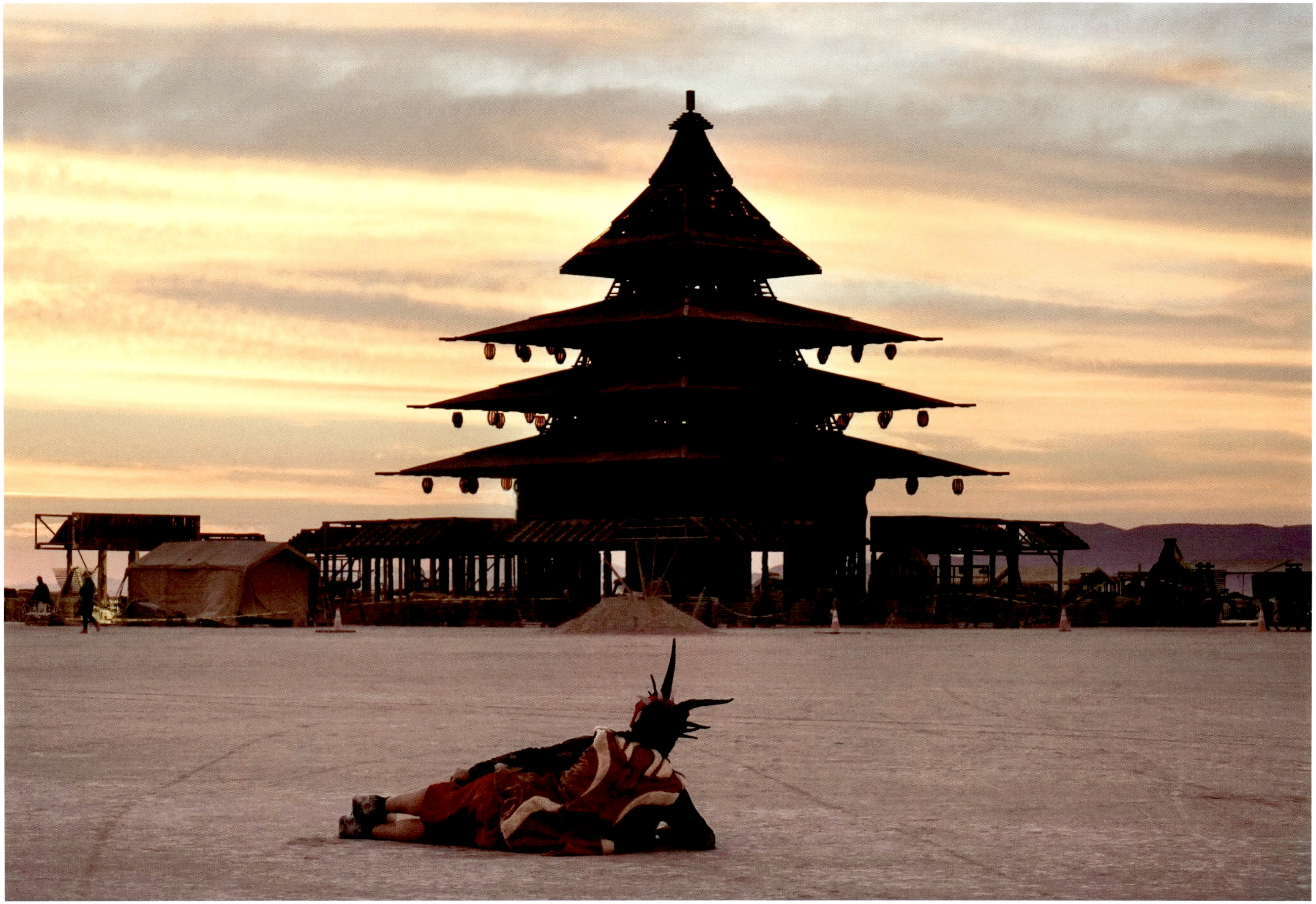

Temple Anticipation, 2016

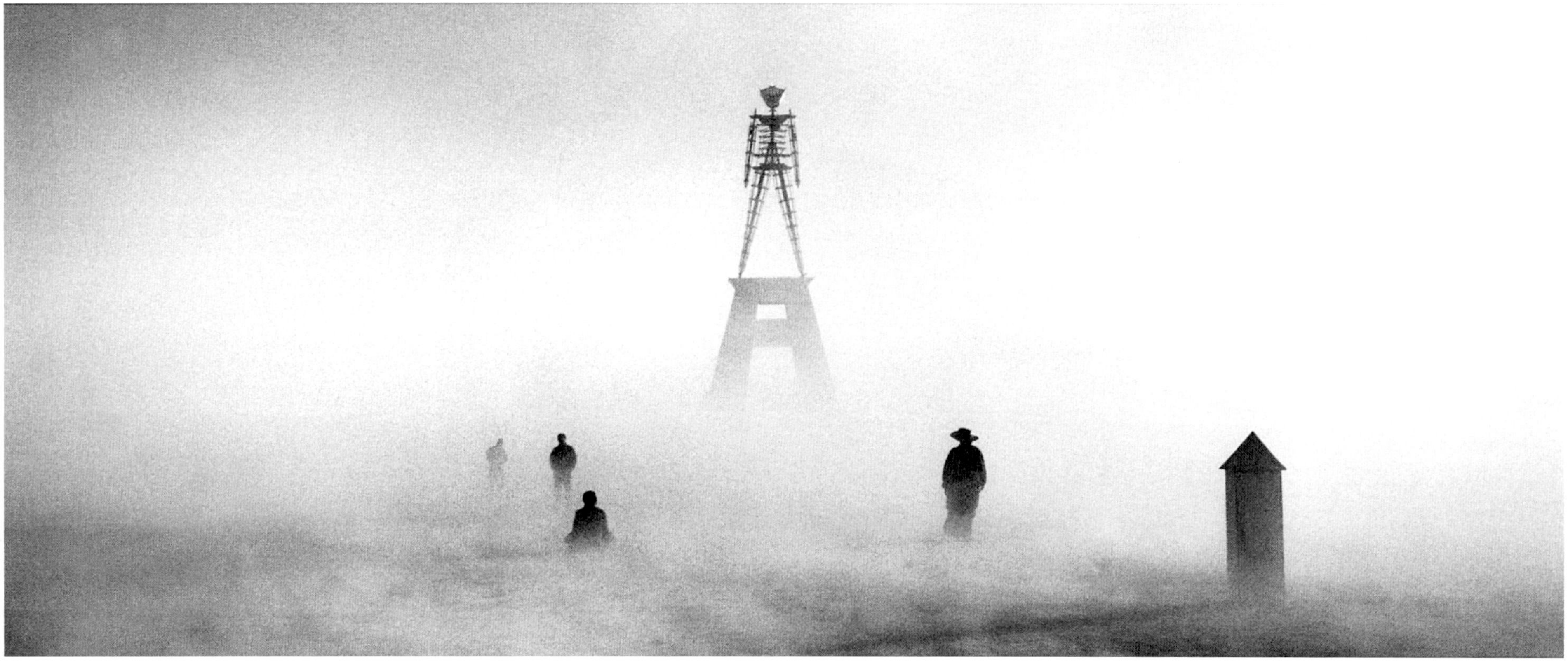

Figures and Dusty Man, 2001

My brother talks about the sacred as being "a profoundly other place." People instinctively understand the first time they set foot on the playa that this is one of nature's "cathedrals," and it can inspire Burners to meditate and indulge their spiritual inclinations. Sunrises are a magnet to many. The playa is a near-perfect environment for an event that has at its core a tapestry of death and renewal. There is no dogma, no theological underpinnings, but none are needed. This is a pageant as old as being and as universal as consciousness.

We Burning Man photographers take our moments where we can find them, and often splendid opportunities are hidden in the event's least dramatic moments. Experience is our mentor, and yet a genuinely moving image may lurk within the unexpected or be concealed in the mundane. Unique opportunities rarely appear as part of a staged ceremony; rather, we are forced to venture into the swirling dust and hope for a momentary revelation in the fog. There a concealed entity may burst forth like a phantom monster, or the thick clouds may dissipate, providing us a glimpse of an unanticipated treasure.

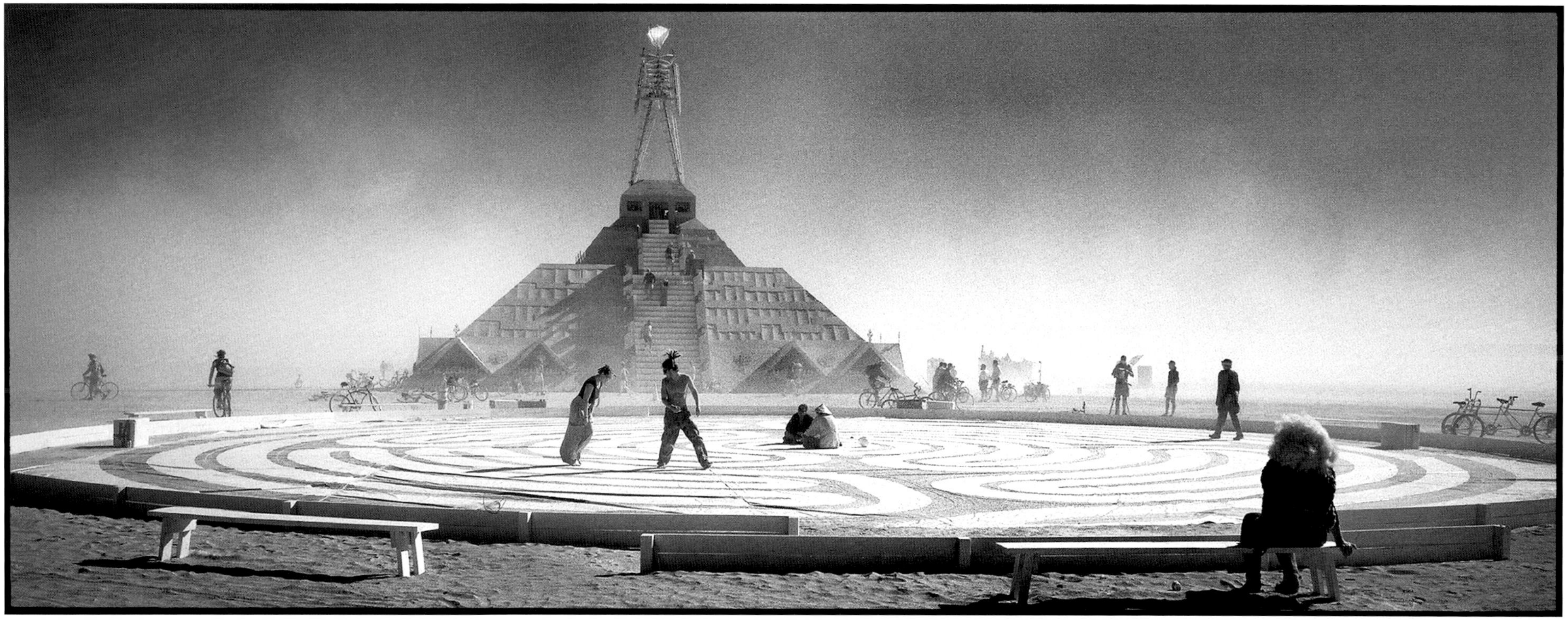

Labyrinth, *2003*

Dusty Man and Woman, 2001

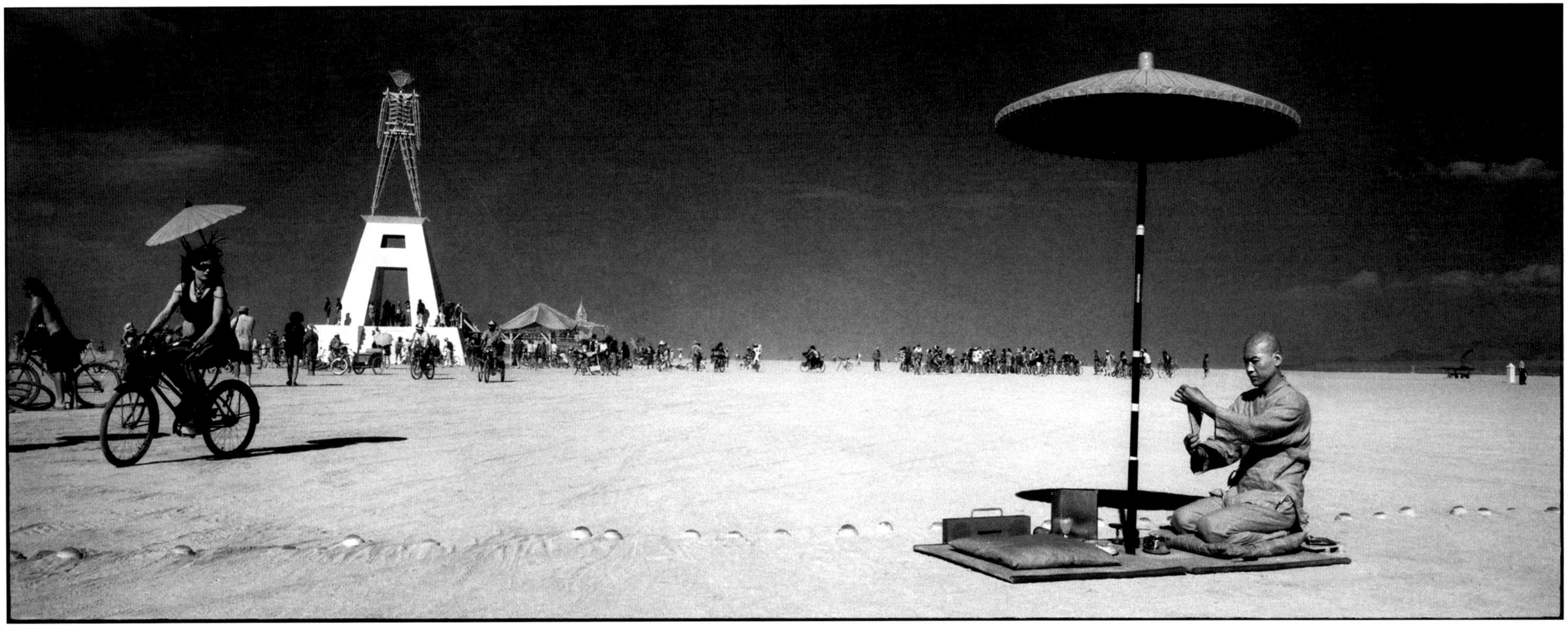

Ken Hamazaki, 2001

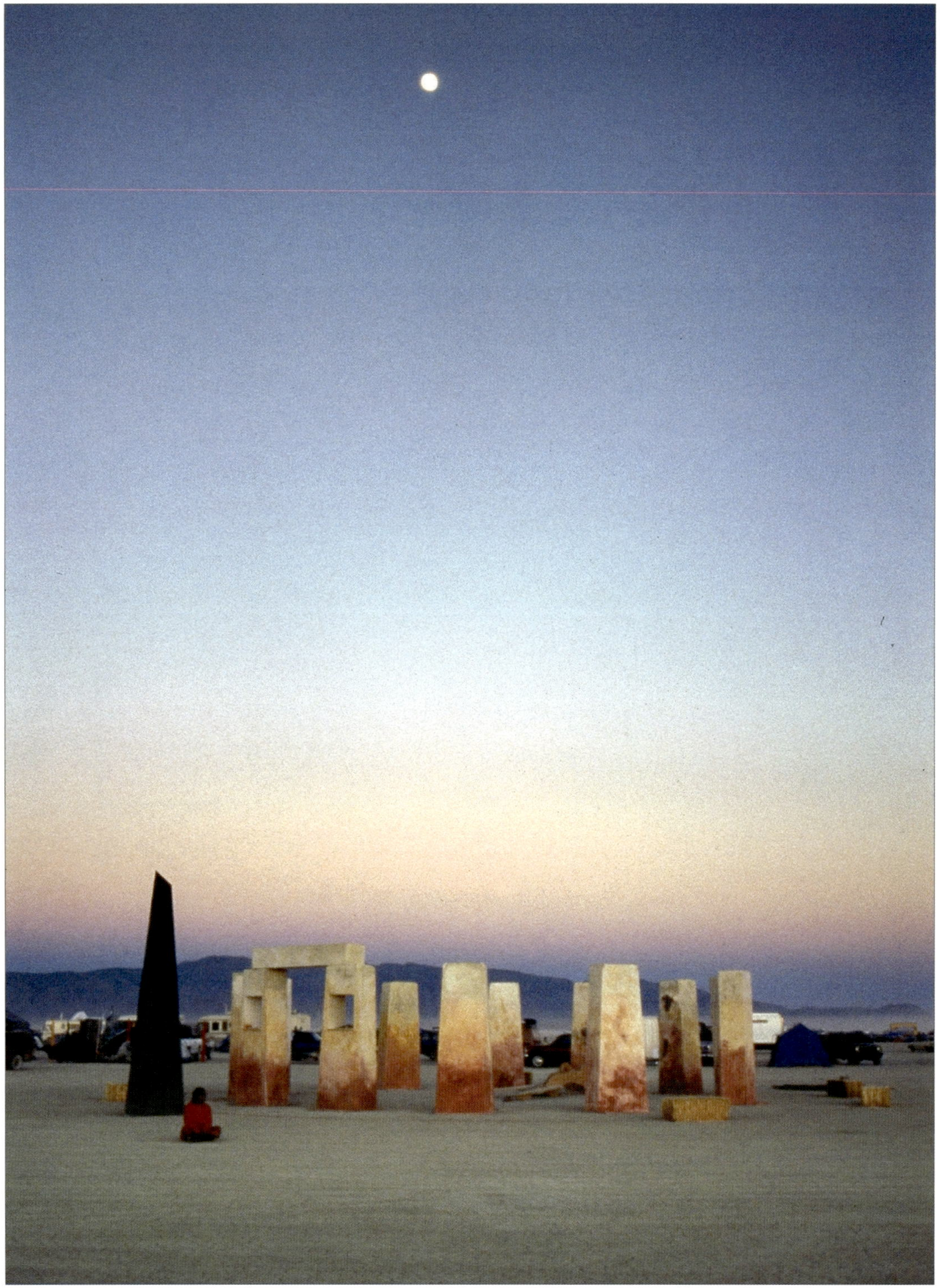

MudHenge *Morning, 1996*

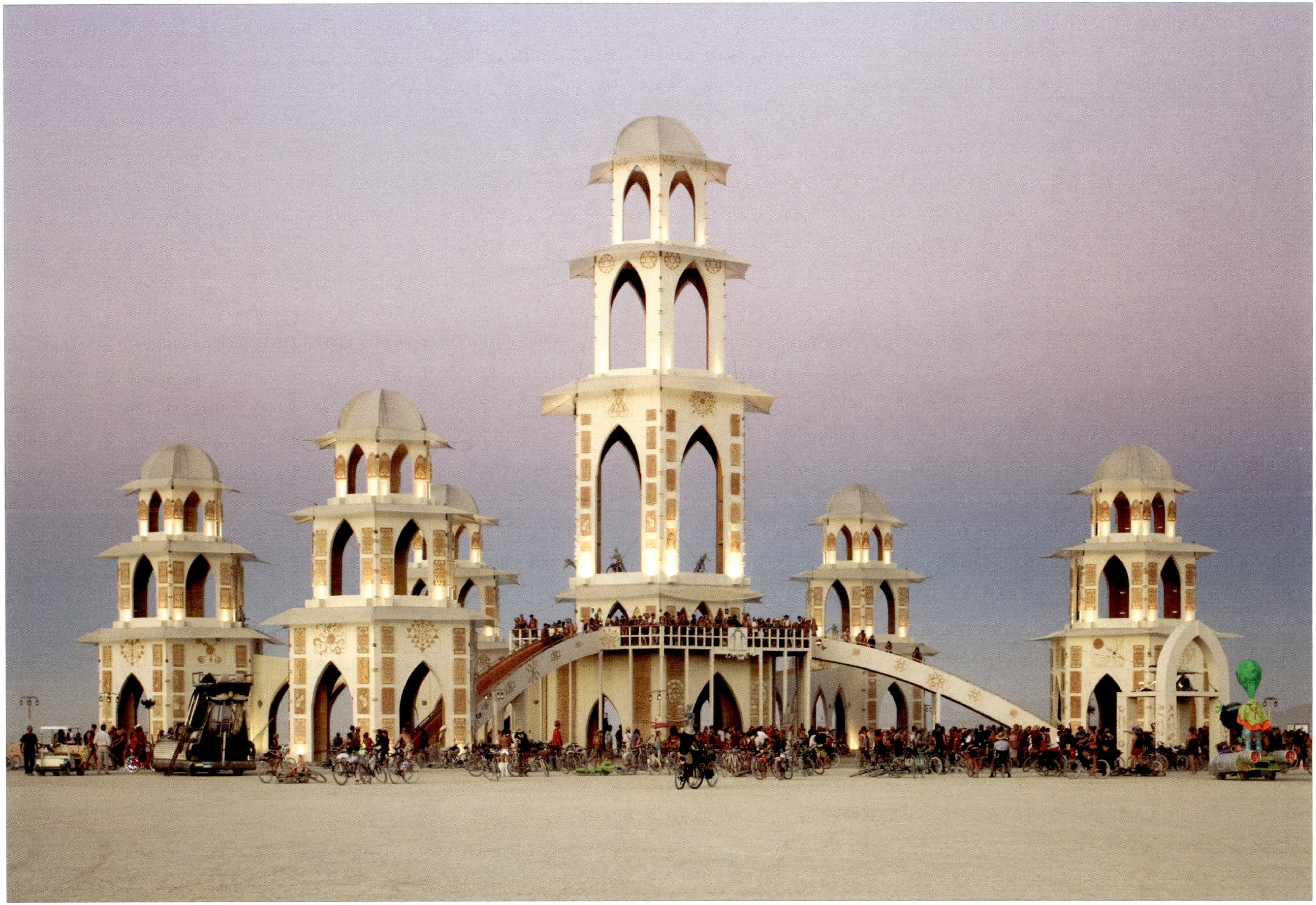

Temple of Transition, *2011*

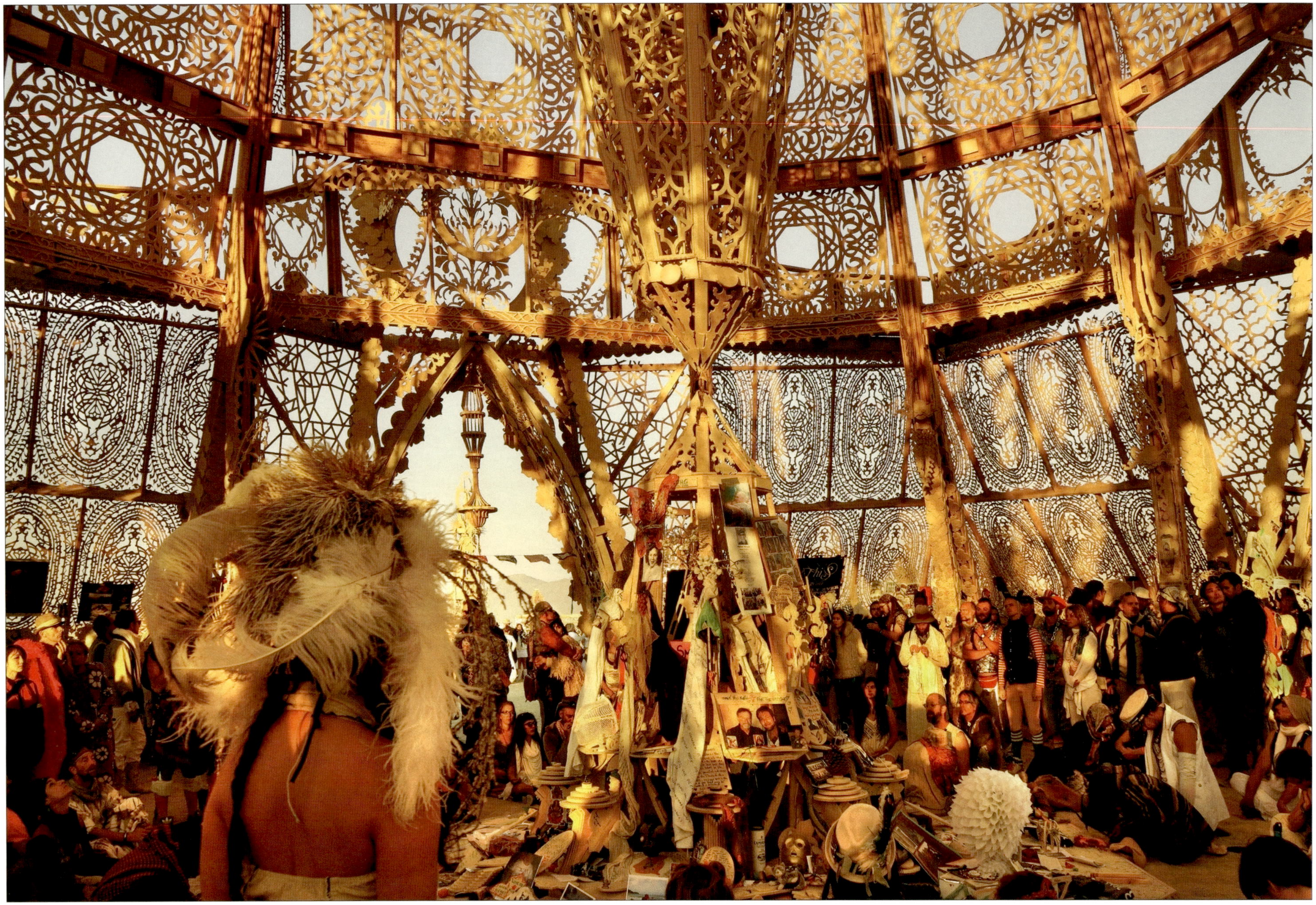

Temple Altar, 2014

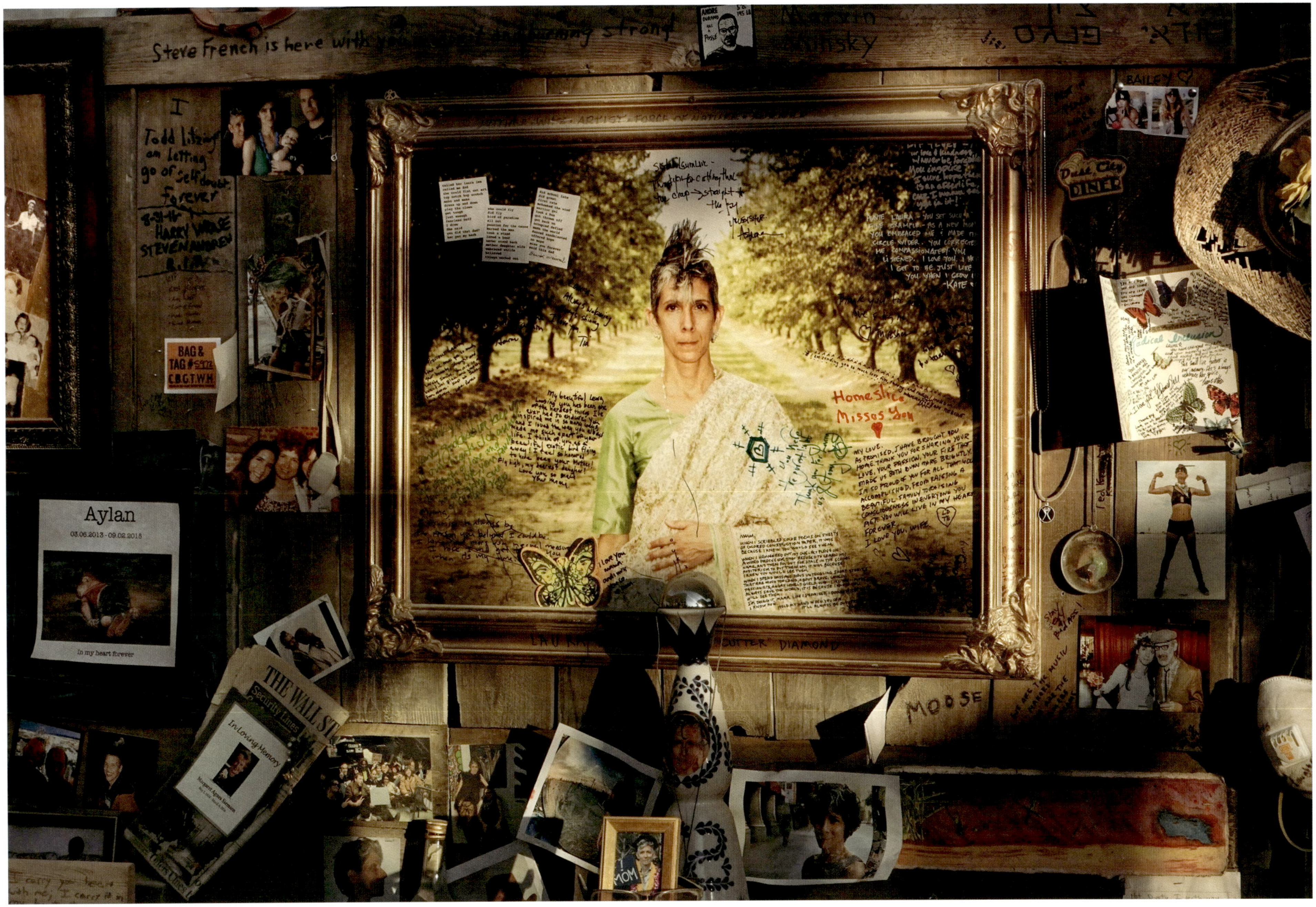

Temple Memorials, 2016

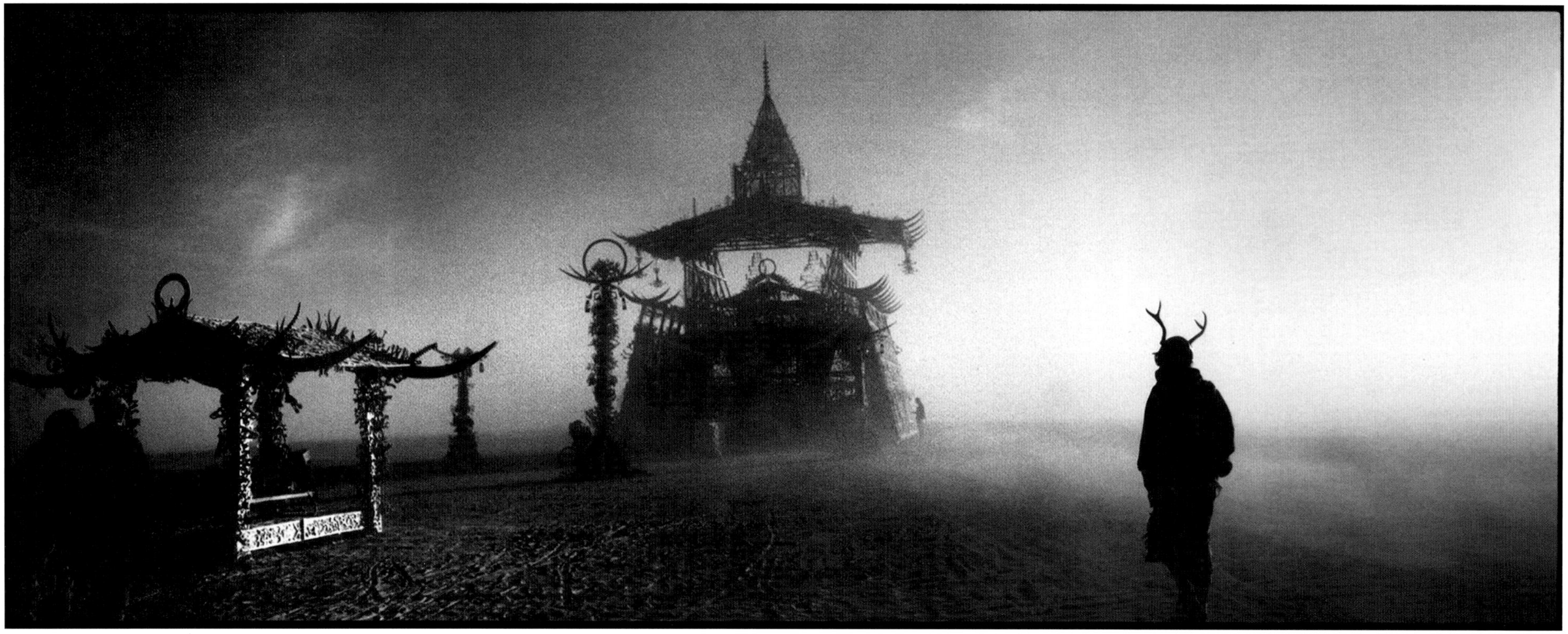

Temple of Tears, *2001*

When Burning Man asked David Best to build his *Temple of Tears* for the "Seven Ages of Man" theme, it altered the event in ways that are still reverberating. Elements of spirituality and the metaphysical had been part of the event's aura from the moment a hundred of us first stepped into the "Zone," but it had never had a clear focus. Temples took the instinctive sense that the playa was a sacred space and provided a place to invest those sensibilities.

At the center of Burning Man there has always been a primal pageant—the saga of death and renewal. We reenact that timeless drama in our lives, and it is at the very core of our mortality. Some people believe we are the only animal that understands it's going to die. I don't happen to believe that particular bit of human arrogance, but we are probably the only animal that's preoccupied with that knowledge. Deep in our being is the longing to resolve the severed ties that death visits upon us, and we hunger for a fitting tribute to our beloved departed. The temples provide an opportunity to focus and reflect upon our loved and lost—and that is a gift that transcends cultural boundaries.

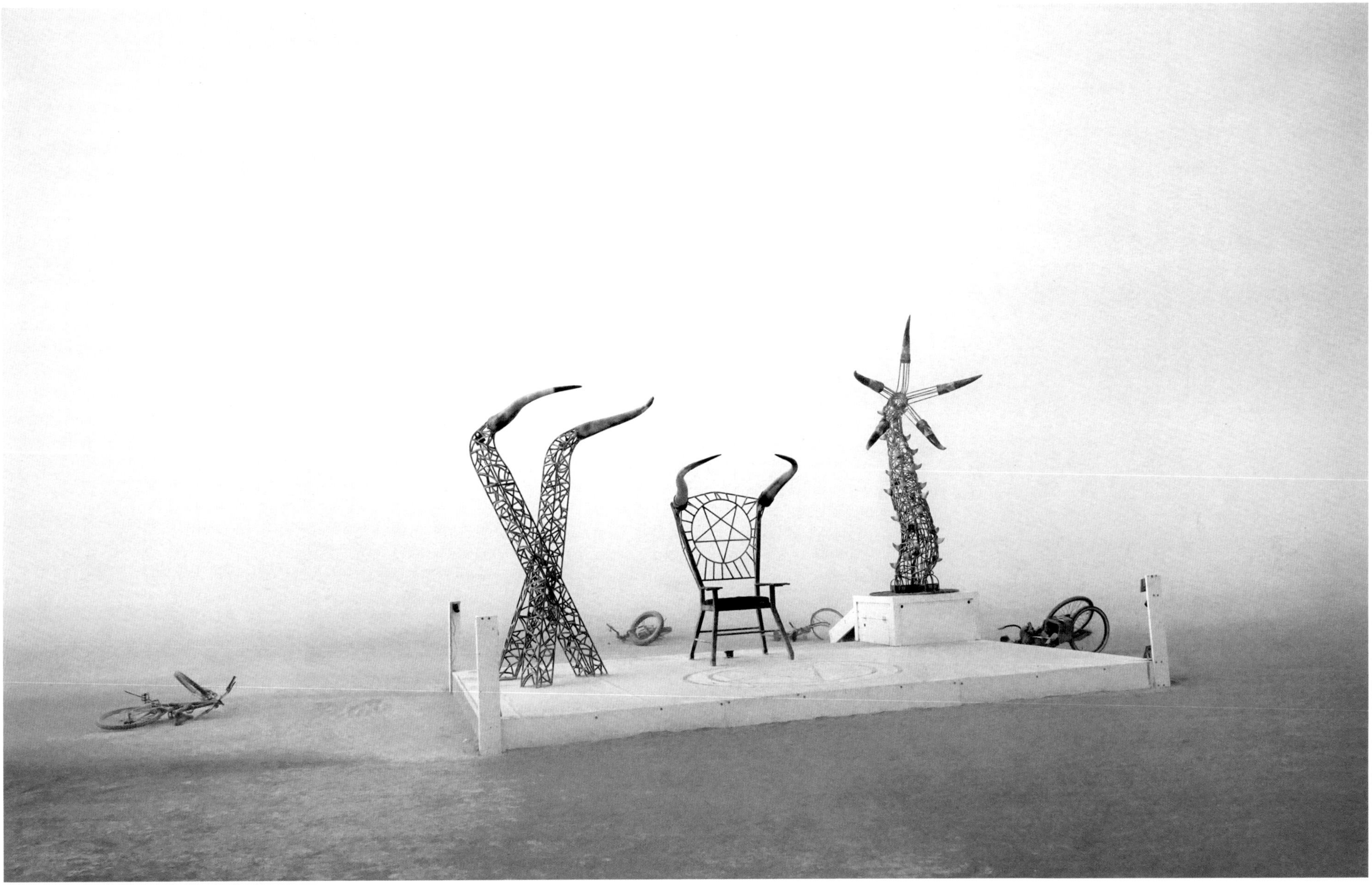

Sinner Stage, *2016*

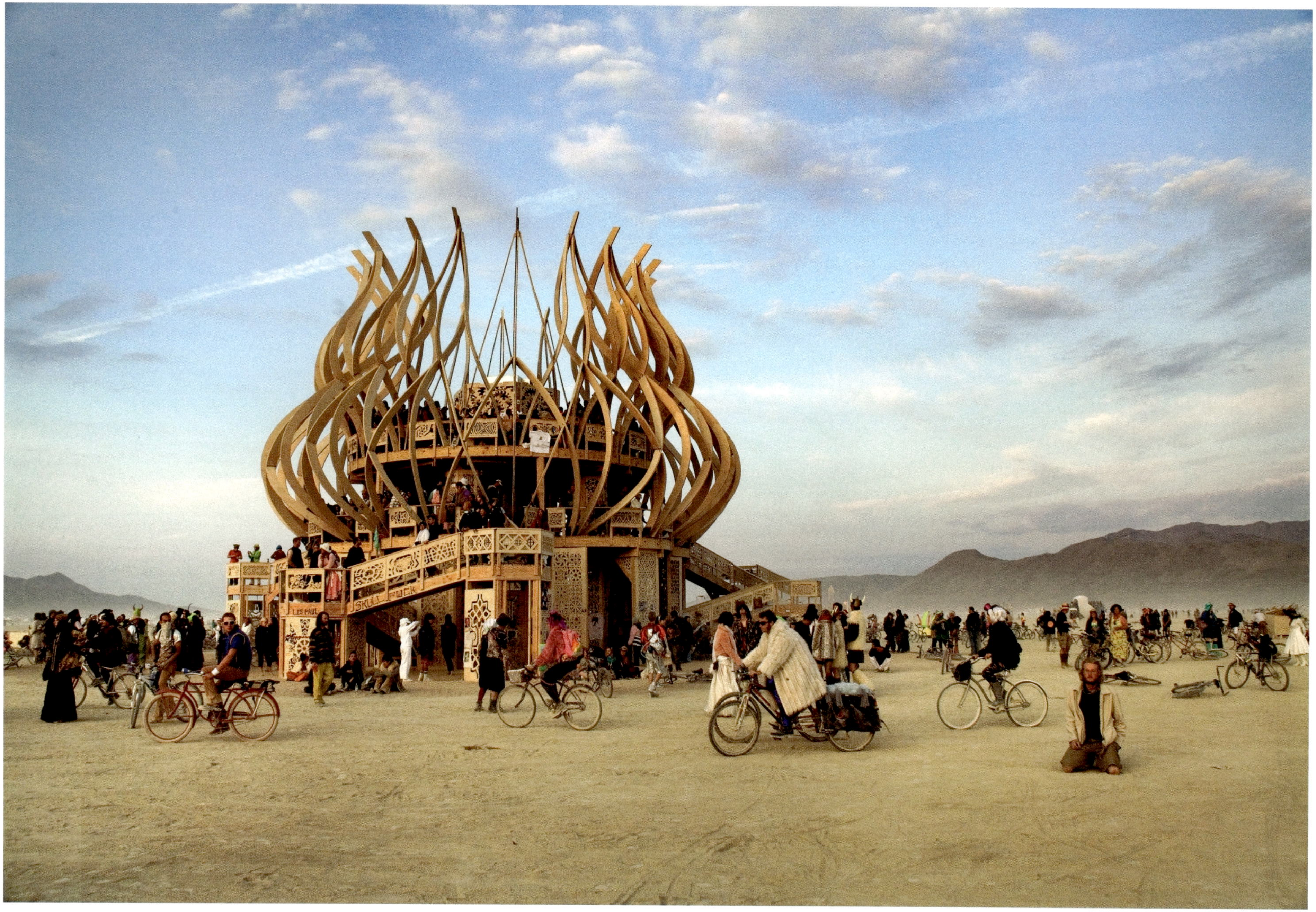

Temple Morning, 2009

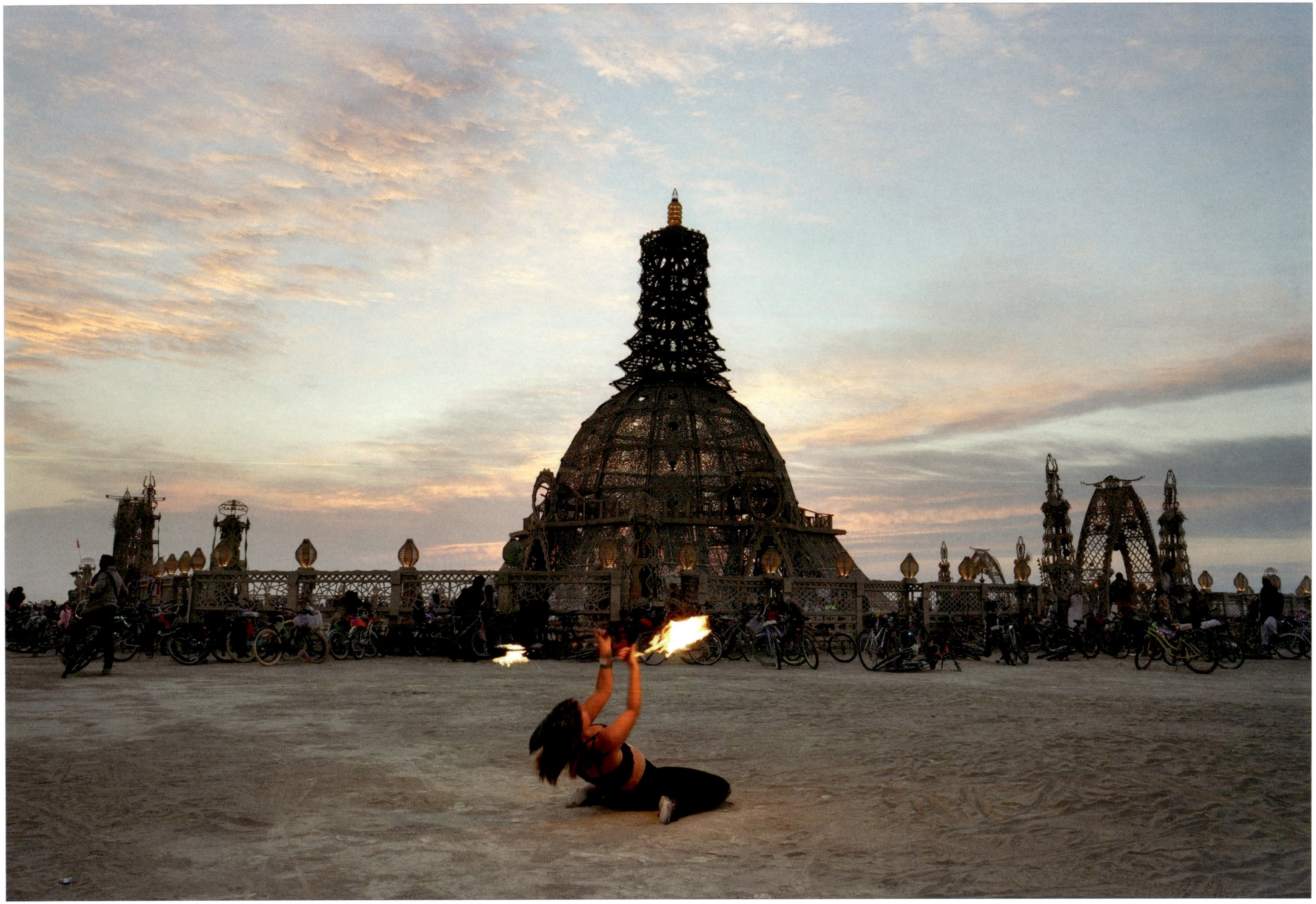

Temple of Grace, *2014*

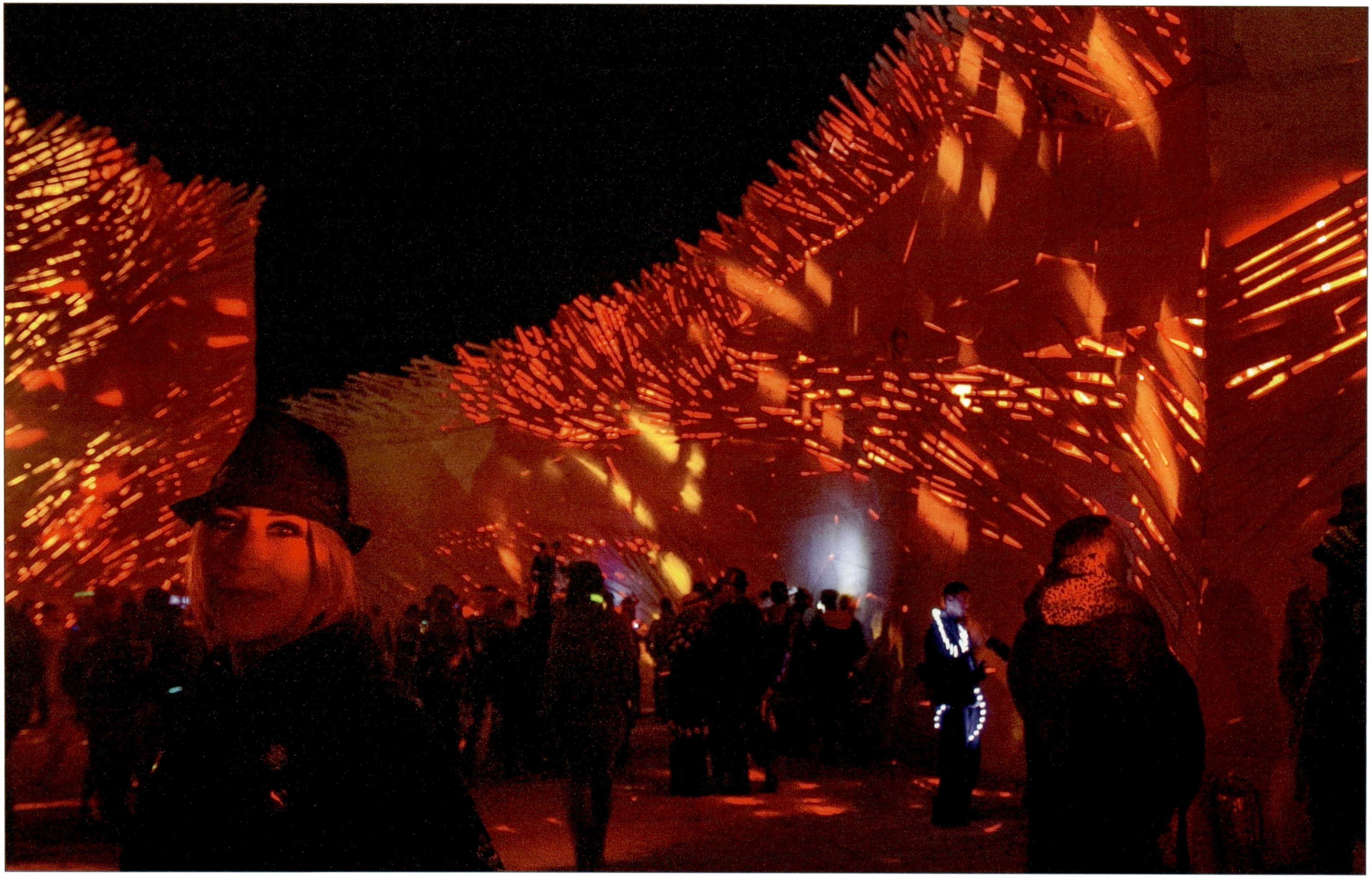

Temple of Flux *Interior, 2010*

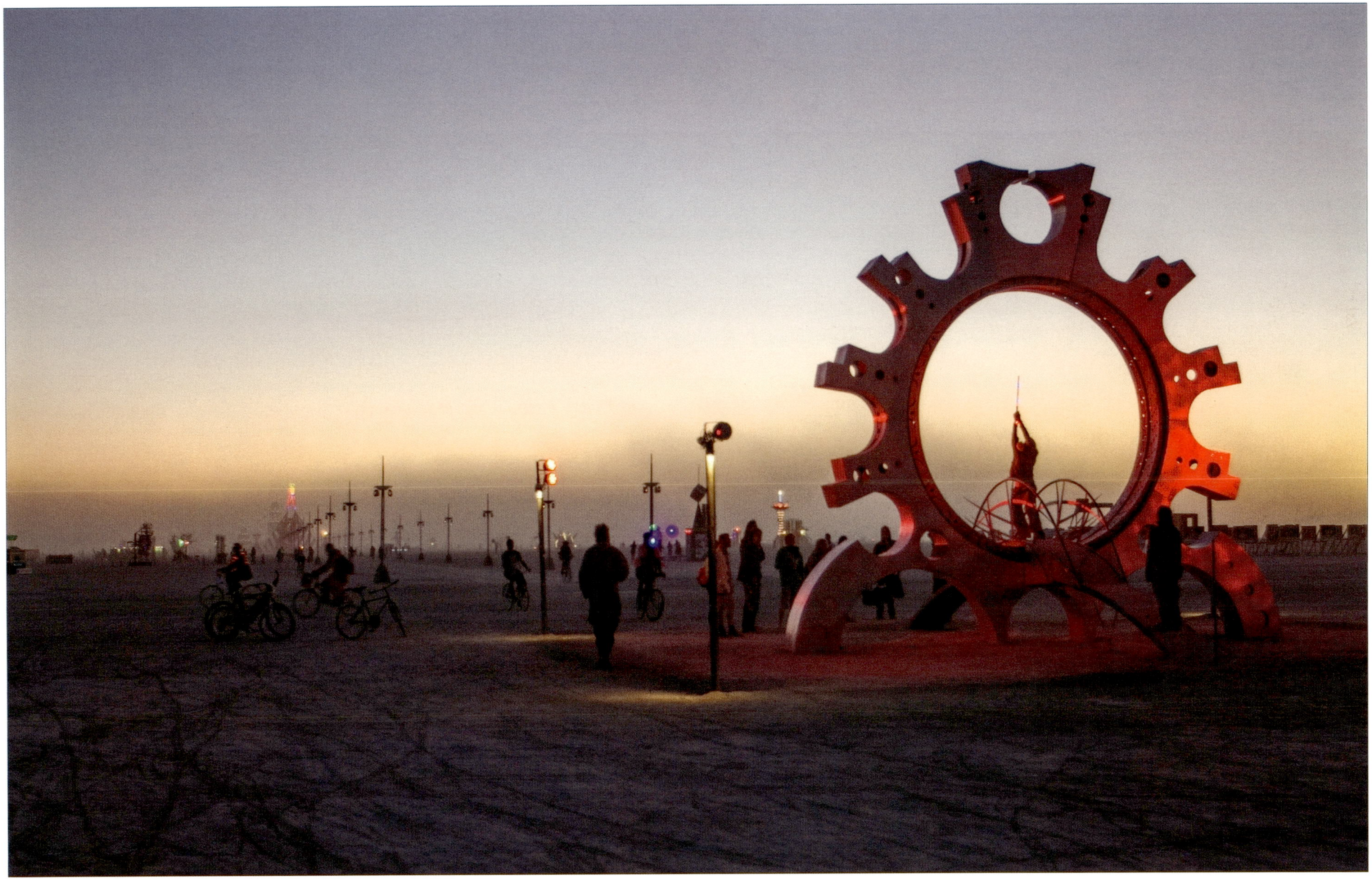

Exsuscitare Traiectus, *2011*

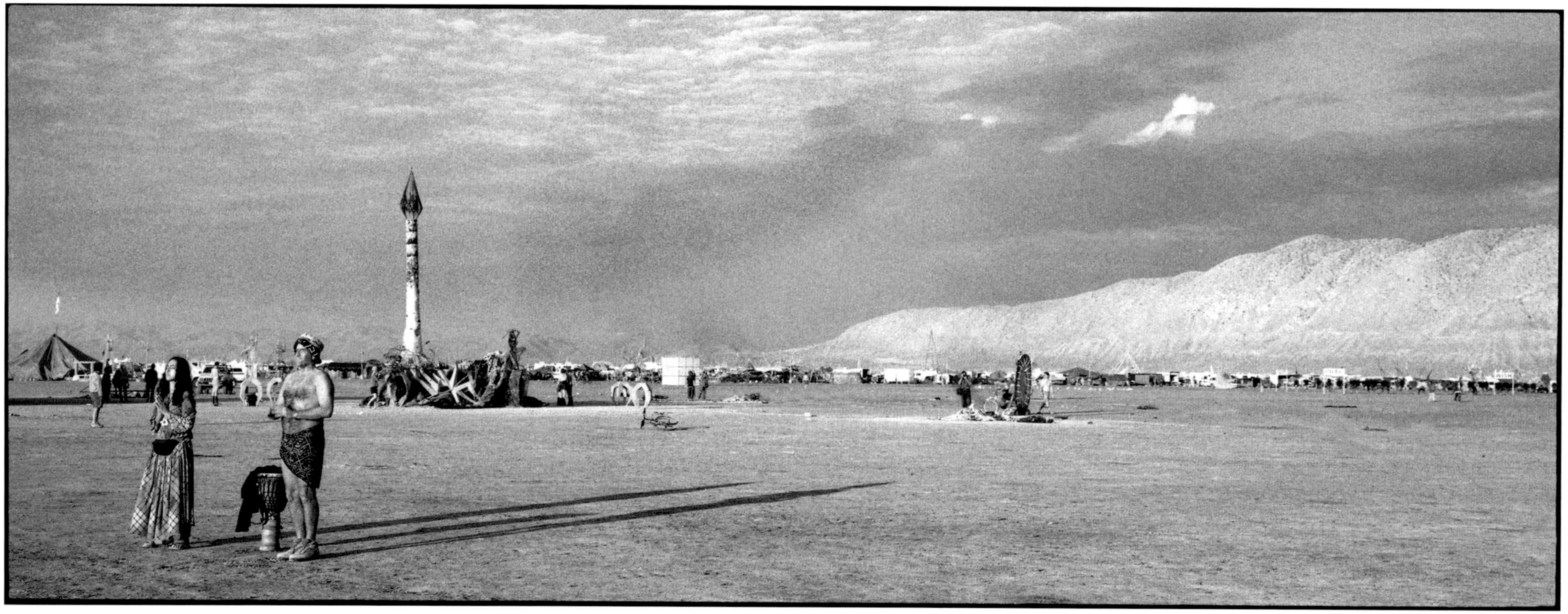

Morning Prayers, 1998

Though much ritual activity at Burning Man is generated spontaneously by individuals or camps, one can often see spiritual acts that follow the forms of traditional religion, especially at the temple. All such gestures are exclusively at the whim of those people who chose to do so, as no form of spiritual expression is either encouraged or discouraged by the event itself. The Ten Principles embrace all forms of expression—radical or not. While the heavy hand of traditional religion's moral authority is sometimes satirized harshly at the event, that is in keeping with the open invitation for people to indulge expression on as personal a level as they might. What is readily apparent is that the playa itself is an inspirational environment for such practice.

While censorship is not something one finds at Burning Man, deeply felt spiritual engagement is everywhere. What I've noticed is that while going to that "hippy-dippy art festival" is still high on many peoples' bucket lists, veterans of the event—those who have been more than two or three times—keep coming back to the playa because it fills a personal void that simply is not ministered to in their daily lives. Traditional religious practice simply doesn't work for a great many freethinkers, but the need for spiritual understanding may still boil deep within them. People do not have to be religiously inclined to hunger for a deeper understanding of their being, and the playa provides a time-honored opportunity to explore that urge. It's one of earth's many natural cathedrals, and like the Grand Canyon or the Great Barrier Reef, you know it the first time you lay eyes on it.

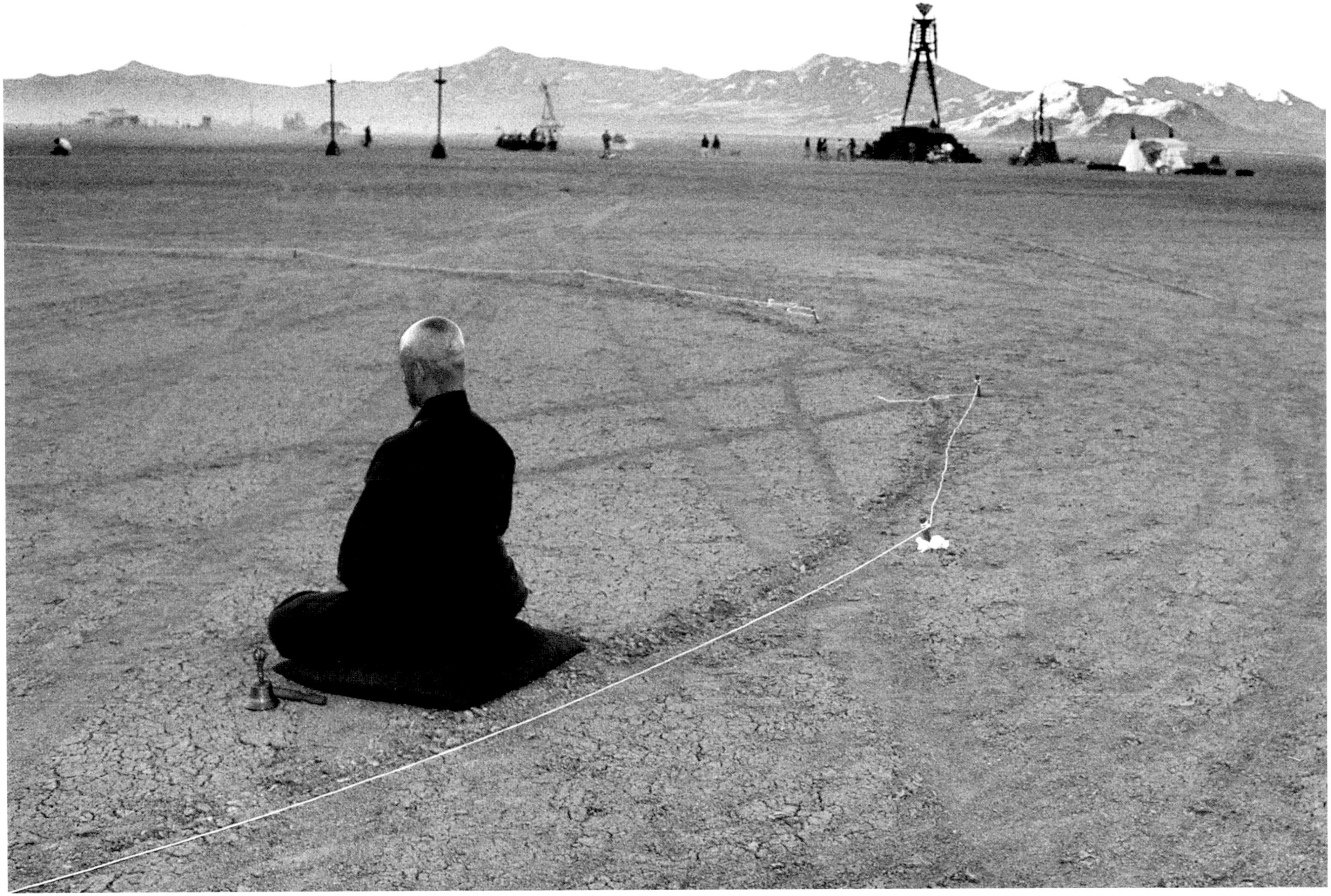

Early Meditation, 1997

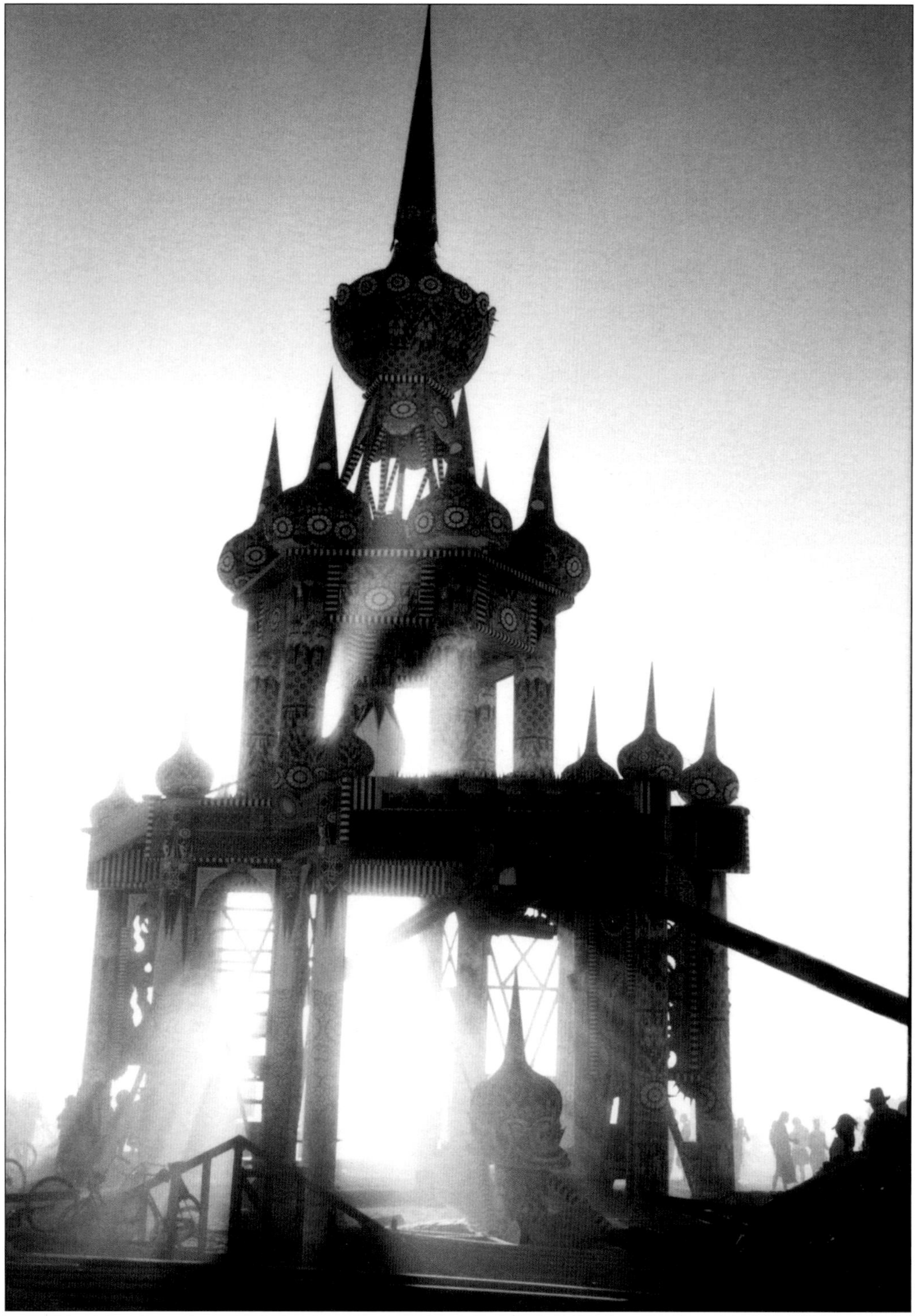

Temple of Honor, *2003*

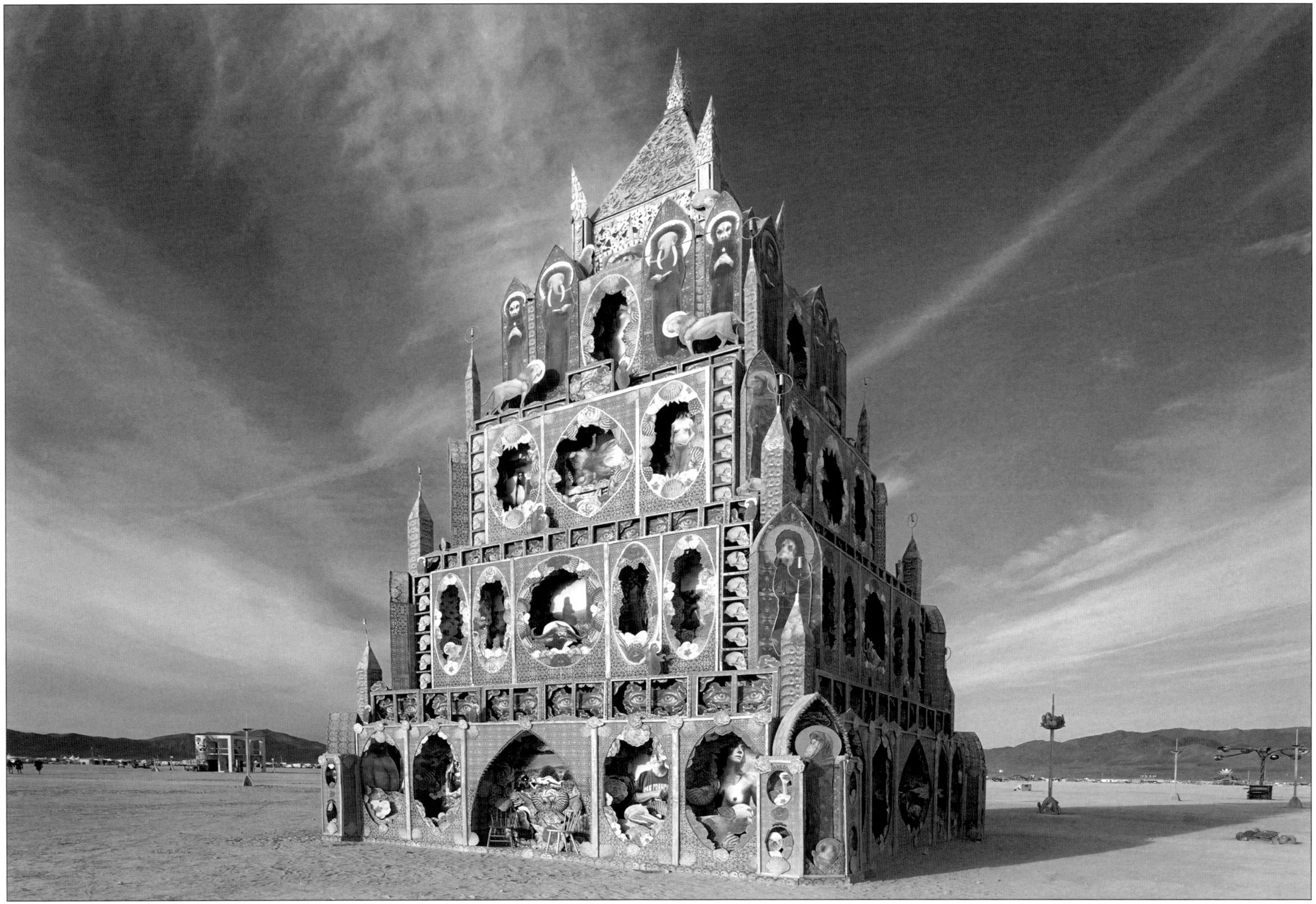

Totem of Confessions, *2015*

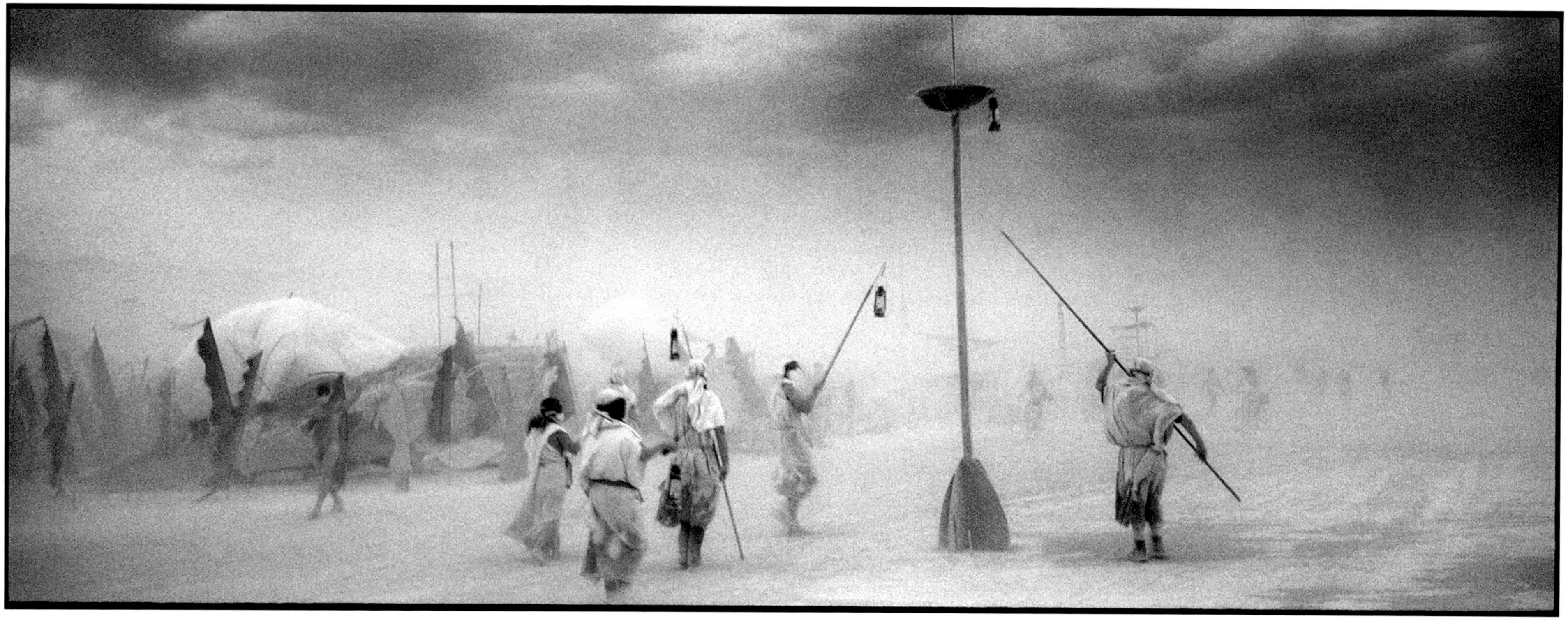

Lamplighters, 2003

Without a doubt the most revered of the legendary Burning Man volunteer crews are Steve Mobia's flame-robed Lamplighters. In the evening, these stalwarts march from Center Camp, bearing shoulder poles lined with kerosene lanterns, to hang these lamps on the spires that border all the roadways leading to the Man. The Lamplighters work silently to the haunting beat of a drum or another percussive instrument, and it is not uncommon to hear Burners applaud as these robed servants pass by. Lamplighters perform their rounds faithfully in every kind of weather, quite often buffeted by the gusting winds and swirling clouds of dust. They are to Burning Man what a color guard is to Arlington Cemetery, and they herald the city's transition from dusty day to illuminated night.

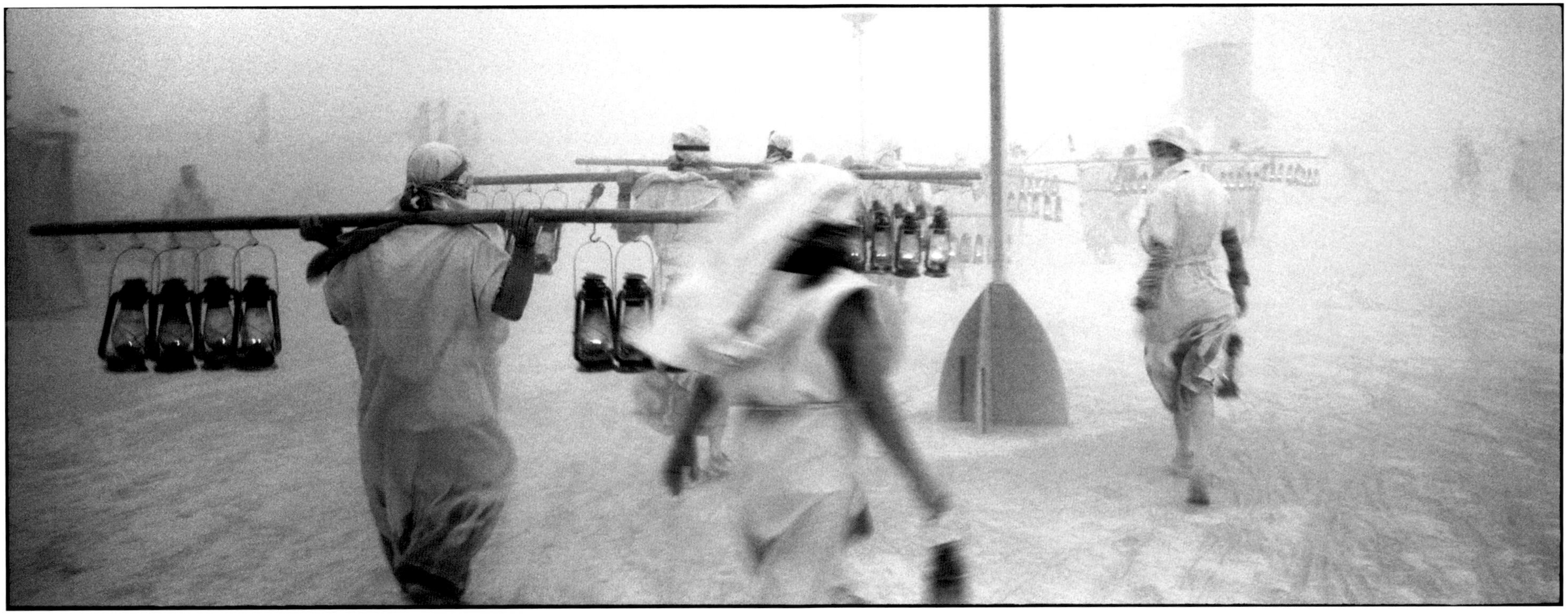

Lamplighters, 2002

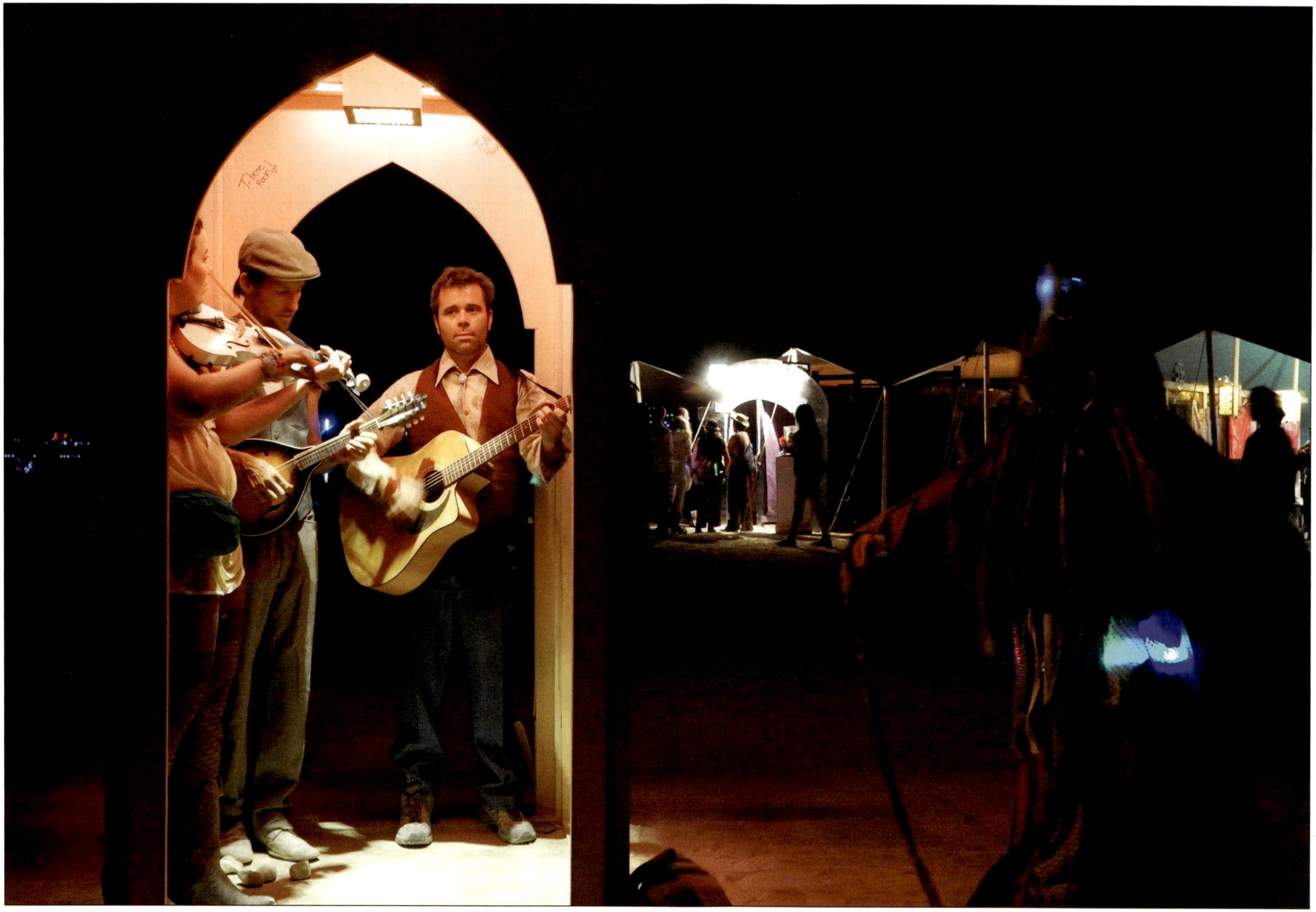

Souk Players, 2014

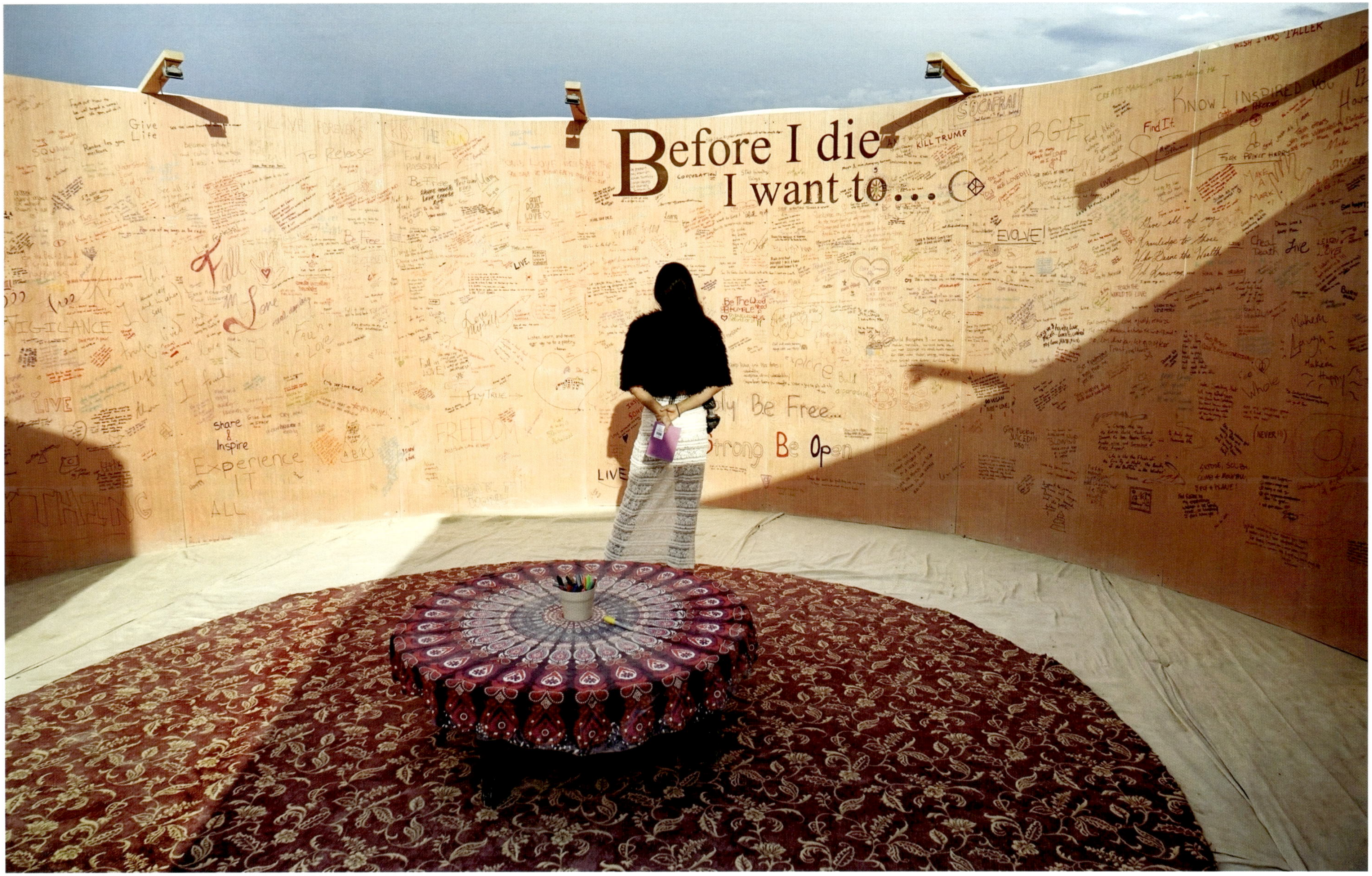

The Before . . . Project, *2016*

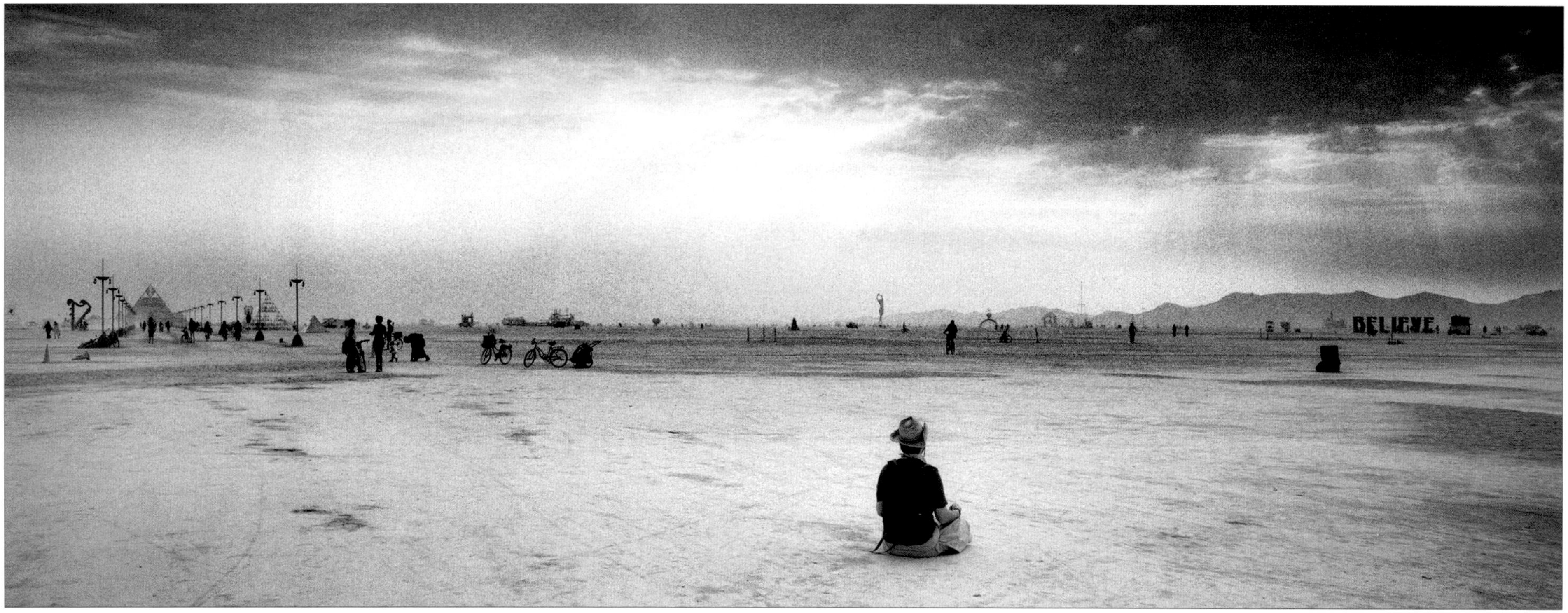

Playa Sitting, 2014

One of the most rewarding experiences you can have at Burning Man is to walk out alone in the early morning light, plop your butt onto the playa, and wait for the sun to peek over the horizon. It needn't be an act of meditation or part of any conscious ritual practice. In fact, I would argue it's better if it isn't. I do my playa sitting as an act of solidarity with the universe. It is a unique opportunity to sit and contemplate your part in a greater context—for the universe is something that may be keenly felt in this wide, flat expanse where all manner of cosmic kinship seems to be hidden just behind the ever-changing skyline.

The playa is a busy place so early in the morning, and you become acutely aware of the myriad movements all around; yet there is a sense that you are utterly protected by a spatial privacy that is all-encompassing. In this land of many thousands, you will have your own intimate turf, and people here will respect and understand your desire for privacy. Often there's a peace that settles in, a stillness of suspended time, and for brief moments the distant people and objects resemble stars in a constellation of undetermined shape. Here you become the center of your own galaxy. The broad playa and its odd-shaped stars seem to orbit around you, and for a few blessedly undisturbed minutes there is nowhere else more important to be.

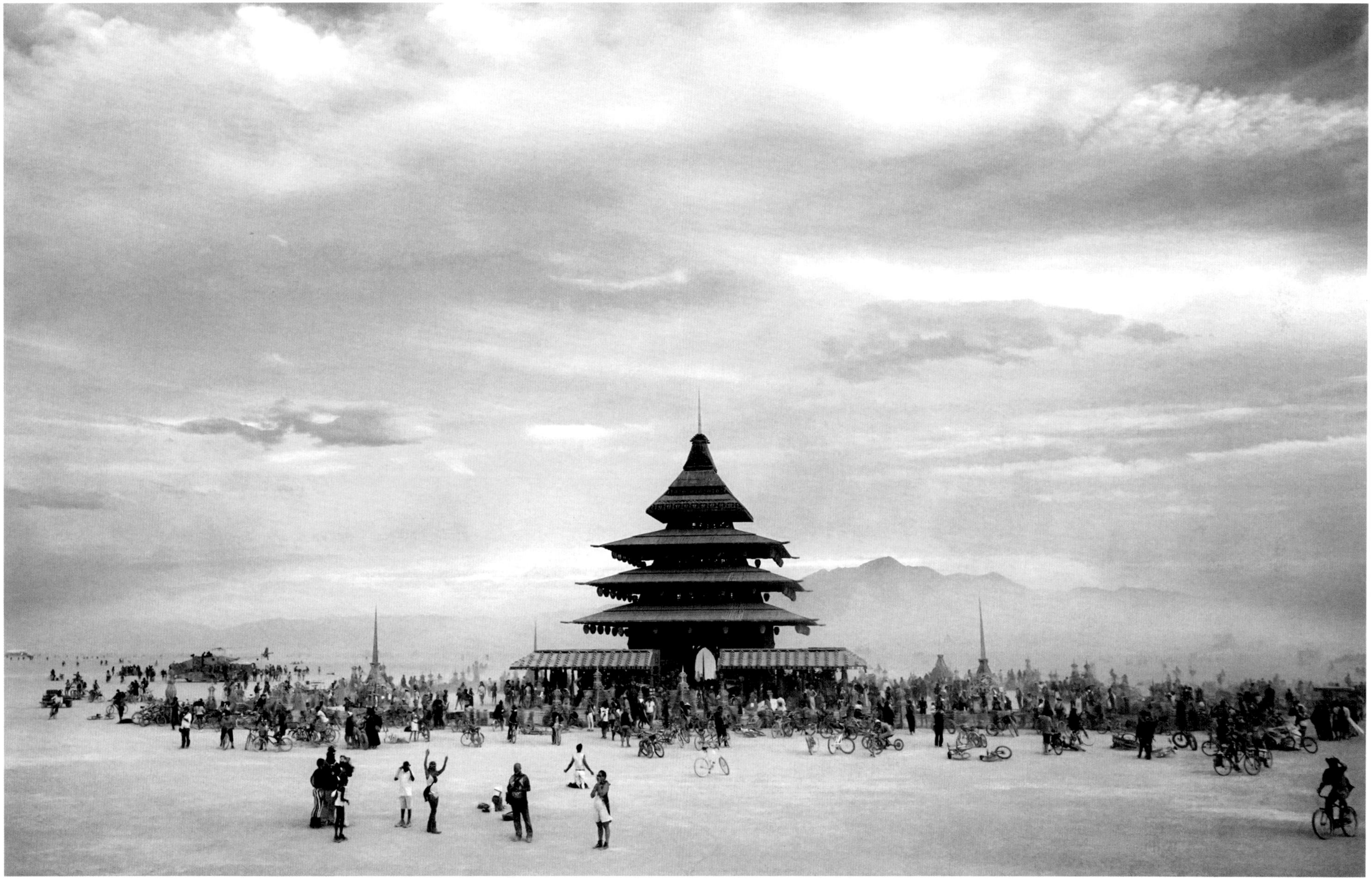

Temple View, 2016

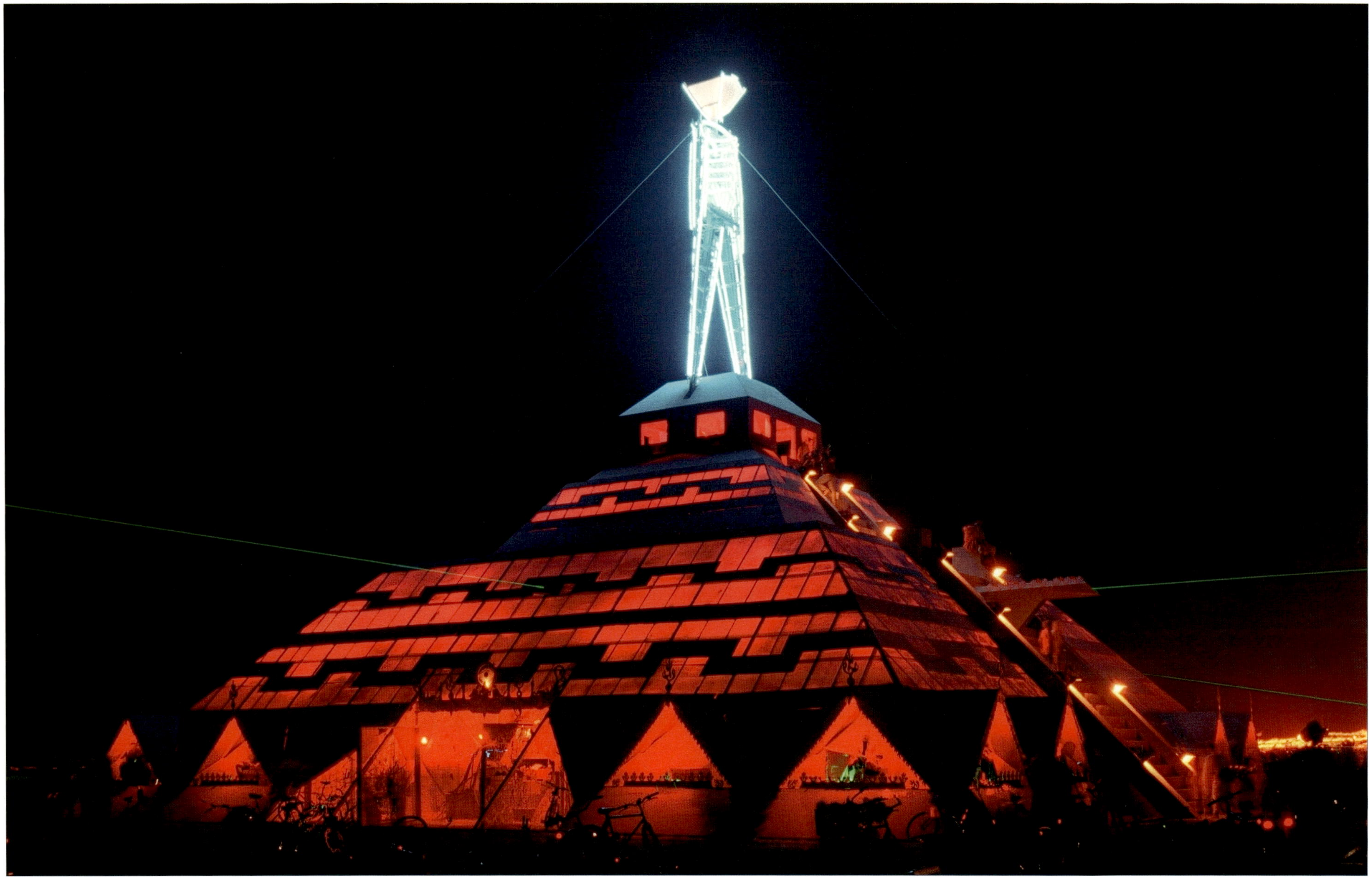

"Beyond Belief" Pavilion, 2003

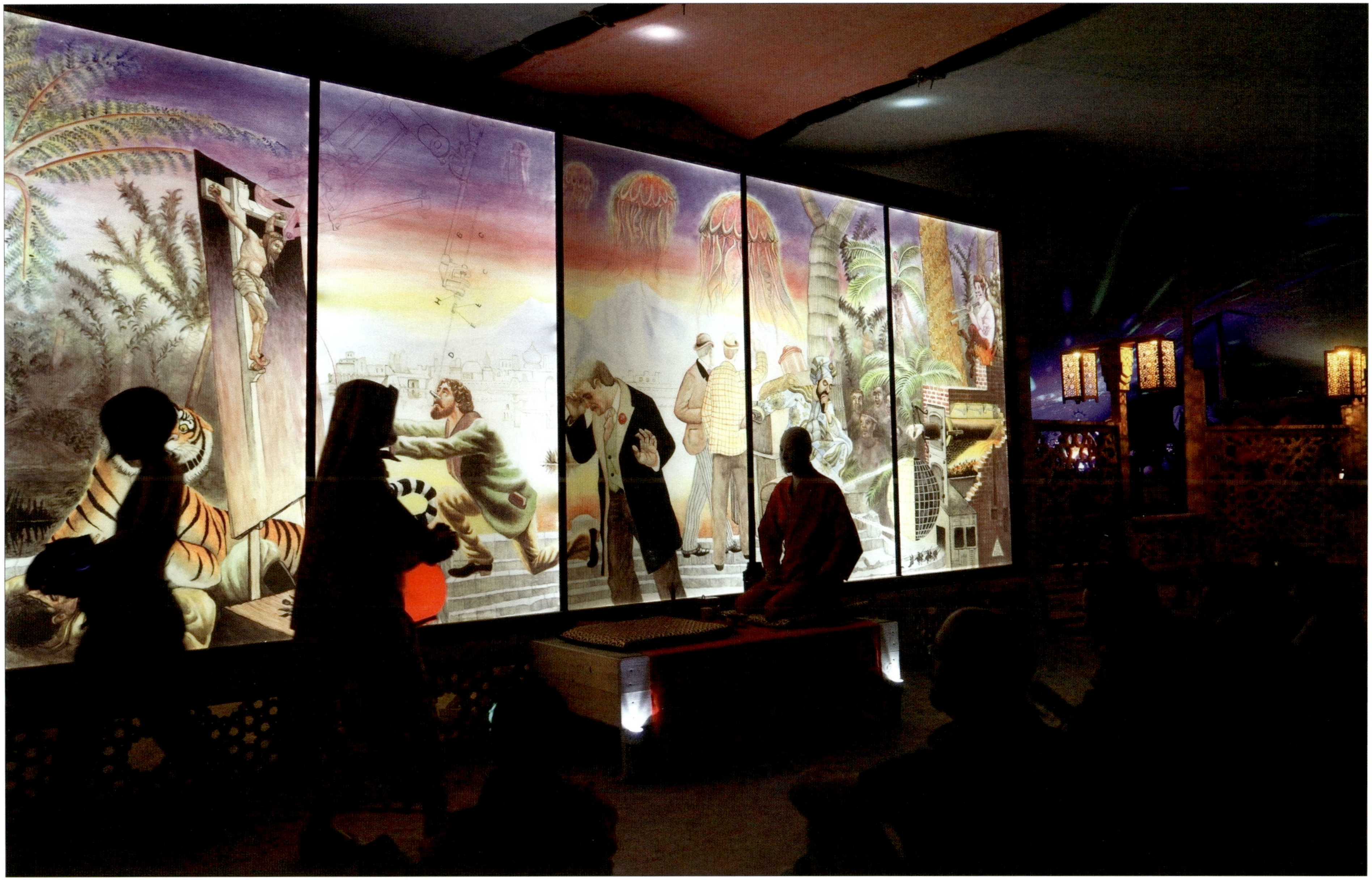

Souk Tea Ceremony, 2014

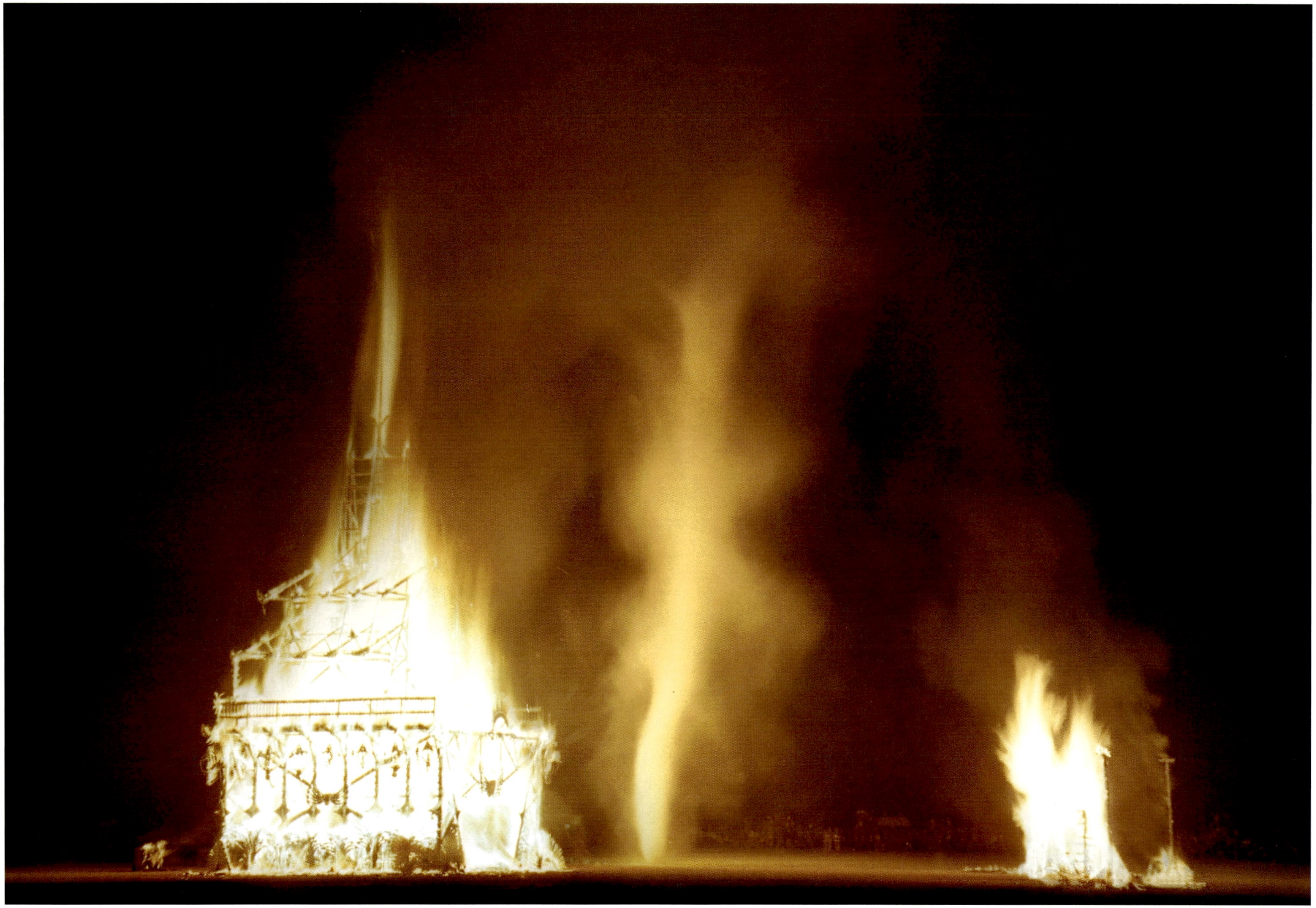

Temple of Joy, *2002*

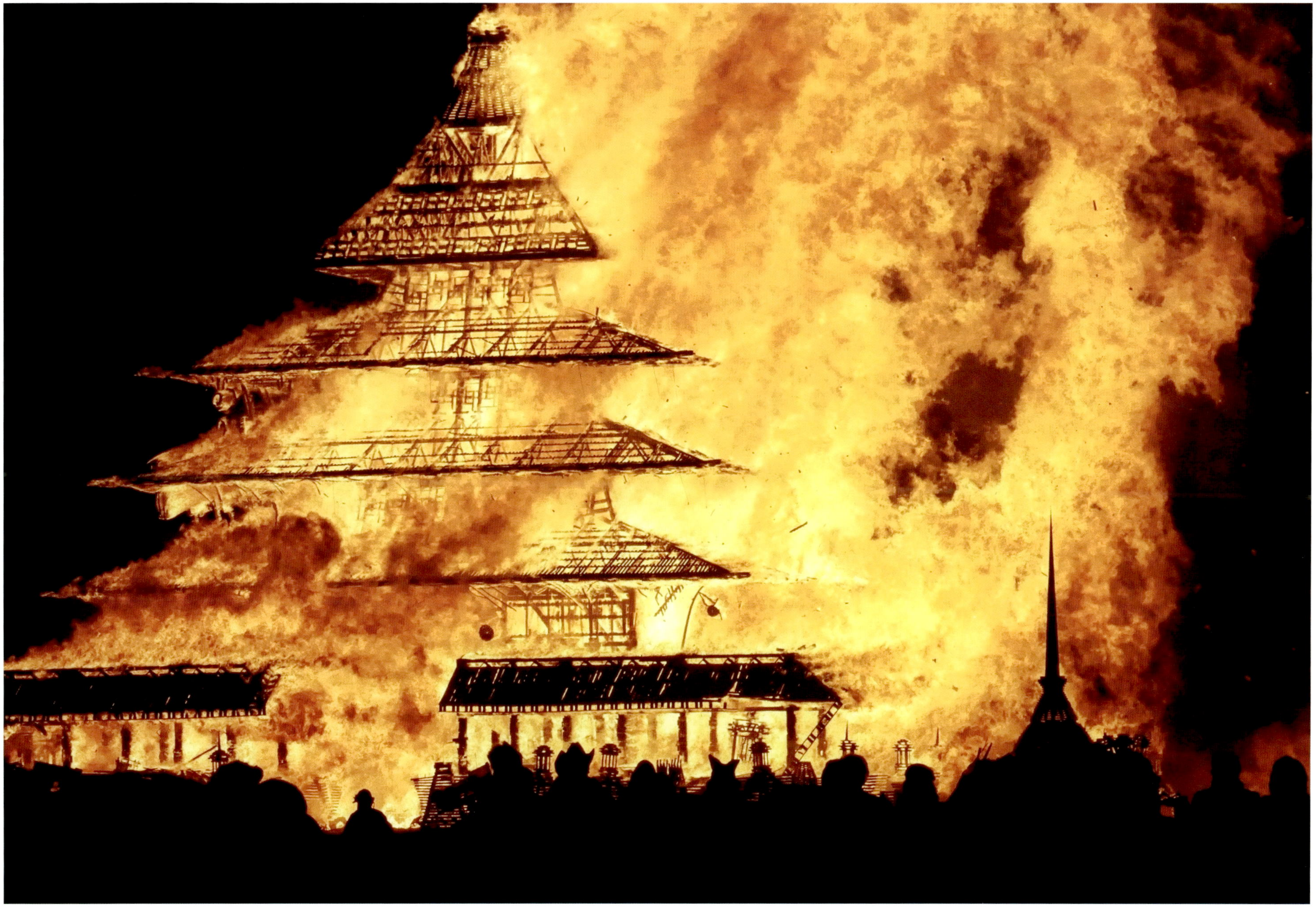

Temple Fire, 2016

CHAPTER 11

ART AND PRINCIPLES: 2005–2010

When my brother penned the Ten Principles in 2004, he was driven by a desire on the part of himself and the other five founders to spread Burning Man culture around the world. Something extraordinary was happening out on the playa besides nudity and big art. It had to do with the way Burners were behaving toward one another, and the sheer cooperative energy they seemed to arrive with in their packs. It also had to do with an elusive bond that formed between Burners. Larry began to speak about it as a broad spirit of community. It's a little bit like when strangers with a common nationality meet by chance in a foreign land. They are bonded not only by a common language but also by a shared history of beliefs and customs.

By this time, many regional Burner groups had formed around art projects, art cars, theme camps, and, more importantly, around the desire to develop their own regional events. It was the latter phenomenon that necessitated a formal articulation of the core values of Burning Man. The organization had long held that it would support regional Burns without demanding anything in return so long as that regional event demonstrated the constructive elements of Burning Man culture, and the Ten Principles articulate the warp and woof of its philosophical foundation.

It's important to repeat that rather than fashioning a constitution or legislating a set of bylaws, Larry set about describing the important attitudes and behaviors that were already in practice at the event. Many of these had been part of the Cacophony culture but were filtered and refined by the constraints and logistics of living in an arid and volatile topography. In that context, it can also be said that at least half or more of these values probably would have developed quite naturally within an environment where civic responsibility and common courtesy are important for survival. It's all well and good to be a jerk at a concert when at the end of the event you simply grab a ride home, but if you had to stay in that concert venue for days in the sweltering heat, well, then you check your attitude in the lobby. There is no doubt in my mind that the most honorable traits of Burning Man culture were forged on the sunbaked playa.

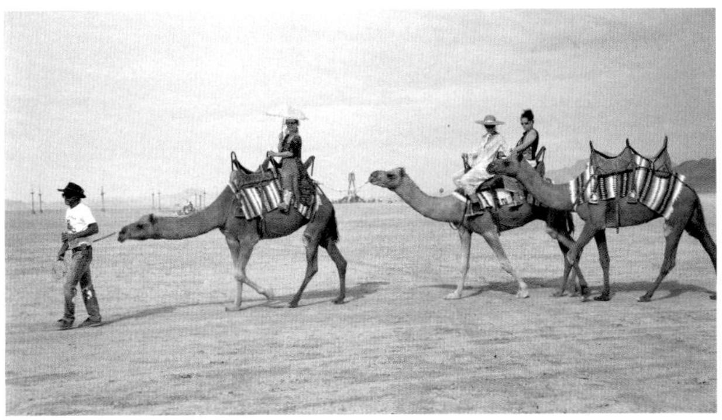

Tocka Wilson brought Pucka, Milagro, and Saddam to teach us the ten principles of camel.

Radical Inclusion

Anyone may be a part of Burning Man. We welcome and respect the stranger. No prerequisites exist for participation in our community.

Radical Inclusion grew out of a serious disagreement between early Burners in the 1990s about whether to restrict Burning Man to people who "got" the ideas behind the event. Some of those ideas came from the Cacophony Society tradition that everyone in the group was expected to generate an activity for the group. In other words, full participation by all was an organizing principle. Some early Burners feared being overrun by gawkers and tourists. Larry countered that restricting the event would turn it into a members-only club and thus limit its creative future. He reminded everyone that Cacophony had always been open to all, and its mantra was "You may already be a member."

Potential snobbery wasn't the issue for my brother. He wanted Burning Man to continue to evolve as an international community, and requiring the world society to "get it" would inevitably be a serious limitation. I remember the days when the scourge of the playa was fat frat boys and drumming circles. Now community resentments include plug-and-play luxury camps and the "one percent." But none of these things are real threats to the culture of community at Burning Man. Rather, being inclusive has infused Burning Man with a cornucopia of unexpected international and homegrown riches.

In 1998, a taciturn Aussie by the name of Tocka Wilson contacted Burning Man about bringing camels to the desert event. Wilson thought he could make a few dollars by giving people camel rides. When informed that there was a firm "No vending" policy at the event, Wilson decided to come anyway. He arrived with three of the dromedary (single-humped) variety of camels—Pucka, Milagro, and Saddam. Once he got over the culture shock of seeing *blokes* walking around naked, Tocka spent the weekend trading for camel rides. "You'd be surprised what I've been offered!" he joked.

Wilson isn't the only person to have mistaken the playa for a potential sales opportunity. Captain Jim Peterson and his crew of fishermen from the Charleston area of Oregon also came to Burning Man in 1998 seeking to unload a trailer full of iced tuna. When they discovered to their chagrin that there was no vending allowed, they spent the weekend cooking and giving away their catch. Then they came back year after year to feed tuna to the multitudes and became a playa legend. I got to know the good captain a bit, and I must say Tuna Camp became one of my favorite haunts and a must-visit each year. They'd change the menu each day, and we'd line up with our plates to receive that great Pacific bounty. The Tuna Guys became a sterling example of the first two principles on Larry's list (the second being Gifting). As roguish and independent fishermen from a small town in Oregon, they might not have been anyone's idea of Burner material, but after *including* them, they turned out to be the epitome of what *gifting* ought to encompass at Burning Man: free-spirited, inventive, and delicious.

Captain Jim lost his life in 2011. He and a small crew had been hired to ferry crab pots out to a fishery. Their small boat began taking on water, and Jim was trapped inside the cabin. He kept the boat afloat long enough so his two crewmen could be rescued. In a moving tribute, his friends built and burned a boat just before the burning of the Man in 2012. We were all standing in First Camp, waiting to proceed out to the Man, when we were startled to see at the southern edge of the playa a line of law enforcement vehicles, all with their red and blue lights ablaze. There looked to be at least twenty rigs, and I must admit it was an unsettling sight. Just then Burning Man's longtime attorney Terry "Lightning" Gross ran up to us and exclaimed, "Is it a raid?" We looked out at the line of flashing lights for a few minutes. "No," Larry said finally, "I think they're participating!" What they were participating in was a salute to Captain Jim just before they set his memorial boat on fire. That's right, Radical Inclusion might have to extend also to the fuzz—at least to some of them, anyway.

Gifting

> **Burning Man is devoted to acts of gift giving. The value of a gift is unconditional. Gifting does not contemplate a return or an exchange for something of equal value.**

Commerce is so engrained in our DNA that it's hard for many people to wrap their heads around an economy based on unselfish giving. But it's not an economy at all; it's a *culture of generosity*. Our parents used to tell Larry and me this story every time our mother fixed hamburger gravy over toast: During the Depression era of the 1930s they were living in an apartment house in Jerome, Idaho. Upstairs from them lived a young couple with two small children. The couple was unemployed. Dad would work a full day for a dollar. On Fridays he would stop at the corner store and, for twenty-five cents, buy a quart of milk, a pound of hamburger, and a loaf of bread. By adding a little flour and an onion, Mom could make enough hamburger gravy to feed themselves and the neighbors. They would then take the hot food upstairs, and after dinner the four adults would play pinochle until late. It happened every payday that winter. That's Gifting.

Giveaways come in every form and value. Sometimes it's a tangible item like an artist-made necklace or pin, but it can be a necessary service or food and drink. Most theme camps have something to give away. One of my favorite camps from the early days was called Sunscreen Massage Camp. People were invited to contribute a tube of sunscreen, but regardless of whether you contributed, you could lie on one of the tables

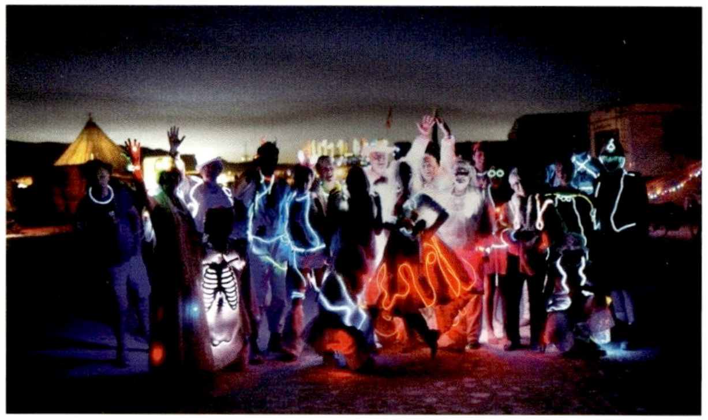

It's hard to imagine how drab the nighttime playa would be without el wire.

and get a full massage using sunscreen. It was the ultimate in practical luxury. My good friends the Children of Chaos always print up dozens of bandanas to give away—very useful in dust storms. Each year they choose a new color, and I know people who have collected several from them over the years.

As a photographer, I like to give away something practical as well. For the past few years, I've been buying a large box of biodegradable lens wipes in individual packets. I then design and print out Burning Man labels that fit the theme for that year and stick them onto the packets. Goggle and lens cleaner is an absolute blessing on the dusty playa, and everyone seems glad to have it.

The excessive part of Gifting at Burning Man is that a certain competitive "swag pride" has crept into the mix. Artisan designers often show up with very beautiful and relatively expensive Burning Man jewelry to give away. Some of the pieces are so extraordinary and there have been so many wonderful examples that Karen Christians, Christine Kristen, and George Post collaborated on a nicely illustrated book called *Jewelry of Burning Man*. The pieces are often original, and I must admit to accepting and wearing several of my favorites year after year, but Burning Man swag does sometimes border on the grandiose, and that feels more elitist and precious than it should. In the final analysis, Gifting ought to be about an attitude of generosity, rather than trinkets.

Just as volunteering is the highest form of Participation, the highest form of Gifting is neighborly service. Helping someone with their bike, offering to share an extra pair of goggles, and pitching in to pitch a tent are all forms of Gifting. I've seen virgins arrive woefully underequipped and leave with more gear than they ever knew they needed. Gifting may be the most socially interactive aspect of the event.

Decommodification

> **In order to preserve the spirit of gifting, our community seeks to create social environments that are unmediated by commercial sponsorships, transactions, or advertising. We stand ready to protect our culture from such exploitation. We resist the substitution of consumption for participatory experience.**

Easily the most maligned and widely misunderstood of the Ten Principles is Decommodification. For one thing, spell-checks refuse to accept it as a word, and for another, there's confusion between commerce and commodity, but the general notion is that you shouldn't confuse experience with things. The simple explanation is that going to a Warriors game is an experience, but buying a Warriors jersey is not. What confuses people is that while vending is generally prohibited at the event, everyone who goes spends a ton of money getting prepared to attend. There may be a few down-low transactions that happen on the playa, but nothing that involves the organization. The only vending is of ice, which is necessary to survive for a week on the playa, and coffee and chai, which are social lubricants. It may seem more symbolic than real when you're walking around in a $300 steampunk outfit and you're staying in a $3,500 RV rental, but it's not. There is commerce in the outside world, and that is the proper place to get your steampunk on, but in the middle of the central circle is Black Rock Boutique, where you can try on and model reclaimed castoffs from real punks and shoes straight from the markdown bin, and they're free! Somehow that just feels more like playa wear.

In the early days of adopting the principles there was a definite push to remove any advertising from the sides of rental units. People were expected to paper over the logos or otherwise limit corporate identity. As time went on and the population grew, that idea became simply too doctrinaire and unwieldy. In the end, the term "decommodification" may be more ideal than real. It costs lots of money to go to Burning Man, and entire Internet industries have grown up around the event. Cool Neon and PlayaLung are two outfits whose products are evident at the event, but people use both in very creative ways. Utilikilts out of Seattle is another company that has prospered on the playa, but I haven't worn mine anywhere else. They're what the stylish older gentleman thinks of as playa perfect.

There is often a genuine confusion as to what the appropriate Burner stance is to a given extravagance. Obviously, many people spend thousands producing mutant vehicles or elaborate music and theme camps, but they are encouraged to do so as long as their expenditure produces an interactive experience for the general population. Luxury plug-and-play camps have become more of an issue for Burner bloggers. Hidden behind a wall of containers or RVs, these camps are much maligned, and the party line is that they are un–Burning Man. That sounds too much like un-Islamic for my taste, and not at all in the spirit of Radical Inclusion. The response from the organization has been to mandate that every placed theme camp be open and hospitable to the public at least four hours out of every day. Last year Larry actually went out with a small group disguised as the hoi polloi to see if they would be welcomed into this Burning Man version of a gated community, and he reports they were welcomed with open arms. The issue of commodification isn't about spending money; it's "What did your venture do to benefit the community?"

In the end, of course, Burning Man is no more or less an example of private enterprise than Cirque du Soleil, Woodstock, or Broadway. Money changes hands for tickets, much money is spent on preparation, and money is spent getting there and back. That isn't a bad or a good thing. The question is whether there can be more to staging an event than making a profit. Burning Man lost money or broke even for many years, and it continued because the people involved believed they were making a positive impact on American culture. Burning Man today is not only a wildly successful enterprise but also an enterprise that sticks to its Ten Principles, and that makes all the difference.

Radical Self-Reliance

Burning Man encourages the individual to discover, exercise, and rely on his or her inner resources.

The playa is first and foremost a primitive environment. Humankind has been living and dying on this barren plain for thousands of years. Careless Burners are apt to pay a steep price for ignoring the dire warnings on their tickets, but Radical Self-Reliance is much more than camping and comporting oneself with caution; it's recognizing that the challenge of living on the playa is a critical part of experiencing Burning Man.

The weather on the playa shapes the event. If there are persistent dust storms, it is a mystical world, but it also keeps people indoors. If it's dry and hot, the mornings will be grand, but the afternoons are often parched and exhausting. The nights can be cold, and rain can destroy the playa surface. What makes the event an experience is how you manage those vagaries of fortune. In 2005, Bryan and I cobbled together a camp with J-Love that we called H.A.T.S. Camp. For shelter, Bryan had designed a new shade structure based on four-by-four posts strapped together in a circle with a parachute cover. Every post in the web was dependent on others for stability. Once all the straps were in place and the stakes driven, it was a solid unit. We spent the afternoon setting up our camp, and then we went to visit one of our favorite camps for R & R: Martini Village from Reno. As their name implies, Aimee and John Frugoli, Jarl and Donna Nelsen, Aimee's parents Don and Kathi, Karen Toth, and their volunteers spend months preparing and most of Burn week doling

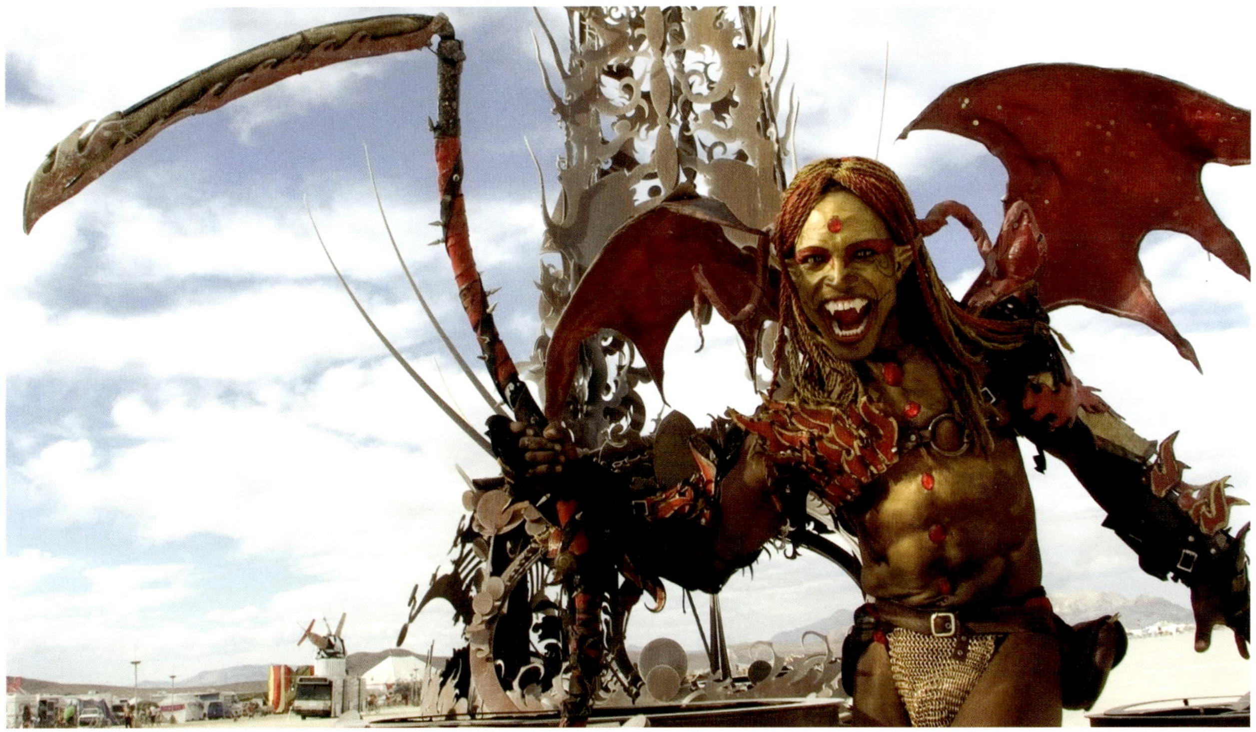

Yes, there are solitary demons at Burning Man roaming the playa in character.

out olive-garnished drinks every afternoon. As a nod to Participation, Martini Village modifies their name and logo each year to address the theme. As I remember during "Beyond Belief" they called themselves Heavenly Martini, and during 2006's "Hope and Fear—the Future," they became Fear No Martini.

We were enjoying ourselves, dancing and drinking dirty martinis, when I looked up and saw a wall of dust at least a hundred yards high heading straight at us. It was a full-on haboob, looking like an exaggerated Hollywood special effect as opposed to the kind of dusty billows that blow across the playa daily. "Uh-oh," I said to whoever I was dancing by, and then I yelled to everyone else, "Batten down the hatches!" We covered our heads and drinks, and danced on. After twenty minutes of blistering winds and blinding dust, I began to worry about our camp. I signaled to Bryan, and the two of us maneuvered our way back to camp, dodging blasts of dust behind trucks and RVs. When we got back to our camp, we were dismayed to see that it had been completely flattened, and everything we owned was covered in an inch of powder. We were grim and it was getting dark. The ones in tents ended up shaking out their gear as best they could and grabbing any bit of couch or chair to bivouac for the night. It was hot and dry the next morning, and we spent another three hours rebuilding our camp from scratch! Radical Self-Reliance often means taking your medicine and making the best of ill fortune. It also speaks as much about overcoming a challenging personal experience as it does about being safe or self-sufficient.

Radical Self-Expression

Radical Self-Expression arises from the unique gifts of the individual. No one other than the individual or a collaborating group can determine its content. It is offered as a gift to others. In this spirit, the giver should respect the rights and liberties of the recipient.

Without a doubt, Radical Self-Expression is the principle that drives the core dynamic of most Burning Man traditions. It

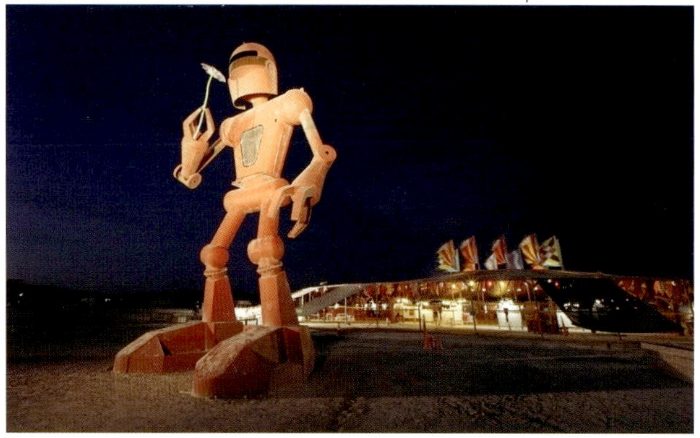

Becoming Human *was a flower-smelling robot that graced the Center Camp Café.*

was there the moment someone showed up on Baker Beach in costume, but it's become a defining mantra at Burning Man, and it inspires everything from massive art installations to some naked dude walking around dangling a daisy. It's also the most controversial principle in that it can appear to overshadow community in its pursuit of individual persona, but there are checks and balances to being too self-focused. Large-scale playa art projects are simply too ambitious to be rendered solo, and established artists like David Best and Bryan Tedrick must assemble large crews. Crews come with their own sensibility, and so most of the big stuff on the playa becomes the product of an ever-growing collaborative interaction. Other artist groups began as interactive teams. The Flaming Lotus Girls are such a collaboration. They've encompassed an evolving cast of characters, numbering over a hundred members, and have created some of the most spectacular examples of flaming steel.

Photographers spend much of their playa time alone. There is little reward in being one of a group of paparazzi surrounding a lone performer; so most of us trudge around the playa alone, looking for that elusive, exclusive image. In that way we mirror the lone practitioners of Radical Self-Expression, but we are solitary observers and they are the stalwarts of the event because they exhibit unmatched dedication and resolve. Often these solitary warriors combine a persona with a vehicle of sorts. They traverse the city from end to end, providing a warm glimpse of what an individual might do by way of creative characterization. There are rewards, I've been told, and in the spirit of supportive community, these lone knights of the playa are often the recipients of much grateful largess.

The most personal of camps and artist vehicles often offer insight into their owners. Some are modest and homegrown, while others are high-dollar fantasies that give off an air of professional construction. In the middle lurk steampunk contraptions or whimsical cartoon camp parodies between like-minded friends. I'm sure such collaborative projects are fun, not to mention collaborating helps spread the costs around. These projects also represent the vital nexus between expression and community. Breaking down any large-scale venture reveals a microcosm of Burning Man itself. Collaboration has always been at the heart of the event. As with many of the Ten Principles, few of them actually stand alone, and for this reason Radical Self-Expression is often partnered with Communal Effort, the next principle on the list.

Communal Effort

Our community values creative cooperation and collaboration. We strive to produce, promote, and protect social networks, public spaces, works of art, and methods of communication that support such interaction.

Not much would be possible at Burning Man without the zeitgeist of the creative community that has become its distinguishing characteristic. All year long in garages and workshops, both here and abroad, groups of collaborators are laboring together to create their latest Burning Man innovation. It could be anything from a butterfly-winged art car to a forty-foot silver Flash Gordon–inspired spacecraft. In the case of their 2009 *Raygun Gothic Rocketship*, the creative team of Sean Orlando, Nathaniel Taylor, David Shulman, and John Manyjohns enlisted a construction crew of ninety-three collaborators. Many of the very large constructions are done at American Steel in Oakland. This six-acre complex was initially rented by Karen Cusolito to build her and Dan Das Mann's mother and child collaboration entitled *Passage*. They returned in 2007 to build the spectacular *Crude Awakening*, which featured a group of figures worshipping a thirty-foot oil derrick for "The Green Man" theme.

Between 2002 and 2003 Burning Man established the nonprofit Black Rock Arts Foundation (BRAF) with the intention of helping Burning Man artists find a home for their work in the outside world, and also to promote Burning Man's cultural values in the community. The result was that not only have several of the most popular playa works been on public view at least temporarily but also community artists have been given grants to at least partially fund works that reflect the Ten Principles of the event. In 2005, BRAF worked with civic leaders to find venues for two longtime Burning Man artists to locate and install their playa-inspired work in the Bay Area. David Best built his *Hayes Valley Temple* in the area known as Patricia's Green, and it inspired the kind of community response that he'd enjoyed with his playa temples. BRAF also worked with the office of San Francisco mayor Gavin Newsom to have Michael Christian's forty-two-foot welded steel alien-looking creature called *Flock* at the Civic Center Plaza across from City Hall.

Over the following decade, BRAF has assisted in the placement of more than forty original or playa-derived installations in various communities in California and Nevada. In addition, it has awarded project grants to artists throughout the nation and to international artists from as far away as Croatia, Czech Republic, Vietnam, China, Ukraine, Mexico, United Kingdom, New Zealand, Ecuador, France, Russia, and South Africa. With the advent of the Burning Man Project in 2012, the activities of BRAF were moved under the umbrella of the new nonprofit reorganization, but the important work of supporting artists with community or environmentally positive projects in the world community continues. Their mission statement reads in part:

> The art experienced at Burning Man invites individuals to interact with both the work itself and with their community at large. BRAF was established to bring this modality of creating and coexisting with art to the rest of the world, with the vision that community-driven, inclusive, and interactive art is vital to a thriving culture.

Civic Responsibility

We value civil society. Community members who organize events should assume responsibility for public welfare and endeavor to communicate civic responsibilities to participants. They must also assume responsibility for conducting events in accordance with local, state, and federal laws.

It's obvious that when Larry drafted the principles in 2004 he was trying to set boundaries of conduct for fledgling regional events that were beginning to gain traction. He was also intent on conveying to a skeptical populace that Burning Man did in fact concern itself with public safety and the rule of law. Burning Man was still battling the widely held perception of the event as primarily attended by riotous naked scofflaws, and there were enough of these types around to keep the image alive. However, they've never made up more than a similar percentage of knotheads in the default world, probably less, but just like the real world, they always get the headlines.

Hurricane Katrina hit New Orleans during the 2005 event, significantly expanding Burners' understanding and interpretation of Civic Responsibility as well as expanding the mission of the BRAF in the process. I got my first glimpse of that newfound perspective on Civic Responsibility while on duty at the Welcome Desk at First Camp. It was a simple Greeter table, and we would direct inquiries and guide visitors to their desired goal. I was manning the table the afternoon following Katrina's landfall when none other than Joan Baez walked up, wearing what looked to be only an apron. "Can you tell me where Lightning's trailer is?" she asked. I pointed out the location of Terry Gross's trailer and then bored her a bit by telling her that Lynda and I were big fans and had been to several

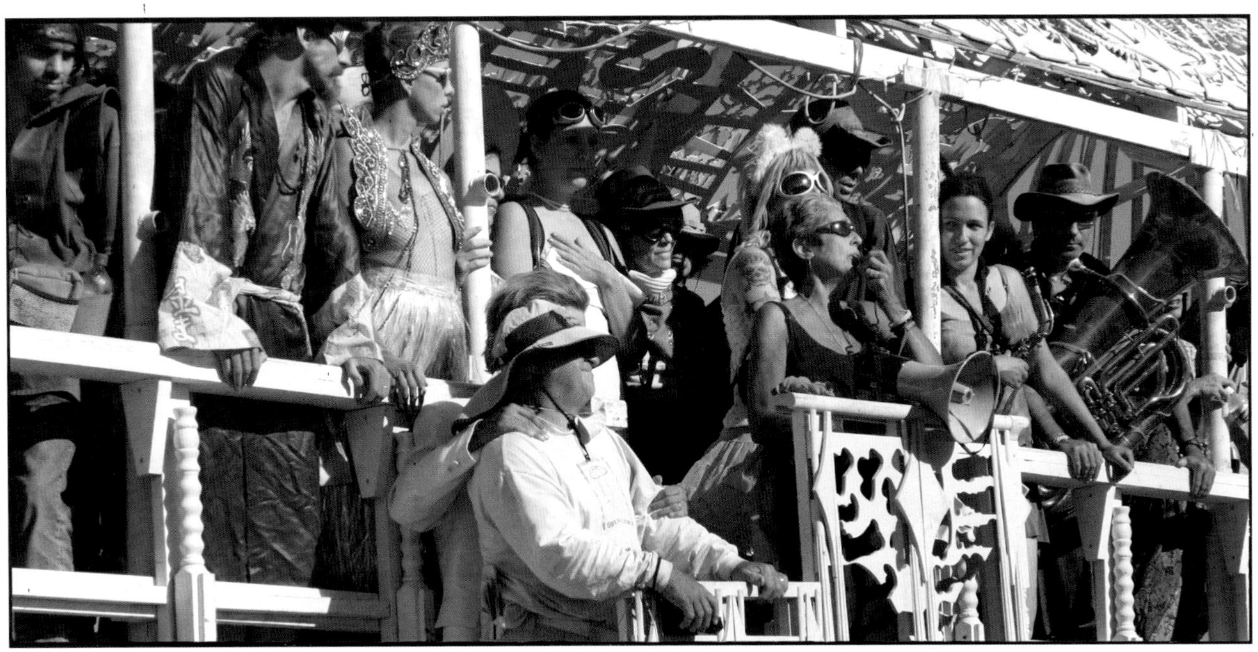

Reverend Billy, Lightning, and Joan Baez raised awareness and money for Katrina relief.

of her concerts, etc. She smiled indulgently and then headed toward Terry's trailer.

I'd been right; the outfit covered only the front half of her underwear. She disappeared into Terry's trailer, and I ran to our camp to find Bryan. "Hey, Joan Baez is in First Camp," I sputtered. "Come over and take a picture of us. Your mom will love it!" Bry joined me at the Greeter table, and we waited there for what seemed to be an hour before Terry's trailer door finally reopened. Joan emerged swathed head to foot in some kind of *Arabian Nights* outfit, complete with a face-covering veil. I turned to Bryan and said, "Forget about the picture. No one will ever recognize who it is!"

It turned out that Reverend Billy, upon hearing the news that was trickling in about Hurricane Katrina, had decided to help raise awareness and money for the people of New Orleans. He borrowed David Best's white *Temple Bus* and began picking up entertainers and other supporters to stage a rally out by the temple. I don't know the inside story on how it all transpired, but by the time they reached Mark Grieve's *Temple of Dreams*, Joan Baez had joined this merry crew of fund-raisers. I was on hand to hear her sing a cappella versions of "Amazing Grace" and "Swing Low, Sweet Chariot." Reverend Billy issued a heartfelt plea for donations, and the crowd broke into a hand-clapping rendition of "When the Saints Go Marching In" as the musicians accompanied them with a few New Orleans–style jazz licks. (It was the Mystic Krewe from New Orleans who had brought *Le Boeuf Gras d'Or* to Burning Man in 1998, and the NOLA Burners have been significant regional art contributors ever since.) By the end of this impromptu concert, Burning Man had effectively expanded its concept of Civic Responsibility to include coming to the aid of the greater Burner community.

The response to Katrina didn't end with the bus rally. Donation stations were established at the exit out of BRC. We were told later that around $30,000 had been donated for Katrina relief by the event's end. A contingent of Burner volunteers headed to New Orleans to assist in the relief effort. I went down there myself, beginning what would eventually be a ten-year photography study of the resilient and colorful people of the city. The collective response by the Burner community to the plight of New Orleans resulted in a significant expansion of the notion of what Civic Responsibility might entail. This was the beginning of Burners Without Borders. Burning Man expanded its involvement in regional Burner events, and Civic Responsibility has become as much about the building of culture and community as it was about safety and art.

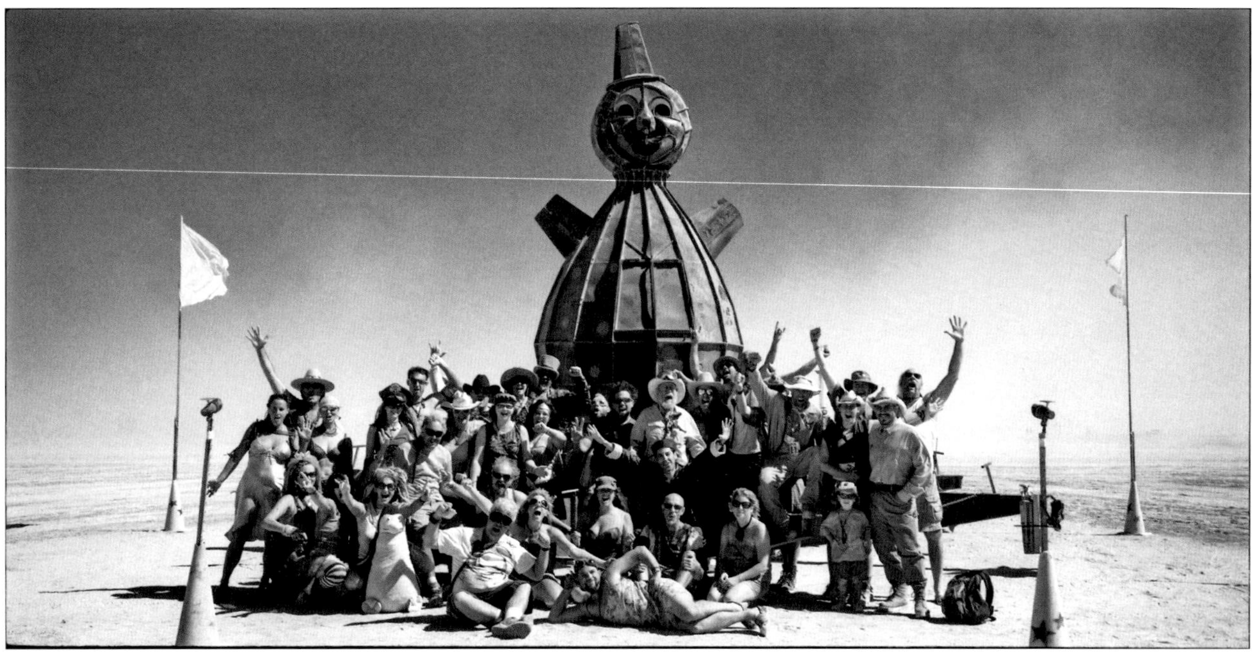

Harley's crews can be motley, but they are the lionhearts of Black Rock City.

Leaving No Trace

Our community respects the environment. We are committed to leaving no physical trace of our activities wherever we gather. We clean up after ourselves and endeavor, whenever possible, to leave such places in a better state than when we found them.

Leaving no trace has always been a component of Burning Man's philosophical allegiance to the environment as well as part of its contract with the BLM. The principal concern with a large event on public lands is the potential for serious environmental damage, and Burning Man has taken that responsibility to heart. Indeed it takes a full month following the event for Tony "Coyote" Perez and his DPW crew to completely remove all the structures and dispose of all the debris. What most Burners don't know is how much is also accomplished prior to the event through careful planning and proper setup. Early Burns were fairly indiscriminate; people often set fire to anything in their path. Afterward the scorched playa sand was removed. What was discovered was that the resulting scorch marks went deeper than anyone realized, and after a rain the burn scars could return to the playa surface. The BLM now mandates that a wide layer of shielding material be spread underneath all objects destined for the fire. Thus all burning must be planned and coordinated prior to the event.

Sometimes the burn shields are incorporated into the sculpture, as was the case with the Flaming Lotus Girls' *Angel*

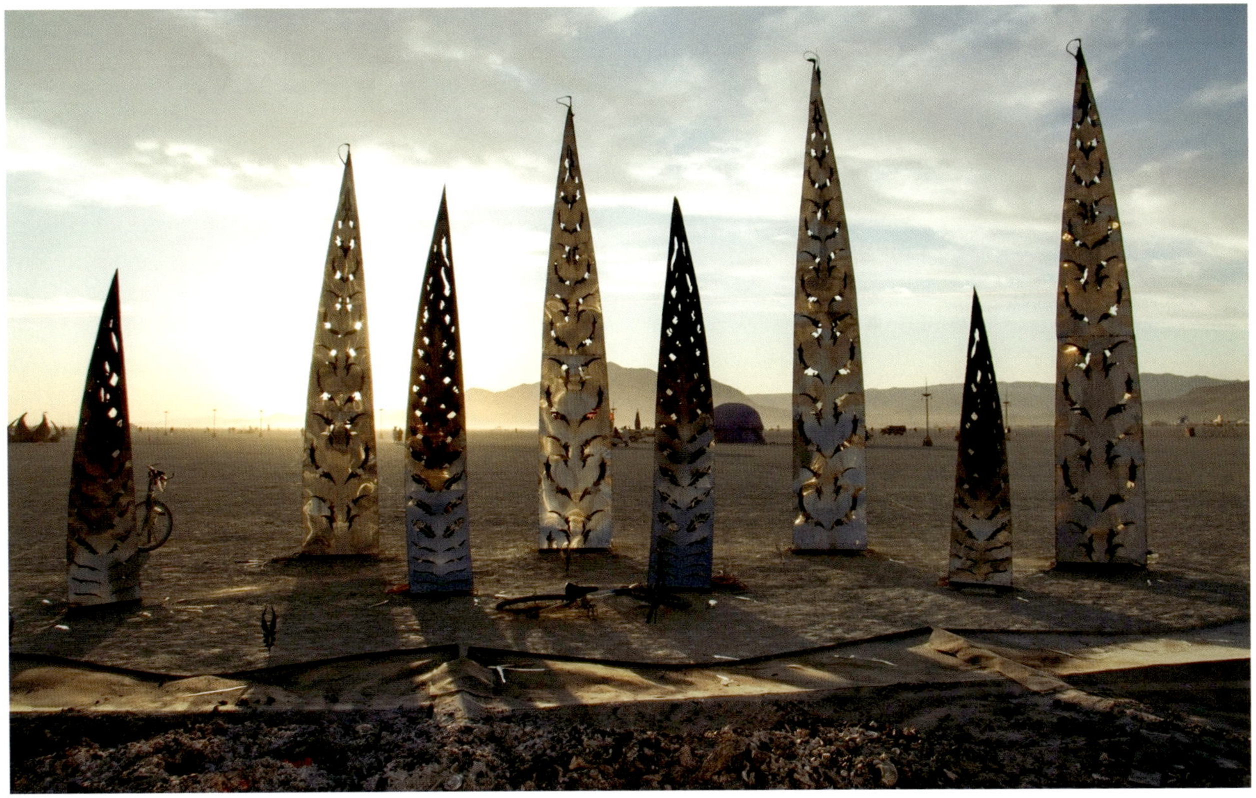

Angel of the Apocalypse *used a large shield to protect the playa as its figure burned.*

of the Apocalypse, which featured a figurative driftwood bird torso laid flat on a protective platform. But controlling the effects of multiple fires is only a small part of Leaving No Trace. The real challenge is what to do with the random effects of having seventy thousand people camping on the windswept playa. One of Burning Man's first acts following its return to Black Rock in 1998 was to install the perimeter fence. Originally conceived as a trash fence to catch windblown flotsam, it has grown into a fully functional security fence, which not only catches trash but also keeps people from crossing the desert from the east and thus avoiding the gate. Coyote Perez and his crew install this nine-mile barrier in less than a day. It's a feat that impresses veteran Burners and Gerlach locals alike. Coyote is an accomplished writer, and he relates in his chapter of *Playa Dust: Collected Stories of Burning Man* that he was having a beer at Joe's, one of Gerlach's five bars (and no churches!), and one of the local cowboys drinking there was giving him a cold stare. Coyote had had more than one altercation with locals over the years, and he could feel this one coming. As the cowboys were leaving, that one stopped in front of Coyote and said, "You know I don't give a fuck about your Burning Man. I tolerate it at best, and I don't give a fuck about art or your crazy naked hippie party. But I do respect that you put up that nine-mile fence in one day like you do." With that the cowboy touched the brim of his hat, nodded, and left the bar.

The population of Black Rock City is as widely diverse as any metropolitan area, although there is a strong percentage of green-minded people. Leaving No Trace is akin to a religious conviction with many West Coast Burners. As a result, there is much discussion and even a few impromptu lectures on the avoidance and management of MOOP—matter out of place—a term coined sometime in the early days of the event to describe trash and personal items left behind when people depart the event, but Burning Man, in concert with the BLM, began publishing a yearly MOOP map in 2006. It uses a color code to evaluate remaining trash after the event has been dismantled: red represents high-impact trace; yellow for moderate trace; green for little or no trace. Ironically, though the population has grown, the percentage of green on the BLM report has generally improved, though it fluctuates.

Coyote says it takes around two weeks to dismantle all the structures, such as the huge Center Camp tent, pack the pieces up, and haul them to the two-hundred-acre property Burning Man bought a few years ago to store the recurrent infrastructure buildings and the earth-moving equipment. After the structures have been put away, MOOP leaders and their crews do line sweeps of the entire city area by quadrants. The crew literally walks seventy abreast in a line, making sure that everything they encounter is picked up and bagged. It's a massive operation, but it's the only way to minimize trace remnants. This effort involves much more than picking up bits of MOOP. The crew also repairs the playa surface from tent peg holes, burn scars, tire marks, and other irregularities caused by structure shapes. Leaving No Trace is a serious endeavor.

Most people who attend the event understand that "You pack it in, you pack it out" has always been a Burning Man mantra. Camp waste has never been cool to leave behind, nor tent stakes, burn debris, wood from shade structures, or playa-muck-covered carpeting, furniture, etc. What people have had to learn is to recognize other MOOP-producing materials. Colorful costume embellishments like feathers, sequins, and glued-on sparkly glitter—"playa herpes"—are abundant examples of MOOP. So are many of the small items people like to stick on their bikes or RVs to add flair. When the wind blows hard, as it often does, that stuff flies everywhere. As a result, you will regularly see small Burner groups doing MOOP patrols. It's an unwritten rule, but just like people are

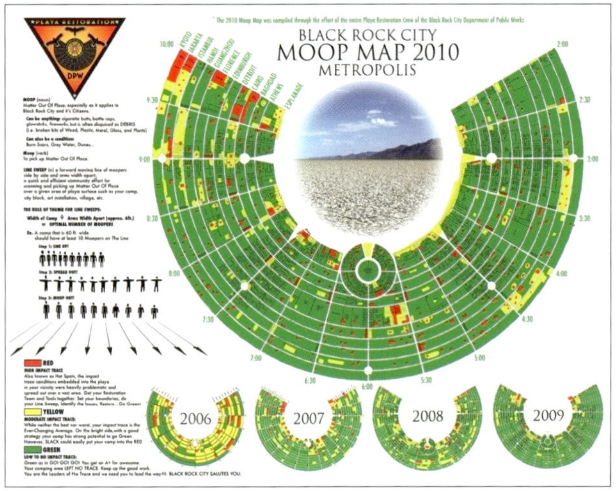

required to pick up after their pets, when you spot a MOOPY thing bouncing along the playa, you're supposed to stop it, pick it up, and take it back to your camp.

Participation

> Our community is committed to a radically participatory ethic. We believe that transformative change, whether in the individual or in society, can occur only through the medium of deeply personal participation. We achieve being through doing. Everyone is invited to work. Everyone is invited to play. We make the world real through actions that open the heart.

"No Spectators" has been associated with Burning Man from its beginning, and collective Participation is the philosophy behind that sentiment. On the simplest level it speaks to doing more than gawking, but how much more is up to the individual. At the very least, it's an impromptu team of friends grabbing on to ropes to get Peter Hudson's *Charon* to animate. Peter has been making zoetrope sculptures for several years, and they are one of the highlights of playa art. The first one I remember was *Sisyphish* from 2003, which was a fixed series of a swimmer positioned in the sand and animated by strobe lights. With the strobes going, the figure appeared to swim in a circle. Hudson's later pieces have been much larger and more ambitious. Most are carousel-based, requiring participants to peddle or pull ropes to make the piece turn. At night the strobe lights complete the animation.

The idea that Burning Man is about doing rather than watching became, over the years, a mandated response to life on the playa, but simply walking around in a funny outfit grew trite, and unique and more expressive ways of participating became the norm. The most obvious method of participation is to volunteer on a crew. As city manager, Harley K. Dubois oversees a complex of disparate entities: DPW builds the city, Black Rock Rangers protect the city, Center Campers entertain the city, Greeters are the face of the city, Lamplighters illuminate the city, Earth Guardians care for the city's environment, Temple Guardians secure the temple, and the Artery Council and Fire Conclave volunteers support artists and performers. Of course the artists and performers are for the most part volunteers as well. Volunteers inhabit every level of Black Rock City's infrastructure, interacting with and assisting attendees on a daily basis.

Of course these are only the most visible centers for volunteerism. Virtually every aspect of the city—medical facilities, communication centers, media and broadcast facilities, commissaries, truck drivers, crane operators, and every kind of mechanic and hammer swinger—involves volunteer labor. That's just the city's infrastructure, but hundreds of volunteers are also part of the vast array of theme camps that provide all manner of Burner entertainment, postal services, nourishment, drink, and activities. There are even volunteers who assist other, more experienced volunteers, and they are called Fluffers.

At its heart, Participation involves an attitude of complete commitment to the event. While volunteering for BRC ser-

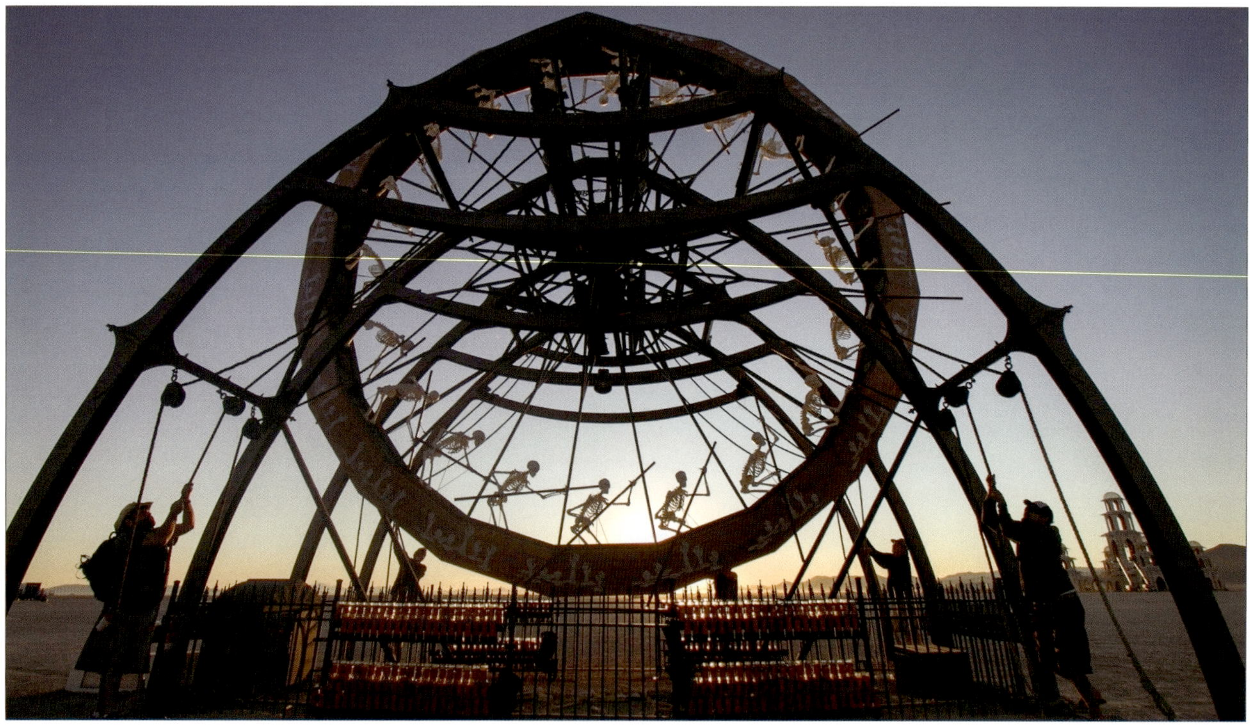

Interactive art creates a symbiotic relationship between artists and participants.

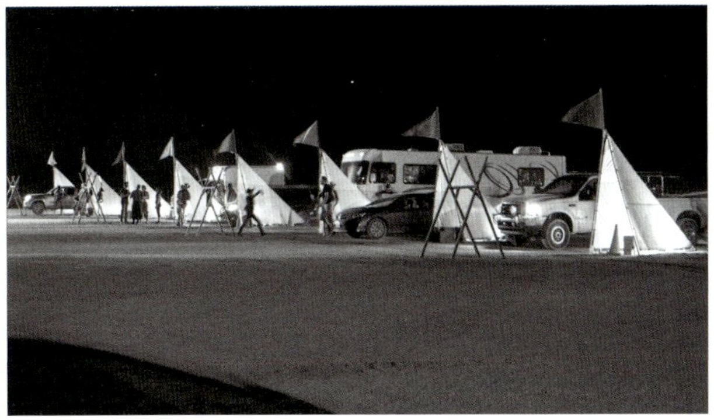

Greeters are the gateway to Burning Man, and they set the tone and welcome us home.

vices may be the most selfless and necessary example, the vast majority of participants are people who pay for their tickets, spend weeks at the thrift stores costuming up, spend hours at the computer designing their camp, spend more money and more hours coordinating with others who will be in their camp to build their camp components, load up their camp, and transport their camp, and then spend even more hours setting up their camp, making it a worthy destination for that year's Burning Man. They come in all shapes and sizes, they pack in pounds of goodies and loads of entertainment, and they all have one thing in common: they're doing what they're doing for the benefit of all, and virtually all are paying, in one way or another, to be there.

Sometime around 2010 Bryan and I stumbled onto the Black Rock Bijou. At Burning Man you regularly hear rumors about some awesome and radical camp that's got everybody buzzing. Most of the rumors turn out to be hype, or the camp can't be found because the person telling you about it has the address all messed up. The camp rarely turns out to be as interesting as it's been made out to be. The Bijou was an exception. Cute as kittens and way, way out in deep playa, this little jewel box would start showing its feature film after midnight and keep it running until everyone went home or to sleep.

The most singular act of participation is unsolicited interplay with strangers. Often it takes the form of Gifting. People will walk around with water cannons and offer to spray down any hot and dusty playa walker who is willing. They will pull around wagons of water or beer for the same purpose. Gifting is a time-honored form of Participation because it's so interactive. It's also one of the most spiritually driven, I think. I remember meeting a fellow named Pippen out by the afterburn ash field in 2012. He was roasting marshmallows with friends by the heat of the Man's smoldering embers and passing them out to whomever was interested. It was a simple act by any measure; in fact, there were others proffering coffee and scones, but it modeled what lies at the heart of Participation, Gifting, and virtually every form of unsolicited sharing: the smallest act of generosity builds community. It also bonds strangers to a person-to-person ethos that continues long after the event is over. It's why there's a bond between Burners that stretches beyond borders and nationalities. We are brothers and sisters of the playa experience—"In dust we trust," naturally.

Playa parading is a signature move at Burning Man. Many parades are scheduled, but even more are spontaneous or hastily planned. People march out onto the playa and interact with strangers. Usually they are Gifting something, or else corralling some unsuspecting dupe and doing a bit of clownish business with them to the delight of their friends. Every once in a while mutant vehicles—which are a kind of parade unto themselves—will hook up with two or three other mutant vehicles for an impromptu spin around the playa in unison. Some parades, like the White Parade to the temple on Sunday morning or the Billion Bunny March, are longstanding traditions. But whatever the reason, there seems to be a hardwired parade gene in most every Burner.

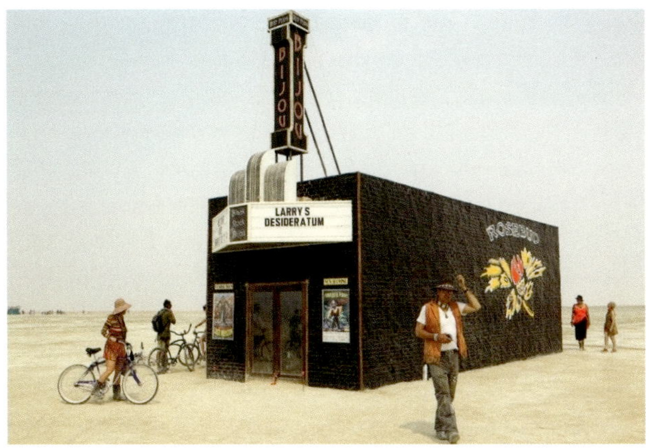

The Black Rock Bijou was a small gem in deep playa that showed us cinema lives.

So why bother? What's all the fuss? Sixty to seventy thousand people going to all that effort to get dressed up, march out to the Man or the temple, hand out candy or cheap Mardi Gras beads to strangers, get all sweaty and dusty, and now they are going to simply walk back to celebrate, like they just won the parade bowl!? Yup, that's Participation. It doesn't matter if the performance is fantastic or banal. It only matters that you're in it. Once you're back at the camp bar, no one says, "Wow, that was a swell parade." They are already mentally down the road to the next adventure. Participation means being an active part of each distinctive moment, and the next moment after that—it all counts. That's sometimes called "immediacy."

Immediacy

Immediate experience is, in many ways, the most important touchstone of value in our culture. We seek to overcome barriers that stand between us and a recognition of our inner selves, the reality of those around us, participation in society, and contact with a natural world exceeding human powers. No idea can substitute for this experience.

The most esoteric of the principles, Immediacy suggests to me "being in the moment," but of course that's an equally elusive idea to put into practice. The minute you start wondering whether you're in the moment, you're not. There are wonderful riches to discover on the playa, and the only way to embrace them is to get away from camp and explore. People are often open and eager to share, and kismet is sometimes just on the other side of the next art piece. I think the wonderful benefit of Larry articulating the Ten Principles is that they empower attendees to interact with one another and to feel encouraged to do so. Most of us subscribe to these ideals, and that constitutes an open invitation. People reach out to the community, and in that solicitation, they are opening themselves up to something novel and exciting. There may be an invitation to an upcoming party, a ride on an amazingly articulated machine, a hot tip on the best place to watch the sunrise, but whatever the encounter, it's your opportunity to engage in a new experience. Immediacy's the secret sauce of being at Burning Man, and while the experience must ultimately be yours alone, community is often the guide to discovering that opportunity.

In 2012, campmate Geoffrey Silver and I were atop the giant thumbs-up *Like 4 Real* sculpture, talking to Michael Holden, who's another veteran Burning Man photographer. Standing on top of a piece of playa art can be a great way to catch a break and enjoy an early morning view. Below us, a lone blond young woman was peddling along on her bicycle. She stopped and asked us how the view was from up there and if we'd mind if she joined us. "Come on up," we shouted in unison. So she did.

Australian Rachael Wright turned out to be one of those plucky types who make the trip to Burning Man solo. Evidently, the friends she had originally made plans with withdrew for various reasons, and she bravely decided to come alone. We spent several minutes enjoying the view from the top of *Like*, and she told us the story of her journey from Sydney to the playa. As she prepared to move on, I mentioned I was having a birthday party at the Children of Chaos camp on the upcoming Thursday afternoon and she should come join us. My birthdays have always been a playa non-event, but this one was a more significant milestone, so Bryan had decided we should have a bourbon tasting as the central attraction. I ended up inviting most everyone I met, especially several random single riders I'd had conversations with on the open playa. The party was a great success, and the most fun of all was that many of those "random encounters" showed up to have a drink and offer best wishes. Rachael came and was introduced to several of the Chaos Krewe, and they ended up trading contact info. The following year, Rachael, her brother, and two of their Aussie friends were camping with Children of Chaos! I think the part of this story that relates to Immediacy regards staying alive to the moment. Burning Man is as much a social model as it is an insular event. Strangers start out with little more than Ten Principles in common, and warm and lasting friendships transpire. We never know what kismet awaits beyond the next piece of playa art, or in the midst of an approaching dust storm.

The Ten Principles have been a wonderful agent for grooming an inspired and proactive culture, and especially in the volatile era of the aughts, they helped shape Burning Man's shift to themes that offered constructive criticism of contemporary events. There never was a shortage of satirical or politically driven art at the event, but the era immediately following Hurricane Katrina seemed to be especially ripe for political nose tweaking. The advent of these more social and political themes were in part a reaction to the failure of the administration to deal with the crisis in New Orleans, then on to the Gulf oil spill, the ever-escalating war in Iraq, and finally leading to themes exploring the United States' struggles with the environment and policy. "Hope and Fear—The Future" in 2006 and "The Green Man" in 2007 were directly concerned with both these struggles. Likewise, "American Dream" in 2008 was a clear reference to the financial crisis of that year. In 2009 and 2010, the themes "Evolution" and "Metropolis—Life of Cities" explored volatility in the human condition. During this period theme art pieces grew both in message and in scale. People began to flock to the event in ever-increasing numbers. By the end of the first decade of the twenty-first century Burning Man attained full maturity both in organization and in world recognition. The days of "What's Burning Man?" had been replaced by "Burning Man . . . I've always wanted to go."

The outside world had taken notice, and there were supporters and detractors of the event on both sides of the political spectrum. And the outside world had decided that not only was Burning Man here to stay but also there was money to be made. Small towns along the north–south routes to the event had become economically dependent on the yearly influx of Burner faithful, and BURNERS WELCOME signs had replaced the curious or hostile stares.

My brother's yearly theme became more and more vital in stimulating both art and community involvement. "The Green Man" theme in 2007, addressing ecology and the ongoing battle to save the environment, is a good example. Center Camp and First Camp were both powered in part by Bill Brooks and Matt Mynttinen's thirty-kilowatt array of solar panels on the playa. It was the beginning of Black Rock Solar, a Burning Man nonprofit group dedicated to reducing the event's carbon footprint through solar power and education. After the event, the solar panels were donated to the Gerlach schools. The panels' capacity has been expanded over the years, and the grid currently provides the school system with 30 percent of its power. I saw the solar field this summer, and it's still humming. Black Rock Solar has joined BRAF and Burners Without Borders as part of Burning Man's bourgeoning community outreach.

David Best returned in 2007 and, along with Tim Dawson, produced one of his most elegant designs: the *Temple of Forgiveness*. Its spare simplicity and open reversed-arch tower suggested Shinto influence, and there was an airy quality to it. That year's environmental theme resulted in two other substantial theme art installations: Mike Ross's *Big Rig Jig*, which consisted of two full-size oil tankers welded into an S shape, and *Crude Awakening*, the full-scale oil-drilling platform fronted by a cadre of giant energy-hungry worshippers.

"The Green Man" was one of those model themes that fit snuggly into the average Burner's wheelhouse, and many environmentally oriented artist groups responded with inspired ideas. *Tasseograph: The Trash TeaHouse Temple*, from a Portland-based crew headed by Shrine and TukTuk, certainly qualified. Here was a Hindu-referenced design made of 90 percent recycled materials, framed windows, and architectural flotsam that hosted meditation and, I would assume, tea drinking. Whatever its purpose, it clearly spoke to the theme and complemented David Best's nearby *Temple of Forgiveness*.

The first decade of the twenty-first century came to a close with an explosion of large-scale installations at the event. Artists like Marco Cochrane, the Pier Group, Michael Garlington, the Flaming Lotus Girls, and Michael Christian

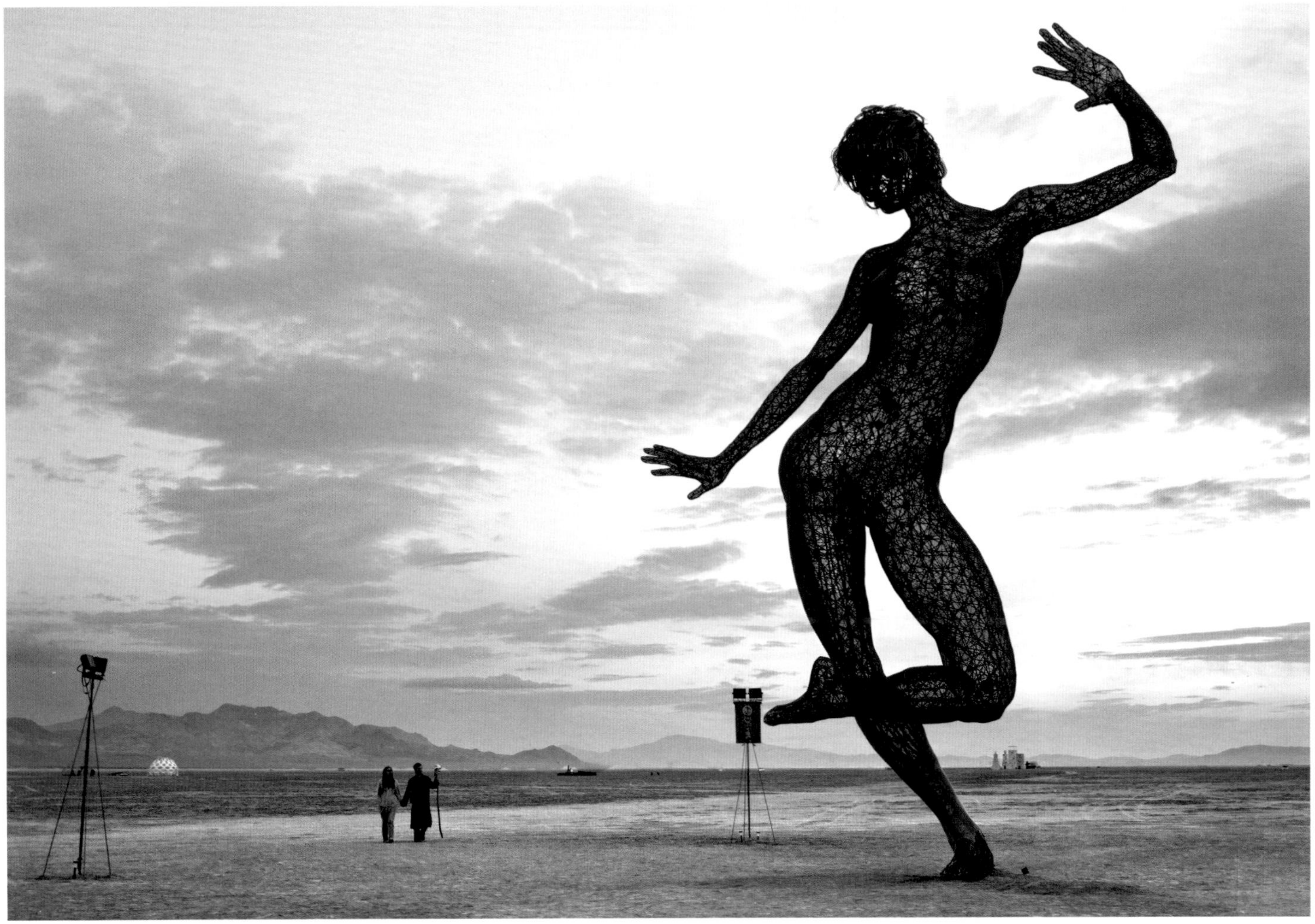

Marco Cochrane's Bliss Dance *in 2010 epitomized a new spectacular scale in playa art.*

set a new standard for just how large, graceful, or intricate playa sculpture could be. Cochrane's *Bliss Dance* was an unapologetic playa sensation, and it lifted the bar for not only scale but also ambitious engineering. Cochrane was certainly not alone; nor was he the first to build something huge and graceful. That honor probably goes to Michael Christian, with his *Flock* or perhaps Jan Kriekels and Arne Quinze for their *Uchronia* (aka *The Belgian Waffle*) a few years earlier, but neither of those projects could approach the jaw-dropping cantilevered majesty of *Bliss Dance*. I never judge the critical merits of Burning Man art. It ranges from didactic to kitschy, but its ability to stimulate and involve the observer is rarely matched in the default world. In the second decade of our new century large-scale audacious art would become the defining image of Burning Man around the world. Today, when corporate stuffed shirts or suburban naysayers complain about sex, drugs, and rave music at the event, the Bay Area CEO or suburban parent can tell the critics, "Oh, yes, Burning Man. I go for the art."

Frankly, I've never gone for the art, although I love much of it and admire the tremendous effort it takes to bring a fully realized piece to this impossibly difficult venue. The media still mostly portrays the event as a pop culture curiosity or sometimes as a business model for a successful countercultural enterprise, but rarely in the way veteran Burners see it: as a place to experience personal renewal. It's much more than that—as if that weren't enough—although it's what keeps me coming back. First timers commonly rave to their friends about the art, perhaps as a legitimizing reason for attending, but I would go if there were never another piece of art on the playa. Don't get me wrong. I'd miss it. But it's not the reason I go. I don't go for the community either, although I would dearly miss seeing my longtime friends in the Burner community. I go for the mysterious alchemy that transpires between the event and the playa, and despite rumors to the contrary, that alchemy just keeps getting better year after year.

Here's my simpleminded view of it all: The organizers at Burning Man are trying to bake a cake, and they've spent three decades fiddling with the recipe. The thing about baking a cake is you can change the ingredients and their proportions all you want, but sooner or later it needs to go into the oven, because without the heat from that playa oven, you just have a pan full of batter. That oven is mysterious and ornery and not all that predictable, but when the time and temperature are just right, it bakes a cake like no other you'll ever taste. I go to Burning Man because of the potential for cake.

CHAPTER 12

THE ART OF INTERACTION

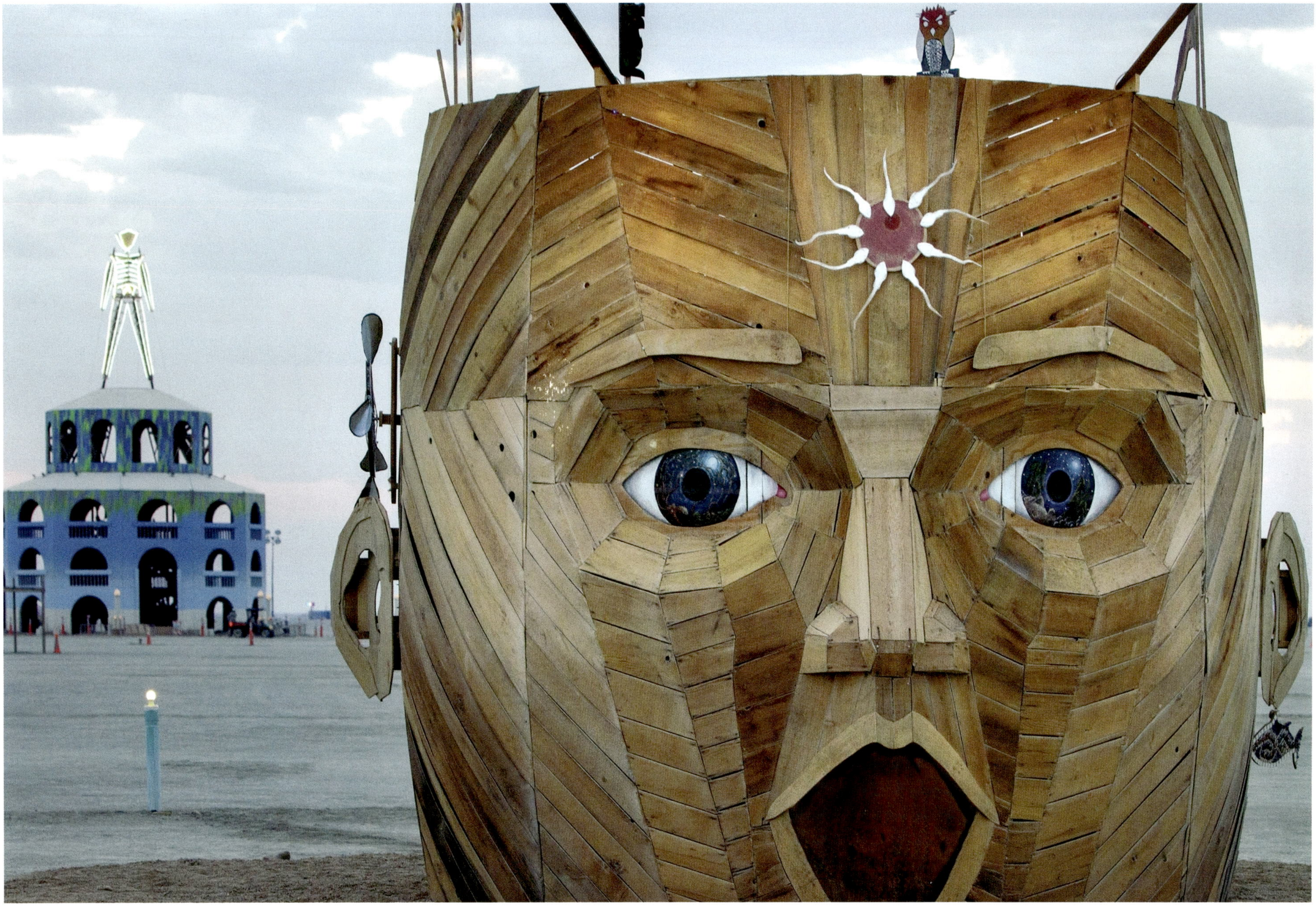

PsychoPhilia, *2012*

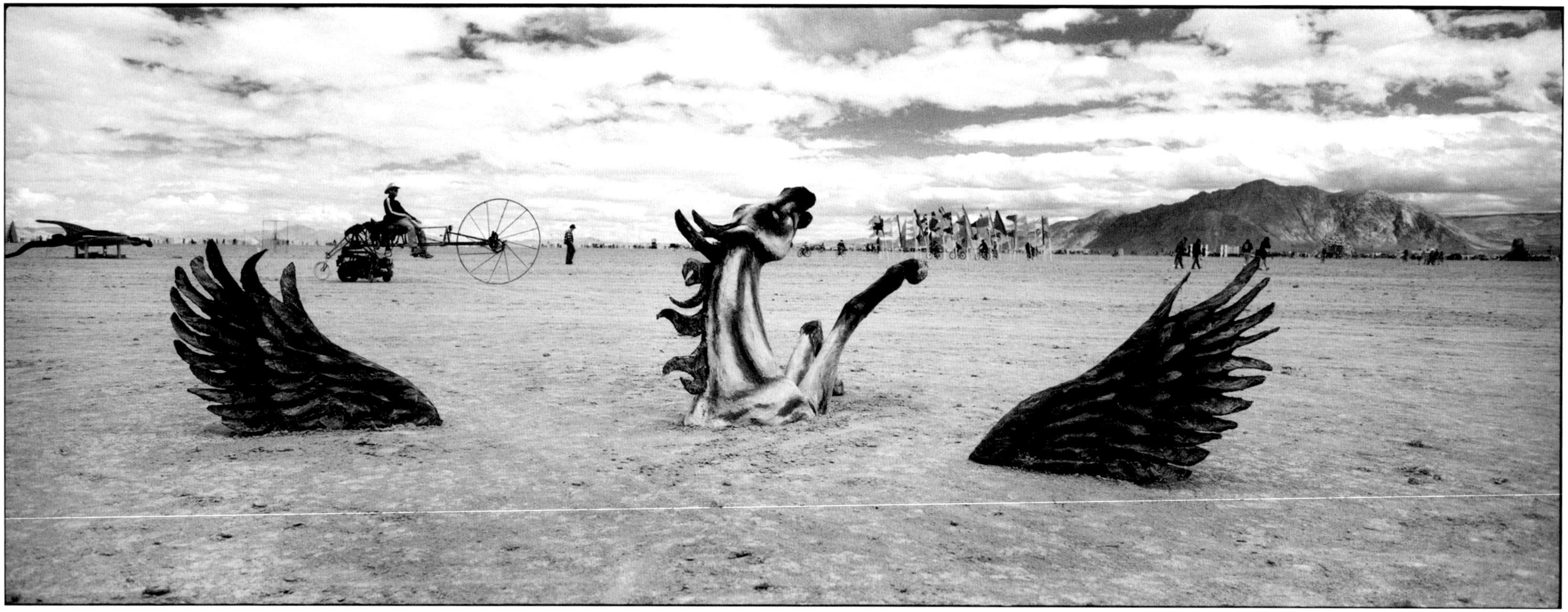

Emergence, *2000*

Interactive art is more than sculptural objects for people to climb on; it is a vital part of the mise-en-scène of the event. Here, works of art and personal expression create the setting for all activities. And the idea of artful expression extends to Black Rock City center, theme camps, indeed to every Burner who passes through the gate. Art influences every aspect of playa life, and it comes from individual artists, artist co-ops, and Burning Man regional organizations around the world. The Circle of Regional Effigies (CORE) in 2012 created thirty-four wooden structures that came from as far away as Lithuania and South Africa.

Early in the history of Burning Man a vital decision was made. I remember during the first couple of years entrepreneurial Burners showed up with T-shirts and other items to sell from the trunks of their cars. The organizers of the event had three choices: allow unlimited free enterprise, take control of all sales and reap a profit percentage (the business model for most festivals), or eliminate all vending. They chose the latter, and it's been the ethical high watermark of the event. While some theme art receives at least a partial grant to support its construction, most theme camps and vehicle art are privately funded and intended purely for the enjoyment of everyone. As a result, artists and attendees alike engage in an ongoing dialogue that can be both playfully public and intensely personal.

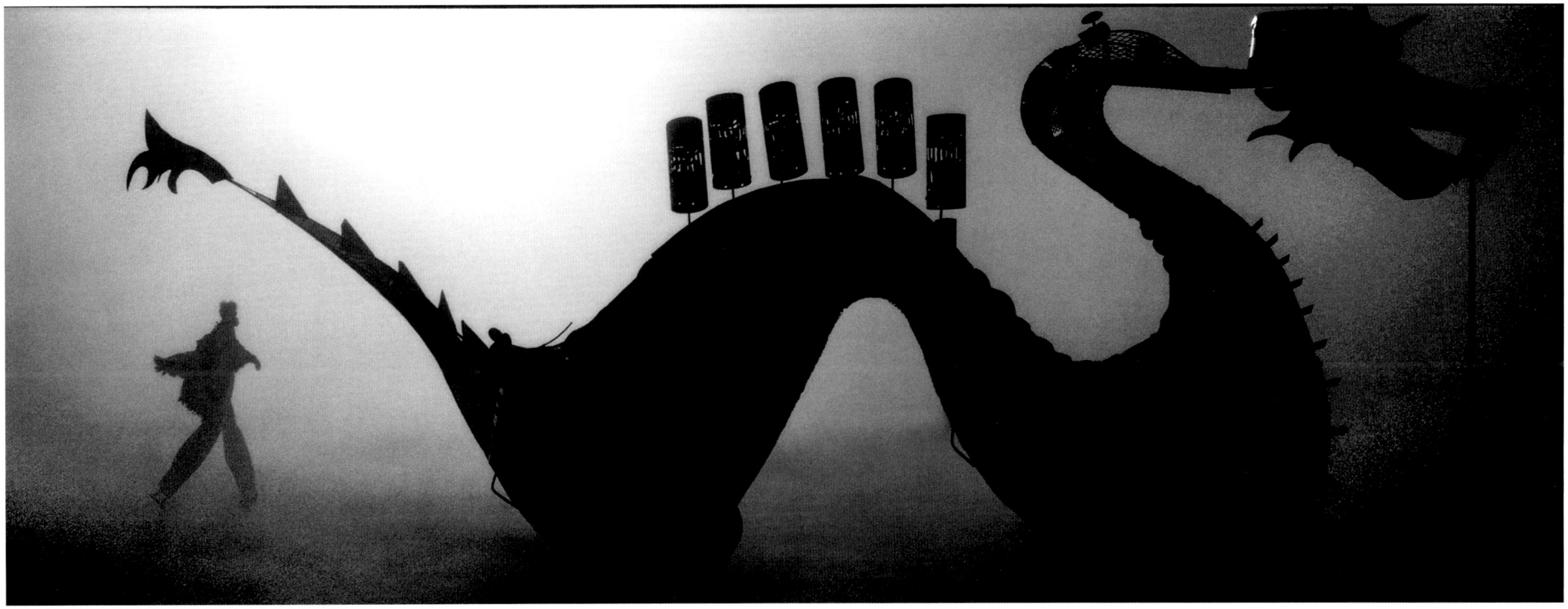

Prayer Dragon, *2009*

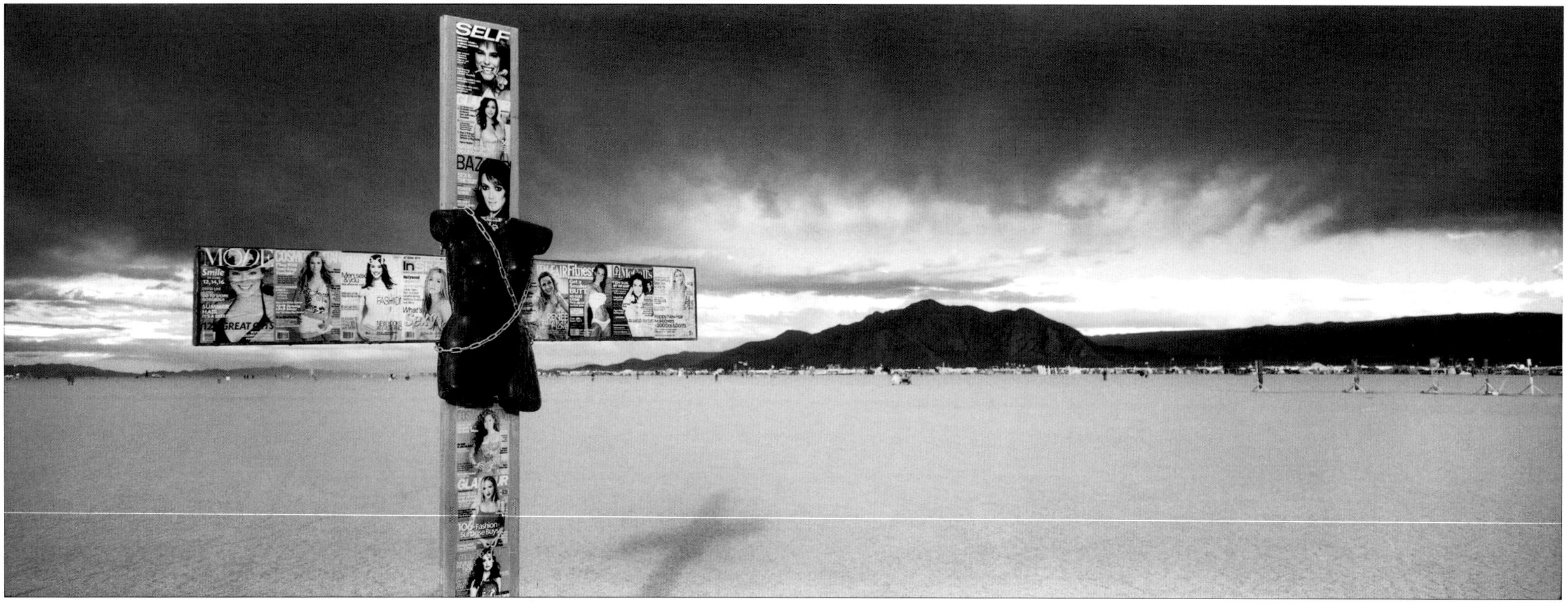

Crucified SELF, 2000

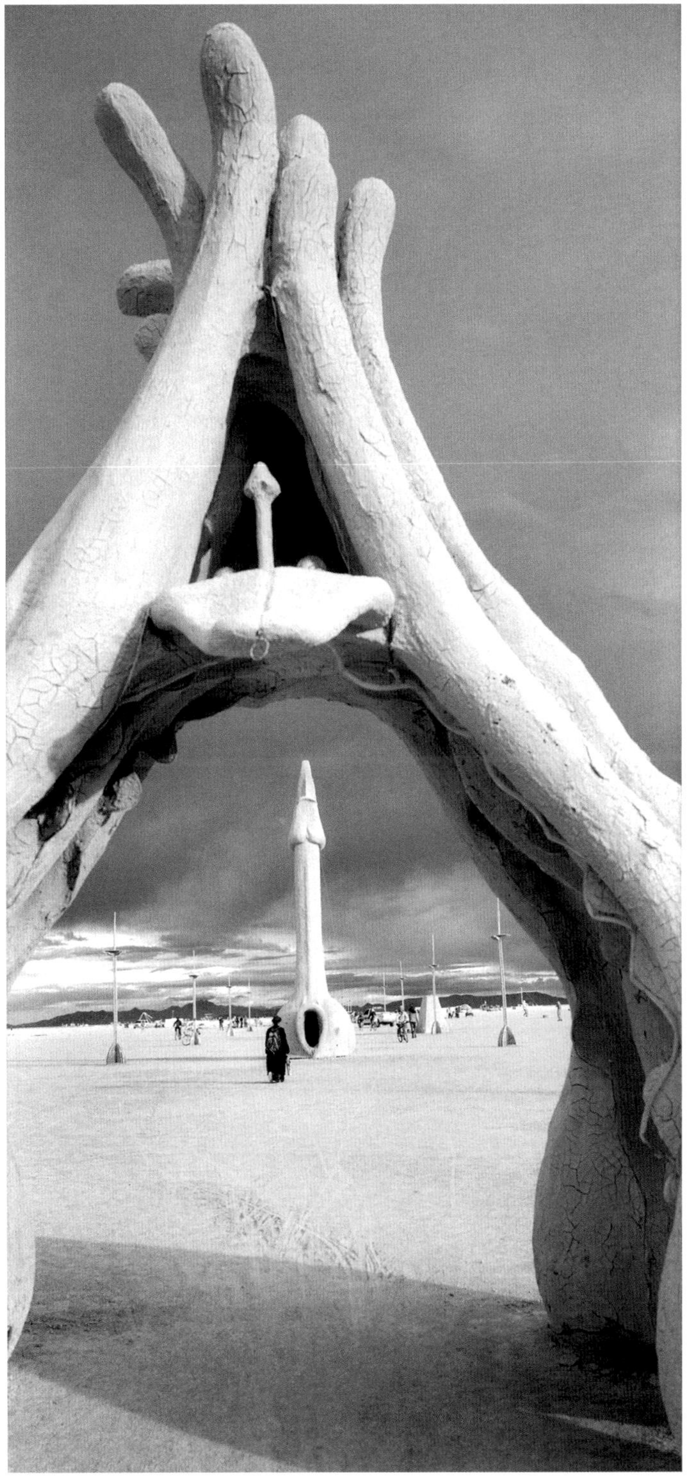

Phallus and Yoni Gate, *2000*

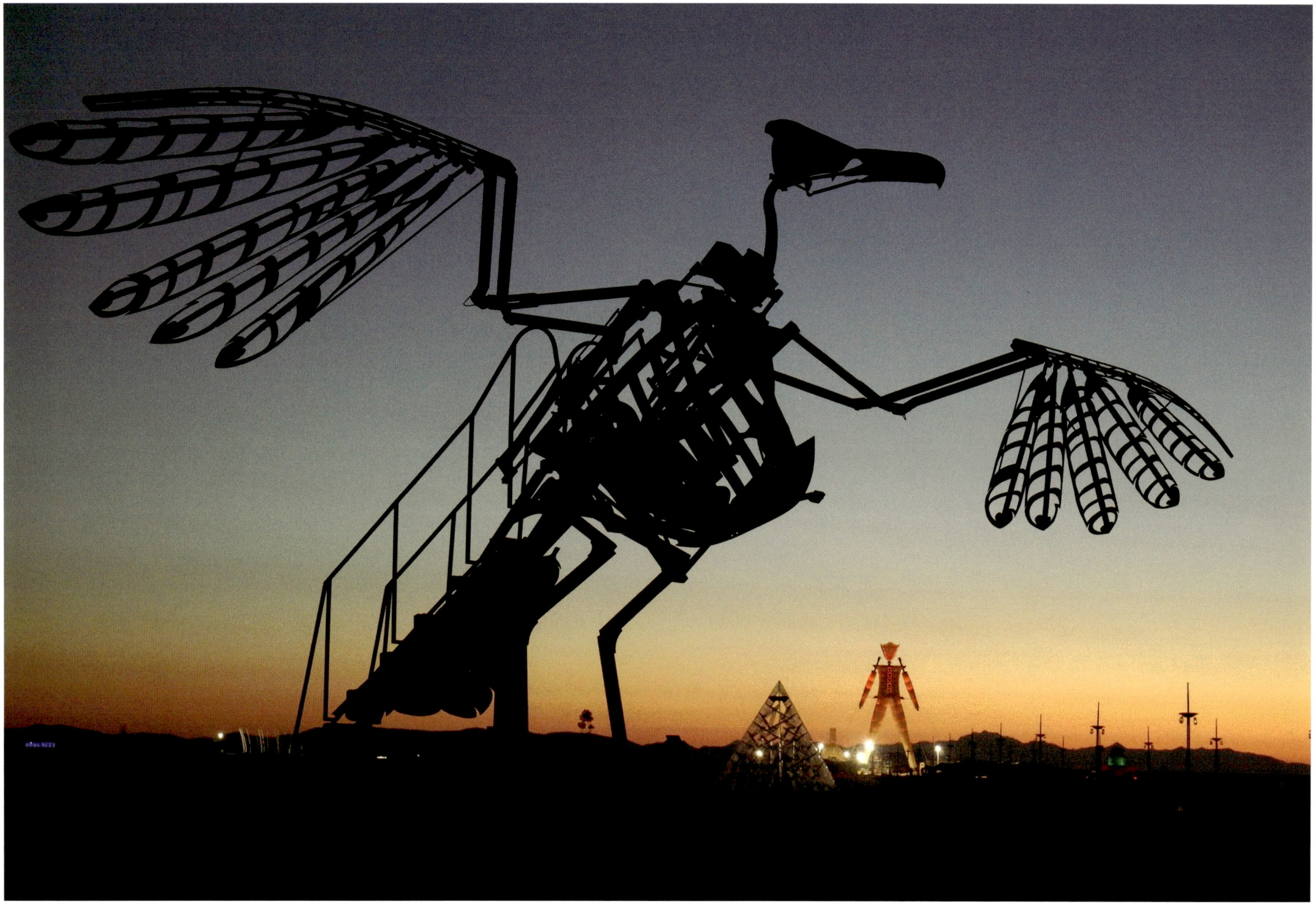

Fledgling, *2014*

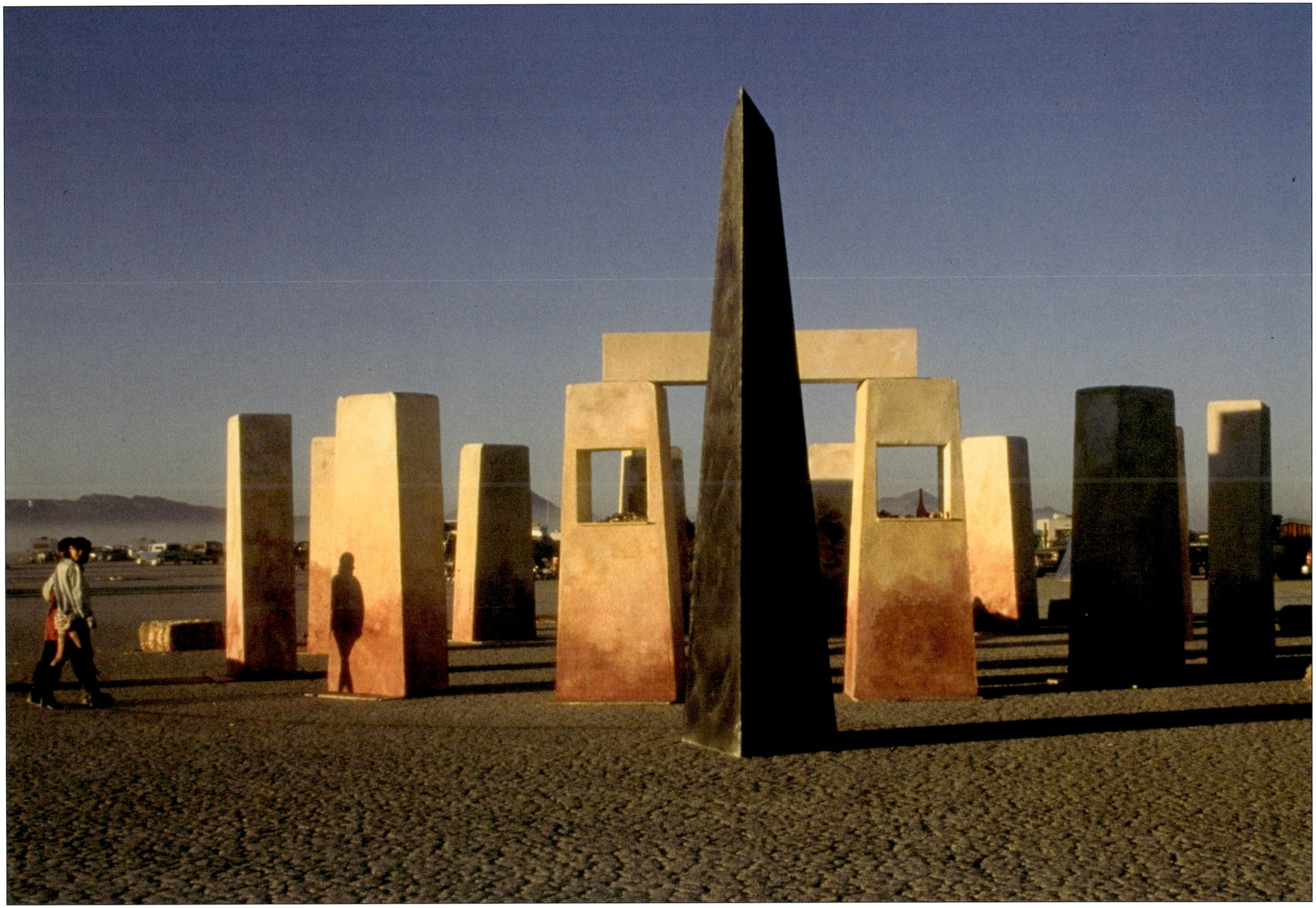

MudHenge *Couple, 1996*

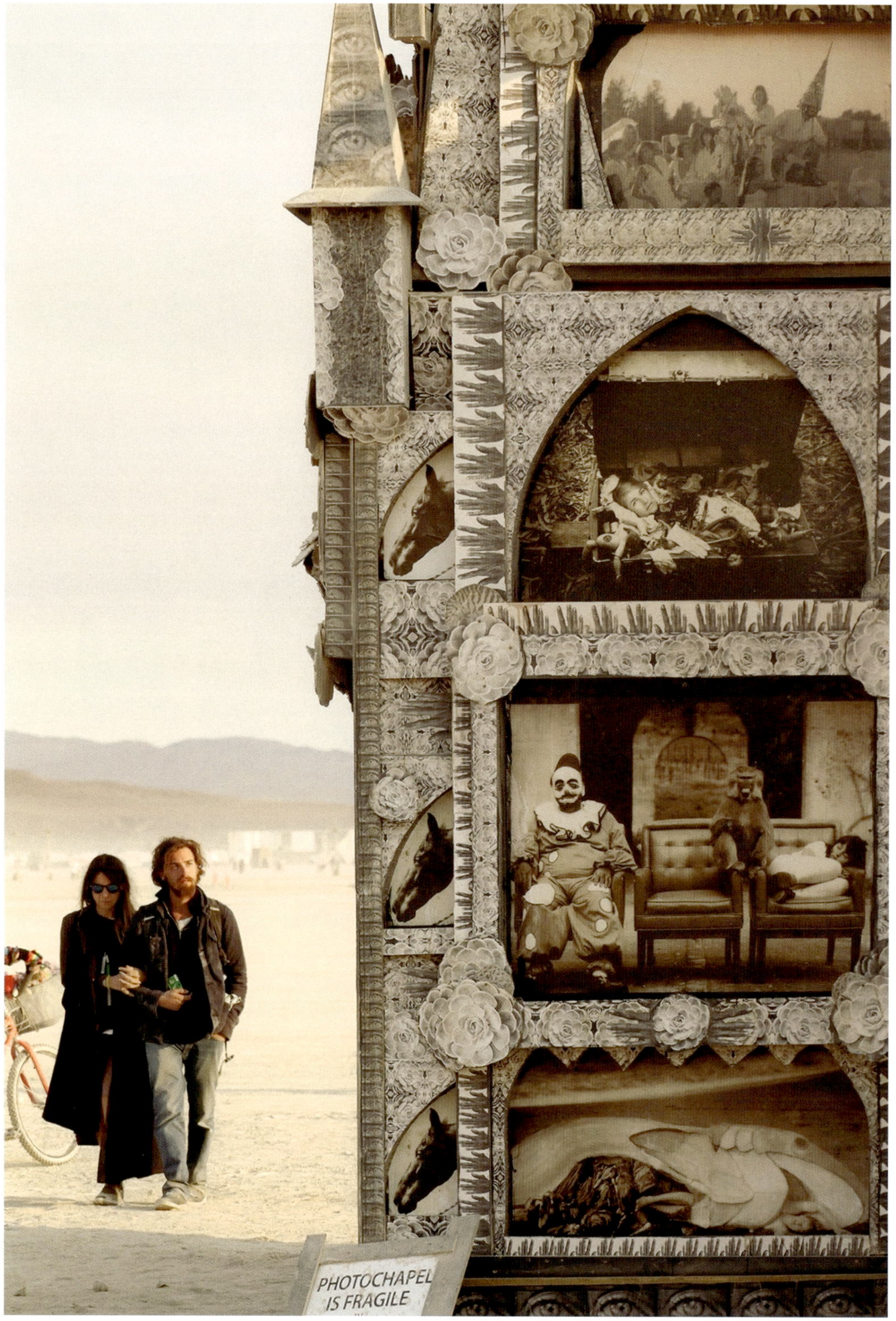

Photo Chapel, *2013*

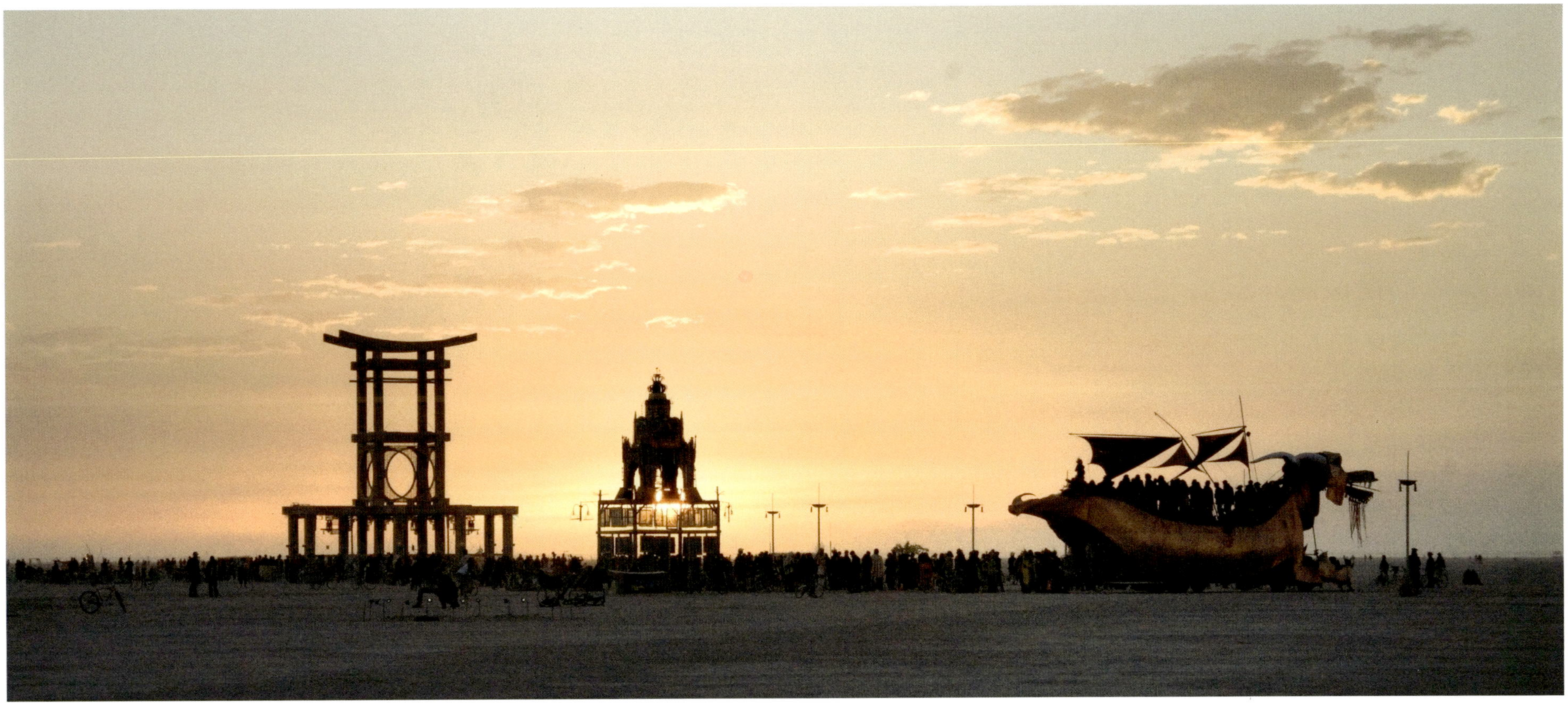

Temple Horizon, 2007

Burning Man funds more art projects than many states. While there is no mandate that funded art address that year's theme, each funded piece must have a degree of interactivity. Honorarium art is juried and constitutes a cornerstone attraction of the event. Most major installations are spectacularly interactive. People often climb in, on, or around them at will. Many of the mechanical pieces require human energy to function or invite the viewer to either contribute a bit of writing or provide some form of input.

But interactivity can also mean engaging the minds of the observers, and the most prominent forms of expression at Burning Man involve parody, satire, and politics—outsized objects that poke fun or rage against the default world. Unfunded art is ubiquitous and appears in a wide variety of shapes and sizes. Most of it is idiosyncratic or hidden in the decor and embellishments of a theme camp. A surprise element is often hidden in deep playa for only the most adventurous to discover. Such gestures are priceless gifts.

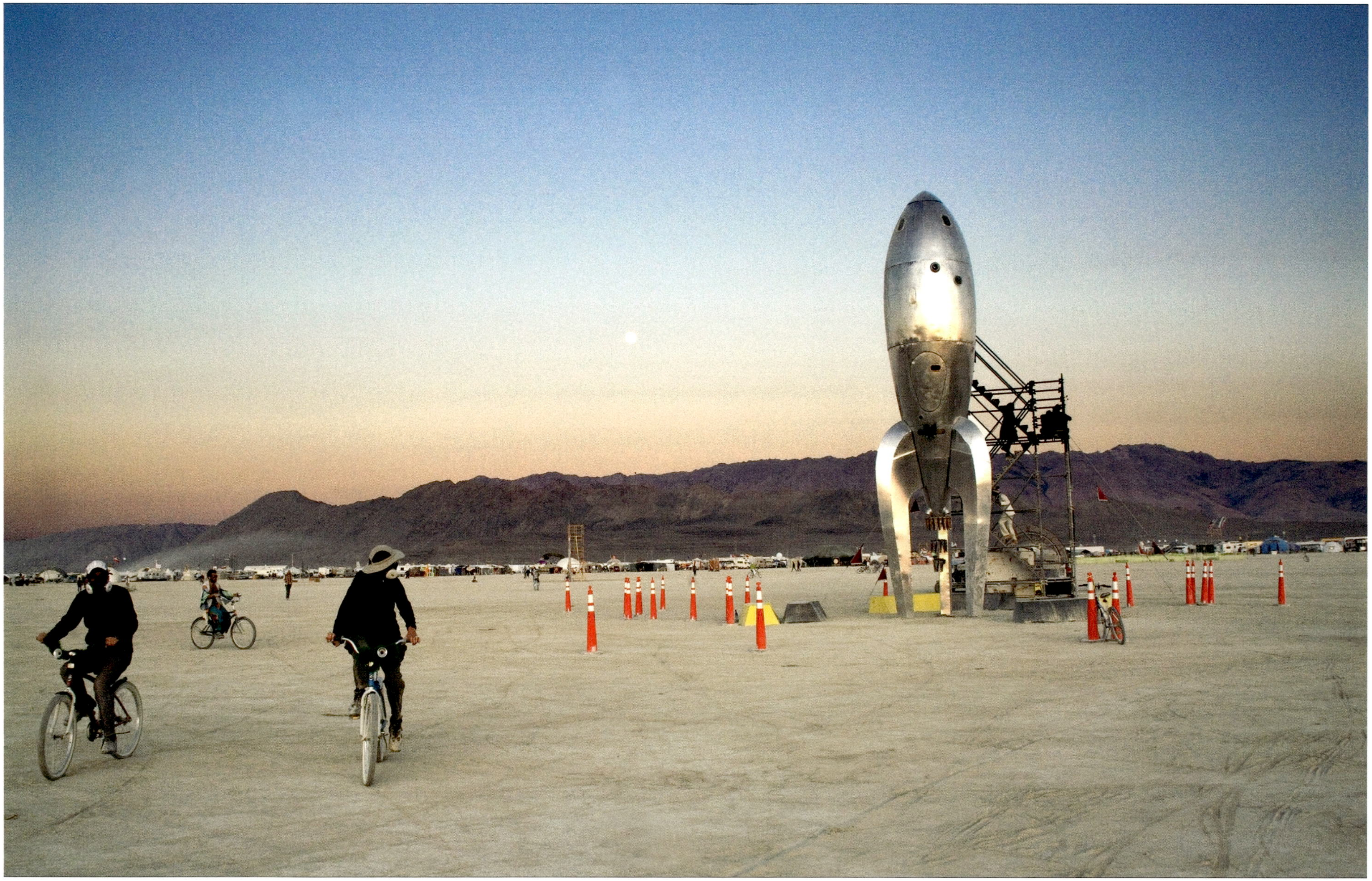

Raygun Gothic Rocketship, *2009*

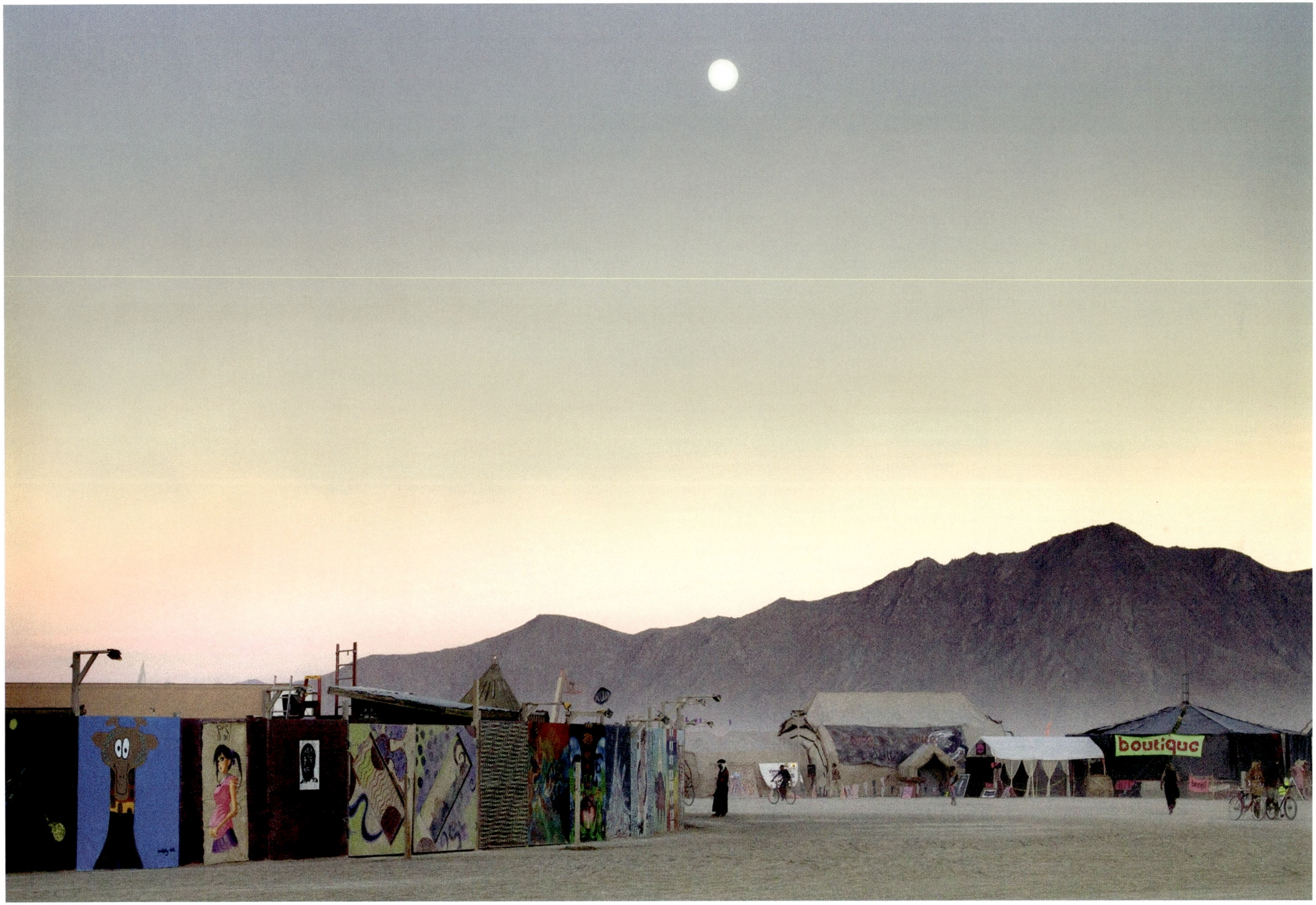

Pastel Center Camp, 2012

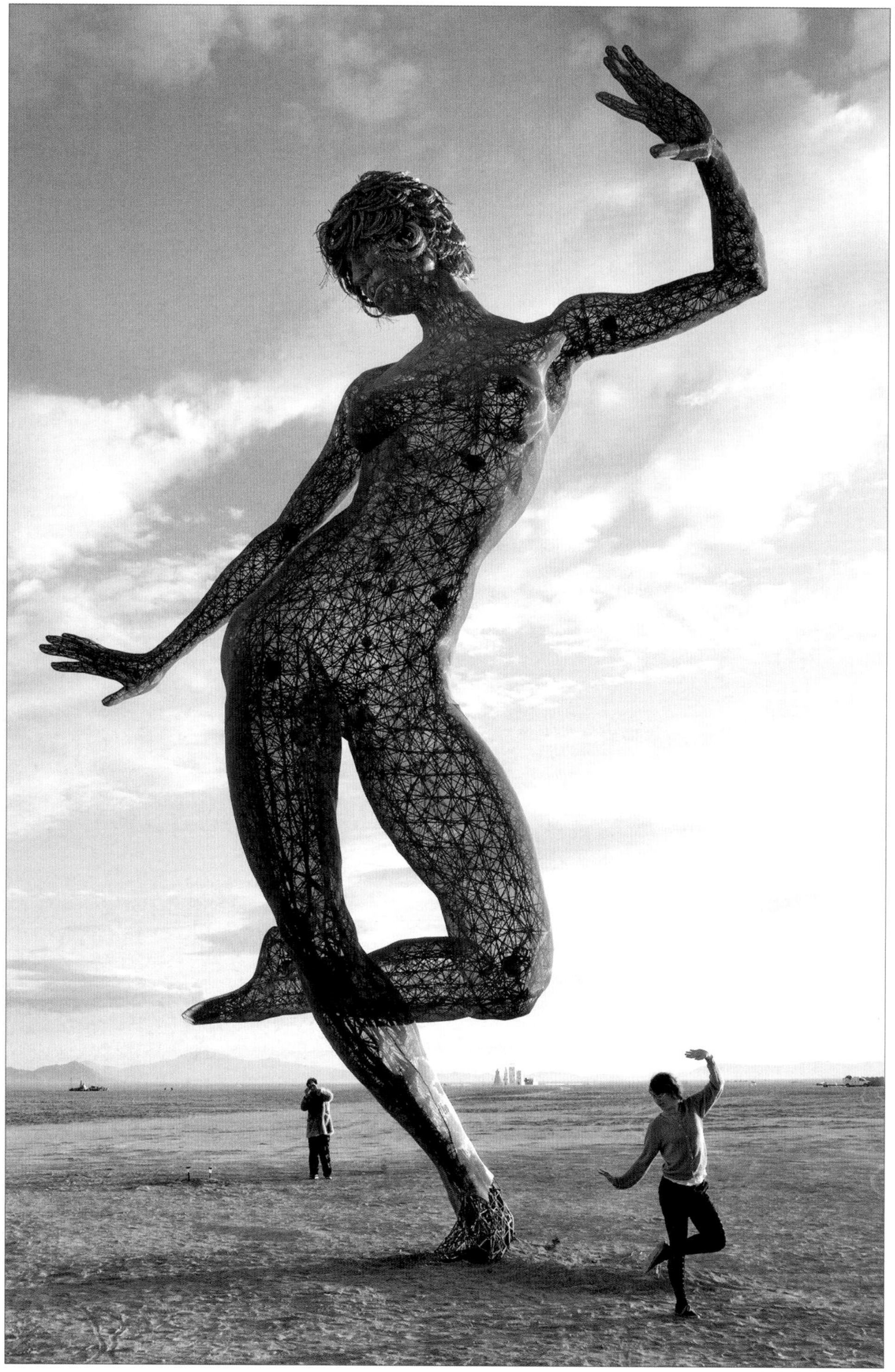

Bliss Dance *X2, 2010*

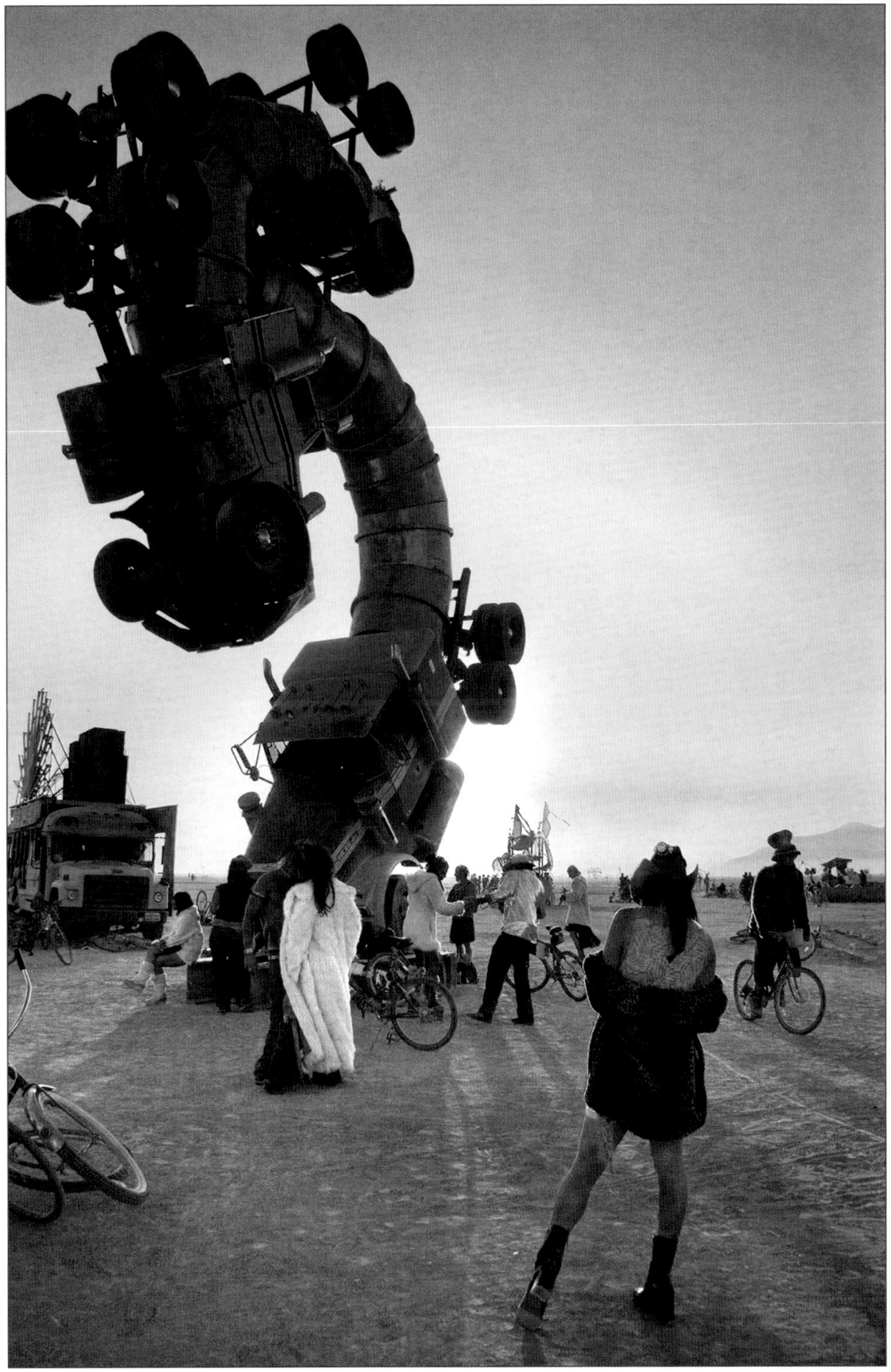

Big Rig Jiggin', 2007

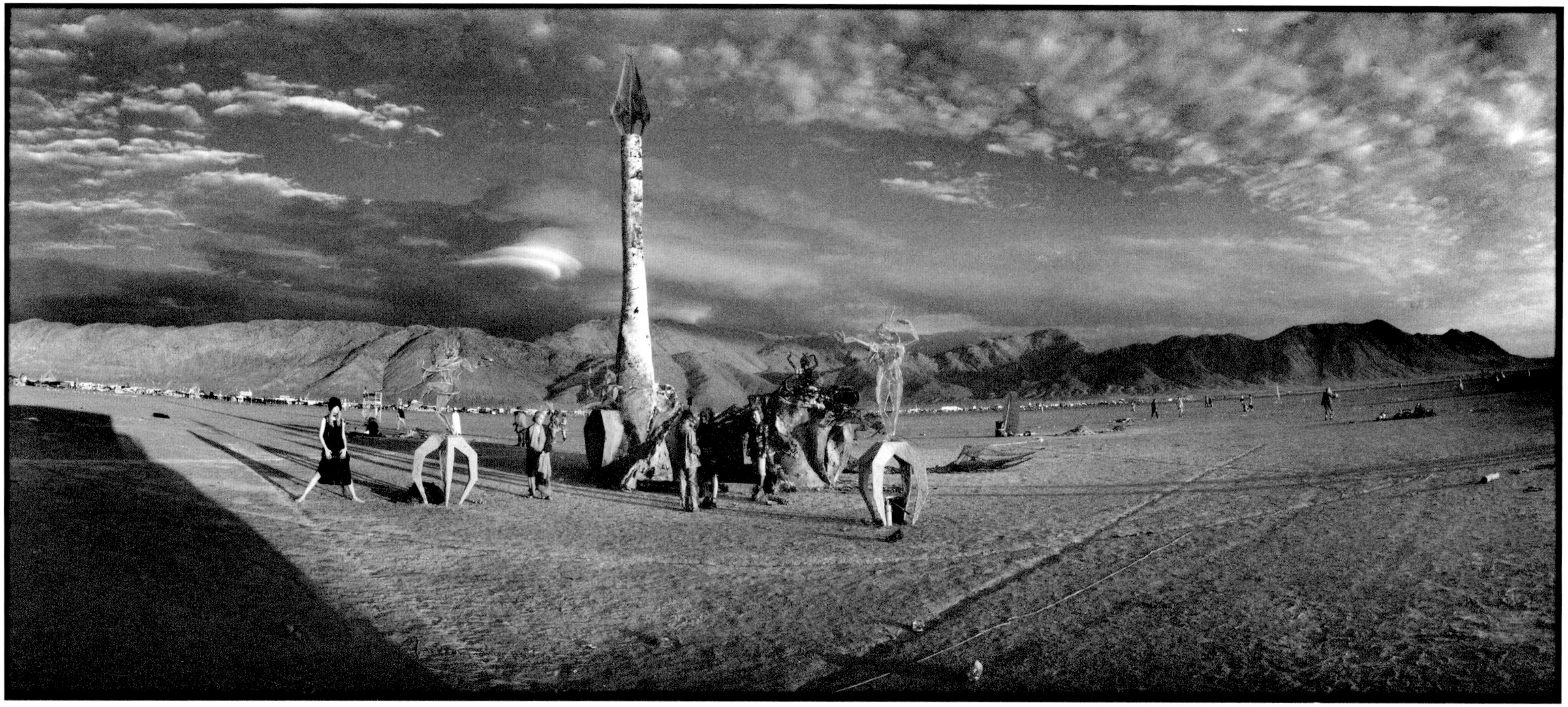

Temple of Rudra *Afterburn, 1998*

I remember walking out to the remnants of Pepe Ozan's *Temple of Rudra* in the early morning of 1998. By then, Pepe had been producing sculpture involving wire frames and mud for several years, and these had morphed into opera stages by 1996. The opera and subsequent burning had occurred the night before, and a few people were rummaging through the ashes. Parts of the scorched set stood like relics of war. One thing that distinguished Pepe's sculptural sets was that they were often just as visually intriguing after they were burned. One woman in a black dress and cloche hat was performing yoga in the early morning light. Others were wandering through the burned sculpture cluster bearing the somber countenances of mourners. The playa's a grand stage set, I thought. We're actors in a one-act drama that must be viewed from a distance.

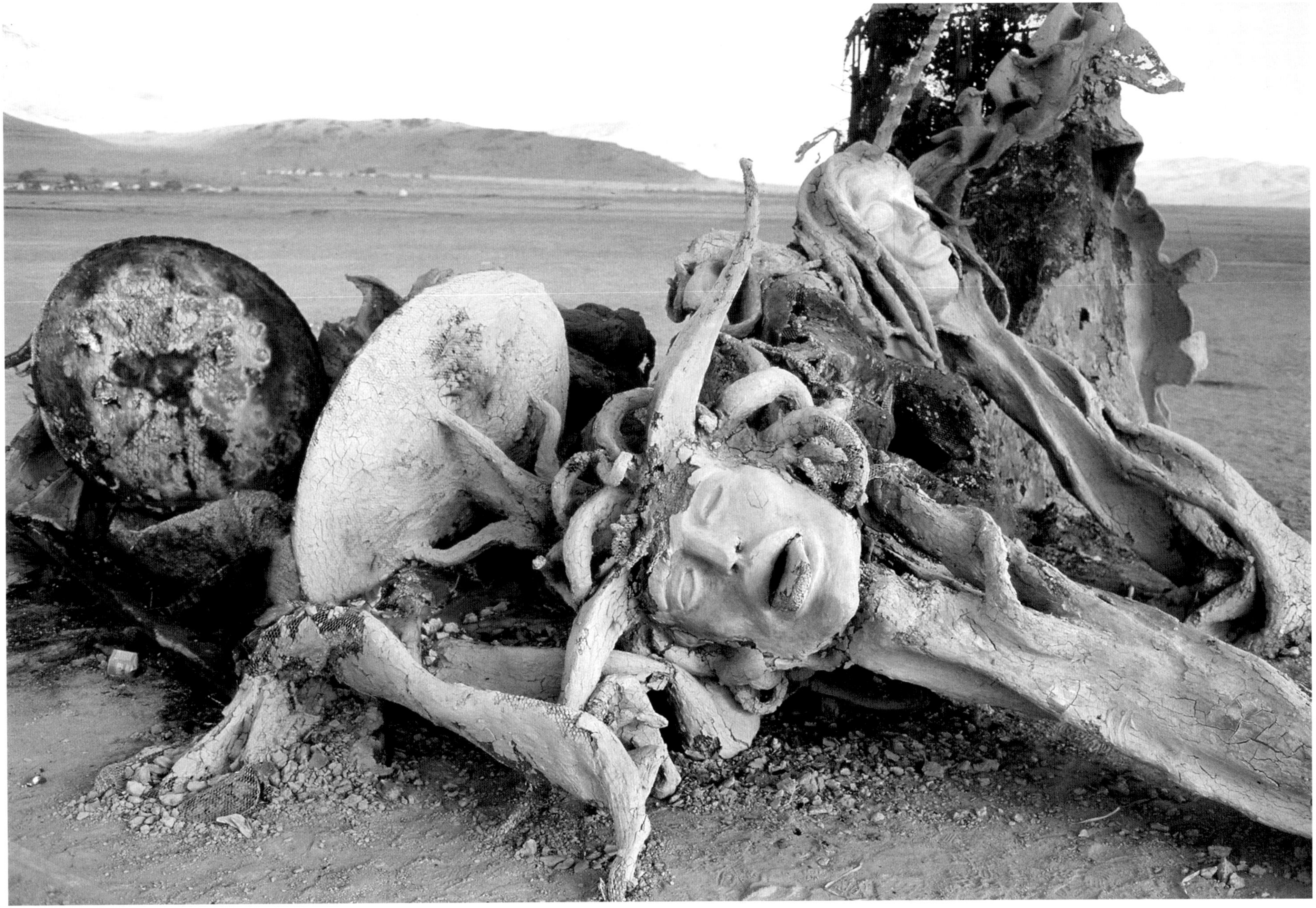

Opera Ruin, 1997

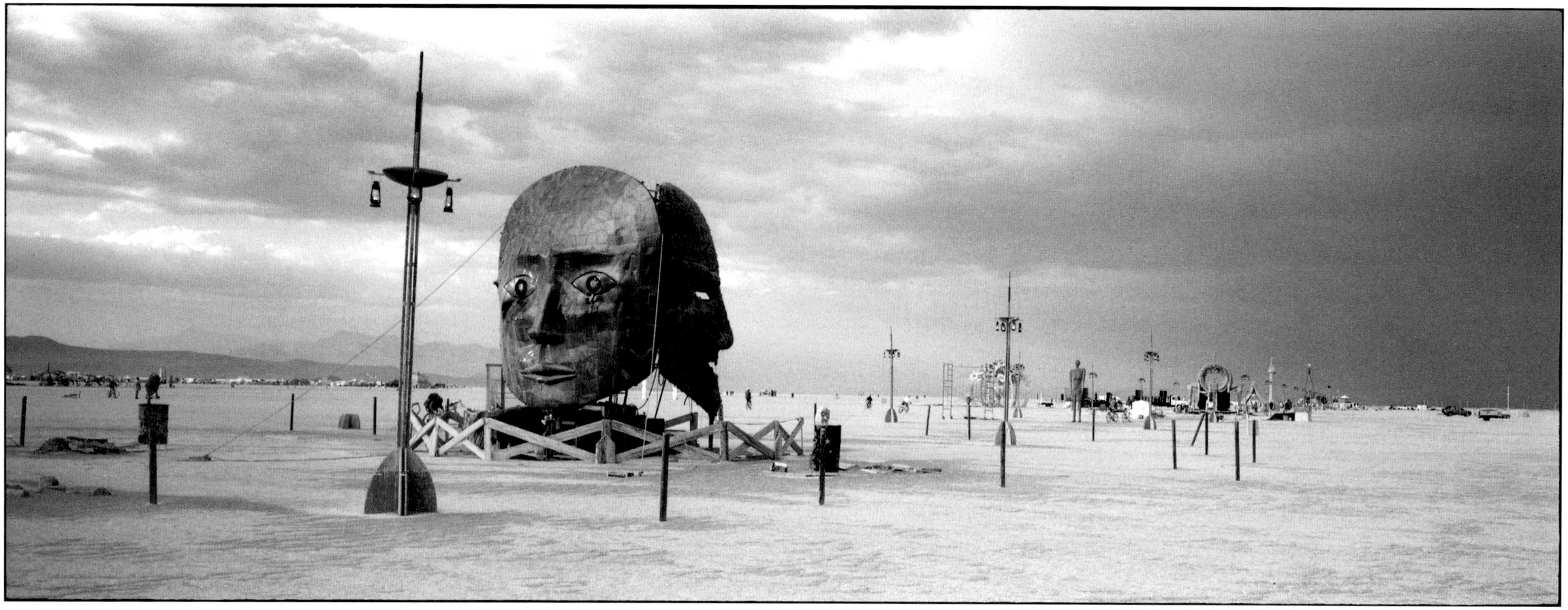

Body Walk, 2000

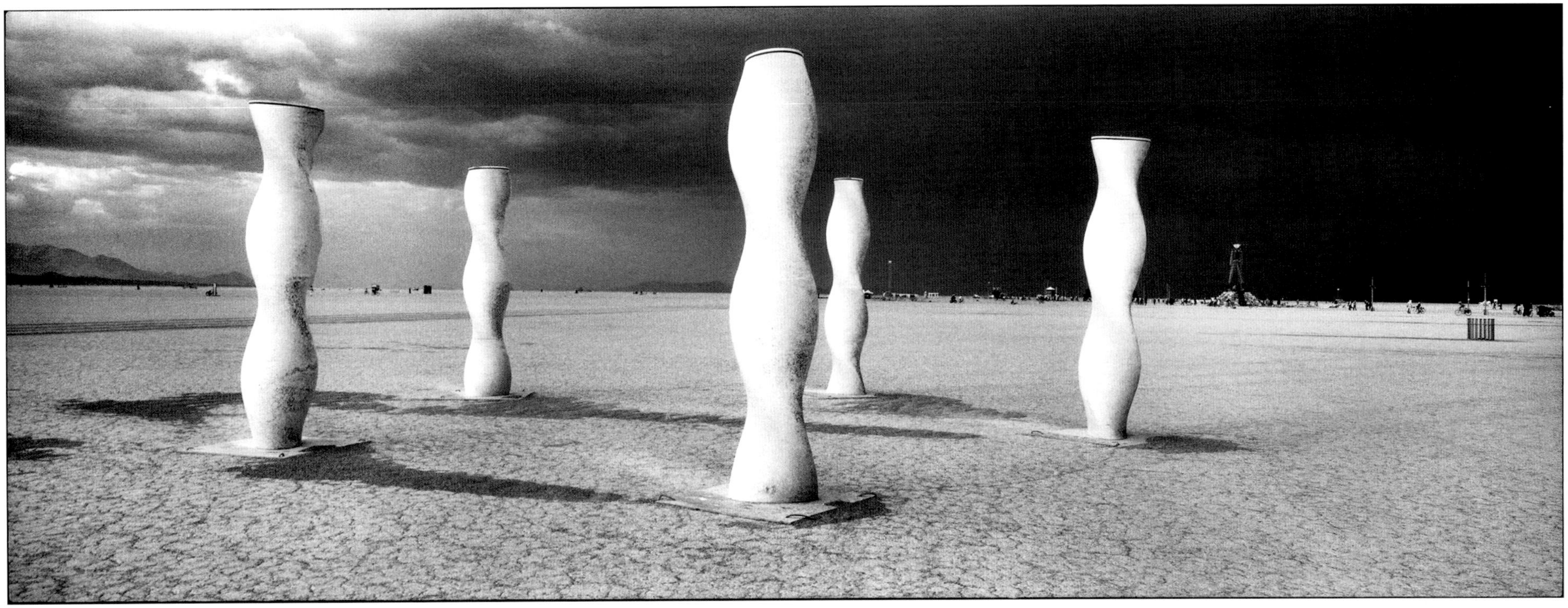

The Temple of Nut, *2000*

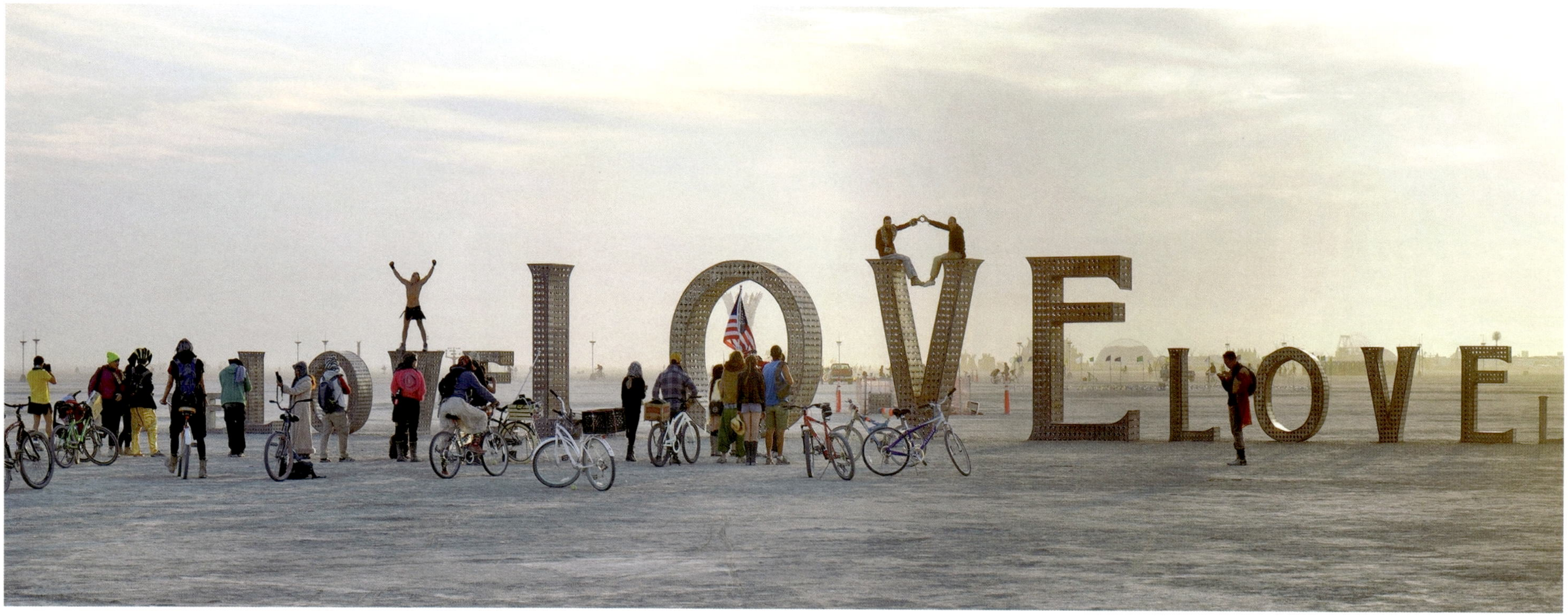

LOVE *Posing, 2014*

Divining the relationship between the Burning Man principles and the Black Rock playa offers a key to understanding the artistic growth and evolution of the event: The desert is an immense blank space with limitless potential for expression. It's a harsh environment, a place where survival is a genuine issue. It also feels boundless. It conjures for us a sense of primal wonder and a deep respect for natural forces. It is an anvil big enough to serve as a smithy for the gods, and everything must be large scale in order to achieve significance. Large scale is a dynamic that affects the viewer in profound ways. A piece that is large enough to be climbed on or requires us to propel its mechanism invites us to participate in a cooperative experiment. We enter into a relationship with the artwork that is unique and momentarily exclusive.

The event, on the other hand, compels us to participate in a vast, instant community and to be expressive. "Here is your big canvas," the event suggests. "Now do something big with it, and while you're at it, craft your art to involve the community as much as possible." The nexus between the two is achieved with the mandate that art should be interactive. Interactive art brings the creative artists into a direct and dynamic relationship with the community at large, and it is this partnership that informs both the design of the piece and the experience of attending the event. Art and audience are in an unspoken conspiracy that promises to allow the installation to achieve its ultimate success. Success isn't measured by the number of people who gawk, or pose, or see it as their personal play structure; it's measured by the number of people who adopt it as their home.

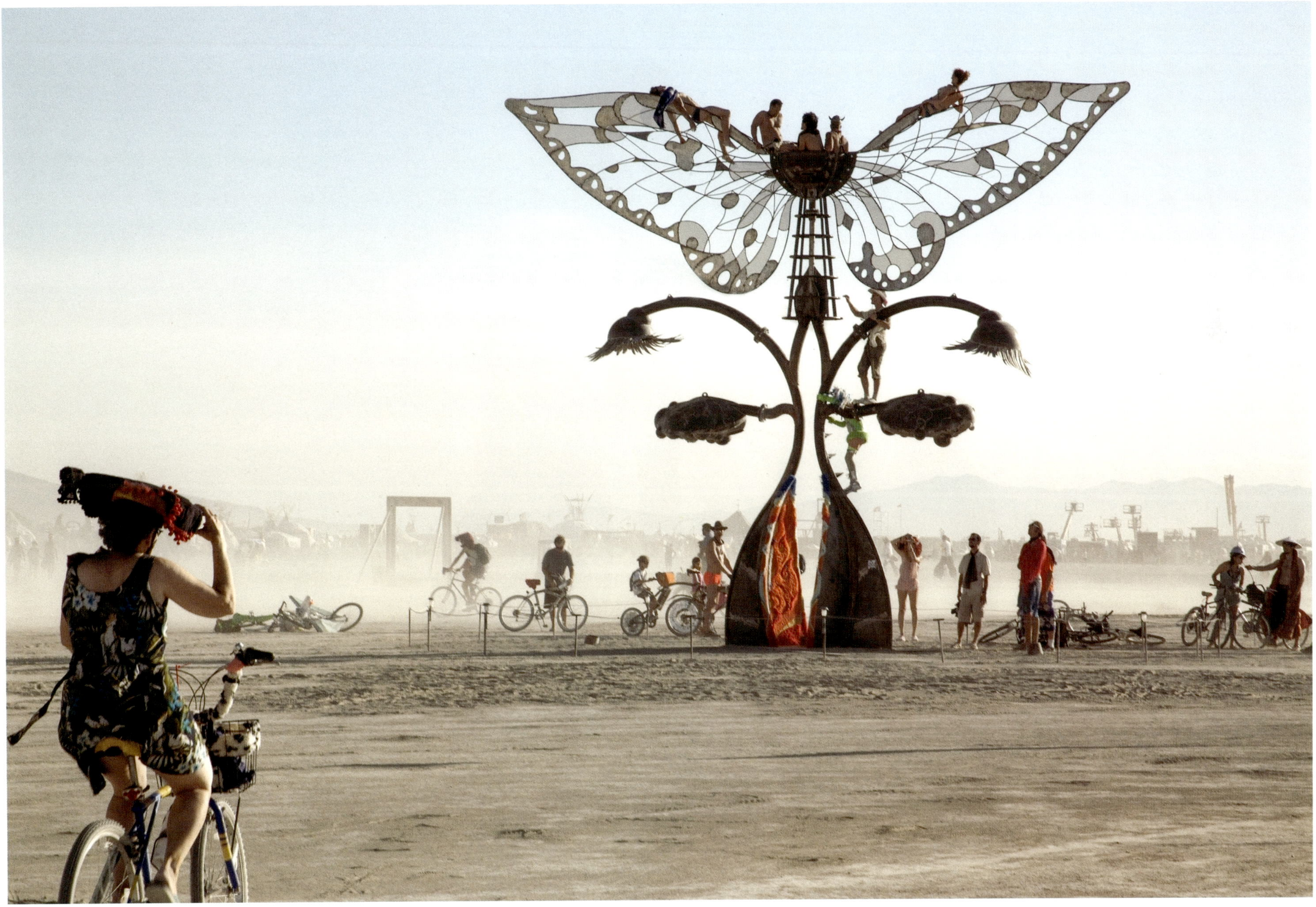

Portal of Evolution, *2009*

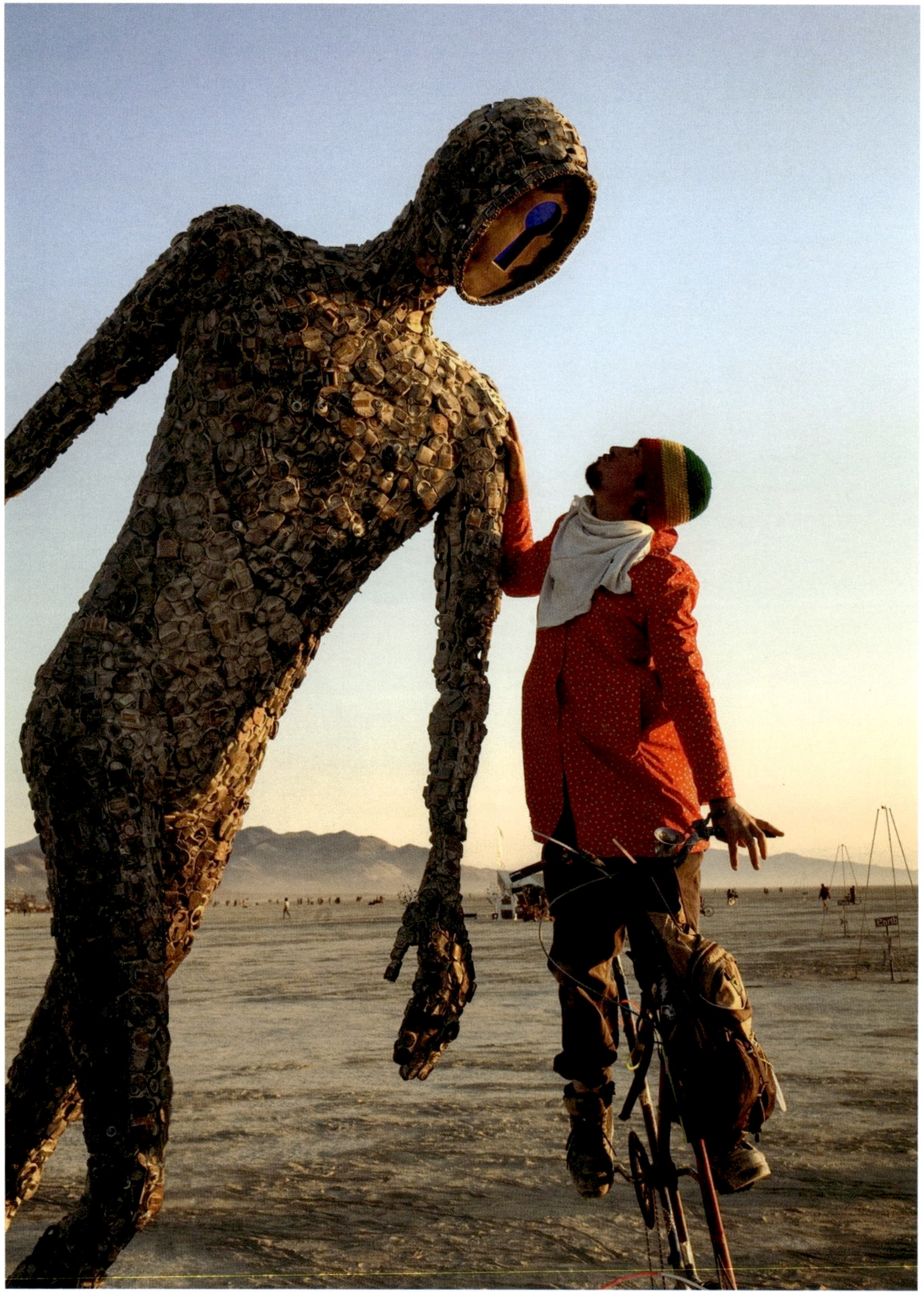

Keynote *Fan, 2009*

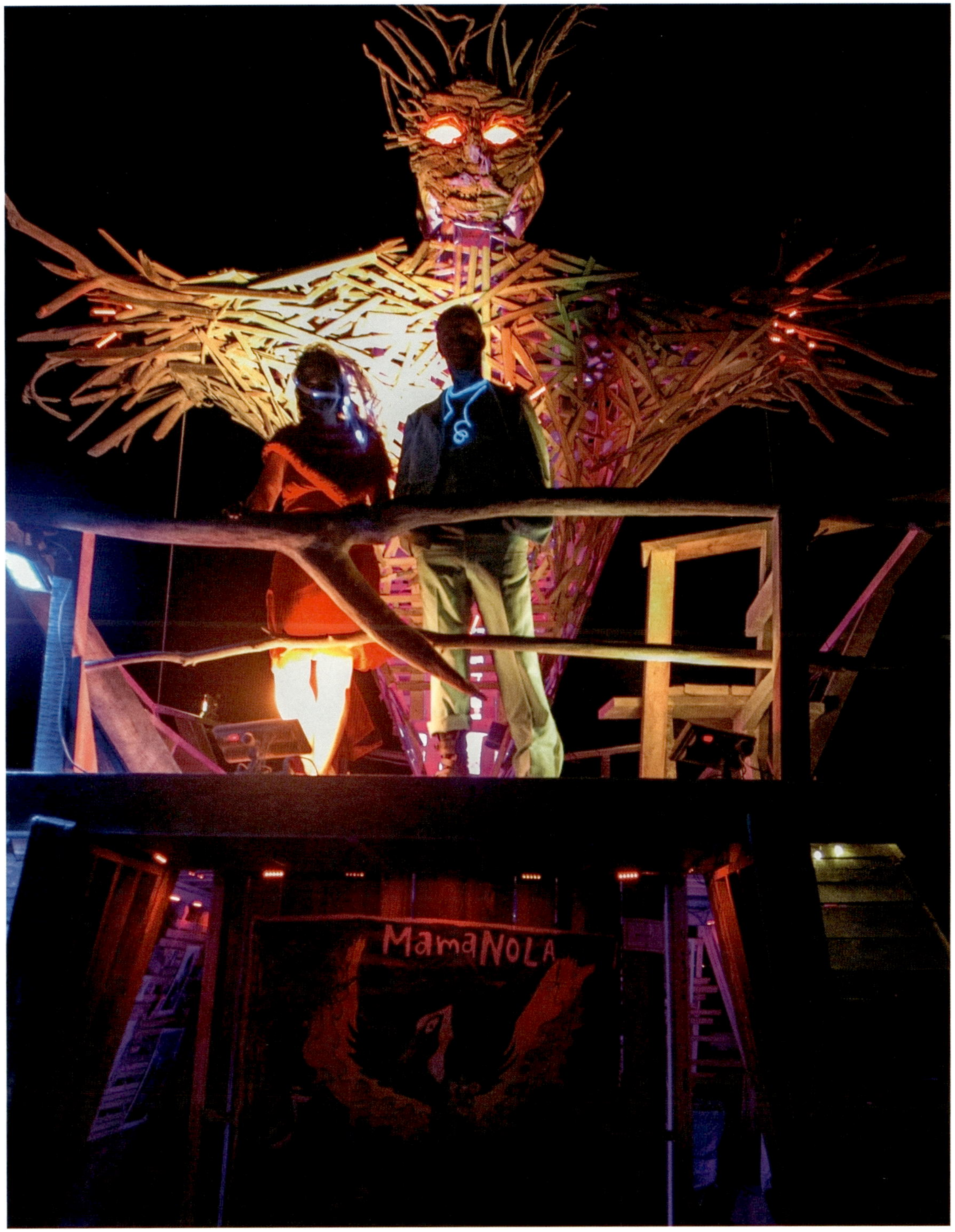

Mama NOLA, *2011*

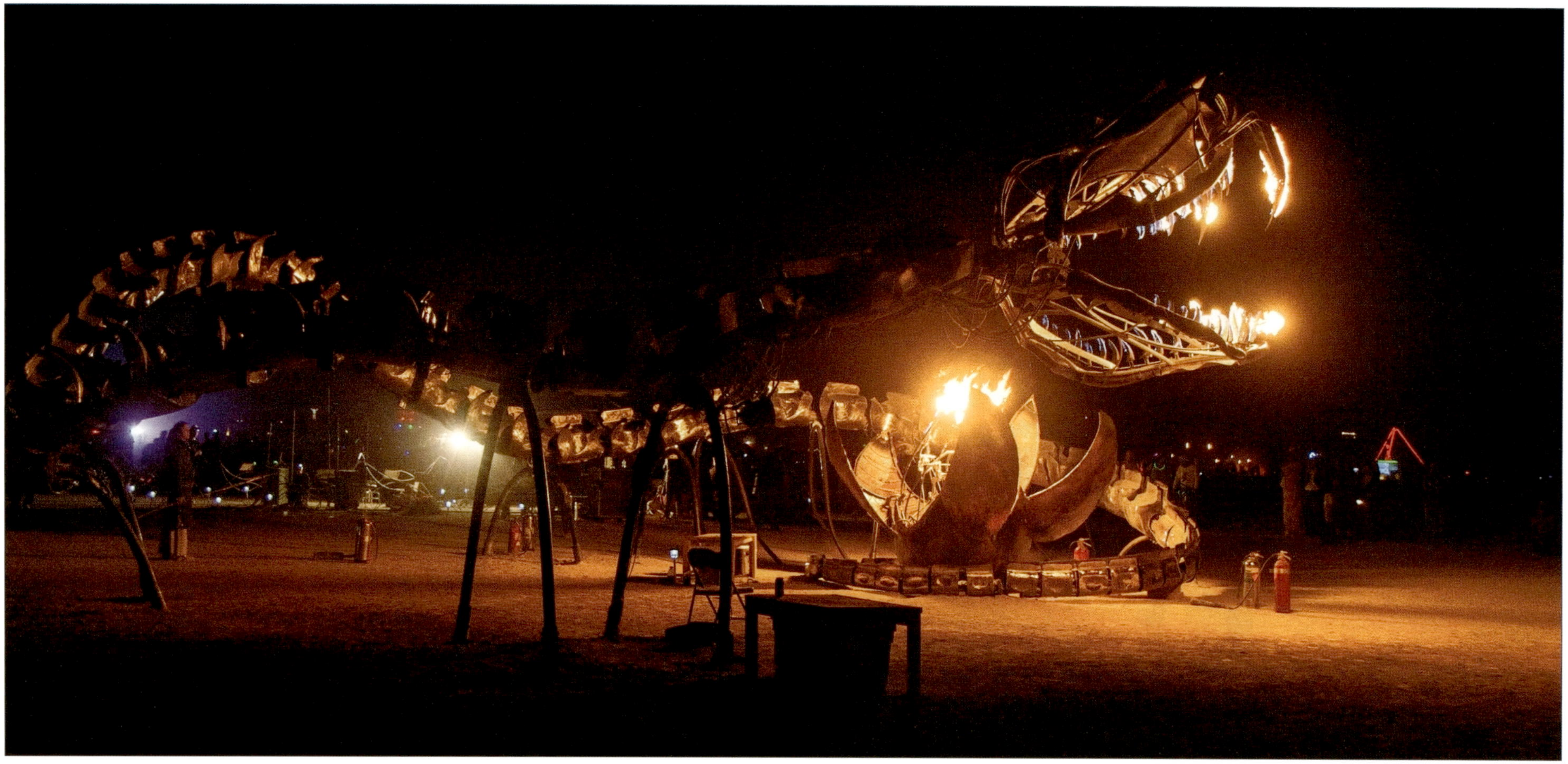

Serpent Mother, *2007*

Much of Burning Man art is designed to have both a day and a nighttime aspect. Some is designed to be burned as well, but often these have a mainly wooden component. Others use both light and sound to make their statement, and more than a few employ fire jets or fire cannons as part of their display. The Flaming Lotus Girls, a group of more than a hundred artists, specialize in large articulated metal sculptures that can belch fire. Many longtime artists have a signature style: Dan Das Mann builds huge iron figures with fire effects; Bryan Tedrick casts large iron animals that move. Laura Kimpton makes word art using big letters. Marco Cochrane creates breathtakingly graceful female figures, which appear to defy gravity and are spectacularly illuminated. Blending medieval architecture and contemporary "Gothic" photographs, Michael Garlington builds Byzantine-style chapels. Peter Hudson creates provocative zoetropes that require several cooperative participants to drive their stroboscopic animation. And pioneering Burning Man sculptor Michael Christian creates tall fluid shapes out of steel. The list of veteran Burning Man artists is long and illustrious.

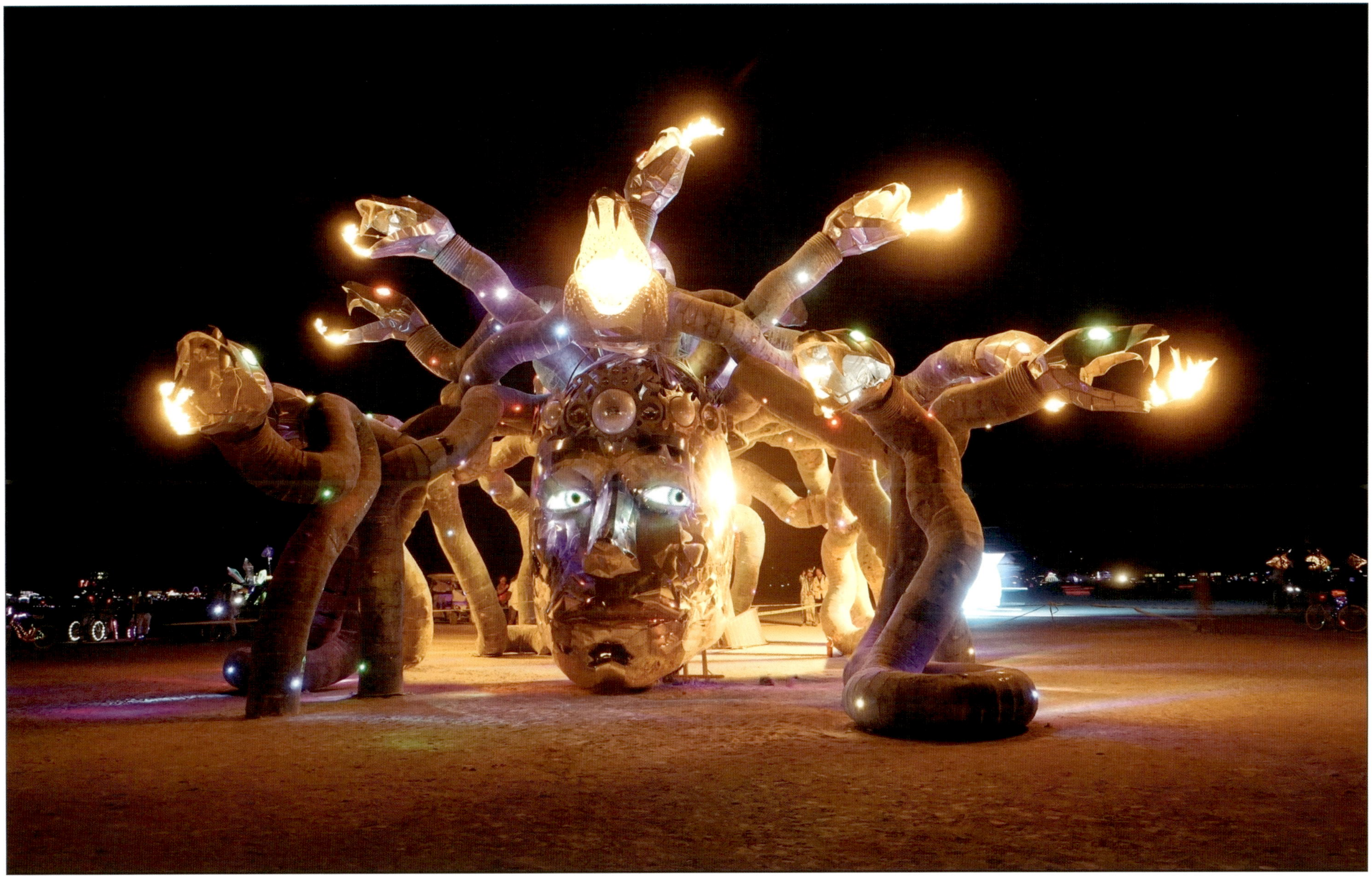

Medusa Madness, *2016*

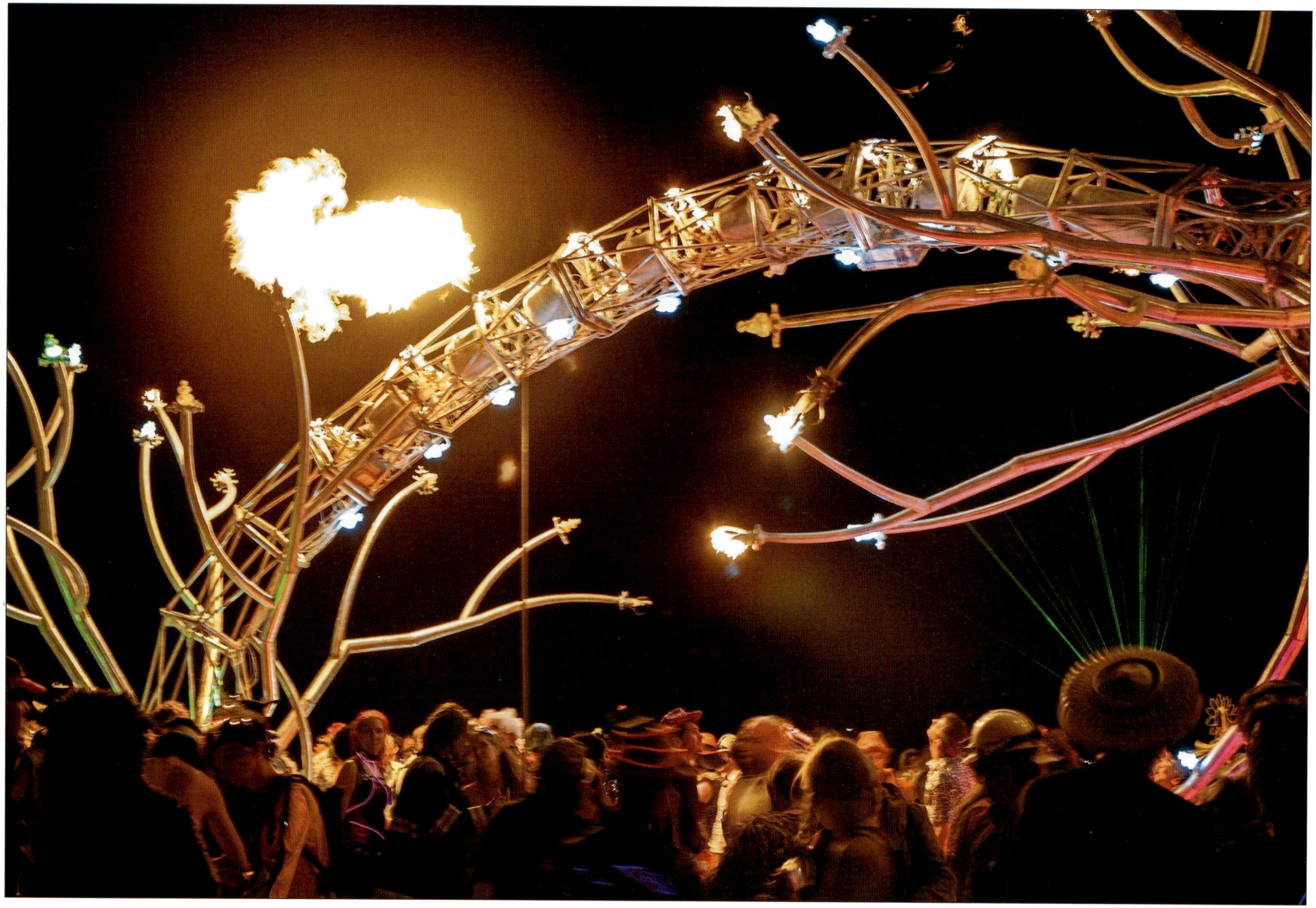

Soma, *2009*

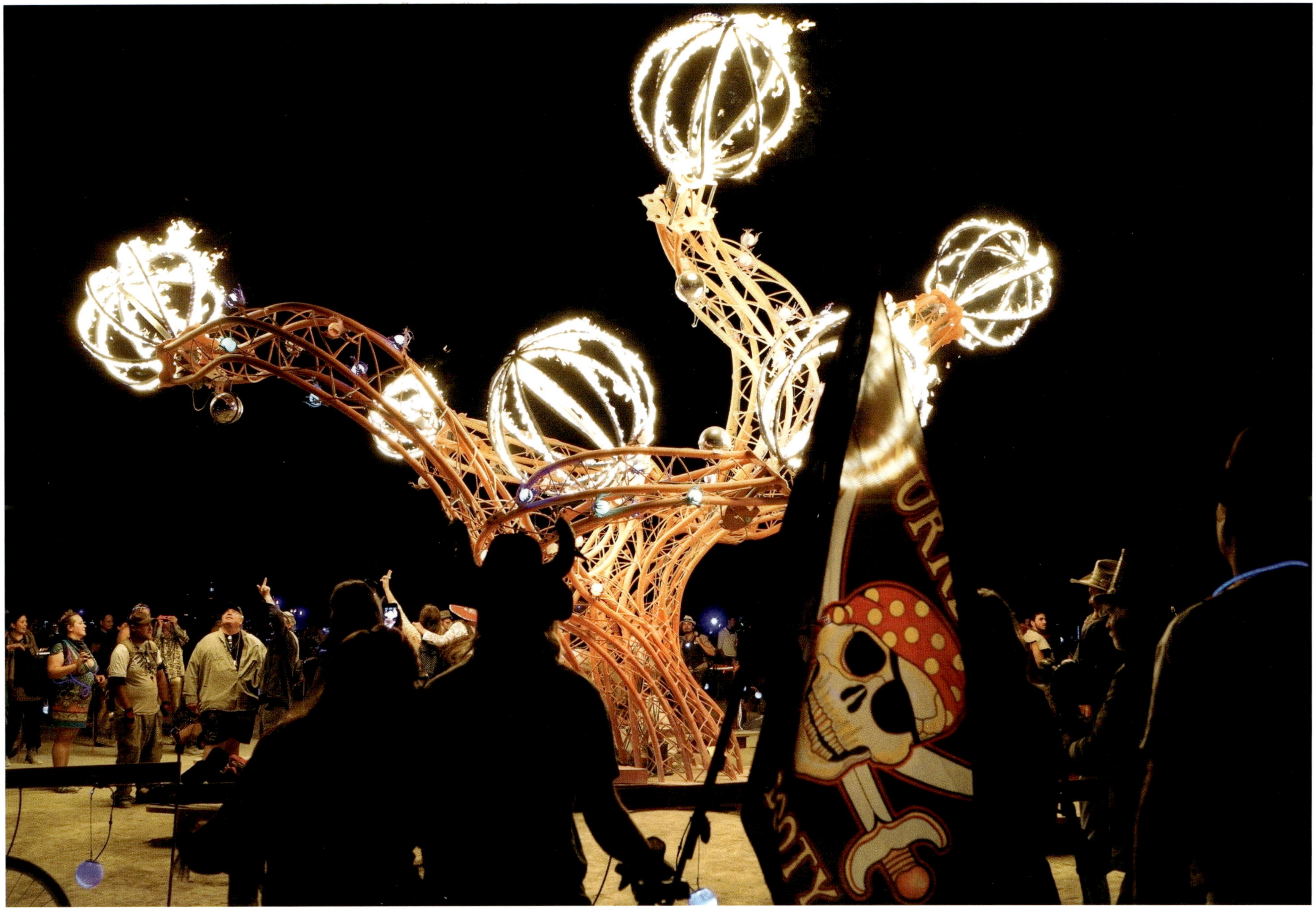

Xylophage, *2013*

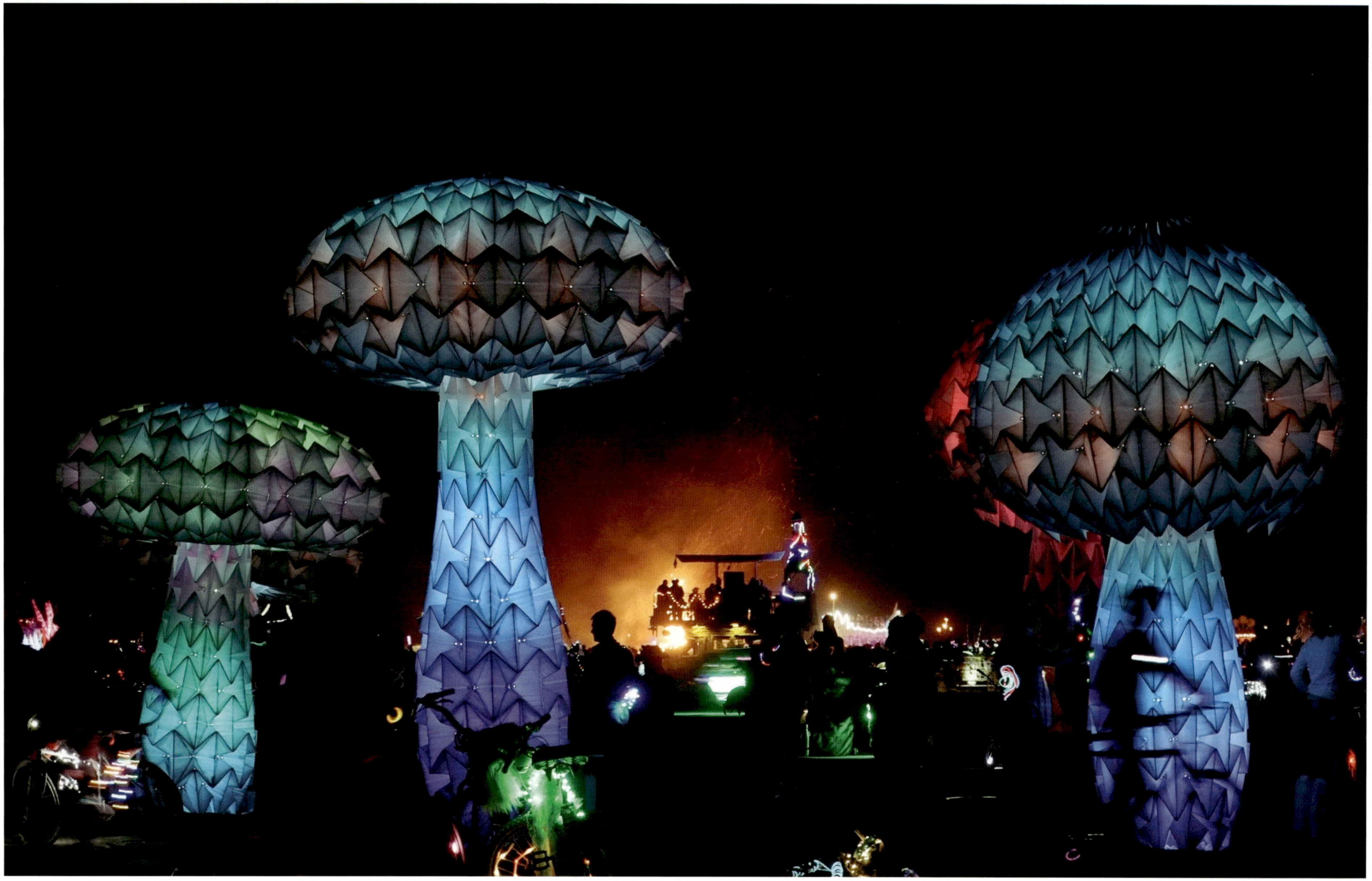

Shrumen Lumen, *2016*

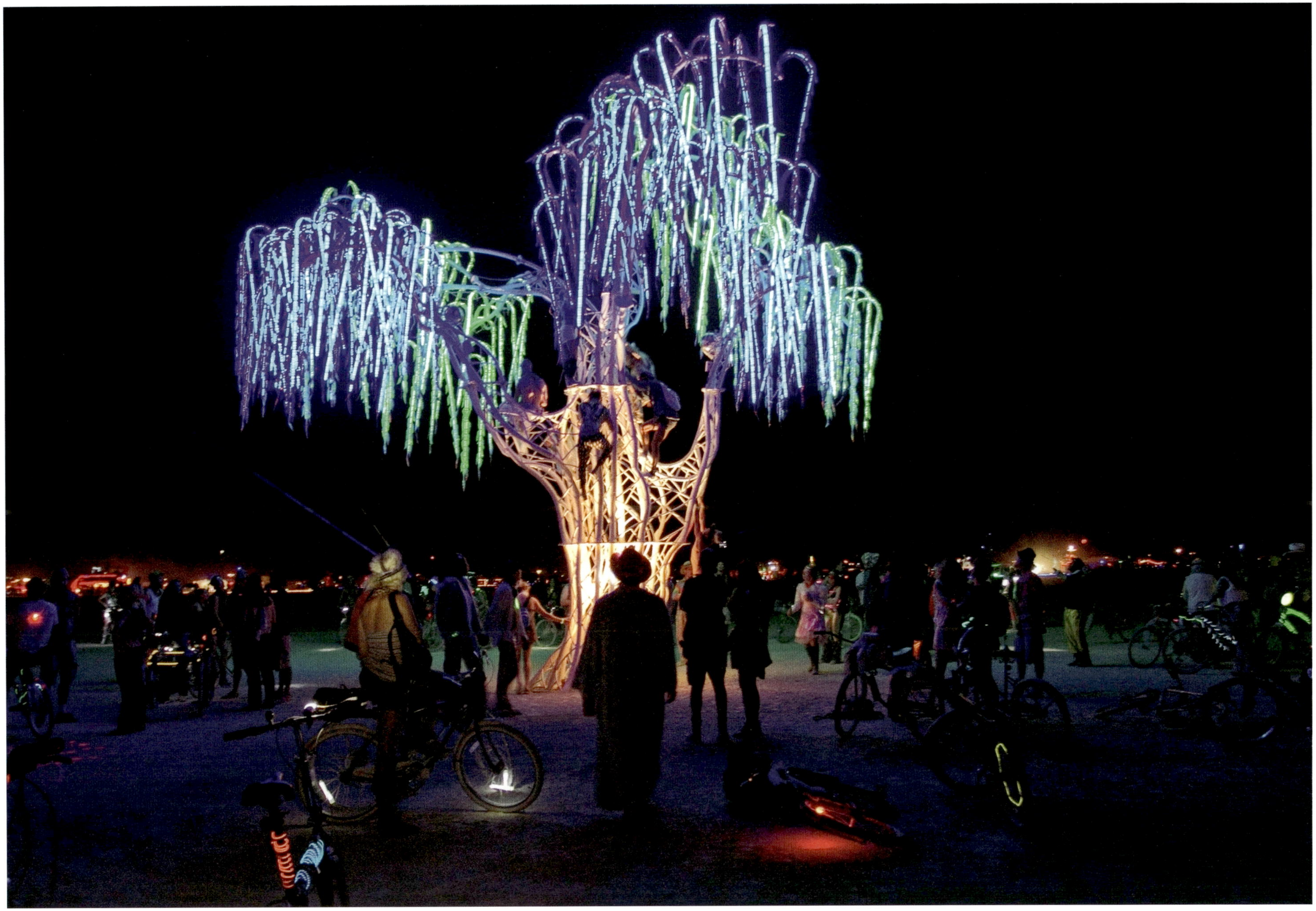

Aurora, *2011*

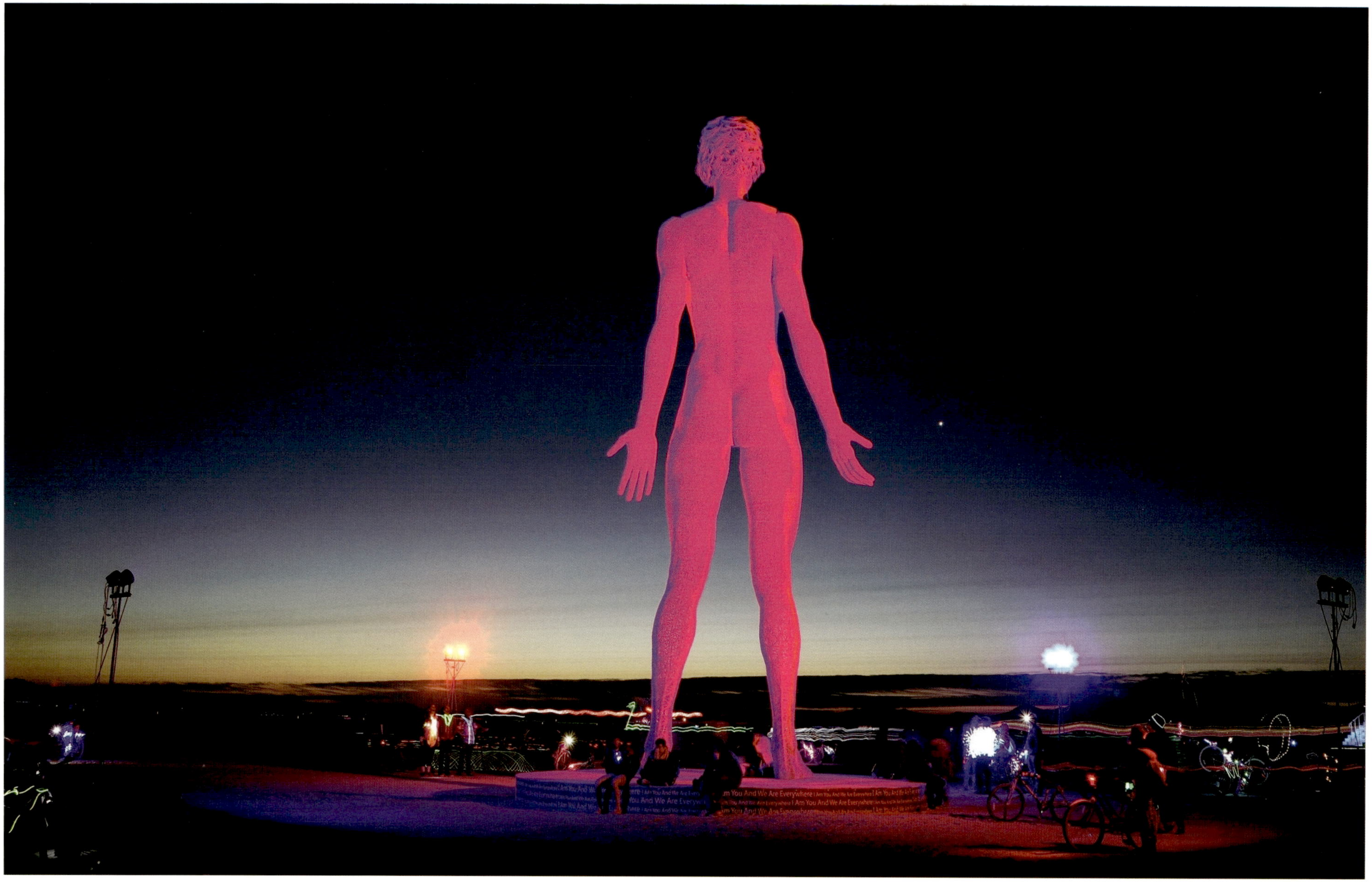

R-Evolution, *2014*

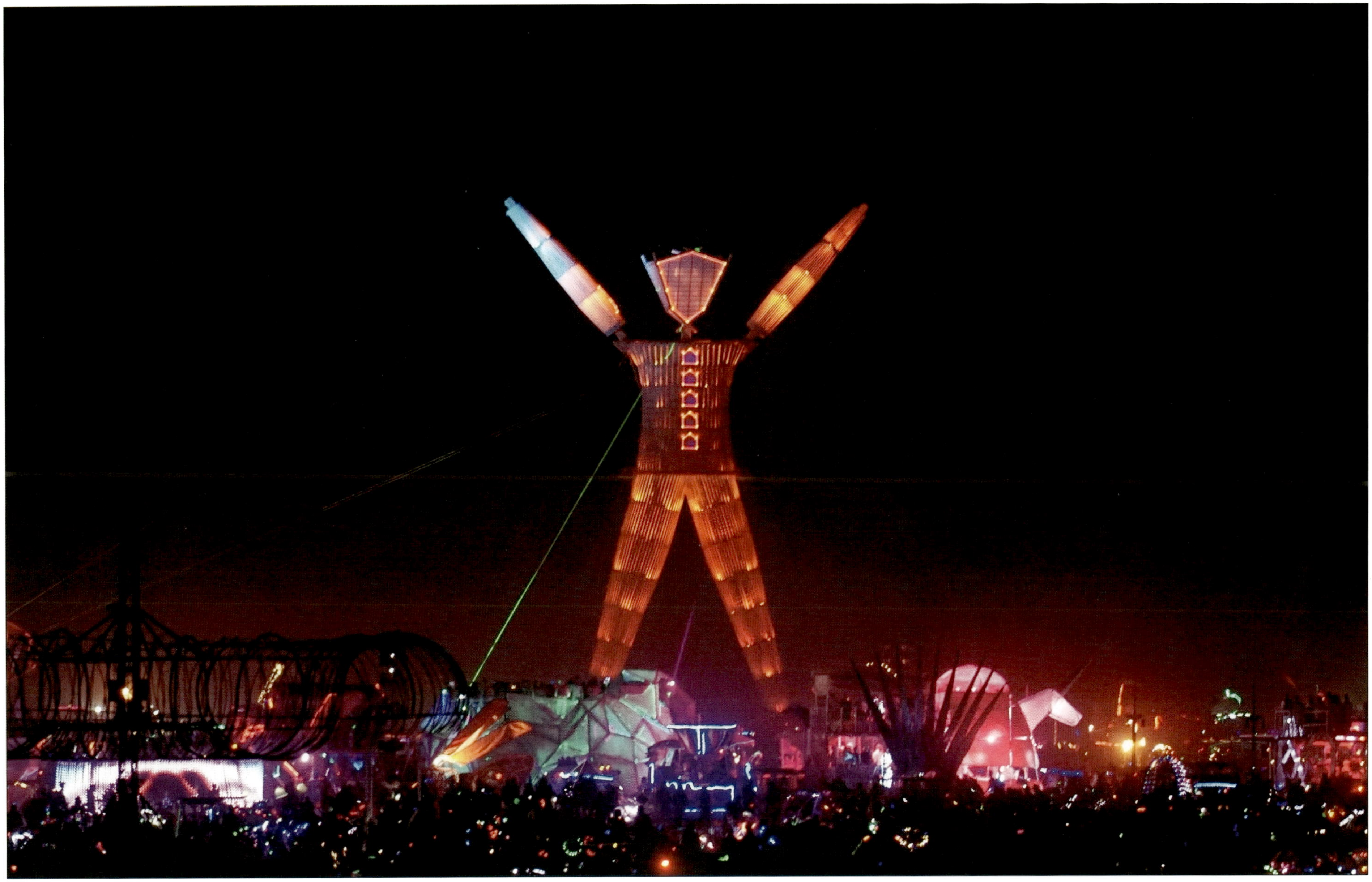

"Caravansary" Night, 2014

CHAPTER 13

THE BIG TENT: 2011–2015

When Rod Garrett drafted his first city design for Burning Man's return to the Black Rock playa, he began in the center of where he envisioned the city to be, and he drew a point on what was probably a BLM map. This is where the Man will stand, and it designates the exact center of Black Rock City. Tony "Coyote" Perez tells me that in the beginning they would put a stake in the ground at that point and draw a circle using a hundred-foot rope tied to the stake. This would form the Burn perimeter.

Legend has it that Rod Garrett positioned the center stake each year so that the sun would rise directly behind the Man—as seen from Rod's chair in First Camp! These days an engineering genius, who goes by the playa handle Bubble Geek, establishes the city's central survey point using GPS averages from thirteen separate orbiting satellites. I'm sure GPS is more accurate, but I like the organic ingenuity of the Rod Garrett method better. Back then, Rod drew a second circle at the 6:00 position, which designated Center Camp.

These days, Center Camp is a massive space devoted to the social aspect of the Burning Man experience, and it is quite an important ingredient to the building of community. But Center Camp began ignominiously as an orange-and-white parachute draped over a rickety steel frame. It didn't look like much, and it barely had a function unless someone was desperate for a modicum of shade. Over the years it's evolved into the kind of recreational hub that every condo association in the United States imagines, but rarely achieves. The parachute transitioned quickly into P. Segal's café, which flourished for a few years until it was literally overwhelmed by the burgeoning cadre of attendees. By the dawn of the millennium, it was obvious the event needed a much larger social space, for Burners to gather for coffee or chai in the mornings, rehearse in the free spaces, nap on the couches, listen to a stream of volunteer entertainers, or browse through displays of Burning Man art and history. In the evenings, there are major league performances or special events, like the infamous Battle of the Bands.

Wandering in for coffee in the late morning is like immersing yourself in a pool of exotic sensations. The lines are often long, but there is so much sensory stimulation going on you

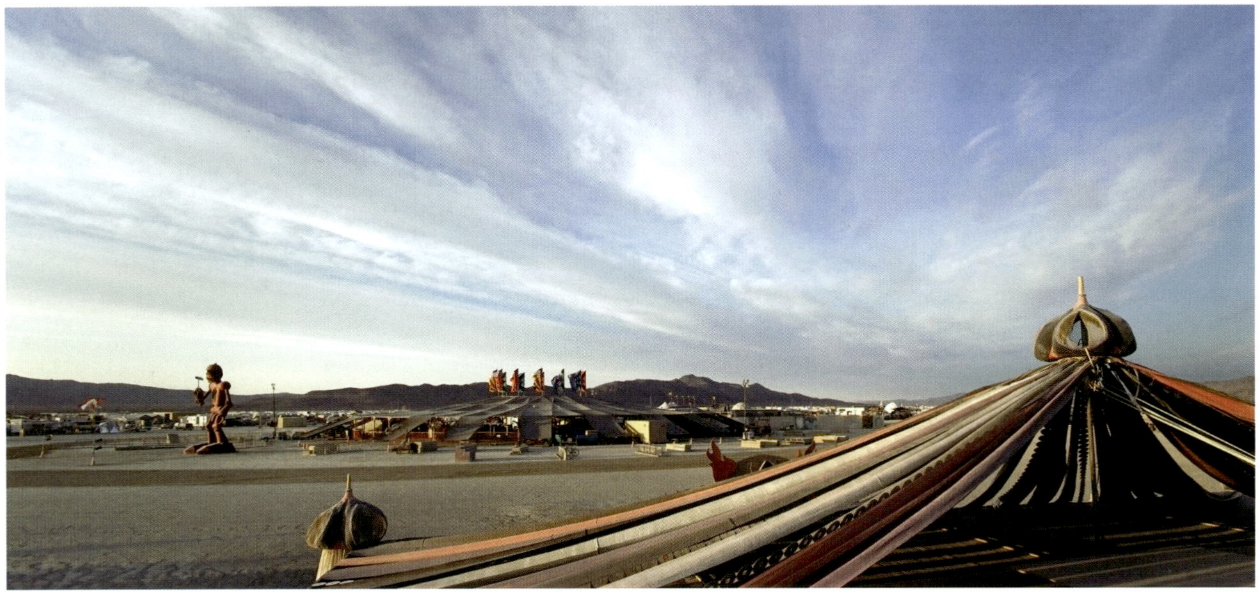

"We've got a big tent."—Grover Norquist (Americans for Tax Reform)
"We've got a big tent too."—Larry Harvey (Burning Man Project)

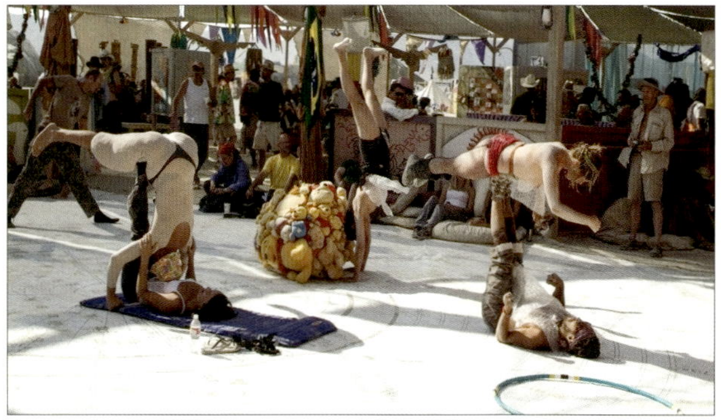

The Center Camp lounge is alive with interactions both social and extemporaneous.

scarcely notice. There is a ceaseless din of laughter amid multilingual conversations. On the small stage, a guitar-strumming troubadour might be trying out an original tune, but he won't manage to rouse the sleeping pile of all-nighters strewn about like pillows atop more pillows. In the back of the tent, a troupe of acrobats might be rehearsing a routine intended for an upcoming performance or a yoga session might be underway. A gang of thirty silver-clad aliens walks in wearing featureless shiny masks. The aliens weave in and around the crowd and disappear outside. Their appearance was an unscheduled gift—unscheduled, but not unexpected. Some people break into applause; others simply say "Thank you."

The Center Camp plaza is laid out in the shape of a keyhole, with the wide part serving as the entry to and from the playa. In the center of the keyhole stands the sprawling big tent. Outside that behemoth of canvas is a circular boundary that is lined on its front with a complex of theme camps, interspersed with the most necessary social services: Information, Media Mecca, Arctica (ice), BRC Hardware, BRC Post Office, *BRC Weekly*, BMIR 94.5 (radio), Medical and Emergency Care, Black Rock Rangers, Black Rock Boutique, and the *Black Rock Beacon*. The road that surrounds the outer circle of the plaza is Rod's Road, named for Rod Garrett, who passed away in 2011. It's a fitting tribute to Rod's memory, but I would submit that the entirety of Black Rock City is a monument to his design genius.

By any measure, 2011 was a monumental year. It began

solemnly with Rod's death, and that summer, several of his friends and associates met on the catwalk between the pillars supporting the "Striding Man." For the first time the figure of the Man wasn't standing stoically with his arms at his sides but stepping forward into the future. We stood there on the catwalk listening to Will Roger Peterson tell stories about his longtime friend. He had worked for Rod, and then he and Crimson had bought an apartment in an Oakland building Rod owned. It was Will who had introduced Rod to Larry and the staff in 1997 and suggested that he would be the ideal person to design their "little city" on Hualapai Flat. After a few stories and a period of quiet reflection, we went our separate ways, but not before we took a moment to look up at the Striding Man, who glowed in brilliant red and yellow neon above us all. "Rites of Passage" was the theme for 2011—and it couldn't have been more perfect for the occasion.

In 2011, the event sold its full allotment of sixty-eight thousand tickets, and it thoroughly altered the dynamic of attendance. The organization responded to the ticket demand by holding a lottery, and it threw the veteran hierarchy into a panic. Imagine a theme camp of fifty, half of whom didn't get a ticket. How would they be able to transport and build their camp? Social media exploded with dire predictions of yet another example of why Burning Man was going to hell. Heretofore being a theme camper was a calling; you and your mates began to plan the design and logistics of your next camp within weeks of the previous Burn. But how do you do that if a crucial segment of your tribe may not get a ticket? In an inspired moment of anticipation, Marian decided to hold back ten thousand tickets. These were allotted to theme camps, artists, and mutant vehicle makers, but also staff, staff support camps, families, and spouses. It was a master stroke that rescued crucial longtimers, but the yearly demand for tickets continues to exceed supply.

The upside to all the Burning Man popularity was that by 2011, playa art and theme camps in Black Rock City had reached an international and institutional zenith. Artists from around the world were able to propose extremely ambitious projects, and the increased revenues allowed the organization to at least partially fund them. "Build it bigger, build it bolder, build it better" had never been more of a reality, and professional artists and ordinary Burners alike responded with oversize ambition and unprecedented determination.

No project made a bigger visual impact that year than the *Temple of Transition*. Arabesque, stately, and articulate, this multi-towered beauty graced the playa as nothing before. New Zealander Chris "Kiwi" Hankins designed and directed an international crew that fabricated and installed a temple complex of five three-story towers surrounded by an elegant 120-foot central tower. These towers were connected by walkways from the circular balcony at the central first-floor level. The sheer visual splendor was breathtaking. David Best's temples, while elaborate and imposing, always had a rough-hewn, barbaric sort of majesty. This temple was Xanadu embellished with *One Thousand and One Nights*. To give some perspective to the scale of the edifice, it would take three of Marco Cochrane's *Bliss Dance* women stacked one on top of another to equal the height of the central tower!

While its six towers presented an astonishing silhouette against the twilit sky, the temple's interior was surprisingly prosaic—betrayed by its CNC (computer numerical control) cutout plywood origins. It was a bit like being on a Hollywood Western set and discovering that the buildings are empty facades. I'm not sure the interior was ever finished, and it certainly wouldn't be the first time a large Burning Man art project ran afoul of its construction schedule. What did work wonderfully was the inclusion of William Close's *Earth Harp*. It was strung from a Gothic archway between the south tower to the central tower, and people would gather at sunset to hear Andrea Brook play like an eerie muse to the windswept playa.

Responding well in a crisis has been a hallmark of Burning Man since the near disasters of 1996–97. The ticket crisis of 2011 spawned much reevaluation at Burning Man HQ, and they began forming strategies for dealing with their exploding popularity, as well as seriously pondering their future. The organization was maturing. Four of the founders were into their sixties, and while their two administrative giants, Marian Goodell and Harley K. Dubois, were and are still in their prime, Michael Mikel and Will Roger Peterson were edging

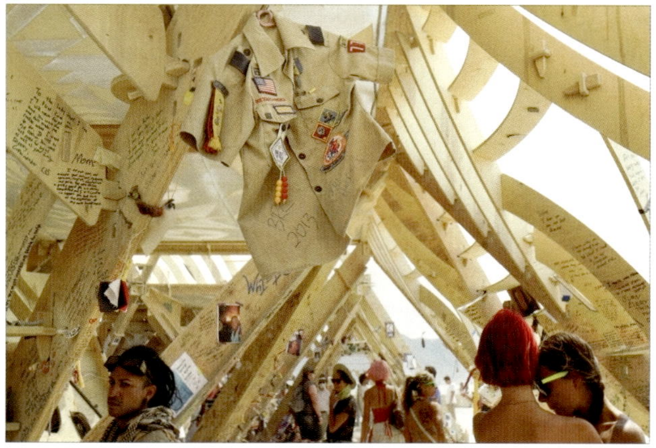

Bryan was an Eagle Scout, and this shirt's implications touched Lynda and me deeply.

into retirement. Larry and Crimson Rose were also in their sixties, and while they showed few signs of wanting to retire, everyone was aware that this was a time to seriously look down the road. So, they decided to look a hundred years down the road! That's called vision, and vision is what has distinguished Burning Man from the beginning.

The question for any successful business entity is what will happen when the founder retires. Despite its renown as a progressive and community-oriented business, Black Rock City LLC was a corporation, and there was no guarantee that a future owner would maintain allegiance to the community, let alone maintain a commitment to the Ten Principles that have been the hallmark of the event. Even though nonprofit boards of directors are notoriously conservative, turning Burning Man into a nonprofit seemed like the only strategy for the long term. The trick was to create a benevolent nonprofit that would not only continue the philosophy that has guided Burning Man for thirty years but also consolidate the various facets of the organization into a more efficient administrative model. It took monumental negotiations, but in 2012 the nonprofit Burning Man Project was established with Larry as president of its board of directors, Will Roger Peterson as chairman, and Michael Mikel and longtime Burning Man attorney Terry Gross as vice presidents. With Marian Goodell as CEO, Harley K. Dubois as chief transition officer (charged with bringing

BRAF, Burners Without Borders, and Black Rock City LLC into the Burning Man Project), and Crimson Rose as secretary of the board, Burning Man is safely in the hands of the people who made it a model for cultural innovation—at least for the time being.

The not-so-modest goals of the project are to further spread the Ten Principles of Burning Man culture internationally and to create a year-round Burning Man Cultural Center in Gerlach, Nevada. They are well underway. Burning Man has been nurturing regional Burner activities around the world for a number of years, and representatives from these regional groups regularly participate in the pageantry of the playa event. There are already regional Burner groups in over thirty countries, and many festivals. These regional Burns include AfrikaBurn in South Africa, Kiwiburn in New Zealand, Burning Seed in Australia, Midburn in Israel, and Nowhere in Spain. Additionally, there are twenty-five regional Burns stateside and three Canadian versions. Recently it was announced that there will be the first sanctioned use of the Burning Man name at a regional event outside of Nevada: Burning Man Netherlands.

One of the most universal elements of Burning Man, best suited to reaching across borders, is its temples. Temples at Burning Man bring a much-anticipated sense of spirituality to the event. Every human experiences loss and pain, and sacred spaces in which to process those are a universal need. I'm prejudiced, as he is a good friend, but I don't feel anyone has created more effective sacred spaces on the playa than David Best. David is unmatched at creating sacred spaces. In addition to being the creator of the first temple, he has been the architect of the majority of them. When I worked on the temple he built in Derry, Northern Ireland, I learned much about his method. His temples have always been elaborate, and they keep getting larger, taller, and more ornate, but they are much more than Byzantine facades covered in DBS (his acronym for "decorative bullshit"). There's soul inside a David Best temple. Regardless of the overall shape, there is always a tall cathedral space under the steeple. In the center of that room is an ornate altar, and often hanging above the altar is a massive wooden pendulum. The crew works very hard to get the points of the pendulum and the altar to meet. Usually the altar becomes covered with tributes. When people visit the altar, they instinctively understand that this is sacred territory, and they behave accordingly.

Another temple that worked better than I imagined it would was 2013's *Temple of Whollyness*. Contrasting with the Byzantine complexity of a David Best temple, this appeared to be a simple pyramid complex from the outside made from interlocking precut triangles. The interior was a large, empty space anchored in the center by an altar made of mammoth black stones. I was initially skeptical of its ability to create sacred space. The interlocking ribs and triangles were joined together with pegs and seemed too much like an enlarged version of a child's building set. I initially didn't like the sparse open interior. But I was wrong. Sometimes sacred space is achieved by the atmosphere created, and this temple used its openness to encourage private meditation in a group setting. There were also open walkways, and these were a magnet for memorials. The open ribs provided abundant places for messages, and by week's end it was filled with thousands of individual memorials.

Lynda and I visited this temple in 2013 with Bryan, and I was surprised at their emotional response. We wandered through and left our personal messages. Most people write or draw on the open walls and beams of the temples, but a significant number bring personal memorabilia too. Photographs are the most abundant, but toys, articles of clothing, or cherished mementos show up, too. We happened on a Boy Scout shirt in the upper rafters. "You are here" was its simple but heart-wrenching message. Bryan had been an Eagle Scout, and we immediately flashed to his cancer ordeal and hoped that wasn't the story. As I was to realize in time, the ultimate test for "templedom" lies not in its architecture but in its ability to engender heartfelt response, and the *Temple of Whollyness* achieved that. It also burned with a fine fury that had the crowd shielding their faces.

In 2014, David Best was called in just two months before the Burn to replace the scheduled temple builder, who had pulled out. It meant he had to design, order material, assemble a crew, and build the modular pieces in about six weeks. When you look at the size and complexity of his *Temple of Grace*, it was an amazing feat. The design was vintage David Best: a bell-shaped filigree body with a tall pagoda-style spire. If it had been a bell, it would have been a school bell, and the spire would have been the handle. Outside there was a courtyard with an ornate perimeter fence and Gothic archways. It was at once spare and complex, and the interior chamber was a symphony of reverence. By the end of the week the central altar was buried in memorials—everything from a mask of C-3PO to a photograph of Robin Williams with John Pedone, one of the mainstays of the Mystikal Misfits theme camp. Around the altar, people instinctively knelt or stood in quiet reflection. It was a masterwork.

David Best's temple designs host deep and highly individualized feelings and provide a sense of the sacred. Not sacred space in the traditional religious sense, though, because there is no focus on worship, and therein lies the difference between a spiritual experience at Burning Man and elsewhere. David and his team create a space that looks and feels sacred because it shares many of the architectural elements of a place of worship while allowing people to claim it and make a portion of it their own. David's original inspiration for designing a temple was the death of a close friend, but he also understood that at Burning Man each person experiences the event in their own way. The marvelous magic he's managed to conjure is that each temple remains simultaneously public and private, somber and jokey, benevolent and self-absorbed. One person might tearfully inscribe a prayer to their parents, but another

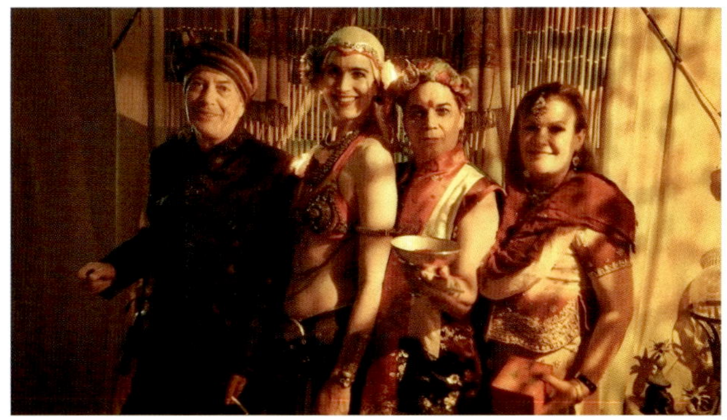

Larry relished being a souk merchant. He'd say, "Let me show you something special."

might wish for love or renew a commitment to winning the lottery. It's all sacred. It's equally profane. And the temple is the perfect place for airing such deeply felt humanity.

Throughout most of the first decade of the new century, there has been a growing rivalry in the minds of many Burners: "Which do you prefer, the Man Burn or the Temple Burn?" Of course, no one would suggest replacing one with the other; it is more a question of sensibilities: "Do you prefer raucous fire or sacred fire?" Behind that, however, exists a persistent rivalry for Burner participation and attention. The temple has the advantage of unlimited size and style. It is only limited by the budget and imagination of its architect. While there have been a few temple designs that have proved to work better on the outside than within, the temple's status as a center for grief and reflection is unmatched as a draw. Conversely, the Man had been the same size since 1990 and in recent years has had to rely solely on his base to provide inspiration and interactivity.

As the popularity of the temple increased, there appeared to be a lessening of the popularity of the Man base. Everyone would visit the Man, to be sure, but the question remained: Which did they prefer to be around? The temple was in deeper playa, and so mobile sound camps could be in the area, whereas they were restricted from hanging out at the Man. Within the organization there was a concern that their Burning Man was in danger of becoming supplanted as the central attraction.

There was an effort with the base designs of 2012 and 2013 to make the Man more interactive. The beehive motif of the base for 2012's "Fertility 2.0" theme was Rod Garrett's final design, and its window-lined three stories could accommodate many visitors, but the saucer-shaped base for 2013's "Cargo Cult" theme was far more interesting from the outside than it was to explore. Meanwhile, the *Temple of Juno* in 2012 and the *Temple of Whollyness* in 2013 proved to be extremely popular. I won't suggest that the Man was losing ground, but the time had come for Burning Man to present something extraordinary in order to pull his shriveling cojones out of the fire, and 2014's "Caravansary" Man did exactly that!

Like many Burners, I needed a history lesson when the 2014 theme was announced. The term "caravansary" rang no bells with me. Larry's accompanying essay made it clear that the theme would address both cultural exchange and an unprecedented opportunity for Participation: "For countless centuries, travelers along the Silk Route crossed paths in caravansaries, a network of oases and sanctuaries that dotted the four-thousand-mile road from Europe to East Asia." It had been prefaced by a phone conversation with Larry in which he waxed poetic on the fact that the Man would be a hundred-foot colossus surrounded by a circular tent complex housing an international marketplace: the Souk.

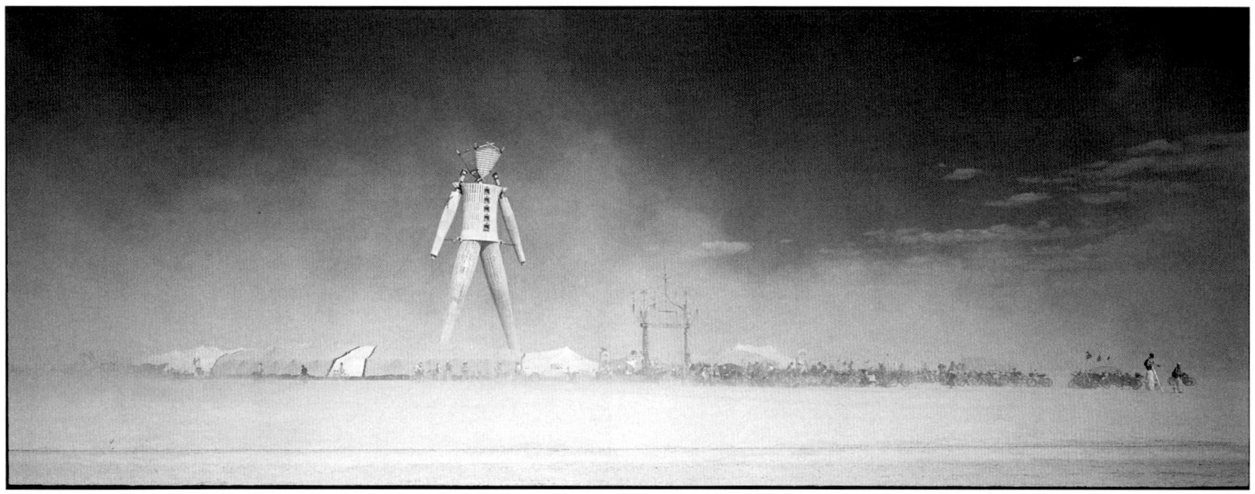

"Caravansary" debuted the largest Burning Man ever in 2014. It took forever to burn.

"Caravansary" was a wonderfully interactive idea. It not only reinvigorated the central area of the Man but also provided an opportunity for regional Burner groups to take a role in the pageantry. After a grand parade with LoveBomb Go-Go, a Northwest marching band, the Souk was open for business. Traders, merchants, and regional representatives offered demonstrations, performances, or "goods" to their visitors. Of course, as the essay makes clear, "anyone may pose as 'merchant' here, and anyone may play a 'customer,' but nothing in this strange emporium shall have a purchase price—no quid, no pro, no quo—no trade at all will be allowed in this ambiguous arcade. According to a rule of desert hospitality, the only thing of value in this 'marketplace' will be one's interaction with a fellow human being."

Larry was in fine form. He and his assistants rounded up two rooms full of bric-a-brac, much of it maimed or broken. They then set about finding just the right item for each "customer." Inquiries would be made as to personal likes and dislikes. The customer would be shown item after item, and if nothing struck a chord, they would be taken into the back room where the special pieces were. In the end, of course, they would be gifted their treasure and politely escorted out the door. It was a treat to see him in full merchant regalia and in character.

The growth of the temple, the increasing population size of Black Rock City, and the complexity of themes like "Caravansary" all marked the maturation of Burning Man as the second decade of the twenty-first century began. The event has indeed come an amazingly long way from its bohemian origins on Baker Beach. Once the Ten Principles were embraced by most Burners, the event in the desert took on familiar patterns and a bit of a patina. Each year holds abundant surprises, and there is usually some sort of yearly crisis (tickets, car searches, turnkey camps, gate shutdowns, sparkleponies, new rules, new charges, etc.), but there is also enough recurrent pageantry that one can understand the complaints about Burning Man losing its avant-garde mojo. Year after year many of the same mutant vehicles prowl the playa, the beat of long-in-the-tooth sound camps keeps us awake, and more than a few familiar pieces of art have been recycled. Certainly the Fire Conclave procession and performance prior to the Burn, while spectacular, is for many veterans déjà vu. Frankly, the Burn itself sometimes goes on too long. It's not surprising that longtime Burners feel they've seen it, done it, and bought the T-shirt (metaphorically, of course!).

But while many familiar attractions have existed for decades, I would argue it's that very continuity that allows for innovation to occur without disrupting the essential core of the community. The familiar is what allows us to relax and feel secure enough to open ourselves to new experience. Every year veteran Burners do their grand bike tours of art and camps. We marvel at the two or three mind-boggling examples of creative audacity, or a colossus of gravity-defying engineering, but we also revel in the warmth of old friends and familiar places. Some of that familiarity takes the form of camps we look forward to visiting anew, like a favorite bistro in a city where we had a wonderful vacation, or art cars we've enjoyed seeing in previous Burns. We walk about the playa and say, "I remember that camp from last year; we ought to check them out." As those dust-covered Greeters remind us each year after we've endured the interminable wait in line, it is indeed a "homecoming."

There have been theme-oriented camps since the mid-1990s, but in the late 2000s their ambition and scale surged in proportion to the playa art that was growing to unbelievable proportions. The term "theme camp" refers to any "placed" camp with a unifying identity, a stimulating appearance, a good MOOP record, and an aim to interact with the Burner population. Harley K. Dubois used placement as a means of encouraging early Burner groups to create interesting camp motifs, or "themes." The concept has generated outrageous—some might say ridiculous—results, but theme camps, whether music- or art-based, are the classy uptown of Black Rock City.

Every camp has its particular story. The Internet is filled with picture albums and blogs about Burning Man camps that have been together for a decade or more. Often the camps are organized around a particular vehicle or activity. Others are centered around performance, art, or service. Bryan and I have created (with many others) and stayed at many different theme camps over the years, but since 2010 I have been staying in the "Feral Colony" with Geoff Silver and his wife, Sallie Edmunds. It was established by Marian Goodell as a friends-and-family bedroom community in a large area near First Camp. Of course the name Feral Colony is more an inside joke, and it's not actually labeled as such on any map. What began as "friends and family" has increasingly become populated by VIPs, but they are a fascinating and friendly bunch, and we've enjoyed sharing their company. The playa is a dusty equalizer, and I'm usually oblivious to any kind of media status. I usually end up making friends with the drivers of the RVs and the mega coaches for those who can afford them, as the drivers often get there first to set up their rigs. The VIPs tend to fly in via Black Rock City Airport, adjacent to the city. During the first few years we were lucky to exchange pleasantries on the way in and out of our campers, but over the past few years Marian has created outdoor lounge areas and an Absinthe Bar, and this has upped the social interaction remarkably.

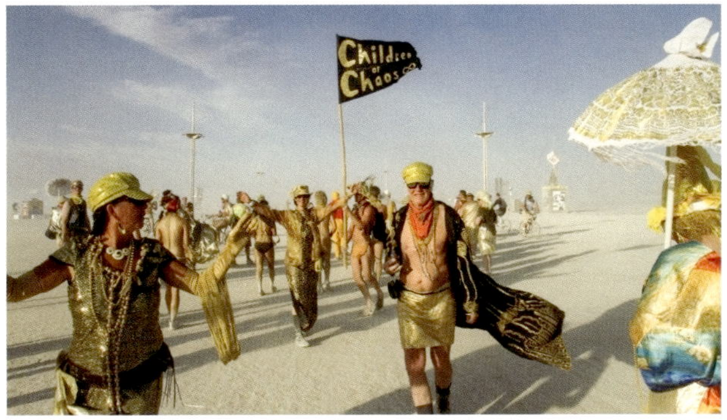

On a weekday afternoon, we don our gold drag, grab a load of beads, and parade.

One thing I enjoy about staying in the Feral Colony is the broad strata of public figures drawn to Burning Man and my brother. I tend to give them polite space, but occasionally we'll engage in conversation. Some of them eat with us in Kalamite's Kanteen or drop by as guests. On a given day you might see contemporary tech entrepreneurs like Sergey Brin and Ping Fu, political opposites like Dennis Kucinich and Grover Norquist, or cultural innovators like Guy Laliberté and Michael Murphy, the founder of the Big Sur retreat center Esalen. Last year, Larry spent a fair amount of time with Murphy, and he and Marian visited Esalen. It may very well influence their future dreams for Fly Ranch.

Burning Man has had an unrequited love affair with Fly Ranch since we all first laid eyes on the Black Rock Desert. The 1997 Burn on nearby Hualapai Flat only intensified that attraction. Will Roger Peterson says that the Caseys offered to sell the organization the ranch back then for $300,000. It was right after the financial debacle with Washoe County. It might as well have been $3,000,000, but the times are a-changin'. Thanks to the generous support of six prominent donors, the nonprofit bought the 3,800-acre Fly Ranch complete with Fly Geyser! I was there recently, and Will took me on a lengthy tour of the property. It was refreshing to take a dip in the hot pool, look out across the water at the old round-topped dormant geyser called the Wizard, and imagine a year-round Burning Man cultural institution nearby, founded on the Ten Principles as opposed to profit.

As I mentioned, the past few years I've been sharing an RV with my good friend and fellow photographer Geoff Silver and his wife. Bryan's childhood friend, Chris White, introduced me to Geoff in 2010. Chris was working at Pro Photo Supply in Portland, where Geoff and I were both customers. Geoff in turn introduced me to Vic Stevens and the Children of Chaos camp. COC is a group of Portland friends who have been doing outings together for years. They named themselves the Children of Chaos after marching in the New Orleans Mardi Gras parade, and when they started coming to Burning Man, it became their camp moniker.

Bryan and the remnants of one of our earlier camps, the Inebriati Camp, were invited to join COC, and the group has grown into an enclave of thirty energetic mixed-age adults. Dan, the oldest, has recently crested his eighties, whereas my nieces, Anna and Monica, are in their early twenties. The middle groups are generally in their thirties and forties. Captain Vic Stevens heads the older bunch and shares the organizational duties with Bryan, who manages the middle- to younger-aged contingent along with his cousin Adam Gorciak. Together they have fashioned an industrious and convivial community that in many ways reflects the diversity of Burning Man itself. Burning Man camps range from a single person to hundreds. Some of the larger camps are sound or art institutions, but I would guess most camps are between twenty and fifty people and are often organized around a common interest.

COC likes to parade in costume and throw parties. They will parade in all manner of playa conditions. Their signature event is the Gold Parade, in which anyone who wants to parade shows up dressed in gold for drinks at four o'clock Wednesday or Thursday afternoon of Burn week. Once everyone is in the mood, the parade begins. We usually wind through the Center Camp lounge, each parader packing a couple dozen gold Mardi Gras beads. It's a loose procession; no one tries to stay in formation. Rather, we weave through the throng of loungers draping beads around willing necks. Some people clap or laugh, and everyone smiles. Once in a while, someone gifts something back to one of us, but it's not expected. People give to one another as the spirit moves them. It's a gift, not a trade.

Children of Chaos has a commitment to the unity of collective activities. That's what makes all theme camps hum. Activities can take many forms, but it's not enough simply to come up with a catchy name and a gaudy facade. Everyone in camp must commit to at least two major functions, and the best camps have a very high level of participation. There also needs to be many creative and cooperative cooks in the kitchen. The more creative and ambitious the camp activity, the more likely it will draw a crowd. Some camps have been putting on parades and doling out goodies to people for decades.

Although they are far from the most ambitious theme camp on the playa, Children of Chaos epitomizes the ideal of theme camps. Yes, they are friends of mine, so I'm biased, but I have my reasons for using them as an example. For one thing, they are an all-ages camp, which means they present an array of ideas and utilize different age-related skills. Captain Vic has

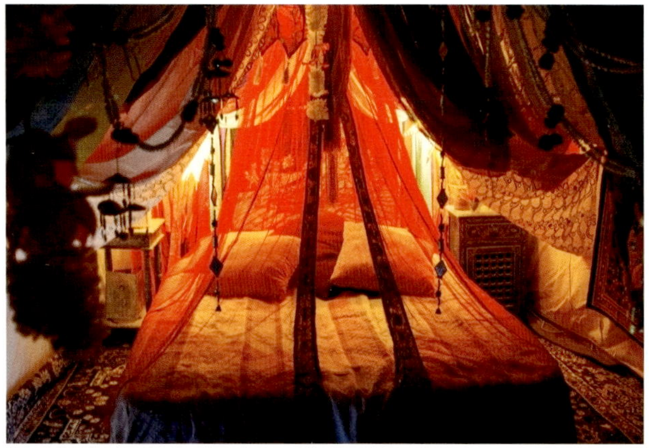

Winning a suite at the Ashram Galactica is an unparalleled playa luxury.

been strict about keeping the camp size to between thirty and forty, and they have vetted one another's suggestions for new members. The younger people have typically been the ones to build the lounge, complete with lights, sound system, and decor. Veteran engineer Dan Willsie designed a wind-driven evaporator for the shower. Restaurateur Lisa Schroeder does a regular advice session as "the Jewish mother you never had." Animation artist Joanna Priestly and her husband, Paul Harrod, typically dream up projects that are startling examples of camp high jinks morphed into performance art. What makes Children of Chaos a success is their solid commitment to group participation.

Many camps aren't abodes in the physical sense but, like Cacophony Society, are groups of people with an allegiance to a common countercultural attitude. A great many camps are simply groups of friends who've adopted an organizing endeavor for the year. Indeed, many interesting camp motifs are these one-offs hidden deep in the burbs.

Sex-themed camps are notorious as Burning Man press fodder. A glance at a selection of recent activity guides lists nearly seven hundred theme camps. A handful of camps have titles that at least on the surface suggest that raunch is the order of the day, or else that they're making a really corny porn flick. Here are a few camp names: Crack Whore, Spank Bank, Spanky's Village, Bloodbath and Beyond, Retro Frolic, Beaverton (women only), Poly Paradise, Flamin' Merkin, Battlestar Erotica, Miso Horny, and the grand dame of erotic theme camps: Orgy Dome, whose proprietors, Lefty and Shade, have been on the playa for eleven years. Like that most elegant of playa hostels, Ashram Galactica, Orgy Dome provides an air-conditioned luxury space for "sex positive" interactions between adult Burners. It's open to all couples or "moresomes" who are interested in being openly sexual. I haven't partaken myself, but I must say their online video portrays polyamorous sex as downright wholesome! Most of the rest of the sex camps just seem like old dusty, lusty, jokey fun while offering novices a glimpse into the world of kink.

I sometimes feel that as an outsider to the San Francisco hipster scene, I'm at a disadvantage when going into veteran Burning Man camps. Of course, everyone at the event is expected to be hospitable, and they are, at least at reasonable hours, but I'm instinctively shy around strangers, and they are sometimes wary of a "snapper" with a pro camera. Geoff and I roam the playa early and late, looking for the elusive moment when all the elements of visual confusion gel into an instant of clarity. While Geoff likes to engage Burners for portraits, I prefer to be a fly on the playa. If I'm with my brother, it's a different—though potentially frustrating—dynamic. People would much rather talk to him, and I'm lucky to get a polite nod and an introduction. On the other hand, he often takes me to places in deep playa that I wouldn't know even existed, and I've met wonderful people from near and far during these excursions.

One of my favorite nights is when Larry and I do an evening tour of the art or sometimes the perimeter. "Out there" in deep playa, where tiny shacks and outposts huddle, Rangers and security workers police the security fences of Burning Man. It takes special volunteers to man these outposts, as you are likely to miss much of the event while on shift. There are compensations, however. In the late stages of twilight, you can sit in one of those camps and gaze out upon a haunting view of the playa in the moonlight with only a fragile line of car lights or a fragile ribbon of dust to indicate the human presence. This is "early Man," and it's a wonderful opportunity to experience personal solitude before the invasion.

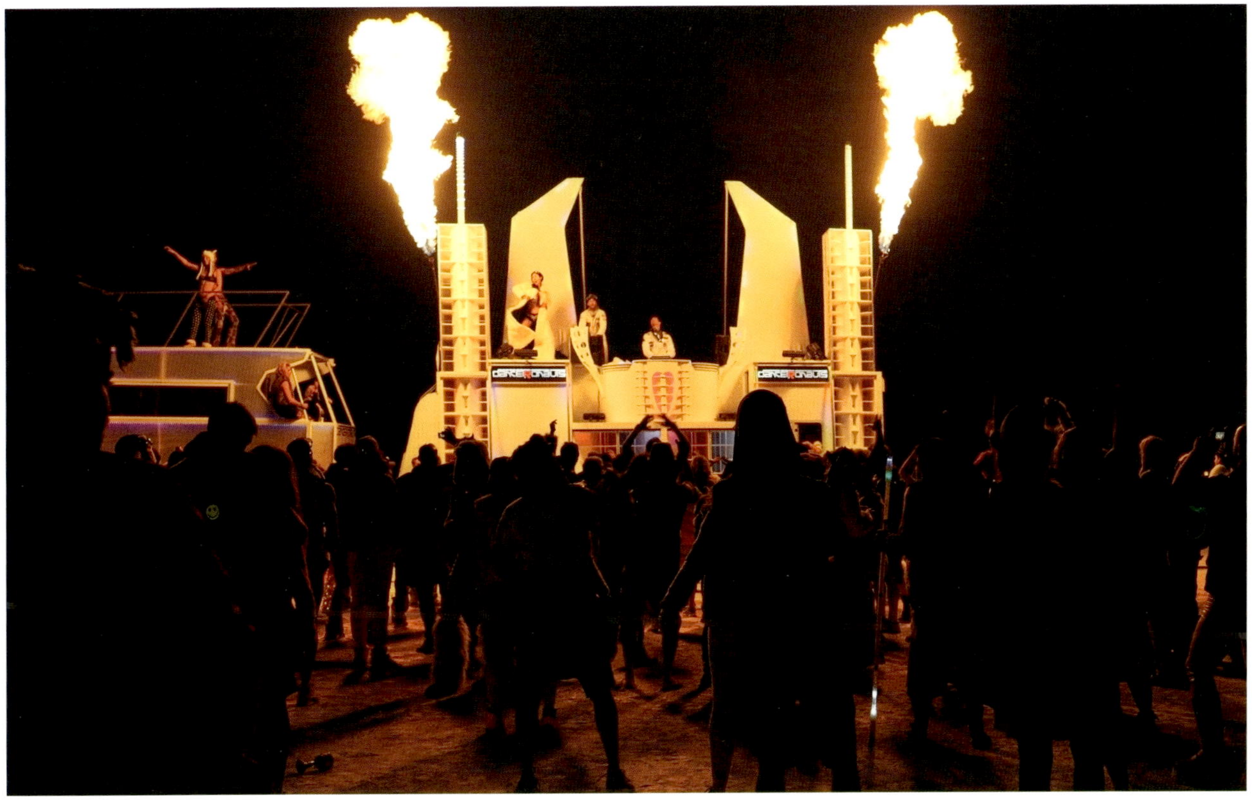

Large mobile sound camps like Dancetronauts have created new issues of placement.

Sometimes a theme camp is great because it has a great concept. The Ashram Galactica—which more than makes up in Middle Eastern elegance for what it may lack in stature—is famous for presenting the cleanest rug-covered social areas on the playa and a snazzy dance floor. Each night the camp holds a drawing for an overnight stay in one of its tented bedroom suites, which are decorated with as much luxuriously appointed detail as is imaginable on the playa. No hint of dust here, and I have no idea how they can maintain such high hostel standards. But the point of theme camps isn't extravagance; it's community. The absolute variety and complexity of individual theme camps is extraordinary, and virtually all of them are self or crowd funded. I call them the core of Burning Man because they constitute the neighborhoods of Black Rock City, and they uniquely celebrate the personalities of their makers. Often they address an attitude, either psychological or political, that you didn't even realize you harbored.

Of course, many of the early mega camps were music based. I remember Emerald City in 2001. It was essentially a three-story dance club fronted by a series of sixty-foot-high green laser-lit towers. The size and extravagance of the installation at that time was breathtaking. That's when we first realized the close relationship between Silicon Valley wealth and the increasing opulence of the Burning Man camps.

Speaking of opulence, the Opulent Temple of Venus, another extravagant techno institution, has been attracting multitudes of dance-crazed Burners since the early 2000s, but it recently dropped out for a year over a placement dispute. There has been a placement struggle between EDM (electronic dance music) camps and Burning Man HQ from the early 1990s, when techno camps were required to set up a mile away from the central complex, but it's not a conspiracy to abolish EDM, as some have suggested; it's really that a great many people at the event really dislike being kept awake all night, and the complaints abound.

EDM was a magnet for bringing new people to the event in the early days, and they will always be welcome, but regulations will also always be an ongoing negotiation, upheld today by the DMV (Department of Mutant Vehicles). In 2015, the DMZ (Deep-Playa Music Zone) was created so nighttime and early morning sound-blasting vehicles would be kept to areas of the playa out beyond the Man. It seems Burning Man's need to regulate the loud music scene is second only to its need to create parody versions of common acronyms.

Placed music camps like the open-air Distrikt and Skinny Kitty Teahouse represent a departure from the traditional techno ghetto scene of the early years. They may offer dancing nightly or throw a huge one-time multi-band bash, but they also exist as community camps. Pinkie's, or the Pink Mammoth as it's called these days, is a popular afternoon disco saloon where people (often in pink outfits) who can't wait for nighttime dance their dusty butts off.

There are some longtime Burning Man attractions that aren't grounded in techno—in fact, one of the most venerable is about as far away from music as you can get. Death Guild's Thunderdome offers veteran Burners the reassurance of seeing a familiar friend each year—assuming your friends are mostly anger-prone freaks. It's been part of Burning Man since the late 1990s and is one of the remaining aspects of the event that evokes its dark early side. It's also a temple of sorts—a big nasty homage to life at its most adrenaline-fueled best. The faithful climb the curved geodesic walls, and root loudly for their gladiatorial champion to perform a rite of passage as old as blood. I've never gone into battle myself, but I've known many who have. It's a lot of Rock 'Em Sock 'Em action, and I look forward to attending a battle or two each year. Although I must admit that lately the battle has been getting close enough to get a good view. Bodies cover most of the geodesic surface, and then the groundlings are stacked in bands of straining eyeballs surrounding the perimeter. Inside the dome, black-clad guardians maintain a semblance of order by exaggerated displays of menace. Just like in the movie, they are there to stage and regulate combat between two padded-club-wielding contestants suspended by elastic harnesses. Only no one actually dies—at least not so far.

For those not from the Bay Area, Death Guild is a long-running goth-industrial dance night that currently runs on Mondays at Club DNA in San Francisco's hip SoMa scene. The story I heard was that David King (DJ Decay) founded Death Guild back in the early 1990s, and that he came to Burning Man the first time in 1997. Decay acquired a *Mad Max*–inspired black Plymouth Sebring Satellite and brought it to the playa with the intention of attending Gigsville's Car-be-que, where they have a tradition of roasting a junker. Once Decay and his team laid eyes on the playa, they decided to construct a Thunderdome to go along with their vehicle. Frankly, there is no shortage of *Mad Max*–influenced mutant vehicles at Burning Man. The visual cues in a seemingly infinite dust-ravaged landscape are simply too obvious to pass up.

Lynda returned to the playa in 2013 to take part in my birthday celebration and to get better acquainted with Naomi, Bryan's future wife. Several of our close friends also chose to attend that year, and one was Lynda's longtime client and almost member of the family Shawn Kelley. Shawn's a small-statured dynamo and world traveler who is always looking for her next great adventure. One day she announced in camp that she and a girl from the camp where she was staying were going to do battle in Thunderdome that night, and she hoped everyone would come to support her. It's a serious matter. Though the truncheons are heavily padded, the fact is, most combatants get very adrenalized and start wailing the bejeezus out of each other. In the early days, it was mostly nasty-looking guys (DPW types) who were into the contest, and there was a lot of unintended mayhem. Bloody noses and kicks to the groin were inevitable. "Two balls enter—one ball leaves" has been an oft-heard riff from the movie's tagline.

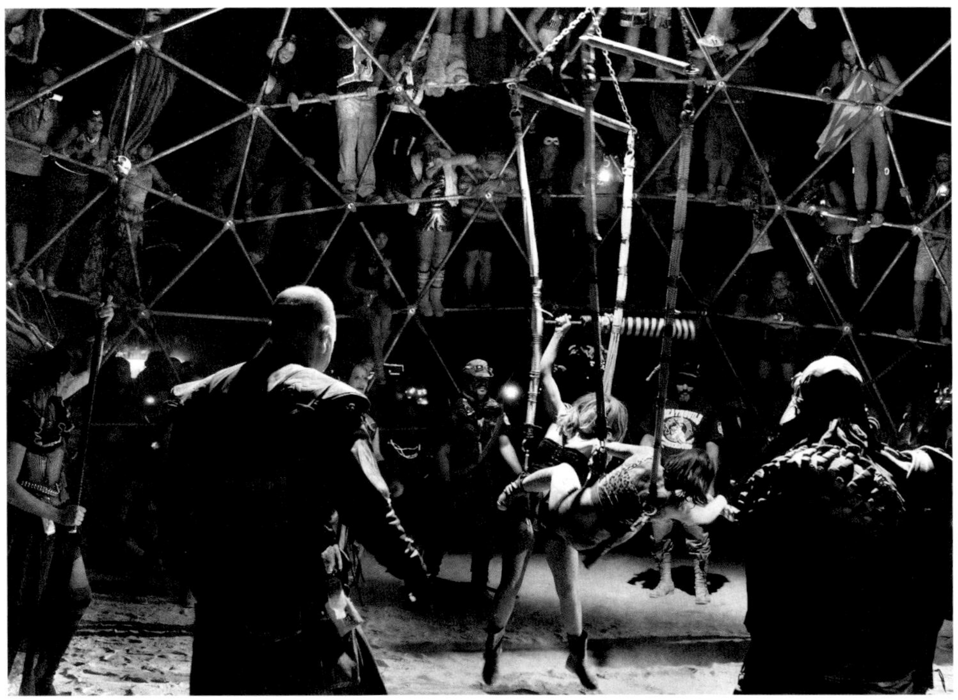

When Lynda's client Shawn Kelley battled in Thunderdome, we all showed up to cheer.

Bryan, Naomi, and several Harvey cousins were already lining the upper reaches of the dome when Lynda and I got to Thunderdome a few matches before Shawn's. It was already three rows deep around the perimeter, and we had to wade closer as people left. By the time we got up front, Shawn and her friend were ready to rumble. As is the tradition with Thunderdome, combatants rise to the occasion. Not that they have a choice. After the handlers strap them into the elastic harnesses, they pull each fighter back and slingshot them into each other. Feet, knees, and padded bats are a-flying. It was quite an enthusiastic melee. After the ruckus subsided, the girls embraced and laughed about the whole adventure, and I took a picture of Lynda and Shawn for posterity.

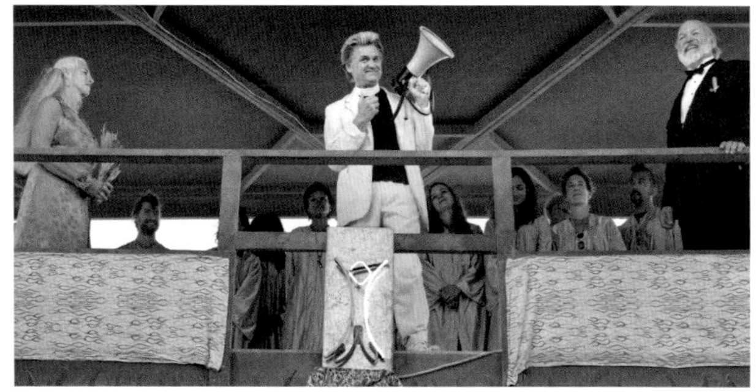

We gathered to celebrate a permanent change to the Burning Man family.

Since the future is the prevailing question on the minds of the organization and Burners alike, it seems fitting to end this chapter with a wedding—two weddings, to be precise—and a death. The first wedding was a culmination of decades and signified both an end and a new beginning. Will Roger Peterson and Crimson Rose have been together for many years. Crimson Rose first brought Will to the playa in 1994, and within a couple of years he was actively building Black Rock City. It was Will who cut the road into Fly Ranch in 1997. We used remnants of it one recent summer to travel into Hualapai Flat, and though it was easy enough to see its former path, I was amazed how much of that wide swath had been consumed by the sagebrush.

In 2012, a few hundred of us assembled in First Camp for their nuptials. Typical of most playa weddings (dozens of couples get married at Burning Man each year), this was a lighthearted affair. It was, however, a real wedding and not some "sham for the Burn." I remember one woman who stood out by the Man one year, offering to marry any man who was willing. She probably got "hitched" a few dozen times. This wasn't like that at all. The groom wore a tuxedo, and the bride wore a "dusty rose" gown. The Stop Shopping Choir sang, and the Reverend Billy presided as he does for many weddings each year—"Playalujah." It was a sweet and solemn occasion filled with the warm promises and goodwill of all present. Most of all, it signaled in no uncertain terms that transition was in the wind.

Virtually everyone involved long term with Burning Man was there, as were some of my favorite photographer friends and Burners from near and far. The bride was serene and aglow, and Will was beaming. They could have been kids, and probably were at heart. Brides always seem like little girls to me at their core, and Crimson Rose was no exception. The ceremony was humorous and heartfelt, but transitions are at the center of all things. Change is the only constant. As they moved to ascend the platform above First Camp, the strains of an acoustic guitar could be heard in soft but resonant tones. David Walker (aka Tom Sawyer) was strumming them into their future together, but sadly he would be lost to us within four years, another casualty of cancer and a life well-lived, playing on the edge.

It was a precipice of change for the Harveys too. Among the attendees at the wedding were Bryan and Naomi. That year was her first Burn, and she had a mixed experience. Everyone had a good laugh when, after the first dust storm, she frantically swept out their tent. "Just wait five minutes," someone joked, only they weren't kidding, which Naomi learned in time. After the nuptial fireworks, the three of us walked out to watch the full moon rising over the playa. In the distance was an artificial tree that had fake dollar bills for leaves. Bryan and Naomi were dressed in their best playa formal wear, and I couldn't help thinking they looked like they had a future together. And in December 2016, we would head to Antigua, Guatemala, to take part in their wedding.

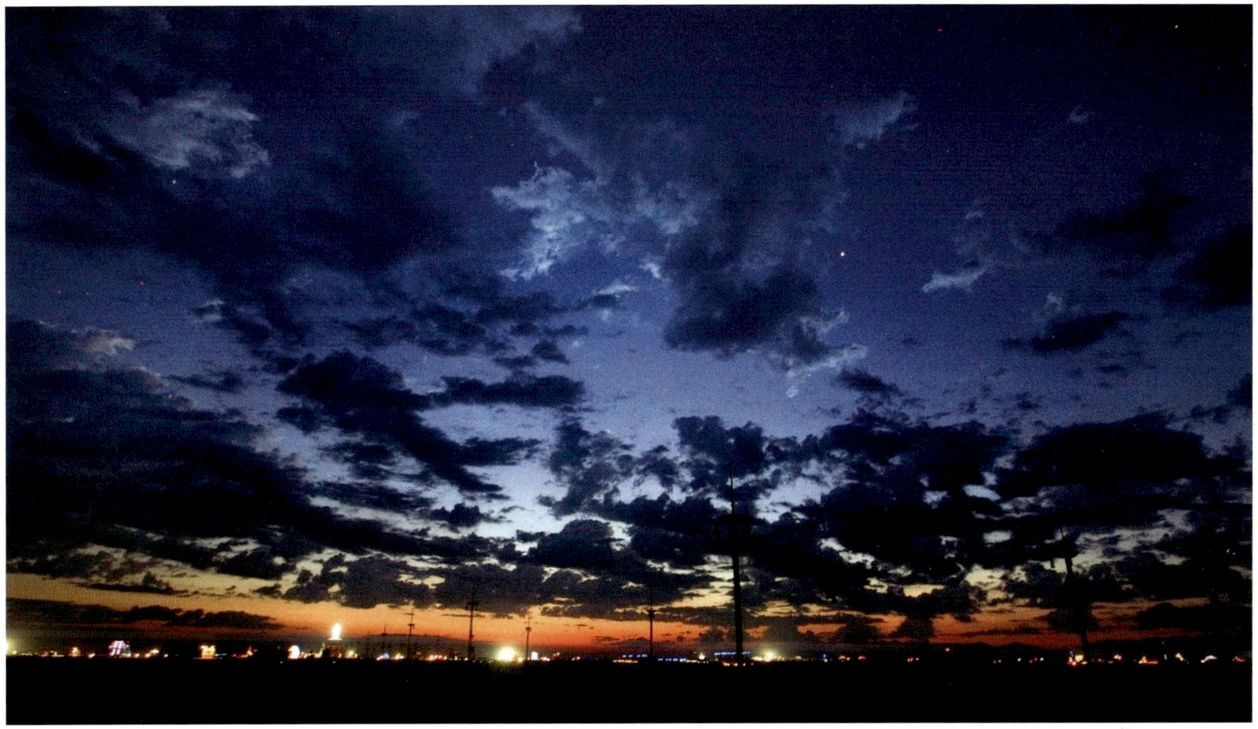

Twenty-seven years later, I still love nothing better than walking the playa at dawn.

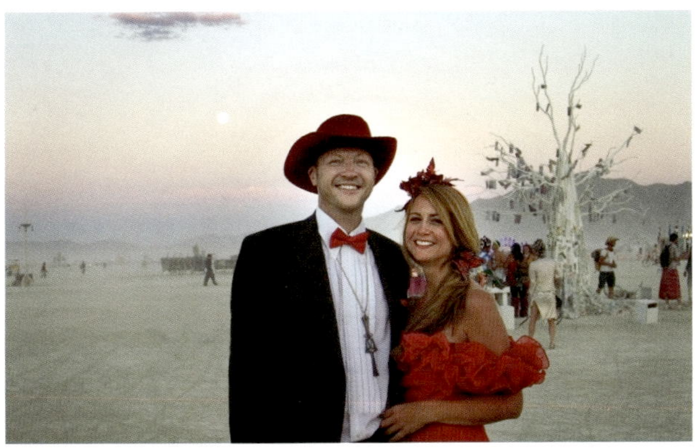

Sometimes on the moonrise playa at twilight you catch a glimpse of the future.

Today, twenty-seven years after Bryan and I first ventured onto the playa, I still enjoy nothing better than wandering out in the predawn to gaze up at the same ocean of stars that filled the sky when the Black Rock Desert was created, those same distant spheres that formed a crystal ceiling over this ancient landscape in the prehistoric world. In those days the desert was covered by the vast waters of Lake Lahontan, in the Pleistocene epoch, back when humans were little more than a cosmic dream. That world is millions of years removed from this one, but you can still feel its presence in the relentless shifting sands and the restless wind. For a week in late summer the arid remains of that once-abundant lake host Black Rock City, the loudest, gaudiest, bawdiest town in northern Nevada and one of its richest. It's a gilded city where your money's no good, but friendships are unlimited and wealth is measured in playa sunrises. It's a genuine experience, something that—in this consumer-driven world—is as fleeting as starlight in the glowing dawn. I trudge about the playa sand in that brief hour, suspended between the utterly ancient and the resolutely contemporary, and even though that old lake water is long gone and the aboriginal totems of first peoples have given way to neon towers, the promise of the playa seems as brilliant today as it did when Bry and I first drove across the alkali sand those many years ago, and the horizon still glows bright with possibilities yet undreamed.

CHAPTER 14

PLAYA ON FIRE

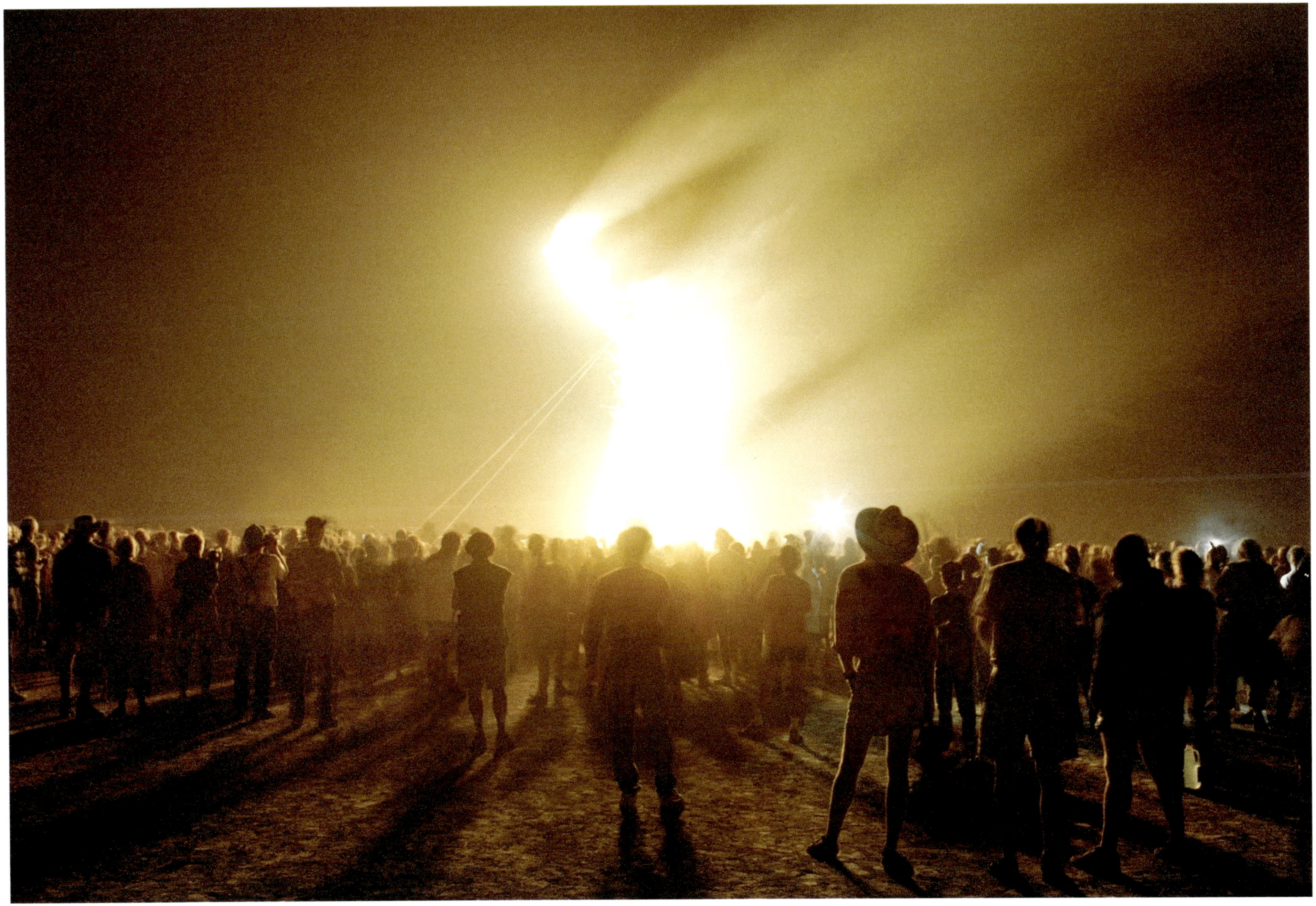

Dust Storm Burn, 1993

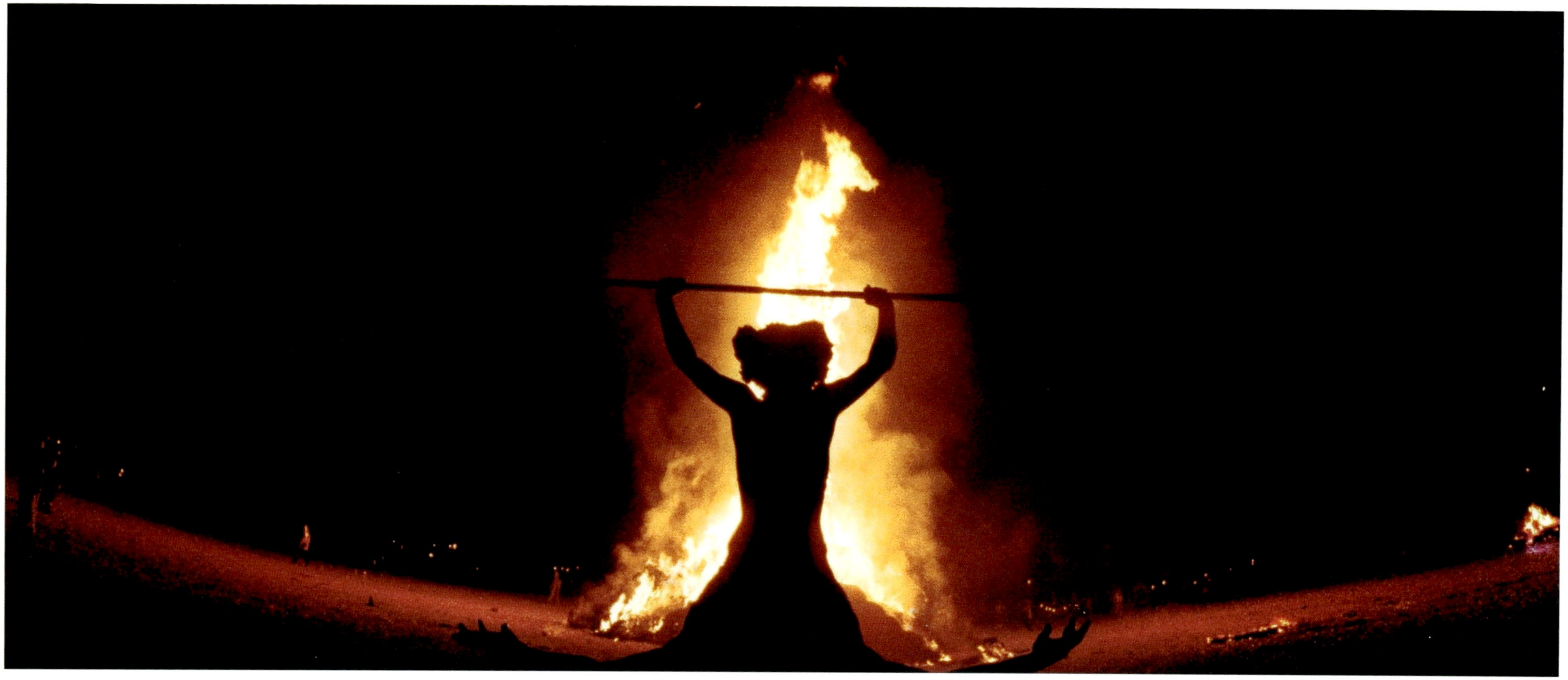

Ritual Gesture, 1998

At its heart, Burning Man's immolation of a giant human effigy is a ritual pageant of death and regeneration. The Man is sacrificed annually with a raucous send-off and the unspoken promise that he will be born anew for the coming year. It is an ancient promise, and it strikes a hopeful chord in the many who are present. It awakens within us the old desire for some assurance that we will not have lived our lives in vain—that there is some purpose to our being, or at least a bit of revelation in having made the journey. What compels people to attend the event each year is two-fold: the first is little more than hipster curiosity, a check on the scoreboard of a life well lived, but the second is the possibility that hidden within this arcane pageantry is a hint about our place in the universe.

But with Burning Man there are no easy answers. There is only a glimpse at the abyss and the perennial hope that within these flames we might discover ancient connections and maybe a personal revelation. Those of us who return again and again to the playa have found that the annual journey itself is a rewarding ritual. For what is ritual if not taking solace in the repetition of the familiar? We are warmed in the glow of renewed friendships, and we pause to remember that which we cherish. We relive a time in our youth when happiness and security were parental gifts. We walk to a far-off temple in the dust and offer up our memories and sorrows to a fire that commemorates love and life experience.

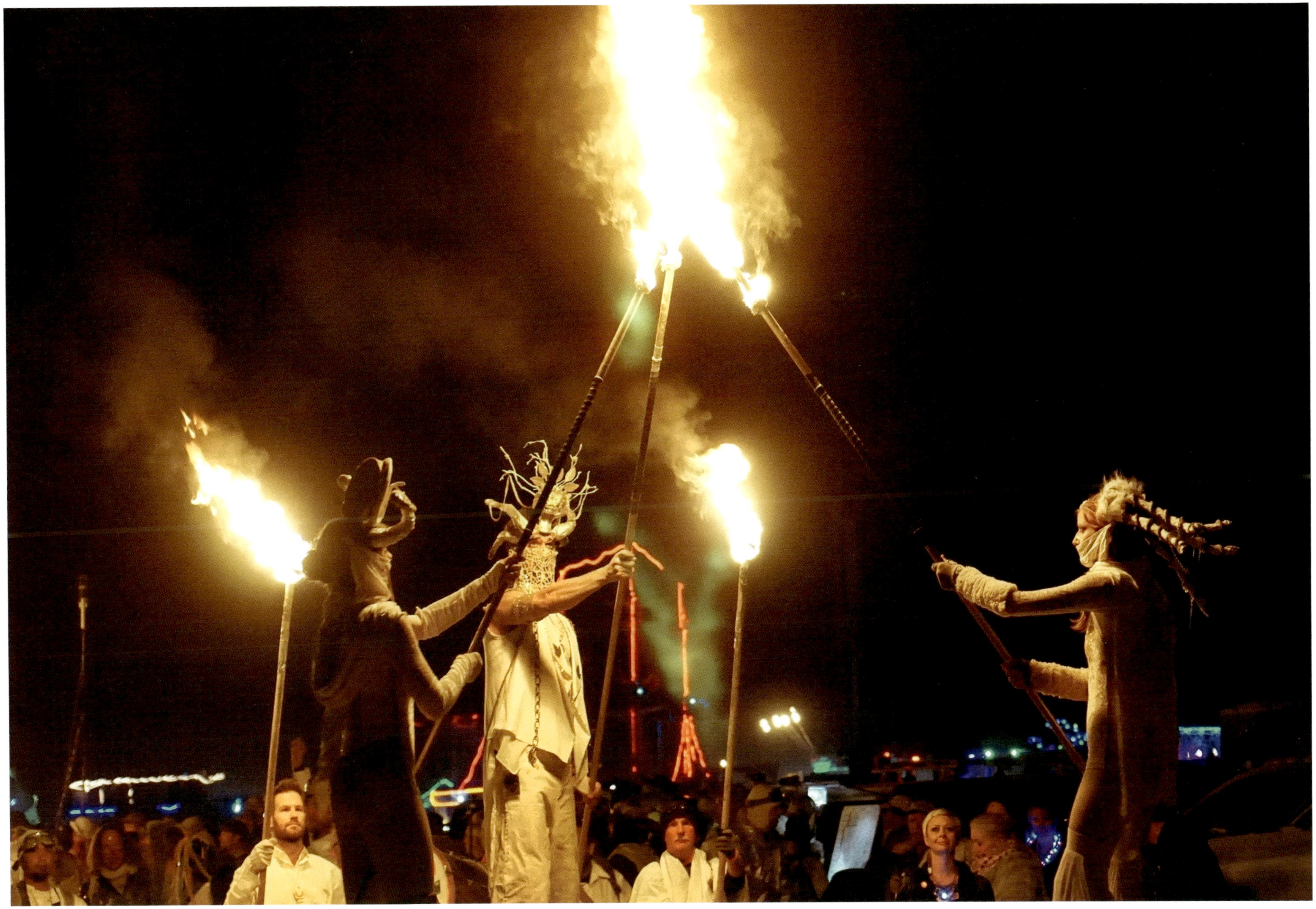

Torch Ritual, 2015

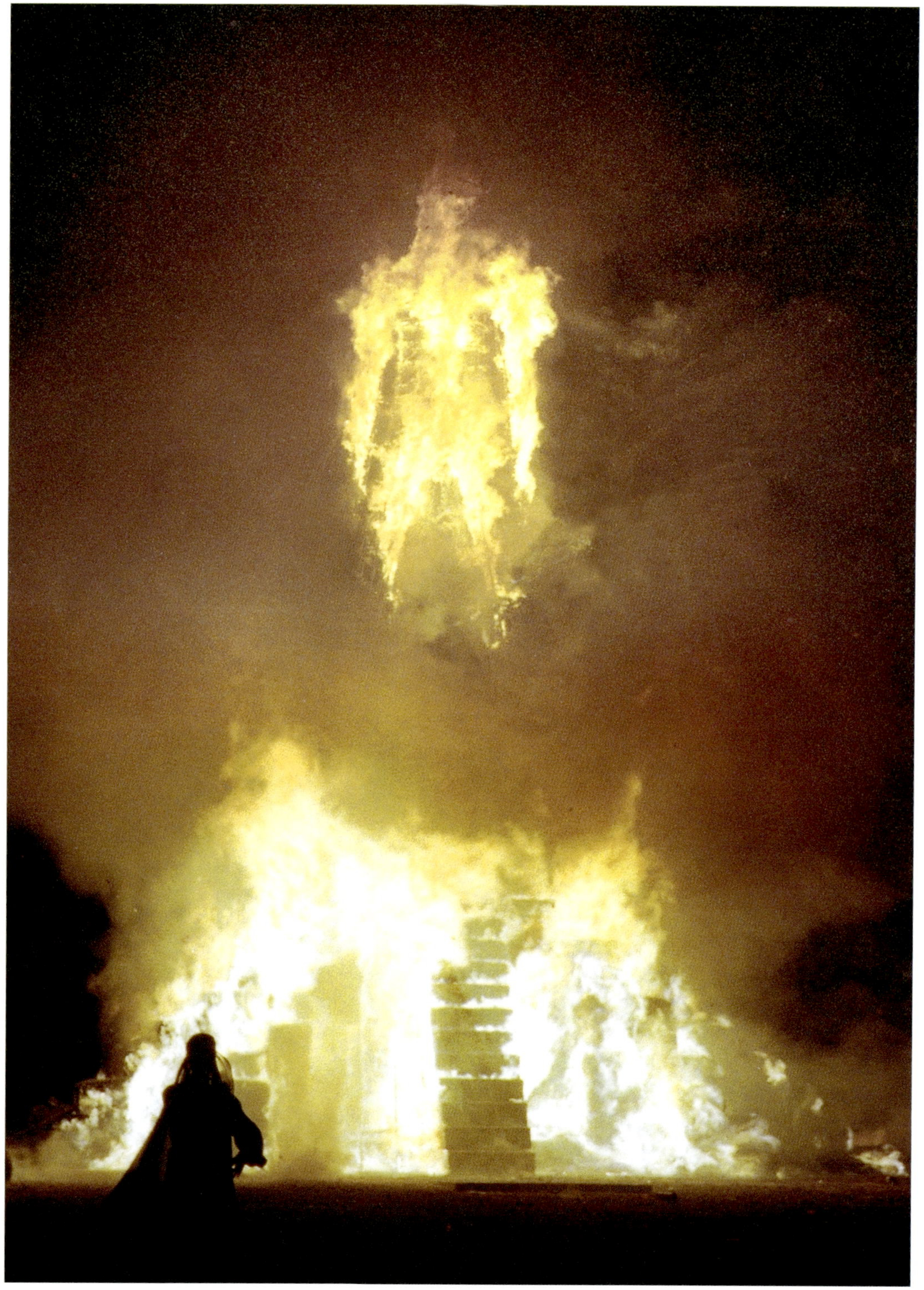

Burn Specter, 1999

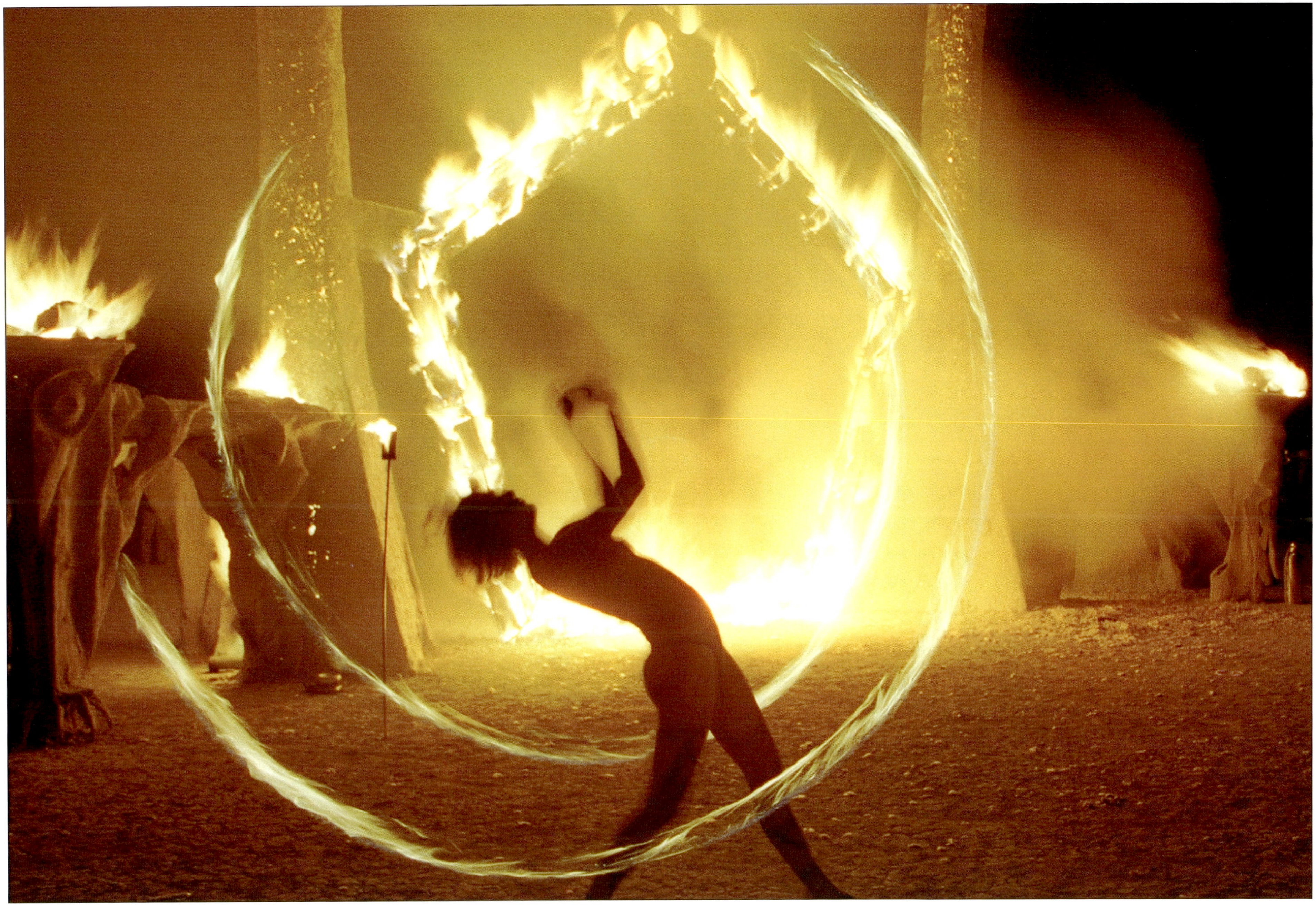

Opera Spinner, 1999

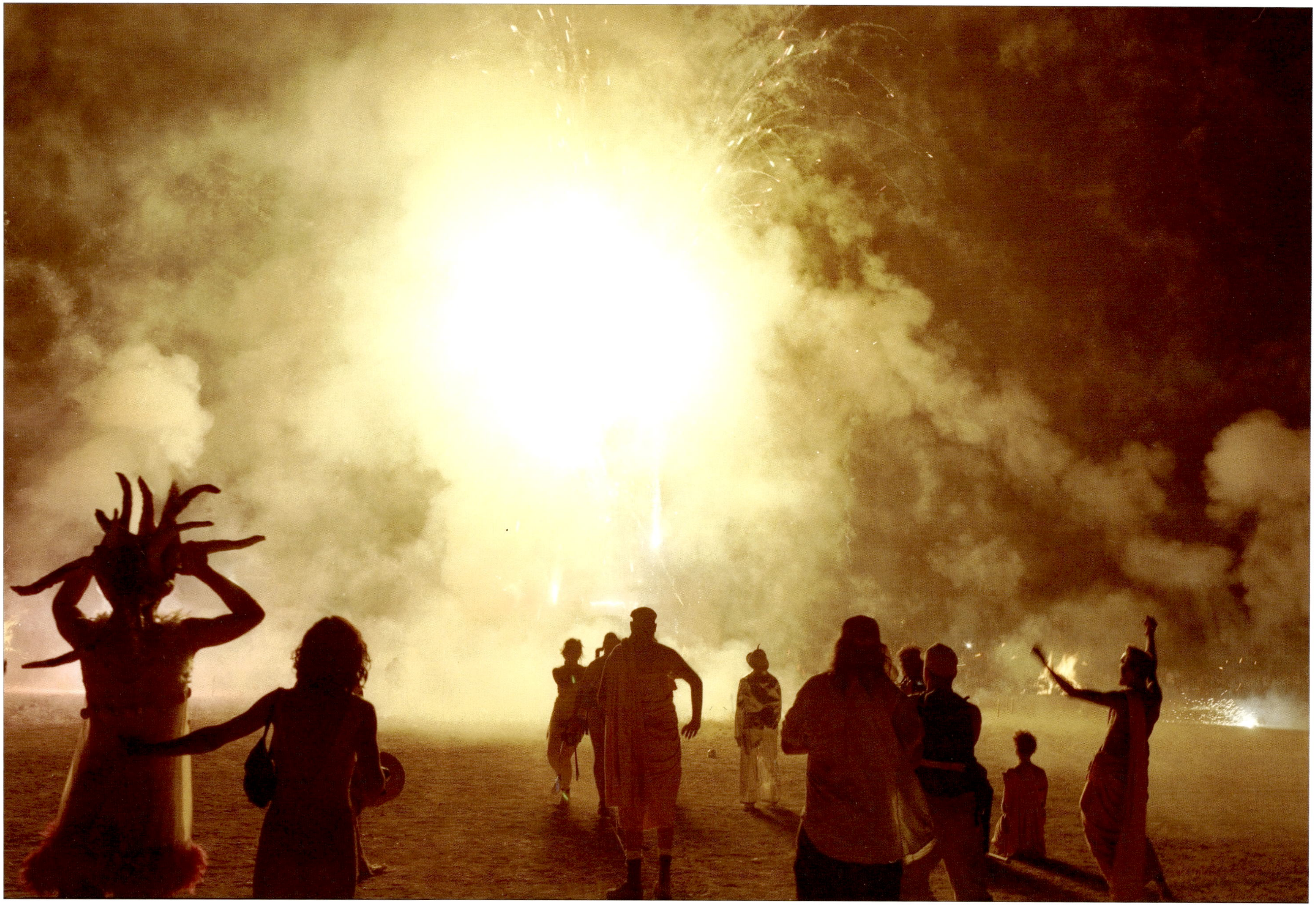

Big Bang, 1998

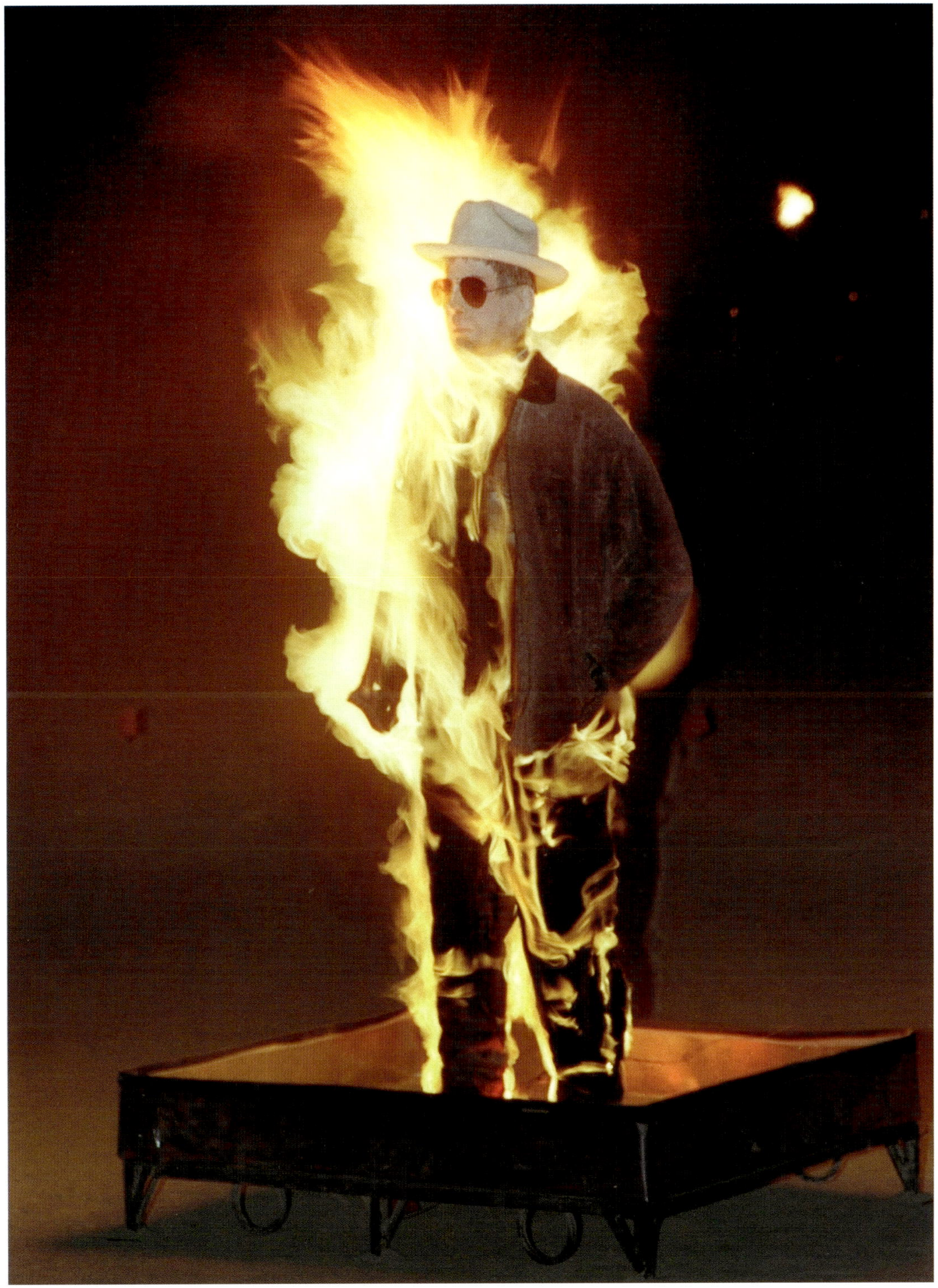

Floating Larry, *2002*

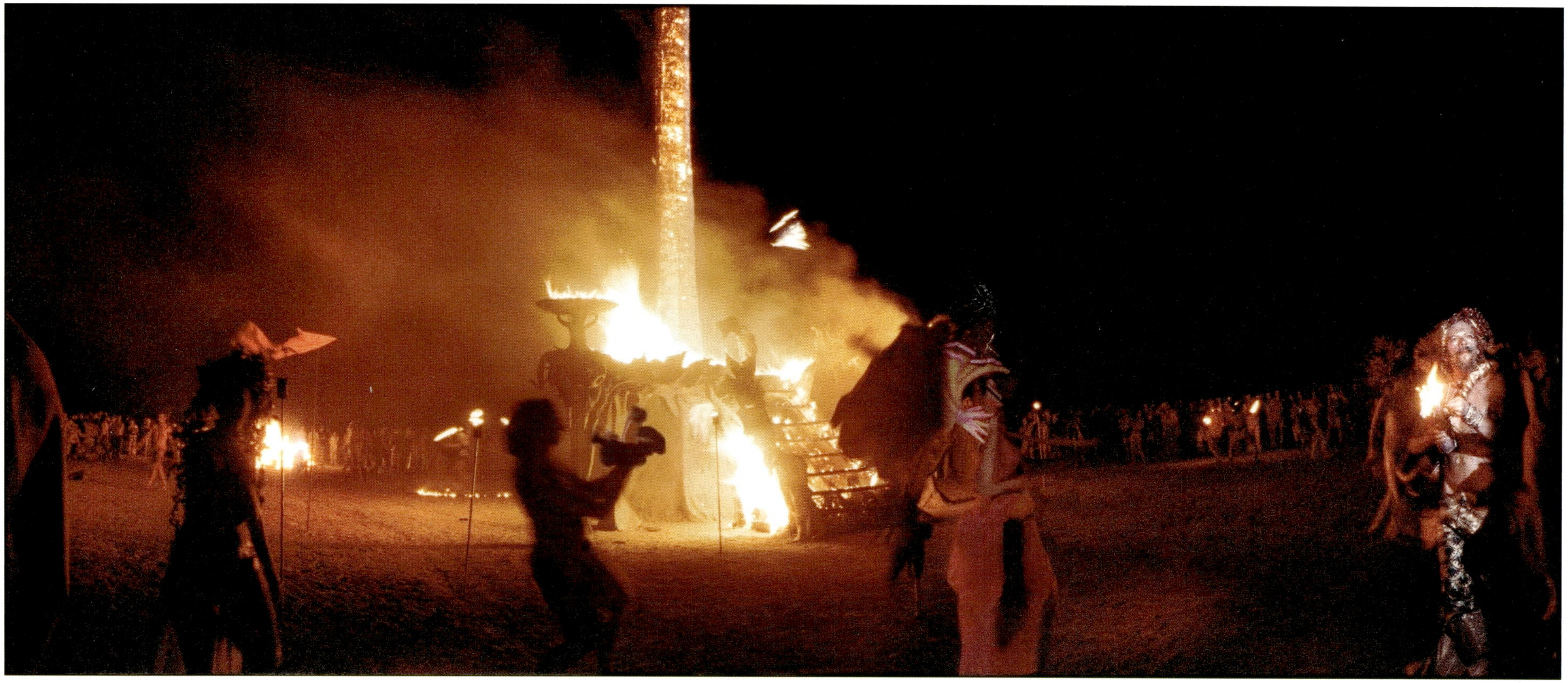

Daughters of Ishtar, *1997*

In the era before the advent of temples, the most dramatic fire ritual other than the Burning Man was Pepe Ozan's yearly operas. These extravagant combinations of playa art and performance were a Friday night fixture in the latter half of the 1990s. Frankly, I could never make heads nor tails of the story, but they always drew a huge crowd and employed many volunteer performers in mythological masks and various states of undress. The music and story often took a backseat to the spectacle, but Pepe was a master sculptor, and his lingam-based stage sets were a Byzantine triumph. Not only were the operas the second most important Burn of the weekend; they also invited participation by dozens of volunteer performers. He even managed to persuade many of the onlookers to get into the act.

While participation is a cardinal principle of Burning Man, there weren't so many obvious opportunities in the early days. I'm not sure when the Lamplighters began, but other than the Black Rock Rangers, volunteer opportunities were more a matter of part-time or occasional work. The operas required a large number of costumed performers to commit to rehearsal and to perform in front of expectant audiences. While I didn't get to know Pepe Ozan very well, I understood that he was a tireless taskmaster, and so being in one of his productions demanded that performers forsake the frivolity of the event and take on the responsibility of a role in the grand pageant—an exquisite regiment of volunteer artists.

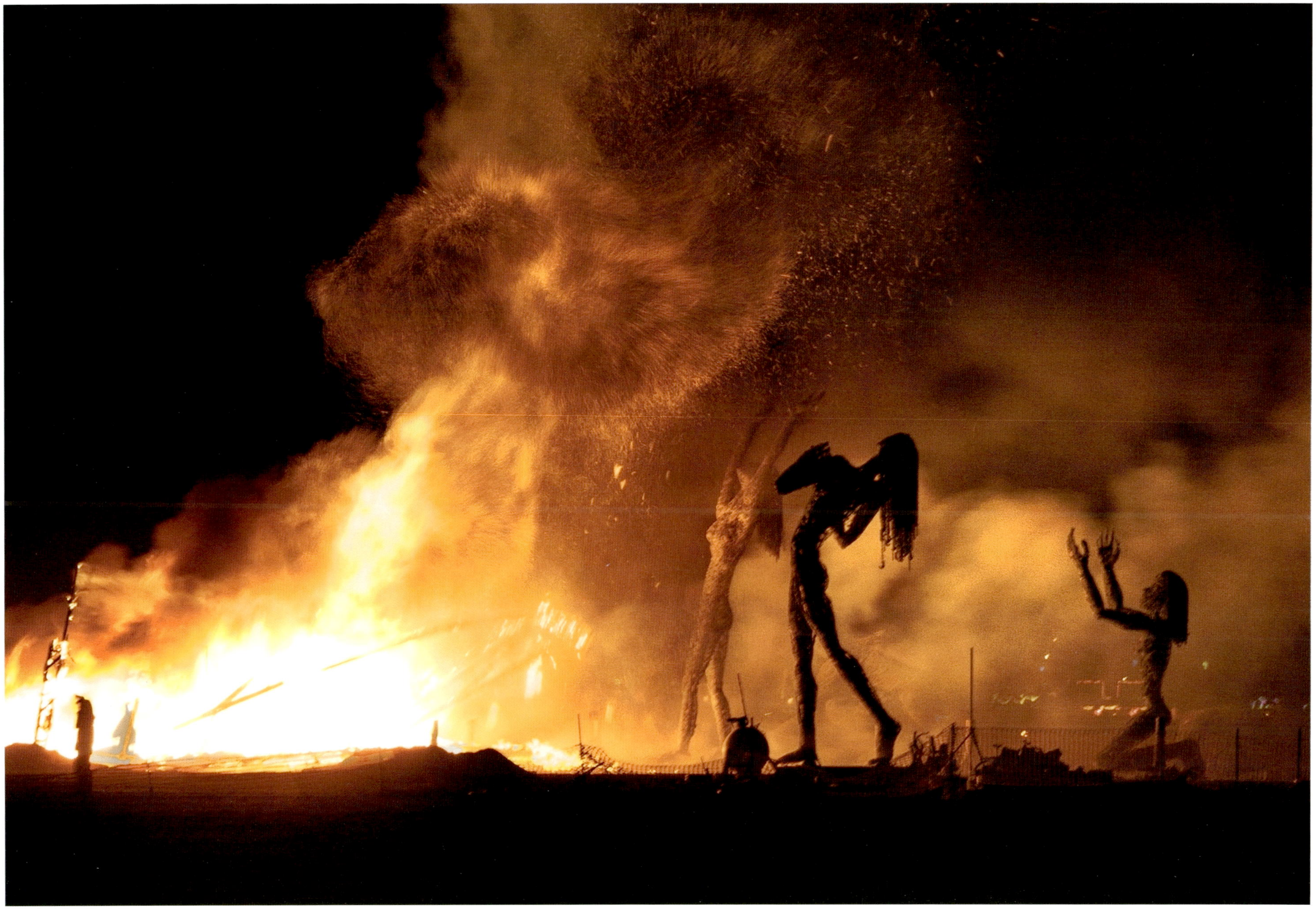

The Collapse of Crude Awakening, *2007*

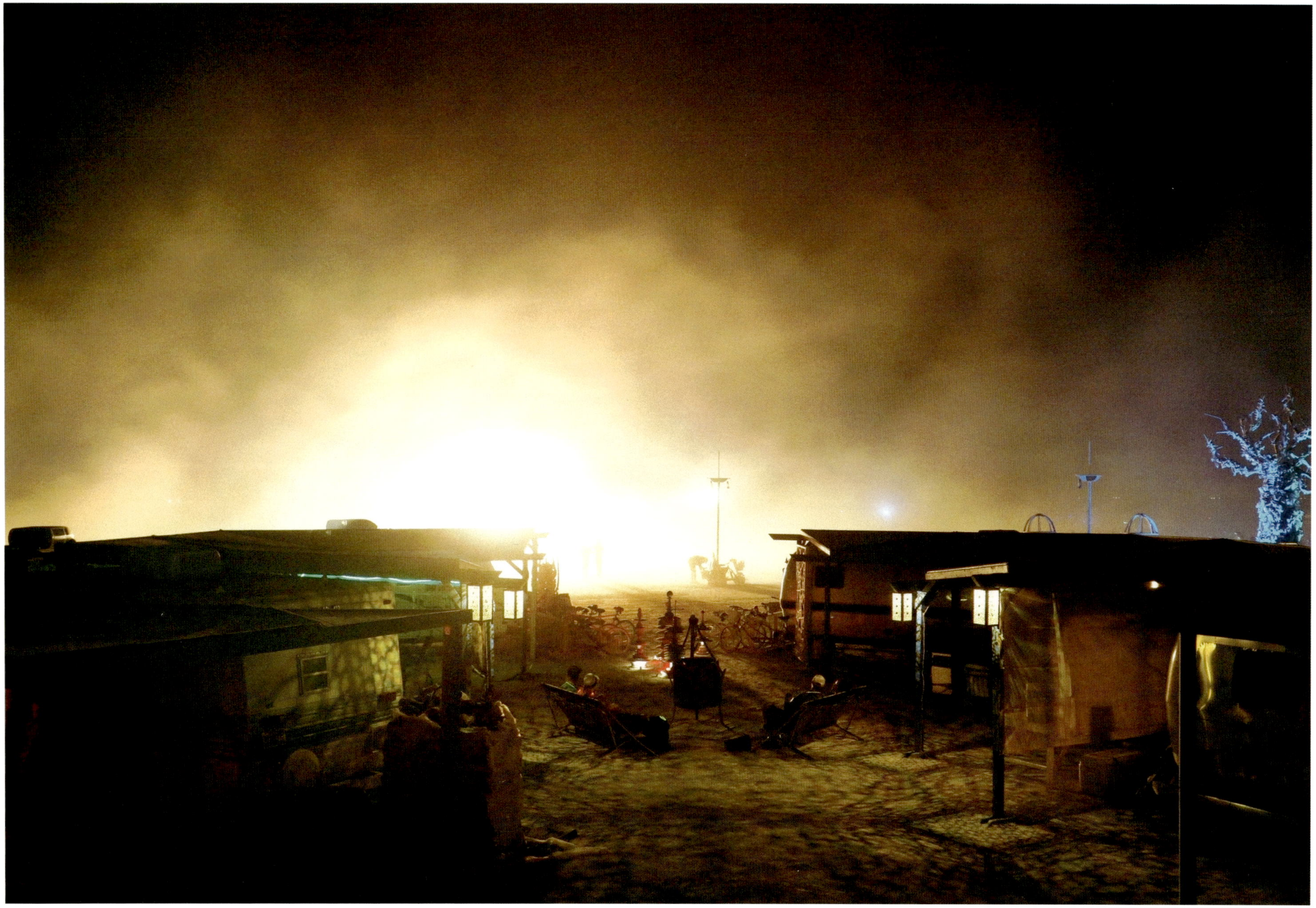

Dust Fire, 2014

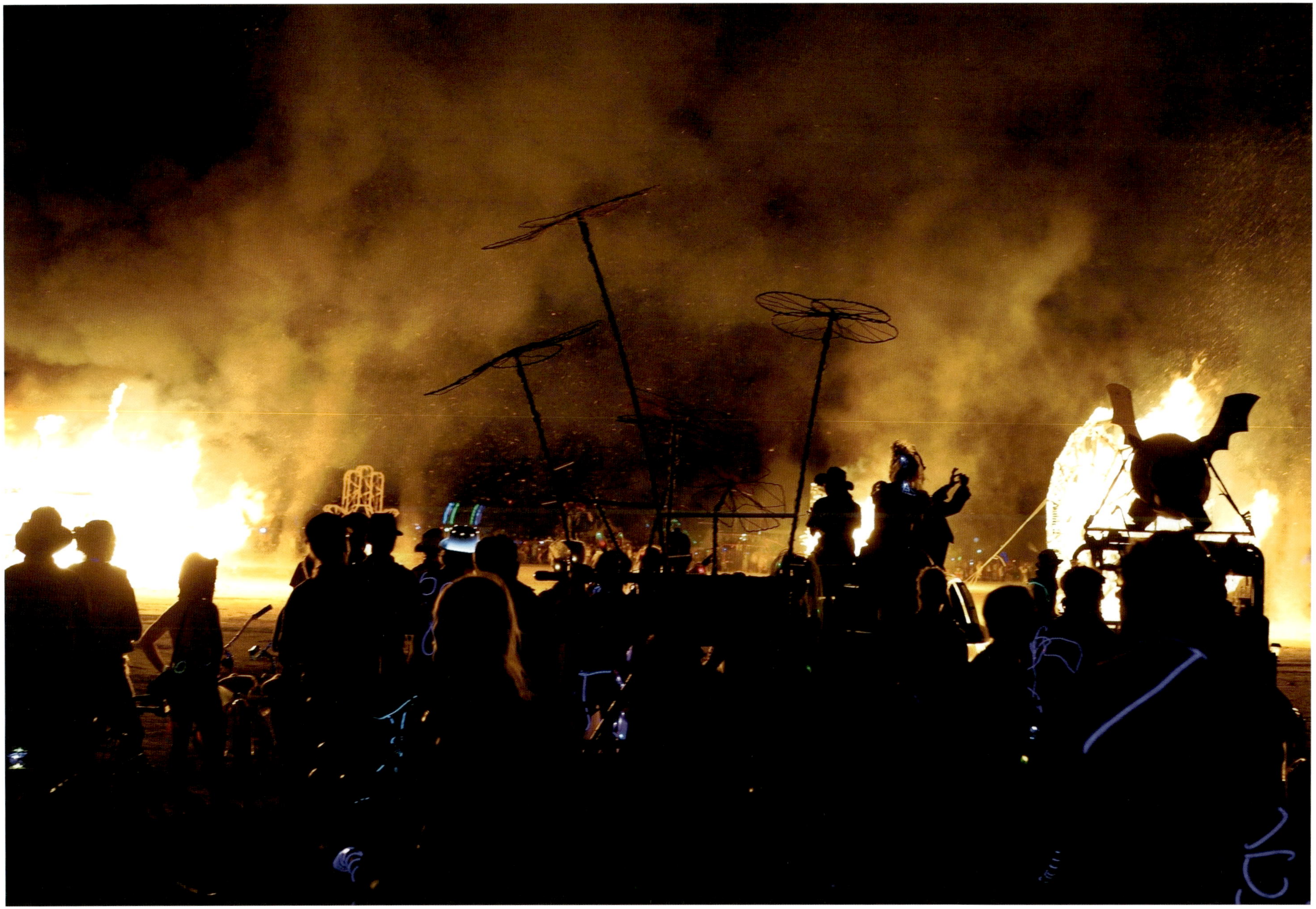

Burning Regional Effigies, 2013

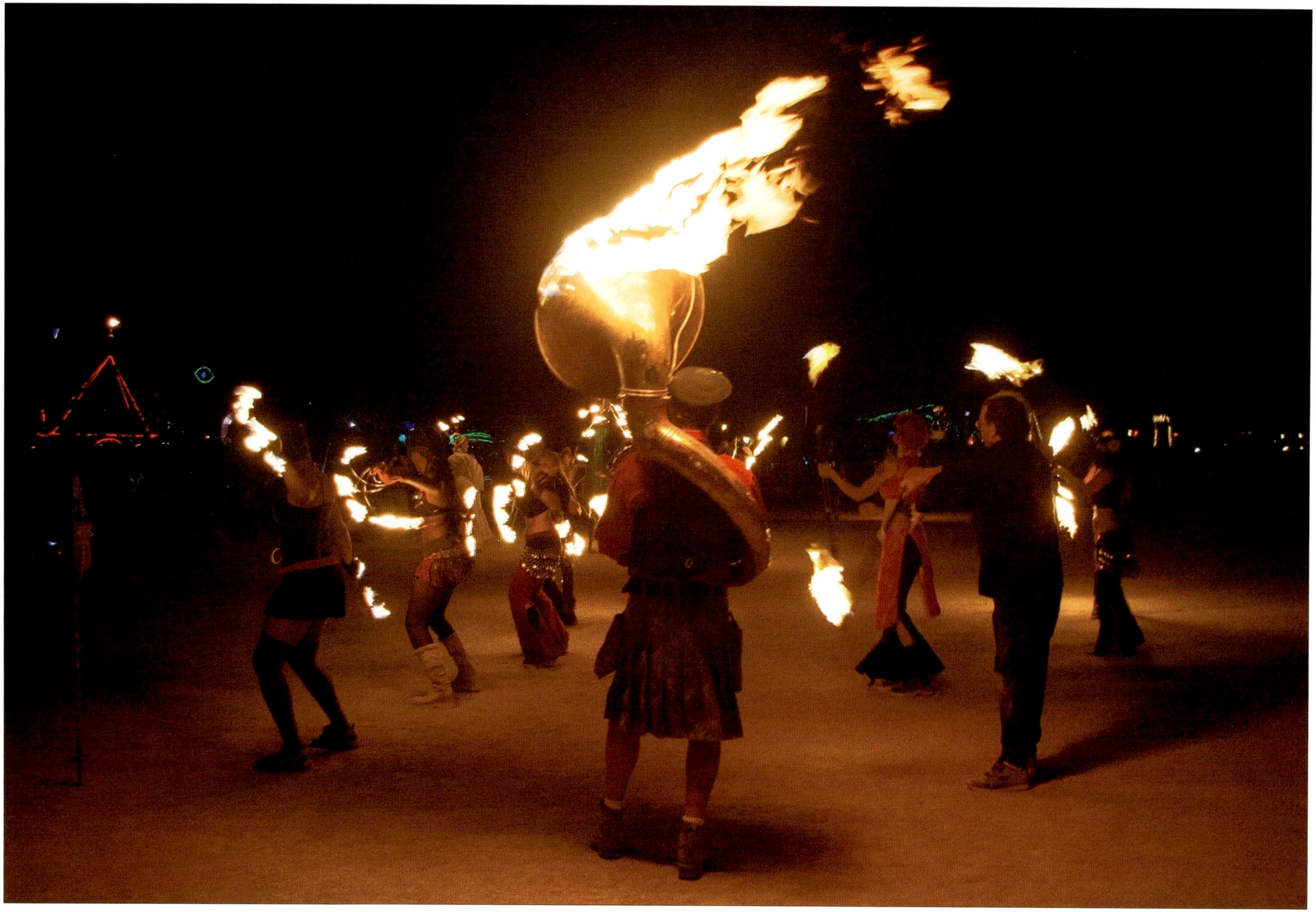

Flaming Tuba, 2007

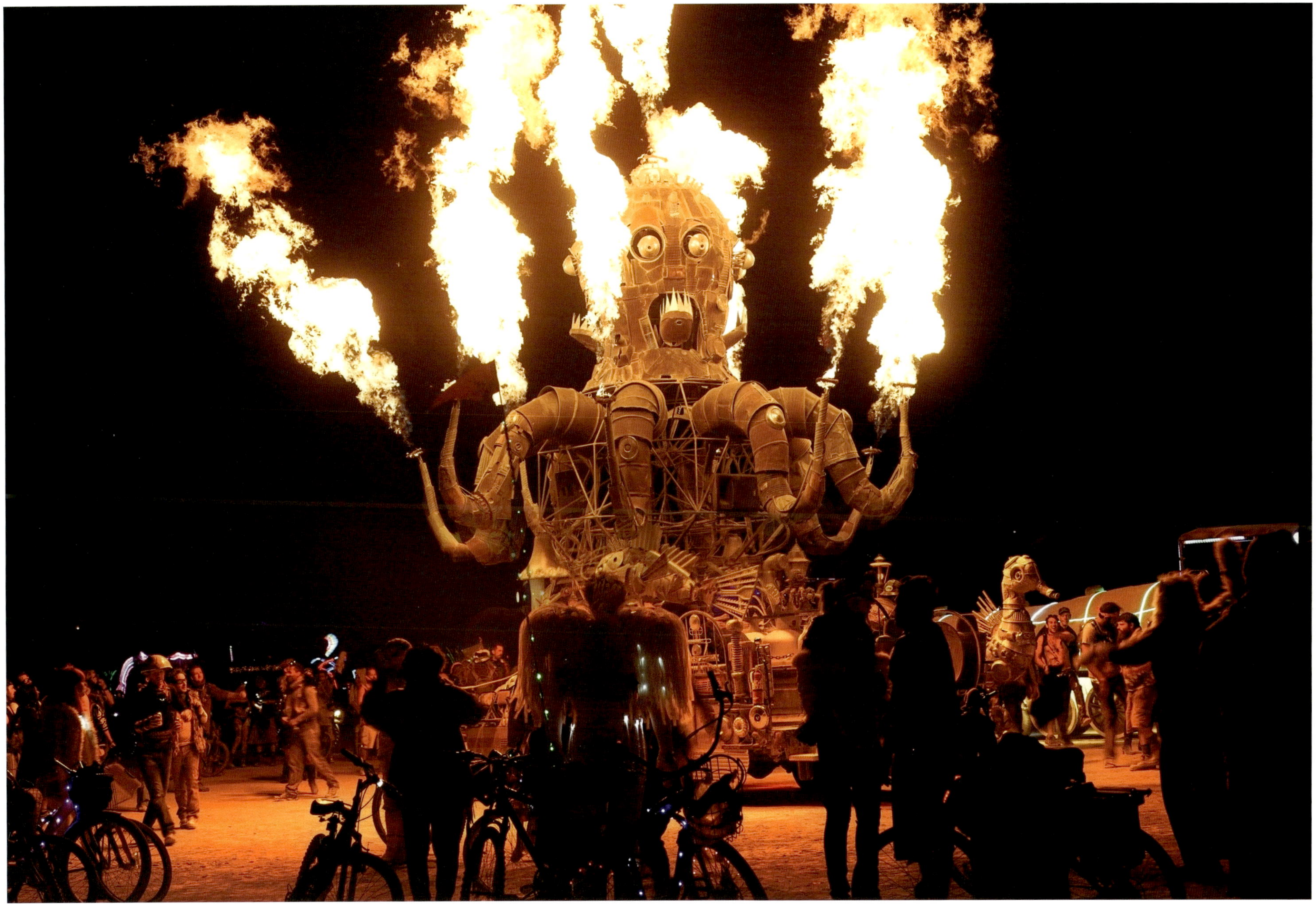

El Pulpo Mecanico, *2016*

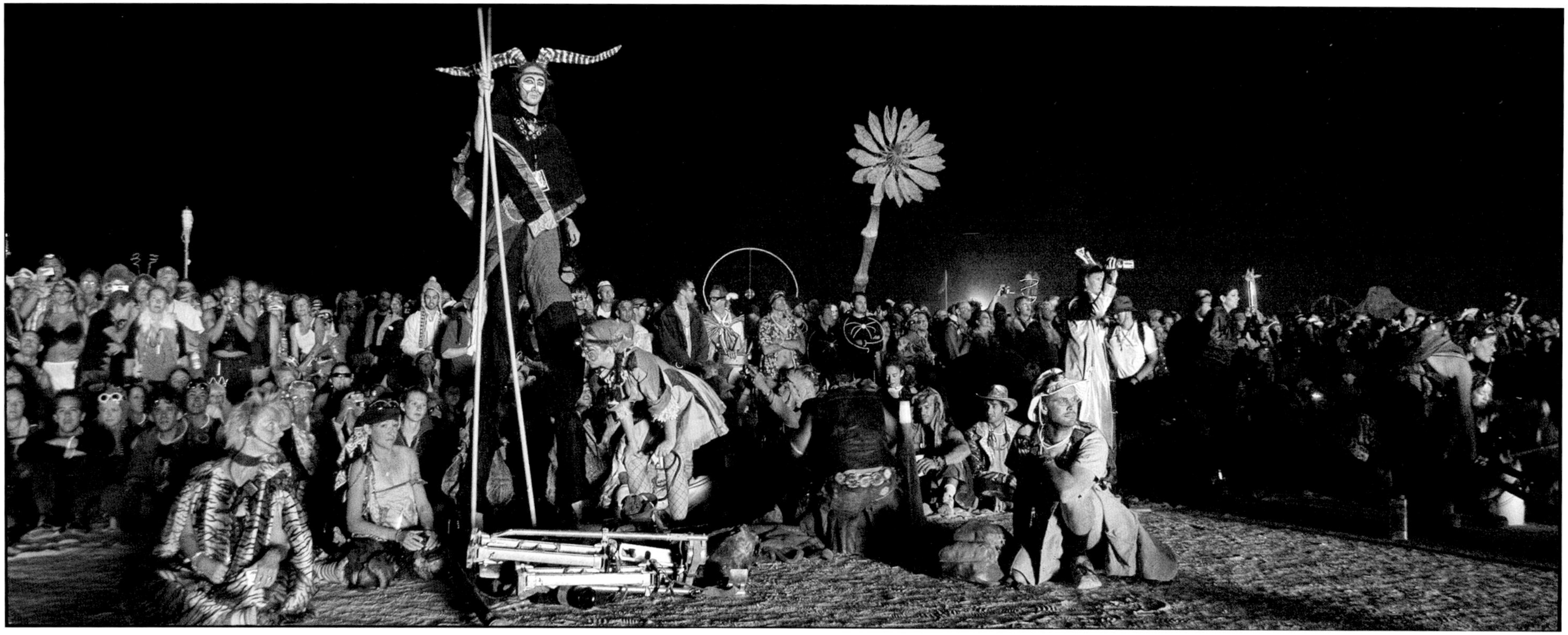

Fire Light, 2005

Fire is a potentially fatal attraction, and an attraction that goes back to the first Burns on the playa, back when the heat from the burning effigy was close enough to scorch your skin. As the disintegration of the Man draws near, the crowd will tense with anticipation. Some will even begin to creep forward on their hands and knees only to be warned back by the fire marshals. All it takes to release that pent-up energy is for the flaming figure to crumble under the relentless onslaught of rapid oxidation and the sheer weight of its half-consumed remains.

The Man is held vertical by guy wires, and in the days when he stood flat-footed on the playa, a weight-bearing cable was attached to his midsection. It could be cut at the critical moment, and down he would go. Sometimes just before that happened, one of Larry's henchmen would jump up and down on a guy wire, causing the Man to shutter and shake. It would drive the electrified crowd into a frenzy. Then the cable would be cut, and the Man would crumble to the ground in a shower of sparks. The crowd of frenzied Burners would rush to the Man and encircle the flaming ruins, and then they would dance. It's a primal dance of mourning and celebration, as old as the playa itself. It still happens every time.

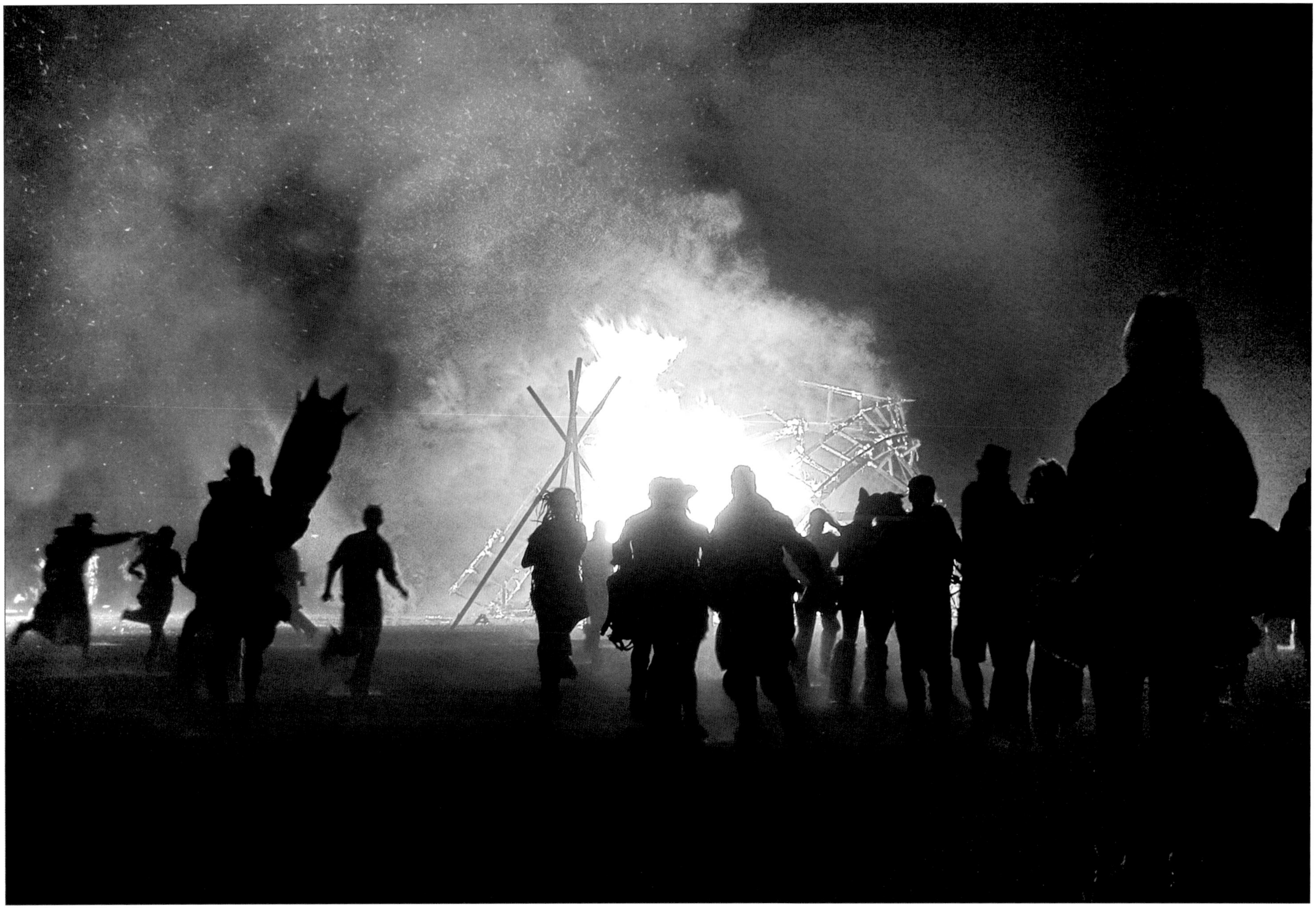

Burn Rush, 2005

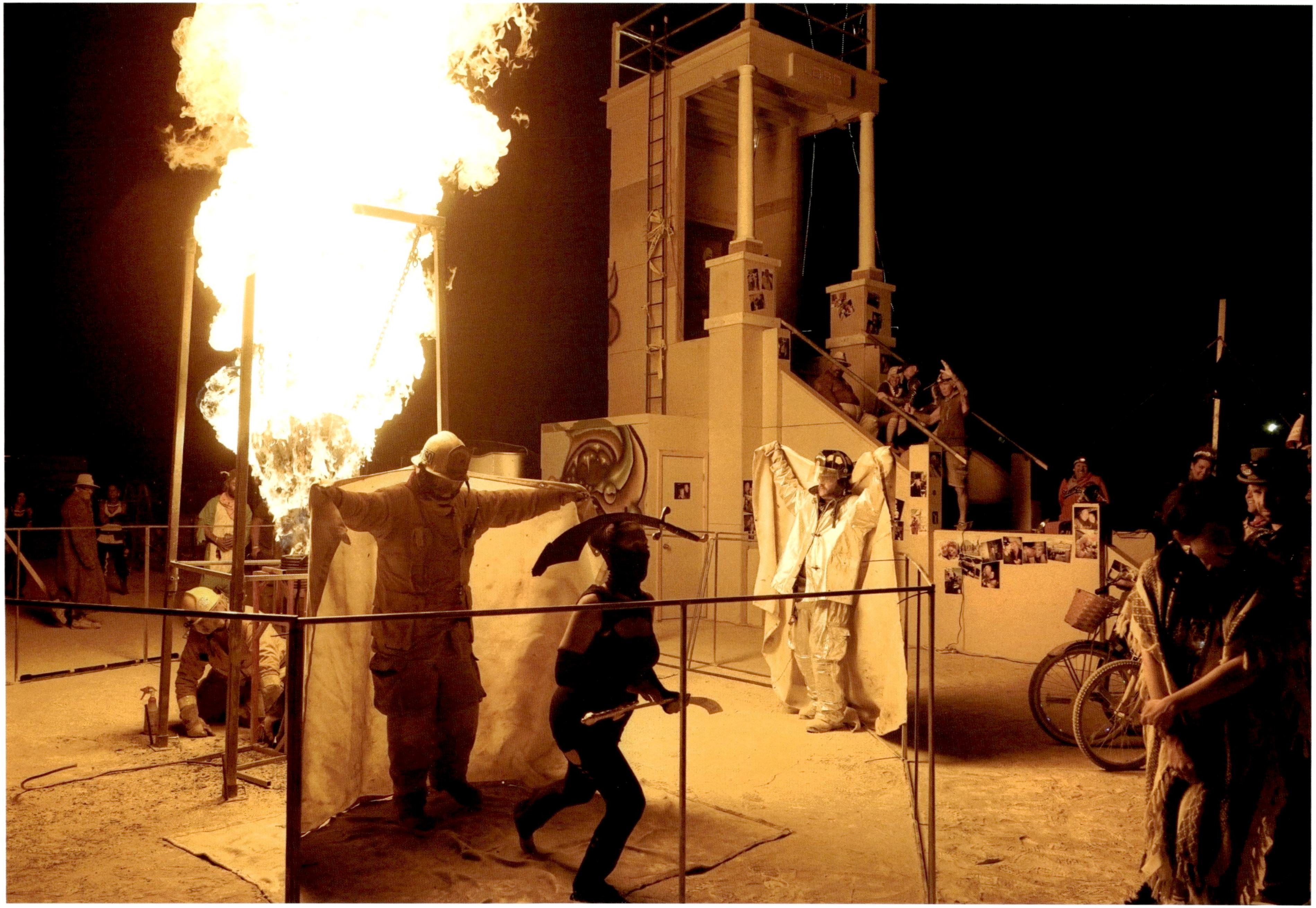

Flaming Slideshow, 2016

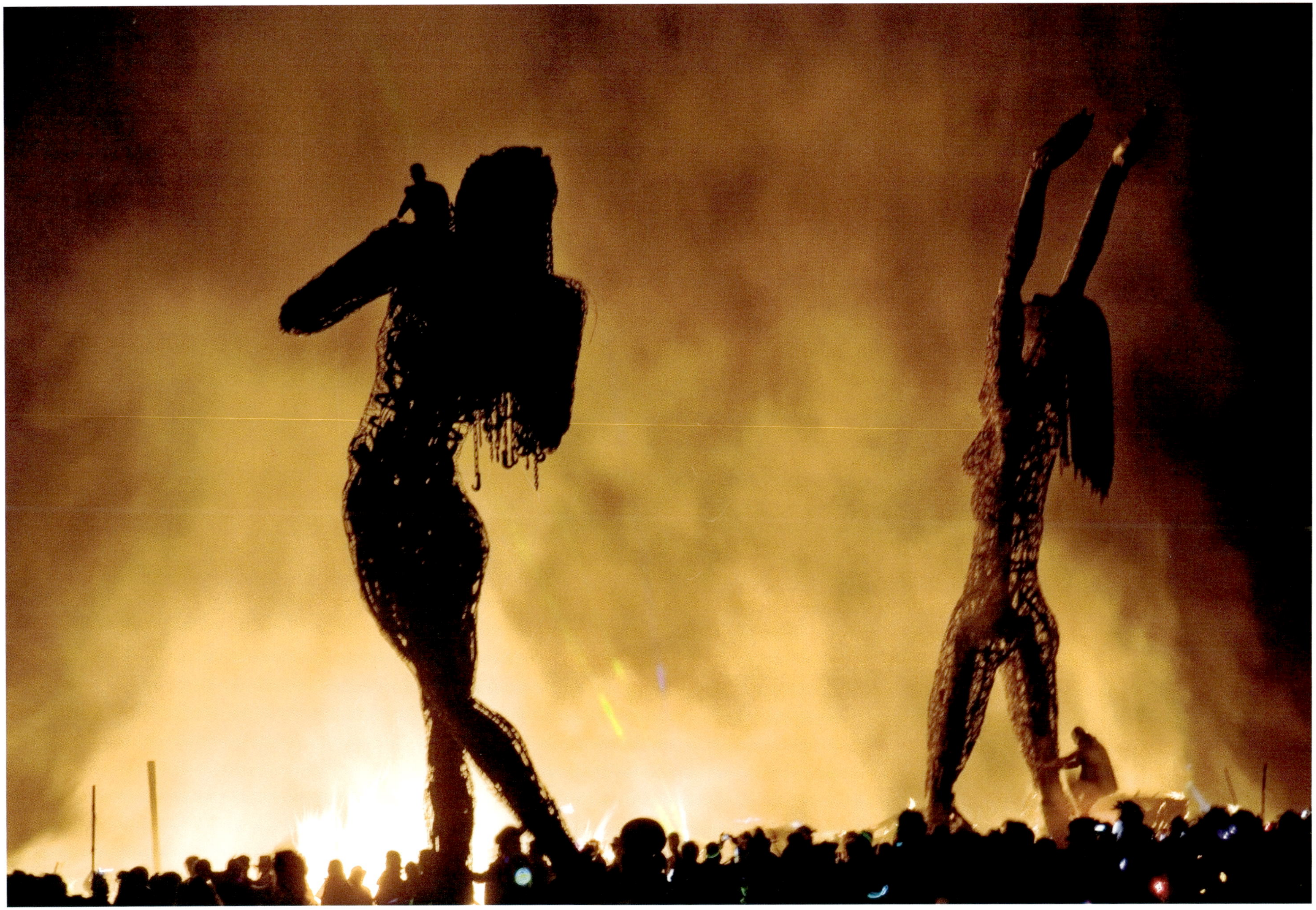

Fire Climb, 2007

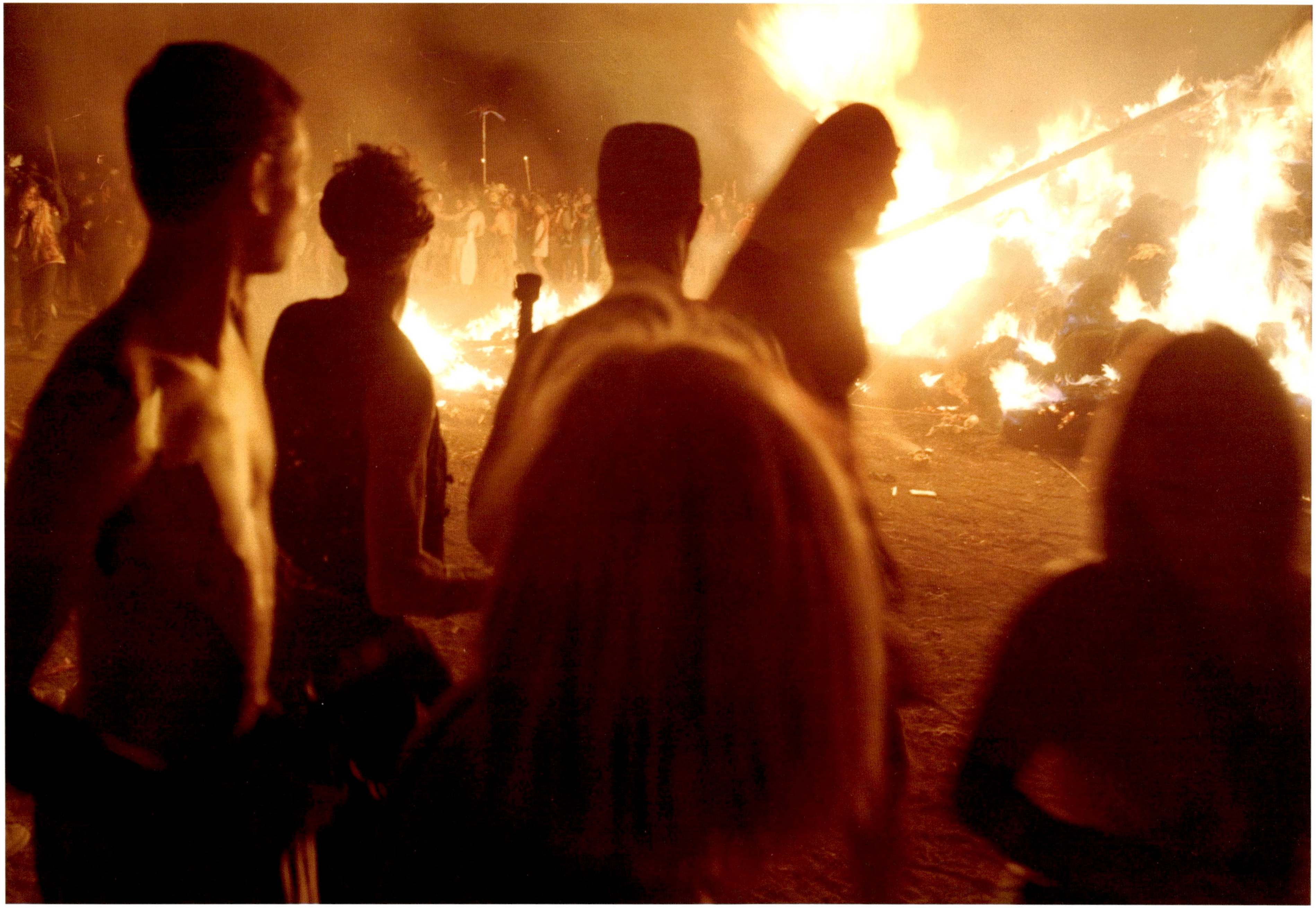

Fire Crowd, 1997

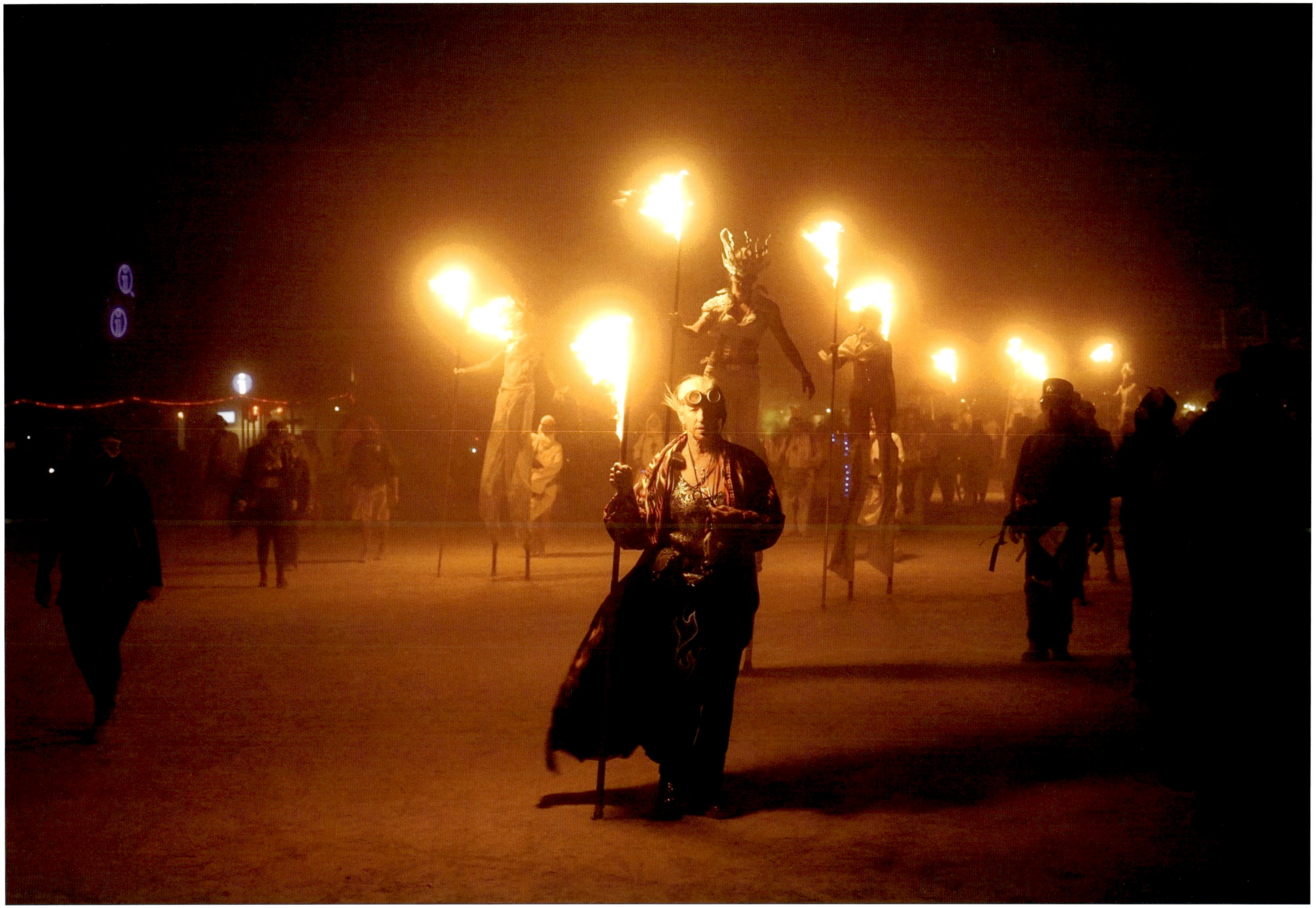

Crimson Rose and the Fire Conclave, 2016

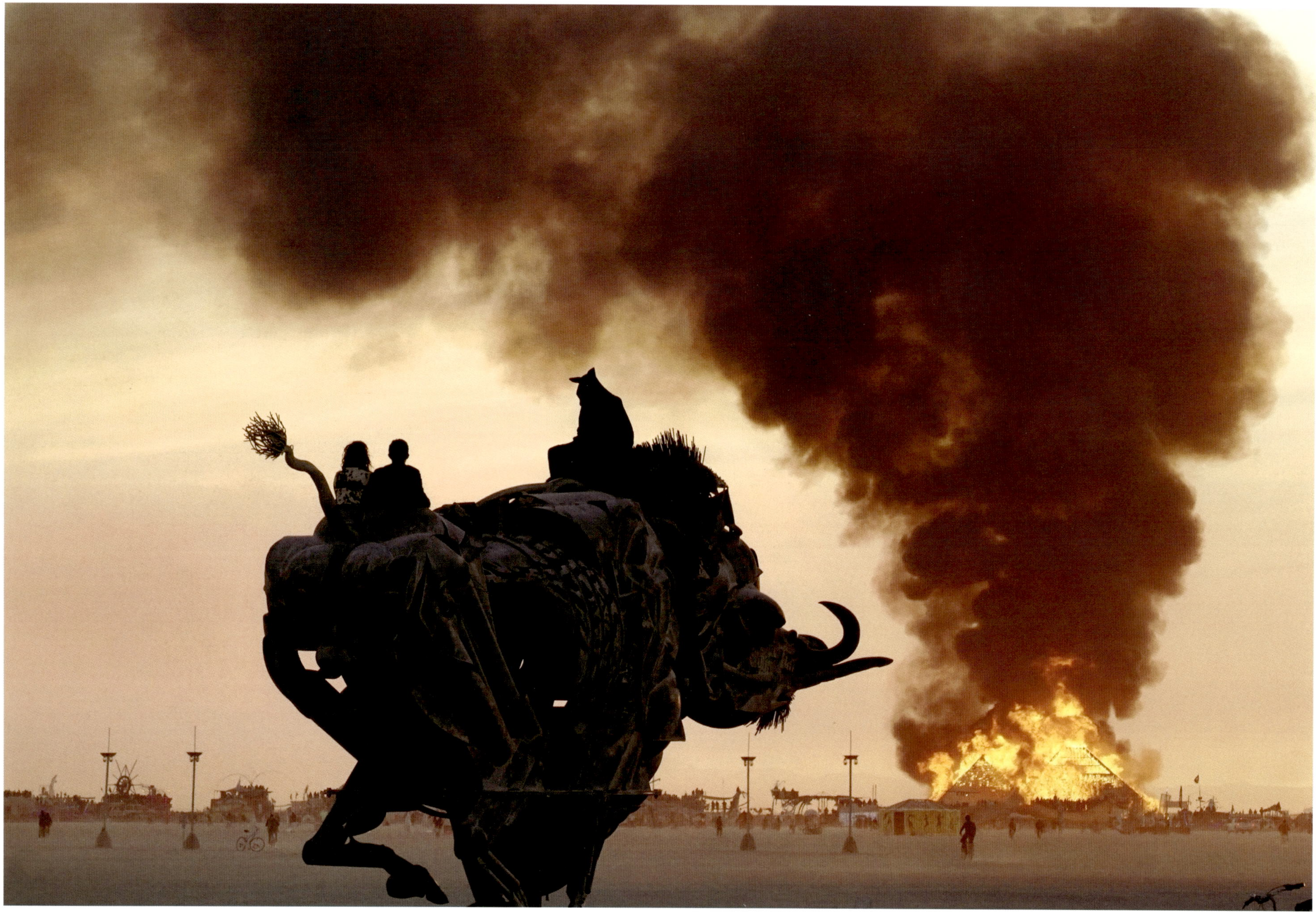

Lord Snort *Ride, 2016*

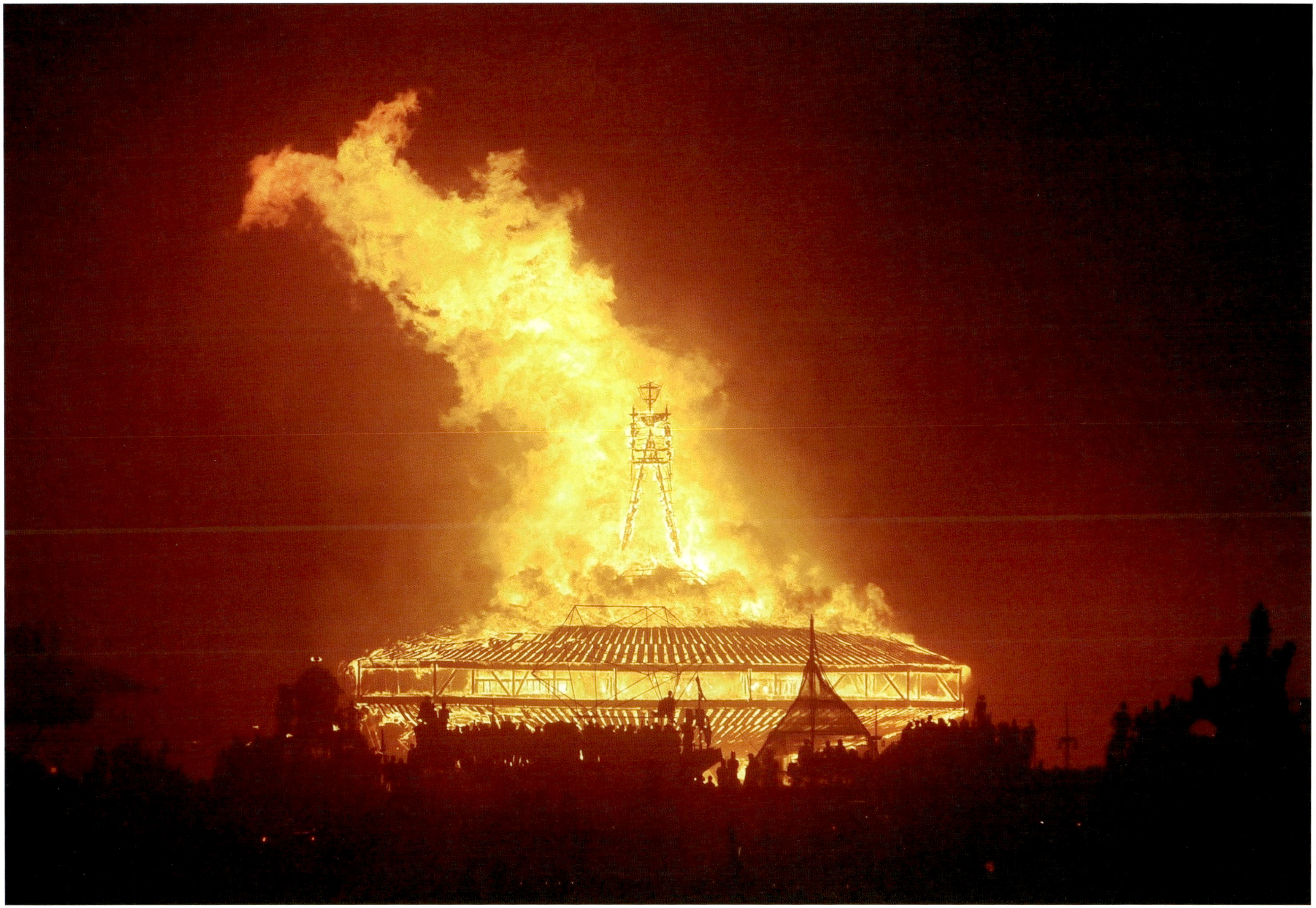

"Cargo Cult" Burn, 2013

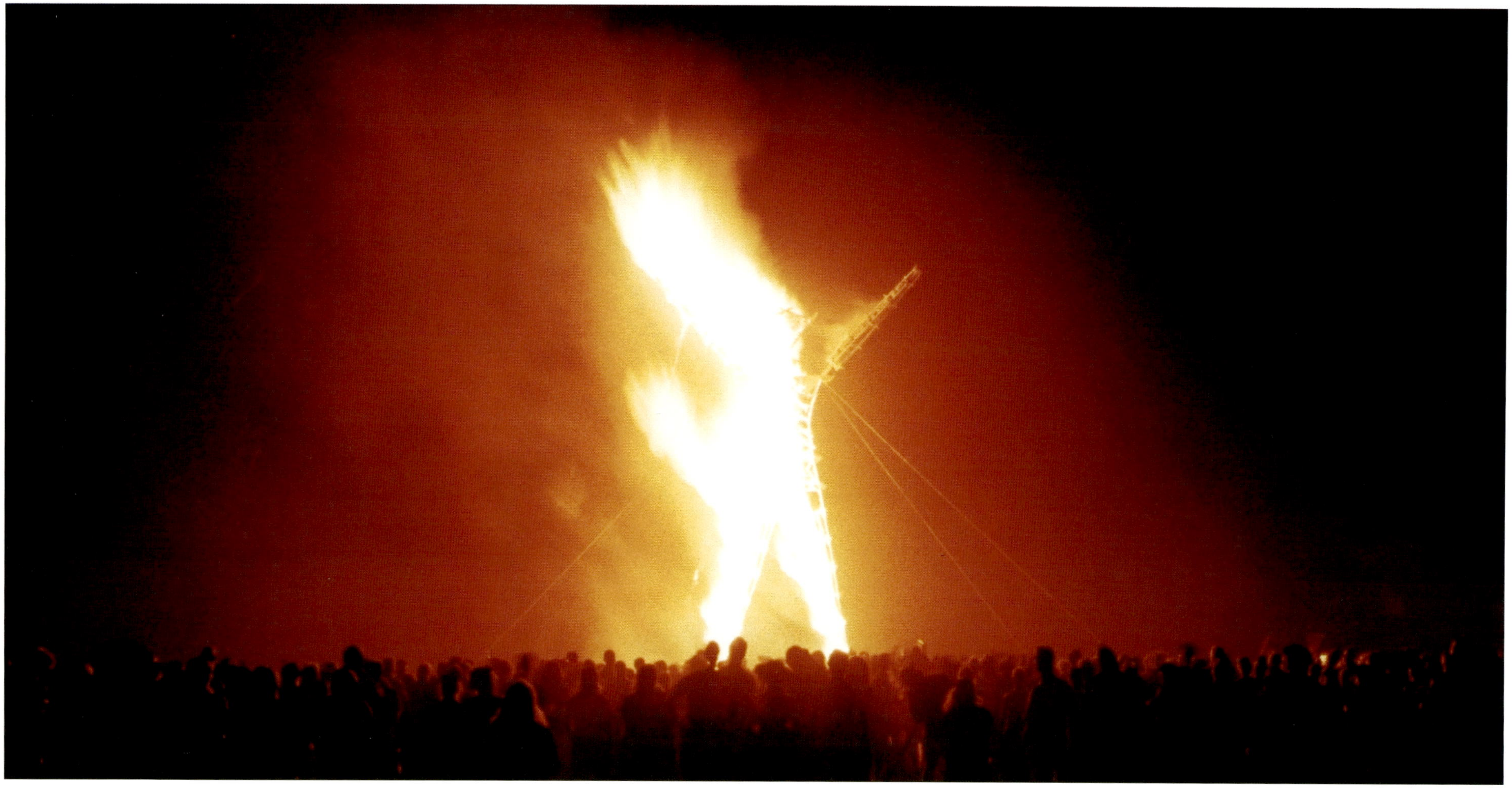

Full Burn, 1993

As it had been on Baker Beach in its formative years, the ritual immolation of a giant figure continues to be the central ceremony that compels thousands to attend Burning Man. Even though the spectacle and gigantic scale of the modern Burn dwarfs anything imaginable in the early years, I will concede that the intimacy of those early Burns was magical. Standing mere feet away from a flaming figure that we had raised by hand from the desert floor is difficult to duplicate, but the central motif of ritual sacrifice is forever powerful, and the core elements of Burning Man today continue to evoke a spiritual component that is as ancient as it is undeniable.

Fire is a living thing, and it quickens sensibilities long muffled by modern life. While the elaborate pageantry may feel redundant after attending a few Burns, the consuming flames are utterly unique each year and continue to re-create specters from a primitive consciousness. The fire crackles, and we are transformed into acolytes of an aboriginal sacrificial rite. It is primal stuff, and for a few very brief, very intense moments, we experience that searing reality that can be felt deep in our being. The pageantry may become familiar, but the visceral impact of the fire transcends both time and memory.

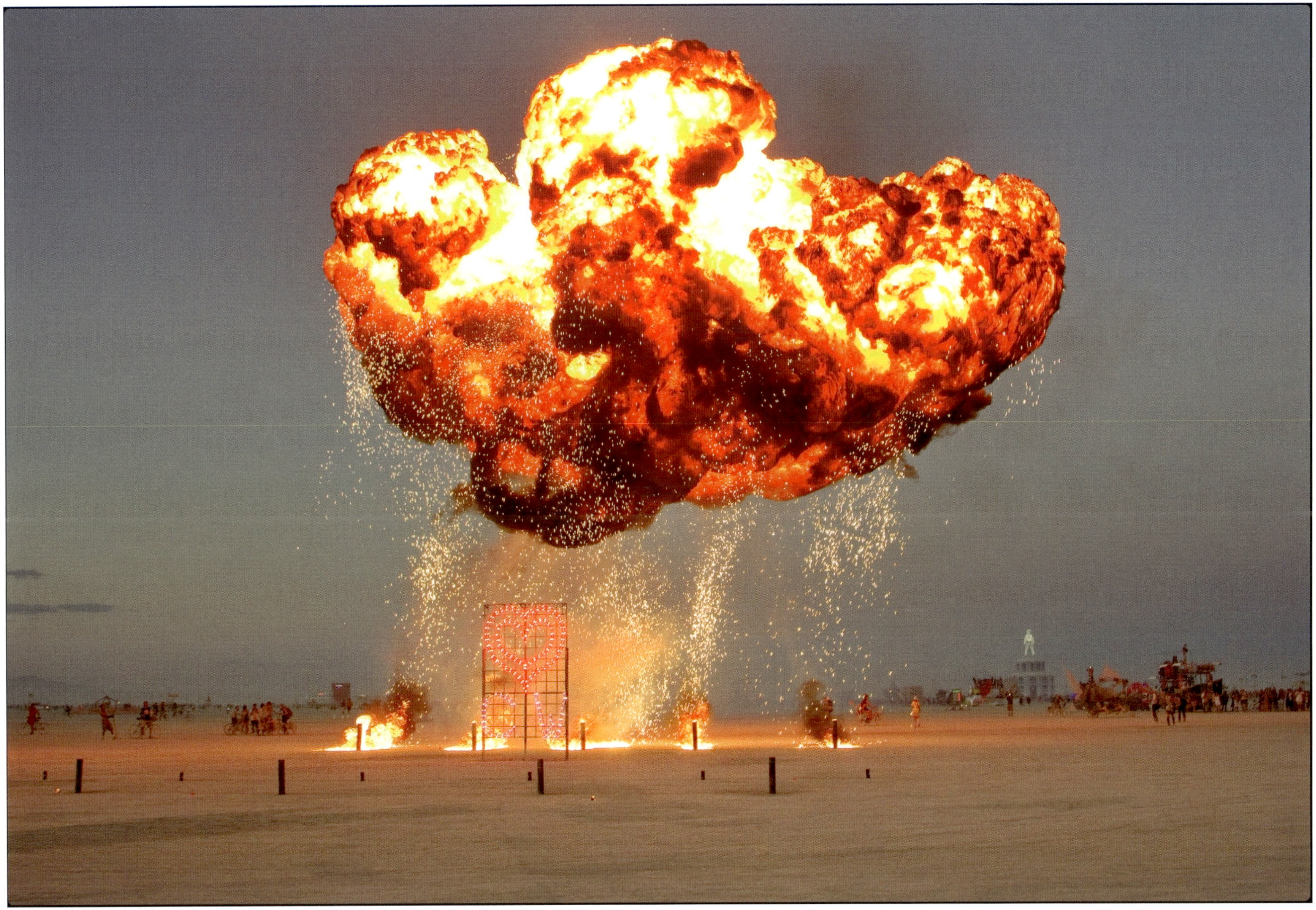

Exploding Heart, 2012

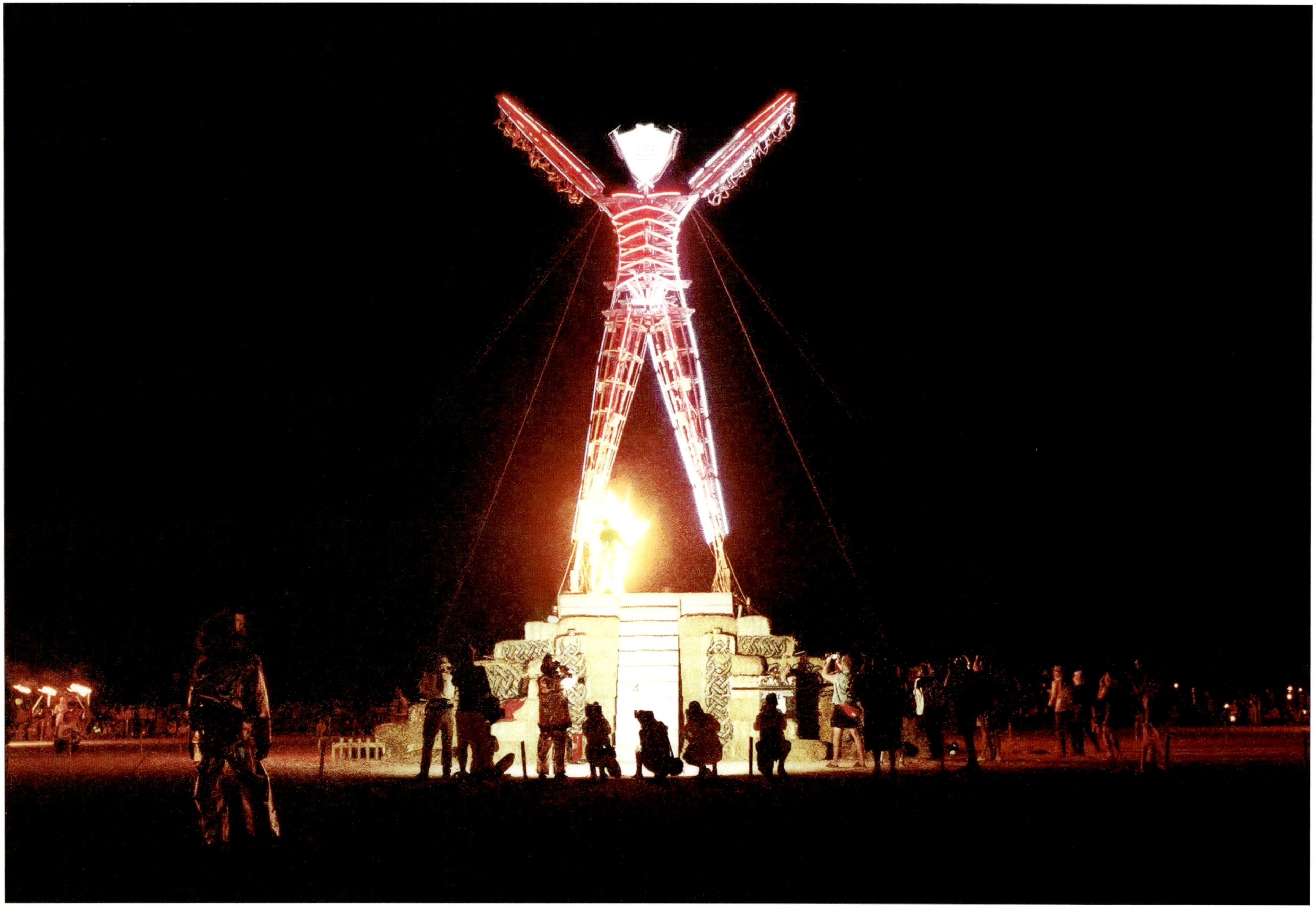

Man on Fire, 1998

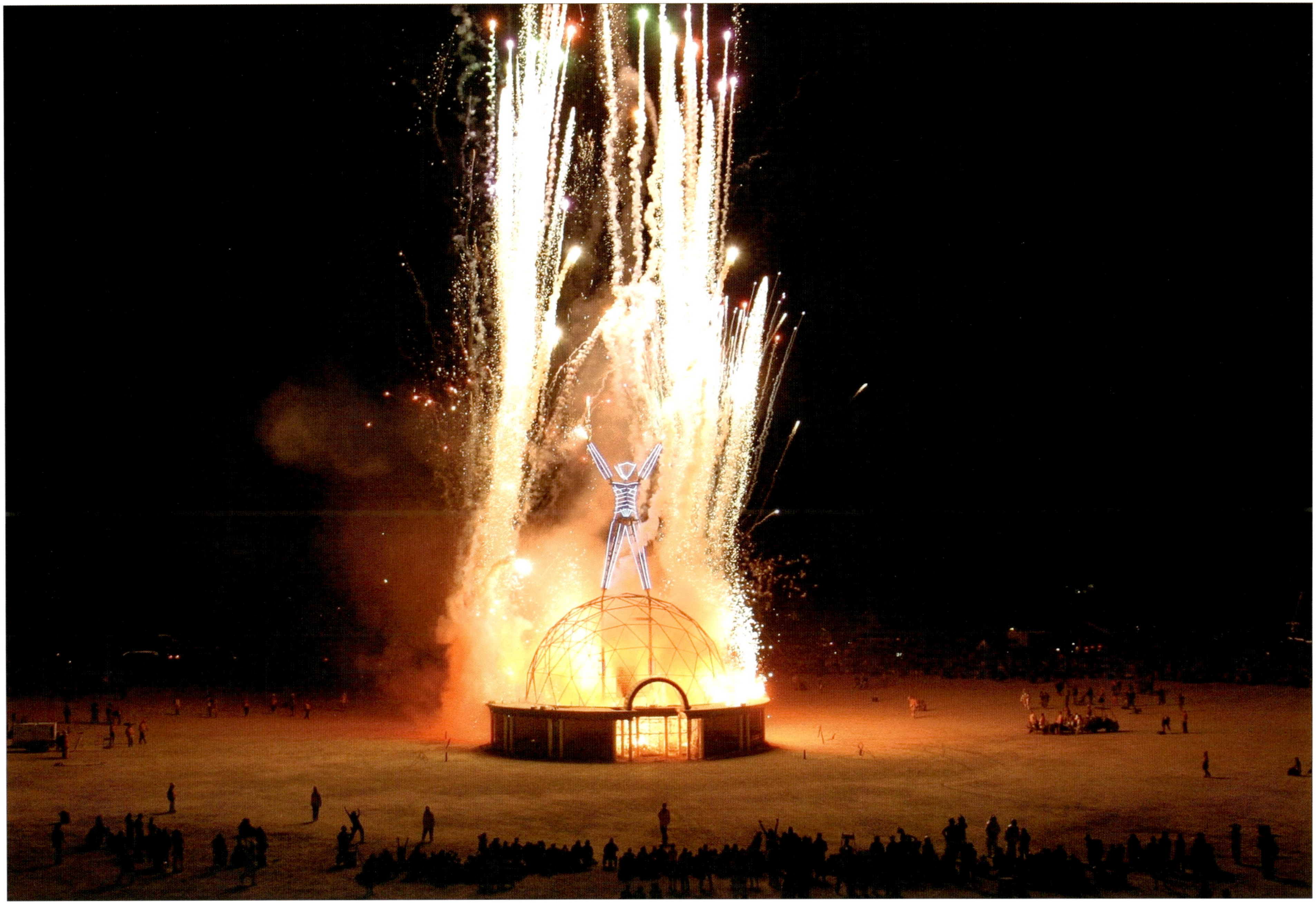

Vault of Heaven, 2004

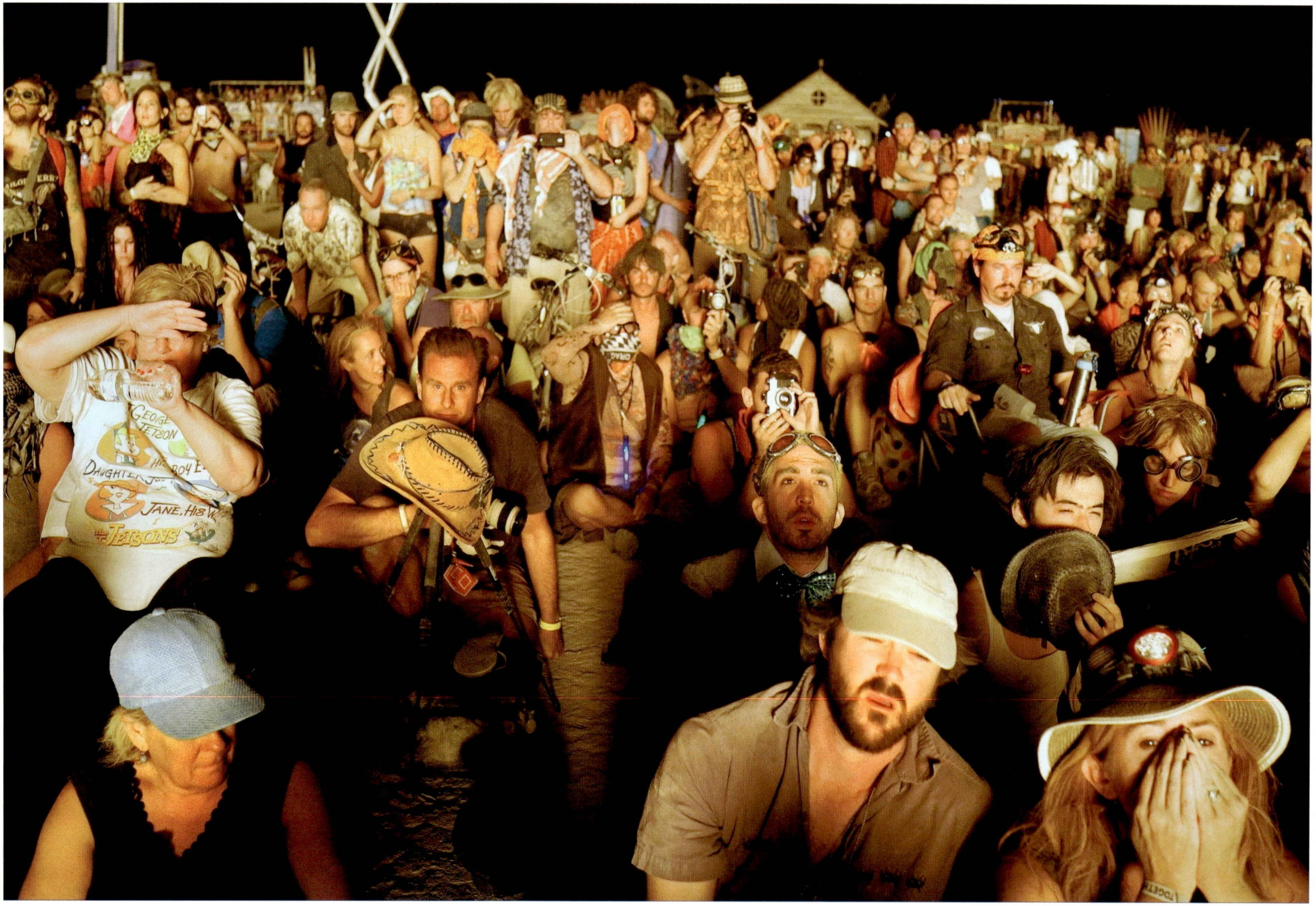

Temple Heat, 2012

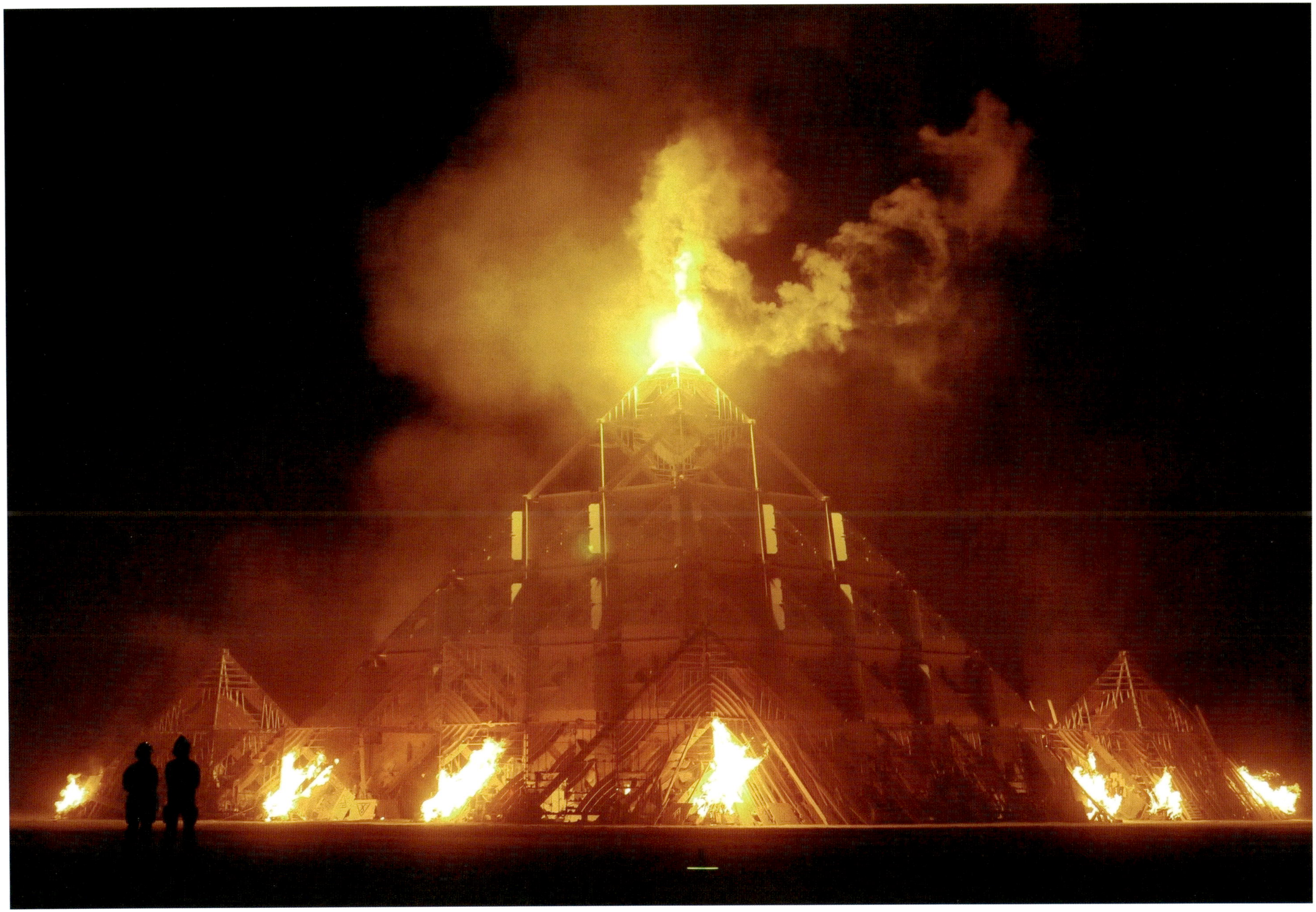

Temple of Whollyness, *2013*

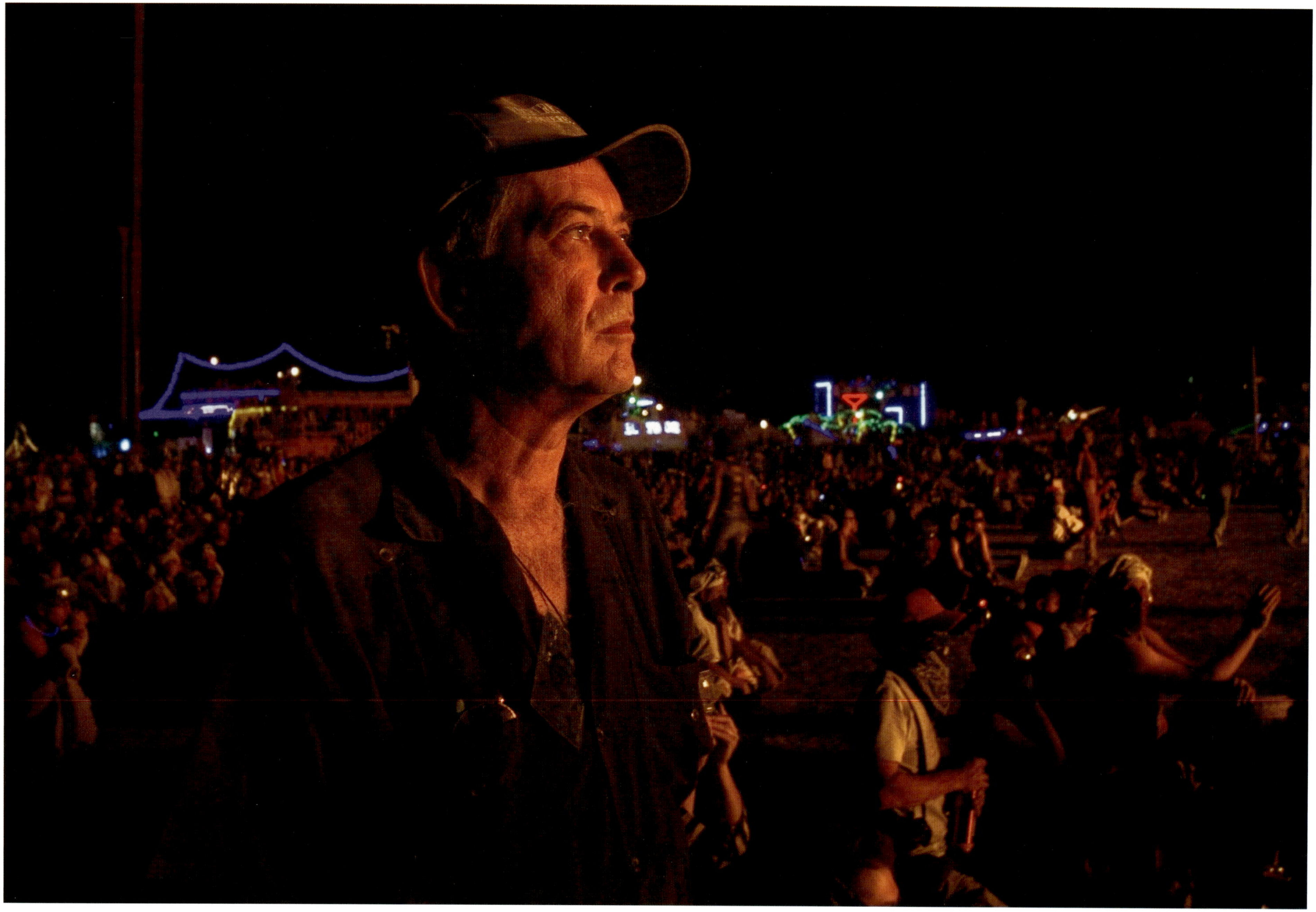

Larry, 2012

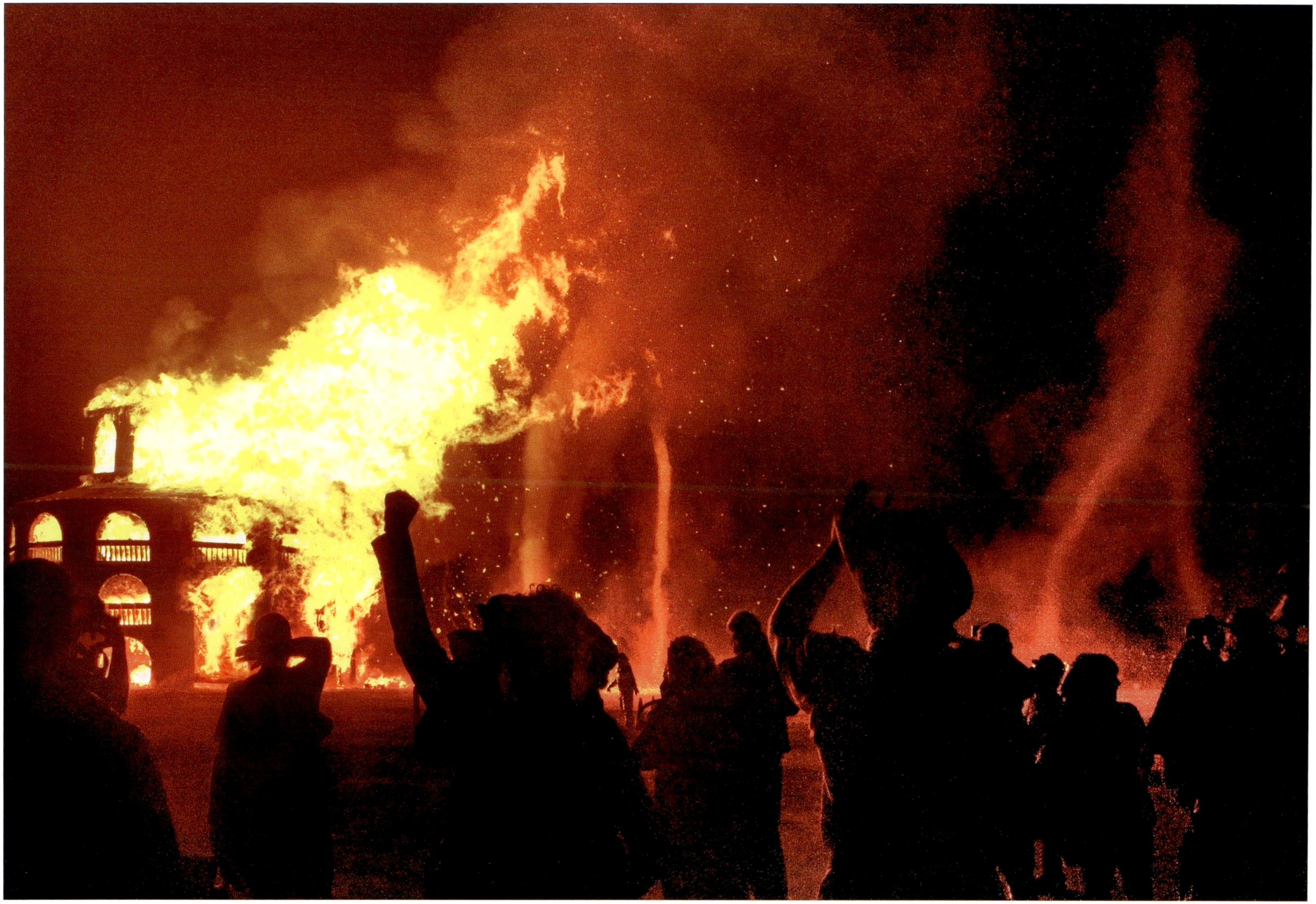

Falling Man, 2012

CHAPTER 15

THE GOLD SPIKE: 2016 AND BEYOND

On a chilly morning thirty days before Labor Day in 2016, I stood on a bluff and gazed out at the shoreline of an ancient lake bed and waited for the sun to crest the distant hills. The playa's a barren surface that proclaims the promise of new beginnings, and later that day a hardy group of us would gather to celebrate the first step in that renewal. There a somewhat shaggy survey crew and their eager cohorts would gather on that expanse and travel several miles out into its vast nothingness, looking for a virtually invisible point in the middle of apparently nowhere. From that spot they would begin a survey to plat out Black Rock City, which reappears like Oz each year in August and disappears without a trace by October. To inaugurate this phenomenon, a hundred workers and guests would gather together for the yearly ritual that marks the occasion. It's called variously the Golden Spike, the Gold Spike, or simply—the Spike.

The spike itself is a simple iron rod about four feet long that has been spray-painted a metallic gold, held in the possession of Tony "Coyote" Perez, who directs the ritual. Standing there at the moment the spike is driven into the ground, it's hard to imagine that somehow this flat emptiness will support anything other than an occasional insect or perhaps an errant crow. The idea that soon this emptiness will host throngs of Burners, dozens of art installations, and a cluster of camps that will stretch for two and a half miles, end to end, seems preposterous. In fact, it is preposterous, and that's exactly what makes Burning Man so interesting.

Will Roger Peterson directed the building of the first Burning Man "city" on Hualapai Flat in 1997, and then Rod Garrett, in 1998, platted the first iteration of the city on the Black Rock Desert. Will is intimately involved with rural Nevada, and he and Crimson Rose have a home in Gerlach. From there, he works with area environmental groups and has been the vital link between Burning Man and the BLM. Retired as an organizing director, Will commutes to San Francisco periodically but spends most of his time working as Burning Man's representative in Nevada. He is vice president of Friends of Black Rock High Rock and leads several campouts and star parties in the nearby hills. An avid outdoorsman, he roams the surrounding area on his ATV and celebrates the spiritual serenity of this rugged sanctuary by walking at sundown the rock labyrinth that he and Crimson Rose created on their property.

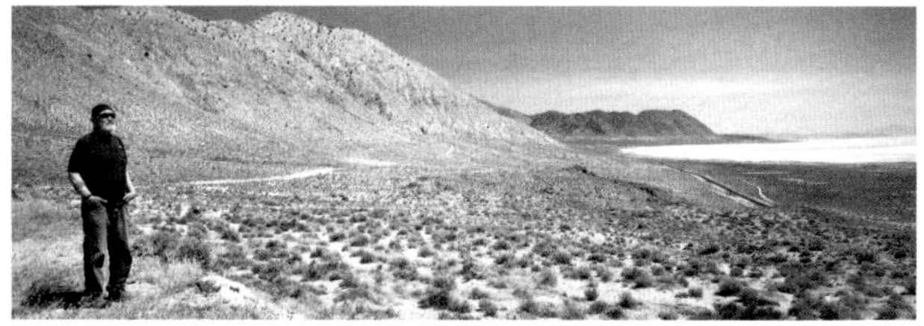

For Will Roger Peterson, the primal terrain of northern Nevada evokes mystery and reverence.

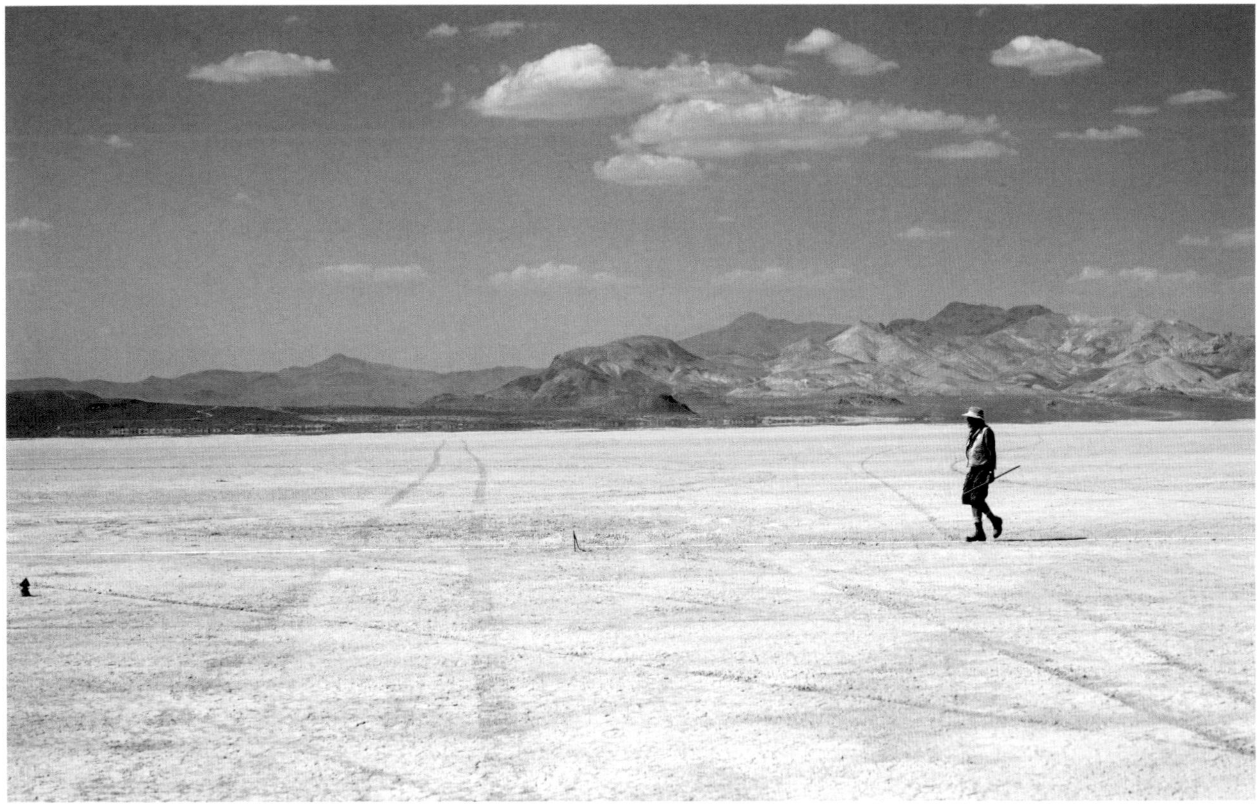

"Out of nothing came everything."
—Larry Harvey

Will created the Gold Spike ritual in 1998 to celebrate the initial survey for a designed city on the playa. "I originally came up with ceremonies like the Golden Spike and the DPW Parade to instill in my workers a sense of self-respect and camaraderie," he told me. "In those days we couldn't afford to pay anyone, and so I got what I got. My crews were often a collection of social misfits or characters that for whatever reason couldn't live on the grid. My job was to weld them into an efficient construction crew, and these ceremonies help to create a team loyalty."

What he found was that people who share a grueling experience develop a tremendous bond with one another. Out of that deep bonding comes a sense of belonging to a higher purpose. It's not an unfamiliar tale. I've met dozens of Burner volunteers who talk of "finding" themselves while laboring at Burning Man. People who haven't ever seemed to fit into conventional society find acceptance and self-worth in this most countercultural of settings.

So when Will called together a core crew of thirty or so to stand in the early morning on the barren playa in 1998, he was onto something seminal. They gathered in a circle around a spot that Rod Garrett had sited to pound a metal stake into the ground. This would be the geographical center of Black Rock City—the place where the Man would stand and from which every annular road and radial street would spread.

I rode out to the Gold Spike ceremony in 2016 with Will Roger Peterson. As more and more arrived, we clustered together and renewed old acquaintanceships. When the anticipated number had arrived, Coyote waved the few dozen of us to gather in a circle. The ritual was simple. First came speeches by dignitaries—Coyote, Will Roger Peterson, Michael Mikel, and other old-timers—and crew leaders made welcoming remarks, then each person took a whack at the stake.

Michael spoke briefly but with passion. He reminisced about the first year on the playa, when there were nearly as many people attending this small ceremony as there were at that first 1990 Burn. Back then he looked out across the open playa and declared they were crossing into a territory that would change them forever, and it has. I imagine he harbors—as I do—the belief that it was an extraordinary bit of celestial good fortune that Burning Man found this meager garden, because it grew the culture of the event as few other places could.

In many ways Michael has been the most elusive of the founders, especially in recent years. There is something anachronistic about the way he dresses: Cabela chic with a slouch camo hat, baggy cargo pants, and high boots. It's a worn Western look with a tinge of world-weariness, as if he belongs to an era of rustic prospectors and Nevada saddle tramps. At the event, he prefers to camp on the periphery of the city near the remote walk-in road. I sometimes see him at First Camp receptions, but he's not one to hang out much with the other founders. Always a private person, Michael seems to prefer in these later years to pursue his own interests rather than the broader issues of the organization. He's also been working on slide presentations to a variety of arts organizations on the history of Burning Man, but he seems to set his own agenda.

After Michael, several veteran Burners spoke—those who felt compelled to elaborate on the occasion, which I realized would include almost everyone. At its heart, the ceremony was a sharing of experiences that provides exactly the kind of unified bond that Will envisioned. Several told of the hardships they'd had to overcome to be there, or of the change in their lives that being on the survey and construction crew had wrought. A particularly moving story came from a lanky fellow in a black suit coat, burnt-orange shirt, black jeans, and a black cowboy hat—its DPW patch front and center. He was known as Slim, and he talked of going back to resume chemotherapy as soon as the survey was complete. He'd been warned that venturing into such a harsh environment was a substantial risk, but he allowed that he would not have wanted to miss this opportunity to be with his comrades. "Don't worry," he admonished. "I fully intend to be back here next year!" There was something about his conviction, something about his audacity for wearing a dark, sharply tailored outfit on the hot, parched playa that made me a believer.

There followed a series of teams, each representing different aspects of the build. Some were DPW. Some were transportation or support staff for the workers. Some were office workers led by Fireball, who coordinates between the teams and the powers that be in San Francisco. One particularly amusing group was comprised of women who work as "servers" in either the cafeteria or at the Black Rock Saloon. The women of DPW are a hardy, lusty bunch regardless of whether they sling hash or a hammer. To quote one of them, who shall remain nameless, they can on occasion be "lewd, rude, and crude." The term "cunt" gets tossed around freely and is applied to whomever seems appropriate without

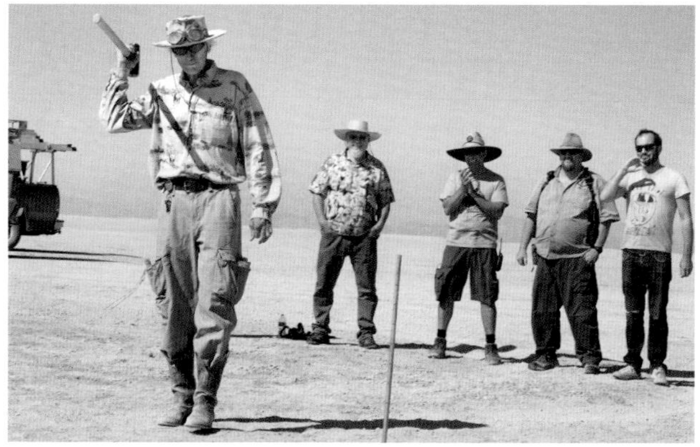

Seeing Michael Mikel hammer the Golden Spike implied a continuum old as the "Zone."

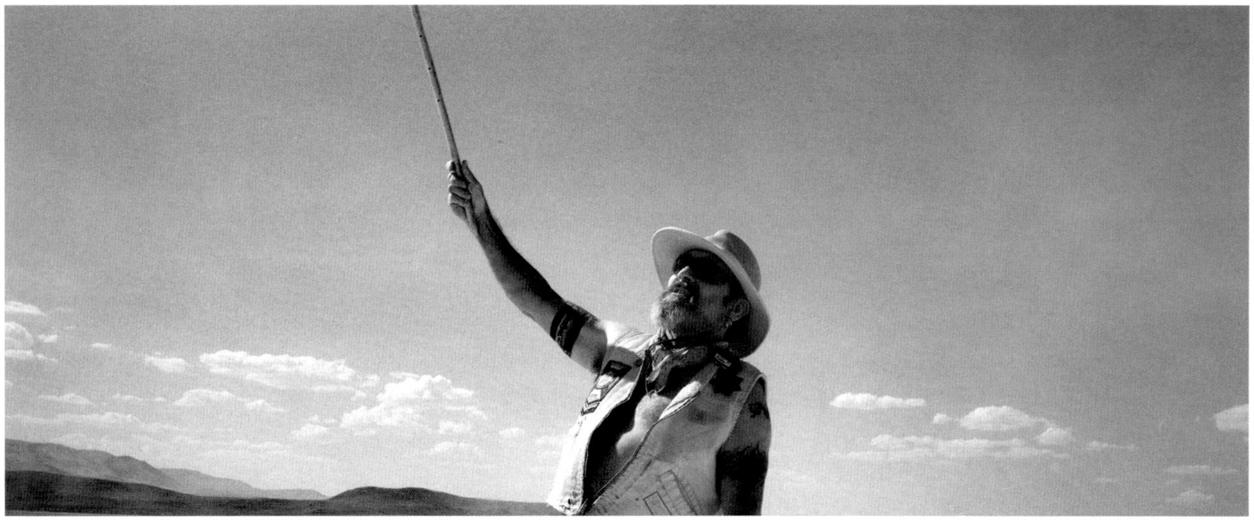

Tony "Coyote" Perez waved the spike like a wand and changed our loose gathering into a ceremony.

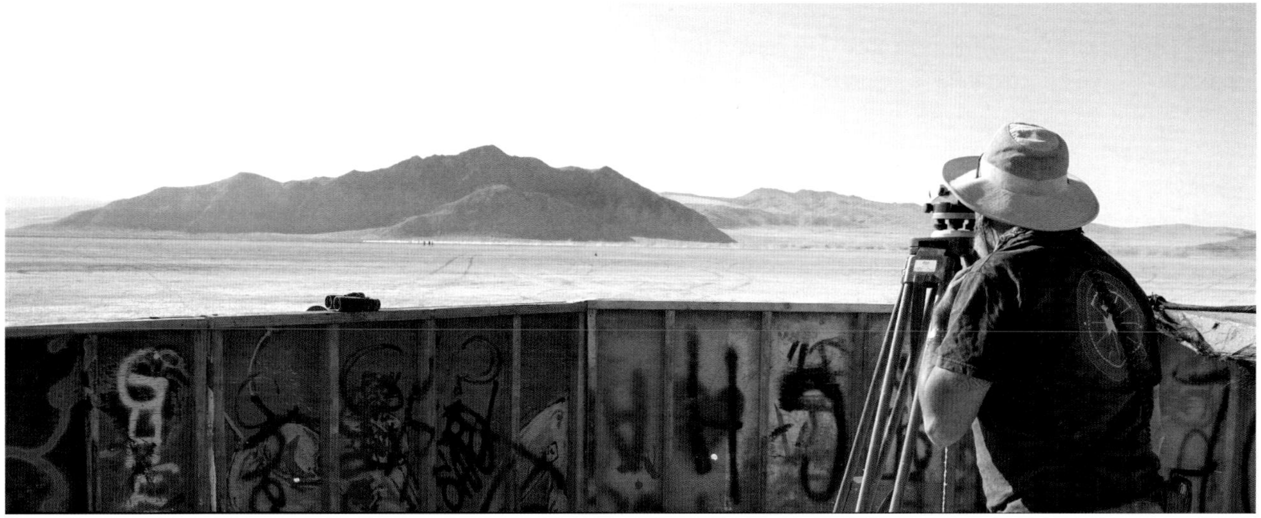

Behind the graffiti-spattered walls of his octagon, Coyote chased an elusive wiggle.

regard to gender. One of these maids of mayhem was able to take three sledgehammer swings while balancing a two-thirds-full bottle of sparkling wine on her head, and she never spilled a drop!

When the speeches were finished, Coyote called upon anyone who hadn't yet struck the spike to come forward and take a lick. There were about half a dozen of us "outsiders" who ventured into the circle to participate in what has become a hallowed tradition. I took my swing, feeling the pleasure at having been asked to join. Tony christened the spike by breaking a bottle of champagne on top of it, and everyone rushed forward to pick up a shard as a souvenir, or maybe it was to MOOP the playa—I couldn't tell. The annual building of Black Rock City was once again underway, and this communal swelter in 104°F was the perfect raggedy kickoff.

Those of us who were leaving gathered our stuff together for the journey back to Gerlach. Coyote and his crew began to prepare for the next morning's survey. They would spend the night in a temporary encampment and the next two weeks staking out Black Rock City. Will and I returned to the lovely house he and Crimson were busy expanding, but I told Coyote I'd be back in the morning to watch the beginning of the survey. I had struggled over whether to sacrifice four days of valuable writing time to come down for the ceremony. I left the playa that afternoon feeling I had made the right decision. This was an encounter at the front lines of Burning Man—something I could never experience at First Camp. "If you want to know about the army," I had told myself, "don't just talk to the Pentagon. Hang with a platoon."

The following morning I returned to the survey site. Tony and his team had built an octagon-shaped surround for the transit that also doubled as a windbreak for sleeping. The transit's plumb bob would swing in the wind as well, so the surround helped keep it steady. All the roads and camps in the city would radiate from the significant center point of the Man. "Degrees and distances magnify as they spread outward," Coyote explained to me. "If I'm off a half degree at center, by the time you get to the Esplanade someone loses thirty feet off the end of their campsite."

It was nearly nine o'clock when I got to the survey area, and already the temperature was nearing 90°F. As I headed back over to Tony in the octagon, I tipped my hat toward Slim and his team. How is it that someone in a battle with cancer would find this brutish task so compelling as to further risk his frail health? What instills such devotion? More than any other factor, this level of volunteer commitment is the vital engine of Burning Man's achievements. But why is it there? It was a question I hoped to answer.

Tony, meanwhile, was in the flow of the survey. He would talk on the radio to three different teams and compare their individual positions relative to himself and to one another. He was tense and preoccupied. If he gets these cardinal positions right, everything else falls into place relative to them and is true. Occasionally, he pulled out a magnifying glass to make sure he was reading the fine adjustments on the transit correctly and then adjusted his position. Something was slightly off, and it bedeviled him. Two of the three positions were solidly in line, but one leg was off by a bit. "There's a wiggle," he declared and got back on the radio. After many back-and-forth adjustments by the team, he was ready to compromise. "The wiggle is still there," he said, "but it's small and won't make much of a difference." The sun was rising higher and hotter. It was time to move along.

The tiny hamlet of Gerlach, Nevada, sits on the shore of the ancient Lake Lahontan and is surrounded on three sides by the alkali remnants of that primordial water. To the west is the Smoke Creek Desert, a small portion of which you cross on the way south to Empire and onward eventually to Reno, over a hundred miles away. To the east is the Black Rock Desert, home to the Burning Man festival and Gerlach's best hope of surviving the twenty-first century. When you arrive in Gerlach from the south, a cheerfully lettered sign proclaims the area to be the CENTER OF THE KNOWN UNIVERSE. The sign also rates the town's attitude as GOOD, and the population is listed as WANTED.

At its peak, in the 1950s, Gerlach boasted a relatively healthy township of a thousand, some of whom worked as ranchers or for the Western Pacific Railroad, but most as employees of the U.S. Gypsum plant in nearby Empire. It's always been a hardscrabble, rock-strewn area with gnarly sagebrush and little arable land. Typically, such remote communities are dominated by a handful of entrepreneurial figures, and Gerlach was no exception. In the 1930s and 1940s, J. J. Thrasher's company provided a variety of local services,

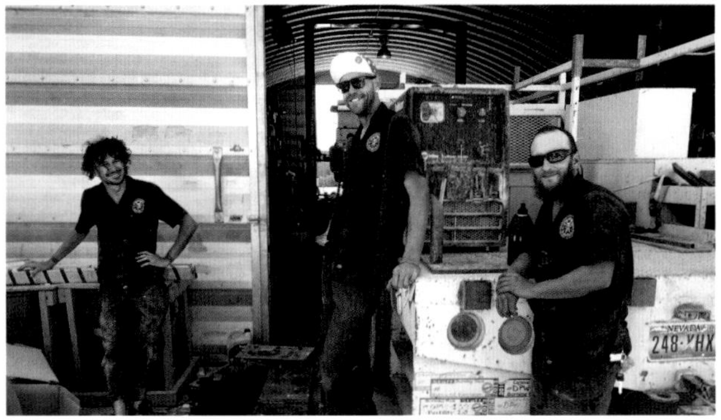

Will Roger Peterson introduced me to Nine Volt, Lil Friend, and Yoder at the Work Ranch auto shop.

including electricity; in the contemporary era, Bruno Selmi put his stamp on much of the town's retail services, including the legendary Bruno's Country Club, which modestly claims to be a motel, café, casino, and saloon. By the time Burning Man arrived in 1990, the town's population had dwindled to four hundred, and that eventually plummeted to a meager one hundred full-time residents after the gypsum plant closed in 2011.

Each May, however, the Burning Man office—housed in what was once the J. J. Thrasher Company building—opens, and the population of Gerlach begins its seasonal transformation. Burning Man has in many ways taken over the town. Besides maintaining the office, they own properties to house and support the crews that build Black Rock City. Over the weeks following the Gold Spike ceremony, a steady stream of workers invades the tiny town. Many are on the survey and build crews, but others concentrate on repair and transportation for the myriad city structures and official vehicles that will constitute BRC. Most of these activities happen at the two-hundred-acre Work Ranch north of Fly Geyser.

The Burning Man Work Ranch is a collection of ramshackle buildings that serve as support offices, rows of vintage art cars, old trailers to accommodate workers on the playa, time-honored sculptures that are often placed around First Camp, and fenced off containers filled with building components that will become Center Camp and other facilities in Black Rock City. There are also several mechanical and wood shops, where skilled workers build, repair, and refurbish the vital logistical elements of the city. *Bone Tree* and *Narwhal* are there, as well as others, like a tall, rusted fire sculpture by David Best and a dragon-inspired fire breather by Dan Macchiarini. The Work Ranch provides logistical support and long-term storage for the entirety of BRC, and it makes building that bustling complex in less than a month possible.

Soon after the city survey has begun, the Work Ranch coordinates with the Burning Man office in Gerlach to employ the heavy equipment needed to transfer city components to the shoreline of the playa. Strategically, the building of Black Rock City is akin to a military operation. Troops of workers are brought into Gerlach, housed and fed in temporary quarters, and then marshaled into the field in teams specific to each task. The marvel is that the entire enterprise functions without much input from Burning Man headquarters in San Francisco. It is one of the more ingenious aspects of an event that still subsists on a significant amount of volunteer labor. The generals may have been planning for months back at headquarters, but the entire success of the operation in the field depends on the dedication of trusted lieutenants and squad leaders, and central to it all is a belief by the legion of workers that their mission is worthwhile—and that doesn't happen overnight.

Part of troop support for the build involves providing a number of free or nearly free accommodations. A cafeteria is essential, as is a place to sleep. A place to drink is also mandatory. Although there are several bars in Gerlach, many workers arrive without much money to spend. Burning Man acquired the Black Rock Saloon in order to provide a place for DPW workers to unwind and, in the spirit of Decommodification, to drink for free. The effect on the local economy is mixed. Estimates place Burning Man's current economic contribution to the town's annual revenue at around 20 percent. In the early days Burning Man relied on local vendors for much of their worker support, but over the decades the organization expanded its food and beverage services, and when it purchased the Black Rock Saloon a few years ago, that took a bite out of the neighboring bars. Early on there were five Gerlach bars, but the Jalisco Club closed in 2001 when owner Joe Pineda died, and that building now houses the Friends of Black Rock High Rock headquarters. To date, Bruno's, Joe's Gerlach Club, and Bev's Miners Club remain in local hands.

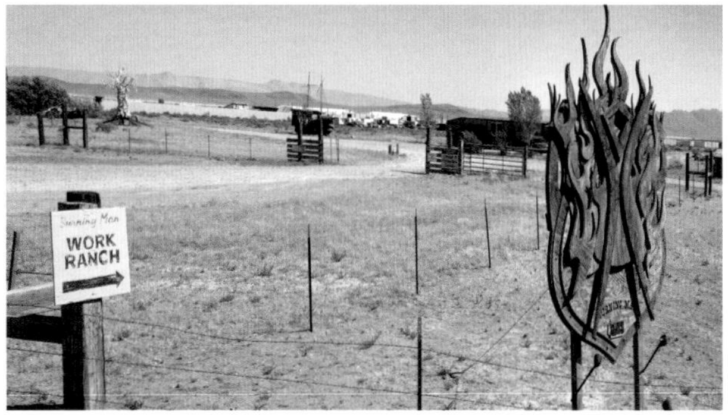

From the Work Ranch gate I could see Dana Albany's Bone Tree *and Pepe's* Narwhal.

Attending the Gold Spike ceremony was an eye-opening glimpse at the raw devotion and steadfast loyalty that comes from offering an opportunity to people who are often marginalized by society. Some are artists, mired in the stagnation of low-wage employment. Some are simply wandering youth looking for a level of personal achievement. Others are lost souls looking for some sort of meaning after years of poor choices. All are hoping to enrich their lives, and that's one of the fundamental attractions to the event. People are drawn to the spirit of Burning Man, and that spirit resides in the myriad selfless acts of generosity and toil that help turn this empty desert into a dusty metropolis. It resides in quiet moments of reflection or in private conversations with a person who a week ago was a total stranger and to whom you now feel a deep kinship. It exists in the hearts and minds of all our fellow travelers to Black Rock City, because people come to the event consciously or unconsciously on a quest for validity and fulfillment.

There is an aspect to attending the event year after year that is no more than seeing old acquaintances. The yearly Burn is the time I look forward to seeing principal contributors and playa friends like Flash, Sting Rae, Nurse Jess, Lightning, Syn,

Haggis, Dustbunny, Lady Bee, Stuart Mangrum, Mags, Chip Martzall, Jeannie Schulz, and on and on. I got to see Flash this year with Larry and Haggis, or Andrew Johnstone if you prefer given names as I usually do, but certain playa names make sense, and Haggis suits this burly Scot to a tee. I used to see him out on the playa wailing on his bagpipes long before I knew his name. Of course, Flash was Flash long before there were playa names, so his name doesn't count, but he and Dan Miller were there in the days before there was a there, and that history counts. Haggis is the chief builder of the Man, and 2016 was a rough year, as construction did not go smoothly. He's a bonny fellow, however, and I was privileged to attend his wedding to the lovely Jeri in 2014 in front of his "Caravansary" Man.

After the Gold Spike ceremony and before I prepared to leave for home, Will and I made a final visit to the area around Fly Ranch and Hualapai Flat. He pointed out the potential not only for creating a year-round Burning Man center but also for staging a series of smaller events there. As 2016's event would prove, the constituency is getting decidedly international, and the idea of creating a center for regional culture is clearly part of the discussion. In less than a month Geoff, Sallie, and I would return for "Da Vinci's Workshop" and my twenty-sixth Burn, but not before taking one last walk around the labyrinth that Will and Crimson had built in their side yard. Crimson Rose lives primarily in their Oakland home, as her principal duties are still carried out at Burning Man headquarters in San Francisco, but she is a student of labyrinths and spent many hours studying traditional designs.

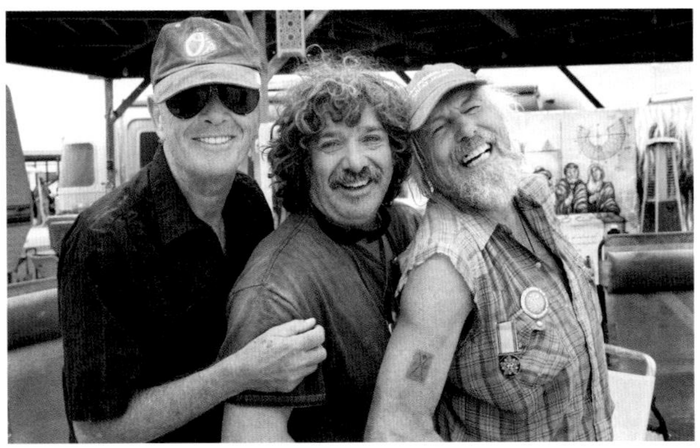

Larry, Haggis, and Flash making like the Three Amigos at a karaoke bar.

She finally settled on the pattern used in twelfth-century Chartres Cathedral. Crimson laid out the design, and Will spent considerable time gathering rocks and sacred objects to form the boundaries of its pathways. In the center, he placed a vertical shard of selenite, which is a crystalline form of gypsum, the material that was once the lifeblood of Gerlach's economy. This example was nearly three feet high and glowed a rosy hue in late-afternoon light. During my stay, Will walked the labyrinth nightly at sundown, and I joined him each evening. Several of their friends have walked the labyrinth, and many have left little sacred objects lodged in the stones. I added a partial cow femur that had been attached to *Bone Arch* on Hualapai Flat in 1997. The repetition of walking these loopy switchbacks combined with the arid atmosphere created a tranquil respite, and I could almost feel the tension fall from my shoulders into the crunching gravel at my feet.

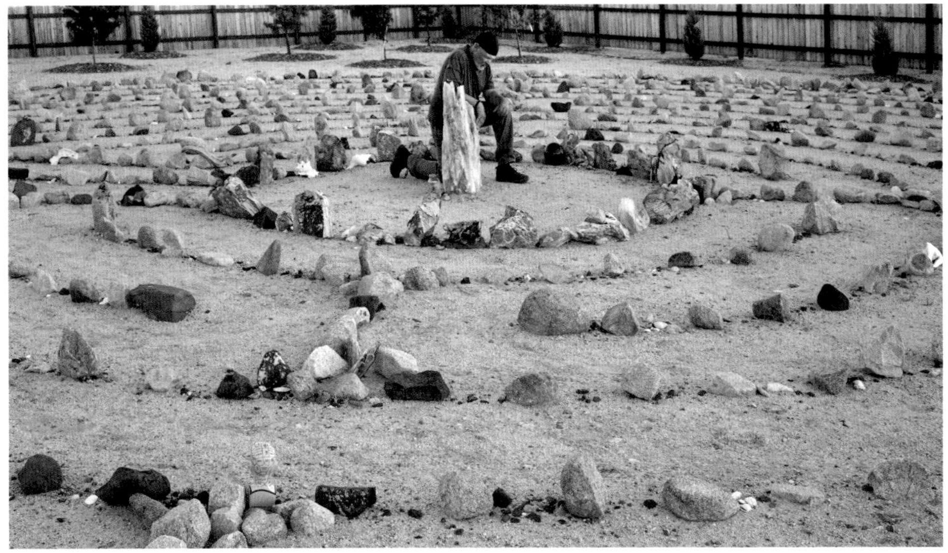

I envied Will's nightly walk in their labyrinth, and I aspire to build one of my own.

Will and Crimson are spiritual souls, and one of the pleasures of staying in their home was seeing how they've responded to the beauty and serenity inherent in a place far away from urban dissonance. Marian Goodell once remarked that one of the oddities of Burning Man's evolution is that none of the current founders were particularly well qualified to grow and manage what has turned out to be a cultural juggernaut. "A venture capitalist would have thought we were a joke," she said, laughing. "Imagine, a nude model [Crimson], a photographer and grip [Will], a guy who mows lawns [Larry the landscaper], a guy who makes neon signs [Michael], an aerobics instructor [Harley], and a person who does web work [Marian] are going to pull this shit off for fifteen years!" She was exaggerating for effect, of course, as each of them possesses extraordinary drive and the ability to explore uncharted territory. They all sacrificed job security for a higher purpose—a characteristic that is essential when reinventing and elevating the cultural ceiling of a fire festival.

Crimson Rose first saw the Man in a grainy video that Louis Brill showed her after the 1990 Burn. Louis was one of the first chroniclers of Burning Man and an old friend of Larry's. Crimson was initially unimpressed, but later that year she saw the Man displayed on a barge at Fort Mason. "When they started pulling up the Man, something hit me," she remembered. "And later when a man [Flamo LaGrande] lit the Man with a dragon's breath, I thought, 'My God, I have to go. I have to go.'" She went to the desert in 1991 and volunteered to assist with the lighting ceremony. "I happened to bring my sixteen-foot silk wings," she continued, "and you captured that great photo." It had also been a seminal moment for me.

It was the first image at Burning Man I'd made that felt like more than a documentary—it felt like a revelation.

These days I love to proceed out to the Burn with Crimson's Fire Conclave. It feels like being part of the show, and it connects me with the Burn. Crimson works with over thirty groups of fire artists from all over the world, and when these sixteen hundred souls come together for this pageant, they become instruments for transporting the crowd of Burners into an open and receptive head space. The processioners begin by lighting their torches from a cauldron in Center Camp, and they follow this lone woman, who takes slow, measured strides through all manner of crowd confusion and blinding dust. Over the years Crimson and her dancers have brought fire to the Man, and that time-honored ritual elevates the sacrifice of our humanoid mentor.

Spending four days reconnecting with Gerlach and these denizens of the desert renewed my affinity for long shadows and old stones. In the morning I headed down the road to Reno and the flight home, but I was taking back more than I had hoped to find. To overcome the overused oxygen of the city, one needs from time to time to take in the rarefied air of the remote and unspoiled. Even if that air is 104°F and dust laden. I came away from Gerlach and the Gold Spike refreshed by the knowledge that much of the soulful magic of Burning Man was already present in the rocks and hardscrabble existence of life on the edge of next-to-nowhere—all it had needed was a few hundred hardy souls with hopeful hearts and boundless determination.

Though the spectacle of the death and subsequent resurrection of the Man is seductive and timeless, I'm becoming increasingly convinced that the burning of the effigy is not the most important thing that happens at Black Rock City.

Don't get me wrong. It's the raison d'être of the event, and it's very powerful as a spiritual touchstone, but it's not where the magic hides—at least not the magic I crave. I felt some of that magic as a dedicated few whacked on a gold-painted stake in the middle of nowhere, and I felt some magic walking among Will and Crimson Rose's labyrinth, and I felt it in the swirling sand while talking with a bunch of sun-bedeviled individualists who'd just spent the day on the griddle-hot surface of the playa in a concerted effort to extend its true center—it's the sense that nothing is impossible. I've also seen it on faces during a playa sunrise, on the faces of temple builders, and on the faces of dust-covered volunteers at the gate. It's a look, really, a sense that something has changed, and though it's never clear what that alteration is, even the slightest variation from routine life as usual is a good sign. As I see it, Burning Man's magic flows to and from everyone who believes in the promise of transformational experience and who willingly and unselfishly gives of their time and energy to turn that promise into a reality. The inspiration for that devotion may flow from the top down, but the magic flows from the ground up.

As Burns go, 2016 was a mixed year. The theme, "Da Vinci's Workshop," generated many inspired attempts to blend science and art; however, unfortunate circumstances prevailed. The pavilion under the Man was designed as the workshop courtyard, an homage to the Renaissance master's ingenuity. The Man was splayed on a wheel that had been incorporated into a series of wooden gears like a mill wheel, which was intended to be turned via ropes and a wooden transmission. In theory, participants pulling on the rope mechanism would cause the Man to rotate. The idea was plausible; the execution was not. During initial testing, a major bolt kept sheering off, and consequently interactivity with the Man was thwarted. More seriously, trying to repair the malfunction caused a three-day delay in opening the pavilion. Without its planned interactivity, the entire complex was reduced to the level of a da Vinci display at a science fair.

Fortunately there were many high-level art installations, and David Best's temple was another masterwork, this time evoking the sacred aura of Tibet. It was perhaps his most passionate

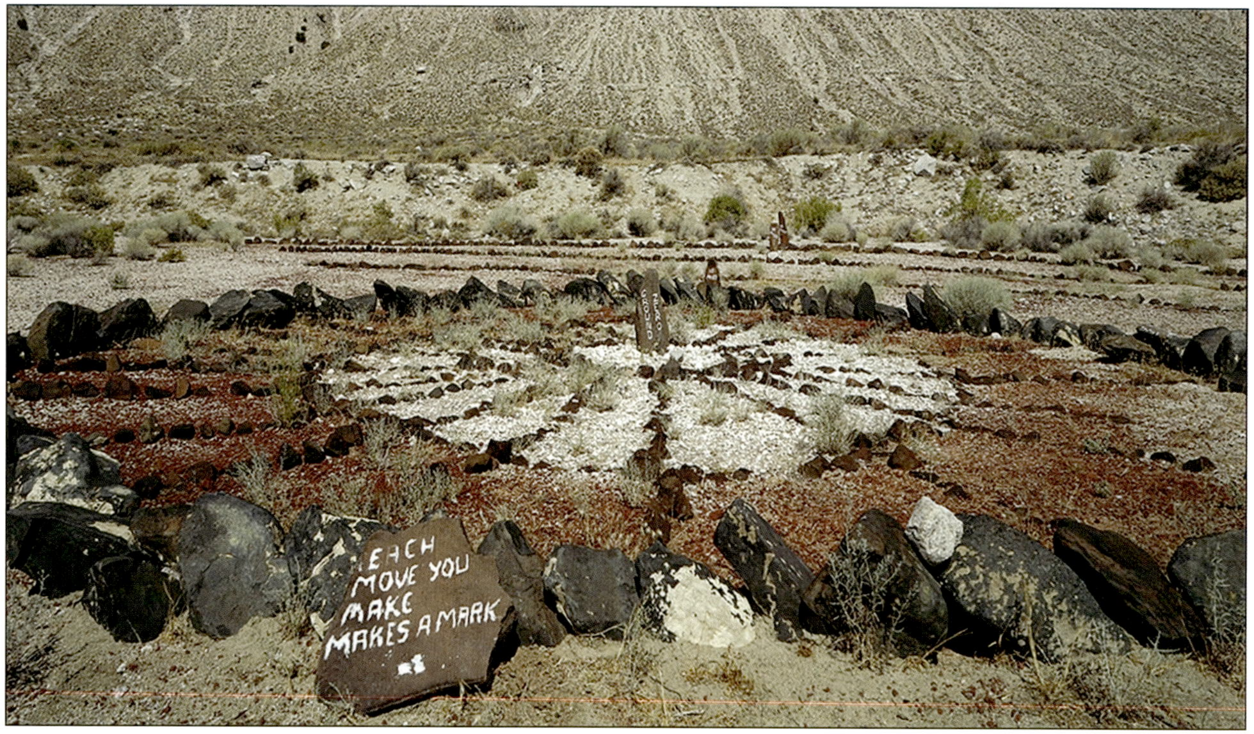

Much of the message of Burning Man was already present in the rocks around Gerlach.

and inspiring effort. Its tall pagoda shape was surrounded by a series of basket-shaped sentries with gold spires, all of which were stained like dark tea, using gallons of vinegar and steel wool. The temple towered before the glowing sky like a holy relic from an ancient age. It inspired instant reverence, and the memorial response by people was overwhelming. Hundreds of Burners were waiting for it to open, and they spent hours lost in memory and private grief. David said it would be his last playa temple, and though he's said that before, I suspect he means it this time. If so, he's going out on a very high note.

I had hoped this year's theme would generate the kind of interactive interest that "Caravansary" did, but while that never happened, the theme did inspire many da Vinci–esque installations and activities, including *The Last Supper* renderings, flying machines, and a splendid profile casting of Leonardo's head partially buried in the playa. Titled *Inside the Mind of da Vinci* (by Phoenix Rising and Wrecking House), it featured some of his drawings and sketches on the back side of the head. Other popular pieces featured Leonardo's design for the solar system, a spiral helicopter, and a museum of Renaissance-style paintings.

Several theme camps produced activities designed around Leonardo, and Children of Chaos was a prime contributor. Portland animator Joanna Priestly came up with the idea of a tableau vivant of Leonardo's *Last Supper* called *The Last Summer*. Here the position and expression of each apostle was carefully rendered to mimic the painting except that Jesus and his disciples were all played by women in 1950s swimwear. The lone female (the alleged Mary Magdalene) was played by Bryan. The twelve gathered together behind a table in an area in front of the Man. Placers, accompanied with reference copies of Leonardo's original, helped pose each of the "disciples" in the clusters of three that are part of the famous original. Once everyone was in position, lead photographer Michael Holden directed the exposures. Geoff and I did backup duties, as neither one of us could commit to the original schedule of the evening before. I'm proud of the way Children of Chaos participates in the yearly theme, and yet they are far from alone. As iconic as large playa art has become over the years, I would argue that it's the volunteer parades, pageants, camp themes, and costumed events that are the secret surprises awaiting attendees each year and that truly capture the essence of what Participation at Burning Man is about. At the end of the tableau, only a lucky few that happened by got to see what had taken weeks of planning and preparation to achieve, and yet it was this unheralded glory of doing a performance for its own sake that made it a pure act of Participation.

So, where does it all come from, and where is it going? Artists, of course, have vision and determination and construction plans, and then they fund-raise and gather crews to fulfill those visions. But art is simply the most visible and obvious reason why people might come to Burning Man. It's not just about the Burning Man organization either, because even though they are the driving force for the event, and more importantly, they are the stewards of the event's future, they can only account for the planning and logistical details. What they can inspire but never control is the extraordinary loyalty and determination of the servants to the cause. The more pertinent question is where does the energy come from, the will to create this city of roads and plazas, with its nearly one thousand placed theme camps, its central complex of walkways and roads with lighted spires? And what's its ultimate destination as a cultural phenomenon?

The acquisition of Fly Ranch in the spring of 2016 broadened the vista for the future of Burning Man, and at this writing, virtually every scenario is under discussion. The most common notion is that an educational center might be established at the ranch, but there is wide disagreement as to what kind of physical presence that might entail. Each of the founders has their own ideas on the matter, but all are adamant that what they don't want is an elaborate conference facility, nor do they want a complex of buildings—no Burning Man Institute, at least not in the conventional sense. Most envision a gradual evolution into year-round activities and structures that fit seamlessly into the landscape.

Will Roger Peterson, the founder most involved in relations with Nevada, is excited by the prospect of helping to revive the local economy of Gerlach. What Fly Ranch could represent is the opportunity for a permanent staff and an

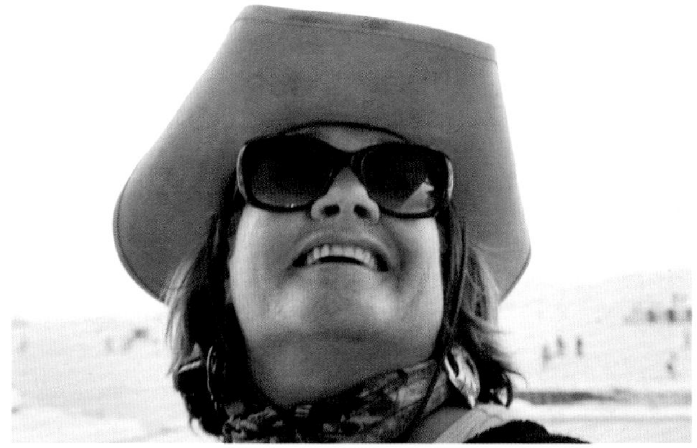
Harley is the chief transition officer.
Marian says Burning Man's always in transition.

annual series of events that would generate local business several months in the year. Winters can be tough in the area, but adding education programs or smaller events in the spring and fall would be a tonic to an economy that has been in recession for decades. He also sees potential for long-term expansion onto other areas of BLM land that aren't being used for much of anything. It's all speculation, of course, but Burning Man is uniquely situated to pioneer an innovative arts and cultural vortex in a region that has heretofore been in decline.

The chief area of concern for Will and all the founders is how to develop a viable arts and educational center within an ecosystem that is extremely fragile. The area around Fly Ranch and Fly Geyser is a mixture of grassland, sagebrush, warm water, light crusted playa, and wildlife. There are genuine questions concerning the number of people that could inhabit this delicate region without doing significant harm. True, there was a Burning Man held on Hualapai Flat in 1997, but there are remnants of that event still present, and the attendance then was around ten thousand, not the seventy thousand of today.

What most of the founders can agree on is furthering the advancement of Burning Man culture—a global arts and civic philosophy based on the Ten Principles. All of them have come to believe that what has evolved on the Black Rock

Desert over the past thirty years is worth sharing. It is to that end that the nonprofit Burning Man Project was founded. Harley K. Dubois effected the transfer of responsibilities from Black Rock City LLC to the nonprofit, a convoluted task that required the consolidating and shuffling of departments. Harley has been managing the departments in BRC since the late 1990s onward. In many ways that's her highest and best calling. She began by getting people enthusiastic about creating their own theme camps, and she has continued in that vein by finding out what people most want out of their jobs, then making sure it's a good fit for both them and the group. Harley is a boots-on-the-ground manager, and her strong suit is helping people rise to their full potential and realize their own best and highest calling to service.

Going to the Black Rock Desert is for many people a powerful and life-altering experience. Most of them have never witnessed the coming together of both uninhibited exhilaration and unbridled generosity, and it may seem like a blending of heretofore opposing values. Many hold to the traditional ecclesiastical view that you could either be a wastrel or a righteous person of service, but not a "wastrel in service." Burning Man suggests that being individually expressive and self-reliant need not be at the expense of civic concerns and generosity. In other words, selflessness is not a prerequisite to being of service. I would argue that it's only a person who has a firmly developed sense of self who can be truly generous. That's

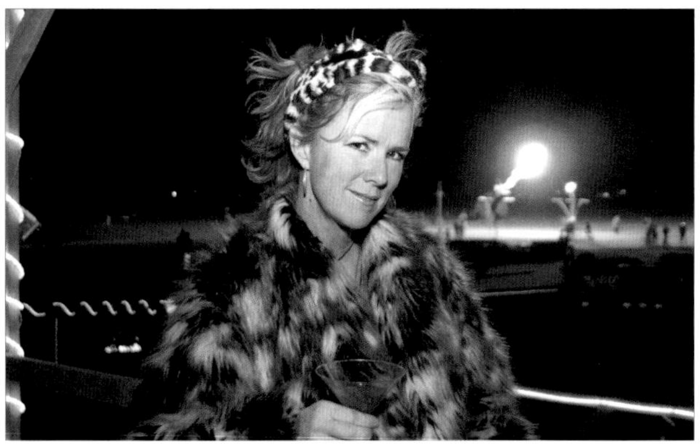

Maid Marian is the CEO (chief engagement officer) of the Burning Man Project.

a notion I inherited from Shorty Harvey. He called it having character.

The revelation of the playa is that while some people have transformational personal experiences in the midst of random acts of kindness, they do so without sacrificing their autonomy. It's a delicate balance, maintaining equilibrium between individual autonomy and the needs of the community, but it's possible. When the individual and the communal merge, it can become transformational. Harley maintains that Burning Man's highest goal is to "provide an opportunity for transformation."

She also mentioned that Burning Man has a hundred-year goal. When I asked what that was, she declared, "Our goal is to still be transforming lives in a way that is relevant to where the world is at in a hundred years." It's an ambitious goal, but not impossible, because the event has always moved forward in thoughtful and measured ways.

"How do you see the future of Burning Man?" I asked Harley.

"Do you mean the event in the desert or Burning Man?" she responded. "I call the event in the desert BRC, as it's clearer," she continued. "There are a lot of ways we could lose the event in the desert: we could lose our contract with the BLM or we could have terrible weather, and that might kill the event temporarily, but if we reach the point when people can have an anonymous experience at the event and not engage with the community or the culture, then we've lost much more. The goal really is to spread the culture globally, and that isn't dependent on BRC."

"Yes," I chimed in. "I think the regional events are the most exciting thing to happen in the past decade."

"'Regional' is too limited a word," she countered. "We were thinking too small when we developed that lexicon. We hope to foster opportunities for transformational experience around the world."

When I asked her how transformation happens, she resorted to a gardening metaphor. "Each year we look at what worked at the event and what didn't. We've been tending this garden for many years, and our job is to separate the flowers from the weeds. Each year it becomes harder and harder to tell the healthy plants from the weeds. If we get to the point when we can't tell one from the other, it'll be time to quit." She laughed. "One thing we're doing is codifying what we've learned about creating an opportunity for transformation. Everything we've learned about putting on the event for so many years is being written down and being made available online for people to read. We've created a Philosophical Center on our website so that people in a hundred years can read about what we've learned and apply it to their own lives." When I asked how she sees her role in the organization, her answer was simple and straightforward. "I'm where the rubber meets the road in terms of what I do on a daily basis," she offered in a matter-of-fact voice. "I hold us to our values."

The most exciting news for the Burning Man Project was clearly the purchase of Fly Ranch, but what is equally clear was that no agreement has been reached as to what Fly Ranch means to the future of the event. "I tell people we bought this piece of property in advance of knowing what it was going to do," CEO Marian Goodell has said. Speculations aside, what gets assimilated into Burning Man is a study in the slow evolution of ideas and the school of hard knocks. The success of the event in the desert has been nothing if not a process of trial and error. Harley's metaphor of the event as a garden seems apt: Flowers are what works over the long haul; weeds are what inhibit that growth. One nurtures the flowers and plucks the weeds.

Talking to Marian reinforces that model. The contemporary era of Burning Man was nurtured by six people who, for the most part, learned by doing. Larry thought to burn a figure because he understood the importance of primal symbolism in stimulating a deeply felt response, but he was working mostly on an artistic impulse. Over the succeeding thirty years that simple act of whimsy has grown into a worldwide celebration of individual creativity and the power of a generous and supportive community to effect cultural change. Marian would say that Larry provides "the spark," and the rest provide the structure and administration. Original thought is an ultra-rare phenomenon, and it only happens occasionally in a generation, but that's what my brother contributed and continues to contribute. I'm quite sure there would have been no Burning Man without him, and I'm not sure it will remain a force for innovative culture without him. On the other hand, his thinking wouldn't have amounted to much more than table talk without the steadfast support and organizational skills of all the people who have come to Burning Man and left their considerable marks.

Each of the original founders, going all the way back to Jerry James, has added something vital to the legacy of the event by way of their personal energy and ideas. Ironically, almost none of them had experience with festival culture prior to becoming involved with Burning Man, although one could certainly argue that the Cacophony Society provided the blueprint for the intertwining of radical expression with crowd dynamics. In a conversation with two of the best minds of the modern organization, Stuart Mangrum and Caveat Magister (Benjamin Wachs), I was happy to discover that subversive attitude—so much a part of the Cacophony years on the playa (1990 to 1996)—is still alive and well. Caveat would be the first to say that Burning Man has absolutely no intention or ability to provide anyone with a transformative experience, and he's right. Experience isn't a gift you dole out like Mardi Gras beads. People may have a life-altering moment at Burning Man, and many have made the claim, but it's their personal experience, and they're responsible for it having happened. No event can choreograph a significant emotional reaction. At most, it might be able to create an exquisite opportunity.

As Caveat puts it, "'Transformative' and 'transformational' were useful words at one point, words which sometimes did good work. But because Burning Man is hard to describe we leaned on these words too heavily, and eventually even came to frequently confuse an effect that Burning Man culture has (it transforms people) with a primary characteristic of the thing itself (What's Burning Man? It's transformational)."

Overseeing what Caveat describes as a "master class in social transformation" is Marian's team at Burning Man headquarters. There are upward of seventy full- and part-time staff members who handle everything from choosing grant artists to overseeing the production of each year's event. Coordinating such a massive undertaking is a complex task, and Marian and Harley are the generals in charge of the command center. Marian is very much a hands-on CEO. She's a tireless whirling

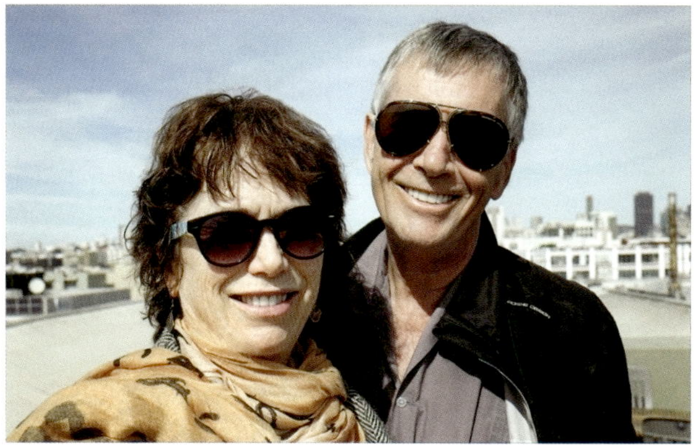

Forty years after moving to San Francisco, Larry and Jan still enjoy a warm friendship.

dervish who is seemingly everywhere at once. Her life is a never-ending series of meetings, and she oversees virtually every aspect of the event. Her sense of dedication to the event is seconded only by her dedication to the Ten Principles. Equal responsibility is at the heart of her managerial style, and she has ruffled the feathers of more than one playa VIP or lazy relative at the Burn by insisting that they roll up their sleeves and help with the chores.

Larry's "spark," as Marian puts it, typically begins with creating the theme for the coming year's event. It's the sacred seed of creative stimulation. These days Larry works with Stuart and Caveat to refine the theme and decide what it is that they hope it will accomplish. They understand that stimulating participation and engagement is the surest route to providing the possibility of transformative experience. The most successful themes have been the ones people respond to in large numbers and with a high degree of enthusiasm and creativity. A genuinely moving experience isn't simply a matter of happenstance. A lot of effort goes into establishing an environment where people can come away feeling personally moved, as if they've been *somewhere* instead of just *anywhere*, and that's no small feat.

While Caveat correctly states that Burning Man has "no ability to provide anyone with a transformative experience," I think he might readily admit that the crafters of the event work very hard to provide the opportunity for such a change. To imply that it may be no more than an existential accident is to deny the forces that stimulate and provoke our deepest thoughts and feelings. Larry's 2017 theme, "Radical Ritual," seems to be perfectly in tune with that tradition. Burning Man has been evoking ancient mysticism in its central ceremony from the very beginning. I think the not-so-small miracle of my brother's inspiration in 1986 is that it has led to an experiential banquet and a metaphysical smorgasbord. It has become a bold celebration of individual initiative and a site for creative adventuring. It has stimulated the development of a wise, supportive, and compassionate community. And finally, it has enabled individuals to engage their longing for the ethereal without an accompanying mythology or dogma. To me, that's the trifecta of human aspiration.

Marian talked to me about what first attracted her to Burning Man and then eventually to my brother: "I came to Burning Man because a woman brought some incredible shots of the first year on the playa to a photo class at the Academy of Art in 1992. These pink and orange sunsets with this wooden structure—I'll never forget them. Me and this other guy were really excited by them. 'Where is that?' we both said in unison." The other guy turned out to be Joe Maggiore, whom Marian once dated and who took her to her first Burning Man in 1995. "I went to Burning Man with Joe," Marian continued, "and I had this amazing reaction, and a vision that I needed to know why I was having this incredible experience. From the moment I arrived till the moment I left, I was completely stimulated by the environment, by the people, by the sounds, by the weather, by the engagement with other people." She paused. "Joe and I went back in 1996, and I made it a mission to find out everything I could about why I had had this amazing experience. I sought out the founders and introduced myself, and then back in San Francisco I met Larry again at a party at Miss P.'s, and we started dating." She paused again. "I had never dated someone so interesting, and I had dated a lot of really interesting people, but Larry was the most intelligent, quirky, brilliant, and deep thinking, and broad—like broad! Larry's mind is full of history and philosophy and urban planning and literature and politics, and all those things together made it so compelling for me to be there with him."

Marian's arrival in the fall of 1996 coincided with the breakup of the triumvirate and the splintering of the relationship between Burning Man and Cacophony. John Law not only left the group but also took several of the principal players with him, including Stuart Mangrum, who had been doing the newsletter and who had created the first web presence for the event. Marian added, "I came along in the middle of a crisis, but I was working for a web design company, and I thought, 'I can help fix this.'" It was Marian who suggested Burning Man register its own domain, and she created *The Jackrabbit Speaks*, which remains the official newsletter of Burning Man. "We rolled out the first BurningMan.com website in true Cacophony style on April 1, 1997. With Rusty Hodge, Scott Beal, who is now Laughing Squid, and Eric Waterman," she recalled. "Of course I had to prove myself." She laughs. "People would ask 'Who's that girlfriend?'"

As I look down the road, it is apparent that many of these intertwining relationships have played and will continue to play a pivotal role in Burning Man's future. The six donors, who made the acquisition of Fly Ranch possible, are simply the tip of a very broad ice floe of Burning Man support. People from all over the globe are becoming part of their future strategy. This spring a contingent from the organization, including Stuart Mangrum (who returned to the fold a few years ago) and Crimson Rose, were invited to attend the centuries-old Las Fallas fire festival in Valencia, Spain. What is abundantly clear from the success of global Burning Man events is that the "event in the desert" is no longer the sole vehicle for spreading the culture of the Ten Principles.

Like Harley K. Dubois, Marian Goodell was equally adamant that the future of Burning Man and the event in the desert are not necessarily one and the same. "I could foresee a day when we would no longer depend on the event on the Black Rock Desert for our identity," she mused. "Our discussions these days all center around what's the best way to spread the culture, and that may not always be tied to Black Rock City or even to the name Burning Man." I'm not sure I'm convinced, but with the clamor for limited tickets the need for associated events is pressing. Fly Ranch, with its proximity to a wondrous geyser and diminutive playa, seems to me to be the logical place to host these kinds of events, but the future of Fly Ranch remains a matter for prolonged discussion.

Having no official standing whatsoever, I see no harm in my looking down the road at possibilities or at what seems most likely to me at this early stage of the conversation. First of all, there is a need for additional smaller events throughout the year in order to absorb some of the pressure for tickets to the main event, and Fly Ranch and the adjacent Hualapai Flat are logical, if fragile, sites. A number of suggestions include an educational center, artist-in-residence programs, a place to invite representatives from around the globe for seminars, and curated art events, which might replicate the BRC experience. Larry also sees a fairly broad spectrum of possibilities and feels strongly that Black Rock City is still the proven site for fostering cultural experience. For me, the most interesting glimpse into the bubbling stew of his ruminations came near the end of a recent conversation when he said offhandedly, "You know, we could build a temple out there."

John Law reportedly joked back in the mid-1990s that the next thing that would happen was Burning Man would become a religion. In my opinion, this underscores the core of the philosophical differences between Larry Harvey and John Law. Law saw Burning Man as a place for crafting a temporary radical utopia freed from societal conventions, and Larry always saw Burning Man as an instrument of social change. As an "atheist by conviction," founding a religion would be as alien to my brother as it would be to the adherents of Hakim Bey's notion of a Temporary Autonomous Zone, but a temple? Now, a temple is quite another matter. David Best has proved that an edifice that ministers to universal grief and memorializes loss can speak to most of humanity. I immediately envisioned a contemplative space like the Rothko Chapel in Houston or maybe something as provocative and arty as Michael Garlington's *Photo Chapel* from 2013.

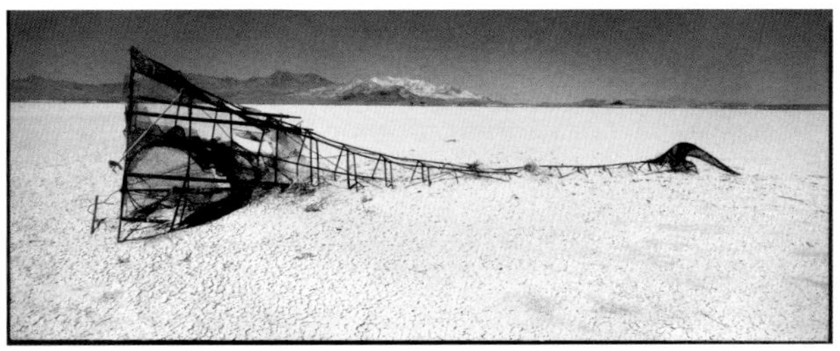

In 1997, on diminutive Hualapai Flat,
Burning Man inaugurated a city and left a trace.

The Burning Man presence on Black Rock Desert provides two essential elements to the human spirit: a place to aspire and a place to feel at home. Those are the twin desiderata of life on Earth. Without them we are forever hopeless and in pain. With them all things are possible and bearable. This is the spirit of the promise and the soul of the legacy of Burning Man—a genuine experience and an opportunity for transformation. Yes, thousands of people attend the Burn each year and come away with little more than blisters and a hangover. As Caveat pugnaciously suggests, spiritual renewal is not the point of Burning Man; it is utterly pointless. Yet I warm to the idea of a temple near Fly Geyser; I think it would be fitting and powerful.

This narrative began as a story about two adopted kids from a small farm in the outskirts of provincial Portland, Oregon, who did all right. Stewart met and married Lynda, and they were rewarded with a wonderful son. Larry visited San Francisco for the Summer of Love and discovered a thriving bohemia that promised to sate his long-sequestered dreams. Eventually, he and his companion, Janet Lohr, moved to the Haight-Ashbury district to satisfy the creative longings of a child of meager means and lofty principles. The spawn of this twisty odyssey turned out to be nothing short of a cultural lodestone, and though they separated in 1981, their relationship has remained intertwined and supportive. It was Jan who helped take care of Tristan when he was an infant, and she provided much-needed support in the early iterations of Burning Man. I'm glad their continuity survives.

In February of 2016 I visited Larry and spent time at Burning Man headquarters. It was a bit intimidating. It's a dervish of a place with a high-efficiency atmosphere, and it's abundantly clear that Burning Man has its administrative act together. I left with mixed feelings, and mixed feelings are not unfamiliar in my long sojourn with Burning Man. There have always been moments when, after the Man has collapsed in a shower of sparks and the crowd has rushed forward to dance and whoop it up, I would disengage from photography to wander the coolness of the empty playa. I'd walk out into the darkness and feel truly alone for the first time in a week. Occasionally I'd pause to look back at the fading flames and listen to the muffled throb of the crowd, and I'd feel a mixture of awe and sadness. I have always been in awe of what my brother and the other founders have wrought; this is a significant moment in the evolution of American radical culture, and I am fortunate to have been a witness. But there is also a sadness that I never joined the crew. I guess it's the lot of most photographers; we witness history but rarely make it. It's why I joined David's temple crew in Derry last year, and will again.

When Will Roger and I walked out on Hualapai Flat in June of 2016, we encountered several relics from the 1997 Burn. It presented us with a psychological dilemma. No responsible Burner would leave trash or, worse, MOOP behind. But I have to admit, it was nostalgic to see these fragile remnants of our having been present there those many years ago. It felt a bit like discovering a long-hidden cave of primitive drawings, or shards of pottery from an aboriginal culture. Leaving No Trace has been a dictum of Burning Man since it first set foot on the playa, but to leave *utterly* no trace introduces its own conundrum. If you actually leave no trace at all, has your being there been of any value? I guess I would say it depends on the nature of the trace you leave behind, and Fly Ranch allows for the possibility of leaving behind examples of enlightened thought, creative achievement, and bold cultural influence. I would take pride in leaving behind that kind of a trace.

In 1990, when Bryan and I drove ten hours from our home in Portland, Oregon, to the dust-covered wasteland called the Black Rock Desert, we brought with us naive curiosity and little more. The playa was an intimidating and utterly foreign environment, and yet I felt at home in the presence of the alien effigy that would perish in the flames there—he so easily inhabited the horizon and his place on Earth. The desert's boundaries appeared limitless and suggested that anything you could imagine making would belong there. Burning Man has always had a soul at its core, and soul begets spirit, and spirit is released through genuine and deeply felt experience. When Michael Mikel drew that line in the playa sand that first year and said, "On the other side of this line everything will be different. Reality itself will change," perhaps he might have added, "and all things will be possible."

The morning I left Gerlach, after the Gold Spike had been hammered deep and the survey crew were busy at their work, I drove Will's truck back up to Hualapai Flat. I sat for a time and looked out at what might be the future center for Burning Man and thought about its past. Not with nostalgia for 1990s Black Rock or Baker Beach, or for the many miles Bryan and I had traversed through barren land to get there, or even for my thirty years of aging and adventuring in the proximity of such a cultural juggernaut. No, I was thinking of the long-ago past. I've been to ancient sites, recently the ruins of Tikal and Teotihuacán, and when Lynda and I stood atop the Pyramid of the Sun, I felt a vague urge to reconcile the long span of human history with the brevity of human life. Here we stood on a temple of extraordinary majesty, amid a city complex as accomplished as the Greeks', and yet precious little is known about the people who built it.

I've been in touch with Burning Man from the moment the idea first popped into my brother's head thirty years ago, but the truth is, I didn't truly "get" Burning Man until I traveled to Derry to help David Best build a temple. I had gone as a photographer, the endless observer, but one can only learn so much from observation, and taking repetitive pictures all day long is a waste of pixels. David tolerates only so much standing around, and he hates it when one person waylays another in conversation. I soon learned that if I wasn't making photographs, I'd better be productive in another way. So, I picked up a nail gun and pitched in.

It was there, in an ancient land of carefully laid stones and centuries of faith, where I came truly to embrace the possibility of individual healing and change. Of course no change is permanent—change itself is a constant in our lives—but the fact that change is possible even for a little while is a comfort. What I discovered in Northern Ireland is that no amount of knowledge or observation can substitute for rolling up your sleeves and participating, and that lesson was reinforced by the rough-hewn hammer swingers of the Gold Spike. I'd like to think that offering that opportunity to people mired in the mundanity of their lives is itself a noble pursuit. I've come to realize that after witnessing the evolution of Burning Man, I'm only just beginning to glimpse its cultural potential. While great value lies in providing a unique opportunity for cultivating personal change, it is abundantly clear that real transformation is also a mysterious and elusive process.

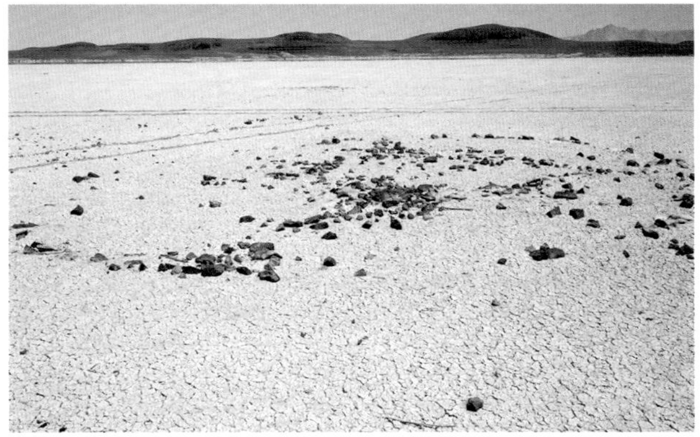

There is an anomaly to Leaving No Trace, as it's dependent on the trace you leave.

When Will and I ventured out onto Hualapai Flat a couple of days before, I had found an oddly circular cluster of stones. We thought it might be the remnants of an art piece from 1997 or perhaps evidence of some transient campers from more recent times, but neither of those notions was satisfactory. The stones seemed arranged in a deliberate pattern that defied easy explanation, and yet there was also a randomness that defined them as well. Likewise, when I stare at their photograph, it's like looking at one of those optical-illusion puzzles. At moments the clustered stones resemble a swirling nebula; at other times I see Black Rock City with its dense central community and radiating outward, flowing art installations, theme camps, and the occasional lone individual biking or jogging the perimeter fence. It's how I imagine the future of Burning Man: a galaxy of possibility. It follows their tried-and-true mixture of deliberately orchestrated design mated to inspired happenstance. Prolonged staring into those deftly scattered rocks feels to me like gazing toward dark stars in an infinity of bright space or at prescient tea leaves sprawled across the bottom of a vast celestial cup.

CHAPTER 16

A TEMPLE IN DERRY: A POSTSCRIPT

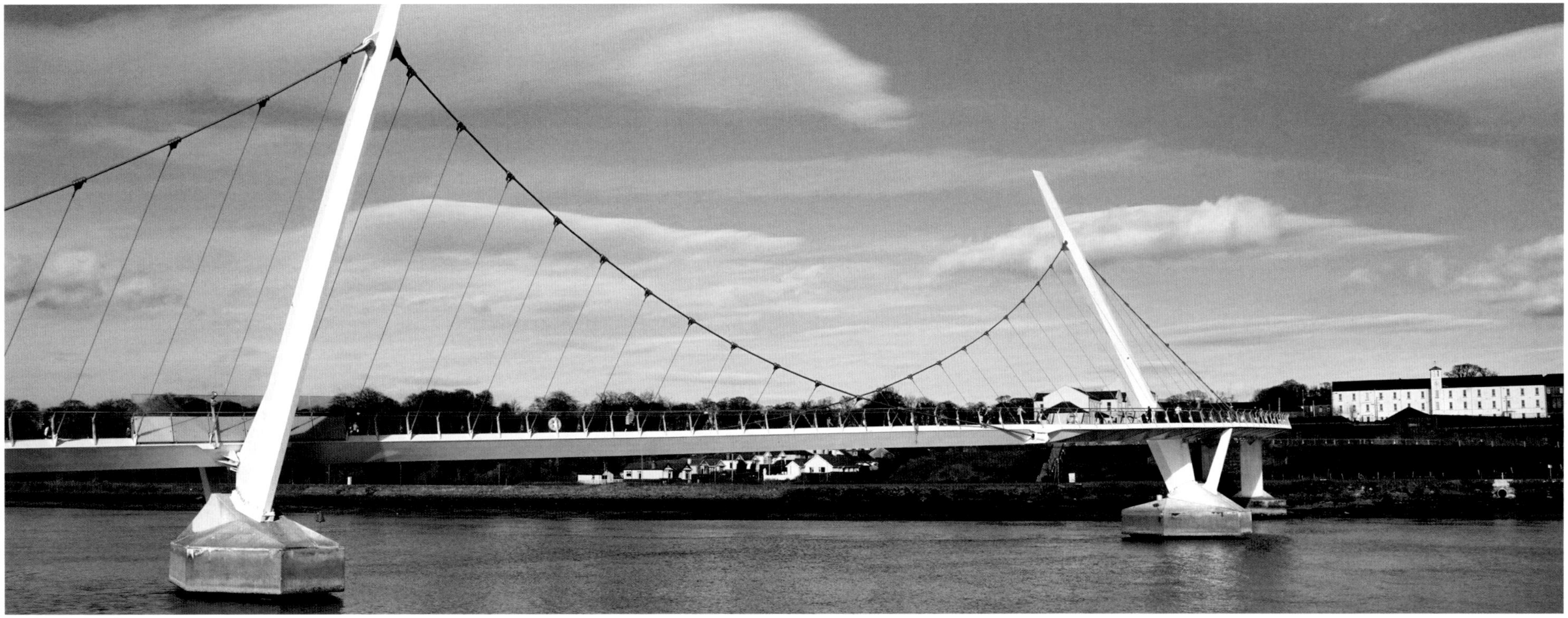

Derry Peace Bridge, 2015

In Derry, Northern Ireland, the S-shaped pedestrian Peace Bridge spans the River Foyle to a road leading up through Ebrington Barracks on the Protestant-dominated Waterside. In 1969, the Battle of the Bogside (a dense, working-class Catholic neighborhood north of the city center) was the first of many clashes between Catholic (Republican) IRA rebels and Protestant (Loyalist) factions, and an opening salvo to the thirty-year "troubles" of Northern Ireland.

Today, ideological suspicions and resentments continue, and in an effort to heal those wounds, Helen Marriage and her London-based Artichoke Trust commissioned David Best to build and burn one of his art temples in hopes of unifying the citizens of Derry (few locals refer to it as "Londonderry"). The hope was that citizens would embrace the Burning Man tradition of inscribing memorials and personal messages on the temple walls. David assembled a crew of stateside builders plus forty Irish artisans to construct one of his most elegant designs. It was to be a challenging build in volatile weather.

The site was a Catholic property overlooking the Foyle and Derry's downtown Cityside. As I got into the taxi to ride over to where we were staying, the driver looked at me and said, "You must be one of them Yanks." I nodded. "Well," he began, "it's a fine idea, but they built it the wrong place!" I stayed silent. "Ya see," he continued, "the Waterside is mostly Protestant; the Catholics aren't going over there, but that property on the hill belongs to an old IRA Catholic family, so the Protestants aren't going up there neither. Nobody's gonna come!"

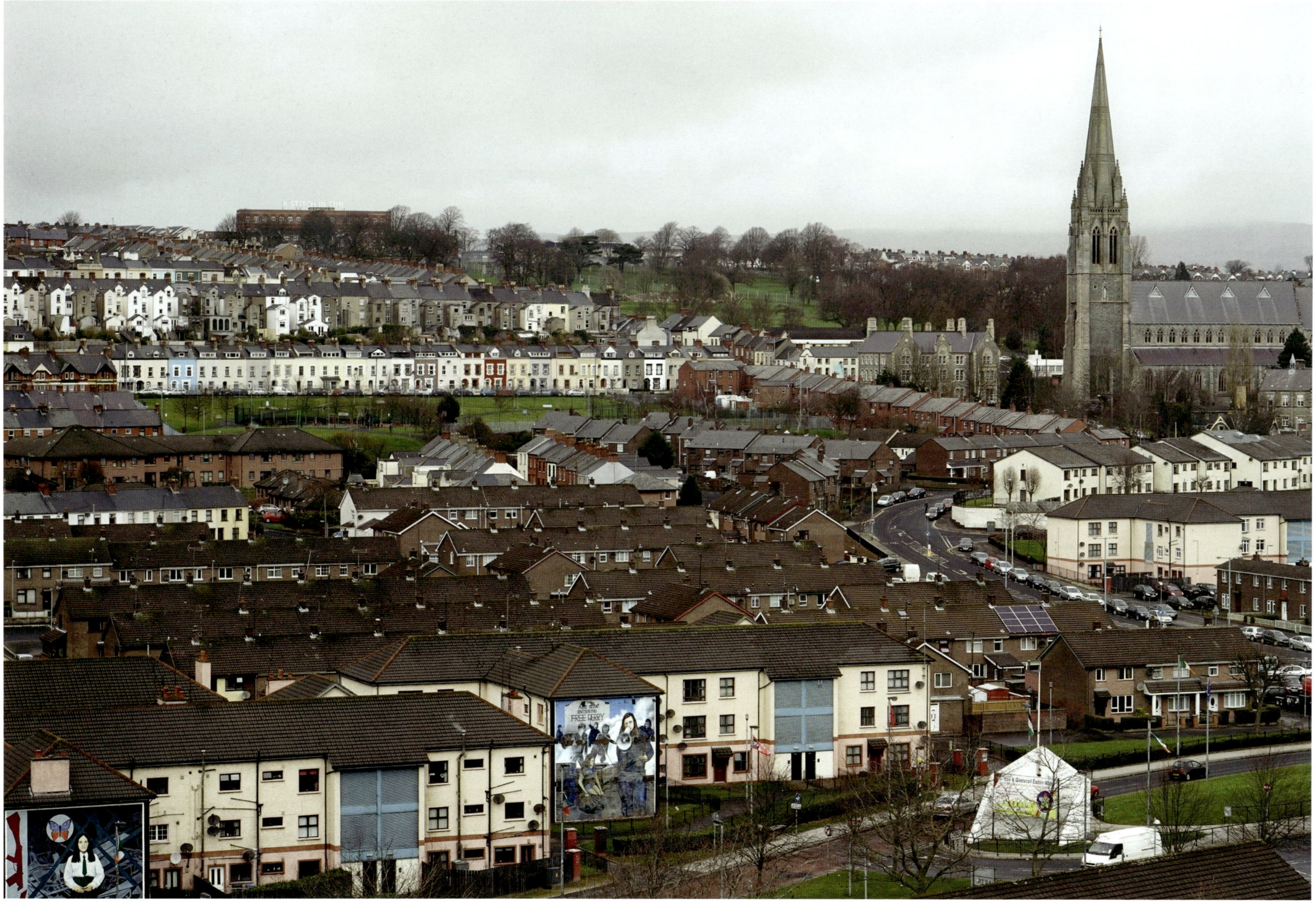

Bogside Murals, 2015

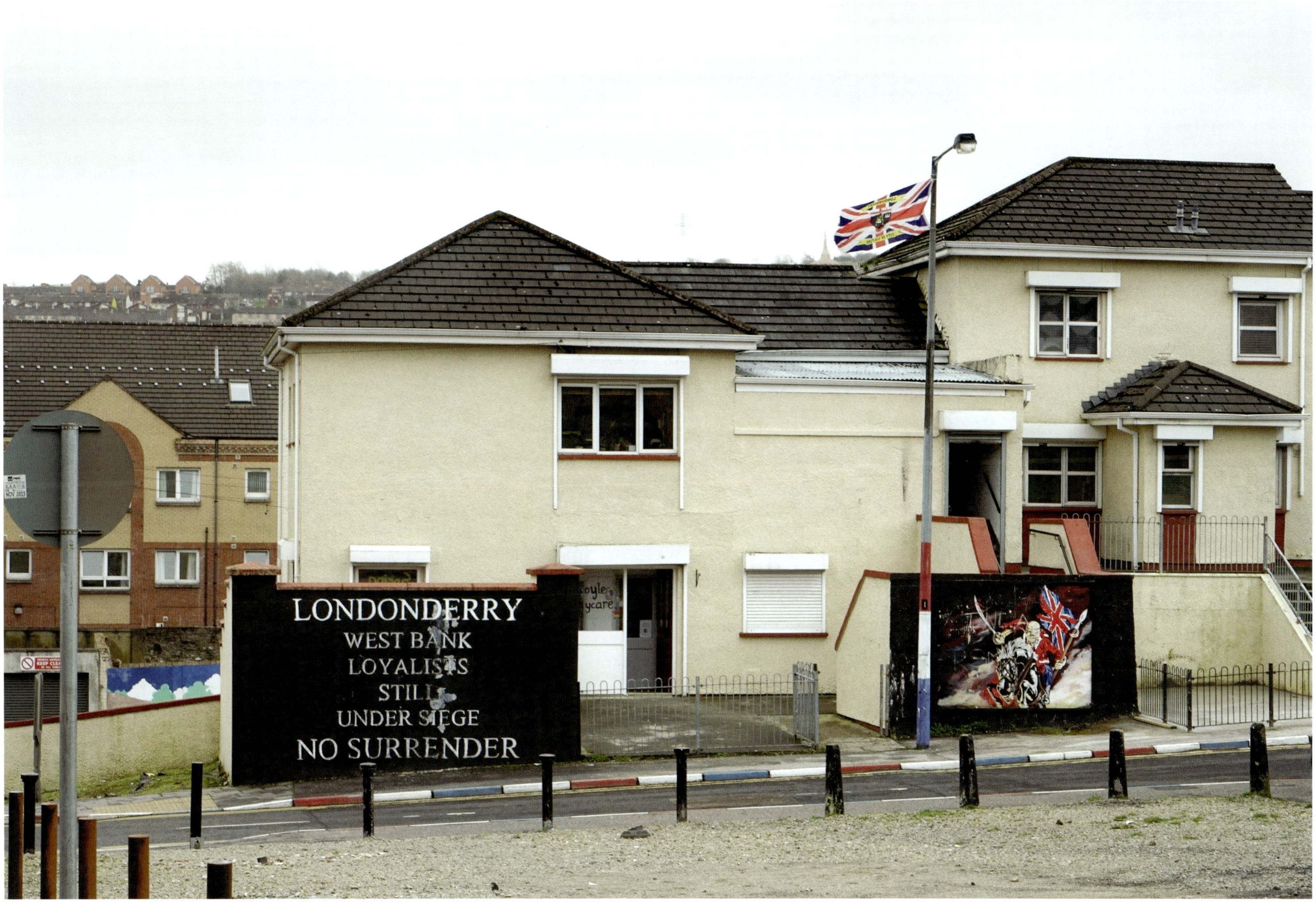

West Bank Loyalists, 2015

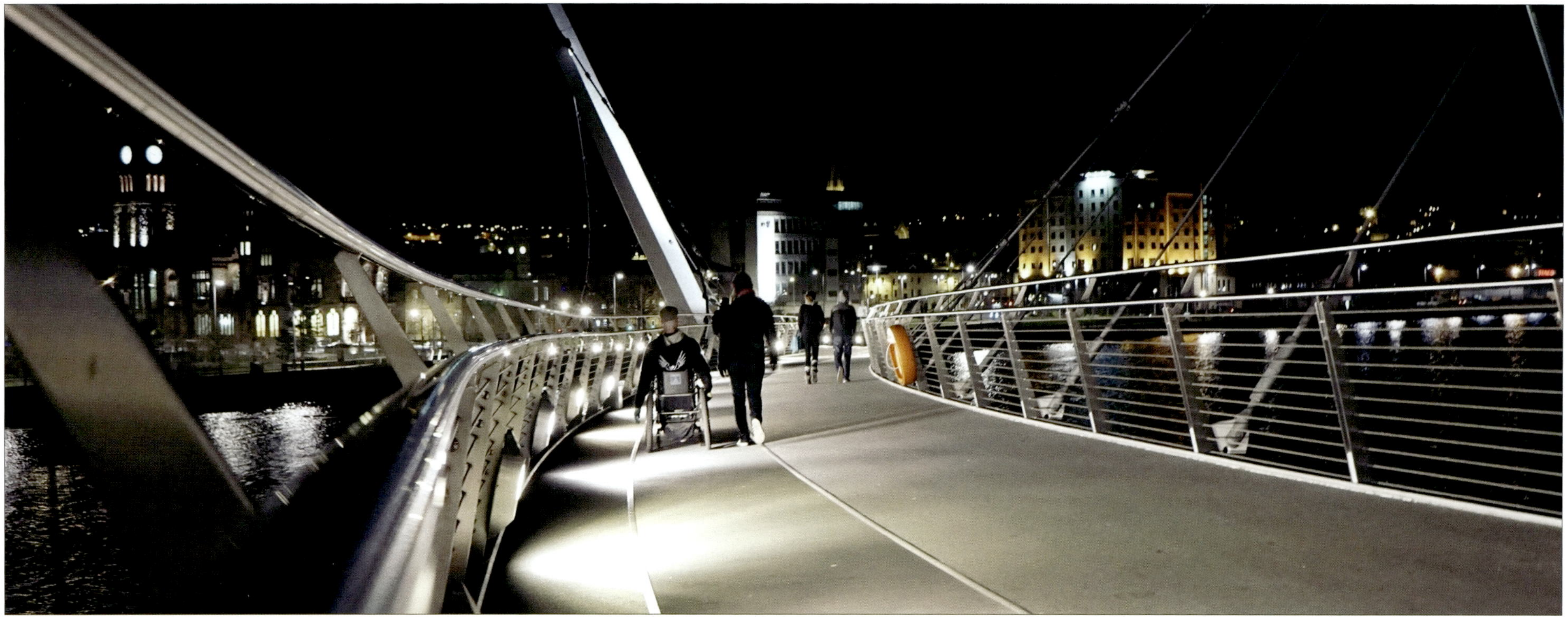

Sandino's Bound, 2015

Derry is one of the most beautiful of Ireland's great cities and sits regally on the Foyle as the jewel of Northern Ireland. We were staying in St. Columb's Park House, which in the eighteenth century had been the manor of the Hill estate. The estate was sold and turned into a sylvan parkland, which continues to host wildlife, street urchins, and dog walkers. Saint Columb is the patron saint of Derry, and there is a grand cathedral on the Cityside that bears his name.

On my first night at St. Columb's, I met one of the many good friends I would make on this adventure: Paul Walker. Paul is a lovely soul who unfortunately became paraplegic from an accident a few years ago. Not that it's held him back. The first thing he said to me once I'd settled into the dorm was "I was thinking of going to Sandino's for a drink tonight. Care to join?" In no time six of us were hustling our way down through the park and over the Peace Bridge to the city. I grew to marvel at his dexterity with his chair, especially navigating through the mud at the build site. Paul's a playa temple builder, and they're a rugged lot.

At the boundary of the park sits the empty Ebrington Barracks, which were the home to British and U.S. forces in World War II, and the base for British forces employed to quash Derry's Republican rebels in the late 1960s and early 1970s. Today they sit empty—a haven for street kids—but there are many signs that the wounds from the troubles still fester. Several of the homes on the Bogside sport murals depicting scenes from the conflict. Likewise on the Cityside you find Loyalist sentiments and fluttering Union Jacks. These old conflicts still bubble just beneath the surface, but if Derryites were to squint over the next few nights, they might just see the glow of an ambitious wooden spire rising skyward on the hillside beyond the River Foyle.

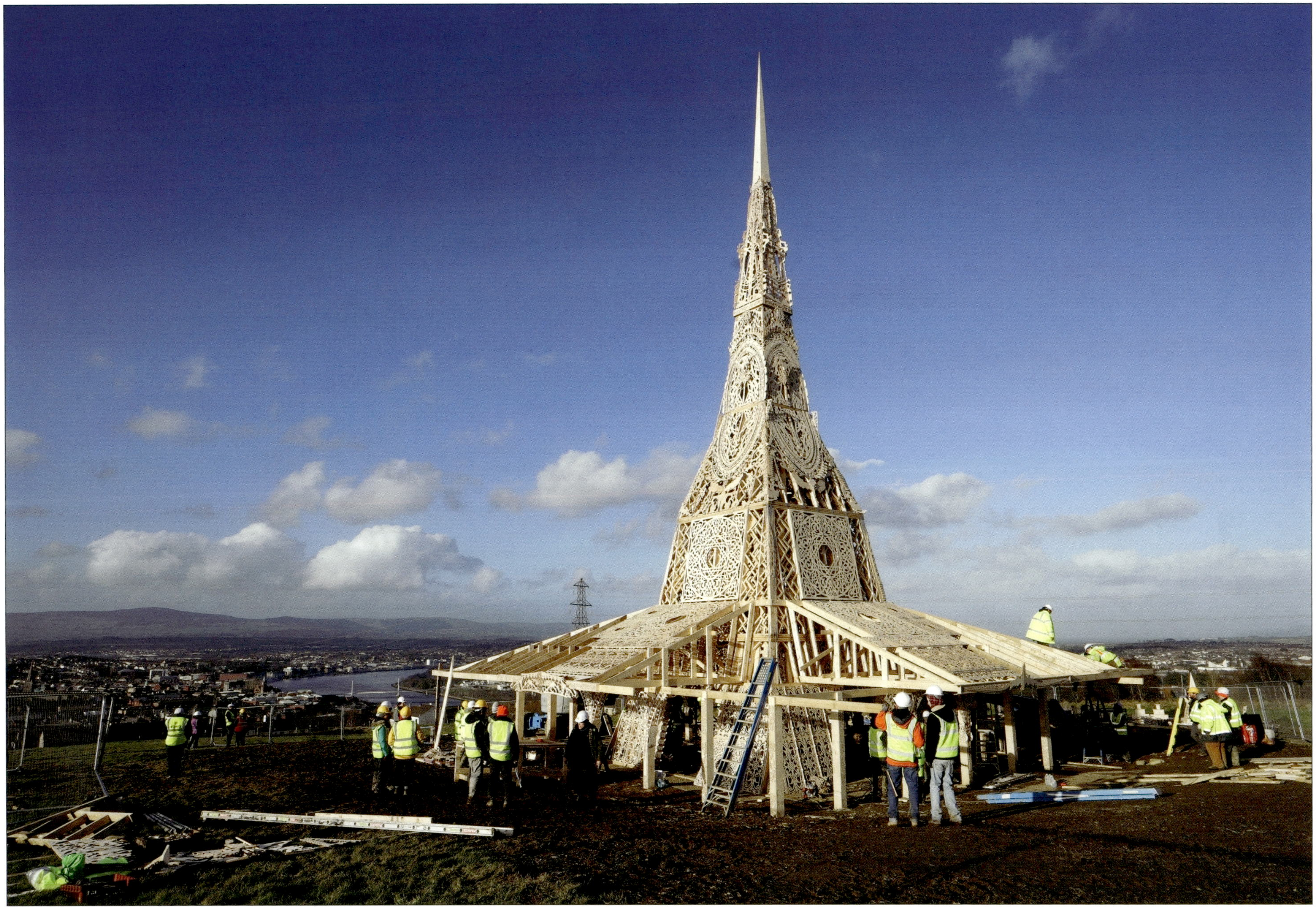

Derry Temple *Build, 2015*

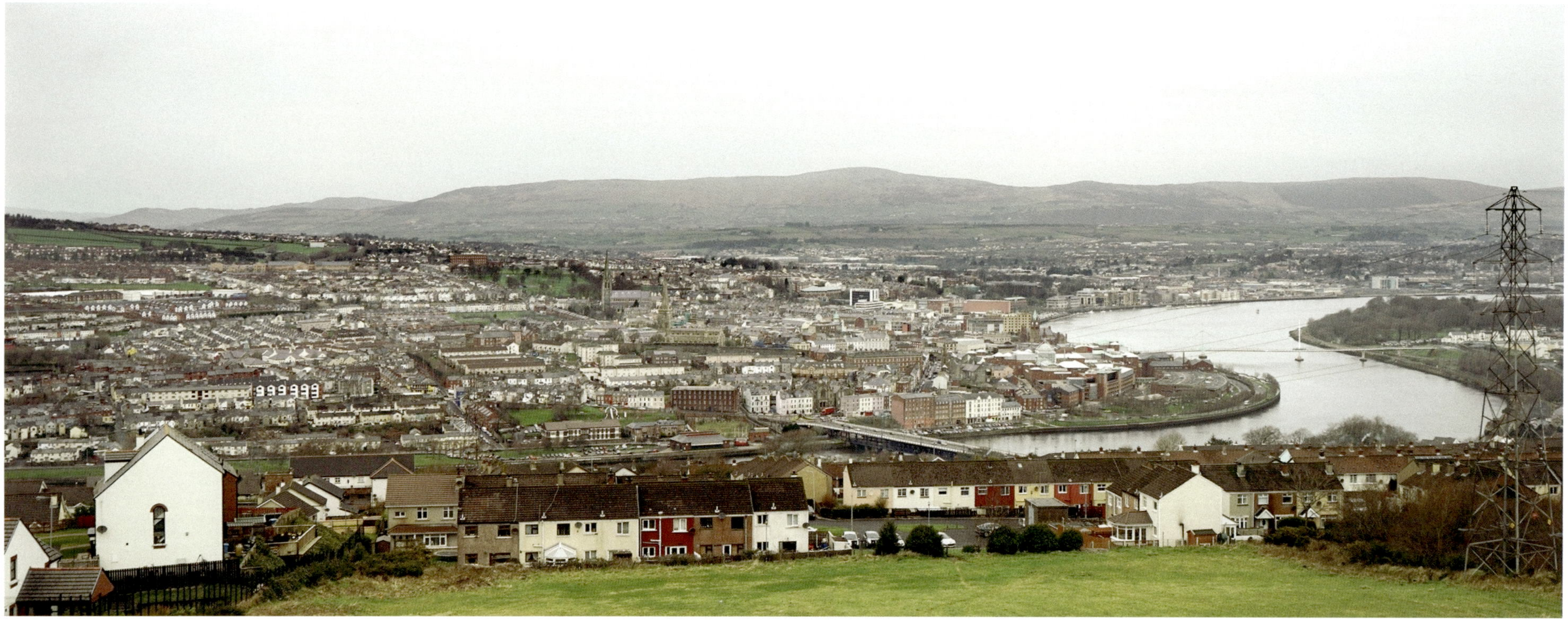

Derry Vista, 2015

Derry glows softly in the misty Irish air. The temple was being built on a hilltop property chosen because it was one of the few sites that could be seen from virtually any location in the city. The weather in April was unpredictable and could change on a dime. Mostly it alternated between overcast and bluster as everyone labored hard to finish the project by the coming Saturday.

I had arrived on Tuesday—a latecomer to the party. In truth, I was under the impression that my role was to be a volunteer photographer, but that changed in a hurry. The build was running behind schedule for several reasons. The property sloped toward the River Foyle, and it became obvious that there would need to be a concrete foundation. The temples of Black Rock City sit on the flat, smooth playa, but this was neither flat nor smooth. As a consequence, they had started out behind schedule. Then the weather turned ugly—torrential rains, even a spate of snow. The ground around the temple transformed into a boggy mire.

I began to document the build, but photography is swift and construction is slow. Soon I found myself standing around waiting for something to happen. Bored, I began holding ladders for people working higher up. Eventually I learned to use a nail gun and got pretty good at layering wooden embellishments—David's DBS (decorative bullshit). Then something happened. I became personally invested in the temple and its outcome. After decades of being an observer, I now felt like a member of a creative team. I was cold and muddy, but I was a temple builder, and it felt good.

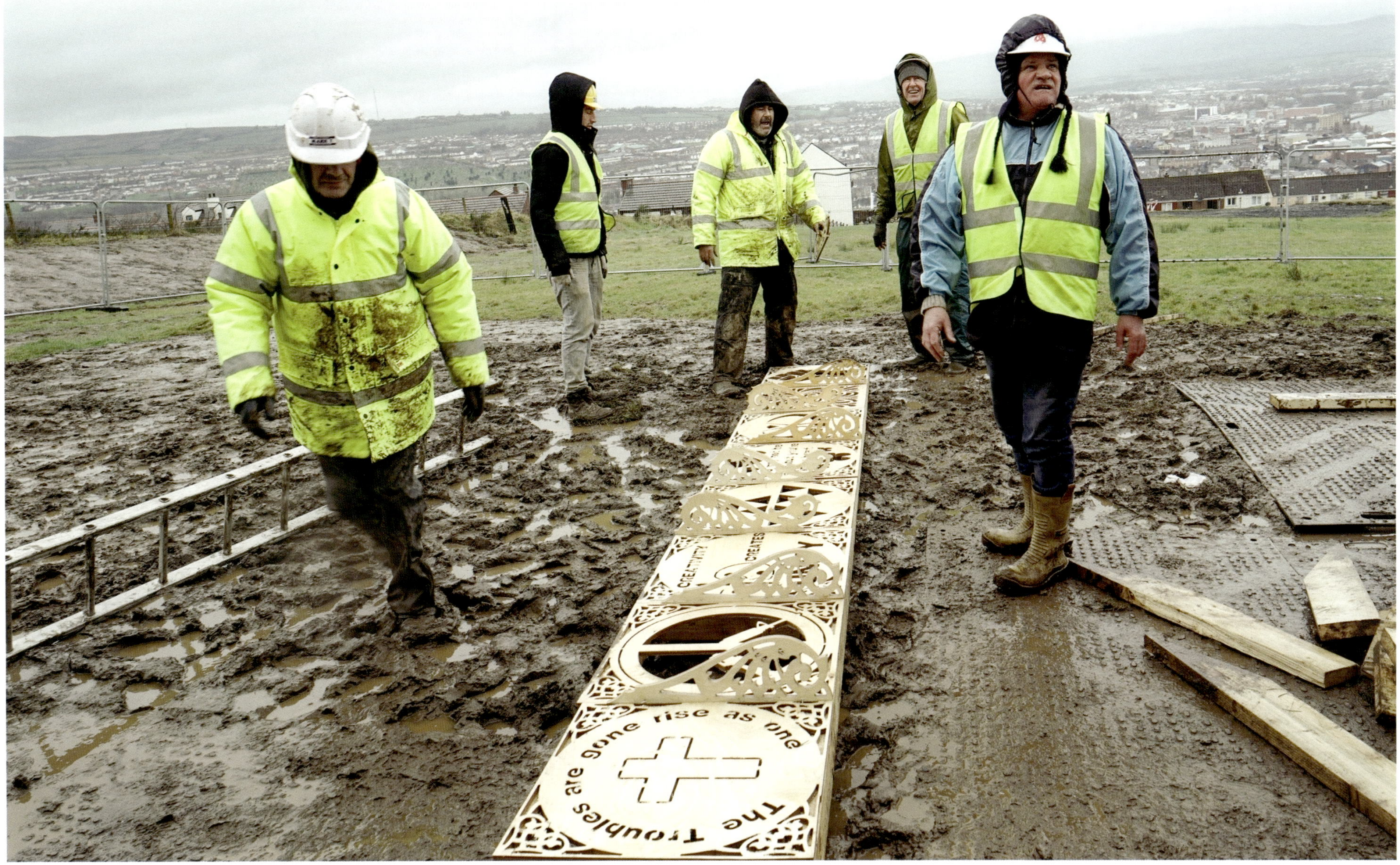

Muddy Slog, 2015

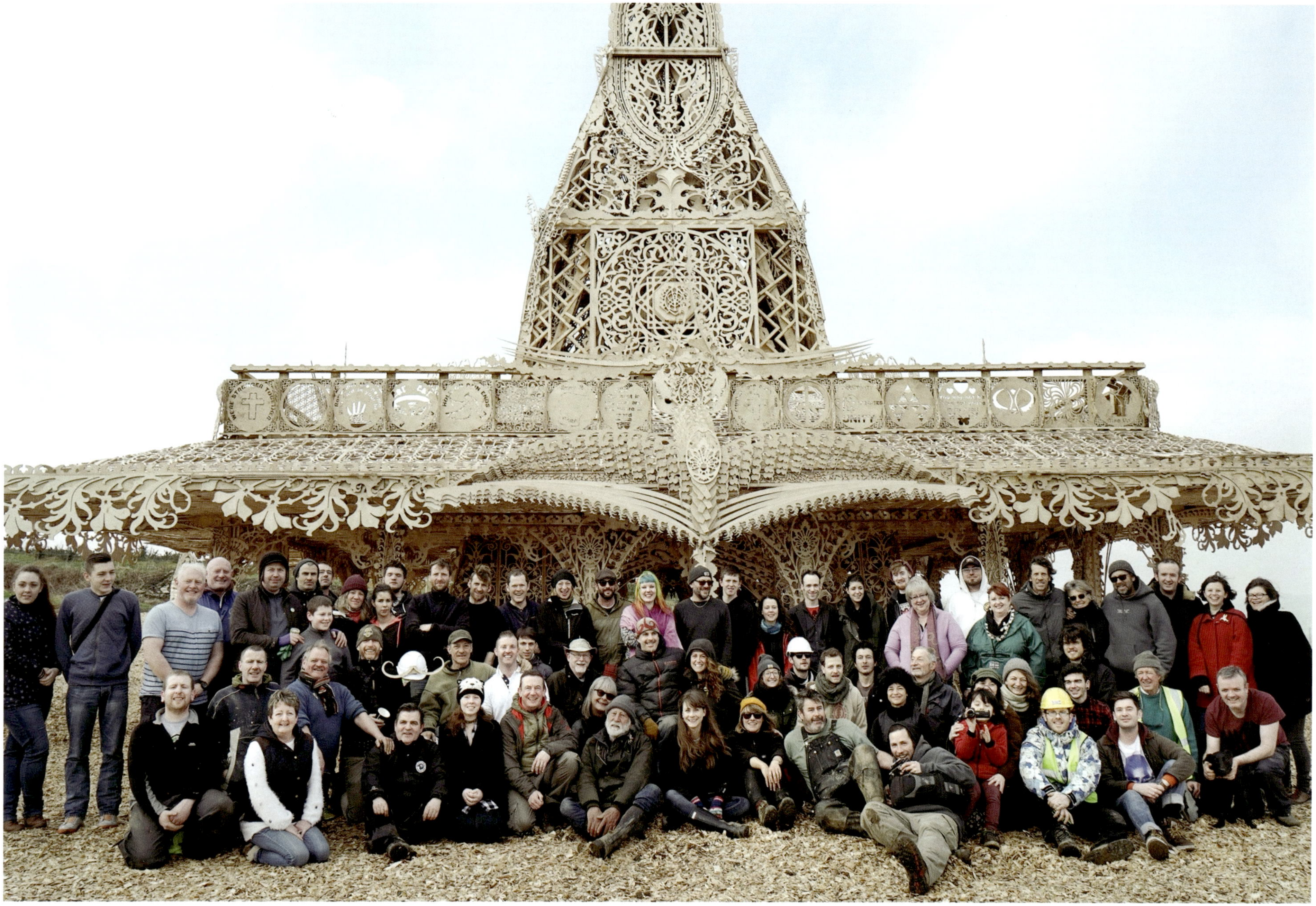

Temple Crew, 2015 (Photograph by N. K. Guy)

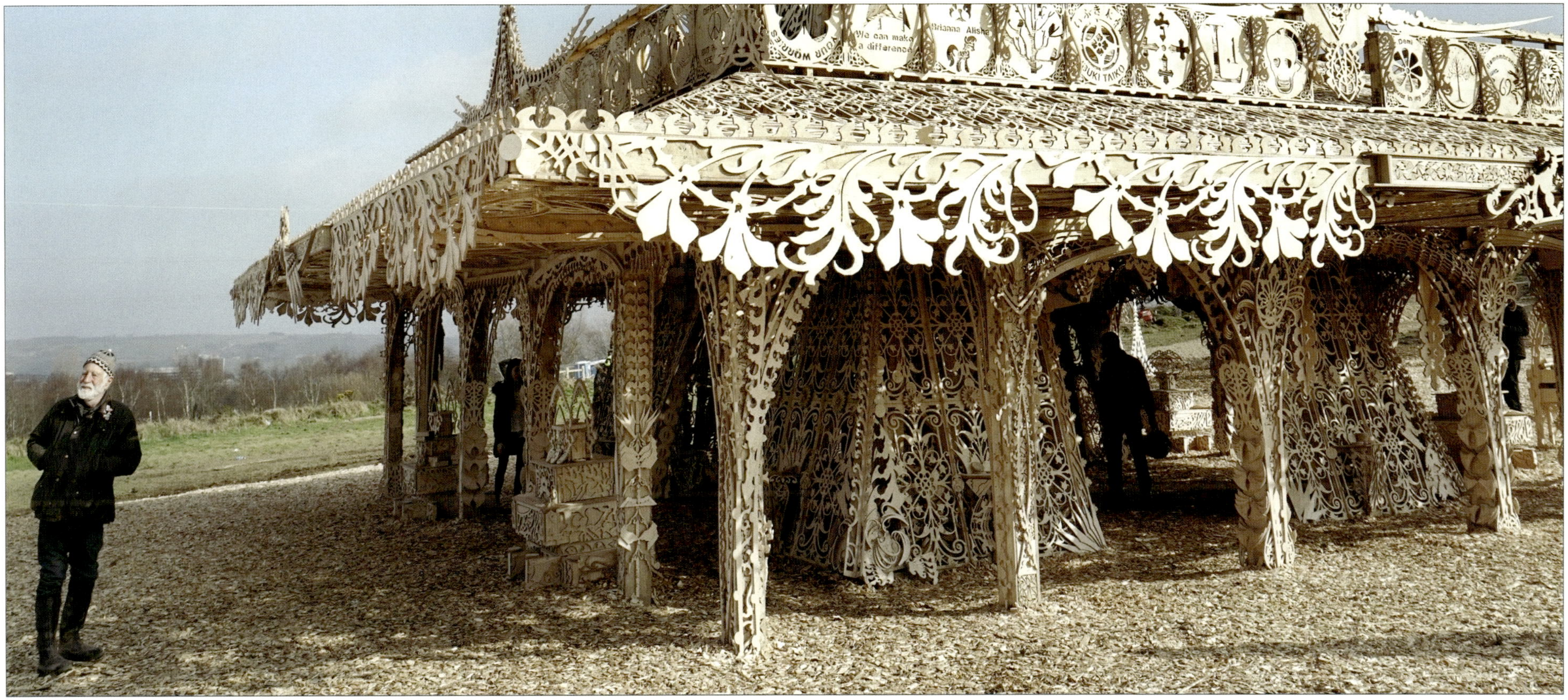

David Best, 2015

David Best is a remarkable man, and I've known him as a friend for several years. His artist's acumen is without peer. I've warmed myself at his spiky fire sculptures and ridden the playa in his famous *Rocket Car,* and if he had done nothing more than introduce "the temple" concept to Burning Man in 2000, his legacy would be secure. To date, he has built nine temples on the playa and in the process has transformed the event. The temple is a principal reason many people return to the playa each year. Yet this achievement alone is not what makes him remarkable in my eyes.

Like most committed artists, he gives himself entirely to his current endeavor, and he has little patience with those who can't follow suit. He is also the most generous and warmhearted of individuals. His unerring sense of compassion has fostered a unique art form that speaks to the universality of loss and hope. It's why he is invited to build his memorial temples in faraway places, and it's why he came to Derry, where political mistrust was a cultural legacy.

For me, the most remarkable thing about David Best is the loyalty he inspires in the talented temple builders who willingly follow him around the world and give of themselves unselfishly so that others might heal deep wounds. His is a vital mission and speaks to the humanity in all people. Burning Man artist crews are all dedicated and hardworking, but temple builders are a special lot. They will follow David to the ends of the earth, and I believe it's because they feel the personal rewards of performing worthy work. It's not simply dedication; it's a calling.

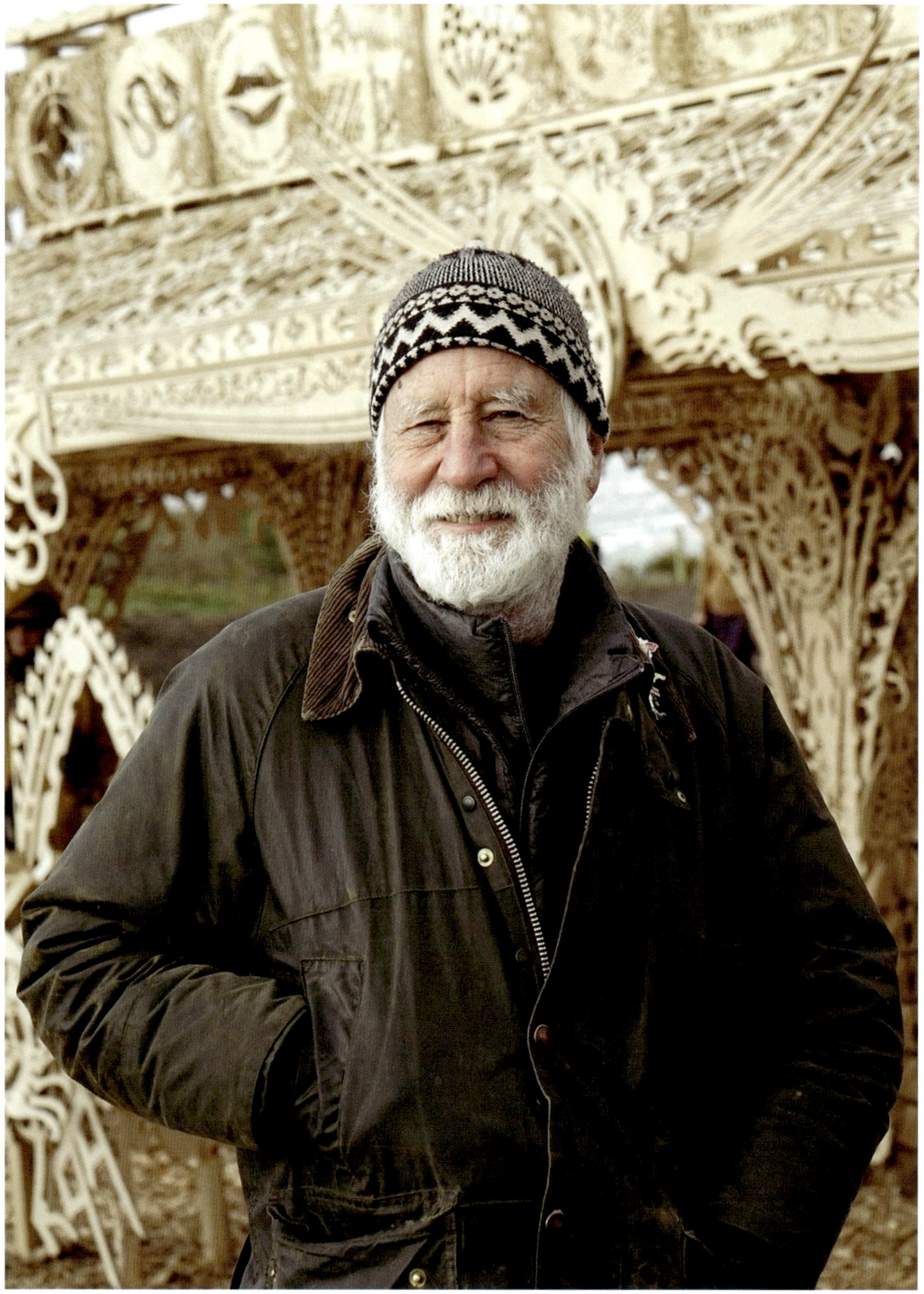

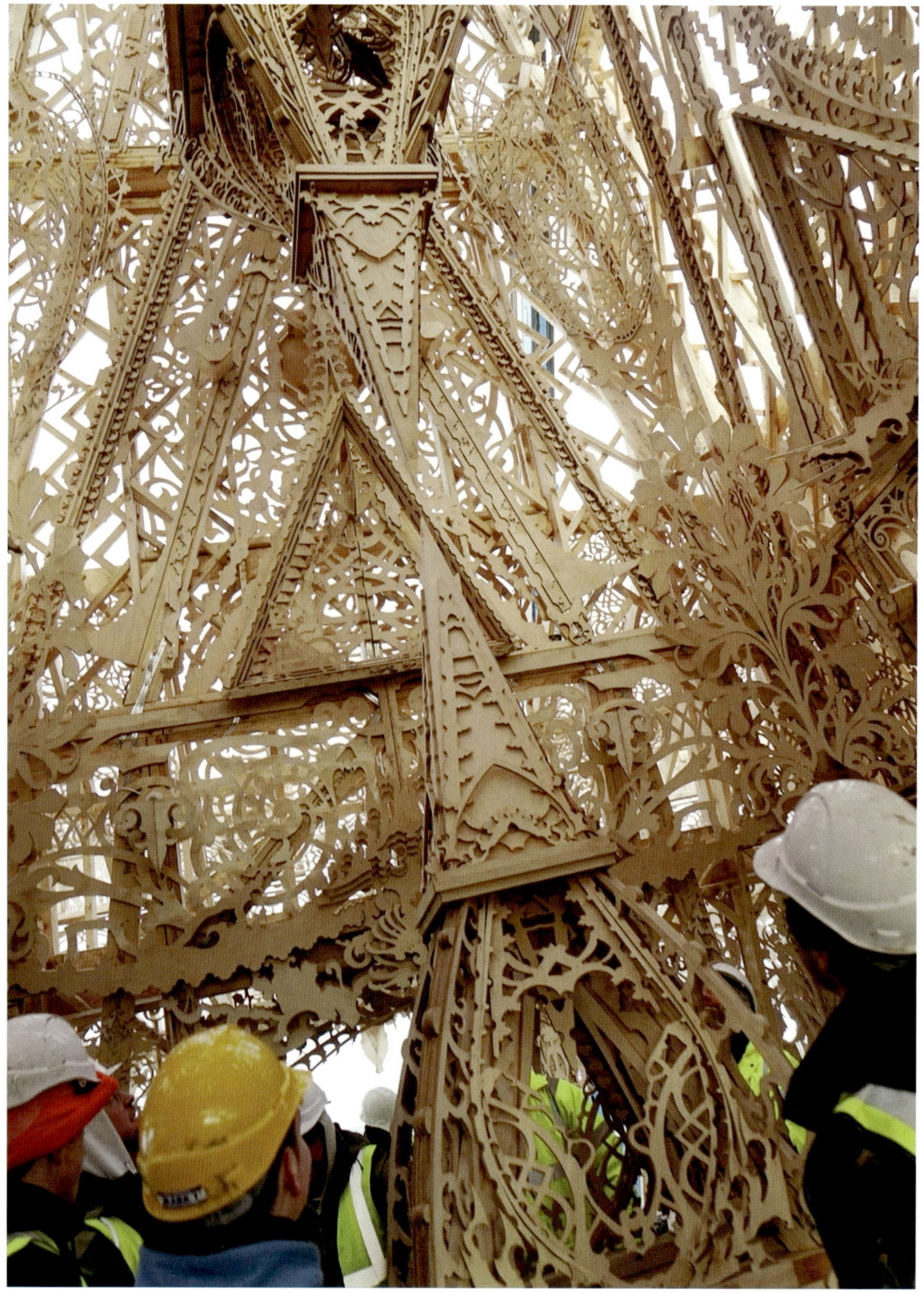

David Best and Crew, 2015

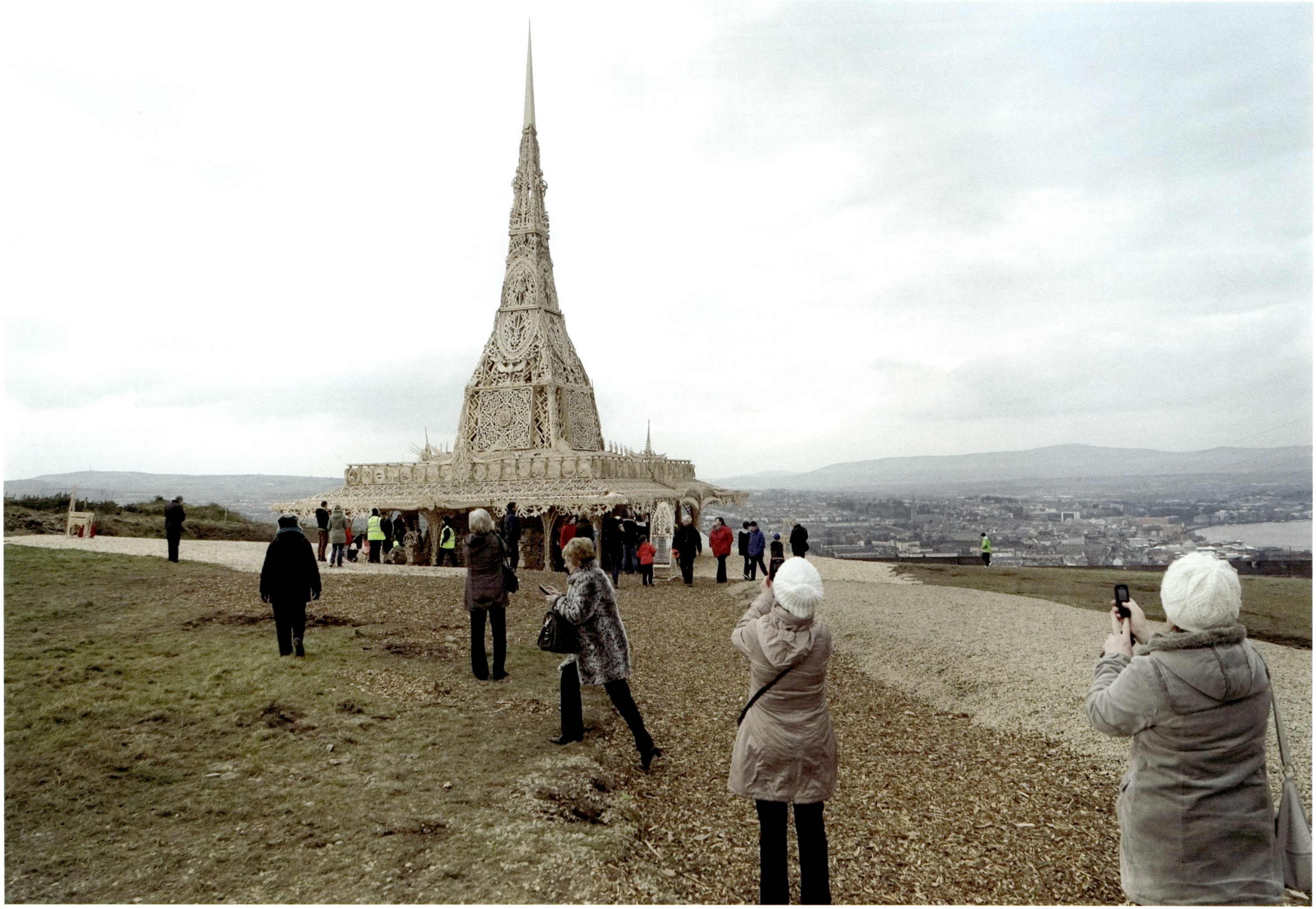

Temple Opening, 2015

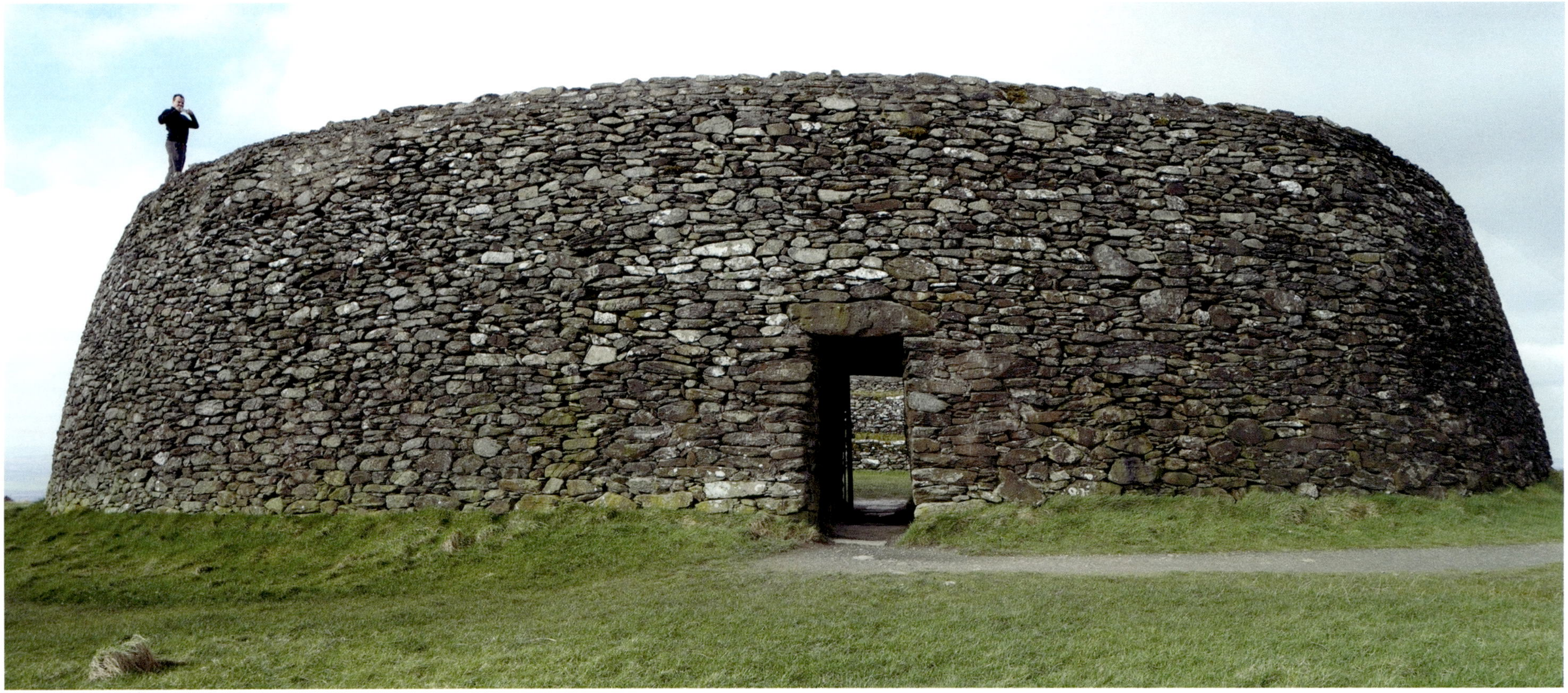

Grianan of Aileach, 2015

After the temple was officially opened, and the dignitaries and first visitors began to appear, the crew was suddenly out of a job. Some simply flew home, but the bulk of us were committed to staying in Ireland for the Burn. I had assumed there would be planned activities scheduled all week long, but there didn't seem to be any. Rather, the gates were opened so that the people of Derry could experience the temple at their leisure and make of it what they might.

Meanwhile, I had been invited by Paddy and John Dunne to drive up to Donegal to see one of the great ring forts that go back to the sixth century and earlier. This particular example was ruled by the UI Neill clan between 789 and 1050, and was destroyed in 1101. It was restored to its present shape in 1878. Paddy claims that the UI Neill chieftain commanded as far as he could see from the top of the fort, which on a clear day might include the coastline of Scotland!

When we returned to St. Columb's, Donnadh Ryan and Diarmuid Hanley proposed making a "roady" down the Donegal coastline, and traveling over to Donnadh's hometown of Glin on the River Shannon. It was a fine opportunity for me to see the Republic and to experience Ireland with the Irish. Our first night was in Ballyshannon, the birthplace of Rory Gallagher, and we dined on homemade Irish stew at Finn McCool's. The next day we visited Yeats's grave at Drumcliff. We then spent two lovely days with the Ryan family. It was an opportunity to discover what everyone who goes to Ireland soon learns—it's an ancient and magical place.

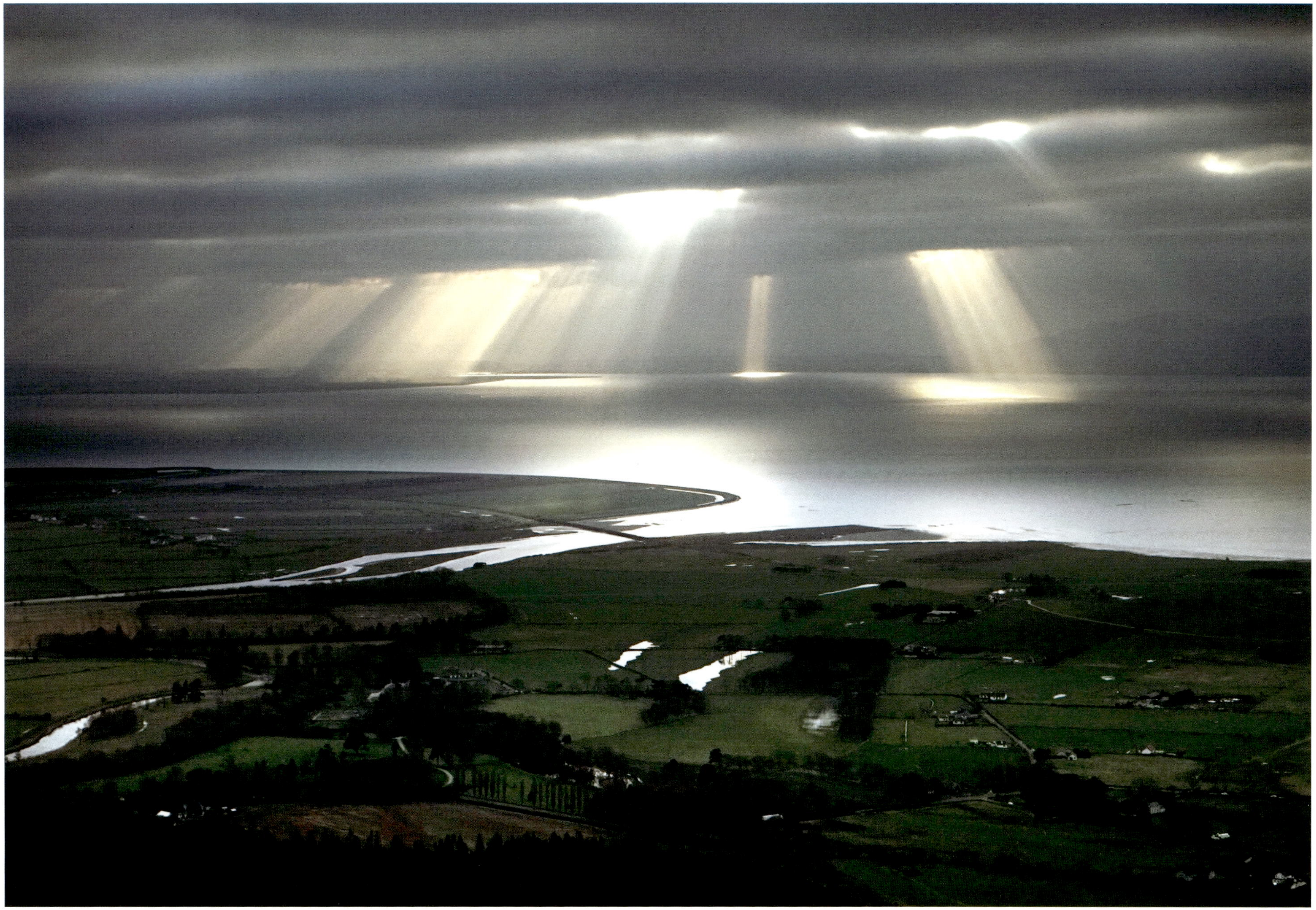

Beyond the Foyle, 2015

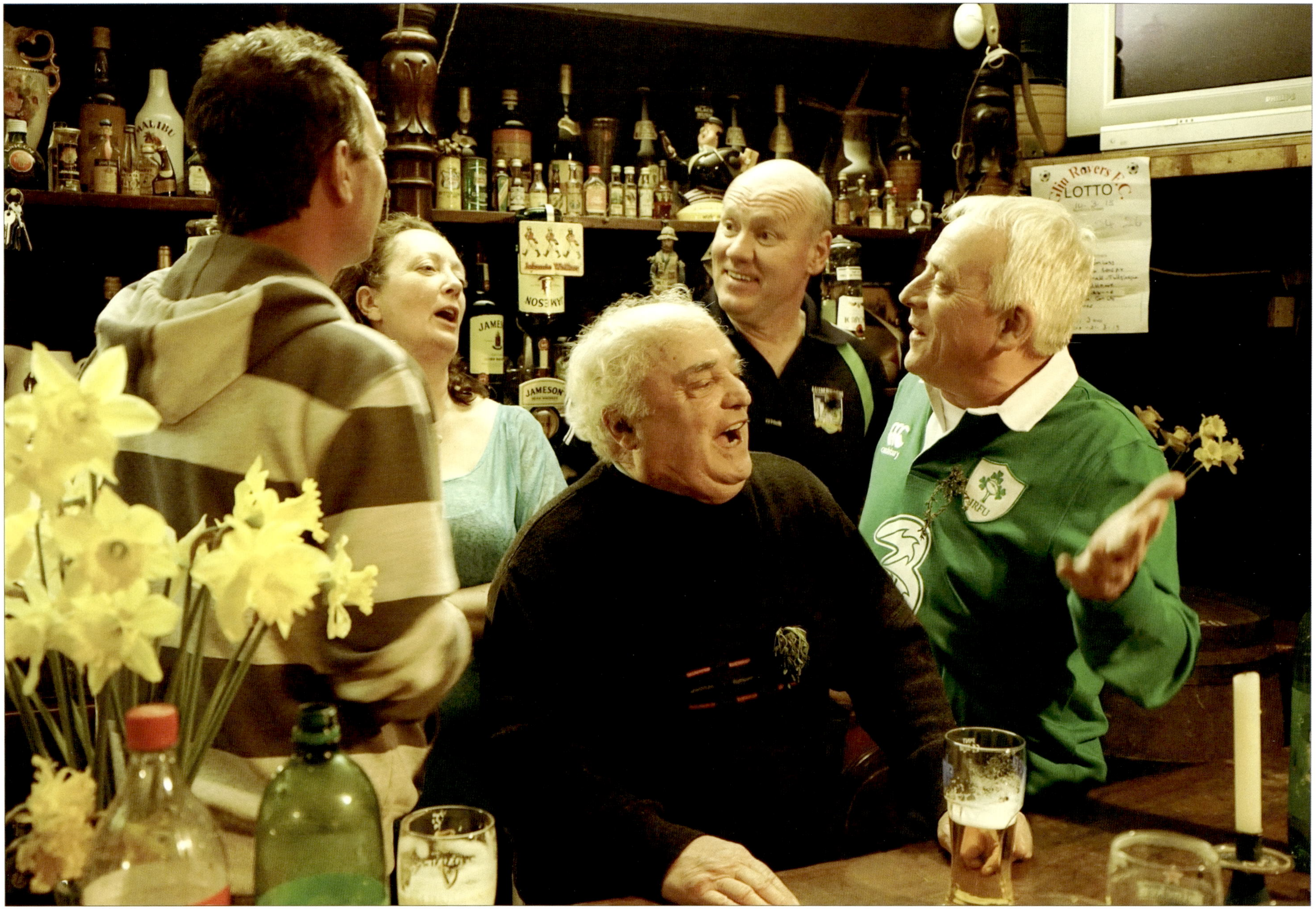

O'Shaughnessy's a Cappella, 2015

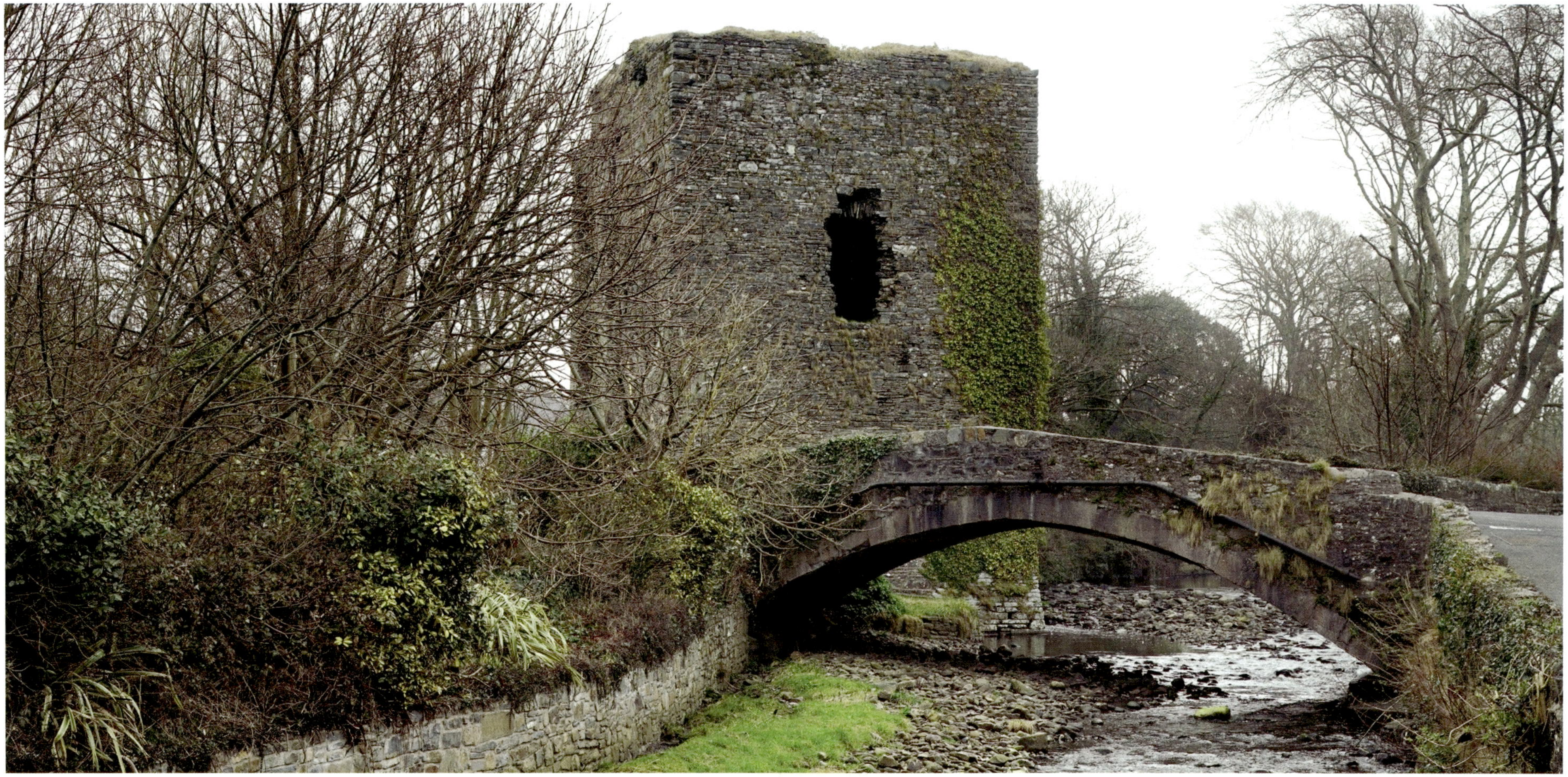

Glin Tower, 2015

We arrived in Glin Village in County Limerick late on St. Patrick's evening. Donnadh suggested that we check out Glin's most renowned public house, the Captain O'Shaughnessy. The pub was packed with patrons wearing bits of shamrock on their sweaters. In a scene that seemed to belong in a John Ford film, patrons Billy Martin and Pat Noonan broke into a rare old Irish tune, and were soon joined by their friends, Billy's high tenor rising above the rest like a vapor.

The next morning, Donnadh showed me a thirteenth-century tower ruin virtually in their backyard. Ireland's seamless blend of ancient and contemporary landscapes reminded me of the chameleon nature of the playa. We had worried whether our Burning Man temple would be accepted by the citizenry of Derry; we needn't have been concerned. After touring the Irish countryside, I realized the obvious. It's a country full of temples of one sort or another.

We arrived back in Derry the night before the Burn. It was dark, but we drove up to the hill anyway, or rather we made an attempt to drive it. The roadway was jammed on both sides with people trudging their way up the hill or back down. That's when we realized that the naysayers had been wrong. The citizens of Derry had come to the temple, lots of them, and they came not just out of curiosity, but to leave messages of sorrow, remembrance, and above all hope.

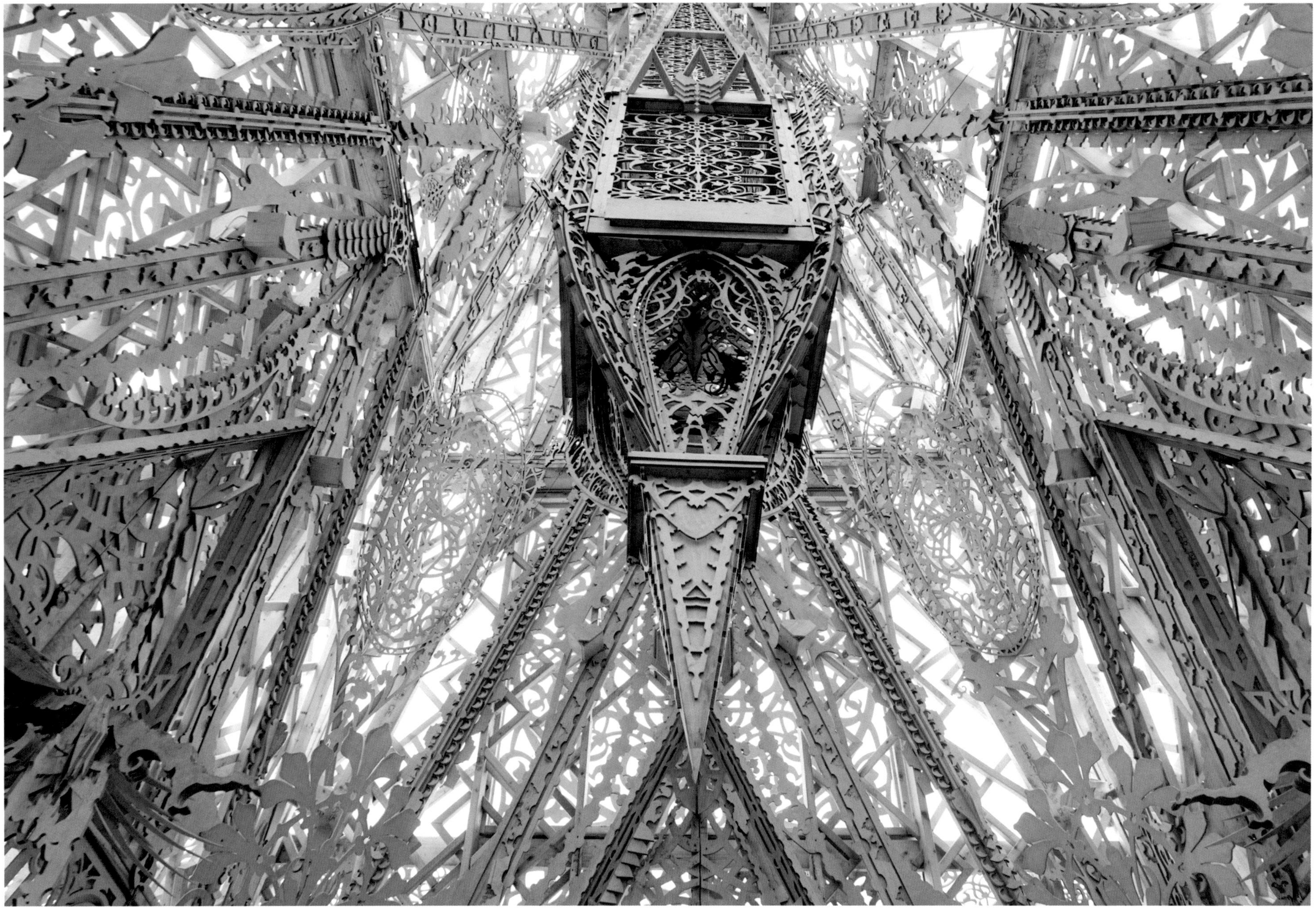

Temple Chandelier, 2015

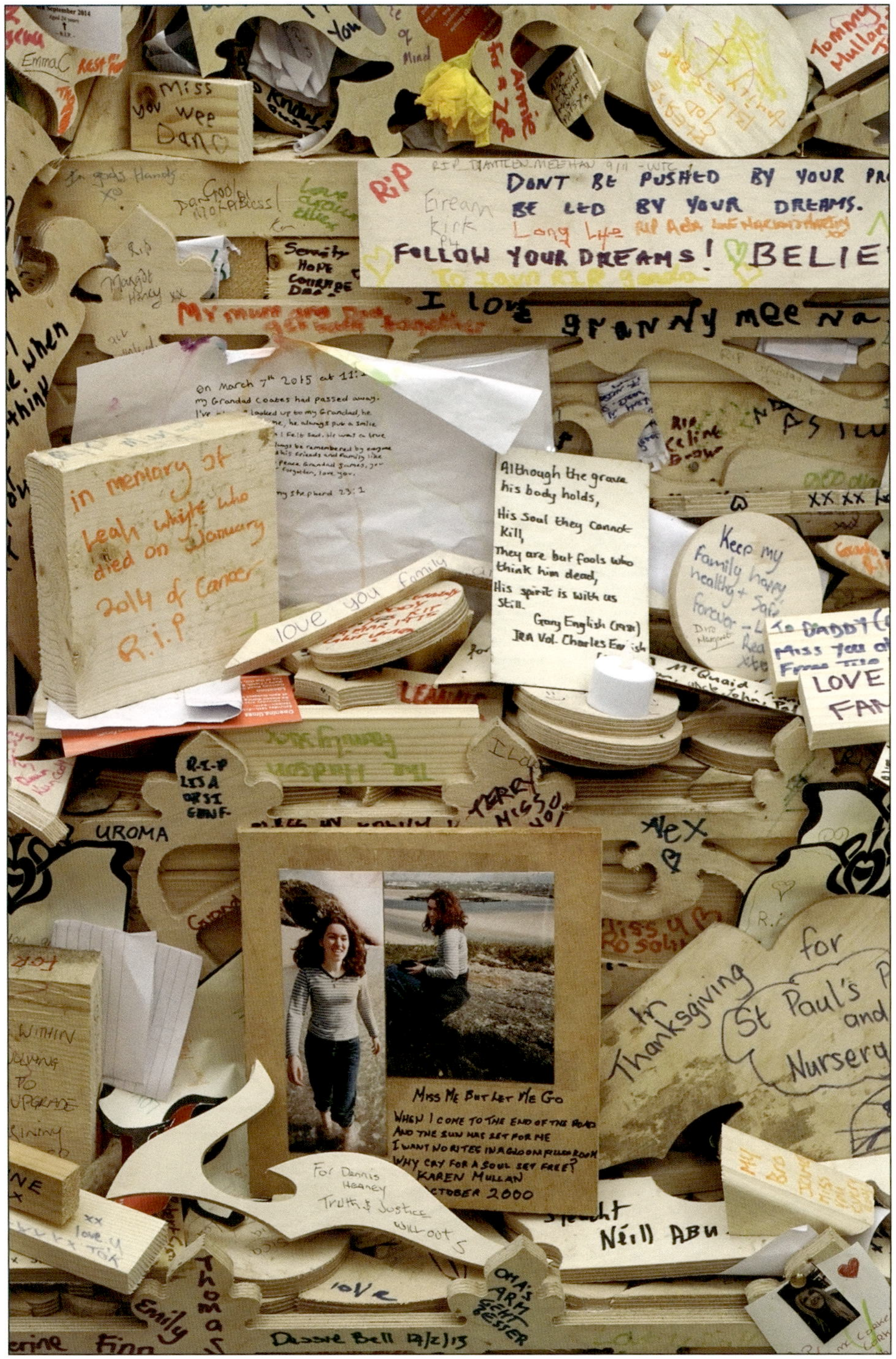

Memorial Messages, 2015

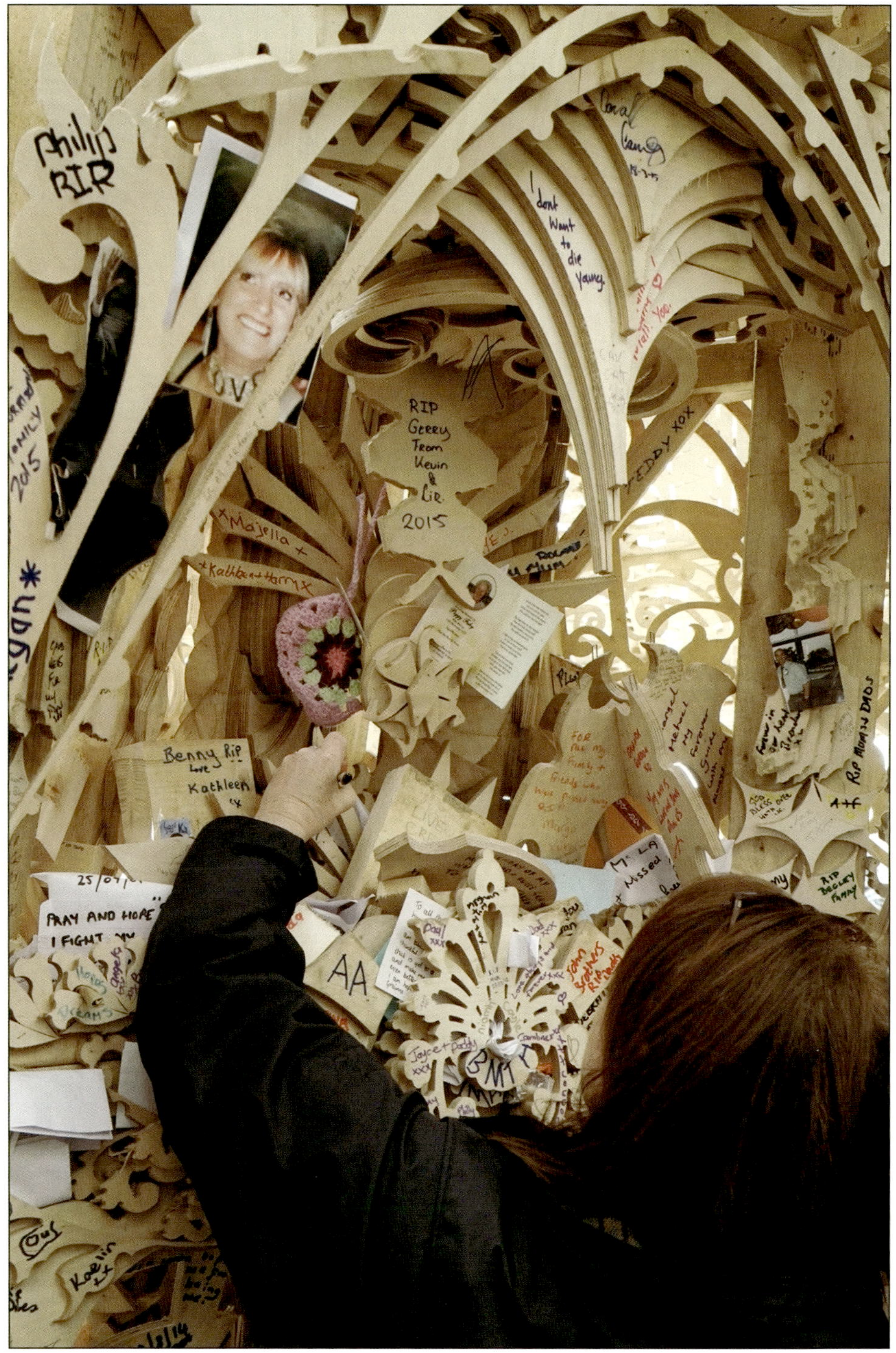

Temple Interior, 2015

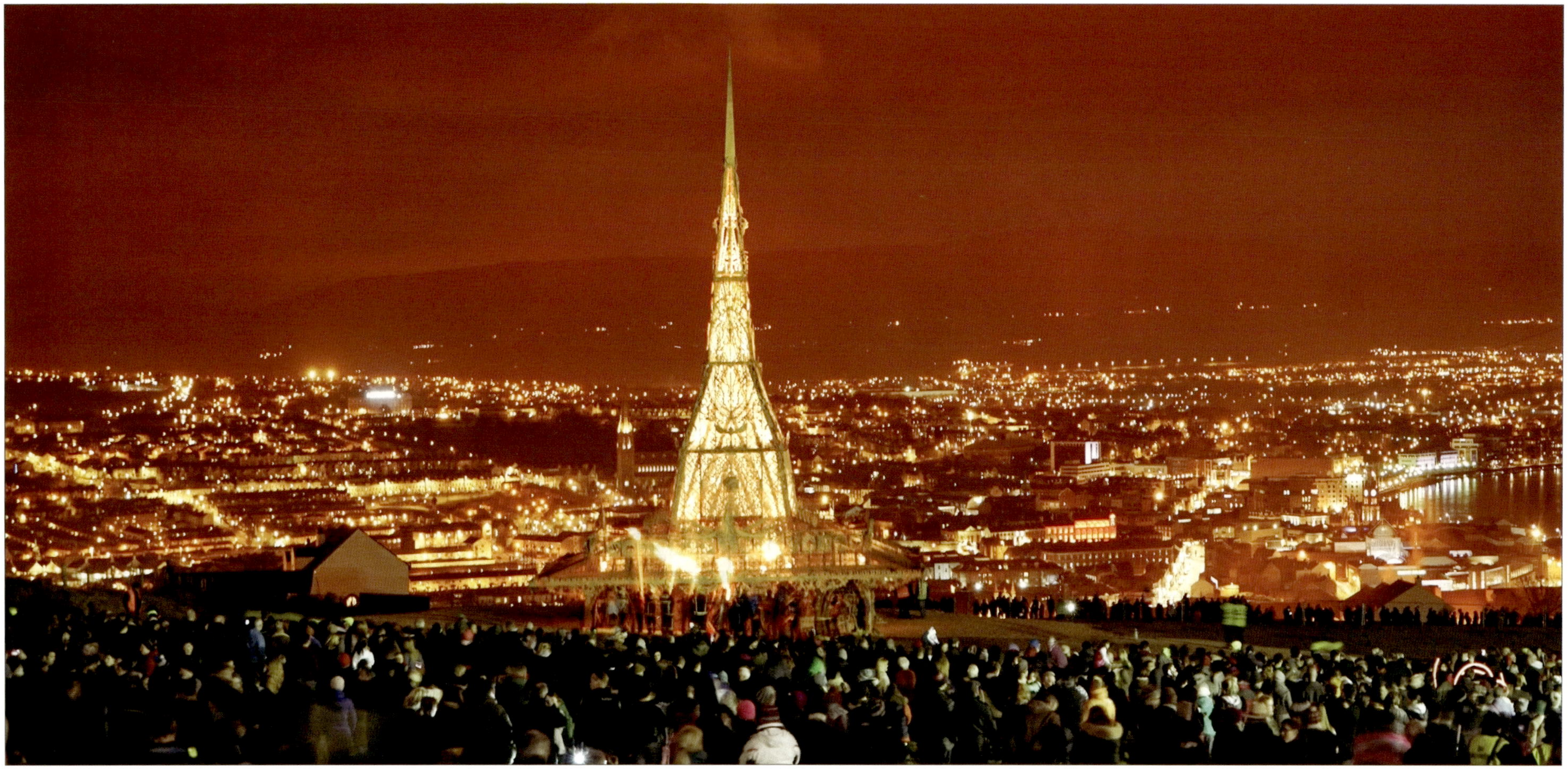

Temple Lighting, 2015

My brother conjures the image of spirit soaring upward, and fire is a natural embodiment. People have been sending flaming aspirations skyward for centuries. But Larry also says soul remains at home, and for years I maintained that the Black Rock Desert was the indispensable repository of soulfulness at Burning Man. Certainly it was a crucial part of the event's development, but Derry taught me that home is more than a landscape; it's a cradle of being. It shapes our consciousness, our culture, and our identity. It's why ritual fire can happen anywhere that constitutes a homeland.

The Derry temple was inherently different than its Burning Man siblings. The playa temples are about individual grief, but David understood from the beginning that the core of this long-standing grievance straddled religious, political, and social lines. This grieving was collective. In fact, one of the reasons Artichoke invited an outsider artist in the first place was the belief that it would take a neutral party to bridge the divide between this centuries-old rivalry.

That night nearly thirty thousand eager souls gathered for the Burn. David adroitly chose his fire setters. They represent both sides of this old conflict. Kevin Strathern, for example, whose father was gunned down in the doorway of his shop, and Tony Doherty, whose father died on Bloody Sunday. On the Protestant side was Graham Warke, a former soldier from Ebrington Barracks. These and other former political enemies lit the flames that would consume the temple and send thousands of healing messages skyward. It was a night when the crimson sky hung like a garland over the old city.

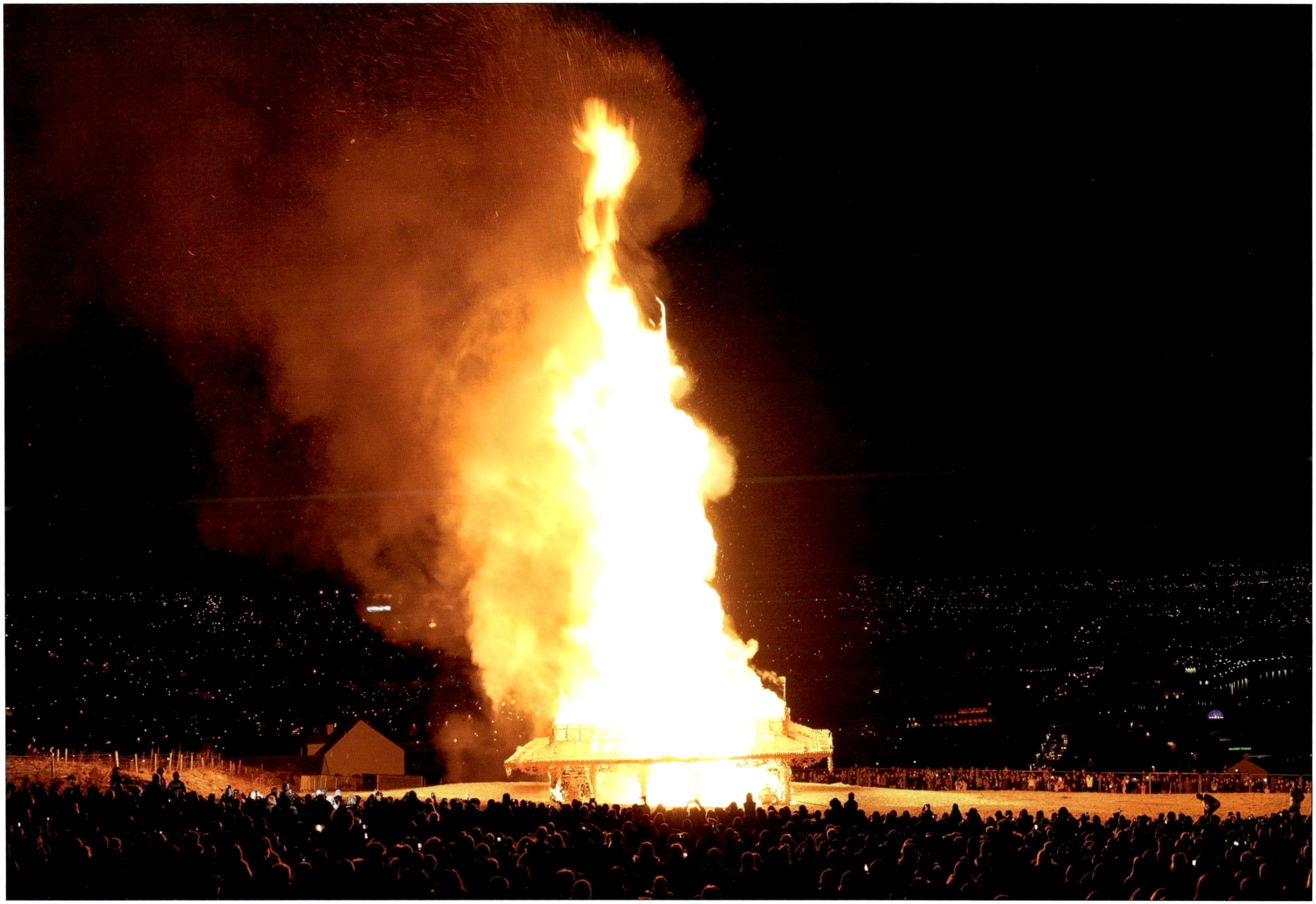

Derry Temple *Burn, 2015*

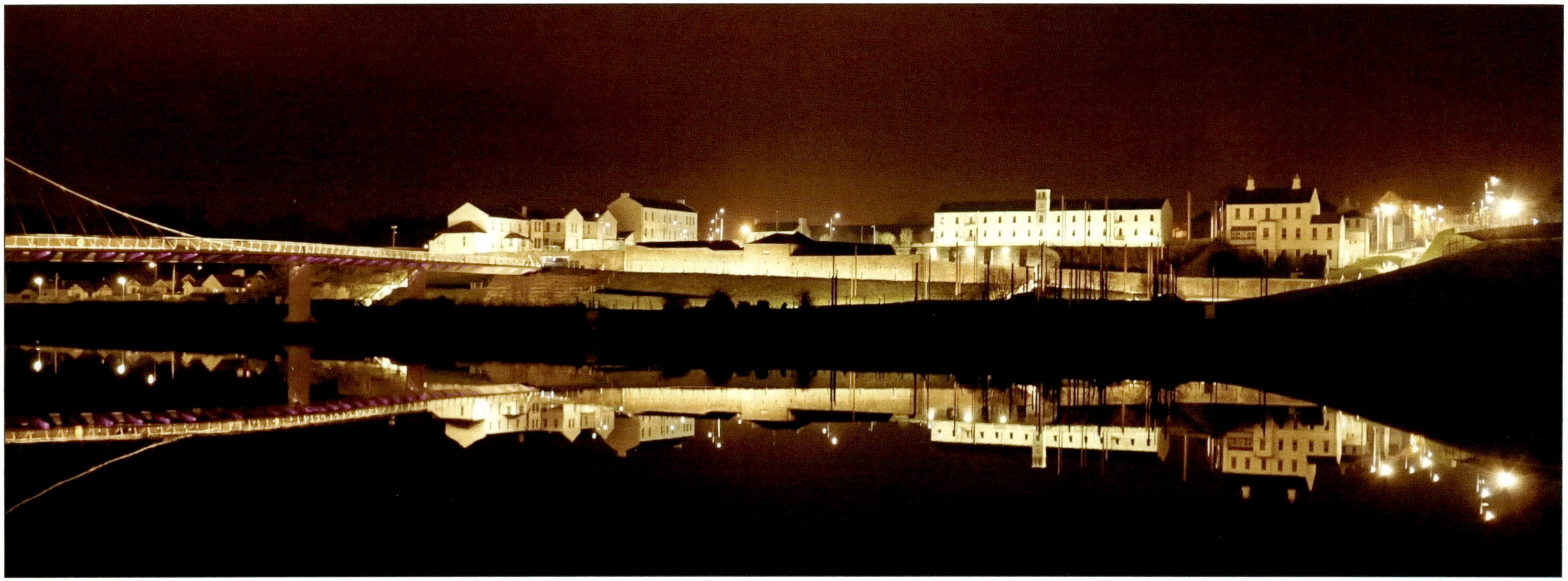

Ebrington Farewell, 2015

After the flames subsided and the crowd thinned, we made our way back across the Peace Bridge to Sandino's for a well-earned celebration. We had been overjoyed by the response. We were hearing that there had been more than thirty thousand at the Burn, and estimates were that more than sixty thousand had visited the temple during the week. David had reserved the entire second-floor ballroom at Sandino's, and we reveled raucously yet wistfully, knowing our time in Ireland was coming to an end.

Derry had been an eye-opening experience for me. After twenty-six Burns and thirty years of interacting with Burning Man, I felt I had just gained a greater appreciation for the potential of cross-cultural expression and global participation. Being even a small part of spreading that culture had been a tonic. I felt grateful for the opportunity, yet there lingered a wee uncertainty. Would our sincere efforts have a lasting impact or be a momentary diversion? You never know.

Sandino's closed around one A.M., and six of us trudged our way back across the Peace Bridge to the dark shore of the Waterside. As we neared Ebrington Barracks, we could see ten or so young couples hanging out in the shadowy confines of those relics of the troubles. As we approached, we eyed one another cautiously. Just as we drew abreast of the youths, the most remarkable thing happened: they burst into applause. I still get emotional reliving that moment.

I hasten to add I was occasionally mistaken for David. We're the same age with white whiskers, but this spontaneous gesture wasn't adulation. It was appreciation. David Best had come to Derry to share his unique art, which has become Burning Man's annual tribute to personal loss and enduring hope. The death of a loved one invokes a universal response, and in honoring that we evoke our brotherhood. In this, *Derry Temple* speaks to all of humanity—without exception.

AFTERWORD

Black Rock City is not an easy place to be a photographer.

The weather's mood swings on a dime. One moment the desert will be deliciously calm and tranquil, the next moment an eye-ripping whiteout will blast in, and then it'll revert to its default state—a sweltering plain of sunbaked clay.

Somehow you have to make your way across this vast cracked wilderness, hauling cases or bags of fragile camera equipment, trying to find or create a compelling visual record of the proceedings in a way that nobody else has done before.

Sixteen times I headed out to that remote patch of Nevada, bent on conveying or capturing a fragment of that magic. And after all those years I still found that translating the incredible experience that is Burning Man into a workable two-dimensional image is a lot tougher than it should be, by rights.

You try to frame a shot, only to find banks of chemical toilets squatting in your angle of choice. Or you end up spending ten minutes shifting the mound of bikes that some thoughtless participants have piled onto that gorgeous piece of art. And, ubiquitous and unemotional, there's the relentless seeping dust, callously undermining your best technical efforts. It's dirty, exhausting work. Sometimes it feels like making art in a vacuum cleaner factory.

Yet among all of us, proud members of this self-appointed club of obsessives and reprobates who have documented Burning Man over the years, Stewart Harvey stands out. The images he records reflect his long and visceral understanding of the event, combined with the uncanny ability to infuse emotion into his shots.

His monochrome photography is a case in point. I've heard the argument that the austere rigors of black and white are ill-suited to playa photography. And there is something in that. Black Rock City is a place bursting with color, not just tonality. This is particularly true with the contemporary playa's bright sunlit costumes and LED-washed nights. But I'd argue that Stewart's work serenely ignores these restrictions. His mastery of the arcane traditions of silver-based chemistry yields frames of high-contrast clarity. There's no murky haze of gray obscuring his stories. He presents stories and splinters of time, set off against the bleak majesty of the windswept American West.

Consider *Java Cow Ritual, 1993*.

It's dawn. The chill of night has been summarily banished by the sharp rays of the rising sun. Clouds, backlit, frame the evocative wooden skeleton of the Man. Cracked clay, striated by the parallel tracks of the odd car, stretches relentlessly to the horizon. And there he is. The Java Cow. A man in rags and a cow skull, striding purposefully to the south.

Perhaps you're familiar with the early history of Burning Man. Perhaps you know about Kimric Smythe's Java Cow. A simple, albeit surreal, performance—a man-cow ritually serving coffee, always black, at dawn. Then you'd know that this photo is a cultural marker for the event. It's a document of an early manifestation of so many Black Rock City touchstones—interactivity, community art, gifting. Stewart's photo tells this story (page 66).

But even if you don't know the official backstory, there's the sheer glory of that mysterious image. A foreground figure, distorted yet recognizably human, alone yet totally at home on that barren plain. The distant Man and the remote hills. Layers of narrative are built into a photographic landscape.

Or take *Raising of the Man, 1993,* taken in the early days when participants would line up and raise the Man off the desert floor by playing tug-of-war. It's a print from a single Widelux negative; the product of a curious mechanical camera that takes in a huge swath of scenery through the expedient of rotating its lens (page 50).

The filtered sky offers a rich contrast to the scattered clouds, and standing below is a row of assembled participants: jubilant, joyful, anticipating the final moment when the Man stands alone. These are photos that capture the instant like an ensemble nineteenth-century painting.

His more recent work records the vast scope of the bustling municipality that is today's Black Rock City and the interwoven traditions and rituals that undergird the week's festivities. The photo of *Crimson Rose and the Fire Conclave, 2016,* is a strong full-color example (page 279). She's one of the founders of the event, and Stewart shows her leading the procession of fire performers into the annual Fire Conclave circle, which marks the beginning of the end for the Man. Clad in her traditional fire-print Burn Night robes, goggles at the ready, she bears a massive flaming torch with fiercely implacable determination. Behind her, a trio of masked white-clad stilt walkers lead a phalanx of mysterious, dark-clad figures. You can feel the leaping, flickering orange heat.

The synthetic fabrics and battery headlights indicate that this shot has to be a record of the late Anthropocene. But there's an essentially primal aspect as well. Fire. A high priestess. Acolytes. Where are they going? What task do they bear?

These are just three examples of Stewart's work—of a person who has spent a lifetime developing the technical and aesthetic skills needed to record such consistently evocative images of a remarkable event.

Today, Burning Man is huge by any conceivable measure. It's a diverse and complicated cultural phenomenon: massive, complex, and manifesting at many different levels. It's essentially become impossible for one person to produce a truly comprehensive and just account of its rise and growth, though goodness knows some of us have tried! But the book you hold is one of the finest records of the mad, ephemeral, and multifaceted string of transitory beauty that is today's playa.

Stewart's been to more Burns than just about anybody short of Larry Harvey. And now, at long last, we get to see his work as it should be seen—a sweeping panorama through time, covering the most comprehensive pictorial account of Burning Man that anyone's ever made. I also believe it's essential for an artist to present his or her own work, both visually and verbally. After all, only one person was there when every single photo in a solo book was taken. Who better to talk about the conditions, the backstory, or narrative behind the work, the artistic and technical decisions that went into making the photo? So to have his photos combined with his intimate accounts of their creation is a fantastic gift indeed, from the playa to the page.

N. K. Guy

ACKNOWLEDGMENTS

For the Harveys, Burning Man has always been a family affair, and acknowledging the invaluable support I've received from family is number one on my list. My brother, Larry, has spent many hours helping me with facts and filling in the gaps in my own recollections. In doing so we've become acutely aware of the vast invisible influences that were passed on to us from our parents, and which we in turn hope to pass on to our sons, Bryan and Tristan. For Bryan and myself, our nearly annual sojourns to the Black Rock Desert over the past thirty years have deepened our love for each other and enriched our bond. Those long drives across barren landscape provided precious time together, and this book is as much a celebration of our father-and-son relationship as it is about the growth of an innovative cultural event. I'm forever grateful for every hour we've gotten to share with each other.

Very special thanks to my lovely wife and resident editor Lynda, and to her ever supportive parents, Johnny and Valeria Seubert. No one who goes to Burning Man does so without trauma, and whether Lynda was going that year or not, she would endure two weeks of staging, shopping, and endless packing. I would also be remiss if I didn't mention the plethora of relatives from Lynda's side of the family, along with various and sundry FOBs (Friends of Bryan), who have graced our camps over the years and kept us in stitches.

In preparing this memoir, I've received valuable information, assistance, and inspiration from many people. Among the most notable: Larry Harvey (Tristan, Dante, and Zan), Marian Goodell, Harley K. Dubois, Crimson Rose, Will Roger Peterson, Michael Mikel, Janet Lohr, Jerry James, Dan Miller, Mike Acker, Kevin Evans, Kimric Smythe, Kelly Anders, LadyBee, Steven Raspa, Nurse Jess, Sting Rae, Camera Girl, Jennifer Raiser, Ping Fu, N. K. Guy, Stuart Mangrum, Caveat Magister, P. Segal, Flash, Koosh, Marti, Dust Bunny, Chip Martzall, David "Tom Sawyer" Walker, Geoffrey Silver, Sallie Edmunds, Tom Sumner, Jaron Aires, Captain Vic Stevens (with co-captains Bryan Harvey and Adam Gorciak), and the Children of Chaos, Martini Village, Jim Bocci and our early Portland campmates, Tony Perez and the survey crew, David Best and the Temple Crew, with special mention to Donnadh Ryan, Diarmuid Hanley, and Paul Walker of the Temple Crew in Derry, Ireland. Special mention as well for two Jims: publisher Jim Leisy, who talked to me about writing a Burning Man book two years before his untimely death, and Jim Lommasson, my longtime studio partner, who has been my critical touchstone for every important design decision. Finally, my invaluable editor Libby Edelson and the fine crew at HarperElixir.

ART CREDITS

Art, art cars, and artists featured in photographs are named below, preceded by the page number on which they appear.

26 *Prairie Wind Chapel* by Robert Hoehn and Wind Tribe
34 *Linguistic Islands* by Travis Ortiz
38 *Flock* by Michael Christian
40 *Temple of Flux* by Rebecca Anders, Jessica Hobbs, Peter Kimelman, and Flux Foundation
42 *LOVE* by Lanna Kimpton and Jeff Schomberg
47 *Grateful* by unknown artist
54 Kimric Smythe as the *Java Cow*
59 *Bone Tree* by Dana Albany
61 Performance by Crimson Rose
64 Performance by unknown artists
66 Kimric Smythe as the *Java Cow*
67 Performance by Ed Joseph
68 Performance by Ed Joseph's Umbrella Dancers
71 *Looking Glassholes* performance produced and directed by Joanna Priestly and Paul Harrod
72 *MudHenge* by Lisa Galli
73 *Awakening* by Ryan Elmendorf and Nick Geurts
74 Performance by unknown artist
75 Performance by MarchFourth Marching Band
80 *Nevada* directed by Spencer Tunick
83 *Transformoney Tree* by Dadara
84 *Cosmic Barometer* by Rob Seiverston
92 *Water Woman* by Ray Cerino
94 *Helco Burn* by Kal Spelletich and Seeman, Christian Ristow, John Law, Maya Hayuk, Serena Irwin, Flynn Mauthe, Kimric Smythe, Robert Burke, Tanya, Nick Spelletich, and many beloved helpers
99 *Rocket Car* by David Best
100 *Bodies in the Wind* by Charley Gadeken
111 Camp art by David Best and crew
113 *Embrace* by Matthew Shultz and the Pier Group
114 *Drifts* by Michael Christian
115 *Space Whale* by the Pier Group with Matthew Schultz, Android Jones, and Andy Tibbetts
118 *The Last Summer* performance produced and directed by Joanna Priestly
119 *The Lost Tea Party* by Alex Wright
121 *Coyote* by Bryan Tedrick
122 *El Pulpo Mecanico* by Duane Flatmo
123 *Bone Tree* by Dana Albany; *Mayan Tricycle* by Robert Marzewski
124 *Star Portal* by Carey Thompson
125 *Leaping Giants* by Dan Das Mann and Karen Cusolito
126 *Thunderdome* performance by the Death Guild Crew
127 Performance by MarchFourth Marching Band
129 *Space Whale* by the Pier Group with Matthew Schultz, Android Jones, and Andy Tibbetts
133 *One Tree* by Dan Das Mann
134 *Bone Tree* by Robert Burke
135 *Body of Knowledge* by Dana Albany
136 *Anus* by David Normal and Max Hunter
137 *Temple of Honor* by David Best and the Temple Crew
139 *Baby Abraxas* by Rob Bell
140 *Neverwas Haul* by Shannon O'Hare; *Enzo the Hovercraft* by Brian Herman
141 *5:04 PM* by Michael Mikel
142 *O My Gawd!* by Harrod Blank
143 *Jesus Chrysler Art Car* by Reverend Linville
144 *Abraxas* by Rob Bell
146 *Daisy Solar Wagon* by Samuel Carter
147 *Pig Pen* by Paul Chaussee and Jeannie Schulz
148 *Sunrise Caddy* by unknown artist
149 *Heart Deco* by Adam Ebel
150 Kimric Smythe as the *Java Cow*
151 *Karma Kar* by unknown artist
152 *Mayan Warrior* by Paldo Gonzalez Vargas, Alex Gray, and crew; *El Pulpo Mecanico* by Duane Flatmo and crew
153 *Lady Sassafras* by James Oroc and the Crown Collective
154 *Wonder Wagon* by Tom Bates and Gretchen Roosevelt
155 *Temple Bus* by David Best
156 *Flaming Metal Dragon* by Lisa Nigro
157 *Mystic Flyer* by Timothy Johnson
158 *Blue Peacock* by Jason Howes
159 *Lepidodgera* by Rachel Norman, Mike Thielvoldt, Lira Filippini, and Jake Haskell
160 *Medusa Train* by Mark Sheets
161 *Shark Car* by Sid Kurz
162 *Tin Pan Dragon* by Duane Flatmo
163 *Teddy Bear Train* by "Fred" from Saline Valley
164 Hood ornament by unknown artist
165 *Big Giant Head* by Dale Huntsman
167 *Tiki Island* by Desiree Barlow

169 Tea ceremony performed by Ken Hamazaki; *Temple of Hope* by Mark Grieve and crew
171 *Fire Cannons* by Jim Mason and Alexander Rose
173 *La Contessa* by Simon Cheffins and crew
179 *Temple Project* by David Best and the Temple Crew
181 *Labyrinth* by Todd Dworman
183 Tea ceremony performed by Ken Hamazaki
184 *MudHenge* by Lisa Galli
185 *Temple of Transition* by Chris Hankins, Diarmaid Horkan, and International Arts Megacrew
186 *Temple of Grace* by David Best and the Temple Crew
188 *Temple of Tears* by David Best, Jack Haye, and the Temple Crew
189 *Sinner Stage* by Matt Walker
190 *Fire of Fires* by David Umlas, Marrilee Ratcliffe, and Community Art Makers
191 *Temple of Grace* by David Best and the Temple Crew
192 *Temple of Flux* by Flux Foundation Crew
193 *Exsuscitare Traiectus* by Orion Fredericks
196 *Temple of Honor* by David Best and the Temple Crew
197 *Totem of Confessions* by Michael Garlington and crew
201 *The Before . . . Project* by Eric Schurman
203 *Temple Project* by David Best and the Temple Crew
205 Tea ceremony performed by Ken Hamazaki
206 *Temple of Joy* by David Best and the Temple Crew
207 *Temple Project* by David Best and the Temple Crew
211 Playa demon performed by unknown artist
212 *Becoming Human* by Christian Ristow
213 *Amazing Grace* performed by Joan Baez
214 *Feeble Flobber* by Charlie Smith and Jaime Ladet
215 *Angel of the Apocalypse* by Flaming Lotus Girls
216 *Charon* by Peter Hudson
217 *Black Rock Bijou* by the Bijou Crew
219 *Bliss Dance* by Marco Cochrane
221 *PsychoPhilia* by Vancouver, B.C., CORE Crew
222 *Emergence* by Mardi Storm
223 *Prayer Dragon* by Ryan Mathern
224 *Crucifixion of the Soul* by Michael Tscheu
225 *Phallus of Man and Yoni Gate* by Pepe Ozan
226 *Fledgling* by Christian Ristow
227 *MudHenge* by Lisa Galli
228 *Photo Chapel* by Michael Garlington
229 *Temple of Grace* by David Best; *Tasseograph* by Shrine and TukTuk; *Abraxas* by Rob Bell
230 *Raygun Gothic Rocketship* by Sean Orlando, Nathaniel Taylor, David Shulman, and crew
232 *Bliss Dance* by Marco Cochrane
233 *Big Rig Jig* by Mike Ross
234 *Temple of Rudra* by Pepe Ozan
235 Art by Pepe Ozan
236 *Faces of Man* by Dan Das Mann
237 *The Temple of Nut* by Bill Stender
238 *LOVE* by Laura Kimpton and Jeff Schomberg
239 *Portal of Evolution* by Bryan Tedrick
240 *Keynote* by Michael Christian
241 *Mama NOLA* by NOLA CORE Group
242 *Serpent Mother* by Flaming Lotus Girls
243 *Medusa Madness* by Kevin Clark and Reared in Steel
244 *Soma* by Flaming Lotus Girls
245 *Xylophage* by Flaming Lotus Girls
246 *Shrumen Lumen* by FoldHaus Artist Collective
247 *Aurora* by Charles Gadeken
248 *R-Evolution* by Marco Cochrane
251 Center Camp performance by unknown artists
252 *Temple of Whollyness* by Synthesis LLC: Gregg Fleishman, Melissa Barron, and Lightning Clearwater III
263 Torch ritual by Crimson Rose's Fire Conclave
265 *Le Mystere de Papa Loko* by Pepe Ozan
267 *Floating Larry* by Steven Carthy
268 *Daughters of Ishtar* by Pepe Ozan
269 *Crude Awakening* by Dan Das Mann, Karen Cusalito, Black Rock FX, Pyrokinetics, Nate Smith, Mark Perez, and MonkeyBoy
272 Performance by David Silverman
273 *El Pulpo Mecanico* by Duane Flatmo
276 Fire performance by unknown artist
277 *Crude Awakening* by Dan Das Mann, Karen Cusalito, Black Rock FX, Pyrokinetics, Nate Smith, Mark Perez, and MonkeyBoy
280 *Lord Snort* by Bryan Tedrick; *Catacomb of Veils* by Dan Sullivan and the Catacomb Crew
287 *Temple of Whollyness* by Synthesis LLC: Gregg Fleishman, Melissa Barron, and Lightning Clearwater III
295 Labyrinth by Crimson Rose and Will Roger Peterson
296 *Guru Road Rock Art* by Dewayne "Dooby" Williams

Derry Temple by David Best and the Derry Temple Crew is featured on pages 307, 310, 311, 312, 313, 318, 319, 320, and 321.